SIXTH EDITION

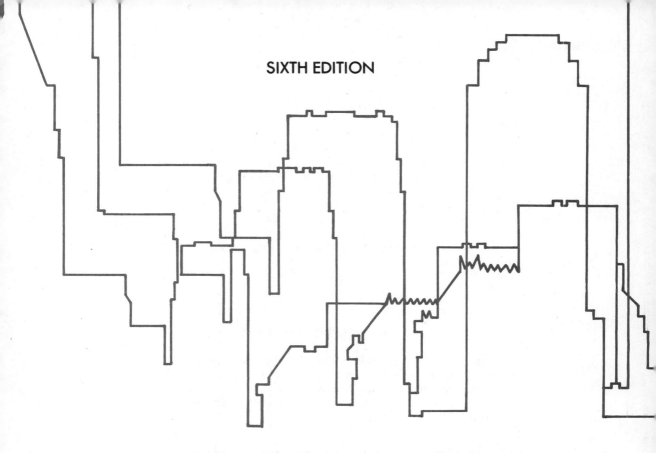

FINANCE
Introduction to Markets, Institutions and Management

MERLE T. WELSHANS
Washington University

RONALD W. MELICHER
University of Colorado

Published by

F15 **SOUTH-WESTERN PUBLISHING CO.**

CINCINNATI   WEST CHICAGO, ILL.   DALLAS   PELHAM MANOR, N.Y.   PALO ALTO, CALIF.

Copyright © 1984

by SOUTH-WESTERN PUBLISHING CO.

Cincinnati, Ohio

ISBN: 0-538-06150-2

Library of Congress Catalog Card Number: 83-61524

1 2 3 4 5 6 7 **D** 9 8 7 6 5 4 3

Printed in the United States of America

Cover Photograph by Francis Hidalgo/The Image Bank

Part Opener Photo Credits

Part I—U.S. Department of Housing and Urban Development
Part II—Photo Courtesy of Celanese Corporation
Part III—U.S. Department of Agriculture
Part IV—Department of the Treasury

PREFACE

This Sixth Edition of *Finance* continues to be designed for the first course in finance. It is our belief that the development of a basic understanding of the complex world of finance should begin with a survey course that covers an introduction to financial markets, institutions, and management. The subject matter of this book includes the whole scope of the financial system and its functions: (1) the markets in which funds are traded, (2) the institutions which participate in and facilitate these flows of funds, and (3) the principles and concepts of financial management which guide the participants in making sound decisions.

This book provides the necessary background for courses in financial management, monetary policy, bank management, government finance, and securities markets. It is especially appropriate for students taking only one course in the field of finance and will prepare them for making financial decisions as consumers. Because the text thoroughly examines the financial structure of our economy, it is also an appropriate text for business students who will eventually be seeking funds for business and other operations.

This Sixth Edition is organized around four major topics or parts. The first is the financial system of the United States. In the second part we focus on business financing and management. Financing other sectors of the economy is covered in the third part. The fourth part covers monetary, fiscal, and debt management policies.

Substantial changes and revisions have taken place in the Sixth Edition of *Finance*. Some of the major developments are summarized below.

Part I has been substantially revised to reflect current developments in the U.S. financial system. Banking structure and banking operations are in the midst of rapid change. Competition among depository institutions and between depository institutions and other financial institutions is being encouraged and fostered by recent legislation. Major provisions and implications of the Depository Institutions Deregulation and Monetary Control Act of 1980 are discussed in Part I and in other chapters where appropriate. The Garn–St. Germain Act of 1982, which allowed increased competition by depository institutions for money market funds, also is covered.

Part II was totally restructured and revised. It now focuses on both financial management topics and business financing sources. First, an introduction to business finance is presented in Chapter 7. Then, students are introduced to the functions of financial planning and working capital management (i.e., the management of cash and marketable securities, accounts receivable, inventories, and current liabilities) in Chapter 8. Sources of short-term business financing are covered in Chapter 9.

Students are introduced to the time value of money concept and related problems early in Chapter 10 of Part II. Then our attention focuses on the management of fixed assets and methods for selecting between capital investment projects. This is accomplished without subjecting students to excessive rigor. The remaining chapters in Part II cover the management of long-term debt and equity funds, sources of long-term business financing, and markets for long-term business funds.

Part III has been revised and reorganized. Government financing at both the federal level and state and local level is covered. This is followed by a three chapter discussion of the financing of consumers. The remaining chapters in Part III cover the financing of agriculture and international finance topics.

Part IV has been substantially revised. Chapter 21 is a new chapter dealing with the policy instruments of the Federal Reserve and the Treasury. Recent developments in the areas of interest rate levels, business fluctuations, international payment problems, and monetary and fiscal policy actions also are incorporated in the Sixth Edition.

The authors have benefitted greatly from discussions with and helpful comments of colleagues at Washington University and the University of Colorado. Comments from students and teachers that have used prior editions of this book also are greatly appreciated. A special recognition goes to Carl A. Dauten who, along with Merle Welshans, was responsible for the first four editions of this text.

Finally, the Sixth Edition continues to benefit from Merle Welshans' experience as Vice President of Finance at Union Electric Company where he served for fourteen years before recently returning to academic teaching.

MERLE T. WELSHANS
RONALD W. MELICHER

CONTENTS

Part I—The Financial System

Part II—Business Financing and Management

Part III—Financing Other Sectors of the Economy

C. FINANCING SPECIAL AREAS

Part IV—Monetary, Fiscal and Debt Management Policies

PART I

The Financial System

1

Nature and Role of Finance in Our Economy

An effective financial system is vital to the operation of a modern market economy such as ours. The essence of economic activity is the production and exchange of goods and services. Large-scale production and a high degree of specialization of labor can function only if there exists an effective means of paying for productive resources and final products. Business can obtain the money it needs to buy capital goods such as machinery and equipment only if the institutions and markets have been established for making savings available for such investment. Similarly, the federal government and other governmental units can carry out their wide range of activities only if efficient means exist for raising money, for making payments, and for borrowing.

Our financial system encompasses not only those institutions that specialize in financial transactions, but also the markets in which they interact with other firms, individuals, and governments. Virtually all economic units are participants in the financial system, both borrowing and supplying funds. The study of finance includes an examination of the decision processes and management principles which guide the behavior of those units in their financial activities. Our economy could not function as it does without an effective financial system, and intelligent participation in that system requires some knowledge of finance.

BASIC REQUIREMENTS OF AN EFFECTIVE FINANCIAL SYSTEM

An effective financial system needs an efficient monetary system, facilities for creating capital by channeling savings into investment, and markets in which to buy and sell claims to wealth to facilitate the investment process.

The financial system must provide an efficient medium for exchanging goods and services. A basic feature of such a system is a unit in which to measure prices, that is, a unit of account, such as the dollar in our economy or the pound sterling in the British economy. This unit of account must be universally accepted in the economy if exchange is to function smoothly. It must also be a reasonably stable unit if it is to be used widely. There must be convenient means for making payments for goods and services purchased, whether the purchase is a pack of chewing gum or a complete business worth millions of dollars. This means that the monetary system must operate with monetary institutions, instruments, and procedures geared to the needs of the economy.

A second essential feature in a highly developed economy is a financial system that makes possible the creation of capital on a scale large enough to meet the demands of the economy. Capital creation takes place whenever production facilities are used to produce buildings, machinery, or other equipment to be used in the production of goods for consumer or producer use. In a simple economy, such as that on a largely self-sufficient, one-person farm, this process, in part at least, takes place directly. The farmer creates capital when taking time during the winter months to build a new barn or to fashion a new ax handle. In a highly developed economy, this process takes place when some individuals, businesses, or governmental units do not spend all of their current income. They save some of it and make the savings available to others who use them to buy buildings, machinery, or equipment. This indirect process of capital creation can work only if the proper legal instruments and financial institutions exist so that savers are willing to transfer the ownership of their savings to businesses and other institutions having a demand for them.

A third essential feature in the financial system of a highly developed economy is that it provides markets and procedures for the transfer of claims to wealth, such as promissory notes and shares of ownership in a business, and for the conversion of such claims into cash. Such markets and procedures facilitate the process of capital creation since savings will be made available for investment in sufficient sums by a large group of investors only when the saver can quickly and easily convert the claim into cash when there is a need or desire to do so. For example, several million individuals are willing to invest billions of dollars in the American Telephone and Telegraph Company because the facilities of the New York Stock Exchange make it possible to sell their shares of ownership to other investors easily and quickly.

FINANCIAL FUNCTIONS IN OUR SYSTEM

In our economy, in order to meet the basic requirements of an effective financial system, the government and private financial institutions of many kinds have developed instruments and procedures to perform the financial functions listed in Figure 1-1. These financial functions may, in turn, be viewed as characteristics of our financial system which evolved to support our modern free-enterprise economy.

Creation of Money

Money may be defined as anything which is generally accepted as a means of paying for goods and services and of discharging debts. One of the most significant functions of the financial system is that of creating the money which

Figure 1-1
Characteristics of an
Effective Financial
System

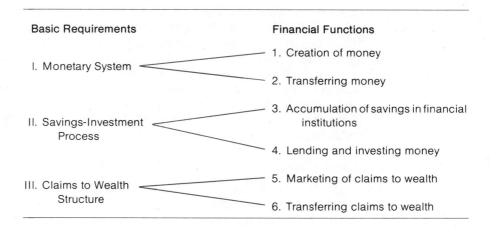

Basic Requirements	Financial Functions
I. Monetary System	1. Creation of money
	2. Transferring money
II. Savings-Investment Process	3. Accumulation of savings in financial institutions
	4. Lending and investing money
III. Claims to Wealth Structure	5. Marketing of claims to wealth
	6. Transferring claims to wealth

serves as a medium of exchange. The value of money lies in its purchasing power. It is the most generalized claim to wealth, since it can be exchanged for almost anything else. Most transactions in any modern economy involve money, and most of these transactions would not take place if at least one of the parties did not have money available. Therefore, a sufficient amount of money is essential for economic activitiy to take place at an efficient rate. On the other hand, if too much money is made available, its value tends to fall, prices go up, and inflation occurs. The Federal Reserve System has primary responsibility for the amount of money that is created, although most of the money is actually created by banks and other depository institutions.

Transferring Money

Individuals and businesses hold money in anticipation of purchases or payments they expect to make in the near future. One way to hold money is in checking accounts and other checkable deposits at banks, savings and loan associations, mutual savings banks, and credit unions. When money is held in this form, payments can easily be made by check. The *check* is an order to the depository institution to transfer the money to the party who received the check. This is a great convenience, since checks can be written for the exact amount of payments, they can be safely sent in the mail, and they provide a record of payment. Institutions can now transfer funds between accounts electronically, with records kept by computer, so that payments can be made without paper checks. Funds transfers can be initiated by telephone or at remote terminals connected to the bank's computer.

Accumulation of Savings in Financial Institutions

A function performed by many different types of financial institutions is the accumulation or gathering together of individual savings. For example, a commercial bank handles the accounts of many businesses and individuals, many of them small. When all are accumulated in one place, however, they are available in amounts much larger than any individual depositor could supply. Banks and other financial institutions conduct continuing advertising campaigns and other promotional activities to secure deposits.

A part of this function of the gathering together or accumulation of savings is that of acting as a custodian of the savings and cash balances of the public. Most individuals, businesses, and organizations do not want to take the risks involved in having large amounts of cash on hand. They, therefore, put them into a bank or other financial institution for safekeeping.

Lending and Investing Money

Another basic function of financial institutions is the lending and investing function. The money that has been put into these institutions may be loaned to businesses, farmers, consumers, institutions, and governmental units. It may be loaned for different purposes, such as to buy buildings or equipment, or to pay current bills. This money may also be loaned for varying time periods. Some financial institutions make loans of almost all types to all groups of borrowers; others specialize in only one or perhaps several types of lending. Some financial institutions invest all or part of the savings that have been put into them in shares of ownership in a business or in debt obligations of businesses or other institutions.

Marketing of Claims to Wealth

Savings may be placed with financial institutions that invest them, or they may be invested directly. For example, a business may want to sell shares of ownership to the general public. It could do so directly, but the process of finding individuals interested in investing funds in that business might be difficult and time-consuming. A type of financial intermediary (referred to as an investment banking firm) has been developed to sell these shares of ownership, or shares of stock as they are called. This function is essentially one of merchandising.

Transferring Claims to Wealth

Several types of institutions or intermediaries facilitate the process of lending and of selling securities. For example, if shares of stock are to be sold to the general public, it is desirable to have a ready market in which such stocks can be resold later if the investor no longer wants to hold them. The several stock exchanges serve this purpose. If lending is to be done effectively, it is desirable to have readily available up-to-date information on the applicants for loans. Various types of credit-checking agencies have been developed to meet this need.

DEVELOPMENT OF FINANCIAL INSTITUTIONS AND INTERMEDIARIES

The current system of financial institutions and intermediaries that exists in the United States, like the monetary system, developed to meet the changing needs of our economy.

Figure 1-2

Major Institutions and Intermediaries in Our Financial System

Depository Institutions

Commercial Banks
Savings and Loan Associations
Mutual Savings Banks
Credit Unions

Contractual Savings Institutions

Life Insurance Companies
Property and Casualty Insurance
    Companies
Private Pension Funds
State and Local Government
    Retirement Funds

Investment Institutions

Investment Companies
Trust Companies
Real Estate Investment Trusts
Money Market Mutual Funds

Finance Companies

Sales Finance Companies
Consumer Finance Companies
Commercial Finance Companies

Facilitating Financial Intermediaries

Mortgage Banking Companies
Investment Bankers and Brokerage Companies
Securities Markets
Credit Reporting Organizations
Government Credit-Related Agencies

Current Institutional Structure

Financial institutions and intermediaries which play active roles in our financial system are shown in Figure 1-2. They are classified into five basic categories. First are the depository institutions, which are commercial banks, savings and loan associations, mutual savings banks, and credit unions. These institutions play an important role in the channeling of savings by individuals into loans to the federal government (by purchasing its debt issues), loans to business firms, and investments such as home mortgages.

The second category relates to contractual savings institutions, which are so classified because they involve relatively steady inflows of money. Insurance companies (life, and property and casualty) receive steady inflows in the form of insurance premium payments. Likewise, pension funds (both private and government programs) receive contributions on a regular basis. These institutions play an active role in supplying funds to business firms by purchasing stocks and bonds, to the housing sector by purchasing real estate mortgages, and to governmental units by purchasing their debt issues.

Investment institutions comprise the third major category in our financial system. These institutions frequently invest in the stocks and bonds issued by business firms and the debt instruments issued by governmental units. While individual investors could invest directly in such securities, the investment institutions offer small investors diversification and experienced management of their funds.

The fourth category consists of finance companies that provide loans directly to consumers and business firms. Sales finance and consumer finance companies lend to individuals. Sales finance companies finance installment loan purchases of automobiles and other durable goods. Small loans to individuals and households are provided by consumer finance companies. Business firms that are unable to obtain financing from commercial banks often turn to business or commercial finance companies for necessary loans. Thus, finance companies constitute an important dimension in our financial system by providing to consumers and businesses loanable funds that are not obtainable from depository institutions such as commercial banks and credit unions.

The fifth category consists of financial intermediaries that provide facilitating activities in terms of the savings-investment process and/or the marketing and transferring of claims to wealth. There are many kinds of facilitating organizations in our financial system and thus it is important to recognize that only selected ones are shown in Figure 1-2. Mortgage banking firms play an important role in the origination of real estate mortgages by bringing together borrowers and lenders. Investment banking firms and brokerage firms often are involved in the marketing of new stock and bond securities issued by businesses. And brokerage houses, along with organized securities markets, facilitate the process of transferring stocks and bonds among investors. The creating or issuing of new securities or other claims to wealth takes place in what is referred to as the *primary* market, whereas the so-called *secondary* market involves the transferring of existing securities from old investors to new investors.

Credit-reporting and -rating organizations aid lenders in deciding whether to extend credit to consumers and businesses. Finally, in recent years government credit-related agencies (such as the Government National Mortgage Association) have taken an increasingly active role in the marketing and transferring of real estate mortgages.

Few of today's financial institutions existed during the American colonial period. Only commercial banks and insurance (life and property) companies can be traced back prior to the beginning of the 1800s. Mutual savings banks and savings and loan associations began developing during the early 1800s.

Trust companies, investment banking firms, and organized securities exchanges also can be traced back to the first half of the 1800s. No major financial institution evolved during the last half of the nineteenth century. Credit unions, pension funds, investment companies, and finance companies had their origin during the early part of the twentieth century. This also was the case for government involvement in terms of credit-related agencies.

Financial Intermediation

The process by which savings are accumulated in financial institutions and, in turn, lent or invested by them is referred to as *intermediation* by financial institutions. In the decade of the 1970s and the first part of the 1980s, the great bulk of all funds flowing into the credit markets was supplied by financial intermediaries. The role of financial intermediaries has been increasing significantly since the early 1920s. In the 1920s somewhat over half of the net increase in the financial assets of households was in the form of securities purchased directly in the credit markets, but by the 1980s such purchases accounted for only a small amount of the financial savings of households. The remainder of the savings of households, except for net additions to the holdings of currency, flowed through financial intermediaries.

The role of intermediaries has grown because they offer savers the kind of investment opportunities they are interested in. The notes, bonds, and shares of stock offered by most of those seeking long-term funds are not the assets which most of the public is willing to purchase and hold. Financial intermediaries offer such qualities desired by savers as safety of principal, liquidity, convenience, and availability in small denominations—one or more of which are often lacking in market instruments. Financial institutions have offered these qualities in increasingly diversified forms to meet the varying needs of savers and have done so at attractive rates of return. Small savers also have a preference for financial institutions because of the relatively high cost involved in making small transactions for securities and also because it is more difficult to effect transactions in such markets than it is to put funds into a financial institution. The development of government guarantees and insurance and the governmental supervision of such institutions has made them more attractive to small savers. The small saver is also attracted to financial institutions because there is a multitude of choices among institutions, each of which is competing for the saver's funds. This has led to a variety of services and conveniences for the saver as well as an attractive rate of return.

This long-run increase in intermediation is not without its problems. In years of strong demand for credit and strong restraint on the money supply, such as occurred in 1973–74 and the beginning of the 1980s, the percentage of funds moving through financial institutions to the credit markets has decreased significantly. These are referred to as periods of *disintermediation*. Such rapid shifts of sources of funds create difficulties in the economy since they impede the flow of funds to such sectors as housing which rely heavily on funds from financial intermediaries.

TYPES OF CLAIMS TO WEALTH

There are many types of claims to wealth currently in existence in our financial system. Claims to wealth may be in the form of real assets or financial assets. *Real assets* would include the direct ownership of land, buildings, machinery, inventory, and even precious metals. *Financial assets* represent claims against the income and assets of those who issued the financial assets and sometimes are indirect claims against real assets. One might hold financial assets that are claims against (obligations or liabilities of) individuals, businesses, financial institutions and intermediaries, and governments. For example, debt obligations issued by business firms are financial assets to holders and represent claims against the issuing firms. Real assets in the form of inventory, machinery, and buildings often support the financial claims or liabilities issued by business firms.

Checkable deposits (checking accounts and share drafts) and time deposits (savings accounts) held in depository institutions, are also examples of financial claims to wealth. In fact, all kinds of promissory notes or "IOU's" represent financial assets or claims to wealth to their holders. Included would be currency issued by the U.S. government (financial liabilities) and held by the public (financial assets).

However, relatively few of the many types of financial claims to wealth actually are involved in the financial markets. That is, only certain financial claims in the form of securities and debt instruments are marketed and transferred in the financial markets. Our financial markets are frequently divided into money and capital markets in addition to the previously mentioned primary and secondary markets. *Money markets* are the markets where debt instruments of one year or less are traded. *Capital markets* thus include longer-term debt securities (notes and bonds) and instruments (mortgages) as well as corporate stocks.

Figure 1-3 indicates the major types of claims to wealth that trade in the financial markets. Since the U.S. government actively borrows through debt financing, its short-term (bills) and longer-term (notes and bonds) financial claims are very important in the money and capital markets. Federal agencies, such as the Federal Land Bank and Federal Home Loan Bank systems, and state and local governments generally issue longer-term financial claims that trade in the capital markets.

Figure 1-3
Claims to Wealth Traded in Financial Markets

Money Market Instruments	Capital Market Securities and Instruments
U.S. Treasury Bills	U.S. Treasury Notes and Bonds
Negotiable Certificates of Deposit	U.S. Government Agency Bonds
Bankers' Acceptances	State and Local Government Bonds
Federal Funds	Corporate Bonds
Commercial Paper	Corporate Stocks
Eurodollars	Real Estate Mortgages

Business firms are active in both financial markets. Some businesses finance a portion of their needs by issuing short-term unsecured promissory notes (referred to as *commercial paper*). Business corporations also issue large amounts of stocks and bonds to meet their financing needs. Real estate mortgages, created to finance residential and other properties, trade in the capital markets.

Negotiable certificates of deposit (CD's) are created and issued by commercial banks and other depository financial institutions. These are in denominations of $100,000 or more and are readily exchangeable in the money markets. *Bankers' acceptances* are created as a result of international trade and also are fully marketable. Federal funds come about because some commercial banks have excess or extra funds that they are willing to lend to other commercial banks for short-term periods. *Eurodollars* are dollar deposits held outside the United

States, usually in European banks. Each of these money market instruments (and capital market securities and instruments) will be described in detail at appropriate places throughout this book.

THE PLAN OF STUDY

The subject matter of this book includes the entire scope of the financial system and its functions: the markets in which funds are traded, the institutions which participate in and facilitate these flows of funds, and the principles and concepts which guide these participants in making the right decisions.

Part I deals with the financial system in the United States economy. Financial functions and the development of institutions and instruments to carry on those functions have been considered briefly in this chapter. The remainder of this part deals with the monetary system of the United States and with the role of commercial banks and the Federal Reserve System in providing money and credit to meet the needs of the economy. The last chapter in this first part focuses on the savings-investment process, which plays a major role in our modern free-enterprise economy.

Part II looks at the financial system as it relates to the business sector of the economy. The essentials of financial management of current and fixed assets are introduced. The first chapter focuses on the nature of business finance and the objectives of financial management. The next chapters discuss the management of short-term assets or working capital and the sources of short-term business financing.

Then the discussion turns to the management of fixed assets and the management of the firm's mix of debt and equity funds. A chapter dealing with the sources of long-term business financing follows. The last chapter in Part II covers the markets for long-term business funds.

We devote so much attention to the financing of business for several reasons. Firms typically look to the financial markets for a large portion of the funds needed for current operations and capital investment. Because business profits are so sensitive to financial decisions, theories and concepts of financial management are highly developed in the business area. Business finance principles also are applicable to other areas of finance, including the management of financial institutions. In addition, a significant part of the financial system is involved in meeting the demands for funds in the business sector of the economy.

Part III is concerned with meeting the demand for funds in other sectors of the economy. Three basic sectors are identified.

Section A of Part III deals with the financing of governmental needs. The first chapter considers the financing of the federal government and the second, of state and local governments.

Section B deals with the financing of the consumer, both for short-term and long-term needs. The initial chapters develop the role of consumer financing in the economy and then discuss the institutions and procedures available for providing short-term and intermediate-term consumer credit. A third chapter focuses on providing long-term credit to finance the purchase of residential real estate.

Section C of Part III covers the institutions and procedures developed to supply short-term and long-term funds in specialized areas. The first to be considered is the financing of agriculture and the second, the financing of international trade and foreign investment.

Part IV focuses on monetary, fiscal, and debt management policies. The first chapter examines the role of the Federal Reserve System in establishing monetary policy and also considers the relationship of the Treasury to the supply of money and credit in the financial markets. Then, attention focuses on the structure and level of interest rates in relation to monetary and fiscal policies. This is followed by two chapters exploring the relationships between monetary policies and price levels, business fluctuations, and international financial equilibrium. The last chapter traces the impact of recent monetary and fiscal policy actions on our free-enterprise economy.

QUESTIONS

1. What are the basic requirements of an effective financial system?
2. Identify and describe the financial functions or characteristics of our financial system that evolved to support our economy.
3. Identify and briefly describe the structure of financial institutions and intermediaries that currently exists in our economy.
4. What is meant by the term *financial intermediation*?
5. How do real assets and financial assets differ?
6. Briefly describe the differences between the money and capital markets.
7. Identify and briefly describe the types of claims to wealth that trade in the financial markets.

SUGGESTED READINGS

Burns, A. R. *Money and Monetary Policy in Early Times.* New York: Alfred A. Knopf, Inc., 1927.

Cook, Timothy Q., and Bruce J. Summers (eds.). *Instruments of the Money Market*, 5th ed. Federal Reserve Bank of Richmond, 1981.

Groseclose, Elgin. *Money and Man, A Survey of Monetary Experience.* New York: Frederick Ungar Publishing Company, 1961.

Harless, Doris E. *Nonbank Financial Institutions.* Federal Reserve Bank of Richmond, 1975.

Kamerschen, David R. *Money and Banking,* 7th ed. Cincinnati: South-Western Publishing Co., 1980. Chapter 1.

The Story of American Banking. New York: Banking Education Committee, The American Bankers Association, 1963.

2 Monetary System of the United States

The essential role of a monetary system in the operation and development of a financial system was explained in Chapter 1. In this chapter, the nature and functions of money are developed more fully, and the nature of the monetary system of the United States is also described and analyzed. Consideration is also given to the monetary standard on which the system is based and to the types of money currently in use to meet the needs of the economy.

NATURE AND FUNCTIONS OF MONEY

In the preceding discussion, money was defined as anything generally accepted as a means of paying for goods and services and of discharging debts. This function of money is generally referred to as that of serving as a *medium of exchange.* This is the basic function of money in any economy, but money also serves other functions, as a store of purchasing power and as a standard of value.

Money may be held as a *store of purchasing power* which can be drawn on at will. This may be done shortly after it is received or after it has been held for a period of time. While money is held, it is a liquid asset for its owner and provides flexibility in the decision to spend or to invest. But the owner pays for this flexibility since it is necessary to forego the potential return that could be earned by investing the money or the satisfaction that could be gained from spending it for goods and services. Money can perform its function as a store of purchasing power only if its value is relatively stable.

The function of serving as a store of purchasing power can also be performed by an asset other than money if it can be converted into money quickly and without significant loss of value. We refer to this property—the ease with which an asset can be exchanged for money or other assets—as *liquidity.* Money is perfectly liquid since it is a generally accepted medium of exchange. Other assets, such as savings deposits held at depository institutions, approach the liquidity of money. The existence of such liquid assets reduces the need for holding money itself as a store of purchasing power.

The third function of money—as a *standard of value*—refers to the fact that prices are expressed in terms of the monetary unit and that contracts for deferred payments are also expressed in this way. Prices and debts are usually expressed in terms of dollars without any statement as to the type of money to be used. The relationship of money as a standard by which to judge the value of goods is a circular one. The value of money may be stated in terms of the goods it will buy, and a change in prices generally reflects a change in the value of money. If money is to perform its function as a standard of value, it is essential that the value of the monetary unit be relatively stable.

DEVELOPMENT OF THE MONETARY SYSTEM

We have answered the question of what money is—but we have not yet said what items serve as money in our system. The answer to this may not be as simple as it seems at first, and a look at the history of money reveals that the answer has changed over time.

Our monetary system developed to meet the changing needs of the economy. Adequate records to trace the early developments of the system do not exist, but we can infer much from the available evidence and from practices still in use in the more primitive economies.

Barter

Primitive economies consisted largely of self-sufficient units or groups that lived by means of hunting, fishing, and simple agriculture. There was little need or occasion to exchange goods or services. Even in such economies, however, some trade took place.

As economies became more developed and some individuals specialized, to a degree at least, in herding sheep, in raising grain, or as goldsmiths and silver-smiths, the process of exchange became more important. To help facilitate such exchanges of goods for goods, or *barter* as it is known, tables of relative values were developed from past experience. For example, the table might show the number of furs, measures of grain, amount of cloth equal to one animal, such as a sheep or cow.

This arrangement helped facilitate exchanges, but the process still had many serious drawbacks. For example, if a person had a cow and wanted to trade it for some nuts and some furs, the person would need to find someone who had an excess of both of these items to trade. The need for a simpler means of exchange led to the development of money.

Early Development of Money

The record of the early development of money is very sketchy. In all probability traders found that some items, such as furs and grain, were traded more frequently than other items. Therefore, they could afford to accept these items in exchange even when they did not have an immediate need for them since they could always trade them for goods they wanted. They probably also found it convenient to figure the value of goods less frequently traded in terms of these more frequently traded items because the system gave them a familiar yardstick with which to value them.

This development took place in much this same way in some American prisoner of war camps in Germany during World War II. Cigarettes were used as a general medium of exchange of goods and services since they could always be traded for other goods. Values of all types of goods were also quoted in cigarettes even when there was no intention of exchanging them.

Records in early economies show many items that were useful for food or clothing which were used as a general medium of exchange and, to some degree at least, also as a unit for measuring value. Included were grain, salt, skins, spices, tea, seeds, and cattle. Some early economies made use of such commodities as beads, ivory, the plumage of birds, gold, and silver because there was a general demand for ornamentation. Some items that were useful as tools or in making tools, such as animal claws, fishhooks, shark teeth, and stone discs, were also used. All of these items were generally accepted in exchange because there was a demand for them since they could be used for further exchange or as food, clothing, tools, or ornament.

Traders accepted these items as long as they felt certain that they could use them again in future trading. This meant that the supply of the item had to be limited in relation to the desires of individuals in the economy to have the item. In early economies this was generally true of such items as grains, cattle, and tools. Items of ornamentation could likewise be used as a general medium of exchange only if there was an unfilled demand for them. For example, the American Indians valued wampum beads as a decoration and were not able to get enough of them to meet the desires of everyone. Therefore, such beads could serve as a general medium of exchange.

Use of Precious Metals as Money

When commodities were used as a medium of exchange, goods could be valued in terms of the item used as money and could be exchanged for it. This process, however, was still clumsy and time-consuming. For example, if furs were used, they were bulky and difficult to carry around. Furthermore, arguments could arise over the quality of the furs. It was also necessary to make a trade of goods equal to one, two, three, or more furs since furs lost their value when cut into pieces.

The transition from the use of such commodities as money to the use of precious metals was probably a gradual one, but the advantages of precious metals eventually led to their general usage. Gold and silver were in great demand for ornamentation due to their durability, malleability, and beauty. The supply of these metals was limited enough so that they had great value, which made them easy to carry around as money. They could also be refined into the pure metal rather easily so that their quality was rather uniform. Various quantities could also be weighed out so that exchanges of varying values could be made. In time, coins with a certain weight of metal in them were developed. Since an unscrupulous trader could cover baser metals with gold or silver or put in short weight, however, this process of coinage needed regulation if coins were to be generally acceptable. For that reason coining money and determining the value thereof has been a governmental function since the earliest days.

Metal coins and other commodities that served as early forms of money are sometimes referred to as *full-bodied money*. They had intrinsic value equal to their value as commodities. Since they were money, they served as a standard of value; that is, the worth of other commodities was expressed in units of the monetary commodity. When governments undertook the function of coining money they formalized the standard, establishing by law the basic money unit in terms of the weight and fineness of precious metals such as gold. This standardization also provided a convenient medium of exchange for trade between nations.

The first monetary act in the United States, which was passed under the new Constitution in 1792, provided for a bimetallic standard. A *bimetallic standard* is one based upon two metals—in practice, silver and gold. The dollar, which was set up as the unit of value, was defined as 371.25 grains of pure silver or 24.75 grains of pure gold. Thus, the metal in the silver dollar was 15 times the weight of the metal in the gold dollar, or there was a ratio of 15 to 1 between the metals at the mint. Provision was made for gold coins in denominations of $2.50, $5, and $10, and for silver coins in denominations of $1, 50¢, 25¢, 10¢, and 5¢. All of these coins contained silver equal to their full face value, the 10¢ piece one tenth as much as the silver dollar, and so on. In addition, provision was made for copper token coins in one-cent and half-cent denominations. Unlike full-bodied coins, *token coins* are worth more as money than the value of the metal they contain.

The bimetallic standard was difficult to maintain because the market ratio between silver and gold, which was about 15 to 1 in 1792, soon changed to about 15½ to 1. Consequently, little gold was brought to the mint for coinage because it was found to be worth more in the open market than at the mint, and the few gold coins that were minted soon disappeared from circulation. In 1834 Congress changed the official mint ratio to 16 to 1; this reversed the situation rather than remedying it. Gold was now overvalued at the mint, so gold coins became abundant but silver coins disappeared from circulation. Officially the bimetallic standard lasted until 1900, but the United States had been on a de facto gold standard since the 1830s. Full-bodied gold coins actually circulated until 1934, and the dollar was defined in terms of gold until the 1970s.

Paper Money

Full-bodied money is a thing of the past. Today the circulating medium, such as the paper in our currency, has little intrinsic value. It has value as money only because it is accepted in exchange and has purchasing power. But this is not a new development.

Since early modern times, governments have issued money in the form of paper. Gold and silver coins are cumbersome to carry around for large transactions. To facilitate exchange, governments issued paper money to represent certain quantities of gold or silver that were kept on deposit by the government to back such paper. The paper was generally accepted as a medium of exchange because the persons accepting it knew they could get the precious metal when and if they wanted it. Banks also issued paper money backed by precious metals. This was done at first without specific authorization by governmental authorities; but, as time went on, governments regulated the issuance of paper money by the banks. Such paper money backed by gold or silver circulated freely. As long as individuals felt certain they could exchange it for the precious metal behind it, there was no inclination to do so.

This early paper money is referred to as *representative full-bodied money*. Each government note or bank note represented a specific amount of gold or silver in storage in a government or bank vault. For localized transactions, the paper was exchanged freely. Holders of the paper rarely had a need to present the paper for redemption in metal. Gradually the paper circulated more widely, and eventually even merchants of different nations would accept the paper money issued by reputable banks and governments. Since only a small number of notes would be redeemed during a given period of time, there was relatively little turnover of the precious metal in the vaults. This situation led to the evolution of modern monetary systems.

Credit Money

Any circulating medium which has little intrinsic value relative to its monetary value is called *credit money*. Almost all money circulating in the world today is some form of credit money—money which does not consist of or represent a specific valuable commodity, but which depends for its value on its general acceptance and, in turn, on the credit of its issuer.

Credit money evolved from representative paper money. One area of its development was in private enterprise. The earliest forerunners of private banks were goldsmiths, specialists in weighing, assaying, and storing precious metals. Individuals would pay to have their gold stored by these early banks for safekeeping. The stored gold would be carefully evaluated, and a receipt issued verifying its weight and fineness. It was often more convenient to conduct a transaction by signing over the receipt rather than handing over the gold itself, since it was cumbersome and dangerous to transport the gold, and the recipients would often have more confidence in the expert evaluation of the weight and fineness stated on the receipt than in their own evaluation of the gold itself. As the receipts or notes circulated more freely, they became some of the first representative full-bodied paper money, as discussed above.

As the paper circulated, the gold sat in the vaults, with only a fraction of it being redeemed during any period of time. Eventually these early bankers went into the loan business, lending either gold itself or issuing additional receipts or notes. In so doing the bankers issued notes for more gold than they actually had in their vaults. As long as the bankers did not experience an unusually high number of customers presenting notes for redemption at the same time, they found this to be a safe and profitable way of doing business. And as long as the depositors were confident that the gold could be redeemed, they were usually content to leave it safely on deposit. This practice not only represents one of the earliest examples of credit money, but also describes the origins of our modern fractional reserve system of banking and money creation, which will be discussed in Chapter 5.

The general acceptance of paper money as a medium of exchange, with no intention of redeeming it for the precious metal behind it, made possible the issuance of paper money with no such backing. From time to time, money was issued based only on the general credit of the government and on the provision that such money was *legal tender*, acceptable to pay taxes and to fulfill contracts calling for payment in lawful money. This is the case today in the United States and in other countries. Since this money is proclaimed to be money by law or fiat, it is sometimes called *fiat money*.

Banks also issued paper money without metallic backing. As such issues were brought under regulation, the banks were required to have some metallic backing for their paper money and to have some form of collateral, such as government bonds, for the remainder of the face value of the money they issued. The privilege of private banks to issue paper money of any type became more and more restricted in all countries and has been abolished in recent years. The only banks that issue any significant amounts of paper money today are central banks, which are owned or controlled by the national government of the country. Paper money issued by central banks under authority of the government is referred to as *fiduciary money*.

Paper Money in the United States

Except for a brief experiment during the War of 1812, the federal government did not itself issue paper money until the Civil War. However, twice during the early years of the country it chartered a national bank authorized to do so. During the years that the First and Second Banks of the United States existed, a reliable paper currency circulated nationally in significant quantities. However, each of these banks was chartered for only twenty years, and for political reasons, neither of the charters was renewed by Congress. Various state-chartered banks also issued bank notes, but except for the years that the national banks existed, the lack of uniform regulation made these state bank issues inconsistent and unreliable. They were frequently accepted only at a discount any distance from the issuing bank, and were sometimes not redeemable even there. Bank-issued money will be discussed in more detail in the next chapter.

To help finance the Civil War, Congress authorized the issue of paper money officially known as United States notes, popularly called *greenbacks*. This was fiat money; the notes were legal tender, but were not redeemable for gold or silver. In addition, in 1863 Congress established the National Banking System, which authorized nationally chartered banks to issue notes. The national bank notes were carefully controlled, and were backed by government securities. In effect, Congress allowed newly chartered banks to issue paper money and lend it to the Treasury. This helped finance the war, and also provided another reliable source of paper money. At the same time notes of state banks, which had been a source of confusion in the economy because of their unreliability, were taxed out of existence. This produced, for the first time in this country, a uniform national currency.

In 1878, the Treasury began issuing silver certificates backed by silver stored in its vault. These certificates continued to serve as the principal small-denomination currency in circulation until 1967. In 1914, the Federal Reserve System began operations, and federal reserve notes replaced national bank notes. In 1967, federal reserve notes also replaced silver certificates. The Treasury had retired some of the United States notes after the Civil War, but about $300 million of these notes still remain in circulation. This is a trivial part of our currency, and they are now issued only as $100 bills. All other paper money has been retired, and, although a few bills may still be in circulation and are legal tender, they are removed from circulation if spotted by the Federal Reserve Banks. Thus federal reserve notes are the only paper currency of significance in the economy today.

Demand Deposits

The process of making exchange more and more convenient did not stop with the widespread use of paper money. Demand deposits have a long history, but their growth was especially rapid after the National Banking System was established and state banks could no longer issue bank notes. Rather than issuing a note in a specific denomination, a bank allows the holder of a deposit to transfer ownership of that deposit by means of a check—an order to the bank to make payment to another party. Today most transactions for any but small amounts are made by checks or share drafts drawn on banks or other depository institutions. Demand or checkable deposits take the advantages of paper money one step further. With these deposits, the holder does not physically hold (or risk losing) anything; checks can be safely sent in the mail and can be used to make payments in any specific amounts. Today, some of these deposits even earn interest. They currently make up the bulk of our money supply.

Electronic Funds Transfer Systems

Though not actually a form of money, *electronic funds transfer systems* (EFTS) greatly enhance the efficiency of the payments mechanisms used in our economy and thus can be considered another evolutionary step in our monetary system. With EFTS, individuals, businesses, and governments can receive and disburse funds electronically instead of through the use of checks. Transfers can be made between deposit accounts even nationwide, with a potential reduction or elimination of the physical handling of checks.

Several EFTS applications are currently in use. Employers can have their employees' wages deposited directly in their checking accounts, rather than issuing payroll checks. Individuals can have regular payments such as mortgage payments or insurance premiums automatically deducted from their accounts. Electronic funds transfers by telephone, for payment of utility bills, credit card balances, and so forth, are increasingly in use. The automated teller machine, which accepts deposits, arranges transfers between accounts, and dispenses cash, has also become commonplace.

THE MONETARY STANDARD AND THE VALUE OF MONEY

One of the functions of money is that it serves as a standard of value. Prices are stated in units of money, and an individual's wealth is frequently expressed in monetary terms. But the value of money lies in its purchasing power. When money was full-bodied, this was unambiguous, at least in terms of one commodity with widely recognized value. This is quite different from the case today, when the monetary unit is not fixed in terms of any commodity.

When gold coins made up the money supply, the value of money was constant in terms of gold. This, of course, did not guarantee a constant purchasing power of gold. For instance, after the discovery of America tons of gold flowed into Europe; prices there rose sharply in terms of gold. Nevertheless, this sudden increase in the availability of gold was an exceptional case. Throughout most of history, the value of gold has been stable enough to provide a useful standard of value. Silver has also served as a monetary standard in the past.

When representative paper money was issued, the standard remained the precious metal which the paper represented. Credit money that is easily redeemable for metal retains the value of that metal as its standard. Until 1900 the United States was officially on a bimetallic standard. However, because differences between the official values and the market values of the two metals made it difficult to keep them both in circulation at the same time, at first silver and later gold served as the de facto monetary standard. As long as people were confident that the paper money issued by the banks was redeemable for gold or silver, it retained the value of a certain weight of metal, and people were willing to hold and circulate the paper.

However, during the Civil War the government printed paper currency and temporarily suspended redemption in metal. We were in effect on an inconvertible paper standard. Although there was an implied promise to redeem these notes at some time in the future, no time was specified, and the U.S. notes became the standard money. National bank notes could be exchanged for U.S. notes, so these had equal purchasing power. However, metal coins virtually disappeared from circulation, and prices in terms of paper money rose dramatically. Although the value of gold and silver remained relatively stable with respect to other commodities, since the money in circulation could not be exchanged for the metals, its value became dependent on its general purchasing power, on its acceptability in trade, and on the amount of goods and services it could be exchanged for. This in turn depends on people's confidence in the monetary authority—confidence in both its restraint in maintaining the relative scarcity of the money and its ability to maintain its legal tender status. The dollars of both the Confederacy and the North lost value as paper money was printed and prices rose during the Civil War, but subsequently the U.S. notes regained their pre-war purchasing power while the value of Confederate money fell to zero.

The de facto gold standard was restored after the Civil War, but after a century of monetary experiments, both gold and silver have now been completely removed from any monetary role in our economy. The Treasury does own some gold and silver, but there is no minimum reserve of these metals backing any of our money. They are traded freely in markets just as are other commodities. Our monetary standard is the paper dollar, issued by the Federal Reserve System. No one doubts the ability of the government to enforce the legal status of the paper dollar; however, its purchasing power, and thus its value, depends on its relative scarcity. It is one of the responsibilities of the Federal Reserve to regulate the supply of money in order to maintain its purchasing power. Some level of growth in the money supply is necessary to support and sustain real economic growth in our free-enterprise system. At the same time, a too rapid money supply growth rate is believed to be inflationary. *Inflation* is a rise or increase in the prices of goods and services that is not offset by increases in the quality of those goods and services. An increase in the general price level of all goods and services in our economy leads to a decline in the purchasing power of money.

The importance of a monetary standard has been especially significant in international trade. Different nations have different currencies. Under a gold standard, all participating currencies are convertible to gold, therefore currency exchange rates are unambiguously determined. However, all major international trading nations have abandoned the gold standard and are effectively on paper standards. Gold does change hands in international trade, but its role is similar to the trading in any other commodity. It still serves widely as a store of wealth, but it is no longer a universal medium of exchange nor a unit of value.

Virtually all international transactions now involve the exchange of currencies or demand deposits denominated in various currencies, either for goods and services, for financial claims, or for each other. The value of one currency relative to another, or their *exchange rate*, depends on the supply of and demand for each currency relative to the other. The supply of a currency in international markets depends largely on the imports of the issuing country (how much of their currency they spend in world markets). Demand for a currency depends on the amount of exports that currency will buy from the issuing country. It also depends on the confidence of market participants in the restraint and stability of the monetary authority issuing the currency. If demand for a particular currency falls relative to its supply (because of, say, domestic inflation, political instability, or an excess of imports over exports) the exchange rate falls and the international purchasing power of that nation's money supply drops. On the other hand, if a currency is widely accepted the demand for it may be increased by the desire of people worldwide to hold it as an international medium of exchange. Such is the case of the U.S. dollar, which is widely held by foreigners because of its general acceptance and its ability to hold its value.

THE MONEY SUPPLY OR STOCK OF MONEY IN THE U.S. TODAY

No full-bodied or representative full-bodied money is in use in the United States today. All of our money is credit money. The Treasury issues token coins, and the Federal Reserve issues paper currency. The rest of the money supply is issued by depository institutions, and is held in checking accounts and similar deposits. As we have seen, the composition of the stock of money has changed over the years—and some of the most dramatic changes have been quite recent. Because of the proliferation of deposit accounts and other financial instruments, the question of how much money there is no longer has a simple answer. Before we can count the money supply, we must define precisely what we want to count.

Defining the Money Supply

There are two things we want to keep in mind in defining the money supply. First, we want to include in our definition those things that perform the functions of money, and exclude anything that does not. Second, we want the definition to be useful. We have already discussed the effect the money supply has on economic activity and the subsequent importance of controlling it. Our definition should correspond to some measurable quantity that is theoretically and observably related to economic activity. This implies that it should consist of a set of categories we can actually measure; it would do us no good to include components which cannot be counted or separated from accounts we want to exclude.

Money serves three functions: it is a standard of value, a medium of exchange, and a store of purchasing power. The standard of value in our system is the dollar. Many assets, including many financial assets, are evaluated in dollar units, but not all are money. (However, anything not measured in dollar units is disqualified— for example, gold is not money in our system.) Many things also serve as a store of value, including financial assets and many real assets. Many of these are preferable to money as long-term stores of wealth, either because they earn interest or otherwise increase in value, or because they provide a flow of services to the owner. However, if we hold an asset as a store of purchasing power, we need to consider its liquidity, or the ease with which it can be converted into other assets. No other asset is as liquid as money, because money is itself a medium of exchange. It does not need to be converted into anything else before it can be spent or used to make a payment. It is this last function that is the most helpful in narrowing our definition of the money supply.

However, even this criterion is not unambiguous in today's sophisticated financial system, where so many financial assets, such as various accounts at depository institutions, are so readily interchangeable. And when we consider the second requirement mentioned above, that our definition include a measurable set of assets which collectively has some relation to economic activity, our choice becomes less certain. Very generally, our reasoning goes like this. The money supply is a measure of purchasing power in the economy; we expect the amount of purchasing power to have some correspondence with the volume of transactions actually made, and this should correspond with other measures of economic activity. Historically we have observed this to be true, in general: too much money in circulation has led to an excessive amount of spending and has been inflationary; too little has restrained the economy and led to recession. We want to define the money supply to include those stores of purchasing power which have a close relationship with spending and other measures of economic activity.

We look to the Federal Reserve System as the ultimate authority in this matter. It has responsibility for controlling the money supply, and is also the source of most monetary data. Using the considerations discussed here, the Federal Reserve has come up with several alternative definitions of the money supply. The basic definition, M1, corresponds to the strict functional criteria above; that is, it comprises those assets which are themselves acceptable in exchange and are normally held with the intention of spending them in the immediate future. The second definition, M2, includes all of M1 plus a number of assets which may be held primarily as savings (for some more distant future expenditure) but which are readily convertible into M1 and thus may be held by some individuals or firms for immediate expenditure. In other words, M2 is a broader definition than M1, and is designed to be a more accurate measure of purchasing power. Although M1 more closely defines what we have traditionally considered money, some observers find M2 to be more consistently related to measures of economic activity. M3 is a still broader measure than M2, and a fourth measure is so broad and so far removed from our functional definition of money that the Federal Reserve designates it L, setting it off as a measure of liquid assets. L is a very broad measure of purchasing power, including everything in the other definitions plus a number of assets which can easily be sold to provide money for expenditures.

Measuring the Money Stock

Even if the Federal Reserve did not define and publish measures of the money supply, it would collect most of the data necessary to do so in performing its central banking functions. Figures collected from depository institutions are aggregated according to the definitions established, and money stock measures are published and released weekly. Since not all depository institutions report to the Federal Reserve every week, some estimation is necessary. These figures are then revised and adjusted as more complete information becomes available. A summary of the definitions of the money stock measures and the relationship among them is shown in Figure 2-1.

M1. The basic definition of the money supply, and the one referred to unless stated otherwise, is M1. It measures transactions balances, those sums of money that can be spent without first converting them to some other asset, and which are held for anticipated or unanticipated purchases or payments in the immediate future. These include currency (coin and federal reserve notes); demand deposits and other checkable deposits at banks, savings and loan associations, mutual savings banks and credit unions; and travelers' checks. Essentially, only those amounts that represent purchasing power of units in our economy other than the federal government are counted. Specifically excluded are vault cash and demand deposits of banks and other depository institutions, the Federal Reserve System, the federal government and foreign banks and governments. (The vault cash and deposits belonging to depository institutions do not represent purchasing power and are therefore not money, but they serve as reserves, an important

Figure 2-1
Definitions of Money
Supply Measures, and
Totals for September,
1982

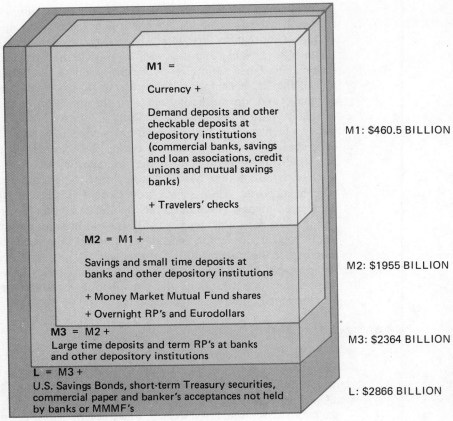

M1 =

Currency +

Demand deposits and other checkable deposits at depository institutions (commercial banks, savings and loan associations, credit unions and mutual savings banks)

+ Travelers' checks

M1: $460.5 BILLION

M2 = M1 +

Savings and small time deposits at banks and other depository institutions

+ Money Market Mutual Fund shares
+ Overnight RP's and Eurodollars

M2: $1955 BILLION

M3 = M2 +
Large time deposits and term RP's at banks and other depository institutions

M3: $2364 BILLION

L = M3 +
U.S. Savings Bonds, short-term Treasury securities, commercial paper and banker's acceptances not held by banks or MMMF's

L: $2866 BILLION

SOURCE: *Federal Reserve Bulletin*, February, 1983, p. A14.

element of our financial system which will be discussed in the next several chapters.) Adjustment is also made to avoid double counting of checks which are being processed.

Figure 2-2 shows the growth of M1 and its components from 1974 to 1982. The stock of money in September, 1982, as defined by M1, was $460.5 billion.[1] Demand deposits at commercial banks make up over half of this amount, but this share has been declining, especially since other checkable deposits were authorized nationwide by the Depository Institutions Deregulation and Monetary Control Act of 1980. Notice that demand deposits took a particularly sharp dip, and other checkable deposits a sharp jump, in the first few months of 1981, as depositors shifted funds to these newly authorized accounts. Other checkable deposits include negotiable order of withdrawal (NOW) accounts and share draft accounts, which pay interest but can be used to make payments by writing a check. The other important component, currency, has grown steadily and makes up just under 30 percent of the M1 money measure.

---

[1] *Federal Reserve Bulletin,* February, 1983, p. A14.

Figure 2-2

Money Stock M1 and
Its Components

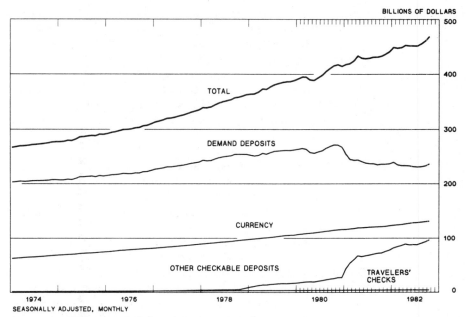

SEASONALLY ADJUSTED, MONTHLY

SOURCE: *Federal Reserve Chart Book,* November, 1982, p. 4.

M2. The Federal Reserve's second definition of the money stock, M2, is a broader measure of purchasing power than M1, and includes all of M1 plus several other types of highly liquid financial assets. Most of these other components are assets that provide their owners with a higher rate of return than would M1 components. These include savings deposits and small (under $100,000) time deposits at depository institutions, money market mutual fund (MMMF) shares, and some other very short-term money market instruments, overnight repurchase agreements, and Eurodollars.[2] Some of the owners of these assets hold them as long-term savings instruments. Since they are so liquid, however, some individuals and firms hold them even though they plan to spend the funds within a few days. M1 thus understates purchasing power by the amount of these M2 balances held for transaction purposes.

The components of M2 illustrate the difficulties the Federal Reserve has faced in drawing the boundaries of these definitions. For example, money market mutual funds provide limited check-writing privileges, and can therefore be used for transactions purposes. Some analysts argue on this basis that MMMF balances should be a part of M1. The Federal Reserve has included MMMF balances in M2 but not in M1, partly because they are so different from our traditional money components, and partly because they are believed to be used

---

[2]A repurchase agreement is essentially a way of making a loan. The lender buys an asset, usually securities, from the borrower, thus providing funds to the borrower. The borrower repays by buying back the asset at a prearranged time and price. Eurodollars are dollars deposited at banks outside the United States. Overnight repurchase agreements (RP's) and Eurodollars are repaid the next day; term RP's and Eurodollars are held for longer periods of time.

more as savings instruments than as transactions balances. On the other hand, it can be argued that small time deposits should be excluded from M2 because they are not, in practice, very liquid. Holders of these deposits who wish to cash them in before maturity are penalized by forfeiting some of the interest they have earned. However, small time deposits are included because they are considered to be close substitutes for some of the other savings instruments included in M2. As Figure 2-1 shows, M2 is over four times as large as M1, and small time deposits make up the bulk of the difference between the two money stock measures.

M3 and L. M3 includes all of M2 plus some large money market instruments, large (over $100,000) time deposits, and term repurchase agreements. These instruments are frequently held by corporations and wealthy individuals, allowing them to earn market rates of interest on large cash balances while still maintaining their liquidity.

L is the Federal Reserve's broadest measure of money available to the public. It adds to M3 a variety of liquid assets, including the public's holdings of U.S. savings bonds, short-term Treasury securities, commercial paper, and bankers' acceptances.[3] All of these represent stored purchasing power of their owners and are thus potentially related to economic activity. The relationship is an uncertain one, because some of the asset owners will hold these liquid assets for years, while others will convert them to cash and spend the funds within a few days. One reason the Federal Reserve defines so many measures of money and liquid wealth is that economists have different opinions as to which measure is most consistently related to spending and other economic activity.

We will see during the remaining chapters in Part I that a major objective of the Federal Reserve System is to regulate and control the supply of money and the availability of credit. The Federal Reserve sets target growth rates for M1, M2 and M3 (but not for L), and attempts to keep actual growth of these money stock measures close to the targets. This task, however, is not an easy one since the banking system has the capacity to expand or contract the money supply. Furthermore, we will see that there are other factors affecting the supply of money which are not under the control of our central bank.

Figure 2-3 illustrates the growth of M1, M2 and M3 during the period 1974–1982. As mentioned earlier, some growth of the money stock or supply is necessary to support and sustain real growth in our economy. However, a too rapid rate of money supply growth may be inflationary. In fact, most economists agree that rapid rates of growth of the money supply contributed to the high rate of inflation during the 1970s and early 1980s. It can be seen that M2 grew more rapidly than M1 by more than doubling in size over the 1974–1982 period, and M3 grew even faster.

Also notice that the M1 measure grew at an unsteady pace since 1980, while the other two measures grew more smoothly. Part of the reason for this is the decreasing regulation and increasing competition among financial institutions

---

[3]Commercial paper and bankers' acceptances are instruments of short-term business credit. They will be discussed in more detail in Chapters 9 and 20.

Figure 2-3

Money Stock
Measures, 1974–1982

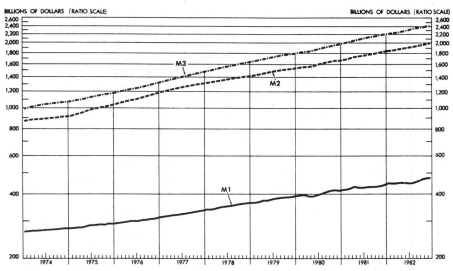

SOURCE: *Economic Indicators*, Council of Economic Advisors, January, 1983, p. 26.

which have led to the growth of new types of accounts. This evolution of the
financial system makes it increasingly difficult to define consistent measures of
the money supply. For example, during 1980 and 1981, money market mutual
funds grew rapidly because they paid a high rate of interest and were highly
liquid. As funds were shifted from demand deposits to MMMF's, M1 declined,
although no real change in purchasing power had taken place. M2 was not
affected by the shift, since both demand deposits and MMMF's are counted in
M2. More recently, beginning in 1983, a reverse shift has taken place as funds
have shifted from MMMF's into Super-NOW accounts, a type of account
offered by depository institutions which pays competitive interest rates and
which is counted in M1. Thus, different growth rates of the money supply
measures may result from the way they are defined. This is another reason why
the Federal Reserve keeps track of several measures of the money supply.

QUESTIONS

1. What are the basic functions of money?
2. Briefly describe the development of money, from barter to the use of precious metals.
3. What is meant by a bimetallic standard?
4. What is credit money? Also define fiat money and fiduciary money.
5. Define paper money and describe its development in the U.S.
6. What are some examples of current electronic funds transfer systems?
7. Describe the historical relationship between monetary standards and the value of money in the U.S.

8. What is the role of a monetary standard from an international trade standpoint?
9. What factors are important in defining the money supply?
10. Describe the M1 definition of the money supply or stock. Indicate the relative significance of the M1 components.
11. How does M2 differ from M1? Which measure is probably more closely related to economic activity?
12. Describe M3 and L measures of the money supply.

SUGGESTED READINGS

Bordo, Michael David. "The Classical Gold Standard: Some Lessons for Today." *Review*, Federal Reserve Bank of St. Louis (May, 1981), pp. 2–17.

Burke, William, and Yvonne Levy. *Silver: End of An Era.* Federal Reserve Bank of San Francisco, 1973.

Dewey, D. R. *Financial History of the United States,* 12th ed. New York: Longmans, Green & Company, 1934.

Friedman, Milton, and Anna J. Schwartz. *A Monetary History of the United States 1867–1960.* Princeton, New Jersey: Princeton University Press, 1963.

Kamerschen, David R. *Money and Banking*, 7th ed. Cincinnati: South-Western Publishing Co., 1980. Chapters 2 and 3.

Laughlin, J. L. *The History of Bimetallism in the United States.* New York: D. Appleton & Co., 1892.

Smith, Dolores S. "Electronic Fund Transfers." *Federal Reserve Bulletin* (April, 1980), pp. 290–296.

Tatom, John A. "Recent Financial Innovations: Have They Distorted the Meaning of M1?" *Review*, Federal Reserve Bank of St. Louis (April, 1982), pp. 23–32.

Wood, John H. "The Demise of the Gold Standard." *Economic Perspectives*, Federal Reserve Bank of Chicago (November/December, 1981), pp. 13–23.

3

Banking Structure and Operation

The importance of the nation's banking system to the processes of a modern industrial economy can hardly be exaggerated. The banking system is an integral part of the monetary system, accumulating and lending idle funds, facilitating the transfer of money, and providing for its safekeeping. An indication of the importance of the banking system to business is that nearly $400 billion was outstanding in loans to business by the banks of the United States at midyear 1983. The banking system also provides part of the long-term financing required by industry, by commerce, and by agriculture. It plays an important part, too, in financing the construction of the nation's millions of homes; and it is an important source for personal loans.

Although the various depository institutions of the nation, namely commercial banks, savings and loan associations, credit unions, and mutual savings banks, display a trend toward providing similar services, there remains enough of the unique character of each to distinguish easily among them. Further, it is through the commercial banking system that the principal influence of fiscal and monetary policy is carried out. It is for this reason that special emphasis is placed on commercial banking in any discussion of the nation's financial system.

In this chapter the development, the functions, and the organization of commercial banks are described, followed by a discussion of bank failures and insurance of bank deposits.

DEVELOPMENT OF BANKING IN THE UNITED STATES

The structure of the modern commercial banking system is the result of historical forces as well as of modern-day banking requirements. Banking, like most forms of economic activity, is more subject to the forces of tradition than to those of innovation. Yet, despite the great influence of early banking practices and legislation on present-day banking, the evolution of commercial banks to meet the requirements of the modern industrial economy has been effective and successful. Nor may we assume that the present structure of commercial banking has achieved permanence. To meet the requirements of a dynamic economy, changes are constantly taking place with respect to banking practices, regulation, and legislation. An understanding of banking in the United States today, therefore, requires an understanding of the development of banking in the economic history of the country.

Banking in America Before the Civil War

Early banking in the United States developed under circumstances that explain much of the apparent confusion and difficulty that accompanied such development. The population lived for the most part on farms; families were self-sufficient; and transportation and communications were poor. The friction between proponents of a strong central government as opposed to state government existed in the early years of our history as it does today. Much controversy raged over the power to charter and regulate banks. The country had little experience in money and financial management.

Early Chartered Banks. During the colonial period, banking took the form of small unincorporated banks that were established to ease the shortage of capital in businesses. Their operations consisted largely in the issue of their own notes. Outside of the larger towns, deposit banking was of minor significance. It was not until 1782 that the first incorporated bank was created along modern lines. The Bank of North America was established then in Philadelphia by Robert Morris to assist in the financing of the Revolutionary War. This bank set a good example for successful banking. Its notes served as a circulating monetary medium, it loaned liberally to the United States government, and it redeemed its own notes in specie upon demand. Two years later the Bank of Massachusetts and the Bank of New York were established. These three incorporated banks constituted the total of such banks until 1790.

The First Bank of the United States. Alexander Hamilton, the first Secretary of the Treasury of the United States, had for several years harbored the idea of a federally chartered bank that would adequately support the rapidly growing economy and would give financial assistance to the government during its crises. His recommendations were submitted to the House of Representatives of the United States in 1790, and in 1791 a 20-year charter was issued to the First Bank of the United States. Although this bank served the nation effectively in the issuance of notes, in the transfer of funds from region to region, in providing useful service to the government, and in curbing the excessive note issues of state banks by presenting such notes periodically for redemption, strong opposition existed to the renewal of its charter; and it ceased operations in 1811. The antagonism of state banking interests was an important cause of the failure of the Bank to have its charter renewed.

Following the expiration of the charter of the First Bank of the United States, the number of state banks increased rapidly, as did the volume of their note issues. Most of the state banks ceased redeeming their notes in gold and silver, and the abuses of banking privileges were extensive.

The Second Bank of the United States. The Second Bank of the United States was chartered primarily to restore order to the chaotic banking situation that had developed after the First Bank of the United States ceased operations. Like the First Bank of the United States, it received a 20-year charter. It began operations in 1816 and, after a short period of mismanagement, set upon a course of reconstruction of sound banking practices. It ably served individuals, businesses, and the government by accepting deposits, making loans, issuing notes, and restraining the note-issuing practices of state banks by presenting periodically the notes of such banks for redemption. The Second Bank of the United States also played a most important and efficient role as fiscal agent for the government.

In 1833 President Andrew Jackson and many of his associates embarked upon such a vigorous campaign against the Second Bank of the United States that it became apparent that its charter would not be renewed upon expiration in 1836. Not until 1863 was another bank in the United States to receive a federal charter.

State Banks from 1836 to the Civil War. Following expiration of the Second Bank's charter, the excesses that had plagued the period 1811–1816 again came into play. This period is characterized as one of "wildcat" banking. Although many state banks operated on a conservative and very sound basis, the majority of them engaged in risky banking practices through excessive note issues, lack of adequate bank capital, and insufficient reserves against their notes and deposits.

Because the notes of even the well-established banks were often of inferior quality, it was easy for skillful counterfeiters to increase the denomination of notes. Also, because of the poor communications that existed between various sections of the country, it was quite often difficult for a banker to be certain of the nature of the notes presented for payment. Skillfully prepared counterfeit notes frequently circulated with greater freedom than did the legitimate notes of weak and little-known banks.

In spite of the many abuses of state banks during this period, New York, Massachusetts, and Louisiana originated banking legislation of a highly commendable nature, much of which provided the basis for the establishment of the National Banking System in 1863.

The National Banking System

In 1863 the National Banking Act again made it possible for banks to receive federal charters. So many amendments were submitted for the improvement of the National Banking Act of 1863 that it was repealed in its entirety in 1864. The National Banking Act of June 3, 1864, represented a complete revision of the Act of 1863. This legislation provided the basis for our present national banking laws.

As for the First Bank and the Second Bank of the United States, the reasons for federal interest in the banking system were to provide for a sound banking system and to curb the excesses of the state banks. Probably an important additional purpose of this legislation was to provide for the financing of the Civil War. Secretary of the Treasury Salmon P. Chase and others believed that government bonds could be sold to these nationally chartered banks, which could in turn issue their own notes based in part on the government bonds so purchased.

Through the National Banking Act, various steps were taken to promote safe banking practices. Among other things, minimum capital requirements were established for banks with federal charters, loans were regulated with respect to safety and liquidity, a system of supervision and examination was instituted, and minimum reserve requirements against notes and deposits were established. These reform measures, in general, were constructive; but, in some instances, they have been regarded as altogether too restrictive, as in the case of forbidding loans against real estate. Much of the criticism of the national banking system, in fact, was derived from the inflexibility of its limitations, many of which were either modified or eliminated in 1913 with the establishment of the Federal Reserve System.

The National Banking Act did not establish a system of central banks; it only made possible the chartering of banks by the federal government. The Federal Reserve Act of 1913 brought to the American economy a system of central banks. The Federal Reserve System was designed to eliminate many of the weaknesses that had persisted under the National Banking Act and to increase the effectiveness of commercial banking in general. It brought with it not only strong central domination of banking practices but also many services to commercial banks. The influence of the Federal Reserve System is described in Chapter 4.

The Depository Institutions Deregulation and Monetary Control Act

The changing character of the economy and the demands placed on the banks and other financial institutions require a constant evolution. The Commission on Money and Credit, created in 1958, was sponsored by those who wanted the nation's financial institutions regulated differently. Although no legislation resulted from the efforts of this Commission, its final report advocated increased regulation and control by the Federal Reserve System.

The Hunt Commission, a special governmental task force created as a result of a recommendation by the President in his 1970 Economic Report, was charged with the responsibility of recommending changes in the existing structure of banking and other financial institutions. The recommendations of this Commission were similar to those of the Commission on Money and Credit and, as in the case of those recommendations, no legislation resulted.

In 1980, President Carter signed into law the Depository Institutions Deregulation and Monetary Control Act. This Act represents a major step toward deregulating banking in the United States, introducing competition on an equal basis in the provision of all types of banking services. The Act is designed to improve the effectiveness of monetary policy by applying new reserve and reporting requirements set by the Board of Governors of the Federal Reserve System for nearly all depository institutions and by generally eliminating distinctions between member banks and other depository institutions. The provisions of the Act (hereafter, the Monetary Control Act) will be referred to frequently as the many areas of its influence are discussed throughout the book.

FUNCTIONS OF COMMERCIAL BANKS

The basic functions of the modern commercial bank are (1) the acceptance of deposits and (2) the granting of loans to business borrowers and to others. In accepting deposits, the commercial bank provides an alternative to the hoarding of funds for future use on the part of the public. Individuals and businesses seldom wish to spend their money as it becomes available; and without the depository facilities of the bank, such funds may lie idle. Having accumulated deposits, the commercial bank puts them to use through loans to persons and businesses having immediate use for them. The result of the pooling of funds by the commercial banks is a more effective utilization of funds.

Corollary to the acceptance of deposits by commercial banks are the functions of (3) safekeeping for depositors, (4) the efficient and economical transfer of claims to deposits through check-writing procedures, and (5) the record of transactions provided the depositor through the regular bookkeeping and reporting procedures of the bank.

In the granting of business loans, the commercial bank accomplishes a desirable objective of (6) selection of risks. The banker's refusal to finance an ill-conceived venture is in the interest of the bank in protecting its assets, but it may also be in the interest of the prospective operators of the new venture, preventing them from engaging in an activity that will result in loss to them. Furthermore, the careful apportionment of loan funds to those businesses with the best apparent chances of success makes possible the development of the nation's resources to the greatest possible advantage.

COMMERCIAL BANK ASSETS AND SOURCES OF FUNDS

The assets of the typical commercial bank and the sources of the funds with which these assets are acquired are shown in Figure 3-1.

Bank Assets

The principal assets of a commercial bank are cash, securities, and loans.

Cash. Cash includes funds in the bank's vaults, in a federal reserve bank, and in correspondent banks. A bank must keep a certain minimum of vault cash to meet the day-to-day currency requirements of the bank's customers. The amount of such cash requirements may be small relative to the total of a bank's resources for the simple reason that the typical day's operation will result in approximately the same amount of cash deposits as cash withdrawals. A margin of safety, however, is required to take care of those periods when for one reason or another withdrawals exceed deposits.

The appropriate amount of cash that a bank should carry depends largely upon the character of its banking operations and on the distance of the bank from its depository for legal reserves. For example, a bank that has a few very large accounts might be expected to have a larger volume of unanticipated withdrawals

Figure 3-1
Commercial Bank
Assets and Sources
of Funds

Commercial Bank Assets	Commercial Bank Sources of Funds

Cash:
    Vault cash and cash items in
        process of collection
    In Federal Reserve Bank
    In correspondent banks
	Deposits:
	    U.S. government deposits
	    Other demand deposits
	    Savings and time deposits

Securities:
    U.S. government securities
    Other public securities and bonds
    Capital stock of the Federal
        Reserve Bank
	Other Liabilities and Deferred Credits:
	    Discounts collected but not
	        earned
	    Funds borrowed from Federal
	        Reserve Bank

Loans:
    Secured loans
    Unsecured loans and discounts
    Real estate loans on first mortgages
	Bank Capital Funds:
	    Capital stock
	    Surplus
	    Undivided profits

Other Bank Assets:
    Accrued interest on bonds and
        notes
    Bank buildings and furniture
    Prepaid expenses	

(and deposits) than a bank that has only small individual accounts. An erratic volume of day-to-day withdrawals requires, of course, a larger cash reserve. A bank that is located a great distance from its depository for legal reserves also must maintain larger cash reserves than a bank that can in a matter of minutes or hours draw on such reserves.

The second cash item, designated "in Federal Reserve Bank," is considerably greater than vault cash. Members of the Federal Reserve System are required to keep a percentage of their deposits as minimum reserves either with the federal reserve banks of their districts or in the form of vault cash. As withdrawals are made and total deposit balances decrease, the amount of the required reserves also decreases. These reserves that have been freed may be used by the bank to help meet withdrawal demands.

The Monetary Control Act referred to earlier provides for the imposition of uniform reserve requirements on all depository institutions in order to enhance monetary control as well as competitive fairness. Nonmember depository institutions are being phased up to a full reserve requirement over an eight-year period.

Cash "in correspondent banks" refers to the common practice of keeping substantial deposits with other banks, particularly banks in large cities. Such correspondent relations with other banks facilitate the clearing of drafts and other credit instruments, and provide an immediate access to information regarding the money markets of the large cities.

Securities. Securities comprise the second major group of bank assets. These securities held by the bank include those of the United States government, those of state governments, and of municipalities. Also included are other bonds and capital stock of the Federal Reserve Bank. The bonds owned by this bank are held as investments. The capital stock of the Federal Reserve Bank owned by the bank is a requirement for all member banks of the Federal Reserve System.

Loans. The third group of asset items includes several classifications of loans: first, those loans that are payable on demand and which are secured; second, those secured loans that have definite maturities; third, and by far the most important, unsecured loans and discounts with definite maturities; and finally, real estate loans on first mortgages.

In a *secured loan*, specific property is pledged as collateral for the loan. In the event of the failure of the borrower to repay the loan, the bank has recourse to the assets pledged as collateral for the loan. In all cases, the borrower is required to sign a note specifying the details of the indebtedness; but unless specific assets are pledged for the loan, it is classified as unsecured. An *unsecured loan* represents a general claim against the assets of the borrower. It is the typical arrangement between the businesses of the community and the bank whereby periodic amounts are borrowed for the purposes of meeting a payroll, accumulating an inventory, or for other short-term working capital purposes. This section reflects the most important single activity of the commercial bank and, except for the real estate component, it has often been thought to be the sole type of activity in which the commercial banks should be permitted to engage. Through these loans, the bank has gained its reputation as being the most important single source of short-term funds for businesses. During World War II, however, banks were encouraged to purchase large quantities of United States government securities. In the period immediately following World War II, United States government obligations constituted 72 percent of bank loans and investments. There has been a strong trend toward loans relative to investments since that time, and since the mid-fifties, loans have again been the largest category of bank assets. The sharp increase in loan proportion since 1973 is reflected in Figure 3-2. Earnings from interest on loans account for approximately 65 percent of total banking earnings.

The distinction between a loan and a discount is an important one. A loan customarily includes a specified rate of interest that must be paid with the principal amount of the loan at the maturity of the loan contract. With a discount arrangement, a deduction is made from the face amount of the note at the time the money is loaned. The borrower receives less than the face of the note, but repays the full amount of the note when it matures.

A given discount rate means a higher real cost of borrowing than an interest loan made for the same rate. This is true because under the discount arrangement less actual money is received by the borrower, although the amount paid for its use is the same. For example, if $500 is borrowed on a loan basis at an interest rate of 10 percent for one year, at the maturity of the loan $500 plus $50 interest is repaid. On the other hand, if the $500 is borrowed on a discount basis and the rate is 10 percent, a deduction of $50 from the face of the note is made and the

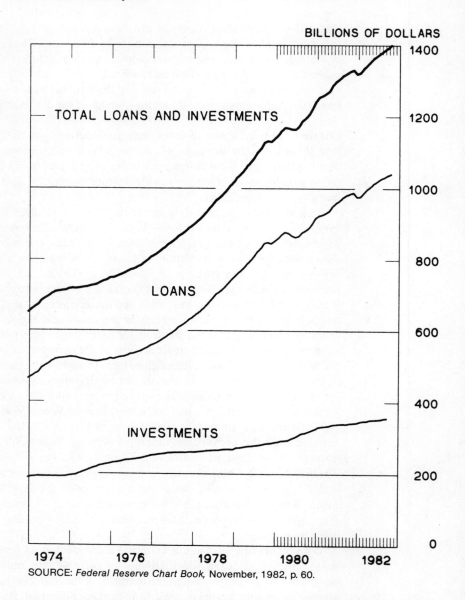

Figure 3-2

Loans and Investments
of Commercial Banks

SOURCE: *Federal Reserve Chart Book,* November, 1982, p. 60.

borrower receives only $450. At the end of the year, the lender pays the face amount of the note, $500. In the first case, the borrower has paid $50 for the use of $500; in the second case, $50 has been paid for the use of only $450. The effective rate of interest, therefore, on the discount basis is approximately 11.1 percent in contrast with the even 10 percent paid when the $500 was borrowed on a loan basis.

Other Bank Assets. The remaining assets are of less importance than the foregoing groups. They include interest accrued on bonds and notes earned but not yet received, bank buildings and furniture, and prepaid expenses such as insurance premiums paid in advance and the purchase of supplies.

Commercial Bank Sources of Funds

There are two major sources of the funds with which banks acquire their assets. Capital funds represent the initial investment and accumulated profits of the owners of the bank. Liabilities represent the funds owed to depositors and others from whom the bank has borrowed.

The most important liability of a commercial bank consists of its deposits of various kinds, but a bank's other liabilities should be understood also.

Deposits. Several types of deposits—traditionally grouped as demand, savings, and time deposits—make up the principal liabilities of all commercial banks. Demand deposits are the regular checking accounts of individuals, businesses and other institutions. Such deposits may be withdrawn on demand; that is, the bank agrees to pay the depositor immediately when requested to do so. The depositor normally requests the bank to make payment to another party, by means of a check.

In practice, banks also make savings deposits immediately available to depositors on demand, but they are legally permitted to require written notification up to thirty days in advance of withdrawal. All savings deposits, as well as time deposits, earn interest. Most time deposits are represented by printed receipts called *certificates of deposit* (CD's) which have a stated maturity and either pay a fixed rate of interest or are sold at a discount. A smaller category of time deposits is time accounts, which include special club accounts such as Christmas and vacation savings clubs.

Although records reveal that commercial banks issued certificates of deposit as early as 1900, a major innovation in the early 1960s has resulted in a vastly increased importance for them. This innovation was the issuance of "CD's" (certificates of deposit) in negotiable form. The negotiability feature was not totally unknown before that time; but negotiable CD's were so seldom issued that it was difficult to sell them in the general money markets. Along with the vastly increased use of negotiable CD's in the 1960s there came into existence a secondary market for them. Today, CD's as issued by banks are purchased and sold in the money markets as readily as most forms of debt obligations. The commercial banks of the nation have used negotiable CD's as a means of attracting vastly increased sums of deposits of business corporations and other institutions.

Until recent years there was a precise and easily identified distinction between noninterest-bearing checking account deposits and interest-bearing savings and time deposits. This distinction has now been significantly modified. In the early 1970s nonbank thrift institutions in New England were permitted to issue "negotiable orders of withdrawal" referred to generally as NOW's. These check-like facilities had the effect of providing a near substitute for interest-bearing checking accounts. They resulted in such effective competition for bank deposits that banks resorted to such devices as the automatic transfer of funds from savings to checking accounts under certain conditions. Thus, checks written by customers for amounts in excess of their checking account deposits could be covered by the automatic transfer of funds in their savings account to their checking account. These adaptations of commercial banks to meet the competition of interest-bearing check-like facilities by nonbank depositories came to an end with the enactment of the Monetary Control Act. Effective December 31, 1980, banks and nonbank depositories alike were authorized to issue NOW accounts for individuals and not-for-profit institutions. "Automatic transfer savings account" (ATS) and "share drafts" at credit unions were also authorized. The rapid growth of these interest-bearing checking instruments has resulted in intense competition among depository institutions for deposits.

Another landmark banking law, signed by President Reagan on October 15, 1982, provides for even greater attraction of funds by banks and certain thrift institutions. Known as the Garn–St. Germain Depository Institutions Act of 1982, the legislation provides the opportunity to offer a money market deposit account that is "directly equivalent to and competitive with money market mutual funds." These accounts have no interest-rate ceilings and, since they are insured up to $100,000, the competition for funds against money market mutual funds which are not insured should be most effective. This legislation provides for a host of other important changes in the regulation of financial institutions; it is difficult to exaggerate its importance.

Other Liabilities and Deferred Credits. The second category of liabilities is represented by items having a far smaller dollar significance than that of deposits. In brief, these include liabilities not yet payable and the receipt of fees and other charges for which service has not yet been rendered. Funds borrowed from the Federal Reserve Bank or other banks are also reflected here.

Bank Capital Funds

The capital funds category includes capital stock, surplus, and undivided profits. At the time a bank is formed capital stock is purchased by the promoters of the bank or by the public. From time to time additional stock may be sold to accommodate bank expansion. Surplus is accumulated from the sale of stock at a price above its par value and may include a part of retained earnings. When dividends are paid, the undivided profits section is reduced. These capital accounts constitute the total capital funds of a bank.

On the balance sheets of many banks today, there is to be found in the capital funds section an item designated as *capital notes*. These notes, always subordinated to the claims of bank depositors, reflect long-term borrowing on the part of the bank for purposes of bolstering the capital section. Although, like deposits, they are liabilities of the banks that issue them, reserve requirements do not apply to them. The Comptroller of the Currency of the United States, in its regulation of national banks, and the bank regulatory authorities of many states consider capital notes to be a part of the capital accounts in determining the adequacy of bank capital. The Board of Governors of the Federal Reserve

System, on the other hand, has taken a far less liberal view of such long-term debt and generally ignores capital notes in the measurement of capital adequacy.

Although a large volume of assets and deposits makes possible greater earnings for the stockholders of the bank, the larger the volume in relation to the capital contribution of the stockholders, the smaller the margin of safety for depositors. While the initial function of bank capital is to provide for the buildings and equipment necessary for operations, it serves also as a cushion for possible bank losses. The depositors of a bank, in fact, are creditors and hence have a claim prior to that of the stockholders in case of liquidation. The depositors of a bank lose nothing until the entire stockholder contribution and accumulation is exhausted.

When the assets or deposits of a bank are high in relation to capital funds, it may be said that the stockholders are assuming a small proportion of the risk of the bank and the depositors a large share of the risk. When the deposits of a bank are low relative to its capital funds, the bank will probably be in a poor position to pay satisfactory dividends to the stockholders unless the assets of the bank provide an unusually high yield.

The composition of a bank's earning assets is more important than the simple relationship between the volume of deposits and its capital funds. For example, if the bulk of a bank's deposits and capital is invested in government bonds, high-grade municipal securities, and government guaranteed real estate mortgages, the high ratio between total deposits and capital funds is not so serious as would be the case if the bank had the bulk of its funds invested in less secure assets. By the same token, if a bank has most of its earning assets invested in extremely safe securities, the yield from such investments will be rather modest; and a high ratio between total deposits and capital funds will be necessary in order to avail the stockholders of a competitive rate of return on their investment. For regulatory purposes, authorities now place primary emphasis on a careful examination of the quality of bank assets rather than on a simple application of such ratios as assets at risk to capital or deposits to capital. Irrespective of quality, however, banks are under regulatory pressure to maintain capital in an amount equal to at least 5 percent of total assets.

CONCENTRATION IN BANKING CONTROL

Concentration in banking control has taken a number of forms as banks, like other businesses, have increased their scope and volume of operations to accommodate the growing economy. The changes in the structure of the American banking system have been especially significant since 1970. Yet commercial banks in the United States are typically single-unit organizations, each bank having its own board of directors and stockholders, exercising no control over branch offices, and in turn being responsible to no parent organization. At midyear 1982, of the 14,752 commercial banks in the nation, 7,917 were independent units. The trend, however, is strongly toward branch banking or bank holding company arrangements. These two forms of banking concentration are discussed below.

Branch Banking

Branch banks are those banking offices that are controlled by a single parent bank. One board of directors and one group of stockholders control the home office and the branches. Some of our branch banking systems are very small, involving perhaps only two, three, or four branches. Others are quite large, extending over an entire state and having many branches. The laws of some states prevent the operation of branch banking. Other states permit the operation of branch offices only within limited areas, and still others permit branch operation on a statewide scale.

One of the most important merits of branch banking is that branch banking systems are less likely to fail than are independent unit banks. In a branch banking system, more adequate diversification of investments can be made, and the temporary reverses of a single community are not so likely to cause complete failure of the entire banking chain. This would be true primarily of those branch systems that operate over wide geographical areas rather than in a single metropolitan area. The independent bank cannot rely on other banks to offset local economic reverses.

It is on this score that branch banking operations appear to have their strongest argument, for the record of bank failures in the United States has been one of which the banking system as a whole cannot be proud; but there have been few failures in those systems of banks that have engaged in branch banking practices. Opponents of this form of banking have pointed out, however, that failure of a system of banks, although less frequent, is far more serious.

In addition to the matter of safety, a system of branch banks may provide more adequate banking service to the local community than the independently owned bank because it may draw on the resources of its other branches. The independently owned unit bank, of course, may have access to larger banks for assistance when requests are made for loans beyond the capacity of the bank.

Other advantages claimed for branch banking systems are the greater convenience to customers that results from the prompt placement of branches in newly developed centers of population, the greater uniformity of interest rates throughout the areas of branch banking activities due to the mobility of funds from branch to branch, and the operational advantages of bigness in business activity. For example, it may be possible to achieve economies through the large-scale purchase of bank supplies, through the establishment of elaborate operating systems, through the extensive training of personnel, and through the employment of more competent management.

Among the objections to branch banking are the fear of concentration in control of banking operations, the lack of sincere interest in community affairs of branch managers who may be transferred to other areas, the possibility of loan delays while awaiting approval from main offices, and the possible withdrawal of funds from small towns and rural areas for the benefit of larger cities.

These objections lack substance in the light of experience both in this country and in Canada. Although branch banking does result in some degree of concentration of control, competition remains intense in branch banking areas. With respect to delays in loan approvals, most branch bank managers have the authority to approve practically all loan applications coming to them and can facilitate approval of most of the remaining applications by telephone. Since branch managers establish a successful record of operations through cooperation with and service to the communities which they serve, it is doubtful that lack of interest in local affairs would exist. Finally, the flow of funds from rural areas to the cities is contrary to normal expectations; typically, the higher interest rates prevailing in rural areas result in a flow of funds from the cities to these areas.

The importance of branch banking has grown rapidly in several states. At the end of 1951, branches accounted for only 26 percent of all bank offices. At year-end 1980, branches accounted for nearly 75 percent of all banking offices. The change in the number of banks and branches is shown in Figure 3-3.

Figure 3-3
Banks and Branches
Since 1915

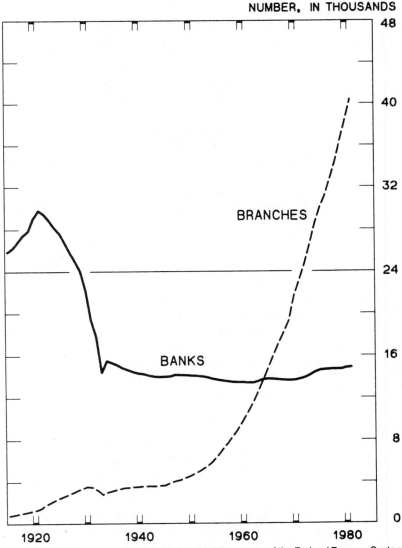

SOURCE: *1982 Historical Chart Book*, Board of Governors of the Federal Reserve System, p. 82.

In contrast with banking in the United States, the branch banking system is predominant in Canada and Britain. Canada's five largest chartered banks, through their thousands of branches, hold approximately 90 percent of all bank assets in that country. England has approximately 13 incorporated banks, of which 5 account for most of the deposits of that nation. These incorporated banks operate more than 8,000 branches throughout that country. The record of bank failures in both Canada and England is far superior to the record in the United States in spite of the fact that those countries have also been subject to extreme economic pressures.

Bank Holding Companies

The bank holding company is a device whereby two or more individual banks are controlled through a company that holds the voting control of the individual banks. The policies of banks thus controlled by such a holding company are determined by the parent company and coordinated for the purposes of that organization. The holding company itself may or may not engage in direct banking activities, and the banks that are controlled by the holding company may operate branches.

Little control was exercised over bank holding companies until the depression years of the early 1930s. Bank holding companies did not come within the jurisdiction of either state or federal control unless they also engaged directly in banking operations. The Banking Act of 1933 and the Securities Acts of 1933 and 1934 imposed limited control on bank holding companies, but it remained for the Bank Holding Company Act of 1956 to establish clear control of such operations. This Act defined a *bank holding company* as one which directly or indirectly owns, controls, or holds the power to vote 25 percent or more of the voting shares of each of two or more banks. The Bank Holding Company Act Amendments of 1966 established uniform standards for the evaluation of the legality of bank holding company acquisitions. But it remained for the Bank Holding Company Amendments of 1970 to provide the base for modern-day bank operations. These amendments provide that bank holding companies can make acquisitions of companies having activities "closely related to banking." Such closely related activities include mortgage, finance, credit card, or factoring subsidiaries. They can have industrial bank or industrial loan company subsidiaries. They can have subsidiaries that service loans, conduct fiduciary activities, or lease personal property. They can have subsidiaries that make equity or debt investments in corporations designed to promote community welfare. They can have subsidiaries that provide bookkeeping or data processing services or that furnish economic or financial information. They can have insurance agency subsidiaries and can underwrite credit life and credit accident and health insurance. And they can have subsidiaries that act as investment or financial advisors to mutual funds and mortgage or real estate investment trusts.

By the end of 1980, 74 percent of domestic commercial banking assets were held by subsidiary banks of bank holding companies. The total number of banks controlled by multibank holding companies increased from 723 in 1969 to 2,426 in 1980. The number of multibank holding companies increased from 86 to 361 during this period. The increase in the number of subsidiary banks was concentrated in a relatively small number of unit banking or limited branching states. Figure 3-4 shows the percent of commercial banking deposits held by multibank holding companies, and also shows branch banking provisions by state.

BANK FAILURES AND DEPOSIT INSURANCE

Like all forms of business enterprise, the commercial bank is subject to failure when improper management or unfortunate economic conditions prevail for a long enough period of time. Furthermore, the commercial bank must enjoy the complete confidence of the public. Commercial banks secure their profits largely through the investment of funds that have been deposited with them for safe-keeping. These invested funds are necessarily unavailable for a period of time; and immediate withdrawal demand by a large number of depositors, because of a lack of confidence or other reasons, inevitably would lead a commercial bank to insolvency unless help were forthcoming from other quarters. It is necessary, therefore, for the sound and continued operation of a bank that its customers retain confidence in the bank.

The failure of one bank in a community may precipitate the loss of confidence in other banks in the same area, giving rise to panic and demands for withdrawals. Bank failures not only present a hardship to individual depositors but also materially affect business within the community. The smooth flow of business intercourse is interrupted by bank failures through the loss of confidence on the

Figure 3-4
Percent of Commercial Banking Deposits Held by Multibank Holding Companies and Branch Bank Limitations by State, 1980

SOURCE: *Federal Reserve Bulletin,* February, 1982, p. 81.

part of the bankers themselves in their ability to meet withdrawals. Few new business loans may be made, and many existing loans may be called or renewal refused.

Whatever the causes of bank failures, until recent decades the rate of failures in the United States was as high as, or higher than, that in any other highly industrialized country of the world. This had been an intolerable situation for the simple reason that a smoothly operating and highly efficient system of commercial banks is essential to the development of our industrial potential.

Early State Plans for Insurance of Bank Notes and Deposits

The federal system of deposit insurance has been in existence for fifty years, but state plans of insurance date back more than a century before that. New York adopted such a plan in 1829, and several other states followed shortly thereafter. The emphasis of these early plans was the insurance of notes issued by the banks, since bank notes played a dominant role as the circulating medium of the period. Several states, however, also provided insurance for the deposits of bank customers. These early state plans disappeared after the passage of the National Banking Act, when the federal government placed a prohibitive tax on state bank notes and thereby ended their issuance. State bank failures still occurred, however, and several states established bank insurance plans for the protection of depositors after the banking panic of 1907.

Each of the state plans raised funds to cover the losses of banks that failed by collecting a contribution or assessment from all participating banks. In some cases, the participating banks were permitted to retain their proportionate contribution until funds were actually needed to cover the liabilities of a failed bank. In other cases contributions were collected to establish a safety fund administered by an agency of the state.

All of these various state plans of deposit insurance failed. Among the reasons for their failure is the fact that supervision of the plans was generally faulty. Also, generally distressed conditions caused more bank failures than had been anticipated, which created an undue strain on the rather meager resources of the insurance plans. Finally, in most of the states that established deposit insurance plans, there was economic dependence primarily upon one agricultural crop with little diversification to offset the risk resulting from a poor year or two for that crop.

Following the stock market crash in 1929 and the accompanying large number of bank failures, there again developed an insistent demand for some form of deposit insurance. This demand followed each such period of major bank failures. A total of 150 bills for guaranty or insurance were introduced in Congress from 1886 to 1933. The proponents of a federal system of deposit insurance finally exercised considerable influence. They contended that in spite of the failure of the state plans of deposit insurance, a plan established on a national basis would prove successful as a result of the diversification it would entail—diversification that would permit one or more sectors of the economy or geographical areas to experience difficulty, while the system of deposit insurance would remain sound.

The proponents also argued that, if established on a federal basis under very strict supervision and with liberal provision for the accumulation of a reserve from which losses could be met, the chances of success on the part of the deposit insurance fund would be considerably enhanced. Also, they alleged that many of the difficulties which the commercial banks of the country faced resulted from the intense competition between national banks and state banks. A federal system of deposit insurance that would permit participation by both state banks and national banks would tend to eliminate much of this competition and provide a sounder basis for banking operations.

The Federal Deposit Insurance Corporation

The forcefulness of the arguments by the proponents of a national plan of deposit insurance and the intense demand of the general public for such protection caused the Congress to adopt a temporary form of deposit insurance to become effective in 1934. The plan, which resulted from the Steagall Amendment to the Glass Bill of 1933, received the support of a large majority in both houses of Congress. This first plan of federal deposit insurance provided protection of deposits up to $2,500 for each depositor. It continued in effect until 1935, during which time the various interested parties in Congress managed to reach agreement on the form of operation of a permanent plan of deposit insurance. The permanent plan provided for the establishment of a corporation to be known as the Federal Deposit Insurance Corporation. The stock was to be held jointly by the United States Treasury and the federal reserve banks.

Sources of Capital. The Secretary of the Treasury subscribed to $150 million of stock of the Federal Deposit Insurance Corporation (hereafter referred to as the FDIC), and each federal reserve bank was required to subscribe for an amount equal to one half of its surplus on January 1, 1933. The total stock purchased by the Treasury and the federal reserve banks was approximately $290 million. This stock did not provide for voting privileges nor for the payment of dividends. For the purpose of meeting emergency financial claims against it, the FDIC was authorized to issue debentures in an amount aggregating not more than three times the sum of its paid-in capital stock plus the amount received as assessments from insured banks. All capital stock of the FDIC has now been retired. Although part of the original stock of the FDIC was purchased by the federal reserve banks, the Corporation is not a part of the Federal Reserve System. The FDIC has its own board of directors of three members. One of these is the Comptroller of the Currency of the United States Department of the Treasury, and the other two are appointed by the President with the advice and consent of the Senate. The term of office is six years.

Deposit Protection. Until 1950 the maximum amount of deposit insurance afforded each account under the permanent plan of deposit insurance was $5,000, and this limit has been increased periodically since then, most recently on March 31, 1980, to $100,000. The costs of such deposit insurance are borne by the member banks of the insurance system.

Although membership in the FDIC is necessary for all banks holding national charters and for member banks of the Federal Reserve System, membership is available for state banks that are not members of the Federal Reserve System. On

December 31, 1982, 97 percent of the nation's banks were insured by the FDIC. To protect depositors in state banks from having insurance withdrawn arbitrarily without notice to the depositors, it is provided that although the insured status of a bank is terminated when it ceases to be a member bank of the insurance system, for two years thereafter the bank remains liable for assessments and retains the insurance on insured deposits held by it when it ceased to be a member bank. Deposits received by such a bank after its insured status has been terminated are, of course, not protected under this provision.

The FDIC serves not only to minimize and eliminate the hardships resulting from bank failures, but also to establish sound banking practices and to minimize the chance of such losses developing in the first place. It is empowered, among other things, to pass on applications for deposit insurance, to examine and supervise the general operations of member banks, and to make loans to insured banks or facilitate mergers or consolidations of banks when such actions are in the interest of the depositors.

Evaluation of the Federal Deposit Insurance Corporation. The FDIC has served a very useful purpose. Having minimized the hardships of loss to depositors in the banks that have failed during the history of the FDIC, the Corporation has also contributed to the present high degree of public confidence in the banking system in general. Such confidence is an essential factor in the successful operation of any banking system.

Among the criticisms of the present system of deposit insurance are the claims that the premiums paid by the banks are too high, that the FDIC could not withstand the financial pressure resulting from a major depression, and the fact that a large part of the average bank's assets today are either direct or indirect obligations of the federal government anyway. With respect to the first and third points, only future events will determine whether the FDIC is accumulating too great a volume of reserves to meet periods of economic distress on the part of the banks. The recent rash of bank failures and the fact that FDIC reserves relative to insured deposits is only slightly more than one percent has, in fact, raised the question of whether reserves are high enough rather than too high. In any event, it is doubtful whether the FDIC could withstand the financial pressure of an economic depression similar to that of the early thirties. It has been suggested that the support given to the banking system by the FDIC during the course of depression may actually prevent economic conditions in general from deteriorating as much as would otherwise be the case. There is little doubt that the depression of the early thirties was made all the more burdensome by the accompanying failure of many banks.

A more fundamental criticism of the system of deposit insurance as it now exists relates to the need for additional bank regulation. It is claimed that deposit insurance gives insured bankers an incentive to undertake more risk than they would in an unregulated and uninsured free market. They can benefit privately by undertaking risks that society as a whole considers excessive. Thus, restrictive bank regulations may be necessary to undo the distortive impact of deposit insurance. There seems to be no question that small depositors need and desire deposit protection, but such protection doesn't justify the frequent increases leading to the present $100,000 limit. It has been suggested that reducing the limit of deposit protection would shift risk back to bank management. Another suggestion for reform would make the insurance premiums paid by banks vary according to the riskiness of their portfolios. Just as automobile insurance companies charge more to insure unsafe drivers, riskier banks would pay a higher price for insurance than safe banks.

Loss Experience of the Federal Deposit Insurance Corporation. From the beginning of deposit insurance on January 1, 1934, to December 31, 1981, the FDIC made disbursement to protect depositors in 578 insured banks. Disbursement for the protection of depositors totaled approximately $6 billion.[1] The FDIC in turn has recovered approximately 90 percent of its disbursement through the liquidation of assets taken over from closed banks.

QUESTIONS

1. Compare the operations of commercial banks during the nation's colonial period with those of today's modern banks.
2. How vital a role did commercial banking play in the development of the United States economy? Has its importance decreased or increased with industrialization?
3. Comment on the general objectives embodied in the Monetary Control Act.
4. Describe the principal functions of commercial banks.
5. Why do regulatory authorities insist on certain minimum capital requirements on the part of banks before they may begin banking operations?
6. What are the sources of capital for a bank? Why would the bank wish to increase its capital after operations had begun and its initial capital requirements had been met?
7. Increasing emphasis by regulatory authorities in recent years has been placed on the riskiness of assets rather than on the deposits-to-capital ratio of banks. Explain the reasons for this change in attitude.

8. How do you explain the relative decrease in bank investments relative to bank loans since World War II?
9. To what extent is concentration in banking control in the United States increasing? Do you anticipate a degree of concentration comparable to that of Canada and Britain during the twentieth century?
10. Compare the relative merits of independent unit banking as opposed to branch banking.
11. What are the principal causes of bank failures? Have bank failures been unusual in the history of United States commercial banking? Are bank failures frequent at the present time?
12. It has been suggested that the Federal Deposit Insurance Corporation could not survive the financial pressure of a major economic depression. To the extent that this may be true, why not strengthen it to the point where it could withstand such pressure?
13. Evaluate the significance of the Federal Deposit Insurance Corporation to commercial banking in the United States.

---

[1] *Annual Reports* of the Federal Deposit Insurance Corporation, supplemented by correspondence with FDIC.

SUGGESTED READINGS

Dewey, D. R. *Financial History of the United States,* 12th ed. New York: Longmans, Green & Company, 1934.

Flannery, Mark J. "Deposit Insurance Creates a Need for Bank Regulation." *Business Review,* Federal Reserve Bank of Philadelphia (January/February, 1982), pp. 17–26.

Hammond, Bray. *Banks and Politics in America from the Revolution to the Civil War.* Princeton, New Jersey: Princeton University Press, 1957.

Kamerschen, David R. *Money and Banking*, 7th ed. Cincinnati: South-Western Publishing Co., 1980. Chapter 2.

"Monetary Control Act." *Sixty-Sixth Annual Report,* Federal Reserve Bank of New York (For the Year Ended December 31, 1980), pp. 33–35.

Ritter, Lawrence S., and William L. Silber. *Principles of Money, Banking, and Financial Markets,* 4th ed. New York: Basic Books, Inc., Publishers, 1983. Chapter 3.

Savage, Donald T. "Developments in Banking Structure, 1970–81." *Federal Reserve Bulletin* (February, 1982), pp. 77–85.

Varvel, Walter A., and John R. Walter. "The Competition for Transaction Accounts." *Economic Review*, Federal Reserve Bank of Richmond (March/April, 1982), pp. 2–15.

Watkins, Thomas G., and Robert Craig West. "Bank Holding Companies: Development and Regulation." *Economic Review*, Federal Reserve Bank of Kansas City (June, 1982), pp. 3–13.

4 The Federal Reserve System

The Federal Reserve Act of 1913 was the culmination of a long series of bills, proposals, and public debates arising from dissatisfaction with the National Banking Act. Although the National Banking Act resulted in substantial improvement in banking practices, certain weaknesses persisted; and new problems developed as the economy expanded.

WEAKNESSES OF THE BANKING SYSTEM

One of the principal weaknesses of the banking system late in the nineteenth century appeared to be the inappropriate arrangement for the holding of reserves. A large part of the reserve balances of banks was held in the form of deposits with the large city banks, in particular with large New York City banks. During periods of economic stress, the position of these large city banks was precarious because they had the problem of meeting deposit withdrawals not only by their own customers but also by their correspondent banks. The frequent inability of the large banks to meet such deposit withdrawal demands resulted in extreme hardship for their correspondent banks whose reserves they held.

Another weakness of the banking system under the National Banking Act was the inflexibility of the note issue system. In an effort to provide the nation with a sound national currency, no provision had been made for the expansion or contraction of national bank notes with variations in business activity. The volume of national bank notes was governed not by the needs of business but rather by the availability and price of government bonds.

The National Banking Act provided that national banks could issue their own notes only against deposits with the Treasury of United States government bonds. Note issues were limited to 90 percent of the par value (as stated on the face of the bond) or the market value of the bonds, whichever was lower. When bonds sold at prices considerably above their par value, it meant that the advantage of purchasing bonds for the issue of notes was eliminated. For example, if a $1,000 par value bond were available for purchase at a price of

$1,150, the banks would not be inclined to make such a purchase since a maximum of $900 in notes could be issued against the bond (90 percent of par value in this case). The interest that the banker could earn from the use of the $900 in notes would not be great enough to offset the premium price of the bond. When government bonds sold at par or at a discount, on the other hand, the prospective earning power of the note issues would be quite attractive and encourage purchase of bonds for note issue purposes. The volume of national bank notes, therefore, depended on the government bond market rather than the seasonal or cyclical needs of the nation for currency.

In addition to the foregoing two weaknesses of banking under the National Banking Act, the collection of out-of-town checks continued to be a cumbersome process. The Federal Reserve System has contributed much to the improvement of the check clearance and collection process.

CENTRAL BANKING

In the last analysis, the financial system of the United States during this period appeared to suffer not so much from the shortcomings of the National Banking Act as it did from the lack of an effective banking structure. Yet throughout the welter of proposals and counterproposals that preceded the enactment of the Federal Reserve Act ran a single theme: that of opposition to a strong central banking system. Although the nation had experienced central banking under the First and Second Banks of the United States, the national banking system itself did not provide for any form of central banking. The opening of the vast western frontiers along with the local autonomy of the southern areas presented an atmosphere of distrust of centralized financial control. This distrust was made all the more pointed by the experience, during the years immediately preceding enactment of the Federal Reserve Act, of an era of trust-busting under President Theodore Roosevelt. Many of the practices of the large corporate combinations were at that time being made public through legislative commissions and investigations.

Although the United States was one of the last major industrial nations to adopt a system of central banking, many financial and political leaders had long recognized the advantages of such a system. These proponents of central banking were given immense assistance by the dissatisfactions arising out of the panic of 1907. It must be acknowledged, however, that the central banking system adopted by the United States was, in fact, a compromise between the system of independently owned unit banks in existence in this country and the central banking systems of such countries as Canada, Great Britain, Spain, and Germany. This compromise took the form of a series of central banks, each representing a specific region of the United States and hence being more responsive to the particular financial problems of that region.

In many respects, a central bank resembles the commercial bank with regard to services performed. A central bank lends money to its members; it is required to hold reserves; it is given the responsibility of creating credit, generally through bank notes and deposits; and it has stockholders and a board of directors as well as other characteristics of the commercial bank. In contrast with the commercial bank, a central bank does not necessarily operate for a profit, but it has a primary responsibility for influencing the cost, the availability, and the supply of money. It facilitates the operations of the commercial banks in their relationships with the business community and with the government.

THE FEDERAL RESERVE SYSTEM

Under the authority of the Federal Reserve Act, twelve federal reserve districts were established. Each federal reserve district is served by a federal reserve bank, and the activities of the twelve banks are in turn coordinated by a Board of Governors in Washington, D.C. The members of the Board of Governors are also members of the Federal Open Market Committee. The Federal Advisory Council provides advice and general information to the Board of Governors. The organizational structure of the Federal Reserve System is shown in Figure 4-1.

The Federal Reserve System did not supplant the system that existed under the National Banking Act but rather was superimposed upon it. Certain provisions of the National Banking Act, however, were modified to permit greater flexibility of operations.

Federal Reserve Membership

The Federal Reserve Act provided that all national banks were to become members of the Federal Reserve System. In addition, state-chartered banks, as well as trust companies, were permitted to join the system upon the presentation of evidence of a satisfactory financial condition. It was provided further that all member banks would be required to purchase capital stock of the federal reserve bank of their district up to a maximum of 6 percent of their paid-in capital and surplus. It has been necessary, however, for the banks to pay in only 3 percent; the remainder is subject to call at the discretion of the Federal Reserve System. Member banks are limited to a maximum of 6 percent dividends on the stock of the federal reserve banks that they hold. The federal reserve banks, therefore, are private institutions owned by the many member banks of the Federal Reserve System.

State chartered banks and trust companies are permitted to withdraw from membership with the Federal Reserve System six months after written notice has been submitted to the federal reserve bank of their district. In such cases, the stock originally purchased by the withdrawing member is canceled and a refund is made for all money paid in.

As of mid-1982, of the nation's 14,752 commercial banks, 5,558 were member banks. Compared with the 97 percent of all commercial banks that carry insurance under the provisions of the Federal Deposit Insurance Corporation, this appears to be a rather small coverage of banks by the Federal Reserve. These member banks, however, hold approximately 70 percent of the deposits of all commercial banks. Even this figure understates the importance of the Federal

Figure 4-1
Federal Reserve System

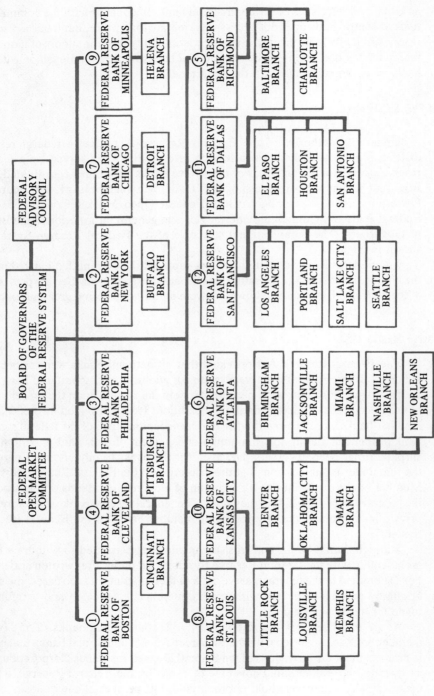

SOURCE: Board of Governors of the Federal Reserve System.

Reserve in the banking system, since many of its services and some of its regulatory powers extend to all depository institutions.

Structure of the Federal Reserve Banks

Directors and Officers. Each federal reserve bank has corporate officers and a board of directors. The selection of officers and directors, however, is unlike that of other corporations. As in the case of member banks, each federal reserve bank has its own board of directors. These nine directors must be residents of the district in which they serve. The directors serve terms of three years, the appointments being staggered in such a way that three directors are appointed each year. In order to assure that the various economic elements of the federal reserve districts are represented, the nine members of the board of directors are divided into three groups: Class A, Class B, and Class C.

Both Class A and Class B directors are elected by the member banks of the federal reserve district. The Class A directors represent member banks of the district, while the Class B directors represent nonbanking interests. These nonbanking interests are commerce, agriculture, and industry. There is a further subdivision of Class A and Class B directors to represent the small banks, the medium-sized banks, and the large banks. Each of these groups is permitted to elect one Class A director and one Class B director. We have, therefore, a wide diversification of interests on the board of directors of each federal reserve bank. The Class C directors are appointed by the Board of Governors of the Federal Reserve System, and it is provided that these persons may not be stockholders, directors, or employees of existing banks.

Although the majority of the directors of the federal reserve banks are elected by the member banks of each district, the three members of each board appointed by the Board of Governors are in a strategic position relative to the other board members. One member appointed by the Board of Governors is designated chairperson of the board of directors and federal reserve agent, and a second member is appointed deputy chairperson. The federal reserve agent is the Board of Governors' representative at each reserve bank, and is responsible for maintaining the collateral backing federal reserve notes issued by each bank.

Each federal reserve bank also has a president and first vice-president who are appointed by the board of directors with the approval of the Board of Governors. A federal reserve bank may have several additional vice-presidents. The president is responsible for the execution of policies established by the board of directors and for general administration of the affairs of the federal reserve bank. All other officers and personnel of the federal reserve bank are subject to the authority of the president.

Federal Reserve Branch Banks. In addition to the 12 federal reserve banks, 25 branch banks have been established. These branch banks are located for the most part in geographical areas not conveniently served by the federal reserve banks themselves; hence, the geographically large western federal reserve districts have a majority of the federal reserve branch banks. The San Francisco district has 4, the Dallas district has 3, and the Atlanta district has 5 branch banks. The New

York federal reserve district, on the other hand, has only 1 branch bank, while the Boston district has no branches. The federal reserve districts and the cities in which federal reserve banks and their branches are located are shown in Figure 4-1.

The Board of Governors

The Board of Governors of the Federal Reserve System, previously known as the Federal Reserve Board, is composed of seven members. Each member is appointed for a term of fourteen years. The purpose of the fourteen-year term undoubtedly was to make possible as little partisan political pressure on the Board as possible. This Board need not be bipartisan in nature, nor is there any specific provision with respect to the qualifications a member must have. All members are appointed by the President of the United States with the advice and consent of the Senate, one member being designated as the chairperson and another as the vice-chairperson.

The primary purpose of the Board of Governors is to give direction and coordination to the activities of the twelve federal reserve banks under its jurisdiction. The Board of Governors is also responsible for passing upon the applications of state-chartered banks applying for membership in the system and for recommending the removal of officers or directors of member banks because of infraction of rules established by the Federal Reserve System and other regulatory authorities. The Board of Governors must approve changes in the level of the rediscount rates of the federal reserve banks, and it implements many of the credit control devices that have come into existence in recent decades.

The Federal Open Market Committee

As early as 1922 efforts were made to coordinate the timing of purchases and sales of securities by the federal reserve banks in order to achieve desirable credit objectives. The Banking Act of 1933 formalized the early committees that had been established to coordinate these activities by the creation of the Federal Open Market Committee. This Committee, with the additional powers granted to it by the Banking Act of 1935, now has full control over all open market operations of the federal reserve banks.

The Federal Advisory Council

In an effort to keep the members of the Board of Governors in close contact with local business conditions, the Federal Advisory Council was created. This organization meets at least four times a year to consult with and to advise the members of the Board of Governors in matters relating to general business conditions, banking operations, and general questions of policy.

FUNCTIONS OF THE FEDERAL RESERVE SYSTEM

The primary responsibility of a central bank is to regulate the supply of money, and therefore the cost and availability of money as well. By exercising such influence on the monetary system of the United States, the Federal Reserve System performs its most unique and important function—the promotion of economic stability. The functions of the Federal Reserve System that relate directly to the control of the cost, the availability, and the supply of money are the establishment of reserve requirements for member banks, loans and discounts to member banks, and open market operations. It is through the buying and selling of securities in the open market that it exercises its most direct control of the money supply. In addition, the Federal Reserve System exercises selective controls, such as the regulation of credit available for the purpose of purchasing listed stocks and the payment of interest on time deposits of member banks. The Federal Reserve System has also at times exercised control over consumer credit. These responsibilities involve policy decisions. Other functions of the System, such as collection of checks and issuance of currency, are regarded as services or chores.

In the remainder of this chapter we shall divide the functions of the Federal Reserve System into those that relate directly to member banks and those that relate to the economy in general.

The functions to be discussed are as follows:

Bank-Related Functions	General Functions
Issuance of Currency	Open Market Operations
Bank Reserves	Selective Credit Controls
Loans and Discounts	Government Fiscal Agent
Clearance and Collection of Checks	Reports, Publications,
Supervision and Regulation	and Research

The services provided by the Federal Reserve System, described in the following pages, have traditionally been made available to member banks at no charge. The noninterest-bearing reserves that member banks are required to hold have been thought to be adequate to cover the cost of providing these services. The Monetary Control Act, however, has changed this situation and now requires that the Federal Reserve provide services on an equal basis to all depository institutions, and further requires that the Federal Reserve charge both member and nonmember institutions for services provided. This change is only one of the major changes resulting from the institution of the Monetary Control Act.

BANK-RELATED FUNCTIONS OF THE FEDERAL RESERVE SYSTEM

Two of the bank-related functions of the Federal Reserve System are of a policy nature and are discussed in greater detail in Part IV. They are the establishment of bank reserve requirements and the setting of rates on loans and discounts. In this section these two policy functions are described briefly along with the functions of currency issue, clearance and collection of checks, and supervision and regulation.

Issuance of Currency

The federal reserve banks are the main source of currency in the United States. Individuals usually receive paper money and coin by making withdrawals from a bank or from the sale of merchandise or services. In either case the bank must provide such money, either directly or through the intermediary of the purchaser of goods or services. Although the flow of currency from the banks to the public is usually matched by a flow of currency deposits, at times the demand for currency by the public may exceed the bank's available supply. At such times banks depend upon the federal reserve banks for replenishment of their supply. As currency is ordered from a federal reserve bank, the reserves of the bank ordering the currency are charged.

The federal reserve banks maintain large stores of paper money and coin on hand at all times to meet the demands of member banks. Over 90 percent of all currency in circulation is federal reserve notes, the remainder being made up of United States Treasury paper money and coin. Federal reserve notes are the obligations of both the United States government and of the issuing federal reserve banks, and they are backed by specified collateral, such as notes and government bonds.

As additional coin is required by the federal reserve banks for distribution to member banks, it is received from the mints, and the deposit balances of the Treasury with the federal reserve banks are credited. The cost of issuing federal reserve currency, as well as all transportation costs involved in the shipment of paper money and coin to or from the federal reserve banks, is borne by the banks so served.

The issuance of currency by the federal reserve banks, therefore, eliminated one of the major weaknesses of banking under the National Banking Act prior to the establishment of the Federal Reserve System, that of an inflexible monetary system. As the demand for additional currency is now made by the public and by the banks of the nation, the federal reserve banks increase the flow of such currency from their reservoir of funds. Such increased demands for currency usually accompany an expansion in general business activity. As the economy contracts and the large additional supplies of currency are no longer required, the unnecessary currency is shipped back to the federal reserve banks.

Bank Reserves

One of the basic measures provided by the Federal Reserve Act was the institution of a more appropriate system of maintaining reserves by the banks of the nation. The shortcomings of the system of holding reserves as permitted under the National Banking Act had been recognized, and it was apparent that a remedy would have to be provided before substantial progress could be made toward stabilizing the banking system of the country. To accomplish this, member banks were to keep on reserve with the federal reserve bank of their district a specified percentage of the volume of deposits of the bank.

Although all member banks were subject to the same minimum reserve requirements on time and savings deposits, the member banks were divided into three groups for purposes of determining reserve ratios on demand or checking deposits. These three groups were based on the division established earlier by the National Banking Act: central reserve city banks, reserve city banks, and country banks. The importance of cities as national or regional money centers provided the basis for their classification. Under the provisions of the Federal Reserve Act, a part of the minimum reserves was permitted to be held as cash in the member bank's own vault. This provision was changed in 1917 by an act of Congress that required all legal reserves against time and demand deposits to be kept with the federal reserve banks. This requirement was modified in late 1959; and since November, 1960, all vault cash has been considered as part of a bank's legal reserves.

The Monetary Control Act has radically changed the nature of reserve requirements. In addition to establishing reserves based on the amount of deposits rather than by bank classification, such depository institutions as mutual savings banks, savings and loan associations, credit unions, and agencies and branches of foreign banks are now required to maintain reserves with federal reserve banks. Although member banks of the Federal Reserve System must maintain reserves either as vault cash or as deposits with federal reserve banks, nonmembers may maintain reserves with certain approved institutions.

Loans and Discounts

It was believed that if the federal reserve banks were to serve effectively as bankers' banks, they would have to provide facilities for lending to their member banks at times when additional funds were required by the banks. Such a lending arrangement was to meet one of the principal objections to the National Banking Act, that of an inflexible currency system. Loans to member banks by the federal reserve banks may take two forms: first, the member bank may receive an "advance" secured by its own promissory note together with eligible paper it owns; or second, the member bank may "discount" its eligible paper with the federal reserve bank. *Eligible paper*, which is defined in considerable detail by the Board of Governors, includes such items as the promissory notes, bills of exchange, and bankers' acceptances of customers. Bonds and notes of the United States government and obligations of instrumentalities of the United States government that carry the guarantee of the government are also acceptable as collateral for advances.

The use of eligible paper as collateral for a loan from a federal reserve bank involves a contingent liability on the part of the member bank in the case of either a discount or an advance. In discounting eligible paper, the member bank is required to endorse each item. For an advance, the bank must sign a promissory note in addition to submitting eligible paper as collateral. The promissory note, of course, represents a general claim against the bank over and above the value of the eligible paper.

Member banks have generally found that in borrowing from a federal reserve bank the use of the advance arrangement, as opposed to the discount arrangement, is more convenient since the maturity of the various items of eligible paper may not coincide with the needs of the member bank. Under the advance arrangement, paper held by the federal reserve bank as collateral that matures before the due date of the advance is simply replaced by other eligible paper. Also, under the advance arrangement, a single interest rate is calculated on the loan while discounted eligible paper may require varying discount rates, depending upon the quality, length of maturity, and general character of each item. Because of the large bank holdings of United States government securities in recent years, however, and because of their convenience, member banks have generally used these securities instead of eligible paper as collateral for federal reserve bank advances.

The Monetary Control Act provides access to loans and discounts for non-member banks and other depository institutions as well as for member banks. As of early 1983 the rate charged for loans was 8½ percent. The rate may be lowered or raised from time to time to encourage or discourage, as may be desired, depository institutions' participation in the loan program. Also, at times the rate will vary from one federal reserve bank to another. Such variations in rates between reserve banks generally result from a desire to equalize the general flow of credit.

Until late in 1952, the volume of lending operations of the federal reserve banks had reached significant proportions only during World War I and the period thereafter and during the stock market boom of 1928 and 1929. Late in 1952, and again in 1969 and 1970, member banks obtained over $1.5 billion in loans from the federal reserve banks. In 1974 loans to member banks reached an all-time high of nearly $3.5 billion.

Clearance and Collection of Checks

One of the important contributions of the Federal Reserve System to the smooth flow of financial interchange has been that of facilitating the clearance and collection of checks of the banks of the nation. Each federal reserve bank serves as a clearinghouse for all banks in its district, provided that they agree to remit at par on checks forwarded to them for payment. The importance of this service to the banking system of the United States can be readily understood by a brief review of clearance practices prior to the Federal Reserve System.

Although local clearinghouses made it possible for banks within the same city to effect an efficient exchange of customers' checks, it was often difficult and time-consuming to provide for the settlement of claims when checks were drawn on out-of-town banks or when checks drawn on the local banks were presented to out-of-town banks for payment. In addition to the time consumed in routing checks from one bank to another for payment, many banks on which checks were drawn made payment only at a discount; that is, instead of remitting the face value of the check, they would deduct ⅛ to ½ of 1 percent of the face value of the check as a clearance charge. This practice resulted in the establishment of correspondent banking relations between banks in the important commercial centers of the United States.

Correspondent arrangements generally provided that checks exchanged between the two banks would be accepted at par. In this way, a local bank that had received a check drawn on a bank in another community, in order to avoid having the other bank remit at less than par, would send the check instead to a correspondent bank in the same community as the bank on which the check was drawn. That bank, in turn, would either send the check directly to the bank on which it was written, if it were a correspondent of that bank, or pass it on to another bank that might have correspondent relations with it, thus avoiding the penalty. As such checks were forwarded to correspondent banks, the reserves of the forwarding bank were increased because deposits with correspondents were considered to be part of required reserves. The days required to clear checks meant that reserves were greatly padded, increasing their potential for bank lending.

Although it may seem that the bank on which the check was originally presented would be able to pass on such charges to its customers, such practice was avoided if at all possible because of the intense competition for the accounts of businesses and other customers at that time. Hence, banks frequently attempted to absorb these costs, when they could not otherwise be avoided, rather than to pass them on to their customers.

Check Clearance Through the Federal Reserve Banks. Member banks of the Federal Reserve System and nonmembers alike may utilize the check-clearance facilities of the federal reserve banks. Nonmember participating banks, however, like member banks, must remit at par on checks presented to them for payment and must keep a deposit with the federal reserve bank for check-clearance purposes. For the vast majority of commercial banks, the federal reserve banks provide an efficient and economical system of check clearance. For member banks the service is particularly appropriate since they must hold legal reserves with the federal reserve banks anyway. As checks are sent through federal reserve banks for collection, the reserve balances of participating banks are decreased or increased, depending upon the day's total of checks drawn against or in favor of a particular bank.

An example of the check-clearance process through the federal reserve banks will demonstrate the facility with which these clearances are made at the present time. Assume that the owner of a business in Sacramento, California, places an order for merchandise with a distributor in San Francisco. The order is accompanied by a check drawn on the owner's bank in Sacramento. This check is deposited by the distributor with its bank in San Francisco, at which time the distributor receives a corresponding credit to its account with the bank. The distributor's bank will then send the check to the federal reserve bank of its district, also located in San Francisco, which will in turn forward the check to the bank in Sacramento on which the check was originally drawn. The adjustment of accounts is accomplished at the federal reserve bank through an alternate debit and credit to the accounts of the banks concerned in the transaction. The San Francisco bank, which has honored the check of its customer, will receive an increase in its reserve with the federal reserve bank, while the bank in Sacramento will have its reserve decreased by a corresponding amount. The bank in Sacramento will reduce the account of the business on which the check was written. Hence, the exchange is made with no transfer of currency.

In the event that the Sacramento bank found its legal reserve reduced below the point required by its total deposits, it would then be necessary, in one way or another, to supplement its reserves with the federal reserve bank. For the vast amount of check clearance that takes place, however, a negligible amount of cash shipment is required. Although the distributor in this case received an immediate increase in its account for the amount of the check deposited with its bank as is customary, the bank did not receive an immediate increase in its reserves with the federal reserve bank on which it could draw. Had the bank on which the check was drawn been located in San Francisco, there would have been an immediate credit to the account of the depositing bank. The length of time that a bank must wait before checks deposited with a federal reserve bank are added to its active accounts depends on its distance from the federal reserve bank. A schedule of zones exists in which these waiting periods for various geographical areas are specified. In no case, however, is a bank required to wait more than two days before a check deposited with the federal reserve bank will be entered to its credit.

Check Clearance Between Federal Reserve Districts. If at the time the owner of the business placed the order with the San Francisco distributor, an order was also placed with a distributor of goods in Chicago, Illinois, the check would be subject to an additional step in being cleared through the Federal Reserve System. The Chicago distributor, like the San Francisco distributor, deposits the check with the bank of its choice and in turn receives an increase in its account. The Chicago bank deposits the check for collection with the Federal Reserve Bank of Chicago, which in turn forwards the check to the Federal Reserve Bank of San Francisco. The Federal Reserve Bank of San Francisco, of course, then presents the check for payment to the bank on which it was drawn. There are, therefore, two routes of check clearance: the *intradistrict* settlement where the transaction takes place entirely within a single federal reserve district, and the *interdistrict* settlement in which there are relationships between banks of two federal reserve districts.

The Interdistrict Settlement Fund. Just as the federal reserve banks are able to minimize the actual flow of funds by increasing or decreasing reserves of the participating banks, the federal reserve banks are able to avoid the flow of funds between the federal reserve banks to effect interdistrict settlements. This is accomplished through the Interdistrict Settlement Fund in Washington, D.C.

The Interdistrict Settlement Fund has a substantial deposit from each of the federal reserve banks. These deposit credits are alternately increased or decreased, depending upon the clearance balance of the day's activities on the part of each federal reserve bank. At a certain hour each day, each federal reserve bank informs the Interdistrict Settlement Fund by direct wire of the amount of checks it received the previous day that were drawn upon banks in other federal reserve districts. The deposit of each federal reserve bank with the Interdistrict Settlement Fund is increased or decreased according to the balance of the day's check-clearance activities. The Interdistrict Settlement Fund also makes it possible for large sums to be transferred from member banks to banks in other federal reserve districts through the deposit balances of the federal reserve banks with the Fund.

Check Clearance Through Federal Reserve Branch Banks. Branch banks of the federal reserve banks enter into the clearance process in a very important way. If the check is deposited with a bank located nearer to a federal reserve branch bank than to a federal reserve bank, the branch bank, in effect, takes the place of the federal reserve bank.

Check Routing Symbols. The magnitude of the task of assisting in the check-clearance process by the Federal Reserve System is attested to by the fact that over one quarter of the total personnel of the twelve federal reserve banks are engaged in this function. Great effort has been exercised to make this task easier, and much time-saving machinery has been introduced into the operation.

Basic to the clearance process is a machine that has the ability to "read" a system of symbols and numerals. Although these symbols are slightly different from conventional numbers, they are easily read by human eyes as well. Information relative to the clearance process is printed on the lower part of the check form in magnetic ink (ink containing iron oxide). This information can be read directly from checks by the processing machines. The system has been named Magnetic Ink Character Recognition (MICR). In addition to the clearance symbol, banks with compatible electronic accounting equipment include a symbol for each customer's account. This makes possible electronic processing of checks for internal bookkeeping purposes. See Figure 4-2.

Banks continue to include the older check routing symbol in the upper right-hand corner of their checks. This check routing plan was jointly sponsored in 1945 by the American Bankers Association and the Federal Reserve System and is useful for physically sorting checks that are torn or otherwise unsuitable for electronic sorting.

Federal Reserve Transfer of Credit. The Federal Reserve System provides for the transfer of hundreds of millions of dollars in bank credit about the country daily. In 1953 the Federal Reserve System put into operation a near-automatic system of teletype through which bank credit can be transferred. The communication system, referred to as the *federal reserve leased system*, spans approximately 11,000 miles and makes it possible for the 12 federal reserve banks and their 24 branches to maintain facilities for almost instantaneous transfer of bank credit. Headquarters for the communication system is in Culpeper, Virginia.

The tremendous growth of the check-clearance function dictates an entirely new approach to the payment process. While the use of credit cards has taken some pressure off of check-clearance facilities, the problem remains. Credit cards, of course, permit the payment for many transactions to be completed with a single check at the end of each billing cycle. The payments system of the future is usually seen as one that combines modern electronic technology with what is known as the *giro transfer system*. Its characteristics make it especially suitable for the use of computers.

Figure 4-2
Check Routing
Symbols

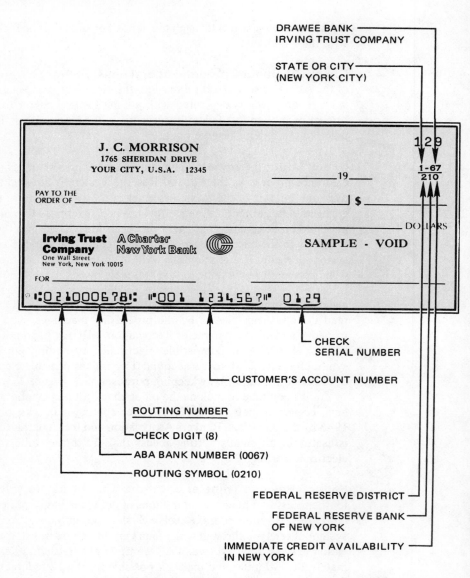

Like the check payments system, the giro system involves deposit balances held by individuals and businesses at a financial or governmental institution, and some systematic arrangement for the transfer of ownership of these balances from payer to payee. Unlike the check system, in the typical giro transaction the payer delivers to the drawee institution an electronic order directing it to transfer a specified sum from the payer's account to that of the payee. This system is more direct and involves less time and paper handling than ordinary check transfers. There are a number of projects in cities around the country aimed toward development of a system of paperless transfers.

Supervision and Regulation

Few fields of activity are so strongly regulated and supervised as the banking system. This regulation, of course, results in part from the strategic role played by the commercial banking system in the nation's economy and the sensitivity of business conditions in general to undue disturbances in the banking system. Regulation and supervision are exercised by several different agencies. For example, national banks are subject to examination by the Comptroller of the Currency, and because all national banks must be members of the Federal Reserve System, they are also subject to examination and regulation by the Federal Reserve System. Also, since members of the Federal Reserve System must be insured by the Federal Deposit Insurance Corporation, they are subject to possible examination by that organization.

Regulation of State-Chartered Banks. If a member bank is a state-chartered institution, although not subject to the supervision of the Comptroller of the Currency, it is subject to the laws of the state in which it is chartered as well as the regulation of the Federal Reserve System and the Federal Deposit Insurance Corporation. Insured state banks that are not members of the Federal Reserve System are subject to examination by the Federal Deposit Insurance Corporation, while nonmember uninsured state banks are subject only to state examination.

Delegation of Federal Reserve Examination Responsibilities. Examination of member banks by the Federal Reserve System is generally delegated to the regional federal reserve banks; however, the Board of Governors of the Federal Reserve System is authorized by law to examine member banks if it so chooses. In practice, national banks are seldom examined by the staff of the Federal Reserve System since they are normally subject to examination also by the Comptroller of the Currency. National bank examiners, responsible to the Comptroller of the Currency, generally submit a copy of the examination report of each national bank to the examination department of the district reserve bank, and normally no further examination is made by the federal reserve bank. The federal reserve bank may, however, dispatch its own examiners to one of the national banks to secure information not covered by the examination of the national bank examiners. The principal activities of the examination department of the federal reserve banks is that of examining state-chartered member banks of the district.

As in the case of national banks and the national bank examiners, federal reserve authorities cooperate closely with the state banking authorities in an effort to minimize the burden of bank examination on banking operations and in order to simplify the procedure. In many states, state bank officials accept the report of the federal reserve examiners and concentrate their own examination activities on nonmember state banks. State and federal reserve bank examiners may appear jointly for purposes of examination to minimize the inconvenience to bank operations. The Federal Deposit Insurance Corporation confines its examination activities largely to insured state banks that are not members of the System.

GENERAL FUNCTIONS OF THE FEDERAL RESERVE SYSTEM

Two additional functions of a policy nature are carried out through nonbanking institutions as well as through banks. These are open market operations and selective credit controls. As is the case with bank-related policy functions, these two functions are discussed in greater detail in Part IV. They are described only briefly here, along with the provision of fiscal services and the preparation of reports, publications, and research.

Open Market Operations

Open market operations are regarded as the most important single instrument available to the Federal Reserve System for purposes of credit control. By purchasing large quantities of securities in the open market, the federal reserve banks increase the flow of funds in circulation. By selling securities, the banks withdraw funds from circulation. Obligations of the United States government are the principal kind of securities that the federal reserve banks buy and sell. The Open Market Committee is responsible for such activities.

As an example of an Open Market Committee action, assume that the Committee decides to buy $50 million of United States government securities. These securities are purchased in the open market from whatever source may be available. A check drawn on the federal reserve bank making the purchase is delivered to the seller of the securities. The seller deposits the check with a member bank, which in turn delivers the check to the federal reserve bank. The seller of the securities has had a deposit balance increase with the member bank, and the member bank in turn has increased its reserves with the federal reserve bank. On the basis of the expanded reserves of the member bank with the federal reserve bank, loans and investments may also be expanded. The net effect, therefore, of the purchase of securities is to expand the reserves of member banks and in turn their credit-creating potential.

If it is the desire of the Federal Reserve System to restrain credit expansion and growth in money supply, the federal reserve banks may sell securities in the open market. The purchasers of the securities pay for them by drawing checks on their balances with member banks. This, in turn, reduces the reserves of the member banks with the federal reserve banks, and they must adjust their loan and investment operations to the lower level of reserves on deposit with the federal reserve bank. In this way pressure is brought to bear on the loan and investment activities of commercial banks.

Until October, 1979, Open Market Committee actions were directed to the control of short-term interest rates. At that time the Federal Reserve announced a significant change in operating procedures aimed at more consistent achievement of money supply targets. This change, apparently influenced by the growing acceptance of "monetarist" ideas, emphasized controlling the money supply by focusing on the supply of bank reserves rather than on short-term interest rates. While the result has been a closer control of the money supply, it has also meant much greater short-term fluctuations in interest rates, and although this change has contributed to the reduction in general price inflation, it has also perpetuated higher interest rates than otherwise expected due to the variability of interest rates. Late in 1982 the Federal Reserve authorities announced a temporary de-emphasis of the money supply approach due to difficulties in money supply measurement.

Selective Credit Controls

To supplement the general methods of regulating the flow of funds, the Federal Reserve System has special powers to regulate the credit terms on which transactions in stock market securities are financed. The terms of consumer credit and certain real estate credit have also been regulated by the Federal Reserve System from time to time. In contrast with the other methods of monetary control, selective credit controls act directly on credit rather than on the reserves of member banks. They are also directed to specific lines of business activity to the exclusion of all others. Much controversy has existed as to the merits of a system of monetary control that imposes special restriction on individual segments of the economy.

Margin Requirements on Stock Market Credit. Since 1934 the Board of Governors of the Federal Reserve System has had the responsibility of curbing the excessive use of credit for the purpose of purchasing or carrying securities. It discharges this responsibility by limiting the amount that brokers and dealers in securities, banks, and others may lend on securities for that purpose. Brokers are limited in their lending for the purpose of purchasing or carrying any type of security. The restriction on banks applies only to loans for purchasing or carrying securities registered on national security exchanges. Such limitations do not apply to loans secured by stocks if the purpose of the loans is for regular business activities. Margin requirements are discussed in Chapter 13.

Consumer Credit. The Federal Reserve System has resorted to regulation of consumer credit only in times of emergency to supplement general credit measures. Its first use in 1941 was for the purpose of curbing the use of credit for the purchase of automobiles, household goods, and other such consumer durables. The problem faced by the nation at that time was one of an acute shortage of consumer goods and services accompanied by an increase in consumer purchasing power. Without restrictive measures, such a situation could only bring increased prices. By 1952 all restrictions on the use of consumer credit were eliminated.

The Truth in Lending Act which became effective May 29, 1968, requires the Board of Governors to prescribe regulations to assure a meaningful disclosure of credit terms so that consumers will be able to compare more readily the various terms available and avoid the uninformed use of credit.

Real Estate Credit. Because of the tremendous inflationary pressure on prices in the post-World War II period, it was necessary to restrict the flow of credit for home purchase. Failure to do so would have meant a substantial diversion of labor and materials from essential defense requirements. In 1950 the Board of Governors of the Federal Reserve System issued Regulation X for real estate credit. It specified the maximum amount that could be borrowed, the maximum length of time the loan could run, and the minimum periodic payments that had to be made to pay off the principal amount of the loan. Restrictions on real estate credit were removed in 1952, and they have not been utilized since.

Government Fiscal Agent

A substantial proportion of the employees of the Federal Reserve System hold duties that are directly related to the provision of fiscal services for the United States government. These services, provided without charge to the government, include the holding of the principal checking accounts of the Treasury of the United States, assisting in the collection of taxes, the transfer of money from one region to another, the sale and redemption of federal securities, and the paying of interest coupons. These duties, undertaken in addition to the general functions of the Federal Reserve System, make it possible for the United States government, in spite of its increased complexity, to handle the mechanics of its fiscal affairs more efficiently and safely than before the establishment of the Federal Reserve System.

Reports, Publications, and Research

The federal reserve banks publish a weekly statement of condition for each reserve bank as well a consolidated statement for all of the reserve banks. This information has become valuable for purposes of studying business conditions in general and for the formulation of forecasts of business activity. In addition to the weekly statement, all twelve of the federal reserve banks, as well as the Board of Governors, engage in intensive research in monetary matters. The Board of Governors makes available the *Federal Reserve Bulletin*, which not only carries articles of current interest to economists and business persons in general but also offers a convenient source of the statistics compiled by the Federal Reserve System. The *Bulletin* is also a convenient secondary source for certain statistical series and data prepared by other organizations.

QUESTIONS

1. To what extent did the Federal Reserve Act of 1913 supplant bank regulation and operation under the National Banking Act?
2. The Federal Reserve Act of 1913 provided for the establishment of a group of "central banks." How do the operations of a central bank differ from those of a commercial bank?

3. Describe the organizational structure of the Federal Reserve System.
4. Describe the circumstances and conditions under which a commercial bank may become a member of the Federal Reserve System.
5. Banking and large, intermediate, and small business are represented on the board of directors

of each federal reserve bank. Explain how this representation is accomplished.

6. What is meant by a "federal reserve branch bank"? How many such branches exist, and where are most of them located geographically?

7. The Federal Reserve System is under the general direction and control of the Board of Governors of the Federal Reserve System in Washington, D.C. How are members of the Board of Governors appointed? To what extent are they subject to political pressures?

8. Explain the process by which the federal reserve banks provide the economy with currency and coin.

9. Discuss the structure, the functions, and the importance of the Federal Open Market Committee.

10. With respect to their lending power, federal reserve banks have at times been described as bankers' banks. What is meant by this statement?

11. Describe the process by which a check drawn on a commercial bank but deposited for collection in another bank in a distant city might be cleared through the facilities of the Federal Reserve System.

12. What is the special role of the Federal Reserve Interdistrict Settlement Fund in the check-clearance process?

13. Explain the usual procedures for examining national banks. How does this process differ from the examination of member banks of the Federal Reserve System holding state charters?

14. In what way do the federal reserve banks serve as fiscal agents for the United States government?

15. Comment on the effect of the Monetary Control Act on the following:
    a. charges for services provided by the federal reserve banks
    b. bank reserve requirements
    c. loan and discount provisions

16. Explain the major change in Open Market Committee policy made in October, 1979.

SUGGESTED READINGS

Brockschmidt, Peggy and Carl Gambs. "Federal Reserve Pricing—A New Era." *Economic Review*, Federal Reserve Bank of Kansas City (July/August, 1981), pp. 3–15.

Campbell, Tim S. *Financial Institutions, Markets, and Economic Activity.* New York: McGraw-Hill Book Company, 1982. Chapter 10.

"Electronic Funds Transfer and Monetary Policy." *Review*, Federal Reserve Bank of Dallas (August, 1977), pp. 6–12.

Federal Reserve System. *The Federal Reserve System—Purposes and Functions*. Washington: Board of Governors of the Federal Reserve System, 1974.

Klein, John J. *Money and the Economy*, 5th ed. New York: Harcourt Brace Jovanovich, Inc., 1982. Part 2.

Prager, Jonas. *Fundamentals of Money, Banking, and Financial Institutions.* New York: Harper & Row, Publishers, Inc. 1982. Part 2.

Savage, Donald T. "Developments in Banking Structure, 1970–81." *Federal Reserve Bulletin*, Board of Governors of the Federal Reserve System, Washington, D.C., February, 1982.

West, Robert Craig. "The Depository Institutions Deregulation Act of 1980: A Historical Perspective." *Economic Review*, Federal Reserve Bank of Kansas City (February, 1982), pp. 3–13.

5 Expansion and Contraction of the Money Supply

The Federal Reserve System attempts to regulate and control the supply of money and the availability of credit. This is because the size of the total money supply in relation to the demands put upon it influences the supply of funds available for investment. This money supply versus demand relationship in turn affects the level of prices and economic activity in our free-enterprise system. Therefore, the process by which the money supply is increased and decreased is a very important factor in the success of the economy.

This chapter begins with a discussion of the changes in the volume of federal reserve notes and of coins. Next, the process by which deposit credit is expanded and contracted by the banking system is examined. This is followed by a discussion of the factors that affect commercial bank reserves in our financial system. The final sections of the chapter briefly explore the concept of a money "multiplier" and the importance of regulating and controlling the supply of money.

At this point it is important to note that the level of savings is the primary factor which determines the supply of funds available for investment in any given time period. The savings and investment process will be explored in detail in the next chapter.

CHANGES IN THE VOLUME OF FEDERAL RESERVE NOTES AND COINS

Federal reserve notes may be issued by the Federal Reserve System with a backing of gold certificates, SDR's,[1] eligible paper, or United States government and agency securities. Eligible paper in the form of business notes and drafts provides little collateral today. Instead, federal reserve notes have been increasingly backed by government securities. At the end of June, 1982, the backing for

---

[1] As was noted in Chapter 2, Special Drawing Rights (SDR's) are a form of reserve asset or "paper gold" created by the International Monetary Fund in the attempt to provide worldwide monetary liquidity and to support international trade.

$134.2 billion in federal reserve notes was $11.1 billion of gold certificates, $3.8 billion of SDR's, and $119.3 billion of U.S. government and agency securities.[2]

The volume of federal reserve notes has increased to meet the needs of the country for currency. Large increases took place during World War II, although there was a fairly rapid rate of increase beginning in 1933. The increases before 1933, except for a brief period during World War I, were largely to meet the needs of an increasing population and a rising standard of living. Part of the increase after 1933 was due to government efforts to raise the level of economic activity. During World War II a major part of the increase was due to the rapid increases in the volume of payments resulting from war activities, and in the postwar period it was due to inflation.

Before the onset of the 1929 depression, the backing for federal reserve notes was gold and commercial paper (short-term business promissory notes). The volume of commercial paper was large enough and grew rapidly enough to permit increases in this part of the money supply to keep pace with the increasing level of business activity. During the depression, the supply of commercial paper in the portfolios of the federal reserve banks dropped to a level so low that extra gold had to be used as backing for federal reserve notes. When gold flowed out of the country due to the uncertainties of the world economic situation, it became almost impossible to provide sufficient monetary backing. As a result, Congress in 1932 passed the Glass-Steagall Act, which permitted government bonds to be used along with gold and commercial paper as backing for federal reserve notes. Since that time government bonds have been used to an increasing extent as backing for the federal reserve bank currency.

The original requirement for gold backing of federal reserve notes was 35 percent and 40 percent against member bank deposits with the Federal Reserve. This was changed in 1945 to 25 percent against notes and deposits combined. In 1965 Congress eliminated the gold-certificate requirement against deposits and in 1968 against federal reserve notes. This action was made necessary by the increase in currency needed to carry on the expanding volume of economic activity and by the sustained loss of gold which occurred after 1958.

Federal reserve notes still maintain their elastic character even though they are not tied to changes in business volume as directly as when they were backed to a large extent by commercial paper. The supply does expand and contract, however, to meet changes in the demand for currency. For example, when the Christmas shopping season ends, the public has less need for currency; and money accumulated in the hands of business persons is deposited in their banks. The commercial banks turn this excess currency over to their federal reserve bank, which exchanges the excess federal reserve notes for its collateral with the federal reserve agent, thus reducing the supply of federal reserve notes.

The money supply is also increased when coins are issued by the Treasury. When the Treasury issues additional coins in response to the demands of one of the federal reserve banks, it receives a credit to its account at that bank. When the Treasury draws checks on such an account, the funds are transferred to the

---

[2]*Federal Reserve Bulletin,* September, 1982, p. A11.

general public. As these funds are deposited in a commercial bank, they become available to the banking system as additional funds. As banks in turn deposit them in a federal reserve bank, they increase their reserve balances.

EXPANSION AND CONTRACTION OF DEPOSIT CREDIT

Discussion of deposit credit expansion and contraction traditionally has focused on the commercial banking system. This is because until recently only commercial banks were able to offer demand or checkable deposits. Now, of course, the other depository institutions also can offer checkable deposits and thus affect the nation's money supply. While we will continue to refer to the expansion and contraction of deposit credit in terms of the "banking system," generically speaking the banking system now includes the other depository institutions in addition to commercial banks.

The banking system of the United States can expand and contract the volume of deposit credit as the needs for funds by individuals, businesses, and governments change. This ability to alter the money supply and credit is based on the use of a "fractional reserve" system whereby reserves equal to some portion of deposits must be held with the Federal Reserve. An understanding of the credit expansion and contraction process requires the study of the operations of banks as units in a banking system, as well as the study of the relationship of bank loans to deposits and to bank reserves.

In analyzing the process of bank credit expansion, it is helpful to make a distinction between primary deposits and derivative deposits. *Primary deposits* add new reserves to the bank where deposited and generally arise when cash and checks drawn against other banks are placed on deposit in a bank. *Derivative deposits* occur when reserves created from primary deposits are made available through bank loans to borrowers who leave them on deposit in order to write checks against the funds. When a check is written and deposited in another bank there is no change in total reserves of the banking system, since the increase in reserves at the bank where the check is deposited is offset by a decrease in reserves at the bank on which the check is drawn. The deposit of a check drawn on the Federal Reserve, however, adds new reserves to the banking system. Banks must keep reserves against both primary and derivative deposits.

Credit Expansion

When reserves were first required by law, the purpose was to assure depositors that the bank had the ability to meet their needs for the withdrawal of cash. This was before the establishment of the Federal Reserve System which made it possible for a sound bank to obtain additional funds in time of need. Confidence of depositors in the ability of a bank to meet their needs has also developed because of deposit insurance and more thorough and competent bank examinations by governmental agencies. The basic function of required reserves today is to provide a means for regulating the process of credit expansion and contraction.

The process of credit creation takes place as a result of the operations of the whole system of banks, but it arises out of the independent transactions of individual banks. To explain the process, therefore, we will consider the loan activities of a single bank, first without regard to their effects on other banks, and then in relationship to a system of banks. This approach is somewhat artificial since a bank practically never acts independently of the actions of other banks, but it has been adopted to clarify the process. Furthermore, it helps to explain the belief of some bankers that they cannot create credit since they only loan funds placed on deposit in their bank by their depositors. This analysis shows how a system of banks in which each bank is carrying on its local activities can do what an individual banker cannot do.

For illustration, let us assume that a bank which must keep reserves of 20 percent against deposits receives a primary deposit of $10,000. The bank statement, ignoring all other items, would then show the following:

ASSETS	LIABILITIES
Reserves $10,000	Deposits $10,000

Against this new deposit of $10,000, the bank must keep required reserves of 20 percent, or $2,000, so that it has $8,000 of excess reserves available.

It may appear at first glance as if the banker could proceed to make loans for $40,000 since all that is needed is a 20 percent reserve against the resulting demand deposits. If this were attempted, however, the banker would soon be in difficulty. Since bank loans are usually obtained just prior to the demand for funds, checks would undoubtedly be written against the deposit accounts almost at once. Many of these checks would be deposited in other banks, and the bank would be faced with a demand for cash as checks were presented for collection. This demand could reach the full $40,000. Since the bank has only $8,000 to meet it, it could not follow such a course and remain in business.

The amount that the banker can safely lend is the $8,000 of excess reserves. If more is lent, the banker runs the risk of not being able to make payments on checks. After such a loan, the books show:

ASSETS	LIABILITIES
Reserves $10,000	Deposits $18,000
Loans. 8,000	

If a check were written for the full amount of the derivative deposit ($8,000) and sent to a bank in another city for deposit, the lending bank would lose all of its excess reserves. This may be seen from its books, which would appear as follows:

ASSETS	LIABILITIES
Reserves . . . . $ 2,000	Deposits $10,000
Loans. 8,000	

In practice a bank may be able to loan somewhat more than the $8,000 since banks frequently require their customers to keep an average deposit balance of something in the neighborhood of 15 to 20 percent of the loan. The whole of the additional $1,500 to $2,000 cannot safely be loaned since an average balance of $1,500 to $2,000 does not prevent the full amount of the loan being used for a period of time. With an average balance in each derivative deposit account, however, all accounts will not be drawn to zero at the same time; and some additional funds are available for loans.

It may be argued that a banker will feel sure that some checks written against the bank will be redeposited in the same bank and that therefore larger sums can be lent. However, since the bank is only one of thousands of banks, the banker cannot usually anticipate such redeposits of funds; and thus cannot run the risk of being caught short of reserves. Thus, when an individual bank receives a new primary deposit, it cannot lend the full amount of that deposit but only the amount available as excess reserves. From the point of view of an individual bank, therefore, credit creation appears impossible. Since a part of every new deposit cannot be loaned out due to reserve requirements, the volume of additional loans is less than new primary deposits.

What cannot be done by an individual bank is being done by the banking system when many banks are expanding loans and derivative deposits at the same time. To illustrate this point, assume that we have an economy with just two banks, *A* and *B*. This example can be realistic if we assume further than Bank *A* represents one bank in the system and Bank *B*, all other banks combined. Bank *A*, as in our previous example, receives a new primary deposit of $10,000 and is required to keep reserves of 20 percent against deposits. Therefore, its books would appear as follows:

BANK *A*

ASSETS	LIABILITIES
Reserves $10,000	Deposits $10,000

A loan for $8,000 is made and credited as follows:

BANK *A*

ASSETS	LIABILITIES
Reserves $10,000	Deposits $18,000
Loans. 8,000	

Assume that a check is drawn against it almost immediately and deposited in Bank *B*. The books of the two banks would then show the following:

BANK *A*

ASSETS	LIABILITIES
Reserves . . . . $ 2,000	Deposits $10,000
Loans. 8,000	

BANK *B*

ASSETS	LIABILITIES
Reserves . . . . $ 8,000	Deposits . . . . $ 8,000

The derivative deposit arising out of a loan from Bank A has now been transferred by check to Bank B where it is received as a primary deposit. Bank B must now set aside 20 percent as required reserves and may lend or reinvest the remainder. Its books after such a loan would appear as follows:

BANK B
(After a loan equal to its excess reserves)

ASSETS	LIABILITIES
Reserves . . . . $ 8,000	Deposits $14,400
Loans. 6,400	

Assume that a check is drawn against the derivative deposit of $6,400 arising out of the loan by Bank B. This reduces its reserves and deposits as follows:

BANK B

ASSETS	LIABILITIES
Reserves . . . . $ 1,600	Deposits . . . . $ 8,000
Loans. 6,400	

The check for $6,400 will most likely be deposited in a bank, in our example in Bank A or Bank B itself, since we have assumed that only two banks exist. In the American banking system, it may be deposited in one of the approximately 14,000 banks, or in one of thousands of other depository institutions.

This process of credit expansion can take place in the same way when a bank buys securities as when it makes a loan. Assume, as we did in the case of a bank loan, the following situation:

BANK A

ASSETS	LIABILITIES
Reserves $10,000	Deposits $10,000

Securities costing $8,000 are purchased and the proceeds credited to the account of the seller, giving the following situation:

BANK A

ASSETS	LIABILITIES
Reserves $10,000	Deposits $18,000
Investments. . . . . $ 8,000	

Assume that a check is drawn against the deposit and is deposited in Bank B. The books of the two banks would then show:

BANK A

ASSETS	LIABILITIES
Reserves $2,000	
Investments. 8,000	Deposits $10,000

BANK *B*

ASSETS	LIABILITIES
Reserves . . . . $ 8,000	Deposits . . . . $ 8,000

Just as in the case of a loan, the derivative deposit has been transferred to Bank *B* where it is received as a primary deposit.

At each stage in the process, 20 percent of the new primary deposit becomes required reserves and 80 percent excess reserves that can be loaned out. In time, the whole of the original $10,000 primary deposit will have become required reserves, and $50,000 of deposits will have been credited to deposit accounts of which $40,000 will have been loaned out.

Table 5-1 shows a further illustration of the deposit credit expansion process based on a 15 percent reserve requirement. An initial $1,000 in excess reserves is injected into the banking system. Initial checkable deposits of $1,000 will occur with excess reserves of $850 being available for loans and investments, and so forth.

Table 5-1

Multiple Expansion of Deposit Credit by the Banking System—15 Percent Reserve Requirement

	Assets				Liabilities
	Reserves			Loans and Investments	Checkable Deposits
	Total	(Required)	(Excess)		
Initial reserves provided	$1,000	$150	$850	—	$1,000
Expansion—Stage 1	1,000	278	722	850	1,850
Stage 2	1,000	386	614	1,572	2,572
Stage 3	1,000	478	522	2,186	3,186
Stage 4	1,000	556	444	2,708	3,708
Stage 5	1,000	623	377	3,152	4,152
Stage 6	1,000	680	320	3,529	4,529
Stage 7	1,000	728	272	3,849	4,849
Stage 8	1,000	769	231	4,121	5,121
Stage 9	1,000	803	197	4,352	5,352
Stage 10	1,000	833	167	4,549	5,549
.	.	.	.	.	.
.	.	.	.	.	.
Stage 20	1,000	961	39	5,448	6,448
.	.	.	.	.	.
.	.	.	.	.	.
Final stage	$1,000	$1,000	$ 0	$5,667	$6,667

SOURCE: Federal Reserve Bank of Chicago, *Modern Money Mechanics.*

The multiple expansion in the money supply created by the banking system through its expansion of deposit credit also can be expressed in formula form as follows:

$$\frac{\text{Initial Excess Reserves}}{\substack{\text{Reserve Requirement} \\ \text{Percentage}}} = \text{Changes in Checkable Deposits}$$

In the example presented in Table 5-1, the maximum expansion in the money supply (checkable deposits component) would be:

$$\frac{\$1,000}{.15} = \$6,667$$

which is the same as the final stage figure shown for checkable deposit liabilities. In our complex economy, however, there are several factors or "leakages" that reduce the ability to reach the maximum expansion in the money supply depicted in our simplified example.

Offsetting or Limiting Factors

The process of credit creation can go on only to the extent that the activities described actually take place. If for any reason the proceeds of a loan are withdrawn from the banking system, no new deposit arises to continue the process. A new deposit of $10,000 permits loans of $8,000 under a 20 percent required reserve; but if this $8,000 were used in currency transactions without being deposited in a bank, no credit could be created. It is the custom of carrying on business by means of checks that makes credit creation possible.

In the examples above, no allowance was made for currency withdrawal or cash "leakage" from the system. In actual practice, as the volume of business in the economy increases, some additional cash is withdrawn for hand-to-hand circulation and to meet the needs of business for petty cash.

Money may also be withdrawn from the banking system to meet the demand for payments to foreign countries, or foreign banks may withdraw some of the money they are holding on deposit in American banks. The United States Treasury may withdraw funds it has on deposit in banks. All of these factors reduce the multiplying capacity of primary deposits.[3]

Furthermore, this process can go on only if excess reserves are actually being loaned by the banks. This means that banks must be willing to lend the full amount of their excess reserves and that acceptable borrowers must be available who have a demand for credit.

Contraction of Credit

When the need for funds by business decreases, this process can work in reverse. Expansion takes place as long as excess reserves exist and the demand

---

[3]The nonbank public's decisions to switch funds between checkable deposits and time or savings deposits also will influence the ability to expand the money supply and credit. This will be explored later in this chapter.

for new bank loans exceeds the repayment of old loans. When old loans are being repaid faster than new loans are being granted and banks are not immediately investing the funds so freed, contraction of the supply of deposit credit will take place.

Let us assume that Bank *A* has no excess reserves, and see the effect of the repayment of a loan. Before the borrower began to build up deposits to repay the loan, its books were as follows:

BANK *A*

ASSETS		LIABILITIES	
Reserves	$ 2,000	Deposits	$10,000
Loans	8,000		

The borrower of the $8,000 must build up his or her deposit account by $8,000 in order to be able to repay the loan. This is reflected on the books as follows:

BANK *A*

ASSETS		LIABILITIES	
Reserves	$10,000	Deposits	$18,000
Loans	8,000		

After the $8,000 is repaid, the books show the following:

ASSETS		LIABILITIES	
Reserves	$10,000	Deposits	$10,000

If no new loan is made from the $10,000 of reserves, credit contraction will result. This is true because $8,000 of funds have been taken out of the banking system to build up deposits to repay the loan and are now being held idle by Bank *A* as excess reserves. The result of taking out $8,000 of reserves may be cumulative on the contraction side just as it was during expansion.

Assume that the $8,000 of deposits built up to repay the loan came from Bank *B*, which before these funds were withdrawn had no excess reserves and showed the following situation on its books:

BANK *B*

ASSETS		LIABILITIES	
Reserves	$ 2,000	Deposits	$10,000
Loans	8,000		

The withdrawal of $8,000 of deposits would require a sale of securities that might be held by the bank or a loan from its federal reserve bank or from another bank that might have excess funds to lend. If we assume a loan was made, its books would show:

BANK *B*

ASSETS		LIABILITIES	
Reserves	$ 400	Deposits	$ 2,000
Loans..............	8,000	Loan from federal	
		reserve bank......	6,400

Reserves must remain at $400 since this amount is the required reserve on the $2,000 of deposits. In order to pay off its debt to the federal reserve bank, this bank will probably refuse to renew the $8,000 loan when it comes due. In order to pay the loan, the borrower builds up her or his deposit by $8,000. The books now show:

BANK *B*

ASSETS		LIABILITIES	
Reserves	$ 8,400	Deposits	$10,000
Loans..............	8,000	Loan from federal	
		reserve bank......	6,400

This enables the bank to pay its loan to the federal reserve bank as follows:

BANK *B*

ASSETS		LIABILITIES	
Reserves	$ 2,000	Deposits	$10,000
Loans..............	8,000		

After the $8,000 loan from the bank is repaid, the situation is as follows:

BANK *B*

ASSETS		LIABILITIES	
Reserves	$ 2,000	Deposits	$ 2,000

In building up the $8,000 deposit to repay the loan, the lender took $8,000 out of another bank in the system. This in turn led this bank to refuse to renew loans for this amount; and in building up deposit balances to repay the loans, funds were withdrawn from other banks. This process of contraction is thus cumulative just as the process of expansion is and it cannot be stopped if a bank sells securities to meet a demand for funds when it does not have excess reserves. When someone buys the securities, it is customary to withdraw funds from some bank in the system to pay for them, thus leading to contraction just as when the adjustment to a deficiency in reserves is a loan from the federal reserve bank that is repaid by reducing the amount of loans outstanding.

FACTORS AFFECTING BANK RESERVES

The extent to which the process of credit expansion or contraction can and does take place is governed by the level of excess reserves which a bank has, that is, reserves above the level of required reserves. This is true for an individual bank and also for the banking system as a whole. Therefore, the factors which affect the level of bank reserves are of basic significance in determining the size of the money supply. *Total reserves* in the banking system consist of reserve deposits and vault cash. Reserve deposits are deposits held at the federal reserve banks by commercial banks and other depository institutions; vault cash is currency, including coin, held on the premises of these institutions. There are two kinds of factors which affect total reserves: those which affect the currency holdings of the banking system and those which affect deposits at the Federal Reserve. Currency flows in response to changes in the demand for it by households and firms. Reserve deposits are affected by a variety of transactions involving the Federal Reserve and banks, which may be initiated by the banking system or the Federal Reserve, by the Treasury or by other factors. Although the Federal Reserve does not control all of the factors which affect the level of bank reserves, it does have the ability to offset or overpower any fluctuation, and thus it has broad control over the total reserves available to the banking system.

Changes in the Demand for Currency

Currency flows into and out of the banking system affect the level of bank reserves of the banks receiving the currency for deposit. Let us assume that individuals or a business find that they have excess currency of $100 and deposit it in Commercial Bank *A*. Deposit liabilities are increased by $100 and so are the reserves of Bank *A*. The bank now has excess reserves of $80, assuming a 20 percent level of required reserves; and these reserves can be used by the banking system to create $400 in additional deposits. If the bank does not have a need for the currency but sends it to its federal reserve bank, it will receive a $100 credit to its account. The volume of federal reserve notes is decreased by $100, and this frees the collateral backing them. These transactions may be summarized as follows:

1. Deposits in Bank *A* are increased by $100 ($20 in required reserves and $80 in excess reserves).
2. Bank *A*'s deposit at its federal reserve bank is increased $100.
3. The amount of federal reserve notes is decreased by $100.

Just the opposite takes place when the public demands additional currency. Let us assume that a customer of Bank *A* needs additional currency and cashes a check for $100. The deposits of the bank are reduced by $100, and this reduces required reserves by $20. If the bank has no excess reserves, it must take steps to get an additional $80 of reserves either by borrowing from its federal reserve bank, calling a loan or not renewing one which comes due, or by selling securities.

The reserves of the bank are also reduced by $100; and if it replenishes its supply of currency from its federal reserve bank, its deposits with this bank are reduced by $100. These transactions may be summarized thus:

1. Deposits in Bank A are reduced by $100 ($20 in required reserves and $80 in excess reserves).
2. Bank A's deposit at its federal reserve bank is reduced $100.
3. The amount of federal reserve notes is increased by $100.

Federal Reserve System Transactions

Transactions of banks with the Federal Reserve System and changes in reserve requirements by the Federal Reserve also affect either the level of bank reserves or the degree to which credit can be expanded with a given volume of reserves. Such transactions may occur at the initiative of the Federal Reserve when it buys or sells securities, at the initiative of a bank or other depository institution when it borrows from its federal reserve bank, or from a change in Federal Reserve float arising out of the process of collecting checks. These are examined in turn, and then the effect of a change in reserve requirements is described. Finally, we will look at Treasury transactions that affect reserves in the banking system.

When the Federal Reserve, through its open market operations, purchases securities, such as government bonds, it adds to bank reserves. The Federal Reserve pays for the bonds with a check. The seller deposits the check in an account and receives a deposit account credit. The bank presents the check to the federal reserve bank for payment and receives a credit to its account. When the Federal Reserve buys a $100 government bond, the check for which is deposited in Bank A, the transactions may be summarized as follows:

1. Bank A's deposit at its federal reserve bank is increased by $100. The federal reserve bank has a new asset—a bond worth $100.
2. Deposits in Bank A are increased by $100 ($20 in required reserves and $80 in excess reserves).

Just the opposite takes place when the Federal Reserve sells securities in the market.

In contrast to the other transactions that affect reserves in the banking system, open market operations are entirely at the initiative of the Federal Reserve. It is for this reason that they are the most important policy tool of the Federal Reserve in controlling reserves and the money supply. Open market operations are conducted virtually every business day, both to smooth out fluctuations caused by other transactions, and to implement changes in the money supply called for by policy directives of the Federal Open Market Committee.

When a bank borrows from its federal reserve bank, it is borrowing reserves; and so reserves are increased by the amount of the loan. Similarly, when a loan to the federal reserve bank is repaid, reserves are reduced by the amount so repaid.

The transactions when Bank *A* borrows $100 from its federal reserve bank may be summarized as follows:

1. Bank *A*'s deposit at its federal reserve bank is increased by $100. The assets of the federal reserve bank are increased by $100 by the note from Bank *A*.
2. Bank *A*'s excess reserves have been increased by $100. It also has a new $100 liability—its note to the federal reserve bank.

This process is just reversed when a debt to the federal reserve bank is repaid.

Changes in Federal Reserve float also affect bank reserves. Float arises out of the process of collecting checks most of which are cleared in one way or another at federal reserve banks. Checks drawn on nearby banks are credited almost immediately to the account of the bank in which they were deposited and debited to the account of the bank on which the check was drawn. Under Federal Reserve regulations, all checks are credited one or two days later to the account of the bank in which the check was deposited. It may take longer for the check to go through the collection process and be debited to the account of the bank upon which it is drawn. When this happens, bank reserves are increased, and this increase is called *float*. The process in which a $100 check drawn on Bank *B* is deposited in Bank *A* and credited to its account before it is debited to the account of Bank *B* may be summarized:

1. Bank *A* transfers $100 from its Cash Items in the Process of Collection to its account at the federal reserve bank. Its reserves are increased by $100.
2. The federal reserve bank takes $100 from its Deferred Availability Account and transfers it to Bank *A*'s account.

Thus, total reserves of banks are increased temporarily by $100. They are reduced when Bank *B*'s account at its federal reserve bank is reduced by $100 a day or two later.

Changes in reserve requirements change the amount of credit expansion which is possible with a given level of reserves. With required reserves of 20 percent, excess reserves of $80 can be expanded to $400 of additional loans and deposits. If required reserves are reduced to 10 percent, it is possible to expand $80 of excess reserves to $800 of additional loans and deposits. Additional expansion also takes place because when reserve requirements are lowered, part of the required reserves becomes excess reserves. This process is reversed when reserve requirements are raised.

Bank reserves are also affected by changes in the level of deposits of foreign central banks and governments at the federal reserve banks. Such deposits are maintained with the federal reserve banks to settle international balances and also at times as part of the monetary reserves of a foreign country. A decrease in such foreign deposits with the federal reserve banks increases bank reserves; an increase in them decreases bank reserves.

Treasury Transactions

Bank reserves are also affected by the transactions of the Treasury, being increased by expenditures and other payments and decreased when the Treasury increases the size of its accounts at the federal reserve banks. The Treasury makes almost all of its payments out of its accounts at the federal reserve banks, and such spending adds to bank reserves. The recipient of a check from the Treasury deposits it in a bank. The bank sends it to the federal reserve bank for collection and receives a credit to its account. The federal reserve bank debits the account of the Treasury. When a Treasury check for $100 is deposited in Bank A and required reserves are 20 percent, the transactions may be summarized as follows:

1. The deposits of Bank A are increased by $100, its required reserves by $20, and excess reserves by $80.
2. Bank A's reserves at the federal reserve bank are increased by $100.
3. The deposit account of the Treasury at the federal reserve bank is reduced by $100.

Treasury funds from tax collections or the sale of bonds are generally deposited in its accounts in banks. When the Treasury has a need for funds for payment from its accounts at the federal reserve banks, it transfers funds from commercial banks to its accounts at the federal reserve banks. This process reduces bank reserves. When $100 is transferred from the account in Bank A and required reserves are 20 percent, transactions may be summarized as follows:

1. The Treasury deposit in Bank A is reduced by $100, required reserves by $20, and excess reserves by $80.
2. The Treasury account at the federal reserve bank is increased by $100, and the account of Bank A is reduced by $100.

The Treasury is the largest single depositor at the Federal Reserve, and the volume of transfers between the account of the Treasury and the reserve accounts of banks is large enough to cause significant fluctuations in reserves in the banking system. For this reason the Federal Reserve closely monitors the Treasury's account and often uses open market operations to minimize the disturbance, buying securities to provide reserves to the banking system when the Treasury's account increases, and selling securities when the account of the Treasury falls to a low level.

The effect on bank reserves is the same for changes in Treasury cash holdings as it is for changes in Treasury accounts at the federal reserve banks. Reserves are increased when the Treasury decreases its holding of cash, and reserves are decreased when it increases such holdings.

Summary of Transactions Affecting Bank Reserves

The previously discussed transactions which change the volume of bank reserves or the ability of banks to expand credit are summarized in Figure 5-1.

Figure 5-1
Transactions Affecting
Bank Reserves

Nonbank Public	Federal Reserve System	United States Treasury
Change in the nonbank public's demand for currency to be held outside the banking system	Change in reserve requirements Open market operations (buying and selling government securities) Change in bank borrowings Change in float Change in foreign deposits held in federal reserve banks Change in other Federal Reserve accounts	Change in Treasury expenditures out of accounts held at federal reserve banks Change in Treasury cash holdings

Important roles are played by the nonbank public in deciding currency holdings, the Federal Reserve System, and the United States Treasury. The Federal Reserve, of course, provides the major impact. First, the Federal Reserve establishes the reserve requirements (fraction or percentage) that banks must hold against their deposits. The impact of a 15 percent reserve requirement on checkable deposits was illustrated in a simplified example earlier in this chapter. In addition to changing reserve requirements, the Federal Reserve can alter bank reserves through its open market operations and its loan policies to banks. Loans are encouraged or discouraged on the basis of the discount rate charged and the willingness of the Federal Reserve to make loans.

Bank reserves are also affected by other transactions involving the Federal Reserve System. Included would be changes in the amount of float, foreign deposits held in federal reserve banks, and various other Federal Reserve accounts.

Finally, Treasury transactions also can influence the level of reserves in the banking system. Treasury expenditures from its accounts held in federal reserve banks, transfers of funds to those accounts from the banking system, and changes in its holdings of cash all alter bank reserves.

THE MONETARY BASE AND MONEY MULTIPLIER

Earlier in this chapter we examined the deposit credit multiplying capacity of the banking system. Recall that in Table 5-1 $1,000 in initial reserves were introduced into the banking system and that a 15 percent reserve requirement on deposits could result in a deposit expansion of $6,667. This also can be viewed as a 6.667 deposit or money multiplier in the following framework: bank reserves times (1/reserve requirement percentage) equals the checkable deposits component of the money supply. Using the data in our example, 1/.15 equals 6.667, thus $1,000(6.667) = $6,667.

Today, however, it is more useful to focus on the relationship between the monetary "base" and the money supply in order to better understand the complexity of the money multiplier in our financial system. The *monetary base* is defined as banking system reserves plus currency held by the nonbank public (a basic component of the money supply). More specifically, the monetary base consists of reserve deposits held in federal reserve banks, vault cash or currency held by banks and other depository institutions, and currency held by the nonbank public. The monetary base (MB) times the money multiplier (m) produces the M1 definition of the money supply and can be expressed in formula form as: MBm = M1.

As of October, 1982, the money multiplier was approximately 2.7 as determined by dividing the $468.3 billion money stock by the $172.9 billion monetary base.[4] In our financial system, the money multiplier can fluctuate over time depending on actions taken by the Federal Reserve plus actions not under the Federal Reserve's direct control. These latter actions include decisions by the nonbank public and the U.S. Treasury.

The M1 money multiplier in today's complex financial system can be expressed as:[5]

$$m = \frac{1 + k}{r(1 + t + g) + k}$$

where

1. r is the ratio of reserves to total deposits (checkable, noncheckable time and savings, and government)
2. k is the ratio of currency held by the nonbank public to checkable deposits
3. t is the ratio of noncheckable deposits to checkable deposits
4. g is the ratio of government deposits to checkable deposits.

Let's illustrate how the size of the money multiplier is determined by returning to our previous example of a 15 percent reserve requirement. Recall that in an uncomplex financial system the money multiplier would be determined as $1/r$ or $1/.15$ which equals 6.667 or a rounded figure of 6.7. However, in our complex system we also need to consider leakages of money into currency held by the nonbank public, noncheckable time and savings deposits, and government deposits. Let's further assume that the reserve requirement applies to total deposits, a k of 30 percent, a t of 25 percent, and a g of 5 percent. The money multiplier then would be estimated as:

$$m = \frac{1 + .30}{.15(1 + .25 + .05) + .30} = \frac{1.30}{.495} = 2.6$$

---

[4]*Federal Reserve Bulletin*, December, 1982, pp. A13 and A14.

[5]The reader interested in following how the money multiplier is derived will find a discussion in most money and banking textbooks. A concise treatment is provided in: S. Kerry Cooper and Donald R. Fraser, *The Financial Marketplace* (Reading, Mass.: Addison-Wesley Publishing Company, 1982), pp. 120–122.

Of course, if a change occurred in any of the components, the money multiplier would adjust accordingly.

IMPORTANCE OF CONTROLLING THE MONEY SUPPLY

At this point we should ask why is it important to regulate and control the supply of money? The historical relationship between changes in the growth rate for money supply or stock and economic activity has been examined extensively. Downturns or recessions in economic activity have been preceded by sharp declines in the short-run (six-month) growth rates of money stock relative to the long-run or trend (five-year) growth rates. This observable link between changes in the growth of money supply and economic activity provides an important foundation for regulating and controlling the supply or stock of money in our financial system.

At the same time, evidence suggests that movements in the long-run money supply growth rates are associated with movements in the rate of inflation. Money growth rates above those levels that are necessary to sustain economic growth in our free-enterprise economy are believed to be inflationary.

It would be naive, however, to believe that regulating and controlling the supply of money and credit is all that is necessary to "manage" our complex economy. As we shall see in later chapters, economic activity also is affected by government actions concerning government spending, taxation, and the management of our public debt.

QUESTIONS

1. Explain how federal reserve notes are supported or "backed" in our financial system.
2. Why is the expansion and contraction of deposit credit by the banking system possible in our financial system?
3. Trace the effect on its accounts of a loan made by a bank that has excess reserves available from new deposits.
4. Explain how credit expansion takes place in a banking system consisting of two banks.
5. Explain the potential for credit expansion when required reserves average 10 percent and $2,000 in excess reserves are deposited in the banking system.
6. What is the process of credit contraction?
7. Trace the effect on bank reserves of a change in the amount of cash held by the public.
8. Describe the effect on bank reserves when the Federal Reserve sells U.S. government securities to a bank.
9. Summarize the factors that can lead to a change in bank reserves.
10. What is the difference between the monetary "base" and total bank reserves?
11. Briefly describe what is meant by the money multiplier and indicate the factors that affect its magnitude or size.
12. Why does it seem to be important to regulate and control the supply of money?

PROBLEMS

1. Determine the maximum deposit credit expansion in a financial system where the reserve requirement is 12 percent, initial excess reserves are $100,000, and there are no currency or other "leakages." What would be the money multiplier? How would your answers have changed if the reserve requirement had been only 8 percent?

2. Assume a financial system has a monetary base of $25 million. The reserve requirement is 10 percent and there are no leakages in the system. What is the size of the money multiplier? What will be the system's money supply? How would the money supply change if the reserve requirement is increased to 14 percent?

3. A complex financial system has the following relationships. The ratio of reserves to total deposits is 12 percent and the ratio of noncheckable deposits to checkable deposits is 40 percent. In addition, currency held by the nonbank public amounts to 15 percent of checkable deposits. The ratio of government deposits to checkable deposits is 8 percent and the monetary base now is $300 million.

    a. Determine the size of the M1 money multiplier and the amount of the money supply or stock.

    b. If the ratio of currency in circulation to checkable deposits were to drop to 13 percent, show the impact on the money supply.

    c. What would happen to the financial system's money supply if the reserve requirement increases to 14 percent while noncheckable deposits to checkable deposits falls to 35 percent? Assume the other ratios remain as originally stated.

SUGGESTED READINGS

Burger, Albert E., and Robert H. Rasche. "Revision of the Monetary Base." *Review*, Federal Reserve Bank of St. Louis (July, 1977), pp. 13–28.

Cooper, S. Kerry, and Donald R. Fraser. *The Financial Marketplace.* Reading, Mass.: Addison-Wesley Publishing Company, 1982. Chapter 6.

Gramley, Lyle E. "Financial Innovation and Monetary Policy," *Federal Reserve Bulletin* (July, 1982), pp. 393–400.

Hamblin, Mary. "Treasury Deposits and the Money Supply." *Monthly Review*, Federal Reserve Bank of Kansas City (February, 1977), pp. 14–20.

Jordan, Jerry L. "Elements of Money Stock Determination." *Review*, Federal Reserve Bank of St. Louis (October, 1969), pp. 10–19.

Kamerschen, David R. *Money and Banking*, 7th ed. Cincinnati: South-Western Publishing Co., 1980. Part II.

Nichols, Dorothy. *Modern Money Mechanics*. Federal Reserve Bank of Chicago, 1979.

Whitehead, David D. "Explaining the Cash Explosion." *Economic Review*, Federal Reserve Bank of Atlanta (March, 1982), pp. 14–18.

Your Money Supply. Federal Reserve Bank of St. Louis, undated.

6   The Savings and Investment Process

Capital formation refers to the creation of physical productive facilities such as buildings, tools, equipment, and roads. The process of adding to the amount or stock of these real assets produces growth in our economy. Investment funds are needed to create real assets and thus carry out the process of capital formation. These funds are provided out of savings. Thus, as we saw in Chapter 1, an effective financial system requires facilities for creating capital by channeling savings into investment. A major portion of the savings-investment process is conducted in the U. S. economy by first accumulating savings in financial institutions. These institutions, in turn, lend and invest the savings.

Savings are the accumulation of cash and other financial assets, such as savings accounts and corporate securities. Changes in the level of savings for individuals and corporations are measured by current income less tax payments and total expenditures. Governments, too, may save insofar as their revenues exceed their expenditures. This definition embraces two types of savings: voluntary savings and contractual savings. *Voluntary savings* are simply financial assets set aside for use in the future. *Contractual savings* include such things as the accumulation of reserves in insurance and pension funds. Contractual savings are not determined by current decision; they are disciplined by previous commitments which the saver has some incentive to honor.

HISTORICAL ROLE OF SAVINGS

As the size of American business establishments expanded, it became increasingly important that large amounts of capital be accumulated and converted to business use. The corporate form of organization provided a convenient and flexible legal arrangement for the mobilization of available investment capital. These advantages of the corporation over the proprietorship and partnership are described in Chapter 7.

Developments in transportation were often too costly and speculative for

86

private promoters to undertake. The magnitude of early canal, turnpike, and railroad construction was such that government undertook much of the task of financing such projects. Until the end of the nineteenth century, governmental units contributed more capital to these efforts than did private interests. Since this government financing was largely through bond issues rather than current revenues, the ultimate source of the funds was the savings of the individuals.

Foreign Sources of Savings

Large proportions of the securities sold by both government units and private promoters were purchased by foreigners. Foreign capital played a decisive role in the development of the nation's early transportation system.

The importance of the role that foreign capital played in the economic development of the United States can be illustrated through a comparison of this development with that of the developing nations of today. These nations now face many of the financial problems that the United States experienced during its early development. Private savings in many of these countries are negligible since almost all current income goes for immediate consumption. Individual nations and such international organizations as the World Bank supply large amounts of capital to the developing nations of the world for purposes of increasing their productive capacity.[1] The flow of development capital not only stimulates economic expansion in these countries but it also makes their capital much more efficient. For example, speedier transportation reduces the amount of goods in transit, thus releasing working capital for other purposes. In due time, as internal capital formation increases, it is hoped that the need for foreign capital will be eliminated and that these countries can then enjoy an autonomous capital formation process.

Domestic Supply of Savings

As capital formation began increasing at a faster and faster rate after the Civil War, the demand for funds also increased. Wealthy individuals and foreigners could no longer provide funds at a fast enough rate. Britain was investing heavily in India because of political commitments, and the other European countries were not of sufficient size and wealth to continue supplying funds in quantities adequate to sustain our growth. The American family soon took over the function of providing savings for the capital formation process. Per capita income had risen to a level where American families could afford luxuries well beyond the subsistence level and also save part of what they had earned. Thus, the United States gradually developed to the stage where it could generate sufficient capital to finance its own expansion. The result was ultimately a change in our status from that of a debtor nation to that of a creditor nation.

---

[1] The World Bank, the popular name for the International Bank for Reconstruction and Development, is a cooperative international organization established for the purpose of promoting long-term capital loans between nations for productive purposes.

CREATION OF FINANCIAL ASSETS AND LIABILITIES

It is common practice today to view the United States' financial system as comprising four basic economic units—individuals, business firms, financial institutions and intermediaries, and governments (federal, state, and local). At any point in time, these units are likely to be holders of real assets and financial assets. They also are likely to have certain financial liabilities or obligations. And, to the extent that their holdings of real and financial assets exceed their financial liabilities, these units will have net worth or owners' equity positions. These concepts will become clearer as we proceed.

In addition to measuring an economic unit's assets, liabilities, and net worth position as of a specific point in time, we also are interested in how these components change over time such as over a one-year period. This is because, for any measured time period, some of the basic economic units may be savings surplus units while others may be savings deficit units.

Savings surplus comes about when an economic unit, such as individuals taken as a group, has current savings that exceed its direct investment in real assets. These surplus savings are made available to savings deficit units. For example, business firms as a group often are unable to meet all of their plant and equipment investment needs out of earnings retained in the business (profits remaining after taxes, and after the payment of cash dividends to stockholders in the case of corporations).[2] This would represent a *savings deficit* situation and thus would make it necessary to acquire funds from a savings surplus unit.

Figure 6-1 illustrates how financial assets and liabilities are created when balancing savings surplus and savings deficit units. The process might begin with a group of individuals placing their savings in time deposit accounts at a commercial bank. The bank might, in turn, loan some of these deposits to a savings deficit business firm that wishes to purchase more equipment. This process of channeling savings into investment through the use of a financial institution or intermediary would result in the creation of two types of financial assets and two types of financial liabilities. The time deposits would represent financial assets to the individuals that saved funds. At the same time, these time deposits would be financial liabilities to the commercial bank. Likewise, the business loan would represent a financial asset to the commercial bank but a financial liability to the borrowing firm. It should be recognized that the total system remains in balance because the increase in time deposits held by the group of individuals would result in a corresponding increase in their net worth and the business loan would be used to increase the firm's real assets.[3]

---

[2]This is referred to as net savings by business firms and corporations. Sometimes reference also is made to gross savings by business firms. This is calculated by adding depreciation charges (designed to reflect the using up of productive assets) to retained earnings. In theory, if depreciation funds were actually set aside, they would be available to replace real assets as they wore out.

[3]The individuals receive safety of principal, liquidity, and a return on their savings over time. At the other end, the business firm anticipates earning a return on its investment in real assets that is higher than the interest cost on the bank loan. The bank, of course, expects to be compensated for facilitating the savings and investment process.

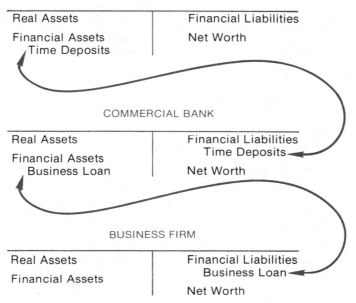

Figure 6-1
Creation of Financial
Assets and Liabilities

At this point we should distinguish between direct securities and debt instruments and those which are indirect. *Direct securities*, such as corporate stocks and bonds, are contracts between the savers and the borrowers themselves. The same instrument represents the financial asset of the saver and the claim on the borrower. Direct financial transactions may be facilitated by brokers or other intermediaries, but the instruments do not represent a claim or obligation of the intermediary. In *indirect* finance, the intermediary creates and is a party to separate instruments with the ultimate lenders and the borrowers. In the above example, the business loan and the time deposits are indirect instruments. The business firm owes money to the bank, and the bank owes money to the individuals, but the firm and the individuals have no direct relationship. Indirect instruments could have been avoided in the above example if the individual had directly supplied funds to the business firm by purchasing bonds issued by the firm.[4] This would have resulted in the creation of one type of financial asset (bond securities held by the individuals) and one type of financial liability (bond securities issued by the business firm).

Transactions involving both direct and indirect securities initially occur in primary markets. Many of these securities can be sold by their owners (the original lenders) in secondary markets. Secondary market transactions allow the

---

[4]There are reasons, of course, why the individuals might not choose to invest directly in the business firm's bonds. If they are small savers, they may be unable to individually purchase a bond. There also is less liquidity and safety of principal in such investments. Thus financial institutions and intermediaries can play an important role in channeling savings into investments.

owners of securities to convert them to cash in order to reclaim their savings for other purposes, prior to the time the original borrower has agreed to repay the indebtedness. Such transactions do not affect the original borrowers except that their debt is now owed to someone else. However, secondary markets provide liquidity to the original lenders, and this feature is important in attracting savings to certain primary markets. For example, the New York Stock Exchange is a secondary market. Its existence makes it easier for corporations to sell new issues of stock in the primary market.

MAJOR SOURCES OF SAVINGS

The most important savings sector in the economy is personal savings. Private individuals provide more than three-fourths of all savings in the United States. It is toward the individual that most financial institutions direct their attention in the capital accumulation processes. Thus individuals as a group consistently represent a savings surplus unit. Corporations also represent an important source of savings. However, their large demand for investment funds (as is the case for unincorporated business firms) generally results in an aggregate savings deficit position. While financial institutions and intermediaries also can save, their primary role in our financial system is to facilitate the savings-investment process. Our governments on balance have operated as a savings deficit unit in recent years. Thus, the ability to provide adequate funds to meet our investment needs is dependent primarily on the savings of individuals and to a lesser extent on the savings of corporations.

Personal Savings

Private individuals maintain savings for a number of reasons. They set aside a part of their current income for the acquisition of costly durable consumer goods. Savings are set aside by individuals to meet unforeseeable contingencies. These savings are not set aside for specific future consumption; instead, they represent emergency or "rainy-day" funds. Individuals may also save for such long-term foreseeable expenditures as children's college education or for retirement. For short periods of time people may save a portion of current income simply because desirable goods and services are not available for purchase.

Persons have open to them a number of media in which to maintain their savings. These media range in liquidity from cash balances to pension funds. The medium that a person chooses is usually a function of the amount of liquidity desired and the degree of safety and return that the particular medium provides.

Cash Balances. The most liquid form of savings that an individual can maintain is cash. Cash savings are generally in the form of checkable deposits and pocket cash. People maintain this liquidity in order to meet current commitments or to make expenditures in the very near future. Cash savings may also be hoarded. Such hoards are not held for specific consumption purposes but rather out of distrust of depository institutions or because the individual wants monetary wealth

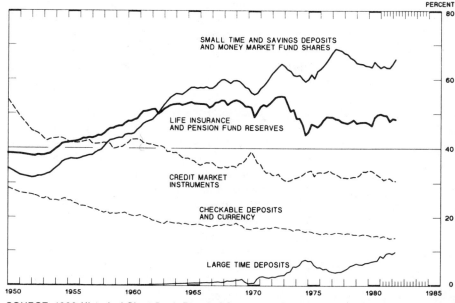

Figure 6-2

Financial Assets Held by Households (Percent of Disposable Personal Income)

SOURCE: *1982 Historical Chart Book,* Board of Governors of the Federal Reserve System, p. 68.

to be close at hand. Funds so hoarded are withdrawn from circulation and add nothing to the capital formation process. Figure 6-2 shows that checkable deposits and currency actually have been declining as a percent of disposable income in recent years.

Time and Savings Deposits. A wide choice of facilities providing both safety of principal and a reasonable yield is available to the individual saver. The combination of ready availability of funds and a regular earning power on time and savings deposits resulted in a substantial rate of growth for such accounts during the 1950s and 1960s. More recently financial assets have been directed towards money market fund shares which offer limited check-writing privileges and returns based on the investment of money market funds in bank certificates of deposit and corporate commercial paper. Household investments in large time deposits (amounts of $100,000 or more) also grew rapidly during the 1970s, as is shown in Figure 6-2.

Insurance Reserves and Pension Funds. The contractual savings embodied in insurance reserves and in pension funds grew rapidly as a percent of disposable personal income during the 1950s. While growth in this area of financial assets has slowed in recent years, Figure 6-2 shows that life insurance and pension fund reserves continue to account for a large portion of total household holdings. Individuals may acquire life insurance through private organizations and may belong to private pension plans or funds. The principal form of individual savings provided by state and local governments are retirement funds. The federal government accumulates reserves for the accounts of individuals through the Old-Age and Survivors Insurance Trust Fund, the Disability Insurance Trust Fund, the National Service Life Insurance Fund, and others. These savings of individuals as represented by government-held reserves are invested primarily in the obligations of federal, local, and state governments. As such, they satisfy a part of the demand for funds of government in general.

Securities. Because of the wide diversity of security forms—corporate stock, corporate bonds, and government securities—private individuals can usually find a security that is well suited to their special savings objectives. For those persons desiring growth of principal, corporate stocks with the promise of growth are available. Such stocks usually provide a lower current income to the saver than is available from most other securities. Other savers may place primary emphasis on stability of principal for liquidity purposes. The stocks of public utilities and other recession-resistant companies are available for this purpose as are high-grade corporate and government bonds. There is a wide spectrum of risk, growth potential, and yield in which virtually every saver who chooses securities as a savings medium can find a place for funds consistent with the saver's own individual objectives and preferences. Figure 6-2 shows the importance of these credit market instruments.

The shares of investment companies add to the importance of common stock as a form of individual savings. These shares have played an especially important role for the saver with limited funds because of their ready availability in small quantities. The investment companies have also instituted convenient procedures for accumulation of shares on a regular basis out of current income.

Corporate Savings

Corporations, broadly described, include not only business enterprises but nonprofit institutions such as colleges, churches, hospitals, and philanthropic foundations. These nonprofit organizations ordinarily acquire their financial assets not through their own saving but through the gifts of individuals and business corporations. The earning power of their endowed funds is usually devoted to their operating expenses, and their savings are small. The savings of the nonfinancial business corporation are defined as the financial assets retained by the corporation out of funds generated through business operations that are neither paid out in dividends nor invested in operating assets of the business. Funds generated through business operations include not only corporate earnings but the conversion of operating assets to financial assets through depreciation allowances.

Corporate saving for short-term working capital purposes is by far the most important reason for the accumulation of financial assets. Seasonal fluctuations create an uneven demand for corporate operating assets, such as inventories and accounts receivable. And because of these seasonal fluctuations, cash inflow is seldom in just the right amount and at the right time to accommodate the increased levels of operating assets. Quarterly corporate income tax liabilities also impose upon corporations the necessity of accumulating financial assets for their payment. Although the short-term accumulation of financial assets on the part of business corporations does not add to the level of long-term savings of the economy as a whole, such funds do enter the monetary stream and become available to users of short-term borrowed funds. As such, these short-term savings serve to meet a part of the demand for funds of consumers, government, and other businesses. These savings are typically held by the corporation in the form of checkable deposits with commercial banks, short-term obligations of the federal government, commercial paper, and certificates of deposit as issued by commercial banks. These financial assets meet the requirements of safety and liquidity.

Corporations also engage in the savings process for purposes of meeting planned expenditures in the future. Reserves are often set up to provide all or part of the cost of construction, the acquisition of equipment, or major maintenance and repairs to existing facilities. Savings committed to these purposes are often invested in securities having longer maturities and higher yields than those acquired for short-term business purposes. Such securities include the debt obligations of both corporations and government and, to a limited extent, corporate stock.

FLOW OF FUNDS FROM SAVINGS INTO INVESTMENTS

Individuals represent the most important source of savings in our financial system. As we have seen, they may invest their savings directly in bonds, stocks, and real estate mortgages or indirectly by placing their savings in financial institutions and intermediaries. We could trace the flow of funds from savings into investments in real assets, including the changes in financial assets and liabilities, in order to have a better understanding of the savings-investment process. In fact the Federal Reserve prepares a flow of funds accounts analysis. This analysis, however, is very detailed and complex. For example, the Federal Reserve prepares a nine-sector (in contrast with our previous discussion of four basic economic units or sectors) flow of funds table or matrix.[5]

As an alternative to the Federal Reserve's complex flow of funds analysis, several private organizations provide basic source and use of funds analysis and projections. We have chosen to use the source (funds supplied) and use (funds raised for investment) approach in this chapter.

Table 6-1 indicates the sources of funds supplied from savings in our economy during recent years. These calculations, estimations, and projections are prepared annually by the Bankers Trust Company. Let's put the table in perspective: individuals may directly invest their savings (as is indicated by the "individuals and others" category) or place their savings in financial institutions and intermediaries. Business firms, particularly corporations, also can supply

---

[5]Quarterly flow of funds data are published by the Board of Governors of the Federal Reserve System. These reports are supplemented once a year by detailed estimates of financial assets and liabilities by sector.

Table 6-1

Annual Source or Supply of Funds. Summary of Financing—Total Funds Supplied (In Billions of Dollars)

	1979	1980	1981	1982 (Est.)	1983 (Proj.)
FUNDS SUPPLIED					
Insurance companies and pension funds					
Life insurance companies	33.6	33.9	38.0	40.8	44.3
Private noninsured pension funds	15.9	20.8	21.5	25.2	26.6
State and local retirement funds	19.4	23.4	23.2	29.4	31.5
Fire and casualty insurance companies	17.5	14.4	12.7	12.6	14.0
Total	86.5	92.6	95.4	108.0	116.4
Thrift Institutions					
Savings and loan associations	51.5	42.1	23.8	18.6	44.0
Mutual savings banks	4.8	5.3	−.2	−.5	6.2
Credit unions	2.0	−2.2	.8	1.2	5.0
Total	58.3	45.2	24.4	19.3	55.2
Investment companies	22.4	22.5	72.9	51.7	47.1
Other financial intermediaries					
Finance companies	24.1	11.8	22.6	3.8	9.1
Mortgage companies	−1.4	2.8	.2	−2.6	1.7
Real estate investment trusts	−1.0	−.7	−1.1	−.8	−.5
Total	21.7	13.9	21.7	.4	10.3
Commercial banks	120.3	100.5	108.7	96.0	107.3
Business					
Business corporations	24.9	14.8	8.2	9.8	15.9
Noncorporate business	1.8	.5	2.7	1.3	1.7
Total	26.7	15.3	10.9	11.1	17.6
Government					
U.S. government	6.2	6.9	4.3	2.4	2.9
Federally sponsored agencies	19.8	18.0	14.0	13.3	10.0
State and local general funds	8.1	14.9	14.4	18.7	21.2
Total	34.1	39.8	32.8	34.4	34.1
Foreign investors	−3.2	28.2	21.9	27.3	30.5
Individuals and others	86.4	69.2	58.9	80.9	81.4
Total gross sources	453.2	427.2	447.7	429.1	499.9
Less: Funds raised by financial intermediaries					
Investment funds	10.0	8.2	−1.1	4.1	6.4
Short-term funds	16.7	5.2	28.4	2.6	9.5
Federally sponsored agency securities, privately held	23.6	24.1	30.1	17.2	14.8
Total	50.3	37.5	57.4	23.9	30.7
Total net sources	403.0	389.7	390.3	405.2	469.2

SOURCE: Bankers Trust Company, *Credit and Capital Markets*, 1983, p. T1.

funds from their savings in the form of retained earnings and by extending trade credit to other business firms.

The primary sources of funds are provided by financial institutions from the savings of individuals. These funds then are lent or invested in the securities issued by corporations and governments and in real estate mortgages. Table 6-1 shows that commercial banks represent the dominant institutional source of funds. The other depository (or thrift) institutions, particularly savings and loan associations, also have been major suppliers of funds in the past. Notice, however, that the high and volatile interest rates of 1981 resulted in a substantial drop in funds supplied by savings and loan associations and mutual savings banks. This disintermediation was similar to that which occurred in 1974–75.

The largest growth in funds supplied in recent years has come from the investment companies, as is shown in Table 6-1. More specifically, the money market funds have been responsible for this rapid increase in funds supplied by investment companies. Also notice that insurance companies and pension funds as a group rank about equal to commercial banks in the annual amount of funds supplied. Funds generated annually by insurance companies and pension funds come primarily from contractual savings while commercial banks depend heavily on the voluntary savings of individuals.

Table 6-2 shows the annual use of funds by nonfinancial sectors in our economy. Funds raised by financial intermediaries are excluded. Thus, the total use of funds corresponds with the total net sources shown in Table 6-1. The activities of financial intermediaries are excluded by the Bankers Trust Company since they do not add to the total supply of, or demand for, credit.

The supply of funds is channeled or grouped into three basic categories or uses: (1) short-term funds; (2) intermediate and long-term funds; and (3) federal government and federal agency securities. Short-term funds usually involve financing for one year or less. Table 6-2 indicates that major annual uses for short-term funds generally are for the extension of credit to consumers, for bank loans to business firms, and in the form of open market paper consisting of commercial paper and bankers' acceptances. Notice, however, the substantial cutback in consumer credit expansion during the economic downturn in 1980. Trade credit extended by some business firms to other business firms, along with commercial or business finance company loans, also represent an important form of business credit, although the amount of funds raised has been affected by economic conditions in recent years.

The U.S. government also plays an important role in the annual use of funds. As budget deficits get larger and larger, the federal government must raise more funds by issuing debt securities. Notice the substantial increase in the funds raised by the U.S. government during the first part of the 1980s. Some economists are concerned that increased competition between the government and private sectors for available funds may adversely affect future economic activity.

Intermediate and long-term funds dominate the annual use of funds, as is shown in Table 6-2. Within this category, the single most important use of funds is for financing real estate through the issuance of mortgages. This is followed by

Table 6-2

Annual Use of Funds. Summary of Financing—Total Funds Raised (In Billions of Dollars)

	1979	1980	1981	1982 (Est.)	1983 (Proj.)
INTERMEDIATE AND LONG-TERM FUNDS RAISED					
Corporate securities					
Bonds	22.5	33.2	23.9	28.7	31.7
Stocks	−3.9	12.9	2.5	2.3	5.2
Total	18.6	46.1	26.4	31.0	36.9
State and local securities	29.8	35.9	32.9	57.3	51.5
Real estate mortgages	164.2	134.0	111.8	88.8	109.3
Foreign securities	4.8	3.1	5.5	5.0	5.6
Term loans					
Commercial banks	17.7	12.5	14.5	16.0	10.5
Banks for cooperatives	.6	.5	.6	.4	.5
Total	18.3	13.0	15.1	16.4	11.0
Total intermediate and long-term uses	235.7	232.2	191.7	198.5	214.3
SHORT-TERM FUNDS RAISED					
Open market paper	21.8	15.8	33.1	7.5	10.8
Consumer credit	45.5	4.9	25.3	12.4	25.2
Policy loans	4.7	6.6	7.3	4.8	3.5
Loans of federally sponsored agencies	4.7	2.8	.8	−1.3	−1.0
Bank loans to business	33.8	21.5	43.2	24.7	11.0
Other bank loans	−.4	12.9	−.9	3.7	5.6
Other business credit					
Net trade credit	17.1	14.0	2.3	3.4	5.8
Finance company loans	10.1	3.4	9.5	−.2	2.5
Total	27.2	17.4	11.8	3.2	8.3
Total short-term uses	137.3	81.8	120.6	55.0	63.4
U.S. GOVERNMENT FUNDS RAISED					
U.S. government and budget agency securities, privately held	29.9	75.7	78.0	151.7	191.5
Total overall uses	403.0	389.7	390.3	405.2	469.2

SOURCE: Bankers Trust Company, *Credit and Capital Markets*, 1983, pp. T1–T3.

the issuance of corporate bonds and stocks to raise funds for investment purposes and by the issuance of debt instruments and securities by state and local governments. Term loans by commercial banks also are an important intermediate use of funds.

FACTORS AFFECTING SAVINGS

Among the several factors influencing the total amount of savings that are forthcoming in any given time period are: levels of income, economic expectations, cyclical influences, and the life stage of the individual saver or corporation. The precise relationship between savings and consumption is the subject of much debate and continuing study, however, and we limit our observations here to broad generalizations.

Levels of Income

For our purposes, savings have been defined as current income less tax payments and consumption expenditures. Keeping this definition in mind, let us explore the effect of changes in income on the levels of savings of individuals. As income falls, the individual attempts to maintain the present standard of living as long as possible. In so doing, the proportion of one's consumption expenditures increases and total savings diminish. As income is further reduced, the individual may be forced to curtail consumption expenditures, and this results in a lower standard of living. Such reduction is reasonably limited, however, since the basic needs of the individual, or family unit, must be met. Not only will personal savings be eliminated under circumstances of drastic reductions in income, but the individual may also *dissave*, that is, liquidate accumulated savings rather than reduce further consumption expenditures.

As income increases, the individual will again be in a position to save. However, the saving will not necessarily begin immediately since it may be desirable to buy many things that had to be foregone during the low-income period. The amount of pent-up demand, notably for durable consumer goods, largely determines the rate of increase in savings during periods of income recovery.

On an aggregate basis, income levels are closely associated with levels of employment. Changes in business activity, in turn, influence employment levels. Downturns in the economy during 1970 and 1974–75 resulted in declines in employment levels and correspondingly impacted on levels of income. Employment also suffered during the first part of the 1980s when unemployment levels rose to post–World War II highs in excess of 10 percent.

Economic Expectations

The anticipation of future events has a significant effect on savings. If individuals believe that their incomes will decrease in the near future, they may tend to curtail their current expenditures in order to establish a reserve for the period of low income. A worker anticipating a long and protracted labor dispute may increase current savings as partial protection against the financial impact of a strike.

Expectations of a general increase in price levels may also have a strong influence upon the liquidity that savers will want to maintain. The prospect of price increases on consumer durable goods may cause an increase in their sales as individuals attempt to make their purchases before such price increases take place. Savings are thus quickly converted to consumer expenditures. Corporate savings too may be reduced as a result of price increase expectations. In addition to the commitment of funds to plant and office equipment before price increases take place, corporations typically increase their inventory positions. And as for the individual, the prospect of an interruption in the supply of inventory by reason of a labor strike or other such cause results in a rapid stockpiling of raw materials and merchandise. The prospect of price decreases and of ample production capacity has the opposite influence of increasing the liquidity and financial assets of a business relative to its operating assets.

The unprecedented inflation or price increases during the 1970s led many individuals to develop the philosophy of "buy it now because it will cost more later." This resulted in a classic example of the impact of price increase expectations on the spend-save decisions of individuals. When the economy began recovering during 1975, employment and income levels also began rising. A savings rate (personal saving divided by disposable personal income) approaching 8 percent was achieved in 1975 before it began declining under the pressure of renewed price inflation during the latter part of the 1970s. After reaching a low of about 5 percent, the savings rate again began increasing until it was at about the 7 percent level by mid-1982.[6]

Cyclical Influences

While changes in levels of income may be brought about largely by cyclical movements in the economy, they do not represent the complete effect that the cycle has on savings. Cyclical movements affect not only the level but also the media or types of savings.

To illustrate this point, let us observe the effect that changes in economic activity have on the shifting of savings from one type to another, notably between time and savings deposits at commercial banks or thrift institutions and other media. Short-term interest rates usually decrease during a period of economic downturn or recession for such money market instruments as United States Treasury bills, commercial paper, and obligations of United States government agencies. This was the case during the latter part of 1974 and into 1975. Short-term money market rates also tend to remain relatively low during the early stages of economic recovery or expansion such as occurred during 1976. However, as the economy continues to expand, short-term interest rates begin to move up rapidly, as occurred during 1977 and 1978. These money market rates usually peak at about the same time that a peak in economic activity occurs. For

---

[6]*Federal Reserve Bulletin*, September, 1982, p. A53.

example, short-term interest rates peaked in early 1980 and in mid-1981 just prior to economic downturns.

Until recently, interest rates paid on time and savings deposits (excluding large negotiable CD's) held at commercial banks and thrift institutions were regulated and thus varied little with economic activity. Financial intermediation took place so long as the interest rates on time and savings deposits exceeded money market rates. However, disintermediation became particularly pronounced in time periods when money market interest rates surpassed interest rate ceilings set on time and savings deposits. Passage of the Depository Institutions Deregulation and Monetary Control Act of 1980 called for the elimination of rate ceilings on time and savings deposits. It is believed that these actions will result in a lessening of cyclical swings between intermediation and disintermediation in the future.

Life Stage of the Individual Saver

The pattern of savings over an individual's life span follows a somewhat predictable pattern when viewed in the aggregate of the total population. An individual saves very little during the youthful years simply because little income is produced. One's income has increased considerably by the time he or she has matured and has begun to rear a family. Expenses, however, have also increased during these early family-forming years; and one's savings are typically limited to those accruing to life insurance reserves. By the time the individual reaches middle age, two factors come into play that result in increased savings. First, income is typically much higher than at any previous time; and second, the expense of rearing children has been reduced or eliminated. It is this middle-aged group that saves the most.

At retirement the individual's income is sharply reduced. He or she may now begin the process of dissaving. Pension fund payments along with accumulated savings now are drawn upon for current living expenses.

The level of savings of individuals is therefore a function of age composition of the population as a whole. Other things remaining the same, a shift in age composition in which the proportion of the young to the elderly increases would cause fewer current savings to be forthcoming. A population shift to a large proportion of individuals in the productive middle-age years would result in a greater savings potential.

Life Stage of the Corporation

Just as the financial savings of an individual are governed in part by age, so the financial savings generated by the business firm are a function of its life stage. It is true, of course, that all business firms do not proceed through a fixed life-stage cycle. To the extent, however, that the firm experiences the typical pattern of vigorous early growth and ultimate maturity and decline, its flow of financial savings is influenced.

During the pioneering and early expansion years of a successful business, the volume of physical assets typically increases rapidly. So rapid is this growth that the firm is unable to establish a strong position with respect to its financial assets. Indeed, it is during these years of the corporate life cycle that heavy reliance is placed on borrowed capital. At this time the corporation is typically a heavy user of financial assets rather than a provider.

More intensive market penetration and expanding geographic areas of distribution make it possible for the firm to continue its growth. Continuing profitable expansion becomes more difficult, however, as the managerial talent of the firm reaches the limit of its ability to direct and control operations and as competing firms in the industry also grow. The combination of a slowdown in expansion and a continuing large flow of cash generation results in financial savings. As the enterprise matures and ceases to expand, it reaches its peak of savings. Earnings are high, and commitment of funds to increased operating assets is reduced or eliminated.

As the firm begins to decline in the final phase of the life cycle, its ability to create financial savings is reduced. During the early years of the decline of a business, however, it may continue to provide a reasonably high level of financial savings. This is true, notwithstanding lower profits, because of the conversion of physical assets to financial assets through depreciation allowances.

As the final stages of decline are reached, the firm is unable to generate further financial savings and is, in all probability, perpetuating itself largely on the basis of the sustaining power of its previously accumulated financial assets.

FINANCIAL MANAGEMENT OF FINANCIAL INSTITUTIONS

Financial institutions exist because they provide economic services such as liquidity, protection of capital, and a return on savings. Other services include life and property insurance and retirement protection programs. Financial institutions must be managed so as to attract the savings surplus units and meet the demand from savings deficit units. This entails packaging their liabilities (savings accounts, CD's, life insurance policies, etc.) so that the needs of savers are met. Futhermore, financial institutions which hold a substantial portion of their assets in the form of loans, such as consumer, business, and mortgage loans, must also effectively package their loans to meet the needs of borrowers.

Financial institutions are constrained both by traditions and laws. Different kinds of institutions originally evolved to meet specific or unique needs. For example, mutual savings banks and savings and loan associations traditionally have specialized in financing residential real estate by providing mortgage loans on homes. In contrast, commercial banks have more varied loan and investment policies and objectives. They provide short-term and intermediate-term loans to business firms, loans to consumers, and mortgage loans on real estate. Life insurance companies provide financial protection against premature death and/or the longevity of policyholders. Some life insurance policies also provide for the accumulation of savings over time.

Commercial banks and thrift institutions are regulated in terms of the types of deposits they can accept, the interest rates they can pay on deposits (these regulations are presently being phased out), and the kinds of services they can provide. These institutions also are regulated in terms of the types and amounts of financial assets which they can hold. For example, commercial banks and thrift institutions are prohibited (with the exception of special situations) from holding common stocks issued by other corporations.

Life insurance companies are regulated by the states within which they operate. In addition to being required to conform to state requirements concerning the selling of life insurance policies, regulation specifies the types of asset investments that can be held. These investments also must meet certain minimum standards of quality. The holdings of corporate bonds, corporate stocks, and real estate mortgages by life insurance companies thus must comply with state laws.

The *principle of hedging* provides the fundamental basis for conducting the financial management of financial institutions. Tradition and legal constraints establish the liability structures for financial institutions. Average liabilities may range from short-term to long-term depending on the type of financial institution. Financial management theory suggests that assets with comparable maturities should be held so that liabilities could be met on demand or when they come due. For example, an institution which accepts a short-term deposit should hedge the liability by also lending on a short-term basis. Thus, the principle of hedging involves the matching of the average maturities of an institution's assets and liabilities.

In actual practice some financial institutions are better "hedged" than others. Table 6-3 shows the estimated maturities of major assets and liabilities held by several different types of financial institutions. Commercial banks hold approximately 76 percent of their liabilities in demand and time and savings deposits which are characterized as having short-term to intermediate-term maturities. These institutions practice the hedging principle rather well, as indicated by the fact that approximately 62 percent of their assets are held in the form of government and other securities and in loans to consumers and business firms. Only about 16 percent of assets are in the form of mortgage loans which generally have long-term maturities.

Savings and loan associations, however, have been major violators of the hedging principle. They hold approximately 80 percent of their liabilities in the form of savings deposits which are short- to intermediate-term in maturity. On the other hand, about an equal amount of assets are held in the form of real estate mortgage loans. Thus, savings and loan associations hold relatively long-term asset investments and relatively short-term liabilities. This often has resulted in liquidity pressures and problems, particularly during periods of disintermediation.

Life insurance companies hold liabilities that are primarily long-term in nature. This permits them to hold assets for long periods of time without being faced with liquidity pressures characteristic of commercial banks and savings and loan associations. Assets are held largely in the form of real estate mortgages and corporate bonds, and to a lesser extent corporate stocks because of legal restrictions.

In recent years a second dimension of the hedging principle also has surfaced. High and volatile interest rates have made it necessary for managers of financial institutions to seek to balance the amount of their rate-sensitive assets with rate-

Major Assets and Liabilities by Estimated Maturities	Percentage of Total Holdings of Assets and of Liabilities		
	Commercial Banks	Savings and Loan Associations	Life Insurance Companies
MAJOR ASSETS			
Short-term and Intermediate-term Maturities			
Cash assets......................	11%	7%	
Government and other securities...	21		7%
Consumer and business loans.....	41		
Long-term Maturities			
Mortgage loans and holdings......	16	80	27
Corporate bonds			38
Corporate stocks			9
Other Assets	11	13	19
Total assets....................	100%	100%	100%
MAJOR LIABILITIES			
Short-term and Intermediate-term Maturities			
Demand deposits	26		
Time and savings deposits.........	50	80	
Long-term Maturities			
Insurance policy reserves..........			81
Other liabilities and equity	24	20	19
Total liabilities and equity.......	100%	100%	100%

SOURCES: These data are based on averages over the past several years compiled from selected issues of *Federal Reserve Bulletin, Savings and Loan Sourcebook,* and *Life Insurance Fact Book.*

sensitive liabilities. That is, if funds are obtained in the form of variable interest rate deposits (liabilities), then loans (assets) containing variable interest rates should likewise be issued. Thus when interest rates rise, higher rates paid on deposits to attract funds will be offset by higher rates being charged on loans, and vice versa. The need to match rate-sensitive assets and liabilities is particularly important to depository institutions because they rely heavily on deposits in the form of money market certificates and other short-term CD's whose rates frequently change. Savings and loan associations have recently moved to alleviate some of their liquidity problems by issuing variable rate real estate mortgage loans with shorter than traditional maturities. Recent legislation, as we will see next, also has been designed to aid depository institutions.

IMPLICATIONS OF THE DEPOSITORY INSTITUTIONS DEREGULATION ACT OF 1980

The Glass-Steagall Act was passed in 1933 as a result of the banking collapse that occurred at the beginning of the 1930s. It provided powers for the Federal Reserve System in addition to those granted under the Federal Reserve Act of 1913. Under the Glass-Steagall Act, the Federal Reserve could set interest-rate ceilings on commercial bank time and savings deposits as long as the banks were members of the Federal Reserve System. Commercial banks were further restricted from paying interest on their demand deposits.

After several years of study, the Depository Institutions Deregulation and Monetary Control Act (DIDMCA) was passed in 1980. It has been heralded by some as the most significant banking and finance legislation since the 1913 and 1933 Acts. The DIDMCA provides for sweeping changes in the Federal Reserve's monetary control procedures and for the deregulation of depository institutions. The powers of thrift institutions are expanded, and increased competition by depository institutions in the financial markets is allowed.

Monetary Control Act

Some of the ramifications of the Monetary Control Act, which is Title I of the DIDMCA, were discussed in Chapter 4. However, a brief overview seems appropriate here. The purpose of the Monetary Control Act was to allow the Federal Reserve to better implement monetary policy by improving its ability to control the money supply. The Federal Reserve's prior authority to set reserve requirements on member commercial banks was extended to include all depository institutions. Reserve requirements will be phased in for nonmember commercial banks, savings and loan associations, mutual savings banks, and credit unions so that equal reserve requirements will be in place for all depository institutions before the end of 1987. It is expected that these actions will lead to improved monetary control of the expansion of checkable deposits by the "banking" system which now includes activities of all depository institutions.

A second provision of the Monetary Control Act now allows all depository institutions borrowing access to the Federal Reserve's discount window. Borrowing at the discount rate can be used to meet reserve requirements or for other special purposes. The Federal Reserve also is permitted to charge a fee for check clearing and collection as well as for other services including the safekeeping of securities and making of wire transfers.

Depository Institutions Deregulation

Title II of the DIDMCA provides for the elimination of interest-rate ceilings on deposits held at depository institutions by early 1986. The law, formally termed the Depository Institutions Deregulation Act, established the formation of a Depository Institutions Deregulation Committee to implement an orderly phaseout of existing ceilings on interest and dividend rates. The committee's voting members include: the Chairman of the Board of Governors of the Federal Reserve System, the Chairman of the Federal Home Loan Bank Board, the Secretary of the U.S. Treasury, the Chairman of the Board of Directors of the Federal Deposit Insurance Corporation, and the Chairman of the National Credit Union Administration Board. The U.S. Comptroller of the Currency is a nonvoting member of the Committee. The Committee will cease to exist by the end of March, 1986, at which time any remaining rate ceilings must be removed.

With depository institutions allowed to compete in the financial markets on an interest-rate basis, savings flows can be expected to become more stable. That is, it is hoped that the removal of rate ceilings will lead to fewer and less volatile swings between periods of intermediation and disintermediation for depository institutions.

Thrift Institution Powers

In order to enhance competition among depository institutions, Title IV of the DIDMCA amended the Home Owners' Loan Act of 1933. Federally chartered savings and loan associations now may invest up to one fifth of their assets in corporate debt securities, commercial paper, and consumer loans. Prior residential mortgage loan restrictions relating to geographical areas and first mortgage lending requirements have been removed. Greater authority also is permitted in the granting of real estate development and construction loans by federally chartered savings and loan associations. In addition, federal mutual savings banks can make small amounts of commercial loans and can accept some demand deposits.

To summarize, the Depository Institutions Deregulation and Monetary Control Act permits both greater competition for deposits and more flexibility in the holding of assets by depository institutions. Thus as institutional differences become more blurred, similarities in the financial management of financial institutions are likely to increase.

QUESTIONS

1. What are savings? Differentiate between voluntary and contractual savings.
2. Briefly describe the historical role of savings in the United States.
3. Compare savings surplus and savings deficit units and indicate which economic units are generally one type or the other.
4. Describe and illustrate how financial assets and liabilities are created through the savings-investment process involving financial institutions.
5. What types of savings media are available to individuals?
6. How and why do corporations save?
7. Indicate which types of institutions provide major annual sources of funds. Also indicate the relative importance of these institutions as suppliers of funds.
8. The supply of funds is channeled into three basic categories or uses. Identify and explain the relative importance of these categories.

9. Describe the principal factors influencing the levels of savings forthcoming from individuals.
10. How do business cycle movements affect the media or types of savings?
11. Why are the financial savings generated by a business firm a function of its life cycle?
12. Explain the principle of hedging and describe which financial institutions practice it effectively and which do not.
13. What are the major provisions of the Depository Institutions Deregulation and Monetary Control Act of 1980? How is this legislation likely to affect the operations of depository institutions?

SUGGESTED READINGS

Corrado, Carol, and Charles Steindel. "Perspectives on Personal Saving." *Federal Reserve Bulletin* (August, 1980), pp. 613–625.

Dougall, Herbert E., and Jack E. Gaumnitz. *Capital Markets and Institutions*, 4th ed. Englewood Cliffs, New Jersey: Prentice-Hall, Inc., 1980.

Economics of Inflation. Federal Reserve Bank of Philadelphia (October, 1974).

Hempel, George H., and Jess B. Yawitz. *Financial Management of Financial Institutions*. Englewood Cliffs, New Jersey: Prentice-Hall, Inc., 1977.

Kemmerer, Donald L., and Clyde C. Jones. *American Economic History*. New York: McGraw-Hill Book Company, Inc., 1959.

Kuznets, Simon. *Capital in the American Economy, Its Formation and Financing*. New York: National Bureau of Economic Research, 1961.

McNeill, Charles R., and Denise M. Rechter. "The Depository Institutions Deregulation and Monetary Control Act of 1980." *Federal Reserve Bulletin* (June, 1980), pp. 444–453.

Robertson, Ross M. *History of the American Economy*. New York: Harcourt, Brace and Company, 1955.

Van Horne, James C. *Financial Market Rates and Flows*. Englewood Cliffs, New Jersey: Prentice-Hall, Inc., 1978.

West, Robert C. "The Depository Institutions Deregulation Act of 1980: A Historical Perspective." *Economic Review*. Federal Reserve Bank of Kansas City (February, 1982), pp. 3–13.

PART II

Business Financing and Management

7

Introduction to Business Finance

All business firms require money to accommodate their operations. Money is needed to provide plant and equipment and to provide the necessary financial support for current operations. Some firms require very little capital, and it is in these industries that there is a vast number of competitors. Any field of activity that requires little investment capital is an open invitation to a host of people who would try to establish their own business. At the other extreme, there are businesses that require huge amounts of money to operate on even a minimum scale. The cement and steel industries, for example, by the very nature of their capital requirements are representative of situations where a few large firms dominate the market.

After discussing the concepts of freedom of entry into business and the choice of form of business organization, we focus on the financial management functions that must be carried out by successful businesses. To perform these functions the financial manager needs an understanding of the basic financial statements and a system for conducting financial analysis.

FREEDOM OF ENTRY INTO BUSINESS

We have freedom to establish the enterprise of our choice if we have, or can arrange, the necessary financing. Since business activities are pursued for profit purposes, the success of the business person in raising funds for operations is governed by the extent to which profits can be produced from operations. This means, of course, that the individual starting a new business must possess either the necessary capital to support initial operations until there exists profit from operations, or the individual must show unusual promise of the prospect of profits. Typically, the would-be business person must possess some initial capital for the creation of the desired enterprise since the prospect of profit is seldom enough to attract financial supporters.

The nation's resources are limited. There is only a certain amount of labor, suitable land, and buildings appropriate for specific purposes, and other factors of production that the business person would like to have under command. Our command over these scarce resources is a measure of the extent to which we engage in successful business operation and financing. The financing of business, therefore, is the process of acquiring the factors of production necessary to conduct the business operations of the firm.

In contrast with controlled economies where factors of production are allocated by central planning authorities, under the market system that process is largely automatic. Resources flow smoothly to those business persons who through their past operations and who through the promise of profitable future operations are able to lay claim to these resources. It is true of course that mistakes are made. Investors often place their funds with business persons only to find that the performance of the firm in which they have invested does not measure up to expectations. The result, of course, is the loss of or decrease in the value of the investment. This is the risk inherent in the free-enterprise system. By the same token, the investor or the financial institution that assumes an unusually large risk in accommodating a business customer does so with the full expectation that if things go well with the firm the rewards for the investment will be very great. Where the prospective risk is very small, the prospective reward is small. It is on this basis that the investment funds flow to risky enterprises as well as to the very safe enterprises. There is simply a difference in the risk and return expectation on the part of the investor. Some investors prefer to maintain a minimum risk; and they must, of course, be satisfied with a modest return on their investment. Other individuals and institutions assume large risks in the hopes of achieving substantial returns.

FORMS OF BUSINESS ORGANIZATION

The choice of a legal form of organization for a business is a strategic matter from many points of view. Managerial lines of authority and control, legal responsibility, and the allocation of income and risk are all directly related to the form the organization takes. Our interest at this time is with the relationship of the legal form of organization to sources and methods of financing and with the allocation of risk.

Sole Proprietorship

The *sole proprietorship* is a business venture that is owned by a single individual who personally receives all of the profits and assumes all the responsibility for the debts and the losses of the business. Although sole proprietorships far outnumber all other forms of business organization, the economic power of these enterprises, as measured by number of employees and amount of payrolls, is far less than that of the corporations of the nation.

The savings of the business person together with the funds that may be borrowed from friends, relatives, and banks may be sufficient for the operation of the typical small business. As the volume of business increases, however, and as larger investments in capital equipment are required, the owner may reach the point where additional funds cannot be borrowed without an increase in equity investment. As increased demands are made for borrowed capital, lenders will generally insist on an increase in the equity capital as well, since the equity of a firm provides a margin of safety for the lender. At this point the sole proprietorship form of organization displays its basic weakness. In many cases, the owner's original investment exhausts personal resources and often those of friends and relatives; and unless profits from the operation of the venture have proved sufficient to meet increased equity needs, the business either is prevented from achieving its maximum growth or is required to adopt a more appropriate form of organization for capital-raising purposes.

The sole proprietor's position as it relates to liability for debts of the business is an unfavorable one. Creditors have recourse not only to the assets of the business for the settlement of their claims but also to the personal assets of the proprietor. Thus, the sole proprietor may find his or her home and personal property under claim by creditors in the event that the assets of the business are not sufficient to meet the demands of creditors. This unlimited liability of the proprietor is, therefore, one of the serious disadvantages of the sole proprietorship.

The Partnership

The *partnership* form of business organization exists when two or more persons own a business operated for profit. Although the partnership resembles the sole proprietorship in a technical sense to some degree, there are many important differences.

Undoubtedly, one of the important reasons for the popularity of the partnership arrangement is the fact that it enables business persons to pool their resources without the complications that often accompany incorporation. In some instances, the partnership form of organization exists from the beginning of business operation, the property, equipment, knowledge, and skills for business purposes being acquired through the joint contributions of two or more persons. In other cases, an enterprise that began as a sole proprietorship may reach the point where additional growth is impossible without an increase in equity capital, and conversion to the partnership arrangement is one method of increasing the equity capital of the enterprise.

Although the number of partners that may be taken into a business venture is theoretically unlimited, the managerial difficulties and conflicts arising as a result of a large number of partners limits effectively the number of such co-owners. The partnership, therefore, like the proprietorship, eventually suffers from a lack of command over large sums of capital because of the practical limit to the number of partners that a business venture may have. Although it is true that some types of businesses have dozens and even hundreds of partners, a modification of the general partnership arrangement is usually utilized. It is extremely rare to find more than a few partners involved in an industrial or commercial enterprise.

Like the sole proprietor, the members of a partnership team risk their personal assets as well as their investments in the business venture. In addition, if one of the partners negotiates a contract that results in substantial loss, each partner suffers loss in proportion to the previously agreed-upon terms of distribution of profits and losses. This is true whether the partner responsible for the loss was pursuing that partner's specified responsibilities or whether the partner's authorized functions were being violated as set out in the articles of copartnership. The other partners may, however, take action against the offending partner because of any violation of the articles of copartnership.

More serious, perhaps, is a partner's liability for the actions of the business. Under partnership law, each partner has *joint and several liability* for the debts of the business, a situation that permits creditors to seek satisfaction from one or more of the parnters if the remaining partners are unable to bear their share of the loss.

The Corporation

In the Dartmouth College Case in 1819, Chief Justice John Marshall described the status of the corporation so explicitly and clearly that this description has since become the generally accepted definition of the corporation. It reads in part as follows:

> A corporation is an artificial being, invisible, intangible, and existing only in contemplation of law. Being the mere creature of law, it possesses only those properties which the charter of its creation confers upon it, either expressly, or as incidental to its very existence... [Dartmouth College vs. Woodward, 4 Wheaton (U.S.) 518 (1819)]

The small corporation that has been in existence only a short time, like most new ventures, usually finds it difficult to attract investment funds from outsiders. It is only after the corporation has become well established and offers attractive prospects for investors that the special features of the corporate form of organization become significant. One of the important reasons for the suitability of the corporate form of organization as a medium through which large sums of capital may be accumulated is that capital stock may be offered to its existing stockholders or to investors in amounts suited to their purposes. The corporate form of organization, however, does not by itself assure the flow of investment funds into the business. Rather, it removes several of the impediments to the flow of capital that exist for other forms of business organization.

One of the advantages to the stockholders is the limitation on liability. Ordinarily creditors and other claimants may look only to the assets of the corporation for satisfaction of their claims; they do not have recourse to the personal assets of the owners. This advantage is particularly appealing to the owner of the business who has built up considerable wealth and has diverse business interests over which complete personal control is not possible. The limitation on liability may also make it possible for the promoters of new ventures to attract the interest of wealthy investors who would otherwise be unwilling to risk possible claims against their personal property. Unlimited liability may be avoided under certain circumstances in some of the noncorporate forms, but the certainty provided by the corporate form is not present.

The limitation on stockholder liability for debts of the corporation is seldom sufficient reason for incorporation of the small business of which there is an individual owner whose personal assets are largely invested in the business. In this situation there is little risk on the part of the owner beyond the personal investment which the individual has made in the corporation. Nor is the corporation form of organization necessarily effective in protecting stockholders from personal risk beyond their investment when the business is relatively new or in a weak financial condition. Creditors may simply require that one or more of the stockholders add their personal signatures to the obligation of the corporation, rendering them personally liable for the obligation. After a corporation has established a good credit reputation, creditors and suppliers seldom insist on personal guarantees on the part of the stockholders.

A further important advantage of the corporation is the ease with which ownership may be transferred. Corporate stock may be transferred freely from one person to another, and the purchaser of such stock thereafter has all the rights and privileges formerly held by the seller. The corporation is not a party to the transfer of ownership and has no power to interfere with the sale or purchase of its stock. By contrast, there must be unanimous approval of all members of a partnership before a new partner can be brought into the business.

Other Forms of Business Organization

In addition to the sole proprietorship, the partnership, and the corporation, there are a variety of somewhat less well-known forms of business organization that combine to varying degrees some of the advantages and the disadvantages of the forms of organization which have been discussed. The *business trust*, for example, also known as the Massachusetts trust, the voluntary association, or common-law trust, combines the advantage of limited liability with convenience in raising capital. Yet, the utilization of the business trust arrangement is limited, for the most part, to the New England states. Under the business trust, assets of the company are held by a trustee, the beneficiaries of the company holding trust certificates as evidence of their beneficial interest. Profits of the company are distributed to holders of trust certificates much as dividends are distributed to stockholders. In spite of the convenience of the business trust arrangement, its general lack of familiarity outside of New England renders it a less desirable form of business organization than the corporation for purposes of raising capital for business operations. Although the business trust arrangement is noncorporate in form, it is subject to federal income taxes at the same rate as corporations.

The *limited partnership*, another minor form of business organization, is a statutory modification of the common-law partnership in which one or more general partners combine with one or more limited partners. The limited partners, much like the shareholders in a corporation, have liability for debts of the business only to the extent of their investment. The general partners are governed by the usual laws relating to partnerships while the limited partners are governed by state statutes. The limited partnership comes into existence only after acceptance and approval by the state of a proper application by the partners.

In addition to the limited partnership and the business trust, there are many other forms of business organization that attempt to combine the advantages of the more common forms, each of which has its particular place and advantages.

These minor forms of business organization include the joint-stock company, the joint venture, the mining partnership, and the partnership association.

Income Tax Considerations

In addition to financing and risk factors, income tax liabilities also may differ according to the form of business organization selected. Income from partnerships and proprietorships is combined with other personal income for tax purposes. Corporations, in contrast, are taxed as separate entities. The Economic Recovery Tax Act of 1981 provided that beginning in 1983 corporations were to be taxed at the following rates on their taxable income:

15% on the first $25,000
18% on the second $25,000
30% on the third $25,000
40% on the fourth $25,000
46% on amounts over $100,000

A corporation with taxable income of $40,000 would have a *marginal* tax rate of 18 percent while another corporation with taxable income in excess of $100,000 would be in the 46 percent marginal tax bracket. The dollar amount of income taxes paid is based on the firm's *average* tax rate. Taxes on the corporation with $40,000 in income would be calculated as follows:

$$15\% \times \$25,000 = \$3,750$$
$$18\% \times 15,000 = \underline{2,700}$$
$$\$6,450$$

Dividing the tax of $6,450 by the $40,000 income produces an average tax rate of 16.1 percent. Of course, as a firm's taxable income gets larger the average tax rate will approach the maximum marginal tax rate of 46 percent. Whether or not an owner would have a lower tax liability if the business is taxed as a proprietorship (or partnership if there is more that one owner) depends on the owner's personal income tax bracket.

Small businesses can sometimes qualify as Subchapter S corporations under the Internal Revenue Code. These organizations receive the limited liability of being a corporation but are taxed as proprietorships or partnerships. A corporation pays taxes on its taxable income and then if cash from profits is distributed as dividends to stockholders they must pay personal income taxes. This double taxation is avoided by the Subchapter S corporation because the business is taxed as a proprietorship or partnership. Whether or not this taxation option is selected again depends on the level of the owner's personal tax bracket.

Business firms also have the opportunity of carrying operating losses backward for 3 years and forward for 15 years to offset taxable income. A new business started as a corporation that loses, for example, $50,000 the first year could only offset taxable income earned in future years. However, initial losses by a new proprietorship or partnership could be first carried back against personal income taxes paid by owners permitting them tax refunds. This could be helpful for a new business that has limited funds.

FINANCIAL MANAGEMENT FUNCTIONS

The overall objective of financial management is to maximize the wealth or value of the owners' investment or equity in the firm. To be successful in this endeavor, the financial manager must effectively carry out the functions of financial planning and analysis, asset management, and the raising of funds.

Financial Planning and Analysis

In order to plan it is necessary to be forward looking. We all have impeccable hindsight but foresight is what determines the success of a business. Long-run plans covering several years must be prepared in terms of growth in sales, assets, and employees. First, a sales forecast needs to be tied to expected developments in the economy and also reflect possible competitive pressures from other business firms. The sales forecast then must be supported by plans for an adequate investment in assets. For example, a manufacturing firm must invest in plant and equipment in order to produce an inventory of products so that sales orders can be filled. Asset investment plans call for, in turn, plans indicating the size of the associated financing requirements. Adequate investment in human resources likewise must be planned for.

In addition to long-run plans or budgets, the financial manager is concerned with near-term cash inflows and outflows associated with operation of the business. Cash flows often are monitored on a daily basis for large firms while small firms may make only monthly cash budgets. As we know from our personal experiences, an unexpected shortage of cash causes financial distress. So it is for the financial manager who seeks a loan from a bank or other lender after the firm is out of money, having failed to plan for such a need in advance.

Financial analysis goes hand in hand with successful financial planning. The established firm must conduct financial analysis of past performance as an aid in developing achievable future plans. The new firm should analyze the performance characteristics of other firms in the same industry before setting plans. Financial analysis is conducted primarily through the examination of financial ratios either historically over time or by comparison against other firms in the industry. Some basics of financial analysis will be discussed later in this chapter. Financial planning will be covered in Chapter 8.

Asset Management

Successful financial planning means that the financial manager must decide on the amount and mix of assets that are necessary to generate the forecasted level of sales and profits. Investments in fixed assets are necessary to support sales. For manufacturing firms, plant facilities and machinery are necessary to produce the firm's products. In addition to fixed assets, the firm must carry adequate amounts of current assets. Inventory must be accumulated for purposes of making sales. Cash balances must be maintained to carry on day-to-day transactions, and receivables may be incurred if sales are made on credit.

The management of current assets will be addressed in Chapter 8, while the acquisition and management of fixed assets will be covered in Chapter 10.

Raising of Funds

Once financial plans have been made and asset needs planned for, the financial manager must acquire or raise the short-term and long-term funds necessary to support the firm's assets. Trade credit may be requested from suppliers, short-term bank loans may be obtained, or other current liabilities may be used. Long-term sources of financing may come from profits, the owners' own equity contributions, or long-term borrowing.

Short-term financing sources are discussed in Chapter 9. Long-term debt and equity funds are covered in Chapters 11 and 12, followed by coverage in Chapter 13 of the merchandising and facilitating agencies involved in long-term business financing.

In smaller firms the operator of the business may take the total responsibility of the finance functions. In fact, in small firms, the owner is usually engaged in the administration of all facets of the business' operations, and it is on this basis that the small business finds itself at a special disadvantage. Few people have the overall ability to effectively perform the many challenging functions of even the small business. The medium and large business, on the other hand, by virtue of size may assign an individual or group of individuals to these special functions and in so doing achieve the efficiency that comes from specialization of talent.

ACCOUNTING AND FINANCIAL STATEMENTS

The financial manager needs a basic understanding of the accounting and financial statements used by businesses in order to carry out the financial management functions. It is important to know both the firm's financial position at a point in time and the change in financial position over time. This financial information indicates the performance of the firm and reflects the success of the financial manager and other officers of the firm.

The Balance Sheet

For purposes of exploring the interrelationship of uses and sources of funds and the allocation of risk for business enterprises, it is very helpful to refer to the balance sheet. The *balance sheet* is a summary or report that shows the assets and the sources of financing of a business at a particular point in time. It reveals two broad categories of information: the properties owned by a business, referred to as *assets*; and the creditors' claims and the owners' equity in the business assets. The creditors' claims, which are the financial obligations of the business, are referred to as *liabilities*.

The balance sheet is in the nature of a snapshot, revealing the condition of a business as of a given date. Like a cutaway section of an automobile motor, however, the balance sheet also reveals much of the dynamic quality of the structure. The various classes of assets indicate at once the result of recent business operations and the capacity for future operations. The creditors' claims and the owners' equity in the assets reveal the sources from which the assets of the business were derived. The term "balance sheet" itself conveys a relationship of equality between the assets of the business and the sources of funds for their acquisition that may be expressed as follows:

$$\text{Assets} = \text{Liabilities} + \text{Owners' Equity}$$

The simplified balance sheet of a manufacturing firm in Figure 7-1 reveals this equality of assets and the financial interests in the assets. The financial interests in the assets, as noted above, comprise the creditors' claims and owners' interests. We shall, in the following pages, discuss the composition of this balance sheet with the specific objective of relating the assets to the sources of funds for their acquisition.

Figure 7-1
Balance Sheet for the ABC Manufacturing Company

Balance Sheet
December 31, 1983

Assets

Cash and Marketable Securities	$ 25,000	
Accounts Receivable	100,000	
Inventories	125,000	
Total Current Assets		$250,000
Gross Plant and Equipment $275,000		
Less Accumulated Depreciation 75,000		
Net Plant and Equipment	200,000	
Land	50,000	
Total Fixed Assets		250,000
Total Assets		$500,000

Liabilities and Owners' Equity

Accounts Payable	75,000	
Notes Payable (Bank, 10%)	20,000	
Accrued Liabilities	30,000	
Total Current Liabilities		125,000
Mortgage Debt (12%)		100,000
Total Liabilities		225,000
Owners' Equity		275,000
Total Liabilities and Owners' Equity . . .		$500,000

Current Assets. The balance sheet of the ABC Manufacturing Company reveals, among other things, that the business had assets as of December 31 of $500,000. The assets of the company have been classified into two groups: current assets and fixed assets.

The *current assets* of a business enterprise include cash and other assets that may reasonably be expected to be converted into cash, sold, or used in the near future through the normal operations of the business. The principal current assets of a business are typically its cash and marketable securities, receivables, and inventories.

Cash and Marketable Securities. This includes cash on hand and cash on deposit with banks along with the holding of marketable securities such as the commercial paper issued by other firms and short-term U.S. government securities.

Accounts Receivable. *Accounts receivable* generally arise from the sale of products, merchandise, or services on credit which reflects an oral promise of the customer to pay. The buyer's debts to the business are generally paid according to the credit terms of the sale.

Some firms also have notes receivable in addition to accounts receivable. A *note receivable* is a written promise by a debtor of the business to pay a specified sum of money on or before a stated date. Such notes are ordinarily made payable to the order of a specified firm or person or to "bearer." Notes receivable may come into existence in several ways. For example, overdue accounts receivable may be converted to notes receivable at the insistence of the seller or upon special request by the buyer. They may also occur as a result of short-term loans made by the business to its employees or to other persons or businesses. These notes may be held until maturity or converted into cash immediately through their sale to a bank or other purchaser.

Most credit sales of goods and services by businesses in the United States are made on the basis of accounts receivable financing. However, for the bank, loan company, or other such financial institution, notes receivable represent one of the principal assets since their customers are required to sign notes as evidence of the loans.

Inventories. The materials and products that a manufacturing enterprise has on hand are shown as inventories on the balance sheet. Generally, a manufacturing firm categorizes its inventories in terms of raw materials, goods in the process of manufacture, and finished goods. Sometimes the balance sheet will reveal the amount of inventory in each of these categories.

Fixed Assets. *Fixed assets* are the physical facilities used in the production, storage, display, and distribution of the products of a firm. These assets normally provide many years of service to the firm. The principal fixed assets are equipment, land, and buildings.

Plant and Equipment. In a manufacturing enterprise large investment usually is required in plant and equipment. As products are manufactured, some of the economic value of this plant and equipment is used up. Accountants attempt to reflect this using up of real assets by charging off depreciation against the original cost of plant and equipment. Thus, the net plant and equipment at any point in time is supposed to reflect the remaining economic value after the gross plant and equipment has been reduced by the amount of depreciation that has been accumulated over time.

Land. Some firms own the land or real property on which their buildings or manufacturing plants are constructed. Other firms may own real estate land for expansion or investment purposes. The ownership of land should be reflected on the firm's balance sheet.

Other Assets. Some businesses occasionally include other assets on their balance sheets. For example, a firm might show some *prepaid expenses* as assets to reflect the prepayment of rent and insurance expenses. These are listed as assets since the time period that has been covered by the rental and insurance payments has not yet expired. Business firms also may list "intangible" assets. *Intangible assets* include patent rights and a firm's "goodwill."

Current Liabilities. The liabilities of a business come into existence through direct borrowing, the purchase of goods and services on a credit basis, and the accrual of obligations for such purposes as wages of employees and income taxes. Liabilities are classified as current and long-term.

The *current liabilities* of a business may be defined as those obligations that must be satisfied within a period of one year. They are the liabilities that are to be met out of current funds and operations of the business. Although the cash on hand plus marketable securities of the ABC Manufacturing Company is only $25,000 compared with current liabilities of $125,000, it is expected that normal business operations will convert receivables and inventory into cash in sufficient time to meet current liabilities as they become due. In addition to notes and accounts payable, there is a third group of current liabilities—accrued liabilities—described below.

Accounts Payable. Accounts payable arise primarily from the purchase of goods by a business on credit terms. The account payable is not evidenced by a note. Although it lacks some of the certainty of the note, its convenience and simplicity have resulted in a considerable popularity in its use. Accounts payable, as well as notes payable, arising from the purchase of inventory on credit terms represent "trade credit" financing as opposed to direct short-term borrowing from banks and other lenders. An account payable shown in our balance sheet is reflected as an account receivable on the balance sheet of the firm from which we have acquired the goods.

Notes Payable. A *note payable* is a written promise to pay a specified amount of money to the order of a creditor on or before a certain date. These notes may arise from the purchase of goods or services on a credit basis, from direct short-term borrowing, or in settlement of accounts payable that have not been satisfied according to the terms of the purchase agreement. The most common situation giving rise to a note payable is the borrowing of money from a bank on a short-term basis for the purchase of materials or for other current operating requirements. The transaction that gives rise to the note payable on our balance sheet is reflected as a note receivable on the balance sheet of the firm to which the money is owed.

Accrued Liabilities. Amounts owed but not yet due for such items as wages and salaries, taxes, and interest on notes are classified as *accrued liabilities* and as such are included in the current liabilities section of the balance sheet. Of special importance is the tax accrual, which often is the largest single current liability of the business.

Long-term Liabilities. Business debts with maturities greater than one year are considered to be *long-term liabilities*. The length of maturity will depend upon the confidence of lenders in the business and the nature of the security that the business may offer for such loans. As a long-term debt approaches the date it is to be paid, ordinarily within a year from its maturity date, the debt is transferred to the current liabilities section of the balance sheet to call attention to the fact that its settlement must be made within the year.

One of the most common methods of obtaining a long-term loan is for a business establishment to offer a mortgage to a lender. A *mortgage* may be described as a conveyance or transfer of title to property given by a debtor to a creditor as security for the payment of the debt, with a provision that such conveyance or transfer of title is to become void on the payment of the debt according to the terms of the mortgage. In the event that the borrowing business fails to meet the obligations of the loan contract, the mortgage may be foreclosed; that is, the property may be seized through appropriate legal channels and sold in order to satisfy the indebtedness.

Owners' Equity. All businesses have an ownership equity in one form or another. This ownership equity initially results from a cash outlay for the purchase of assets with which to operate the business. In other cases, the owners of a business may simply place physical assets, such as machinery, real estate, or equipment, with the firm for its operation. Owners' equity is also increased by allowing profits of the business to remain with the business rather than by making additional contributions of cash or property. On the balance sheet the amount of owners' equity is always represented by the difference between total assets and total debts of the business. It reflects the owners' claims on the assets of the business as opposed to the creditors' claims.

In the case of a corporation, the owners' equity is usually broken down into several different accounts. First is the *common stock* account, which reflects the number of shares of common stock that are outstanding carried at some stated or "par" value. For example, a corporation may have issued 10,000 shares of common stock with a par value of $1 or a $10,000 value on its balance sheet. If the stock actually had been sold for $5 per share, then the $4 above the par value per share would have been placed in a *paid-in capital* or surplus account in an amount of $40,000 ($4 × 10,000 shares). A third account, *retained earnings*, reflects the retention or accumulation of earnings or profits within the corporation. Together these three accounts comprise the corporation's common or owners' equity.

The Income Statement

The *income statement* reflects the change in a firm's financial position over time. Such a statement indicates the extent to which the assets shown on the balance sheet have been used to support revenues or sales for the firm. The expenses incurred in generating the revenues or sales also are shown on the income statement. Finally, the interest costs associated with the financing of some of the firm's assets with liabilities, along with the payment of income taxes, are subtracted in the income statement. The result is the net profit or income (or in some cases the loss) available to the owners of the business. The simplified income statement of the ABC Manufacturing Company is shown in Figure 7-2.

Figure 7-2

Income Statement for the ABC Manufacturing Company

Income Statement
Year Ended December 31, 1983

Net Revenues or Sales......................		$700,000
Cost of Goods Sold........................		450,000
Gross Profit.............................		250,000
General and Administrative Expenses........	$100,000	
Selling and Marketing Expenses	36,000	
Depreciation..............................	25,000	
Interest..................................	14,000	175,000
Net Income Before Income Taxes		75,000
Income Taxes (at 40%)		30,000
Net Income.............................		$ 45,000

Net Revenues or Sales. The starting point of the income statement reflects the revenues or sales generated from the operations of the business. Quite often gross revenues are larger than net revenues. This is due to sales returns and allowances that may occur over the time period reflected in the income statement. Sometimes when customers make early payment on their bills, cash discounts are given by the firm. Also, if customers purchase in very large quantities, trade discounts may be given. Thus, sales discounts also will reduce gross revenues.

Expenses. The typical firm is faced with two types of expenses—variable and fixed. *Variable costs* reflect those types of expenses that vary directly with sales. For example, a substantial part, if not all, of the expense contained in cost of goods sold would be variable. *Fixed costs* would include those expenses such as general and administrative expenses that must be incurred regardless of the volume of sales generated by the firm.

Cost of Goods Sold. The costs associated with producing or manufacturing the products sold to produce the revenues shown on the income statement are contained in the cost of goods sold expense. These expenses are largely variable and reflect the cost of raw materials, labor, and overhead (heating, lighting, etc.) directly involved in producing the products that were sold.

General and Administrative Expenses. These expenses are largely fixed in nature and cover such requirements as record keeping and the preparation of financial and accounting statements. Utility costs not directly associated with the manufacturing of products, as well as the salaries of administrative personnel, are included.

Selling and Marketing Expenses. The costs associated with the selling of the firm's products are included in these expenses. This may reflect salaries and/or commissions generated by the sales force. Also included would be promotional and advertising expenditures.

Depreciation Expense. This expense item reflects the reduction in the economic value of the firm's plant and equipment incurred by manufacturing the firm's products during the time period covered by the income statement. This one time period depreciation is accumulated over time and is reflected in the balance sheet as we have previously noted.

Interest Expense. When a portion of a firm's assets are financed with liabilities, interest costs or charges often result. This would be true for notes payable, bank loans, and mortgage loans, and results in an interest expense being recorded on the income statement.

Income Taxes. Business firms are required to pay income taxes against any profits or income remaining after all other expenses have been deducted from revenues. Effective income tax rates can vary substantially depending on whether the firm is organized as a proprietorship, partnership, or corporation. We use a hypothetical 40 percent income tax rate for the ABC Manufacturing Company.

Net Income. The net income or profits after the payment of income taxes reflects the earnings available to the owners of the business. This income may be retained in the business to reduce existing liabilities, increase current assets, and/or acquire additional fixed assets. On the other hand, all or a portion of the income could be distributed to the owners of the business.

Other Financial Statements

In addition to the balance sheet and income statement, business firms provide a *statement of changes in financial position*. This is also commonly referred to as a *sources and uses of funds statement*. Information is taken from both the income statement and the balance sheet to show how the firm obtained funds during the accounting period and how those funds were used. For example, funds are obtained by making profits, by borrowing, or by selling equity securities. Uses include purchasing fixed assets, building up inventories, and repaying loans.

Another form of useful financial statement is the *cash flow statement*. It differs from the other statements in that only the actual receipt or disbursement of cash is recorded. For example, a sale made for cash would show up immediately in the cash flow statement, whereas a sale made on credit would not be recorded in the cash flow statement until the receivables were actually collected. The cash flow statement is used by firms to manage their day-to-day cash transactions and to forecast short-term borrowing needs that might require bank loans.

FINANCIAL ANALYSIS

Financial analysis is used to evaluate the past performance of a firm through the examination of financial ratios. Two kinds of financial analysis can be conducted. Financial ratios may be compared over several years for the same firm in an effort to identify good and poor trends. This method of comparison is referred to as *trend or time series analysis*. A second method compares the firm's ratios against industry ratios and thus is known as *industry comparative analysis*.

Financial Ratio Dimensions

Financial analysis is designed to cover four areas of the firm. *Liquidity* ratios indicate the ability of the firm to meet its short-term debt obligations as they come due. These ratios focus on the relationship between the firm's current assets and current liabilities. *Asset utilization* ratios show how well the firm uses its assets to support or generate sales. Asset turnover is expressed as net sales divided by total assets.

A third area or dimension is concerned with *financial leverage* ratios which indicate the extent to which assets are financed by borrowed funds and other liabilities. Total liabilities often are expressed as a percentage of total assets or as total liabilities to stockholders' equity. The final dimension focuses on firm profitability. *Profitability* ratios generally are of two types. Net income is expressed as a percentage of net sales to show the degree of income statement profitability. Profitability also is measured by relating net income to total assets or to stockholders' equity.

We will be exploring these various ratio dimensions in greater detail in the remaining chapters of Part II. However, at this time we can increase our understanding of financial analysis by beginning with a financial system that incorporates the profitabilty and asset utilization dimensions.

A Financial Model or System

A system of financial analysis was developed by the Du Pont Corporation which provides a very valuable aid to the financial manager. It can be briefly expressed as follows:

$$\frac{\text{Net Income}}{\text{Total Assets}} = \frac{\text{Net Sales}}{\text{Total Assets}} \times \frac{\text{Net Income}}{\text{Net Sales}}$$

$$\text{Return on Assets} = \text{Asset Turnover} \times \text{Profit Margin}$$

Notice that the model focuses on firm profitability as measured by the rate of return on assets. Two ratio components when multiplied together give the return on assets. The asset turnover component indicates the extent to which assets have been effectively utilized to produce sales. The higher the turnover ratio the more effective the utilization. Income statement profitability is reflected in the size of the profit margin—the higher the percentage, the more profitable the firm.

Firms in some industries are able to achieve high asset turnovers but low profit margins, and vice versa. For example, retail food chains have high utilization of assets (i.e., small asset investments relative to sales generated) but very low profit margins and only average returns on assets. The chemical and steel industries, however, are very capital intensive and thus require large investments in assets to support their sales. Firms in these industries must earn higher than average profit margins to produce average asset returns.

The Du Pont system applied to the data for the ABC Manufacturing Company in Figures 7-1 and 7-2 indicates a return on total assets of 9.00 percent. This is based on a turnover of assets of 1.40 times and a profit margin of 6.43 percent as the following calculations show:

$$\frac{\$45,000}{\$500,000} = \frac{\$700,000}{\$500,000} \times \frac{\$45,000}{\$700,000}$$

$$9.00\% = 1.40 \times 6.43\%$$

This information by itself, however, is of limited value to the financial manager. Prior information certainly would be helpful. For example, the return on assets for 1982 for ABC might have been 10.00 percent based on net income of $40,000 and total assets of $400,000. We might ask why the return on assets declined. If sales were $600,000 in 1982, then the asset turnover had been 1.50 ($600,000/$400,000) with a profit margin of 6.67 percent ($40,000/$600,000). Thus the decline in the return on assets occurred because of a poorer utilization of assets and lower profitability on sales.

ABC's financial manager would want to investigate in greater detail why the performance was poorer in 1983 compared with 1982. He or she might expand the basic model to include the major components of both the balance sheet and income statement. A graphic expansion of the Du Pont system of financial analysis is shown in Figure 7-3. As we will see later, a more detailed examination of individual asset items could have been conducted to determine which ones caused total assets to increase more rapidly than did sales between the two years. Likewise, the various expense items could be examined more closely to identify which contributed to the decline in the profit margin.

The financial manager also should consider comparing ABC's financial performance against industry averages during the same two years to identify whether other firms in the industry had been affected to the same extent. For example, if the industry averages had shown a return on assets of 10.50 percent in each of the two years with asset turnovers of 1.50 and profit margins of 7.00 percent, then there would be reason for concern. The financial manager should determine the specific reasons for ABC's below-industry average performance and then take the necessary steps to improve financial performance in the future.

Figure 7-3
Expansion of the
Du Pont System of
Financial Analysis

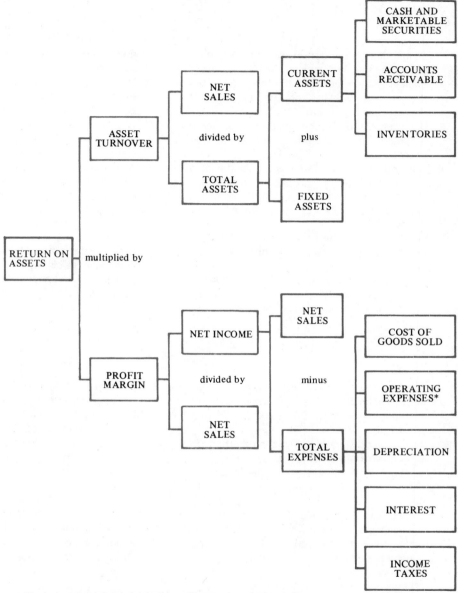

*Includes general, administrative, selling, and marketing expenses.

Financial analysis is an important financial management tool. By calculating and comparing financial ratios, the financial manager can evaluate past financial performance and use this information in planning for the firm's future. Financial analysis also is useful in monitoring the success of financial plans over time.

QUESTIONS

1. How do the financial markets of the nation accommodate the needs of both the very risky business effort and the well-established firm?
2. Explain what is meant by the relationship between risk and return from the standpoint of financial managers and investors.
3. What are the differences in owner liability in proprietorships and partnerships versus corporations?
4. Briefly describe the business trust and limited partnership forms of business organizations.
5. The ability of a business to obtain capital is in part a function of its legal form of organization. Explain.
6. What are some of the income tax considerations in selecting a particular form of business organization?
7. Briefly identify and describe the functions of financial management.
8. Explain and contrast: (1) current assets versus fixed assets, (2) accounts receivable versus notes receivable, and (3) accounts payable versus notes payable.
9. Briefly identify and describe the major types of expenses that must be met or covered by a manufacturing firm.
10. What accounting and financial statements in addition to balance sheets and income statements are used by the financial manager?
11. What kinds of financial analysis comparisons can be made in evaluating a firm's financial ratios?
12. Identify and briefly describe the four dimensions of a firm that are analyzed through financial ratios.
13. Explain what is meant by the Du Pont system of financial analysis. What are the two major components of the system? Also describe how the system is related to both the balance sheet and income statement.

PROBLEMS

1. Determine the marginal and average tax rates for corporations with the following amounts of taxable income: (a) $60,000, (b) $150,000, and (c) $500,000.
2. The Dogwood Manufacturing company had the following financial statement results for last year. Net sales were $1 million with net income of $70,000. Total assets at year end amounted to $800,000.
   a. Calculate Dogwood's asset turnover ratio and its profit margin.
   b. Show how the two ratios in Part A can be used to determine Dogwood's rate of return on assets.
   c. Dogwood operates in the same industry as ABC Manufacturing. Recall from the chapter that the industry ratios were:

   Return on Assets = 10.50%
   Asset Turnover = 1.50 times
   Profit Margin = 7.00%

   Compare Dogwood's performance against the industry averages.

3. Next year ABC Manufacturing (discussed in the chapter) expects its sales to reach $900,000 with an investment in total assets of $600,000. Net income of $70,000 is anticipated.
   a. Use the Du Pont system to compare ABC's anticipated performance against the results for 1982 and 1983. Comment on your findings.
   b. How would ABC compare with the industry if the industry ratios (see problem 2) remain the same the next year?
4. Following are selected financial data in thousands of dollars for the Solar-Genetics Corporation:

	1982	1983
Current Assets	$400	$500
Fixed Assets, Net	600	700
Total Assets	$1,000	$1,200
Current Liabilities	200	250
Long-term Debt	200	200
Common Equity	600	750
Total Liabilities and Equity	$1,000	$1,200

	1982	1983
Net Sales	$1,200	$1,500
Total Expenses	1,100	1,390
Net Income	$100	$110

a. Calculate Solar-Genetics' rate of return on total assets in 1982 and in 1983. Did the ratio improve or get worse?

b. Use Figure 7-3 in the chapter to diagram the expanded Du Pont system for Solar-Genetics for both 1982 and 1983. Insert the appropriate dollar amounts at each stage in your diagrams.

c. Use the Du Pont system to calculate and determine why the return on assets changed between the two years.

SUGGESTED READINGS

Bowlin, Oswald D., John D. Martin, and David F. Scott. *Guide to Financial Analysis.* New York: McGraw-Hill Book Company, 1980.

Carey, Kenneth J. "Persistence of Profitability." *Financial Management* (Summer, 1974), pp. 43–48.

Helfert, Erich A. *Techniques of Financial Analysis*, 5th ed. Homewood, Illinois: Richard D. Irwin, Inc., 1982.

Hill, Lawrence W. "The Growth of the Corporate Finance Function." *Financial Executive* (July, 1976), pp. 38–43.

Johnson, Robert W., and Ronald W. Melicher. *Financial Management*, 5th ed. Boston: Allyn and Bacon, Inc., 1982.

Reiling, Henry B., and John C. Burton. "Financial Statements: Signposts as Well as Milestones." *Harvard Business Review* (November/December, 1972), pp. 45–54.

8 Financial Planning and Working Capital Management

Financial planning is crucial to successful financial management. Sales must be forecasted and assets acquired to support the anticipated sales. The financial manager must decide how to finance the assets with a combination of internally generated profits and external funds. External financing must be planned in terms of the desired mix between debt and equity funds.

The first part of this chapter focuses on planning the asset/sales relationship and the financing mix. We then explore the firm's short-term operating cycle and the link between financial planning and the management of working capital. Broadly defined, *working capital* includes the firm's current assets and current liabilities. Our final emphasis is on management of cash and marketable securities, accounts receivable, and inventories.

FINANCIAL PLANNING

Financial planning begins with a sales forecast for one or more years. Written plans are referred to as budgets. For established firms, sales forecasts usually are based on historical sales data that are extrapolated (using statistical methods) into the future. Adjustments from the past trend then may be made to reflect possible changes in sales growth due to expected economic conditions, new products, and so forth. For example, a firm's sales may have been growing at a 10 percent average annual rate in the past. However, if a slowdown in economic activity is anticipated, management might forecast only a 5 percent growth rate for the next year or two. A booming economic climate might be, in contrast, associated with a 15 percent annual growth rate. New firms without sales histories have to rely on information from the experiences of other firms in their industry. Accurate sales forecasting is essential to the successful completion of the financial management functions.

Asset Investment Requirements

Once the sales forecast has been made, plans must be formulated to acquire the assets necessary to support the new sales level. The relationship of assets and sales is shown in the asset turnover ratio, which was defined in the last chapter as net sales divided by total assets. While firms strive to increase this ratio to improve asset utilization and profitability, the size of the ratio is significantly influenced by the industry characteristics within which the firm operates.

Capital intensive electric utilities might have asset turnovers as low as .33, indicating that they require $3 of investment in assets in order to produce $1 in revenues. In contrast, retail food chains with asset turnovers as high as 10.00 would require a $.10 investment in assets to produce $1 in sales. A typical manufacturing firm would have an asset turnover of about 1.50, or about $.67 invested in assets per $1 in sales.

Recall from the last chapter that the ABC Manufacturing Company had an asset turnover ratio of 1.40 based on 1983 sales of $700,000 and total assets of $500,000. By taking the inverse of this ratio, total assets divided by net sales, we can express assets as a percent of sales which would be 71.4 percent ($500,000/$700,000). This is referred to as the percent of sales method for forecasting asset investment requirements. For example, a 10 percent forecasted increase in net sales of $70,000 ($700,000 × .10) would result in an anticipated new asset investment of about $50,000 ($70,000 × 71.4%).

Figure 8-1 shows each major balance sheet item expressed as a percent of

Figure 8-1
Percent of Sales
Balance Sheet for the
ABC Manufacturing
Company

BALANCE SHEET December 31, 1983		
	Dollar Amount	Percent of Sales ($700,000)
Assets		
Cash and Marketable Securities	$25,000	3.6%
Accounts Receivable	100,000	14.3
Inventories	125,000	17.8
Total Current Assets	250,000	35.7
Net Plant and Equipment	200,000	28.6
Land	50,000	7.1
Total Fixed Assets	250,000	35.7
Total Assets	$500,000	71.4%
Liabilities and Owners' Equity		
Accounts Payable	$75,000	10.7%
Notes Payable (Bank)	20,000	2.8
Accrued Liabilities	30,000	4.3
Total Current Liabilities	125,000	17.8
Mortgage Debt	100,000	14.3
Total Liabilities	225,000	32.1
Owners' Equity	275,000	39.3
Total Liabilities and Owners' Equity	$500,000	71.4%

sales for 1983 for ABC Manufacturing. Notice that the total for all the assets sum to 71.4 percent as we calculated above. Of course, actual asset investment required to support a specific sales increase may be altered if either of two developments occur. First, if ABC could improve its asset turnover ratio to the average of 1.50 times, then assets would be only 66.7 percent of sales. This would mean that a $70,000 increase in sales would require an asset investment of about $46,700, or roughly $2,300 less than the earlier calculation. Second, certain fixed assets such as land or plant investments might not have to be increased each year along with an increase in sales. The deciding factor usually is whether the firm currently has excess production capacity. For example, according to Figure 8-1, if only current assets are expected to increase with sales next year, then the asset investment requirements would be only about $25,000 ($70,000 × 35.7%).

Of course, a greater than 10 percent sales growth would require an even larger investment in new assets. A much lower asset investment would be needed for an expected growth of, say, 5 percent, and existing assets might even be reduced if sales decline.

Let's assume that the $50,000 asset investment scenario will be the proper requirement next year. We now are ready to plan how these assets are to be financed from anticipated profits or external sources.

Internally Generated Financing

Internally generated funds for financing new asset investments must come from the making of profits. Let us return to the ABC Manufacturing Company to illustrate the concept of planning for internally generated funds. Recall from the last chapter that during 1983 ABC earned $45,000 in net income on net sales of $700,000 for a profit margin of 6.43 percent. If net sales are expected to rise by 10 percent next year to $770,000 and the profit margin is expected to hold, then profits would be projected at about $49,500 ($770,000 × 6.43%). This would be adequate, if all profits were retained within the firm, to finance nearly all of the $50,000 investment in new assets.

However, let's further assume that management plans to pay out about one half of the profits or $24,500 to the owners of the company. This would leave only $25,000 ($49,500 − $24,500) in internally generated funds to finance the $50,000 in assets. The amount of profit retained in the firm would show up as an increase in owners' equity, or retained earnings in the case of corporations. The remaining $25,000 in assets would have to be financed with external funds: either short-term debt, or long-term debt, or equity funds. We now are ready to consider how the financial manager might plan for the desired mix of short-term and long-term external sources of funds.

External Financing Requirements

The ABC Manufacturing Company can expect that a portion of its asset financing requirements will be met by almost "automatic" increases in certain current liability accounts such as accounts payable and accrued liabilities. To meet planned sales increases, more credit purchases of materials will be necessary to produce the products to make the sales. Increases also would be expected in accrued wages and taxes. These spontaneous liability accounts reduce the need for other external financing, since they allow the firm to acquire additional inputs without an immediate cash outlay.

Figure 8-1 shows that accounts payable plus accrued liabilities were about 15.0 percent of sales in 1983 for ABC Manufacturing. Based on a 10 percent expected increase in sales, accounts payable and accrued liabilities would be expected to provide about $10,500 ($70,000 × 15.0%) in spontaneous short-term funds. This would leave an external financing need for ABC of about $14,500 ($25,000 − $10,500) in order to cover the asset investment require-ments. Management might choose to borrow the amount from a commercial bank, issue long-term debt, or request more equity funds from the owners.

To summarize briefly, the amount of external funds needed to finance new asset additions can be planned for as follows:

1. Forecast the dollar amount of expected sales increase.
2. Determine the dollar amount of new asset investments necessary to support the sales increase.
3. Subtract the expected amount of internally generated profits from the planned asset investments.
4. Subtract the amount of spontaneous increases expected in accounts payable and accrued liabilities from the planned asset investments.
5. The remaining dollar amount of asset investments indicates the external financing needs (EFN).

For the ABC Manufacturing example we have:

$$EFN = \$50,000 - \$25,000 - \$10,500 = \$14,500$$

Determining the Financing Mix

Figure 8-2 depicts increases in the investment in assets. Increases in the investment in fixed assets and current assets would be consistent with rising sales over time. Seasonal variations in sales in a business also affect the demand for current assets. Inventories must be built up to meet seasonal needs, and receivables will go up as sales increase. This added need for funds will disappear as inventories are reduced by sales as the season progresses and accounts receivable are collected. Thus seasonal variation in sales requires only temporary additional investments in current assets.

A recommended pattern for financing the assets also is depicted in Figure 8-2. Recall from Chapter 6, in our discussion of financial management of financial institutions, that the principle of hedging calls for the matching of average maturities of a firm's assets and liabilities. This implies that fixed assets should be financed with long-term debt and owners' equity funds. At the same time, fluctuating current assets associated with seasonal operations should be financed with short-term liabilities.

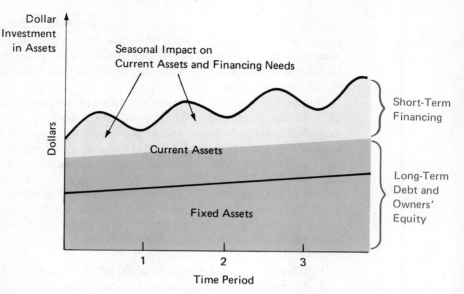

Figure 8-2
Asset Investment and
Financing Relationships

In contrast, the normal level of current assets actually reflects a "permanent" investment in cash, accounts receivable, and inventories needed to support sales. While individual accounts are collected and products sold, they are replaced by others, causing the level of investment in these assets to remain constant. A portion of this investment will be offset by "permanent" levels of accounts payable and accrued liabilities that behave similarly to the permanent current assets. However, the remaining portion of normal current assets requires long-term financing. To finance these assets with a short-term bank loan would be inconsistent with the hedging principle because permanent current assets have in effect long-term maturities.

THE SHORT-TERM OPERATING CYCLE AND WORKING CAPITAL NEEDS

The link between financial planning and the management of working capital, including both current assets and current liabilities, can be described in terms of the firm's short-term operating cycle. Estimation of the time it takes to complete the cycle relative to the level of operations will indicate the size of the investment in accounts receivable and inventories, and the extent to which financing will take place through accounts payable.

Illustration of the Short-term Cycle

Figure 8-3 depicts the short-term operating cycle for a manufacturing firm which presumably has an existing fixed asset investment in plant and equipment. Raw materials must be purchased. If these are credit purchases, then accounts payable are created, providing initial financing for a period. Then, movement through the manufacturing process will result in finished goods. This inventory (raw materials, work-in-process, and finished goods), of course, must be financed.

Figure 8-3
The Short-Term
Operating Cycle
(or Cash-to-Cash
Cycle)

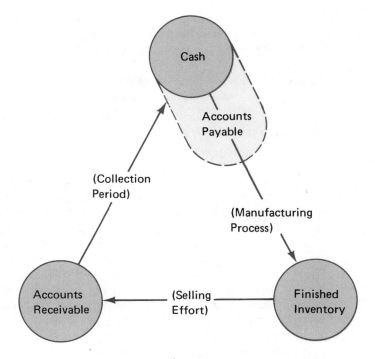

The manufacturing firm also must go through a selling effort which may end in a certain amount of credit sales. These resulting accounts receivable also must be financed. Finally, the firm must conduct a collection effort to turn the credit sales into cash.

As the firm moves through its short-term operating cycle, accrued liabilities (although not depicted in Figure 8-3) also may arise. For example, the manufacturing process is likely to lead to a level of wages payable, and to the extent that the firm is profitable there may be taxes payable. Increases in these accounts provide temporary financing in the same manner as accounts payable.

Working Capital Requirements

The average time it takes the firm to complete its short-term operating cycle will indicate the size of investment needed in accounts receivable and inventories, as well as the amount of financing provided by accounts payable. For example, ABC's production process might require on average 70 days to go from raw materials to finished products and another 30 days before the finished goods are sold. This amounts to an average inventory cycle of 100 days. Let's also assume that ABC Manufacturing extends credit to customers and has an accounts receivable cycle of 60 days. The combined cycle for inventories and accounts receivable now becomes 160 days and would indicate the time it takes on average to complete the firm's short-term operating cycle if ABC did not purchase raw materials on credit.

However, let's assume that materials are purchased on credit terms from suppliers such that accounts payable cycle on average every 70 days (for many firms, the receivables cycle is longer than its payables cycle). Thus the short-term operating cycle would be reduced to 90 days (160 days − 70 days). We can also express the short-term operating cycle in days as follows:

Inventory Cycle	100 days
Accounts Receivable Cycle	60 days
	160 days
Accounts Payable Cycle	−70 days
Short-term Operating Cycle	90 days

Based on the use of a 360-day year, this would imply that ABC's short-term operating cycle would turn over on average about 4 times (360/90) a year.

Now we can develop an idea about the size of the needed investments in inventories and accounts receivable. First of all, the inventory turns over about 3.6 times (360/100) a year based on the use of a 360-day year. If ABC has an annual cost of goods sold of $450,000 associated with producing its products, the average inventory on its balance sheet would be estimated at $125,000 ($450,000/3.6). In essence, we divide the cost of goods sold by the number of times the inventory turns over on average during the year. Accounts receivable turn over on average 6 times (360/60) a year. However, because credit sales include a markup or profit in addition to cost of goods sold, we use credit sales for estimating the investment in accounts receivable. Let's assume credit sales of $600,000. Dividing this figure by the turnover for accounts receivable would provide an average investment of $100,000 ($600,000/6). Thus the combined investment in inventories and accounts receivable would be roughly $225,000.

Accounts payable would turn over 5.1 times (360/70) a year. To estimate the financing provided by accounts payable we would divide the credit purchases of, say, $383,000, by the turnover of 5.1 for an amount of $75,000. This would leave a net accounts receivable and inventories financing need of $150,000 ($225,000 − $75,000). Part of this need likely would be met by the firm's accrued liabilities. Of course, some cash also would be needed to carry on ABC's day-to-day operations. The remaining financing of current assets thus would have to come from short-term bank loans and/or long-term funds.

Net Working Capital

Short-term financing is used primarily to finance part of the current assets of a business. The portion of current assets financed through long-term financing is referred to as the *net working capital*. This amount is determined by subtracting the total of current liabilities shown on the balance sheet from the total of current assets. If short-term financing were relied upon entirely by a business for its current asset requirements, the total current assets of the firm would be equal to the total current liabilities. The balance sheet of a successful nonfinancial business enterprise, however, will reveal an excess of current assets over current liabilities. This excess reflects the extent to which long-term financing has contributed to the support of the current asset requirements of the business firm.

The balance sheet for the ABC Manufacturing Company, shown in Figure 8-1, allows us to examine ABC's net working capital position. ABC has current assets of $250,000 and current liabilities of $125,000 and thus $125,000 in net working capital. This net working capital is supported by the mortgage debt and/or owners' equity.

The net working capital is a measure of the financial soundness of a firm. In general, the greater the net working capital of a firm, the less burdensome are the problems of meeting short-term obligations. So important is the existence of an adequate net working capital to a firm that it has become one of the prime tests of strength, and creditors place great emphasis on it in determining whether or not to extend credit.

Liquidity Ratios

The net working capital or short-term financial position of a firm is expressed not only in terms of dollars but also in relative terms. This relationship is determined by dividing total current assets by total current liabilities, the quotient being the *current ratio* of the firm. Although the net working capital position and the current ratio are simply alternative ways of expressing the short-term financial position of the firm, each has its particular usefulness.

The current ratio concept is particularly useful in comparing the financial positions of firms of varying sizes. For example, the ABC Manufacturing Company has total current assets of $250,000 and total current liabilities of $125,000, in which case the current ratio is 2 to 1 and the net working capital is $125,000. Another firm, engaged in similar business activities, may have total current assets of $500,000 and total current liabilities of $250,000, the current ratio being 2 to 1 and the net working capital $250,000. In this example, the net working capital of the latter firm is twice that of ABC, yet it is clear that it is a matter of proportion, that the latter firm may simply be a larger enterprise doing a larger volume of business. The current ratio of each firm, however, is 2 to 1, revealing the similarity of short-term financial positions.

A second liquidity ratio often is used along with the current ratio in order to better assess the firm's ability to meet its short-term obligations as they come due. This is referred to as the *acid-test ratio* which excludes inventories from current assets because of greater uncertainty as to whether they can be easily converted into cash if needed to pay bills. For comparative purposes, both the current and acid-test ratios are shown as follows for ABC:

$$\textit{Current Ratio}$$

$$\textit{Acid-Test Ratio}$$

$$\frac{\text{Current Assets}}{\text{Current Liabilities}} \qquad \frac{\text{Current Assets} - \text{Inventories}}{\text{Current Liabilities}}$$

$$\frac{\$250,000}{\$125,000} = 2{:}1 \qquad \frac{\$250,000 - \$125,000}{\$125,000} = 1{:}1$$

An acid-test ratio of 1 to 1 is considered good in that current liabilities can be met if needed through the collection of accounts receivable and by the use of cash and marketable securities.

Importance of Adequate Net Working Capital

The importance of providing for part of the current asset requirements of a business through long-term financing may be illustrated by a theoretical and highly improbable situation in which long-term financing has not been provided for this purpose. For example, if in ABC's balance sheet the current liabilities had been $250,000 (each current liability account was doubled and owners' equity was reduced by $125,000), there would be no net working capital.

The current liabilities of such a firm would fall due periodically and would have to be paid out of cash. Since the cash and marketable securities are $25,000, only that much indebtedness could be retired on the date of the balance sheet. It is true, of course, that the accounts receivable and the inventory would in time be converted into cash as the firm moves through its operating cycle. The business would be in an extremely precarious position, however; for, in the event of failure of the conversion of receivables and inventory into cash on schedule, the firm would be unable to meet promptly its current obligations.

The answer to this problem is to provide part of the current asset requirements through long-term financing. With current assets amounting to substantially more than current liabilities, the chance of the business having too little cash to meet its obligations is reduced materially.

An adequate net working capital makes it possible for the firm to meet its debts promptly and to take discounts that may be available if early payment is made for purchases of raw materials and other goods. Also, the firm that is in a position to make cash payments may pay a lower price for its purchases, or it may have access to a better quality of merchandise at the same price because of the better bargaining position it enjoys. Suppliers of materials as well as banks regard more highly the firm with a strong net working capital position, insuring a continuing flow of funds and supplies during peak periods of seasonal activity and making it possible for the firm to take advantage of overall expansion as long-term growth opportunities become available.

FACTORS AFFECTING THE AMOUNT OF SHORT-TERM FINANCING

The determination of the proper proportion between short-term and long-term financing depends upon an evaluation of many factors which affect the business. The nature of the demand for funds is basic and it will be considered first in this section. Then consideration will be given to a series of other factors such as risks, cost, flexibility, the ease of future financing, and other qualitative factors.

Nature of the Demand for Funds

The nature of the demand for funds depends in part on the industry in which business operates and on the characteristics of the business itself. It also depends on such factors as the seasonal variation in sales and output and on the trend of growth of the company. The need for funds also depends upon fluctuations in sales over the business cycle.

Industry and Company Factors. The nature of a company and the industry of which it is a part have a signficant effect on financing decisions. An industry which has a need for large amounts of fixed capital can do more long-term financing than one which has a relatively small investment in fixed assets. Electric power companies, for example, have heavy investments in fixed assets and relatively little investment in current assets. The same is true of telephone companies, railroads, and gas companies. While manufacturing companies often require substantial investments in fixed assets for manufacturing purposes, they also have significant investments in inventories and receivables. Thus, as was the case for ABC, they generally have a more equal balance between current and fixed assets than electric utility and telephone companies.

Large retail stores often lease their quarters but at the same time hold substantial assets in the form of inventories and receivables. Thus, they are characterized by relatively high current asset to fixed asset mixes. At the same time, retail stores are characterized by relatively high total asset turnovers. That is, even though a large portion of their assets are in the form of current assets, it takes a relatively small investment in total assets in order to make $1 in revenues. This high asset turnover, however, is generally offset by low profit margins for many retail operations.

We need to make two points at this time. First, the level of total assets needed to support a given level of sales is significantly influenced by the industry characteristics within which the firm operates. Second, the composition of the asset structure (current assets versus fixed assets) of an industry and of a firm in the industry is a significant factor in determining the relative proportions of long-term and short-term financing done by a firm.

The competitive structure of an industry is also of significance. In an industry in which prices and profits fluctuate widely, as is the case in some of the basic metals industries, it is poor policy to incur a large proportion of debt. The same is true of oligopolistic industries in which price wars can disrupt normal cost and price relationships. In industries in which demand is relatively stable and prices are regulated, such as utilities, a larger proportion of debt financing is generally safe.

The size and age of a company and its stage in its financial life cycle may also be significant in financing decisions. A small, new company may find that its only source of funds is investment by the owner and possibly some friends. Some long-term funds may be raised by mortgaging real estate and buying equipment on installment, and some current borrowing may be possible to meet seasonal needs. As a business grows it has more access to short-term capital from finance companies and banks. Further along in its growth in size and record of profitability a business may be able to arrange longer-term financing with banks or with other financial agencies such as insurance companies. At this stage in its financial development it may also expand its group of owners by having stock held by a wider group of people than the owner and a few friends.

The next stage in financial development is one in which stock is widely enough held and the financial record of a company is such that brokerage houses will sell the stock over the counter. At this stage they may also be willing to sell stock of the company or bonds or notes in a small-scale public offering. The last stage in the financial life cycle is one in which stock is widely enough held that it is listed on a regional and finally also on a national stock exchange. New issues of stock and bonds can then be sold to the general public through a large group of investment banking houses. At these stages in its financial life cycle a company will be able to obtain short-term credit on reasonable terms.

The growth prospects of a company also have an effect on financing decisions. If a company is growing faster than the rate at which it can finance its funds from internal sources, it must give careful consideration to a plan for long-term financing. Even if it can finance its needs in the current situation from short-term sources, it may not be wise to do so. Sound financial planning calls for raising long-term funds under the most favorable conditions, and this may call for such financing at intervals of several years.

Seasonal Variation. Our earlier discussion of Figure 8-2 acknowledged that seasonal variations in sales affect the demand for current assets. Inventories are built up to meet seasonal needs, and receivables go up as sales increase. The peak of receivables will come after the peak in sales, depending on the credit terms and payment practices of customers. Accounts payable will, of course, go up as inventories are purchased, again with a lag depending on terms and payment policies. The difference between the increase in current assets and accounts payable should be financed by short-term borrowing.

The added need for funds will again disappear as inventories are reduced by sales as the season progresses and accounts receivable are collected. When the added need for funds is financed by a short-term loan, such a loan is said to be self-liquidating since funds are made available to repay it as inventories and receivables are reduced.

Trend. The trend of sales of a business also affects the current position. As sales grow, fixed assets and current assets also must grow to support the sales growth as we depicted in Figure 8-2. In fact, the growth rates for sales and assets would be the same as long as the asset turnover ratio remained constant. This need for funds is a permanent one (higher asset levels are necessary to support higher sales levels) unless the upward trend of sales is reversed. If it is met by current borrowing, the loan could not be repaid, except by added investment by the owners, but would have to be renewed indefinitely. The sum of money involved would go up year by year as the trend continued upward. Even if no season existed and, therefore, there was no seasonal need for funds, short-term borrowing could not be used indefinitely to supply the added funds. In time, the current ratio would drop to such a level that no financing institution would provide additional funds. The only alternative then is long-term financing.

Cyclical Variation. The need for current funds is also increased when there is an upswing in the business cycle or the cycle in an industry. Since the cycle is not regular in timing or amplitude, it is hard to predict exactly how long the added funds will be needed or what the extent of the need will be. It will, of course, be estimated for a year ahead in the budget and checked quarterly. When the volume of business decreases, the need for funds will again decrease. If a concern is growing, the need will not return to its former level because of the trend. It is also possible that for a time during the downturn the need will not decrease, but may even increase temporarily because the circular flow of cash is slowed down as receivables are collected more slowly and inventories move more slowly and drop in value.

If cyclical needs for funds are met by current borrowing, the loan will, of course, not be self-liquidating in a year. It may be over a complete cycle except for the increased needs due to the trend. There are hazards in financing such needs on a short-term basis. The lending institution may demand payment of all or part of the loan as business turns down. Funds may be needed more severely than ever at this stage of the cycle, and the need may last until receivables can be collected and inventory can be reduced. A more conservative approach would make use of longer-term financing.

The Effect of Risks on Financing Decisions

The risks which affect all business operations also affect the financing of the business. These risks can be divided into three categories: (1) business risks, (2) purchasing power risk, and (3) interest rate risk.

Business Risks. Some *business risks* arise out of the operation of the business itself; others, from outside economic forces. The extent to which changes in the economy impact on the business operations of the firm and its industry indicates the degree of *macroeconomic business risk*. This business cycle impact, which was just discussed, is reflected in the degree of variability in a firm's sales and profits. In general, the higher the level of this type of business risk, the more risky it is to use debt financing.

Internal business risks arise from several factors. There is a risk of loss of property due to fire, flood, and the like. Such risks can and must be covered by insurance before any financing can be done. There is a risk in small and medium-sized firms of the loss due to the death of a key figure in the business. Such a risk can be covered by insurance on the lives of key officials. In some cases, however, no amount of money will offset the loss sustained if a business does not progress as it did before a key official died. Profits may be too low to attract new capital, or losses may result because of inept management in any area of a business. This is one of the reasons why a small or medium-sized business generally cannot do any significant amount of long-term borrowing except through mortgages on general-use real estate and must rely on short-term borrowing and owners' equity to meet its needs. Suppliers of short-term loans will generally be protected if a reasonable amount of insurance exists since this will allow the business to continue operations and will give the lending institution time to assess the situation. If they feel the risk is too great, they can reduce the loan or call for payment before the business gets into financial difficulties.

Purchasing Power Risk. Some risks which are primarily of a financial nature also have some effect on short-term financing policies, but primarily affect long-term financing. One of these financial risks is the *purchasing power risk* which results from changes in the price level. As the price level increases a business has problems since it takes a larger number of dollars to do the same volume of business. This affects short-term financing almost immediately since part of the purchasing power in cash balances and receivables is lost when the price level increases. This loss is offset to the extent that current assets were financed by current or long-term borrowing since the loan agreement calls for repayment in dollars which now have less purchasing power. But the total dollar amount of current assets to be financed will be greater than before the price rise, and this also means a larger dollar amount of net working capital is needed.

Interest Rate Risk. Another financial risk which has some effect on short-term financing is *interest rate risk*. If interest rates rise significantly in a short period of time, the added cost may affect profit margins unless prices can be raised to offset the added cost. Such increases were especially significant in 1973–74 and at the beginning of the 1980s. Such increases in costs could have been and were avoided by firms that did intermediate- and long-term financing in periods of more moderate interest rates.

Cost of Financing

Another factor to consider is the cost of short-term financing when compared with alternative sources of financing. Short-term interest rates on business loans have generally been lower than long-term interest rates since the depression of the 1930s. This has not always been true, especially in periods of tight money such as 1973–74 and 1980–81. However, when interest rates on short-term borrowing are lower than on long-term borrowing, there is an incentive to use short-term financing as fully as possible.

It is usually less costly to engage in short-term financing than to sell additional equity (ownership) interests in the business. Persons who purchase additional ownership interests in the business, like the existing owners, will share in the profits of the business. During periods of normal business activity, these profits will generally represent a return on investment far greater than the costs of short-term financing. Hence, the existing owners of the business can increase their own earnings through short-term financing to the extent that the earnings on assets acquired through short-term financing exceed the costs of such financing. Both forms of long-term financing, debt and equity, may therefore be more costly than are the usual forms of short-term financing.

Cost can also be a limiting factor in current borrowing. As the percentage of current assets financed by current borrowing goes up, interest charges become higher. If the lending institution feels an increased unsecured loan is not safe, they may lend larger sums on a secured basis, such as an accounts receivable loan or an inventory loan. Not only is the interest charge on such loans higher than on unsecured loans, but the mechanics of the financing arrangement involves added clerical costs, warehouse fees, and the like, and these increase the cost of financing.

Other Factors

Short-term borrowing has several other advantages over other forms of financing. Short-term borrowing has more flexibility than long-term financing. Only those sums needed currently can be borrowed, whereas long-term financing is usually done to take care of needs for some time in the future due to the cost and time involved in getting the funds. If during periods of general business expansion an enterprise obtains its additional current asset requirements entirely through long-term financing, it might be burdened with excess funds during a subsequent period of general business contraction. In using short-term financing along with long-term financing, therefore, a flexibility of operations is possible that does not exist with long-term financing alone. As the need for assets decreases, the firm may simply retire its short-term obligations. Although the long-term obligations of the business may in some cases be retired when the funds provided through such financing are no longer required, such an action may be awkward; and often a penalty must be paid for prepayment of the obligation.

Short-term financing also has advantages that result from establishing continuing relationships with a bank or other financial institution. The firm that depends almost entirely upon long-term financing for its needs will not enjoy the close relationship with its bank that it otherwise would. A record of frequent borrowing from and prompt repayment to its bank by an enterprise is an extremely important factor in sound financial management. Under these circumstances, a bank will make every effort to accommodate its business customers with loans at all times. The enterprise that has not established such a working relationship with its bank will scarcely be in a position to seek special loans during its periods of emergency needs. Also, the credit experience of a business in connection with its short-term financing may be the only basis on which potential long-term lenders to a business can judge the enterprise. Hence, the business that intends to seek long-term loans may wish to establish a good credit reputation based on its short-term financing.

Offsetting these advantages are such factors as frequent renewals and perhaps a greater risk than with more permanent financing. Even though short-term credit is usually easy to obtain, some time and effort must be spent on it at frequent intervals since loans are of short duration. And when business decreases there may be quite a bit of negotiation to get the needed credit.

Frequent maturities also introduce an added element of risk. The bank or finance company can call the loan whenever it is due. Even if a revolving credit agreement is used, it runs for a limited period of time only. A concern may be in a temporary slump due to the business cycle or some internal problem and may be able to work out the problem in time. However, if it is relying heavily on short-term financing, its loans may be reduced or not renewed, which may make it all but impossible to get back on its feet, or may even lead to liquidation. On the other hand, if the concern had raised the money on a long-term basis, it may have worked out of its difficulties, or at least it may have had a chance to do so under more favorable circumstances.

MANAGEMENT OF CURRENT ASSETS

Management of current assets involves the administration of cash and marketable securities, accounts receivable, and inventories. On the one hand, the financial manager should strive to minimize the investment in current assets because of costly financing. On the other hand, adequate cash and marketable securities are necessary for liquidity purposes, acceptable credit terms are necessary to maintain sales, and appropriate inventory levels must be kept to avoid stockouts resulting in lost sales. Successful management thus requires a continual balancing of the costs associated with investment in current assets.

Cash and Marketable Securities Management

Business firms should strive to minimize their cash holdings. Some cash is necessary to carry on day-to-day operations. This is known as a *transactions motive* or demand. If cash inflows and outflows could be projected with virtual certainty, the transactions need for cash could theoretically be reduced to zero. Most businesses prepare cash flow forecasts or budgets in trying to limit necessary cash holdings. However, most firms are forced to hold some cash balances because of cash flow uncertainties, and often because compensating balances are required on loans from their commercial banks.

Marketable securities are held primarily to meet *precautionary motives*. Disruptive developments such as delays in production or shipments, or in the collection of receivables, could cause severe short-term liquidity problems. The holding of marketable securities would serve to cushion such potential developments. In the event of strong seasonal sales patterns, marketable securities also can be used to reduce wide fluctuations in short-term financing requirements.

Marketable securities also may be held in association with *speculative motives*. In certain instances a firm might be able to take advantage of unusual cash discounts or price bargains on materials if it can pay quickly with cash. Marketable securities are easily converted into cash for such purposes.

For an investment to qualify as a marketable security it must be highly liquid, that is it must be readily convertible to cash without substantial price concessions. Generally this requires that it have a short maturity and that an active secondary market exist so that it can be sold prior to maturity if necessary. It also must be of high quality, with little chance that the borrower will default. U.S. Treasury bills offer the highest quality, liquidity, and marketability. Other investments that serve well as marketable securities include negotiable certificates of deposit (CD's) and commercial paper, both of which offer higher rates but are more risky and less liquid than Treasury bills. Business firms also can hold excess cash funds in money market fund accounts, or purchase bankers' acceptances or short-term notes of U.S. government agencies.

Accounts Receivable Management

The management of receivables involves conducting credit analysis, setting credit terms, and carrying out collection efforts. Taken together, these decision areas determine the level of investment in accounts receivable.

Credit Analysis. Credit analysis involves appraising the credit worthiness or quality of a potential customer. That is, should credit be extended? The decision is made on the basis of the applicant's character, capacity, capital, collateral, and conditions—the five C's of credit analysis. *Character* is the willingness of the applicant to pay his or her bills. *Capacity* reflects the ability to pay bills and often involves the examination of liquidity ratios. *Capital* indicates the adequacy of owners' equity relative to existing liabilities as the underlying support for credit worthiness. *Collateral* reflects whether assets are available to provide security for the potential credit. *Conditions* refer to the prevailing economic climate or business cycle state and is an important consideration in assessing whether the applicant can meet the credit obligations.

Once a firm has established its credit quality standards, credit analysis then is used to determine whether an applicant should be granted credit, be rejected, or falls in a "marginal" category. Whether or not credit should be extended to marginal applicants depends on such factors as the prevailing economic conditions and the extent to which the selling firm has excess production capacity. During periods of economic downturn and excess capacity, a selling firm may find it necessary to sell to lower quality applicants that may be slow paying but not likely to become bad debts.

Credit-Reporting Agencies. Several sources of credit information are available to aid the firm in deciding whether to extend credit. *Credit interchange bureaus* exist to obtain information regarding both business firms and individuals. They are nonprofit institutions, established and supported by the businesses they serve. The local mercantile (business) credit interchange bureau provides a central record in the community for credit information on business firms. Bureau members submit lists of their customers to the bureau. The bureau determines the credit standing of these customers by contacting other bureau members who have extended credit to them. Thus, a member firm need only contact its credit bureau for information on prospective customers rather than write or telephone many individual firms.

The exchange of mercantile credit information from bureau to bureau is accomplished through the National Credit Interchange System. Reports of credit exchange bureaus are factual rather than analytical, and it is up to each credit analyst to interpret the facts.

As was the case for mercantile credit, local retail credit interchange bureaus have been established for the purpose of consolidation and distribution of credit information regarding consumers in the local community. These organizations are generally owned and operated by participating members on a nonprofit basis. A central organization known as the Associated Credit Bureaus of America serves as a medium through which local retail credit bureaus in the United States are able to transmit credit information from bureau to bureau.

United States businesses selling to foreign customers encounter all of the problems involved in a domestic sale, plus several additional ones. Among these are increased geographical distance, language barriers, complicated shipping and government regulations, differences in legal systems, and political instability. To help exporters with these problems, the National Association of Credit Management established the Foreign Credit Interchange Bureau. Just as the local credit interchange bureaus increased their knowledge of business credit risks by pooling their credit and collection experience, so the members of the Foreign Credit Interchange Bureau have established a central file of information extending over several decades of experience. The Bureau is located in New York to serve the concentration of export and financial organizations that do business overseas.

Some private firms also operate as credit-reporting agencies. The best known is Dun & Bradstreet, Inc., which has been in operation for well over a century and provides credit information on businesses in all lines of activity. The information that is assembled and evaluated is brought into the company through many channels. The company employs full-time and part-time employees for direct investigation, communicates directly with business establishments by mail to supplement their informational files, and obtains the financial statements of companies being reported on. All information filed with public authorities and financial and trade papers is carefully analyzed to gather bits of information pertinent to a credit analysis. The basic service supplied to the manufacturers, wholesalers, banks, and insurance companies who are subscribers to Dun & Bradstreet, is rendered in two ways—through written reports on individual businesses and through a "reference book."

A Dun & Bradstreet report is typically divided into five sections: (1) Rating and Summary, (2) Trade Payments, (3) Financial Information, (4) Operation and Location, and (5) History. In addition, a composite reference book of ratings on nearly 3 million manufacturers, wholesalers, retailers, and other businesses on which credit reports have been written is published six times per year.

Credit Terms and Collection Efforts. Credit extended on purchases to a firm's customers is referred to as *trade credit*. This credit, of course, appears as accounts payable on the balance sheet of the customer, and as receivables to the seller. (Trade credit as a source of financing for the customer will be discussed in the next chapter.) The seller sets the terms of the credit. For example, the firm might require full payment in sixty days, expressed as net/60. If all customers pay promptly in sixty days, this would result in a receivables turnover of 360/60 or six times a year.[1] Thus, annual credit sales of $720,000 would require an average receivables investment of $120,000. A change in the credit terms or in the enforcement of the terms through the collection effort will alter the average

---

[1] The turnover of current asset accounts such as receivables and inventories, like total assets turnover, are *asset utilization ratios.* Higher ratios imply better usage of assets.

investment in receivables. The imposition of net/50 day terms would lead to an increase in the receivables turnover to 7.2 (360/50) times and the average investment in receivables would decline to $100,000 ($720,000/7.2). If it costs, say, 15 percent to finance assets, then the $20,000 reduction in receivables would result in a savings of $3,000 ($20,000 × .15).

Of course, we are to this point assuming that a reduction in credit terms and thus in the receivables portion of the short-term operating cycle will not cause lost sales. The financial manager must be very careful in not imposing credit terms that will cause lost profits, due to lower sales, to more than offset any financing cost savings.

The collection effort involves administration of past-due accounts. Techniques include sending letters and making telephone calls, and perhaps personal visits for very large customers with past-due bills. If the customer continues to fail to pay a bill then the account may be turned over to a commercial collection firm. The last resort would be to take legal action.

A lax collection policy might result in the average collection period for receivables being substantially longer than the credit period implied by the credit terms. For example, a firm might sell on credit terms of net/60 days but have credit sales of $720,000 and an accounts receivable balance of $150,000. We can determine the *average collection period* as follows:

$$\frac{\text{Accounts Receivable}}{\text{Credit Sales}/360} = \frac{\$150,000}{\$720,000/360} = \frac{\$150,000}{\$2,000} = 75 \text{ days}$$

This shows that the accounts receivable are outstanding on average for 75 days instead of the net/60 day credit period. A tightening of the collection effort might reduce the average collection period to 60 days and the accounts receivable balance to $120,000.

A lowering of the firm's credit standards or customer credit quality also will cause the average collection period to lengthen because poorer quality customers will be slower payers. Thus the financial manager must balance the advantages of increased sales from lower quality customers against higher receivable investments and increased collection costs.

Inventory Management

The administration of inventories is primarily a production management function. The length of the production process and the production manager's willingness to accept delays will influence the amount of investment in raw materials and work-in-process. Finished goods on hand may vary in amount depending on the firm's willingness to accept stockouts and lost sales.

Costs of carrying (financing, storage, and insurance) raw materials need to be balanced against the costs of ordering the materials. Production managers attempt to balance these costs by determining an optimal order quantity in units that will minimize total raw materials inventory costs.

The financial manager is concerned with minimizing the overall investment in inventories in order to hold down financing costs. In other words, it is desirable to increase the utilization of these assets by achieving a high inventory turnover. Let's assume that a firm's cost of goods sold is $600,000 and it has inventories on hand of $100,000. We measure the *inventory turnover* as follows:

$$\frac{\text{Cost of Goods Sold}}{\text{Inventories}} = \frac{\$600,000}{\$100,000} = 6 \text{ times}$$

If the firm is able to increase its inventory turnover to, say, 8 times, then the investment in inventories could be reduced to $75,000 ($600,000/8) and financing costs saved. Of course, if too tight an inventory policy is imposed, lost sales due to stockouts could result in lost profits that more than offset financing cost savings. Thus the financial manager must balance possible savings against potential added costs when managing investments in inventories.

QUESTIONS

1. How can the process of financial planning be used to estimate asset investment requirements?
2. Explain how financial planning is used to determine a firm's external financing requirements.
3. Explain with the aid of a diagram how businesses should strive to finance their asset structures with short-term and long-term funds.
4. Briefly explain and trace through a manufacturing firm's short-term operating cycle. How can its length be determined?
5. Explain the relationship among current assets, current liabilities, and net working capital. Why is it necessary to have adequate net working capital?
6. What factors affect the nature of the demand for short-term versus long-term funds?
7. Describe the various risks that should be analyzed in making financing decisions.
8. Prepare a list of advantages and disadvantages of short-term borrowing relative to other financing decisions.
9. Describe several motives or reasons for holding cash and marketable securities. What characteristics should an investment have to qualify as an acceptable marketable security?
10. What are the five C's of credit analysis?
11. Describe the various credit-reporting agencies that provide information on mercantile or business credit applicants.
12. How do credit terms and collection efforts affect the investment in accounts receivable?
13. How is the financial manager involved in the management of inventories?

PROBLEMS

1. The Watson Company had sales of $1,000,000 and net income of $50,000 last year. Selected year-end balance sheet items were:

Current Assets	$400,000
Fixed Assets	500,000
Total Assets	$900,000
Current Liabilities	$200,000
Long-term Debt	200,000
Owners' Equity	500,000
Total Liabilities and Equity	$900,000

Sales are expected to increase by 20 percent next year.
a. Express each balance sheet item as a percent of last year's sales.
b. Estimate the new asset investment requirements for next year, assuming no excess production capacity.
c. Estimate the amount of internally generated funds for next year, assuming all profits will be retained in the firm.
d. If all current liabilities are expected to change spontaneously with sales, what will be their dollar increase next year?

e. Estimate Watson's external financing requirements for next year.

2. The Marklin Steel Products Company has an average production process time of 30 days. Finished goods are kept on hand for an average of 15 days before they are sold. Accounts receivable are outstanding on average for 30 days and Marklin receives 40 days of credit on its purchases from suppliers.

   a. Estimate the average length of Marklin's short-term operating cycle. How often would the cycle turn over in a year?

   b. Assume that Marklin has credit sales of $1,200,000, cost of goods sold of $1,000,000, and credit purchases of $800,000. Determine the average investment in accounts receivable, inventories, and accounts payable. What would be the net financing need considering only these three accounts?

3. The Novelty Plastics Company has the following current assets and current liabilities for the past two years:

	1982	1983
Cash and Marketable		
Securities	$ 50,000	$ 50,000
Accounts Receivable	300,000	350,000
Inventories	350,000	500,000
Total Current Assets	$700,000	$900,000
Accounts Payable	$200,000	$250,000
Bank Loan	-0-	150,000
Accruals	150,000	200,000
Total Current Liabilities	$350,000	$600,000

a. Calculate the net working capital for Novelty Plastics in 1982 and 1983. What happened?

b. Compare the current ratios between the two years. Also compare the acid-test ratios between 1982 and 1983. Comment on your findings.

4. The Novelty Plastics Company in Problem 3 had credit sales of $1,200,000 in 1982 and $1,300,000 in 1983.

   a. Determine the receivables turnover in each year.

   b. Calculate the average collection period for each year.

   c. Based on the receivables turnover for 1982, estimate the investment in receivables if credit sales are $1,300,000 next year. How much of a reduction in the 1983 receivables would occur?

5. The Novelty Plastics Company in Problem 3 had cost of goods sold of $1,000,000 in 1982 and $1,200,000 in 1983.

   a. Calculate the inventory turnover for each year. Comment on your findings.

   b. What would have been the amount of inventories in 1983 if the 1982 turnover ratio had been maintained?

SUGGESTED READINGS

Gitman, Lawrence J., Edward A. Moses, and I. Thomas White. "An Assessment of Corporate Cash Management Practices." *Financial Management* (Spring, 1979), pp. 32–41.

Johnson, Robert W., and Ronald W. Melicher. *Financial Management*, 5th ed. Boston: Allyn and Bacon, Inc., 1982. Part III.

Lewellen, Wilbur G., and Robert W. Johnson. "Better Way to Monitor Accounts Receivable." *Harvard Business Review* (May/June, 1972), pp. 101–109.

Richards, Verlyn D., and Eugene J. Laughlin. "A Cash Conversion Cycle Approach to Liquidity Analysis." *Financial Management* (Spring, 1980), pp. 32–38.

Smith, Keith V. *Guide to Working Capital Management.* New York: McGraw-Hill Book Company, 1979.

Welshans, Merle T. "Financial Management," *Encyclopedia of Professional Management.* New York: McGraw-Hill Book Company, 1978, pp. 388–396.

Welshans, Merle T. "Using Credit for Profit Making." *Harvard Business Review* (January/February, 1967), pp. 141–156.

9 Sources of Short-term Business Financing

The tremendous resources of the banking system of the nation make commercial banks the largerst provider of short-term loan funds for businessses. Even larger amounts of short-term funds come in the form of trade credit extended between business firms. Other important sources include short-term funds supplied by commercial finance companies, factors, and the Small Business Administration. Short-term financing through the issuance of commercial paper also is discussed in this chapter.

LENDING OPERATIONS OF COMMERCIAL BANKS

The typical loan made by a bank to a business is on an unsecured basis; that is, the prospect for the future of the business is such that the bank believes it to be unnecessary to require the pledge of specific assets of the business as security for the loan. Bankers for many years held the opinion that if a loan did not qualify on an unsecured basis, it should not qualify on a secured basis. In recent years this attitude has been changing, and we find many banks lending on the basis of a pledge of specific assets. The unsecured loan, however, remains the primary type of bank loan arrangement.

The Bank Line of Credit

There is often an agreement between the business and the bank regarding the amount of credit that the business will have at its disposal. The loan limit that the bank establishes for each of its business customers is called a *line of credit*. These lines of credit cost the business only the normal interest for the period for which money is actually borrowed. Under this arrangement, the business does not wait until the money is needed to negotiate for the loan, but rather it files the necessary financial statements and other evidences of financial condition with the bank in order that the credit may be available when needed. The banker, of course, is interested not only in how well the business has fared in the past but also in the probable future of the business, since the line of credit itself is generally extended in advance for a year at a time. The banker may require that other debts of the business be subordinated to the claim of the bank.

Under a line of credit program, major changes in the operation of a business may be subject to the approval of the bank. A major shift or change in management personnel or a major change in the manufacture or sale of particular products can have a material influence on the future success of a company; hence, the bank, having contributed substantially to the resources of the business, is necessarily interested in such business activities. The bank may also seek information on the business through organized credit bureaus, contact with other businesses having relations with the enterprise in question, and other banks.

In the event that the business requires more money than was anticipated at the time the line of credit was established, it may request the bank to increase the limit on its line of credit. It must be prepared, however, to offer very sound evidence not only of the need for additional funds but also of the ability of the business to repay the increased loan from business operations. A request for an increased line of credit frequently occurs when a business is growing and must have increasingly large amounts of capital to make such growth possible. Although banks generally insist that expansion be financed with long-term funds, they may assist such growth by temporarily providing a part of the increased needs. The business that is unable to secure additional credit from its bank on an unsecured loan basis may seek funds from other lenders or from its bank on a secured basis. These other forms of borrowing are discussed later in this chapter.

A *compensating balance* (on deposit by the business) of from 10 to 20 percent of unsecured loans outstanding under bank lines of credit is required by nearly all banks. The most frequently cited justification for this requirement is that since banks cannot lend without deposits, bank borrowers should be required to be depositors also.

Banks usually require their business customers to "clean up" their lines of credit for specified periods of time during the year, that is, to eliminate their indebtedness to the bank for this period of time, generally a minimum time span of two weeks.

The Revolving Credit Agreement

Although the officers of a business may feel rather certain that the line of credit which has been agreed to will provide the necessary capital requirements for the coming year, there is always the possibility that conditions will change to the extent that the bank may have to reduce or withdraw its extension of credit. This possibility is normally part of the original agreement. The bank is obligated to make good on its line of credit only so long as conditions do not change materially.

The well-established business that has an excellent credit rating may find it possible, however, to obtain a commitment in the form of a standby agreement for a guaranteed line of credit. This arrangement is referred to as a *revolving credit agreement*. In addition to paying interest for the use of money for the period of the loan, the business must pay a commission or fee to the bank based on the amount of money it has on call during the agreement period. This additional commission or fee is charged because the bank must provide for such loan demands regardless of changes in business conditions and is, therefore, from time to time denied flexibility in the use of its own funds for other lending purposes.

Accounts Receivable Financing

For the business that does not qualify for an unsecured bank loan or for the business that has emergency needs for funds in excess of its line of credit, a pledge of accounts receivable may be offered as security. This development in banking stems in part from the competition offered the banks by commercial finance companies (to be discussed later) that have come into existence in recent decades.

In extending loans on this basis, banks of course make the same sort of credit investigation as for businesses applying for unsecured loans. Particular attention is given to the collection practices of the company and to certain characteristics of the company's accounts receivable. The bank also spot-checks the receivables of the firm and may in some cases analyze each account to determine the promptness of the customers of the firm in making payments. In addition, the bank will study the type and the quality of goods that are sold, for if the merchandise is of inferior quality, there may be objections from the customers and hence slower payment on the bills. Accounts receivable are of little value as the basis of a loan if large quantities of merchandise are returned and the amount of accounts receivable reduced accordingly. It is also important for the bank to know something of the customers of the business since their ability to pay their debts will have an important influence or bearing on the actual collection success of the business applying for the loan.

Accounts Receivable Loan Limits. The Bank Management Commission of the American Bankers Association recommends that a loan based on the security of accounts receivable should generally be no more than 80 percent of the gross receivables and that this amount should be reduced by any trade discounts allowed to customers and by the normal percentage of the merchandise returns. If there is reason to believe that many of the customers of the business which is applying for the loan are not suitable risks, or if adequate credit ratings are not available, the bank will be inclined to lend a correspondingly lower percentage of the face value of such receivables.

Technical Features of Accounts Receivable Financing. Under the accounts receivable loan arrangement, there is, in addition to the basic interest charge, a fee to cover the extra work that such a loan entails. The banks must periodically check the books of a business that has borrowed on the basis of its receivables in order to see that the business is, in fact, living up to the terms of the agreement. At the time the loan is made, it is generally provided that individual accounts on the ledger of the business will be clearly designated as having been pledged for the bank loan. Only those accounts that are suitable for collateral purposes for the bank are earmarked, and these accounts are replaced by other accounts as they are paid in full or in the event any become unsatisfactory.

Figure 9-1
Promissory Note

$24,744.00   New York   October 15,   19--

Ninety days   _after date_ we _promise to pay_

to the order of Irving Trust Company

Twenty-four thousand seven hundred forty-four no/100---------------- _Dollars,_

_at_ IRVING TRUST COMPANY, NEW YORK. _Value received_

If any maker, endorser or guarantor hereof shall suspend business, become insolvent, offer settlement to any creditors, commit an act of bankruptcy, make any bulk sale, assignment for the benefit of creditors, mortgage, pledge or transfer, of accounts receivable or other property, in trust or otherwise, or any false representation or fail to furnish information or permit inspection of books or records on demand of the Trust Company, or fail to pay any obligation when due, or there be filed by or against it any petition in bankruptcy or proceeding under any law relating to the relief of debtors, or for the appointment of a receiver of any property, or if an execution or warrant of attachment be issued against any of its property, or any judgment be entered against it, or if an individual, he shall die, or if a corporation, it be dissolved or its capital be impaired, or if for any other cause the protection of the Trust Company in its sole discretion so requires, all liabilities of the undersigned to the Trust Company, including this note, shall, at the option of the Trust Company, mature and become due and payable without demand or notice, which are hereby waived. The undersigned further promise(s) to pay to the Trust Company the expenses, including reasonable attorneys' fees, incurred in the collection or attempted collection of this note. If this note is signed by more than one maker they shall be jointly and severally bound.

THE NOBEL CORPORATION

Authorized Signer

In addition to "earmarking" pledged accounts in the ledger of the borrowing firm, the bank also requires a schedule of the accounts so pledged along with a copy of each of the invoices involved in the shipment of goods. The business must also execute an assignment of the accounts involved. A specimen copy of a note for such a loan is shown in Figure 9-1.

As remittances are received by the business on the individual accounts that have been assigned, they must be turned over to the bank separately from other business funds. The bank also reserves the right to make a direct audit of the books of the business from time to time and to have an outside accounting firm examine the books periodically. The accounting firm frequently verifies a certain percentage of the accounts by mail, much as it does in a regular audit. Verification of the accounts in a routine manner leaves customers of the business unaware of the fact that their accounts have been pledged as collateral for a loan.

In this connection, it is interesting to note that businesses utilizing their receivables as collateral for bank loans often prefer to keep such knowledge from their own customers because this may be interpreted as an indication of weakness on the part of the business. Although businesses participating in this form of loan arrangement are frequently in a financially weak condition, this is not always the case. Some firms that are on a sound basis use accounts receivable financing as a permanent arrangement because they feel it has advantages for them which would not be available through other loan arrangements.

Manufacturing concerns appear to be the largest users of accounts receivable financing. In particular, this is true of manufacturers of food, textiles, leather products, furniture, paper, iron, steel, and machinery.

Inventory Loans

A business enterprise may borrow on the basis of its inventory as collateral in much the same manner that it may borrow on its receivables. A study is made by the bank not only of the physical condition of the inventory but also of the general composition of the inventory that the firm owns. Staple items that have a ready marketability serve well as collateral for a loan; style and fashion items do not serve well as collateral except for brief periods of time. Firms that use inventory as collateral are generally not in a position to procure further funds on an unsecured basis.

The bank may protect itself when lending to a business on the basis of inventory as collateral either by having title to the goods assigned to the bank or by taking a chattel mortgage on the inventory. In other cases, a trust receipt instrument may be used. When an assignment of title to the inventory is made to the bank, clear title cannot pass from the business to its customer until the loan is paid off or other collateral is substituted for the merchandise. Under a trust receipt arrangement, the bank retains ownership of the goods until they are actually sold in the regular course of business.

Warehousing of Inventory. In some cases when lending on the basis of inventory as collateral, the bank may insist that the business deposit the inventory in a bonded and licensed warehouse. The receipt issued by the warehouse is then turned over to the bank, which in turn holds it until such time as the loan is repaid. A specimen copy of a warehouse receipt for stored merchandise is shown in Figure 9-2.

It is frequently inconvenient for a business to deliver large bulky items of inventory to a warehouse for storage. This problem is solved through the use of *field warehouses.* A field warehousing enterprise has the power to establish a

Figure 9-2
Warehouse Receipt

LAWRENCE SYSTEMS, INC.

SAMPLE ONLY

ORIGINAL WAREHOUSE RECEIPT

NOT INSURED

NON-NEGOTIABLE

RECEIVED FROM: Wood Lumber and Moulding Company
FOR STORAGE IN Any Town, Any State
LOCATED AT (STREET) 111 A Street

SUBJECT TO ALL THE TERMS AND CONDITIONS CONTAINED HEREIN AND ON THE REVERSE SIDE HEREOF FOR THE ACCOUNT OF AND TO BE DELIVERED WITHOUT SURRENDER OF THIS WAREHOUSE RECEIPT UPON WRITTEN INSTRUCTION OF

FILL IN ▶ First National Bank of Any Town
WAREHOUSE RECEIPT HOLDER

SAMPLE ONLY

RCPT. TYPE	REG. CODE	WAREHOUSE NO.	HOLDER NO.	DATE	RECEIPT NO.	Depositor's Declared Values for which the Warehouseman Assumes No Responsibility
S1-5	02	1218A	S154	11-12-83	51734	

ITEM	CODE NO.	NO. OF UNITS	SAID TO BE OR CONTAIN	UNIT VALUES	EXTENSION (BJH)
	0001	1,151	M. bd. ft. logs pine	105.00	120,855.00
	0002	958	M. bd. ft. logs white fir	80.00	76,640.00
	0003	1,523	M. bd. ft. logs douglas fir	105.00	159,915.00
	0004	621	M. bd. ft. logs cedar	65.00	40,365.00
		4,253			397,775.00
			SAMPLE ONLY		

BJZ

CAUTION: LAWRENCE SYSTEMS, INC. WILL NOT BE RESPONSIBLE FOR THE QUANTITIES SHOWN HEREON UNLESS TOTAL NUMBER OF UNITS IS TYPED BELOW.

TOTAL ▶ Four million, two hundred fifty three thousand board feet

Stored under field warehousing arrangement. Subject to lien for storage, handling and other charges as per contract and lease with the industry served. A general lien is claimed for charges and expenses in regard to other goods deposited by the same depositor. Transfers of merchandise not complete unless made on the books of the warehouse company.

"By agreement goods of same kind or grade may be commingled and where authorized by law unlike units shall be deemed fungible and treated as equivalents."

LAWRENCE SYSTEMS, INC.

BY ▶ SAMPLE ONLY
BONDED WAREHOUSE MANAGER

(Do not accept this warehouse receipt if any corrections or erasures appear hereon.)

bona fide warehouse on the premises of the borrowing business establishment. Field warehouses differ from the typical public warehouse in that they serve a single customer—that customer on whose property the field warehouse is established. The field warehouse could be a cattle ranch, a grain elevator, or a lake on which logs are temporarily stored.

In setting up the field warehouse, it is generally necessary first for the warehousing establishment to obtain a lease on that portion of the property of the business which is to be used for warehousing purposes. It is then necessary to establish fences, barriers, walks, and other postings to indicate clear possession of the property by the warehouse operator in order to avoid accidental or deliberate removal of items by employees of the business during the general course of the business operations. A guard may be posted in order to check on the safety of the goods warehoused, or a room may be sealed and the seal inspected periodically to determine whether or not the company is honoring its agreement.

There must also be a complete statement of the commodities or items that are to be warehoused, and agreements must be made as to the maintenance of the property, proper fire precautions, insurance, and other necessary physical requirements. Under certain circumstances, the warehouse operator is authorized to release a certain quantity of goods by the day, week, or month to make possible a rotation of merchandise. Under this arrangement, periodic physical inventories must be taken.

Extent of Field Warehousing. Field warehouses are in operation throughout the United States with a concentration of such activities in the central and Pacific Coast regions. It is estimated that from 10,000 to 12,000 field warehouses are in existence. Nearly all forms of merchandise that may be safely warehoused have at one time or another been used for this purpose. Canned goods, miscellaneous groceries, lumber, timber, and building supplies fill about two fifths of all field warehouses in this country. Those banks that make commodity loans will generally accept field warehouse receipts as collateral.

Cost of Inventory Loans. Inventory loans are somewhat more expensive than are the unsecured loans. The greater cost is due in part to the cost of the warehousing operation itself and in part to the fact that the borrower's credit rating may be low. Bank interest rates for warehouse loans are ordinarily somewhat higher than unsecured loans; and, in addition, a warehouse fee of from ¾ to 2½ percent of the loan, depending upon size and other factors, must be paid.[1] When warehousing facilities must be utilized anyway, there is little additional cost involved.

Inventory loans, like accounts receivable loans, have become popular due to the increasing demand for working capital additions. Also, business firms are understandably anxious to take advantage of cash discounts on their purchases

---

[1] Inventory loans, like receivable loans, are made also by commercial finance companies. Interest rates charged by these companies are generally higher than those charged by the banks.

when the money for cash payments can be secured at nominal rates. Unemployment insurance taxes under the federal social security laws have made it advantageous for many firms to stabilize both production and employment of labor throughout the year rather than to bear part of the burden of seasonal employment layoffs. Stabilized production throughout the year rather than production just prior to anticipated sales of the products results in the firm's carrying a larger average inventory. In turn, a larger commitment of funds by the company for carrying inventories is required. Such funds for inventory accumulation may be obtained by placing the inventories in a field warehouse, thus using the inventory itself as the basis for a bank loan.

Loans Secured by Stocks and Bonds

Stocks and bonds constitute a very popular type of collateral for short-term loans. Such securities, when pledged as collateral for a loan, are of interest to the banker primarily because of their marketability and their value. If the securities are highly marketable, and if the value is satisfactory to cover the amount of the loan requested and to provide a substantial margin for shrinkage in value, the banker may have little hesitancy in extending such a loan. The banker, of course, gives preference to those securities that are listed on one of the national security exchanges since frequent quotations of the value of such securities are available. Banks will usually lend from 60 to 70 percent of the market value of listed stocks, and from 70 to 80 percent of the market value of high-grade bonds. Since 1934, however, the Board of Governors of the Federal Reserve System has established maximum loan limits when the purpose of the loan is to purchase or deal in listed stocks.[2]

Only assignable stocks and bonds are eligible for this type of collateral financing. This restriction excludes United States Savings Bonds that are not assignable. When assignable securities are placed with the bank, a *stock power* or *bond power* is executed that authorizes the bank to sell or otherwise dispose of the securities should it become necessary to do so to protect the loan (See Figure 9-3.)

Other Forms of Security for Short-term Bank Loans

Security for bank loans may also include such things as the cash surrender value of life insurance policies, guarantee of a loan by a party other than the borrower, notes, and acceptances.

Life Insurance Loans. Small business establishments frequently find it possible to obtain needed short-term bank loans by a pledge of the cash surrender value of life insurance policies. Such policies must be of the assignable type, and many insurance companies insist that assignment forms prepared by the company

---

[2]The operations of the securities exchanges and the limitations on borrowing for purposes of dealing in securities are discussed in Chapter 13.

Figure 9-3
Irrevocable Stock
or Bond Power

IRREVOCABLE STOCK OR BOND POWER

FOR VALUE RECEIVED, the undersigned does (do) hereby sell, assign and transfer to
_____

The Third National Bank of St. Louis, Missouri
_____

	53-0822721
	(SOCIAL SECURITY OR TAXPAYER IDENTIFYING NO.)

IF STOCK,
COMPLETE
THIS
PORTION
— 100 — shares of the Common stock of Black River Timber Company
represented by Certificate(s) No(s). 143001 _____ inclusive,
standing in the name of the undersigned on the books of said Company.

IF BONDS,
COMPLETE
THIS
PORTION
_____ bonds of _____
in the principal amount of $_____, No(s). _____ inclusive,
standing in the name of the undersigned on the books of said Company.

The undersigned does (do) hereby irrevocably constitute and appoint_____
— my — attorney to transfer the said stock or bond(s), as the case may be,
on the books of said Company, with full power of substitution in the premises.

Dated June 17, 19--

IMPORTANT — READ CAREFULLY
The signature(s) to this Power must correspond with the name(s) as written upon the face of the certificate(s) or bond(s) in every particular without alteration or enlargement or any change whatever. Signature guarantee should be made by a member or member organization of the New York Stock Exchange, members of other Exchanges having signatures on file with transfer agent or by a commercial bank or trust company having its principal office or correspondent in the City of New York.

Penelope H. Plack

(PERSON(S) EXECUTING THIS POWER SIGN(S) HERE)

SIGNATURE GUARANTEED

be used for such purposes. Because of the safety afforded the bank through the use of these cash surrender values, such loans usually carry a moderate interest rate compared with loans on other types of business collateral. Another reason for the favorable rates is the fact that the borrower has the alternative of borrowing directly from the insurance company. Bank interest rates in general have been much higher in recent years than the contractual rate at which policyholders may borrow directly from their insurance companies. As a result, there has been a spectacular increase in the number of loans made by insurance companies to their policyholders. Functions and financial operations of insurance companies are covered in Chapter 12.

Comaker Loans. Many small businesses find it necessary to provide the bank with a guarantor in the form of a cosigner to their notes. It is expected that the cosigner would have to have a credit rating at least as satisfactory as and usually far better than the firm requesting the loan.

Discounting Notes and Acceptances. Although the act of discounting a credit instrument with a bank technically may be considered as a sale rather than a pledge of collateral, the fact that such discounted instruments are endorsed by the seller renders the seller contingently liable. The discount of credit instruments by a firm with its bank is a form of bank credit.

The promissory note signed by the customer may be used by a firm when it is not certain of the credit standing of its customer. The use of the promissory note to bind a credit sale, however, as noted earlier, is not common in most fields of business activity. Notes have the advantage to a business of not requiring further proof of the claim against a customer as may be the case for the open-book account. The further advantage of negotiability makes it possible for the business to sell these notes to its bank or other financing agency. Except for the few lines of business activity where the use of the note is customary, however, banks are cautious in their purchase of such instruments because they often arise out of weak credit situations.

Another type of receivable instrument that arises out of the sale of merchandise to a business customer and which may be sold to a bank is the acceptance. An *acceptance* comes into the possession of a business through the sale of merchandise on the basis of a draft or bill of exchange drawn against the buyer or the buyer's bank. The accepted draft or bill of exchange is returned to the seller of the merchandise where it may be held until the date of its maturity. During this period, the business may see fit to discount such acceptances with its bank. Again the seller is contingently liable for these discounted acceptances. The use of the banker's acceptance is shown in detail in connection with an international shipment of goods in Chapter 20.

TRADE CREDIT

The most important single form of short-term business financing is that of credit extended by one business organization to another. The open accounts receivable, together with notes receivable, taken by manufacturers, wholesalers, jobbers, and other business units as sellers of goods and services to other businesses are known as *trade credit*. This discussion excludes credit established as a result of sale of goods to the ultimate consumer, for this is considered in Chapters 16, 17, and 18.

Characteristics of Trade Credit

The establishment of trade credit is the least formal of all forms of financing. It involves only an order for goods or services by one business and the delivery of goods or performance of service by the selling business. The purchasing business receives an invoice stating the terms of the transaction and the time period within which payment is to be made. The purchaser enters the liability as an addition to accounts payable; the seller enters the claim as an addition to accounts receivable. In some situations, the seller of goods or services may insist upon written evidence of the liability on the part of the purchaser. Such written evidence generally takes the form of a note and is carried as a note payable by the purchaser and as a note receivable by the seller. In both situations, through the open account and the use of the note, trade credit as a form of short-term financing has been utilized.

Before a business organization delivers goods or performs a service for another business, it must determine, of course, the ability and willingness of the purchaser to pay for the order. The responsibility of such credit analysis in most businesses belongs to the credit manager.

Terms for Trade Credit

Sales may be made on such terms as *cash, E.O.M.* (end of month), *M.O.M.* (middle of month), or *R.O.G.* (receipt of goods). In other situations, such terms as *2/10, net/30* may be provided, in which case the purchaser may deduct 2 percent from the purchase price if payment is made within 10 days; but if not paid within 10 days, the net amount of the purchase is due within 30 days of shipment. Such discounts for early payment are common and are designed to provide incentive for prompt payment of bills by the purchaser. Occasionally net terms, such as net/30 or net/60 may be provided.

A cash sale, contrary to its implication, does involve the element of credit since the purchaser is generally permitted a certain number of days within which to make payment. For example, a sale of merchandise in which the purchaser is permitted up to ten days to remit may be considered a cash transaction, although credit is outstanding to the purchaser for that period of time. Even for the firm that purchases goods and services entirely on a cash basis of this nature, the volume of accounts payable outstanding on its books at any one time may be large.

Cost of Trade Credit

When trade credit terms provide for no discount for early payment of obligations, there is, of course, no cost for such financing. Even when discounts are available to the purchaser, it may appear that there is no charge for trade credit since failure to take the discount by early payment simply requires the purchaser to pay the net purchase price. An implicit cost is involved, however, when a discount is not taken. For example, with terms of 2/10, net/30 the cost is measured directly by the loss of the discount that might otherwise be taken if payment were made within the first 10-day period. During the first 10-day period, however, the buyer does have trade credit without direct cost.

In order to calculate the comparative cost of trade credit to a business firm as opposed to bank credit, the cost of the trade credit must be reduced to an annual interest rate basis. For example, if the terms of sale are 2/10, net/30, the cost of the trade credit is the sacrifice of the 2 percent discount that the purchaser fails to take if the credit is allowed to run for the full 30-day period. Since the buyer may take the discount if the bill is paid within the first 10 days after purchase, payment on the thirtieth day would result in a sacrifice of the discount for the privilege of extending the payment period by 20 days. The loss of the discount of 2 percent may then be represented as the cost of trade credit for 20 days under terms of 2/10, net/30. Two percent for 20 days is at the rate of 36 percent for 360 days. If we also take into consideration that it is the discount price (100% invoice price — % discount) that is being financed, and use a conventional business 360-day year, the approximate effective cost (EC) is:

$$EC = \frac{\% \text{ Discount}}{100\% - \% \text{ Discount}} \times \frac{360 \text{ Days}}{\text{Credit Period} - \text{Discount Days}}$$

For our 2/10, net/30 example we would have an approximate effective cost of:

$$EC = \frac{2\%}{100\% - 2\%} \times \frac{360}{30 - 10} = 2.04\% \times 18 = 36.7\%$$

This indicates, of course, that the cost of trade credit typically is far in excess of bank rates. Thus it is usually worthwhile to borrow funds to take advantage of cash discounts on trade credit.

Volume of Trade Credit

While it is difficult to come up with a measure of the actual size of outstanding trade credit, approximations can be made. The Federal Trade Commission's records for all manufacturing corporations shows trade accounts in excess of $100 billion, which equals about 10 percent of total assets. Notes and accounts receivable of all nonfinancial United States corporations were in excess of $500 billion as of mid-1982. Trade credit is particularly heavy in the construction industry and in wholesaling operations, and represents a more important financing source for smaller firms relative to larger firms.

Sources of Funds for Trade Credit

Trade credit, unlike other forms of short-term finance, does not involve the conveyance of money to the user. The net effect, however, is very much the same since it enables the user to acquire goods or services without an immediate payment therefor. The firm that provides trade credit must be able to do so from its general resources. If the firm has such a strained financial position that it is unable to extend credit terms in line with other firms of its industry, it operates at a severe if not impossible competitive handicap. Trade credit provided by a firm is reflected in its balance sheet as a current asset, in particular as notes receivable and accounts receivable. Sources of funds for carrying such trade credit are very much the same as for other current assets, namely, purchasing goods and services on the basis of trade credit, short-term borrowing, long-term financing, and retaining profits from operations.

Reasons for Use of Trade Credit

Because the cost of trade credit in most lines of business activity is high, it may be difficult to understand why such a tremendous volume of trade credit would be taken by business. Trade credit is used by financially weak concerns because they have no adequate alternative sources of credit. In any event, it may not be assumed that because of its high cost, trade credit is an undesirable source of short-term financing for the business. It may be, in fact, the most essential form of financing for small and growing business enterprises that are unable to qualify for short-term credit through customary financial channels.

For the firm that does not have recourse to a line of credit with a bank or other financial institution, the question is not the cost of trade credit as compared with unavailable bank credit but rather the profit that can be made from the sale of the goods so acquired as compared with the cost of the trade credit itself. For the firm that does have access to low-cost bank credit and credit from other financial institutions, it appears reasonable to expect a wise management to take advantage of discounts.

The firm in a weak financial condition will find trade credit more readily available than bank credit because the bank as a lender of money stands to gain only the stipulated interest on the loan if repayment is made in accordance with the terms of the agreement. It stands to lose up to the total of the sum loaned if the borrower's obligation is not met. The manufacturer or the merchant, on the other hand, who sells on the basis of trade credit has a profit margin on the goods sold. Failure of the purchaser to meet the obligation results, at most, in the loss of the cost of the goods so delivered to the purchaser.

COMMERCIAL FINANCE COMPANIES

Shortly after the turn of the century, the first commercial finance company was chartered. Since that time, the number of such institutions has increased to more than five hundred. Some of these organizations are small, offering limited financial services to their customers, while others have vast resources and engage in broadly diversified programs of business lending. The *commercial finance company* is an organization without a bank charter that advances funds to business concerns by discounting accounts receivable, makes loans secured by chattel mortgages on machinery or liens on inventory, or finances deferred-payment sales of commercial and industrial equipment. These companies are also frequently referred to as commercial credit companies, commercial receivables companies, and discount companies.

Commercial finance companies, represented by such organizations familiar to the business world as C.I.T. Financial Corporation, the Commercial Credit Company, and Walter E. Heller, International, offer much the same sort of service to business concerns as do the commercial banks in connection with accounts receivable financing and inventory financing. Accounts receivable financing was, in fact, originated by the commercial finance companies and only later was it adopted by commercial banks.

The commercial finance companies gained a foothold in the financial markets and grew to their present size as a result of many factors, including the fact that they were completely free to experiment with new and highly specialized types of credit arrangements, that state laws were generally more favorable to these nonbanking organizations in lending on the basis of accounts receivable, and finally that these organizations were able to charge rates of such a level as to make possible a profitable return for high-risk loans. Frequently these rates were far above those bankers would want or were permitted to charge their own customers.

As noted in the definition of the commercial finance companies, these organizations also lend money on the basis of inventory as collateral and finance the sale of commercial and industrial equipment on a deferred-payment basis. This type of financing is used primarily in fields where there are large numbers of small businesses, such as home appliances, hardware, plastics, drugs, paper, food products, paint, wallpaper, and leather.

Operating Characteristics of Commercial Finance Companies

When a commercial finance company sets up a loan secured by receivables, it enters into a contract with the borrower that provides for the acceptance of the borrower's open accounts receivable as collateral for a loan. The company specifies those accounts that are acceptable to it as collateral and, as a rule, will lend to the borrower an amount less than the total of such receivables pledged for the loan. The excess of the total volume of receivables pledged over the actual amount of the loan provides a margin of safety in the event that the borrower fails to repay the loan, and it also facilitates adjustments in outstanding accounts resulting from the return of goods by customers of the borrowing company.

Terms and Charges of Commercial Finance Companies

The cost of loans offered by the commercial finance companies on the basis of receivables as collateral varies widely with the size of the lending company. In recent years the effective rates per annum on loans by the largest companies have been within the range of 15 to 20 percent. The volume of business of these large companies represents a major portion of all accounts receivable financing by finance companies. Higher rates of interest are not uncommon on business which is handled by small finance companies because these companies generally deal with local firms whose receivables are smaller in amount and more expensive to handle than the receivables of the firms financed by the larger companies. Also, the small finance company cannot achieve the economies of large-scale operation.

Volume of Commercial Finance Company Lending

As of midyear 1982, loans outstanding on accounts receivable by commercial finance companies totaled about $6 billion. These companies also provided a vast amount of credit for businesses through the financing of commercial vehicles, industrial and farm equipment, and other types of business credit. The Board of Governors of the Federal Reserve System estimates the total volume of such business credit outstanding by the commercial finance companies at midyear 1982 to be more than $82 billion.

Sources of Funds for Commercial Finance Companies

The equity position of the commercial finance companies is considerably greater than that of the commercial banks of the nation; however, these organizations do not operate on equity capital alone. Additional long-term capital is acquired through the sale of debenture bonds. In addition, commercial banks lend a large volume of money at wholesale rates to the commercial finance companies, which in turn lend it to business borrowers at retail rates. Banks have been known to refer customers to finance companies for their loans when they do not choose to engage in receivables or inventory financing. Nonbanking financial institutions, as well as commercial and industrial firms, often find it advantageous to invest their temporary surplus funds in the notes of commercial finance companies.

These sources of short-term funds permit the commercial finance companies to meet their peak loan demands without becoming encumbered with long-term debt, only part of which would be used during slack lending periods.

Reasons for Use of Commercial Finance Companies

In view of the average cost of commercial finance company loans as noted above, the question may arise as to why a borrower would under any circumstances utilize the facilities of these companies. As a matter of fact, the business person who has ample current assets and is in a highly liquid position may be well advised to rely on other sources of short-term financing. The business that is without a short-term financial problem at one time or another, however, is the exception rather than the rule. During periods when business is most brisk and growth possibilities most favorable, the need for additional funds on a short-term basis becomes unusually pressing. The business person's first action is to request an increase in the bank line of credit. Failing this, an additional loan from the bank may be secured by pledging either inventory or receivables as collateral.

However, not all banks actively engage in this type of financial arrangement and thus it may be necessary to deal with a commercial finance company. Because the commercial finance companies are able to operate through a system of branches on a regional or on a national basis, unhampered by restrictions on branch operations, they can acquire the volume of business necessary to cover overhead and to provide the needed diversification of risks to undertake high-risk financing. Several bank holding companies have purchased or established commercial finance companies to take advantage of their special operating characteristics.

FACTORS

The *factor*, like the commercial finance company, engages in accounts receivable financing for business enterprises. In contrast with the commercial finance companies, however, the factor purchases the accounts outright and assumes all credit risks. Under this arrangement, customers whose accounts are sold are notified that their bills are payable to the factor. The task of collection of accounts is thus shifted from the seller of the accounts to the factor.

Despite the long history of operations of these companies, their growth has taken place largely within the last thirty years. The origin of factoring was in the textile industry, and since most of the selling agencies and credit-reporting agencies in the textile field are located in New York City, most of the nation's factors are also located there. In addition to serving the textile industry, factors have also proved useful in such fields as furniture, shoes, bottle making, paper, men's clothing, toys, and furs.

Operating Characteristics of Factors

Assume that a business organization in a field which is amenable to the factoring operation finds that for the first time in several years, because of increasing levels of inventory and receivables, the firm is experiencing financial difficulties. Although the firm is well managed and has for several years been able to secure adequate financing through an unsecured line of credit with its bank, in order to take advantage of expanded business opportunities it finds it necessary to supplement its usual sources of current funds. The factor draws a contract establishing the duties and the obligations of each party. This contract includes the conditions under which accounts may be sold to the factor, the responsibility for the payment of all such accounts, the collection procedures to be followed, and the method of reporting balances due. The contract also provides that the daily invoices for sales of goods to customers, together with the original shipping documents, be delivered to the factor and that the accounts so established be assigned to the factor. All proposed sales must be approved by the factor before the delivery of goods, and they are subject to rejection in the event that the credit rating of the customer does not meet the standards of the factor. Daily reports must be rendered to the factor of all credits, allowances, and returns of merchandise. The contract also indicates the charges to be made for the factoring service.

The credit analysis department of the factor is the heart of that organization since it must serve in such a way as to conserve the factor's assets and also to be in constant contact with the factor's clients. Members of the credit department of the factor not only must be extremely prompt and accurate in their credit analyses but also, because they work closely with the firm's clients, must retain the goodwill of the companies that use the services of the factor.

Terms and Charges for Factoring

The charge for factoring is in two parts. First, interest is charged on the money advanced, based on the actual daily net debit balance. Second, a factoring commission or service charge is figured as a percentage of the face amount of the receivables. Such service charges typically range from ¾ of 1 percent to 1½ percent of the face amount of the accounts financed. The commission charge is determined after taking into consideration such things as the volume of sales of the client, the general credit status of the accounts being factored, and the average size of individual accounts.

In addition to the interest and commission charges, the factor will also reserve from 5 to 15 percent of the total amount of receivables factored for purposes of making adjustments, such as for merchandise that is returned to the seller. This is not a charge, however, and is returned to the seller after it has served its intended purpose.

Volume of Factoring

Although the number of firms engaged exclusively in factoring operations has decreased in recent years through merger or acquisition by firms engaged in other commercial financing activities, the dollar volume of factoring operations is increasing and spreading into many lines of business where it was formerly unknown. Several billions of dollars of financing is supplied to American business firms through the factoring of open accounts receivable.

Sources of Funds for Factors

Like the commercial finance companies, factors obtain their funds for operations through a combination of equity capital, long-term borrowing, short-term borrowing, and profits from operations. Although most factors obtain equity capital directly from the small group of persons actively engaged in the factoring operations, at least one factor has sold common stock to the general public.

Reasons for Use of Factoring Services

Although the services of the factor may be used by a firm that is unable to secure financing through customary channels, financially strong companies may also at times use these services to good advantage. In fact, these facilities are of greatest benefit to those companies that are enjoying unprecedented success with respect to sales and growth. It has been noted before that during such periods companies experience extreme shortages of working capital. The sale of receivables without recourse (no contingent liability for their collection) has the effect of substituting cash for accounts receivable, which may make possible even greater growth and profitability in the long run.

Some firms factor their receivables not because it is the only form of financing available to them but because of other considerations. First, the cost of doing business through credit sales is definite and determinable in advance, since the factor assumes all risks of collection. This is in effect a form of credit insurance. Second, it eliminates overhead, including bookkeeping costs, the maintenance of a credit department, and the expenses of collecting delinquent accounts. Unless a firm factors all of its receivables, however, the complete elimination of the expenses of credit department operation could not be accomplished. A corollary of these two advantages, but of a somewhat less tangible nature, is the fact that the management of a business is freed from concern with financial matters and is permitted to concentrate on production and distribution.

In recent years factoring has become increasingly important in supporting export sales. The firm unfamiliar with the problems of financing international shipment of goods is relieved of all such details through the factoring of foreign receivables.

Although factoring services are regarded highly by some business firms, others offer several objections to their use. The two reasons cited most frequently are the cost and the implication of financial weakness. The cost of factoring is admittedly higher than the cost of borrowing from a bank on the basis of an unsecured loan; however, it is difficult to conclude without reservation that the net cost is higher. The elimination of overhead costs that would otherwise be required of a business plus the fact that management need not concern itself with financial matters may completely offset the additional cost involved in the factoring process. With respect to the implication of financial weakness, many borrowers prefer to avoid the factoring plan in favor of the non-notification plan available through the commercial finance companies. In this way they avoid having their customers make their payments to the factor.

Outside the textile field, where factoring has long played an important part, businesses often make every effort to avoid letting their customers know that they are using their accounts in order to secure financing, because of the implication of financial weakness.

SMALL BUSINESS ADMINISTRATION

The Small Business Administration (SBA) was established by the federal government to provide financial assistance to small firms that are unable to obtain loans through private channels on reasonable terms. Created in 1953, the SBA currently operates over 100 field offices through which applications for loans are accepted.

If a firm is able to obtain financing elsewhere, its application to the Small Business Administration for a loan is rejected. An applicant for a loan must prove that funds are not available from the firm's own or a competing bank in an appropriate amount, that no other private lending sources are available, that the issuance of securities is not practicable, that financing cannot be arranged through the disposal of assets of the business, and that personal credit of the owners cannot be used. Such loans may not be used for paying existing creditors nor for speculative purposes.

Operating Characteristics of the Small Business Administration

The Small Business Administration assists in the financing of small enterprises in three ways: it may make direct loans to businesses; it may participate jointly with private banks in extending loans to businesses; or it may agree to guarantee a bank loan. On a direct basis, the SBA can make loans of up to $150,000. When participating with banks in making loans, the SBA's share may not be in excess of $150,000. In guaranteeing loans, the SBA may extend its guarantee to 90 percent of a bank loan or $500,000, whichever is less. The average size of an SBA business loan is $85,000.

Terms and Charges for Small Business Administration Financing

Working capital loans by the SBA are limited to 7 years, while regular business loans have a maximum maturity of 25 years. The SBA sets interest rates on its direct loans and on its share of participation loans. It also sets a maximum allowable rate which banks can charge on guaranteed loans. These rates are adjusted periodically to reflect changes in market conditions.

In addition to the business lending activities of the SBA described above, it has been vested with the responsibility for several corollary financial activities. These include loans to development companies, disaster loans, lease guarantees, surety bond support, minority enterprise programs, procurement assistance, and support for small business investment companies.

Volume of Lending by the Small Business Administration

During the very early days of its operation, the Small Business Administration encouraged lending to small businesses by local credit pools throughout the country. A change in policy, however, resulted in more active lending by the Administration. The amount of loans that the SBA can guarantee is considerably larger than the funds available for direct loans. Several billions of dollars in loans are outstanding, most of which were made on a guaranty basis through commercial banks rather than directly by the SBA.

Sources of Funds for the Small Business Administration

The Small Business Administration operates on a revolving fund provided by Congress. The total of business loans which have been approved far exceeds the revolving fund because of repayments and the fact that a portion of the amount approved is the participation share of commercial banks.

Reasons for Use of Small Business Administration Loans

The reason for the use of Small Business Administration loans by businesses is explained by the stated objectives of the Administration, that is, to enable small businesses to obtain financial assistance otherwise not available through private channels on reasonable terms. When the Small Business Administration was established, it was recognized that the economic development of the nation has depended in large part upon the freedom of new business ventures to enter into active operation. Yet the increased concentration of investable funds in the possession of the large institutional investors, such as life insurance companies, investment companies, and others, has made it increasingly difficult for new and small business ventures to attract investment capital. Through the Small Business Administration it is presumed that deserving small businesses may have access to capital on reasonable terms.

COMMERCIAL PAPER ISSUERS AND DEALERS

Large U.S. corporations of high credit quality can issue or sell *commercial paper*, or short-term promissory notes. These notes are backed solely by the credit quality of the issuer. Commercial paper may be sold directly by the issuer to financial institutions or other holders. Alternatively, commercial paper can be sold to *commercial paper dealers or houses* who purchase the promissory notes for the purpose of resale to holders or lenders. A fee based on the amount of notes purchased, charged to the issuer of the notes, provides the basic income of the commercial paper dealers.

Operating Characteristics of Commercial Paper Houses

The firm that wishes to use the services of the commercial paper house must have an unquestioned reputation for sound operation. If after thorough investigation of the firm's financial position by the commercial paper house it appears that the notes of the firm can be sold with little difficulty, an agreement is made for the outright sale of a block of the firm's promissory notes to the commercial paper house. The commercial paper house will resell these notes as quickly as possible to banks, to managers of pension funds, to business corporations that have surplus funds, and to other investors. The notes are usually prepared in denominations of $100,000 or more with maturities ranging from a few days to 270 days. The size of the notes and the maturities, however, can be adjusted to suit individual investor requirements.

Terms and Charges for Commercial Paper House Financing

The commercial paper house will pay to the borrower the face amount of the notes less the interest charge and a fee often as low as ⅛ of 1 percent calculated on an annual basis. The interest charge is determined by the general level of prevailing rates in the money market and the strength of the borrowing company. When these notes are resold to banks and other lenders, only the prevailing interest rate is deducted from the face value of the notes; hence, the commercial paper house receives the fee as compensation for the negotiation.

Volume of Commercial Paper Financing

The volume of commercial paper has expanded dramatically in recent years. As of the end of June, 1982, nonfinancial companies had outstanding over $57 billion in commercial paper, most of which was dealer placed. At the same time, financial companies had over $36 billion outstanding in dealer-placed paper, and their directly placed paper amounted to more than $84 billion.[3] Less than 10 commercial paper houses, located for the most part in New York City, dominate the dealer-placed market. These dealers serve such borrowing companies as finance companies, manufacturers, wholesalers, retailers, and public utilities.

Reasons for Use of Commercial Paper Financing

The most important reason for directly issuing or using commercial paper dealers is the fact that the cost of such borrowing is generally less than regular bank rates. Also, the need for compensating bank balances is avoided, a factor that adds to stated interest costs on short-term bank loans. Loan restrictions on the amount that can be borrowed from a single bank may also favor the issuance of commercial paper by large corporations.

Industrial firms and other nonbank lenders often purchase commercial paper as a profitable alternative to the purchase of Treasury bills. In recent years, commercial paper has provided a yield above that of short-term government securities. Although commercial banks were historically the principal purchasers of commercial paper, now paper is actively held by industrial corporations,

---

[3] *Federal Reserve Bulletin* (September, 1982), p. A25.

money market mutual funds, and other lenders. Corporations have increased their purchases of commercial paper as a convenient and profitable means of investing their excess cash in marketable securities.

QUESTIONS

1. What is meant by an unsecured loan? Are such loans important as a form of bank lending?
2. Describe what is meant by a bank line of credit. Describe the revolving credit agreement and compare it with the bank line of credit.
3. Describe the nature of accounts receivable lending on the part of commercial banks.
4. What safeguards may a bank establish to protect itself when it lends on the basis of customer's receivables pledged as collateral for the loans?
5. When a business firm uses its inventory as collateral for a bank loan, how is the problem of storing and guarding the inventory accomplished for the bank?
6. Discuss other forms of collateral that a business may use in securing loans from a commercial bank.
7. What is meant by trade credit? Briefly describe some of the possible terms for trade credit.

8. What are the principal reasons for using trade credit for short-term financing?
9. Under what circumstances would a business secure its financing through a commercial finance company?
10. Describe how a factor differs from a commercial finance company in terms of accounts receivable financing.
11. Why would a business utilize the services of a factor?
12. Describe the purpose of the Small Business Administration. How does the SBA provide financing to businesses?
13. What is meant by commercial paper and how important is it as a source of financing?
14. Briefly describe the role and operations of commercial paper dealers or houses.

PROBLEMS

1. A supplier is offering your firm a cash discount on purchases of 2 percent if paid within 10 days; otherwise the bill is due at the end of 60 days. Would you recommend borrowing from a bank at an 18 percent annual interest rate in order to take advantage of the cash discount offer?
2. Assume that you have been offered cash discounts on merchandise that can be purchased from either of two suppliers. Supplier A offers trade credit terms of 3/15, net/60, while supplier B offers 4/10, net/70. What is the approximate effective cost of missing the cash discounts from each supplier? If you could not take advantage of either cash discount offer, which supplier would you select?

SUGGESTED READINGS

Hurley, Evelyn M. "The Commercial Paper Market." *Federal Reserve Bulletin* (June, 1977), pp. 525–536

Jacoby, Neil H., and Raymond J. Saulnier. *Business Finance and Banking.* New York: National Bureau of Economic Research, 1947.

Jessup, Paul F. *Modern Bank Management*. New York: West Publishing Co., 1980.

Johnson, Robert W., and Ronald W. Melicher. *Financial Management*, 5th ed. Boston: Allyn and Bacon, Inc., 1982. Chapter 10.

Moskowitz, L. A. *Modern Factoring and Commercial Finance.* New York: Crowell Publishing, 1977.

Quill, Gerald D., John C. Cresci, and Bruce D. Shuter. "Some Considerations about Secured Lending." *Journal of Commercial Bank Lending* (April, 1977), pp. 41–56.

10 Time Value of Money and Fixed Assets Management

The value of a firm is affected to the greatest extent by the success of the financial manager in making fixed asset investment decisions. These decisions require large financing commitments and impact on the firm for many years. A fixed asset decision will be sound only if it produces a stream of future cash inflows that will cover the investment cost and earn the firm an acceptable rate of return on the investment.

In order to evaluate fixed asset investments, we must first understand the mathematics of finance known as compounding and discounting. These concepts also are used to show how prices or values in debt and equity financial instruments change over time. The first part of this chapter will focus on the time value of money. Then we will turn to the management of fixed assets.

TIME VALUE OF MONEY

Most individuals have experienced the process of compounding by watching a savings account "grow" or increase over time when interest is reinvested. Discounting is the opposite of compounding, as we will see shortly, after we discuss basic compounding concepts.

Compounding to Determine Future Values

Let's begin the discussion with a savings account illustration. Assume you have $1,000 to invest now and a bank offers you an 8 percent interest rate on your money. Another bank will pay 10 percent interest and both banks will compound your money annually. If you were going to invest for only one year, then at the end of the year you would receive $80 ($1,000 × .08) from the first bank, and $100 ($1,000 × .10) from the second bank; in both cases your original $1,000 would be returned. While the $20 difference is important to most of us, the difference is not enormous.

However, to understand the concept of compounding, let's assume that you plan to leave the investment with a bank for 10 years. *Compounding* means that interest earned each year plus the principal will be reinvested at the stated rate. For example, the first bank will accept your $1,000 investment now, add $80 at the end of one year, reinvest the $1,080 for the second year at 8 percent, and so forth. Table 10-1, a partial future value table, shows how a $1 investment will

Table 10-1
Future Value of $1

Year	5%	6%	7%	8%	9%	10%
1	1.050	1.060	1.070	1.080	1.090	1.100
2	1.102	1.124	1.145	1.166	1.188	1.210
3	1.158	1.191	1.225	1.260	1.295	1.331
4	1.216	1.262	1.311	1.360	1.412	1.464
5	1.276	1.338	1.403	1.469	1.539	1.611
6	1.340	1.419	1.501	1.587	1.677	1.772
7	1.407	1.504	1.606	1.714	1.828	1.949
8	1.477	1.594	1.718	1.851	1.993	2.144
9	1.551	1.689	1.838	1.999	2.172	2.358
10	1.629	1.791	1.967	2.159	2.367	2.594

grow or increase in value over a 10-year period. Notice under the 8 percent column that an initial value of $1 or 1.000 will be worth 1.080 (1.000 × 1.080) at the end of one year and 1.166 (1.080 × 1.080) by the end of the second year. At the end of 10 years, the initial 1.000 would have "grown" to a future value interest factor (FVIF) of 2.159. Multiplying this factor by the $1,000 investment gives a future value or worth of $2,159 on your initial investment.

Table 10-1 also shows how a $1 investment will grow in value at a 10 percent interest rate. Notice that the FVIF at the end of 10 years would be 2.594, making your investment worth $2,594 ($1,000 × 2.594) if you use the second bank. Now, of course, the difference between the 8 percent and 10 percent rates is much greater at $435 ($2,594 − $2,159). Thus we see the advantage of being able to compound at even slightly higher interest rates over several years.

The compounding concept can be expressed in equation form as follows:

$$FV = PV(1 + i)^n$$

where FV is the future value, PV is the present value, i is the interest rate, and n is the number of periods in years. For our 8 percent, 10-year example, we would have:

$$FV = \$1,000(1 + .08)^{10}$$
$$= \$1,000(2.159)$$
$$= \$2,159$$

Notice that the $(1 + i)^n$ part of the equation represents the FVIF factor shown in Table 10-1. A more complete table is contained in the Appendix.

Many finance problems actually involve cash flows that occur in several years. When a cash flow stream is constant or level in each time period it is referred to as an *annuity*. For example, suppose you were going to save $1,000 per year for three years at an 8 percent interest rate. This would be called an *annuity due* problem because cash flows occur at the beginning of each time period. The future value of this annuity could be calculated as follows:

$$
\begin{aligned}
\text{FV Annuity Due} &= \$1,000(1.08)^3 + \$1,000(1.08)^2 + \$1,000(1.08)^1 \\
&= \$1,000(1.260) + \$1,000(1.166) + \$1,000(1.080) \\
&= \$1,000(1.260 + 1.166 + 1.080) \\
&= \$1,000(3.506) \\
&= \$3,506
\end{aligned}
$$

Notice that the first $1,000 would earn interest compounded at 8 percent for three years while the second $1,000 would earn interest for two years and the third $1,000 would earn interest for only one year. The future value interest factor for an annuity due (FVIFAD) may be calculated directly by using a financial calculator, or by using the formula and tables given in the Appendix.

Annuity problems also may involve level cash flow amounts that occur at the end of each period starting with the first cash flow at the end of the first year. This type of annuity is referred to as an *ordinary annuity* and can be illustrated for our $1,000, 8 percent rate, 3-year annuity. Only now, the first $1,000 will be invested at the end of the first year. The appropriate calculations would be:

$$
\begin{aligned}
\text{FV Annuity} &= \$1,000(1.08)^2 + \$1,000(1.08)^1 + \$1,000(1.08)^0 \\
&= \$1,000(1.166) + \$1,000(1.080) + \$1,000(1.000) \\
&= \$1,000(3.246) \\
&= \$3,246
\end{aligned}
$$

Table 10-2 is a partial table that can be used for finding future values of ordinary annuities. Notice that the future value interest factor for an ordinary annuity (FVIFA) for 3 years at 8 percent is 3.246 which is the same as we just calculated. We can express the future value of an ordinary annuity in general terms as:

$$
\text{FV Annuity} = \text{Annual Payment (FVIFA)}
$$

Table 10-2

Future Value of
a $1 Ordinary Annuity

Year	5%	6%	7%	8%	9%	10%
1	1.000	1.000	1.000	1.000	1.000	1.000
2	2.050	2.060	2.070	2.080	2.090	2.100
3	3.152	3.184	3.215	3.246	3.278	3.310
4	4.310	4.375	4.440	4.506	4.573	4.641
5	5.526	5.637	5.751	5.867	5.985	6.105
6	6.802	6.975	7.153	7.336	7.523	7.716
7	8.142	8.394	8.654	8.923	9.200	9.487
8	9.549	9.897	10.260	10.637	11.028	11.436
9	11.027	11.491	11.978	12.488	13.021	13.579
10	12.578	13.181	13.816	14.487	15.193	15.937

A more comprehensive table for finding FVIFA factors for ordinary annuities is provided in the Appendix.

Discounting to Determine Present Values

Most financial management decisions involve present values rather than future values. For example, a financial manager who is considering the purchase of an asset wants to know what the asset is worth now rather than at the end of some future time period. The reason that an asset has a value is because it will produce a stream of future cash benefits. However, to determine its value now in time period zero, we have to discount the future cash inflows back to the present. This procedure will be discussed later in the chapter.

At this point let's illustrate the concept of *discounting* with a simple example involving a loan. Assume that a borrower is willing to pay you $1,000 at the end of one year in return for a loan now. If you are willing to accept a zero rate of return you might lend $1,000 now and get back $1,000 one year from now. Of course, most of us would not jump at such an opportunity. Rather, we would require a rate of return on our loan. To receive a return of, say, 8 percent, you would lend less than $1,000 now. The amount to be lent would be determined by dividing the $1,000 that is to be received at the end of one year by one plus the interest rate of 8 percent (i.e., $1,000/1.08) for a loan amount of $926. If you required a 10 percent rate of return, you would be willing to lend only $909 ($1,000/1.10).

Table 10-3, a partial present value table, illustrates the present value of having to wait to receive $1 sometime in the future. Notice under the 8 percent

Table 10-3
Present Value of $1

Year	5%	6%	7%	8%	9%	10%
1	.952	.943	.935	.926	.917	.909
2	.907	.890	.873	.857	.842	.826
3	.864	.840	.816	.794	.772	.751
4	.823	.792	.763	.735	.708	.683
5	.784	.747	.713	.681	.650	.621
6	.746	.705	.666	.630	.596	.564
7	.711	.665	.623	.583	.547	.513
8	.677	.627	.582	.540	.502	.467
9	.645	.592	.544	.500	.460	.424
10	.614	.558	.508	.463	.422	.386

column that a value of $1 or 1.000 to be received one year from now would have a present value of .926. For a $1,000 receipt at the end of one year, the present value would be $926 ($1,000 × .926) which is the same as the figure calculated above. Table 10-3 further shows that if you had to wait 10 years to receive $1 and the discount rate was 8 percent, the present value interest factor (PVIF) would be only .463. A $1,000 future receipt thus would have a present value of $463 ($1,000 × .463).

The discounting concept can be expressed in equation form as follows:

$$PV = \frac{FV}{(1+i)^n}$$

$$= FV\left[\frac{1}{(1+i)^n}\right]$$

where the individual terms are the same as those defined for the future value equation. Notice that the future value equation has just been rewritten to solve for the present value. For the $1,000, 8 percent, 10-year example, we would have:

$$PV = \$1,000\left[\frac{1}{(1+.08)^{10}}\right]$$

$$= \$1,000(.463)$$

$$= \$463$$

Notice that the $1/(1+i)^n$ part of the equation represents the PVIF factor shown in Table 10-3. A more complete table is contained in the Appendix.

Many present value problems also involve cash flow annuities. These usually are ordinary annuities whereby cash inflows are assumed to begin at the end of the first year and each year thereafter for the duration of the cash flow stream. Let's assume that we will receive $1,000 per year beginning one year from now for a period of three years and that we will accept an 8 percent discount rate. The appropriate calculations would be:

$$PV\ Annuity = \$1,000\left[\frac{1}{(1.08)^1}\right] + \$1,000\left[\frac{1}{(1.08)^2}\right] + \$1,000\left[\frac{1}{(1.08)^3}\right]$$

$$= \$1,000(.926) + \$1,000(.857) + \$1,000(.794)$$

$$= \$1,000(2.577)$$

$$= \$2,577$$

Notice that the first $1,000 would be discounted for only one year, the second $1,000 for two years, and the third $1,000 for three years, reflecting when each of the cash inflows is to be received. We can express the present value of an ordinary annuity in general terms as:

PV Annuity = Annual Receipt (PVIFA)

Table 10-4 is a partial table that can be used for determining the present values of ordinary annuities. Notice that the present value interest factor for 3 years at 8 percent is 2.577 which is the same as we just calculated. A more comprehensive table is available in the Appendix.

Occasionally there are present value annuity due problems. For example, leasing arrangements often require the person leasing equipment to make the first

Year	5%	6%	7%	8%	9%	10%
1	0.952	0.943	0.935	0.926	0.917	0.909
2	1.859	1.833	1.808	1.783	1.759	1.736
3	2.723	2.673	2.624	2.577	2.531	2.487
4	3.546	3.465	3.387	3.312	3.240	3.170
5	4.329	4.212	4.100	3.993	3.890	3.791
6	5.076	4.917	4.767	4.623	4.486	4.355
7	5.786	5.582	5.389	5.206	5.033	4.868
8	6.463	6.210	5.971	5.747	5.535	5.335
9	7.108	6.802	6.515	6.247	5.995	5.759
10	7.722	7.360	7.024	6.710	6.418	6.145

Table 10-4
Present Value of a $1
Ordinary Annuity

periodic payment at the time when the equipment is delivered. A financial calculator could be used to directly calculate the appropriate interest factor for an annuity due problem, or the PVIFAD may be found by using the formula given in the Appendix to convert PVIFA values for ordinary annuities.

Determining Annual Payments for Annuities

In addition to finding present values and future values of annuities, there are many instances in which we might want to determine the constant periodic payment. For example, we might want to know the periodic payment amount that will be necessary to pay off or amortize a loan or real estate mortgage. Let's assume that a lender offers you a $20,000, 10 percent, 3-year loan that is to be fully amortized with three annual payments. The first payment will be due one year from the loan date.

How much will you have to pay each year? This is a present value problem because the $20,000 is the worth of the loan now. The annual payment can be solved for by rearranging the present value of an ordinary annuity equation as follows:[1]

$$\text{Annual Payment} = \frac{\text{PV Annuity}}{\text{PVIFA}}$$

We can find the present value interest factor of the annuity (PVIFA) by returning to Table 10-4 and identifying the factor at 10 percent for three years which is 2.487. With this information we now can determine the required annual payment as follows:

$$\text{Annual Payment} = \frac{\$20,000}{2.487} = \$8,042$$

---

[1] Annual receipts or annual payments can be used interchangeably in PV annuity problems depending on whether the problem is viewed from the standpoint of receiving or paying cash flows.

This shows that you will have to pay $8,042 each year for three years to pay off the loan.

Table 10-5 illustrates the repayment process with a loan amortization schedule. The first year you will pay interest of $2,000 ($20,000 × .10). How-

Table 10-5
Loan Amortization
Schedule

Year	Annual Payment	Interest Payment*	Principal Repayment	Loan Balance
0	—	—	—	$20,000
1	$8,042	$2,000	$6,042	13,958
2	8,042	1,396	6,646	7,312
3	8,042	731	7,311**	-0-

*Since the interest rate is 10%, the first year's interest is $2,000 ($20,000 × .10), and subsequent interest payments are based on the remaining loan balances.
**Because of rounding errors, the final repayment of principal is off by $1.

ever, since $6,042 ($8,042 − $2,000) of the first year's $8,042 payment will be used to repay part of the principal, the second year's interest payment will only be $1,396 ($13,958 × .10). The third and final payment will be adequate to cover the last year's interest of $731 and will also pay off the remaining principal balance.

The loan amortization process that has just been illustrated is the same as that used to determine monthly payments on home mortgages. However, the appropriate PVIFA factor must be calculated directly with a financial calculator when the compounding or discounting interval is very short.

Valuation of Long-term Debt and Equity Securities

The values of bonds and stocks also are affected by time value of money concepts. Long-term debt usually provides for a periodic payment of interest plus a return of principal at maturity. Most corporate bonds are issued in $1,000 denominations. To illustrate the valuation process let's assume that a $1,000 face value bond has a stated interest rate of 9 percent and has a 10-year life before maturity. Thus an investor will receive $90 ($1,000 × .09) per year in interest and will receive $1,000 at the end of 10 years.[2]

We wish to determine the present worth or value of the bond. This will depend on the interest rate required by investors on similar quality bonds. For example, let's assume investors require a 9 percent rate of return. We then would discount the $90 annuity portion of the bond at the PVIFA at 9 percent for 10 years which is 6.418 (see Table 10-4). Since the $1,000 will be received only at the end of 10 years, we use the .422 PVIF at 9 percent, year 10 from Table 10-3. Taking these together we have:

---

[2]In actual practice, most bonds pay interest semiannually or twice a year. However, for illustrative purposes we will assume annual end-of-year payments since the value will be about the same in either case.

9% for 10 years

$$\$90 \times 6.418 = \quad \$578$$
$$\$1,000 \times .422 = \quad \underline{422}$$

Bond Value = $1,000

Thus the bond would be worth $1,000. This would be true as long as investors wanted a rate of return equal to 9 percent.

However, what if investors required a 10 percent return or yield on bonds of similar quality? The bond must then fall in price to compensate for the fact that only $90 in interest is still being paid annually. The appropriate discount factors at 10 percent for 10 years from Tables 10-3 and 10-4 would be as follows:

10% for 10 years

$$\$90 \times 6.145 = \$553$$
$$\$1,000 \times .386 = \underline{386}$$

Bond Value = $939

Thus an investor would be willing to pay only $939 for the bond. Although interest remains $90 per year, a new investor would earn a 10 percent return because he or she would pay only $939 now and get back $1,000 at the end of 10 years. We now should have an understanding of why bond prices fluctuate with changes in interest rates. Of course, if investors required less than a 9 percent return for bonds of this quality, then the above-described bond would have a value greater than $1,000.

Stock prices or values, while more complex than bond values, also are influenced by changes in interest rates. In general, investments in stocks are considered riskier than investments in bonds. This is because stock prices fluctuate more widely than do bond prices; also there is greater uncertainty about the returns from stocks. While bond investors depend largely on interest income plus the knowledge that a bond will be worth $1,000 at maturity as long as the issuer does not default, stock dividends plus necessary stock price appreciation are much riskier or uncertain. Thus stockholders must expect, and receive over the long run, higher returns than bondholders. As interest rates rise, stockholders must anticipate even higher returns, and vice versa.

The general risk-return relationship between long-term debt and equity securities is depicted in Figure 10-1. Long-term U.S. government bonds are considered to be riskless because there is little chance of default on the part of the federal government. Investors require only a risk-free rate of return on these bond investments. Corporate bonds are riskier, causing investors to expect higher returns as compensation for assuming greater default risk. Common stocks are even riskier on average, as we just discussed, and investors must be compensated accordingly with higher average returns. Stated differently, we can view the risk-return relationship shown in Figure 10-1 as an investor "indifference curve" for securities of varying degrees of riskiness.

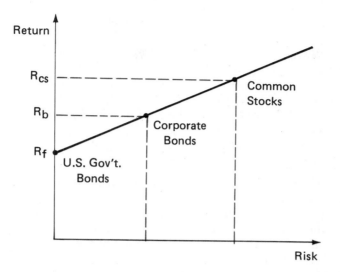

Figure 10-1
Risk-return
Relationship for
Long-term Securities

For a particular firm at a specific point in time, its stockholders or owners will expect a higher rate of return than its long-term debtholders. As we now move to the management of fixed assets, it is important to keep this in mind. The financial manager must set a rate of return which the firm needs to earn on its asset investments in order to cover the cost of debt and still leave an adequate rate of return for the owners. The combined rate necessary to cover the cost of debt and equity funds is referred to as the firm's *cost of capital*.

MANAGEMENT OF FIXED ASSETS

Fixed assets management involves making proper capital budgeting decisions. The financial manager must compare capital expenditures or outlays for plant and equipment against the cash flow benefits that are to be received from these investments over several years. When properly adjusted benefits exceed expenditures, accepted projects will help increase the firm's value.

It is investment in fixed assets that provides the basis for the manufacturing firm's earning power or profitability. Plant and equipment is employed to manufacture inventories that will be sold for profit, produce cash inflows, and make the firm more valuable. Proper capital budgeting decisions must be made by the financial manager for this to occur. The types of decisions include: whether to replace existing equipment with new equipment; whether to expand in existing product lines by adding more plant and equipment similar to that in use; or whether to expand into new product areas requiring new types of fixed assets. Quite often two or more machines that perform the same function may be available from competing suppliers, possibly at different costs and with different expected cash benefits. The financial manager is responsible for choosing the best of these alternatives. Projects that are not in direct competition with one another must be ranked according to their expected returns and a decision made by the financial manager as to how many will be included in the firm's capital budget.

We are able to focus on only a small part of what is a very complex topic. In the remainder of this chapter, we will focus first on determining relevant cash expenditures and cash benefits involved in making capital budgeting decisions. Then we briefly discuss available techniques for evaluating or selecting among fixed asset investments. This is followed by a discussion of risk-related considerations.

Determining Relevant Cash Flows

The decision of whether to invest in a fixed asset begins with the development of a schedule of relevant cash outflows. For many fixed asset investments, all cash outlays occur at the time of purchase. For example, let's assume that a producer will sell to you a machine press for $18,000. It will cost you an additional $2,000 for transportation and installation of the press. The sum of these expenditures is $20,000 and represents the initial outlay now, which is referred to as time period zero.

Potential after-tax cash inflows to be derived from the operation of the machine press are more difficult to assess. The producer's specifications as to output from the machine press will be helpful. If the firm has previously purchased similar machine presses you also can use past experiences in assessing the production of annual inventories and the resulting before-tax cash benefits from the sale of these inventories. Adjustments then must be made for the payment of taxes so that after-tax cash inflows are directly comparable against the initial investment outlays which are payable out of after-tax dollars.

Let's assume that the machine press will have a 5-year life at the end of which it will be discarded. Cash revenues from the sale of inventories produced by the machine press are expected to be $12,000 per year. Cash operating expenses associated with the use of the press are estimated at $5,000 per year. The firm also is entitled to "write off" or depreciate the machine press for income tax purposes. Let's assume that $4,000 ($20,000/5 years) can be depreciated each year and that the firm has a 40 percent income tax rate.

The relevant annual after-tax cash earnings first can be estimated as follows:

Cash Revenues	$12,000
Cash Operating Expenses	−5,000
Cash Earnings before Depreciation	7,000
Depreciation	−4,000
Cash Earnings before Taxes	3,000
Income Taxes (40%)	−1,200
Cash Earnings after Taxes	$1,800

It is important to understand that the $1,800 represents cash earnings after taxes and not the after-tax cash inflows. This is because depreciation does not involve actual cash disbursements; it is only an accounting bookkeeping entry for income tax purposes. To get the cash inflow after taxes we would start with the $7,000 in cash earnings before depreciation and subtract the $1,200 in income taxes which would involve cash payment to arrive at an annual *cash inflow after taxes* of $5,800 ($7,000 − $1,200).

The after-tax cash outflows and inflows now can be combined into the following schedule:

Year	Cash Flow
0	−$20,000
1	5,800
2	5,800
3	5,800
4	5,800
5	5,800

In other words, a $20,000 initial investment in the machine press is expected to produce a stream of benefits amounting to $29,000 ($5,800 × 5) over a 5-year period. This is a net benefit of $9,000 ($29,000 − $20,000). Would you recommend the investment in the machine press? If money had no time value, the answer would definitely be yes. Instead of making a quick decision we must first consider the results of capital budgeting evaluation techniques.

Capital Budgeting Techniques

Methods or techniques for selecting among fixed asset investments provide the basis for making proper capital budgeting decisions. Each technique needs to reflect the fact that cash outlays for plant and equipment occur now, while the benefits occur in the future. Three techniques—payback period, net present value, and internal rate of return—are widely used in practice.

Payback Period. The *payback period* method determines the time it will take in years to recover the initial investment in fixed assets. Let's return to our earlier machine press example that requires a $20,000 cash outlay and will produce cash inflows of $5,800 per year for five years. We will refer to this alternative as Project A. Another machine press investment, Project B, will cost $25,000 but is expected to provide a stream of after-tax cash inflows beginning with $4,000 the first year and ending with $10,000 in the fifth year. The cash flow streams are summarized as follows for the two projects:

Year	Project A	Project B
0	−$20,000	−$25,000
1	5,800	4,000
2	5,800	4,000
3	5,800	8,000
4	5,800	10,000
5	5,800	10,000

The payback period may be used to compare the two investments to determine which one recovers its investment more quickly. In cases where the cash benefits form an annuity, the payback period is easily calculated as follows:

$$\text{Payback Period} = \frac{\text{Initial Outlay}}{\text{Annual Cash Inflow}}$$

For Project A we would have

$$\text{Payback Period} = \frac{\$20,000}{\$5,800} = 3.4 \text{ years}$$

Cash inflows for Project B will total $16,000 ($4,000 + $4,000 + $8,000) for the first three years. This will leave $9,000 ($25,000 − $16,000) still uncovered. It will take an additional .9 of the fourth year ($9,000/$10,000) before the investment is fully recovered. Thus the payback period for Project B is 3.9 years. Based solely on the payback period technique, Project A would be chosen over Project B because it recoups its investment more quickly.

However, the payback period evaluation method suffers from two basic drawbacks. First, the technique does not explicitly consider the time value of money but rather only approximates it. The second limitation is that all cash flows beyond the payback period are ignored. Notice that Project B will return $10,000 in cash inflows in year 5 which is substantially more than the last year's cash inflows provided by Project A. The possible significance of this difference is overlooked by the payback period method.

Net Present Value. The *net present value* method overcomes the shortcomings of the payback period by explicitly considering the time value of money and all expected cash inflows. A project's net present value is calculated as the present value of cash inflows less the initial investment or outlay. When the net present value is positive, then a project is acceptable to the firm.

The financial manager must determine the firm's required rate of return for discounting purposes. This required rate should reflect the cost of long-term debt and equity capital funds. At this time, let's assume that the cost of capital is 10 percent.

We now are ready to apply the net present value technique to the cash flows for Projects A and B. The cash flows are shown in Table 10-6, which also gives the present value of these cash flows when discounted at a 10 percent rate. Notice that there is no discount for the initial outlays because they occur in year zero. Positive net present values are shown for both projects. This means that an investment in either Project A or Project B will provide a rate of return that is greater than 10 percent. Project A with the higher net present value of $1,982 would be preferred over Project B. The value of the firm would be increased more by a net present value of $1,982 than by a net present value of $988.

A short-cut method could have been used to calculate the net present value for Project A. Since the cash inflows form an annuity we could have made use of the FVIFA at 10 percent for five years from Table 10-4, which is 3.791. The net present value then could have been calculated as follows:

Table 10-6

Net Present Value
Calculations

	Project A			Project B		
Year	Cash Flow	× 10% PVIF*	= Present Value	Cash Flow	× 10% PVIF*	= Present Value
0	−$20,000	1.000	−$20,000	−$25,000	1.000	−$25,000
1	5,800	.909	5,272	4,000	.909	3,636
2	5,800	.826	4,791	4,000	.826	3,304
3	5,800	.751	4,356	8,000	.751	6,008
4	5,800	.683	3,961	10,000	.683	6,830
5	5,800	.621	3,602	10,000	.621	6,210
	Net Present Value =		$1,982	Net Present Value =		$988

*The present value interest factors for years one through five are taken from Table 10-3.

$$\$5,800 \times 3.791 = \$21,988 \quad \text{PV Cash Inflows}$$
$$\underline{-20,000} \quad \text{Initial Outlay}$$
$$\$1,988 \quad \text{Net Present Value}$$

The $1,988 figure differs slightly from the $1,982 net present value shown in Table 10-6 due to a rounding of the present value interest factors in Table 10-3. When cash inflows are not in the form of an annuity, the longer calculation process employed in Table 10-6 for Project B must be used to find the net present value.

Projects with negative net present values would not be acceptable to the firm. Such projects would provide returns lower than the cost of capital and if accepted would cause the value of the firm to fall. It is important for the financial manager to make proper capital budgeting decisions by accepting or rejecting projects depending on their expected impact on the firm's value.

Internal Rate of Return. While the net present value method tells us that both Projects A and B provide expected returns that are greater than 10 percent, we do not know the specific rates of return. The *internal rate of return* method is designed to calculate the specific rate by finding the return that causes the net present value to be zero (i.e., the present value of the cash inflows equals the project's investment or initial outlay).[3] A trial and error process must be employed to find the internal rate of return (IRR).

Let's illustrate the IRR process first for Project A. Because the cash inflows form an annuity, the IRR is easy to find. We divide the initial outlay (PV annuity) by the cash inflow annuity amount (annual receipt) to arrive at the PVIFA as follows:

$$\text{PVIFA} = \frac{\text{PV Annuity}}{\text{Annual Receipt}}$$

---

[3]This method also is used to find the "yield to maturity" on bonds. We will discuss bond yields more fully in Chapter 22.

Notice this is simply a rearrangement of the present value of an annuity equation and is the same as the payback period equation. For Project A we have:

$$PVIFA = \frac{\$20,000}{\$5,800} = 3.448$$

We know this PVIFA of 3.448 is for five years. By turning to the Appendix and Table 4, Present Value of a $1 Ordinary Annuity, we can read across the 5-year row until we find a PVIFA close to 3.448. It falls between 3.605 (12 percent) and 3.433 (14 percent) but is much closer to the PVIFA at 14 percent. Thus the internal rate of return for Project A is a little less than 14 percent.

The trial and error process used to find the IRR for Project B is shown in Table 10-7. Discounting the cash flows at a 10 percent rate results in a positive net present value of $988 as we previously calculated. A positive net present value indicates that we need to try a higher discount rate such as 12 percent. The appropriate present value interest factors are taken from the Appendix, Table 3, Present Value of $1. Notice when the cash flows are discounted at a 12 percent rate that the net present value becomes −$514. This indicates that the IRR actually falls between 10 percent and 12 percent. Since −$514 is closer to zero than $988 the specific IRR is a little above 11 percent.

If discounting at a 12 percent rate had still been associated with a positive net present value for Project B, then a higher discount rate would have been applied. This process would be continued until the net present value approached zero and the specific IRR was reached.

The higher IRR for Project A is consistent with the higher net present value we previously found. Both projects are acceptable and would add to the value of the firm because they provide returns that are higher than the 10 percent cost of capital. However, since we want only one machine press, we would select Project A over Project B.

Table 10-7
Internal Rate of Return
Calculations

Year				Project B			
	Cash Flow	× 10% PVIF	= Present Value	Cash Flow	× 12% PVIF	= Present Value	
0	−$25,000	1.000	−$25,000	−$25,000	1.000	−$25,000	
1	4,000	.909	3,636	4,000	.893	3,572	
2	4,000	.826	3,304	4,000	.797	3,188	
3	8,000	.751	6,008	8,000	.712	5,696	
4	10,000	.683	6,830	10,000	.636	6,360	
5	10,000	.621	6,210	10,000	.567	5,670	
		Net Present Value =	$988		Net Present Value =	−$514	

Risk-Related Considerations

The degree of riskiness associated with expected cash inflows may vary substantially across different fixed asset investments. For example, a decision on whether to replace an existing machine with a new, more efficient machine would not be concerned with substantial cash inflow uncertainty. This is because the firm already has some operating experience for the existing machine. Likewise, expansion in existing product lines allows the firm to base cash inflow expectations on past operating results. These types of capital budgeting decisions can be made by discounting at the firm's cost of capital because they are comparable in riskiness to the firm's other assets.

Expansion projects involving new areas and product lines usually are associated with greater cash inflow uncertainty. In order to compensate for this greater risk, financial managers often apply risk-adjusted discount rates to these cash flows. A *risk-adjusted discount rate* contains a risk premium that is added to the firm's cost of capital. For example, let's use the previously presented data for Projects A and B to illustrate the use of risk-adjusted discount rates. Let's assume that Project A involves expansion in an existing product line, whereas Project B is for the production of a new product. The firm's 10 percent cost of capital would be the appropriate discount rate for Project A. Recall that this would result in a net present value of $1,982.

In contrast, a higher discount rate of possibly 12 percent (10 percent cost of capital plus a 2 percent risk premium) might be deemed appropriate by the financial manager for use in discounting Project B's cash flows. Recall from Table 10-7 that this would result in a net present value of −$514. Thus, on a risk-adjusted basis, Project A would still be acceptable to the firm but Project B would be rejected. Making adjustments for risk differences is a difficult but necessary requirement that enables the financial manager to make proper capital budgeting decisions which will increase the value of the firm.

QUESTIONS

1. Describe the process of compounding.
2. What is an annuity? How do ordinary annuities and annuities due differ?
3. What is meant by discounting? Give an illustration.
4. Describe the process for determining the size of a constant periodic payment that is necessary to fully amortize a loan.
5. How is the present value or worth of a corporate bond determined?
6. Briefly describe what is meant by the risk-return relationship for long-term securities.
7. Why is proper management of fixed assets crucial to the success of the firm?
8. What types of cash flows are important in making capital budgeting decisions? What is meant by an after-tax cash inflow?
9. Describe the payback method for making capital budgeting decisions.
10. What is meant by a project's net present value? How is it used for choosing between projects?
11. Identify the internal rate of return method and describe how it is used in making capital budgeting decisions.
12. How are risk-adjusted discount rates used?

PROBLEMS

1. Determine the future values if $5,000 is invested under each of the following situations: (a) 5 percent for 10 years; (b) 7 percent for 7 years; and (c) 9 percent for 4 years.

2. Assume you are planning to invest $100 each year for 4 years and will earn 10 percent per year. Determine the future value of this annuity if your first $100 is invested now. How would your answer change if you waited one year before making the first investment?

3. Determine the present value if $15,000 is to be received at the end of 8 years and the discount rate is 9 percent. How would your answer change if you had to wait 6 years to receive the $15,000?

4. What is the present value of a loan that calls for the payment of $500 per year for 6 years if the discount rate is 10 percent and the first payment will be made one year from now? How would your answer change if the $500 per year occurred for 10 years?

5. Determine the annual payment on a $15,000 loan that is to be amortized over a 4-year period and carries a 10 percent interest rate. Also prepare a loan amortization schedule for this loan.

6. Assume a $1,000 face value bond pays interest of $85 per year and has an 8-year life. If investors are willing to accept a 10 percent rate of return on bonds of similar quality, what is the present value or worth of this bond? How would the value change if investors wanted an 8 percent rate of return?

7. A machine can be purchased for $10,500 including transportation charges but installation costs will require $1,500 more. The machine is expected to last 4 years and produce annual cash revenues of $6,000. Annual cash operating expenses are expected to be $2,000, with depreciation of $3,000 per year, and the firm has a 40 percent tax rate. Determine the relevant after-tax cash flows and prepare a cash flow schedule.

8. Use the information in Problem 7 to determine the machine's relevant cash flows.

a. Calculate the payback period for the machine.

b. If the firm's cost of capital is 10 percent, would you recommend accepting the machine?

c. Estimate the internal rate of return for the machine.

9. The Artic Gas Company is evaluating two projects for possible inclusion in the firm's capital budget. Project M will require a $40,000 investment while Project O's investment will be $50,000. After-tax cash inflows are estimated as follows for the two projects:

Year	Project M	Project O
1	$12,000	$10,000
2	12,000	10,000
3	12,000	15,000
4	12,000	15,000
5		15,000

a. Determine the payback period for the two projects.

b. Calculate the net present value for each project based on a 10 percent cost of capital. Which, if either, of the projects is acceptable?

c. Determine the approximate internal rate of return for Projects M and O.

10. Assume the financial manager of the Artic Gas Company in Problem 9 believes that Project M is comparable in risk to the firm's other assets. In contrast, there is greater uncertainty concerning Project O's after-tax cash inflows. Artic Gas uses a 4 percentage point risk premium for riskier projects. The firm's cost of capital is 10 percent.

a. Determine the risk-adjusted net present values for Project M and Project O using risk-adjusted discount rates where appropriate.

b. Are both projects acceptable investments? If you had to choose between the two projects, which one would be your choice?

SUGGESTED READINGS

Brigham, Eugene F. "Hurdle Rates for Screening Capital Expenditure Proposals." *Financial Management* (Autumn, 1975), pp. 17–26.

Gitman, Lawrence J. and John R. Forrester, Jr. "A Survey of Capital Budgeting Techniques Used by Major U.S. Firms." *Financial Management* (Fall, 1977), pp. 66–71.

Hastie, K. Larry. "One Businessman's View of Capital Budgeting." *Financial Management* (Winter, 1974), pp. 36–44.

Johnson, Robert W., and Ronald W. Melicher. *Financial Management,* 5th ed. Boston: Allyn and Bacon, Inc., 1982. Part V.

Osteryoung, Jerome S. *Capital Budgeting: Long-Term Asset Selection,* 2nd ed. Columbus, Ohio: Grid Publishing Company, 1979.

Schall, Lawrence D., Gary L. Sundem, and William R. Geijsbeek. "Survey and Analysis of Capital Budgeting Methods." *Journal of Finance* (March, 1978), pp. 281–287.

Shao, Stephen P. *Mathematics for Management and Finance,* 4th ed. Cincinnati: South-Western Publishing Co., 1980.

11 Management of Long-term Debt and Equity Funds

The raising of funds to finance assets is an important financial management function. In Chapter 8 we discussed the need to apply the principle of hedging as it related to the matching of the average maturities of the firm's assets and liabilities. This was followed by a discussion of working capital management including the principal instruments of short-term financing.

We now are ready to turn to the coverage of long-term debt and equity funds. Instruments such as stocks and bonds are peculiar to the corporate form of organization and receive much of our attention. Profits that are retained rather than paid out are a form of equity capital because they represent ownership funds reinvested in the business.

We begin with an overview of the relative importance of sources of funds for business corporations. This is followed by a discussion of internal versus external financing. Then characteristics of bonds and stocks are covered. The final section focuses on long-term external financing policies relating to the mix between debt and equity funds.

SOURCES OF FUNDS FOR BUSINESS CORPORATIONS

Business corporations, as a group, rely heavily on internal financing sources to help meet their asset needs. This is shown in Table 11-1, which reflects data compiled by the Bankers Trust Company. Internal sources include after-tax business corporate profits not distributed in the form of cash dividends to stockholders. We often refer to these undistributed profits as earnings retained by the corporations. Capital consumption or depreciation allowances provide a second major source of internally generated funds available to business corporations and are usually viewed as providing for the replacement of worn-out fixed assets.

Short-term funds are made available primarily through short-term loans from commercial banks. In addition, business corporations rely on the issuance of open market or commercial paper and loans from finance companies in order to raise additional amounts of short-term funds. Table 11-1 also shows other short-term sources stemming from tax accruals, U.S. government loans, and direct

Table 11-1

Annual Source or Supply of Funds for Business Corporations

	1979	1980	1981	1982 (Est.)	1983 (Proj.)
			In Billions of Dollars		
Cash flow					
Undistributed profits	97.9	87.4	78.5	40.0	48.7
Capital consumption allowances	134.0	153.1	177.1	205.0	228.0
Total	231.9	240.5	255.6	245.0	276.7
Long-term funds					
Net new bond issues	22.5	33.2	23.9	28.7	31.7
Net new stock issues	−3.9	12.9	2.5	2.3	5.2
Total net new issues	18.6	46.1	26.4	31.0	36.9
Mortgages	1.4	2.0	−1.1	.8	1.2
Industrial revenue bonds	4.2	4.4	6.9	8.5	7.0
Term bank loans	17.7	12.5	14.5	16.0	10.5
Total	41.9	65.0	46.7	56.3	55.6
Short-term funds					
Open market paper	9.7	5.7	16.9	−2.8	2.0
Short-term bank loans	26.2	15.3	28.3	20.5	5.0
Finance company loans	10.2	3.1	8.7	−.2	2.5
Total	46.1	24.1	53.9	17.5	9.5
Other short-term sources					
Unpaid taxes	—	−6.7	−7.6	−10.0	—
Direct foreign investment in U.S.	11.9	13.7	21.3	9.0	9.4
U.S. government loans	1.2	1.5	1.2	1.2	1.3
Total	13.1	8.5	14.9	.2	10.7
Total sources	333.0	338.1	371.1	319.0	352.5

SOURCE: Bankers Trust Company, *Credit and Capital Markets 1983*, p. T26. The Bankers Trust estimates are based on data contained in Federal Reserve Flow of Funds Accounts and U.S. Department of Commerce National Income Accounts.

investment in U.S. business corporations by foreigners. Notice that trade credit does not show up as a separate source of short-term funds. This is because the accounts payable of one corporation would be the accounts receivable of another corporation, and so forth.

Business corporations can meet at least a portion of their annual long-term financing needs by issuing bonds and stocks. The reader should note that corporations annually generate a larger portion of long-term funds from bond issues in contrast with stock issues. The importance of long-term debt financing is further borne out by the significant use of mortgage loans by business corporations. Term loans issued by commercial banks provide important sources of debt funds. Finally, in recent years business corporations have been able to generate a portion of their long-term funds through issuance of industrial revenue bonds by government municipalities or authorities on behalf of the business corporations. The proceeds from these bond issues are used to purchase equipment or construct facilities.

INTERNAL VERSUS EXTERNAL FINANCING

Long-term financing for most businesses is usually made up of, as we have just seen, both internal and external forms. For some types of business, in fact, there may be infrequent occasion to approach the capital markets for any type of financial support. These corporations may rely exclusively upon internally generated funds. Other businesses, by virtue of their rapid rate of growth and of the small amount of funds generated internally, may be forced to go to the capital markets with great regularity to finance their vast financial requirements. But the decision with respect to internal versus external financing is not simply one of resorting to the capital markets only when internal funds are inadequate to serve the needs of the business, but rather to balance these two types of financing in such a way as to provide the best overall financial position for the business.

Dividend Policy

One of the most important policy factors involved in internal financing is that of the firm's dividend policy. A liberal dividend payout may result in a favorable attitude on the part of the stockholders, but it will also result in a reduction of internally generated funds available for investment. It is important for corporate management to adopt a dividend policy that will provide the company with a reasonable amount of retained earnings for internal investment purposes and also hold an appeal to the investor so that public issues of securities will sell at favorable prices.

The company that pursues a policy of paying no dividends and retaining as much of its earnings as possible might find a lack of interest on the part of potential investors in the stock of the company. This is true because many investors depend upon current dividend income to support their personal living expenses. Some investors, in fact, place almost total emphasis on dividend payments in their appraisal of stocks. Other investors may be more interested in the growth of the earnings on their stock.

In general, firms that must approach the capital markets with great frequency find it advantageous to maintain a fairly liberal dividend policy; that is, a policy that provides for a large payout of earnings with a relatively small amount of the earnings being retained in the business. Firms that are able to accommodate a large proportion of their investment requirements through internal financing often find that a conservative dividend policy may be acceptable to the investors. In this case the investor is interested in the growth of earnings and the market price per share.

Keep in mind that the capital markets are made up of a host of investors, each with individual investment goals and objectives. It is the task of the financial manager to so orient the practices of the company that there will be a maximum appeal to a significant group of investors in the capital markets.

Substantial diversity of payout practices occurs among different industries. The aerospace industry was characterized by an average cash dividend payout ratio of less than 40 percent of stockholder earnings over the 1970s decade. Over the same period, the average payout ratio for the electric utility industry was approximately 70 percent. At the same time, there has been substantial variation in payout ratios within certain industries during recent years. Some of this variability is attributable to the volatility of business activity during the 1970s and early 1980s. In some cases, in order to maintain a constant dollar amount in dividends, firms will pay cash dividends in excess of their earnings. This has occurred several times in the automobile industry in recent years. Dividend payout policies also can vary substantially across firms in the same or related industries. Each firm presumably considers all the factors pertinent to its situation and then sets its dividend practices accordingly.

Consistency in Dividend Practices

Once a dividend policy is established by a corporation, investors may be disturbed by departures from such established policy. For this reason corporations tend to move slowly in changing their dividend paying practices. Companies in the same industry may have diverse dividend payment practices and yet pursue these practices with great success. For example, one company may have the reputation of being a liberal dividend payer and enjoy strong support in the capital markets. Another firm in the same line of activity may have a very conservative dividend policy and also enjoy strong support in the market. And yet if each company tried to adopt the policy of the other, it is possible that both of them would experience extreme criticism on the part of their stockholders. Consistency, then, plays an important role in the dividend paying practices of the corporation.

The requirement of consistency also results in a lack of coordination between the generation of funds and their need for investment purposes. If firms could arbitrarily use their earnings as needed, paying out the residual as dividends, the convenience of retained earnings would be far greater. For most firms, it is the retained earnings that is the residual, with dividends having first priority in the administration of the income of the firm.

The ability to generate adequate earnings in order to pay cash dividends and allow for some earnings retention is influenced to a large extent by the firm's profit margin. It should be recalled that the Du Pont system of financial analysis expresses the return on assets as a function of the asset turnover times the profit margin. Changes in the profit margin (net income/net sales), given a stable dollar dividend policy, can cause substantial variation in the retention of earnings from year to year.

The proportion of internal to external financing varies over the business cycle. During periods of economic expansion it is customary for firms to rely increasingly on external funds as investment opportunities outrun internally generated funds. During periods of economic contraction the reverse is true. As profitable investment opportunities diminish, the rate of investment itself is reduced and the reliance on external capital markets decreases.

Dividends and Taxes

Corporate income tax matters also influence the decision of internal versus external financing. Although the corporation must pay a corporate income tax on its earnings, no personal income tax liability is incurred on the part of the stockholders if the earnings are not distributed to the stockholders. The case is often made, therefore, that business should retain a maximum of earnings on behalf of its stockholders since this precludes the creation of a personal tax liability on the part of the stockholders. However, corporate income tax regulations attempt to prevent corporations from using this device as an unfair tax shield. Unless the firm invests retained earnings in due time in business operations, an "undue accumulation of earnings" tax may be levied against the firm. The provision for possible tax penalties is contained in Section 531 of the Revenue Act of 1954.

Not all stockholders may wish to reinvest their funds in the corporations whose stock they hold. Presumably a shareholder is aware of the dividend policies of the companies in which investments are contemplated and therefore the shareholder will choose companies whose dividend practices are compatible with his or her particular tax situation. For the investor who finds a company changing its dividend practice, the alternative is simply to sell the stock. If the company has increased its retained earnings at the expense of the stockholder dividends, the investor who disposes of stock can only hope that the reinvestment of the earnings of the business has been reflected in the market price of the stock.

CHARACTERISTICS OF LONG-TERM CORPORATE SECURITIES

The long-term capital funds for the corporation are of two broad forms: equity capital and debt capital. Equity capital is obtained through the sale of shares of stock in the corporation. These shares may be divided into several classes, each having specified benefits and privileges with respect to ownership status in the corporation. As opposed to the equity capital of a corporation, debt capital represents funds obtained from creditors rather than from owners. Such capital may be obtained through direct negotiations with a lender or the sale of notes or bonds to many lenders.

Equity Capital

Equity capital is the capital supplied by the owners of the enterprise. This ownership claim in a corporation is evidenced by the *stock certificate*. The stock certificate shows the type of stock held by the owner, the name of the company, the name of the owner of the stock, and the names of certain of the company officers. The stock certificate also carries space for its assignment in the event that it is transferred to another person. As a protection against forgery, all signatures on stock certificates must generally be certified by a representative of a commercial bank, a stockbroker, or other authorized person. In the event of the loss of a stock certificate, however, an individual may request a duplicate certificate. The corporation, in turn, will generally require that a bond or surety be posted by the stockholder to protect the corporation in the event that the lost certificate should later be presented.

Stock certificates are generally made out in terms of one hundred shares or multiples thereof. Stock certificates representing less than one hundred shares are generally referred to as *fractional certificates*. The holder of an odd number of shares, as for example, 523, will probably hold one stock certificate representing the ownership of 500 shares and a fractional stock certificate representing an ownership of 23 shares. (See Figure 11-1.)

When the holder of the stock sells the shares, the assigned stock certificate is forwarded to the company by the purchaser, and it is destroyed by the secretary of the corporation. A new certificate is issued to the new owner whose name will then be carried on the stock record. In the larger corporations, an official transfer agent, generally a trust company or a bank, is appointed to accomplish this task. The larger corporations may also have an independent stock registrar to supervise transfer of its securities.

The capital stock of a corporation may be assigned a *par value* (a fixed value) in the certificate of incorporation. If the corporation sells the stock for less than the par value, the owners of the stock may become liable to creditors for the difference between the selling price and the par value in the event of failure of the company. Thus, the limited liability of the stockholders may be defeated. This technicality seldom creates any difficulty, however, since most stock is sold initially at or above its par value. In addition, certain legal devices may be used to protect against such contigent liability even in those instances when the stock must be sold at less than its par value.

Aside from this significance, par value usually bears little relationship to the current price or book value of the stock. Most states permit corporations to issue no-par stock.

Types of Equity Instruments

Equity instruments of the corporation may be grouped broadly into two classes: common stock and preferred stock.

Common Stock. The outstanding characteristic of *common stock* is its complete claim to the profits of the business that remain after the holders of all other classes of debt and equity instruments have received their stipulated returns. Also, it is generally the voting privilege of the common stockholders that governs the selection of the board of directors of a corporation; the board of directors, in turn, exercises general control of the enterprise. For these reasons, the holders of common stock may be regarded as the basic owners of the corporation.

The favorable position of the common stockholders with respect to dividends and control of the corporation is offset by the fact that during periods when profits from operations are low, the claims of others may completely absorb available

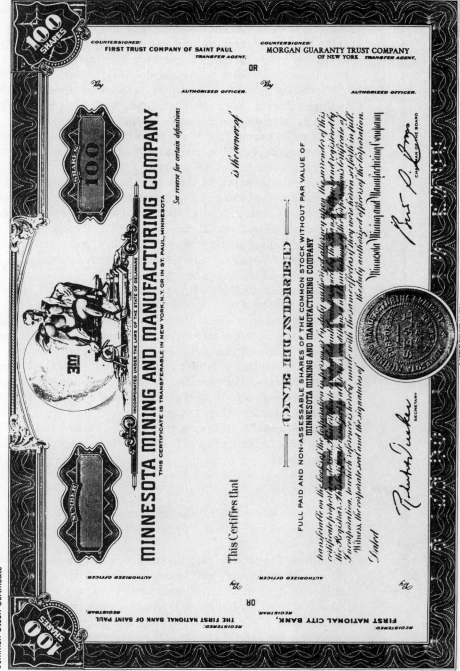

Figure 11-1
Common Stock Certificate

funds, leaving little or nothing for the common stockholders. The common stockholders, therefore, may expect less stability with respect to the amount of their dividends, often receiving considerably greater yield than the holders of other instruments during prosperous periods and generally less than other security holders during periods of distress.

Just as the common stockholders receive dividends only after all other classes of security holders have received their specified return, so they have low priority when a business venture is liquidated. All creditors must receive their claims in full; and preferred stockholders must, as a rule, be paid in full before common stockholders may participate in the proceeds of liquidation. As in the case of dividends, all proceeds of liquidation remaining after the settlement of prior obligations accrue to the common stockholders. It is seldom, however, that an enterprise which has been forced to liquidate because of unfortunate business experience will provide enough proceeds to take care of the claims of creditors and preferred stockholders. Common stockholders generally receive little, if anything, from liquidation proceedings. The common stockholders, therefore, suffer the brunt of business failure just as they enjoy the primary benefits of business success.

Common stock may be divided into special groups, generally Class A and Class B, in order to permit the acquisition of additional capital without diluting the control of the business. When a corporation does issue two classes of common stock, it quite often will give voting rights to only one class, generally Class B. Owners of Class A stock, then, have most, if not all, of the other rights and privileges of the common stockholders. The tendency of some corporations to issue nonvoting equity securities is opposed by some government agencies as well as some authorities in the field of corporate finance on the basis that it permits the concentration of ownership control. The New York Stock Exchange refuses to list the common stock of corporations that issue nonvoting classes of common stock.

Preferred Stock. *Preferred stock*, in contrast with common stock, generally carries a limited dividend, specified as either a percentage of par value or as a fixed number of dollars per year. For example, a preferred stock may be referred to as a 9 percent preferred, meaning that its annual dividend participation is limited to 9 percent of its par or stated value. The dividend priority for no-par preferred stock is stated in terms of a dollar amount, for example, "preferred as to dividends in the amount of $9 annually." The holder of the preferred stock accepts the limitation on the amount of dividends as a fair exchange for the priority held in the earnings of the company.

As has been noted, before the common stockholders receive any dividends, preferred stockholders must be paid the total of their prior claim. The preferred stock, therefore, offers the investor something of a compromise between the basic equity instruments of common stock and credit instruments such as bonds and long-term notes. Because preferred stocks are frequently of a nonvoting nature, the managements of many corporations favor their issuance as a means of obtaining equity capital without diluting the control of the current stockholders.

As in the case of common stock, preferred stock may be classified into Class A, Class B, or First Preferred and Second Preferred. The Class A Preferred or First Preferred usually has priority over other classes of preferred stock of a company in the distribution of dividends and in the proceeds from liquidation.

Preferred stock may have special features. For example, it may be cumulative or noncumulative. *Cumulative preferred stock* requires that before common stock dividends may be paid, preferred dividends must be paid not only for the dividend period in question but also for all previous periods in which no preferred dividends were paid. It is important to remember that since the preferred stockholder technically is an owner of the business, he or she cannot force the payment of a dividend. The preferred stockholder may be made to wait until such time as earnings are adequate for that purpose, the cumulative preferred stock offering protection for those periods during which dividends were not declared. *Noncumulative preferred stock*, on the other hand, makes no provision for the accumulation of unpaid dividends with the result that management may at times be tempted to declare preferred dividends only when it appears that sufficient earnings are available to make possible common stock dividends also. Practically all modern preferred stock is cumulative.

A preferred stock may be participating or nonparticipating. *Participating preferred stock* is stock that participates, on a share-for-share basis with common stockholders, in any residual profits of a corporation after payment has been made of the basic preferred stock dividend and the common stock dividend. Very few issues of preferred stock carry participation clauses today.

Preferred stock also may be callable, in which case the corporation may retire the preferred stock at its option. Preferred stock may also carry a conversion clause that makes possible its conversion to common stock of the corporation at the stockholder's option.

Many special features that preferred stocks may carry exist primarily as an added attraction to investors to permit the sale of securities at times when distribution would otherwise be difficult.

Debt Capital

In addition to the capital provided by the owners of the corporation, funds may be secured also from creditors on a long-term basis. Debt capital, however, must be preceded by an equity investment in the corporation on the part of the stockholders, inasmuch as creditors generally require a contribution on the part of owners before entrusting their own funds to the use of the corporation. Uses for borrowed funds may be the same as the uses for equity funds, for example, the acquisition of additional land, buildings, and equipment. Debt capital, however, has certain rights and privileges not possessed by the holders of equity capital in a corporation. The holder of a debt instrument issued by a corporation may force the business to abide by the terms of the contract even though it may mean reorganization or dissolution of the enterprise. The periodic interest payments due the holders of such debt instruments must be paid, therefore, if the corporation is to survive. The holders of debt instruments have priority over stockholders up to the limit of their claim against the corporation in the event of liquidation of the concern.

Offsetting the advantage of this preferred position, the yield to which the creditors of a corporation are entitled is usually considerably less over a period of years than that available to the owners of the various classes of equity securities. Also, so long as the corporation meets its contractual obligations, the creditors have little voice in its management and control, except for those covenants and restrictions that are a part of the loan contract.

Types of Debt Instruments

Long-term corporate debt instruments may be classified into two categories—secured obligations and unsecured obligations, generally referred to as *mortgage bonds* and *debenture bonds*. In contrast with the stockholder whose ownership of shares of stock may be evidenced by a single stock certificate, the holder of bonds has a separate instrument for each bond owned. On the face of the bond itself appear the facts relating to the rights and obligations of the corporation and the bondholder, including denomination of the bond (generally $1,000), maturity, interest rate, periods of interest payments, and the specific nature of the claim of the bond.

The bond contract is generally rather complicated, and the ramifications are too extensive to be included on the face of the bond. This supplementary information is set out in a document referred to as the *trust indenture*. This document is generally quite voluminous and includes in the greatest detail the various provisions of the loan arrangement. Although the indenture is seldom seen or utilized by the average bondholder, it is available to the creditor who requires its use. The trust indenture, then, provides the basis for the settlement of disputes relative to the responsibilities and the rights of the parties to the contract and hence it is essential that it be carefully preserved, generally by a trustee designated by the corporation. The trustee has a duty to protect the indenture and to enforce its provisions.

When there is a direct loan arrangement established between a borrowing corporation and a single lending institution, corporate notes may be used rather than bonds. Although long-term corporate notes are less formal in nature than bonds, they generally include many restrictive covenants not required in connection with the typical short-term promissory note. Long-term corporate notes may also be used when a group of institutions negotiates jointly with a borrowing corporation.

Mortgage Bonds. The property specifically pledged to secure the mortgage bonds may include all of the assets of a corporation or it may include only a part thereof. As a rule, however, the mortgage applies only to the real estate, buildings, and other assets that are classed as real property. For the corporation that is expanding its plant facilities, the mortgage so offered for expansion purposes usually includes only a lien on the additional property acquired. The opposite has been true of most railway expansions. Originally, railway construction was of a piecemeal nature, providing for extensions of road and facilities over a period of many years. Mortgage bonds issued to finance such extensions of track often included a lien on all of the roadbed previously constructed as well as the additional track.

When a parcel of real estate has more than one mortgage lien against it, the mortgage first filed for recording at the appropriate government office, generally the county recorder's office, has priority; and the bonds outstanding against the mortgage are known as *senior liens*. The bonds outstanding against all mortgages subsequently recorded are known as *junior liens*. Inasmuch as senior liens have priority with respect to distribution of assets in the event of failure of the business, they generally provide a lower yield to investors than do the junior liens. The junior liens of a strong company, however, may be considered by investors to be safer than the senior liens of a less well-established company.

Mortgage bonds may differ to a considerable extent. For example, the mortgage may prevent the issuance of securities over and above those authorized in the initial flotation. The term *closed-end mortgage* applies to this arrangement. Alternatively, the mortgage may provide for continuing sale of bonds against the same mortgage. As a rule when such an *open-end mortgage* exists, there is also a stipulation to the effect that additional real property which the company acquires automatically becomes a part of the property secured under the mortgage.

Debenture Bonds. These bonds are dependent upon the general credit and strength of the corporation for their security. They represent no specific pledge of property, but rather their holders are classed as general creditors of the corporation on a par with the holders of promissory notes and trade creditors that have sold merchandise to the corporation. Debenture bonds are used by governmental bodies and by many industrial and utility corporations as well. Since mortgage bonds would otherwise have a prior claim against the fixed assets of a corporation, even though they are sold subsequent to the debenture bonds, the debenture bonds are sometimes afforded protection against such subsequent sale of senior securities through a covenant of equal coverage. Such a covenant provides that the debenture bonds will be accorded equal rank with any subsequent senior issues of securities.

Like preferred stock, corporate bonds may carry such special provisions as conversion rights and participation rights in order to enhance their original sale.

FACTORS AFFECTING THE LONG-TERM FINANCING MIX

The mix between debt and equity funds used to finance a firm's assets is an important financial management consideration. Because the cost of borrowed funds traditionally is fixed, debt often can be used to increase rates of return to the firm's owners or stockholders in the case of corporations. Of course, this higher potential return must be balanced against higher risk in determining the combined impact on the firm's value. Other factors that impact on the mix between debt and equity capital are: flexibility, control, timing, and availability.

Impact on Return

In Chapter 7 we introduced the Du Pont financial model or system which expressed the rate of return on assets as follows:

$$\frac{\text{Net Income}}{\text{Total Assets}} = \frac{\text{Net Sales}}{\text{Total Assets}} \times \frac{\text{Net Income}}{\text{Net Sales}}$$

$$\text{Return on Assets} = \text{Asset Turnover} \times \text{Profit Margin}$$

Recall that this financial system was applied using financial statements, reproduced here as Figures 11-2 and 11-3, for the ABC Manufacturing Company. The result was a 9.0 percent return on assets for ABC calculated on the basis of the following data:

$$\frac{\$45,000}{\$500,000} = \frac{\$700,000}{\$500,000} \times \frac{\$45,000}{\$700,000}$$

$$9.0\% \quad = \quad 1.40 \quad \times \quad 6.43\%$$

Figure 11-2
Balance Sheet for the
ABC Manufacturing
Company

Balance Sheet
December 31, 1983

Assets

Cash and Marketable Securities	$ 25,000	
Accounts Receivable.	100,000	
Inventories.	125,000	
Total Current Assets		$250,000
Gross Plant and Equipment	$275,000	
Less Accumulated Depreciation	75,000	
Net Plant and Equipment.	200,000	
Land.	50,000	
Total Fixed Assets		250,000
Total Assets.		$500,000

Liabilities and Owners' Equity

Accounts Payable.	75,000	
Notes Payable (Bank, 10%)	20,000	
Accrued Liabilities	30,000	
Total Current Liabilities		125,000
Mortgage Debt (12%).		100,000
Total Liabilities		225,000
Owners' Equity.		275,000
Total Liabilities and Owners' Equity		$500,000

Figure 11-3
Income Statement for
the ABC Manufacturing
Company

Income Statement
Year Ended December 31, 1983

Net Revenues or Sales....................		$700,000
Cost of Goods Sold		450,000
Gross Profit............................		250,000
General and Administrative Expenses.......	$100,000	
Selling and Marketing Expenses	36,000	
Depreciation.............................	25,000	
Interest..................................	14,000	175,000
Net Income Before Income Taxes		75,000
Income Taxes (at 40%)		30,000
Net Income.............................		$ 45,000

In the event that a firm finances all of its assets with equity funds, then the return on assets would be the same as the return to the owners. However, almost all firms make use of current liabilities and many also finance some of their assets with long-term debt. This gives the firm an opportunity to provide the owners with a rate of return on owners' equity that is higher than the rate of return on assets. The use of financial leverage makes this possible.

Financial leverage ratios, as noted in Chapter 7, indicate the extent to which assets are financed by borrowed funds and other liabilities. The *debt ratio*, expressed as total liabilities divided by total assets, is a common way of measuring financial leverage. We can calculate the debt ratio for ABC Manufacturing using its balance sheet data in Figure 11-2 as follows:

$$\text{Debt Ratio} = \frac{\text{Total Liabilities}}{\text{Total Assets}} = \frac{\$225,000}{\$500,000} = .45 \text{ or } 45\%$$

This means that 45 percent of ABC's total assets are financed with debt funds.

As with other ratios, to interpret the significance of the debt ratio we must compare it over time for ABC or against the debt ratios of other firms in our industry. For example, if the industry average is 40 percent, then ABC would be considered to be more risky than the industry. A 50 percent industry ratio would make ABC relatively less risky. When a firm deviates substantially from industry norms it may be severely penalized in the marketplace for its long-term securities. This possible consequence will be covered more fully in our discussion of risk implications.

An alternative way of expressing financial leverage is through the *equity multiplier* ratio, which is defined as total assets divided by owners' equity. The ratio calculation for ABC would be:

$$\text{Equity Multiplier} = \frac{\text{Total Assets}}{\text{Owners' Equity}} = \frac{\$500,000}{\$275,000} = 1.82$$

This means that the owners' investment is levered or multiplied 1.82 times with debt funds to finance ABC's total assets. Notice that the equity multiplier can be found by knowing the debt ratio, and vice versa. For example, if debt is used to finance 45 percent of the total assets, then 55 percent is financed with equity funds. Dividing 1 by .55 gives the equity multiplier of 1.82.

The Du Pont return on assets model can be expanded to a return on owners' equity model by incorporating the equity multiplier ratio as follows:

$$\frac{\text{Net Income}}{\text{Owners' Equity}} = \frac{\text{Net Sales}}{\text{Total Assets}} \times \frac{\text{Net Income}}{\text{Net Sales}} \times \frac{\text{Total Assets}}{\text{Owners' Equity}}$$

Return on Equity = Asset Turnover × Profit Margin × Equity Multiplier

Inserting the appropriate data for ABC from Figures 11-2 and 11-3 gives:

$$\frac{\$45,000}{\$275,000} = \frac{\$700,000}{\$500,000} \times \frac{\$45,000}{\$700,000} \times \frac{\$500,000}{\$275,000}$$

$$16.4\% = 1.40 \times 6.43\% \times 1.82$$

Thus, while ABC was able to earn a 9.0 percent return on assets, the firm provided its owners with a 16.4 percent return on their equity investment because debt funds were used to finance nearly one half of the firm's assets.

The process of using debt funds in an effort to increase the rate of return to owners or stockholders is termed *trading on the equity*. This term is apparently derived from the fact that equity investment must precede debt financing in a business enterprise; hence, the bonds or notes are being sold on the strength of the underlying equity. We now are ready to consider risk implications as they relate to the use of financial leverage.

Risk Implications

Trading on the equity by a firm can either result in positive or negative financial leverage. *Positive financial leverage* will occur as long as the rate of return earned on borrowed funds is higher than the cost of the funds. For example, the cost of long-term debt for the ABC Manufacturing Company was 12 percent, as shown in Figure 11-2. If ABC can earn more than 12 percent on the investment of these funds in assets, then positive financial leverage will result. Since interest is deductible for tax purposes, the return on assets needed is before interest and taxes. ABC had a net income before taxes of $75,000 in 1983 (see Figure 11-3). Adding back interest of $14,000 gives an income before interest and taxes of $89,000. Dividing $89,000 by the firm's total assets of $500,000 gives an average return of about 18 percent. This figure is substantially higher than the 12 percent cost, indicating that positive financial leverage existed for ABC on its long-term debt.

Negative financial leverage occurs when the interest cost of borrowing is more than the rate of return being earned on the assets. Thus the leverage effect of long-term corporate debt should be recognized; as the percentage return to the stockholders is increased substantially during periods of highly profitable operations, so the percentage return to stockholders is depressed during periods of low profits. And, if the earnings before interest fall below the amount needed to meet interest obligations on the bonds, the firm will be insolvent and might be forced into bankruptcy.

A study of the capital structure as reflected in the long-term debt to owners' equity mix for various types of businesses reveals a wide range of practice. In industries subject to only minor operating fluctuations and reverses over the business cycle, we generally find a greater use of borrowed capital than in firms that are subject to wide swings in cyclical experience. The utility companies that have relatively stable revenues can capitalize to a much large extent through borrowed capital than do most industrial corporations.

The capital structure mix between long-term debt and owners' equity is usually expressed on a percentage basis. For example, the capital structure mix for ABC Manufacturing is taken from Figure 11-2 and is expressed as follows:

	Dollar Amount	Percent
Long-term Debt	$100,000	27%
Owners' Equity	275,000	73
Total Capital	$375,000	100%

Long-term debt has a "weight" of 27 percent of ABC's capital structure, with owners' equity constituting 73 percent.

An "optimal" capital structure reflects the ideal mix between long-term debt and equity funds taking into consideration the industry within which the firm operates. Let's assume that ABC Manufacturing is similar to its industry norms from an operating standpoint and that its debt and equity mix is roughly at the industry average. Because firms within an industry are continually striving for the ideal capital structure mix, it is likely that a mix close to the industry average will be optimal, other things being equal.

An *optimal capital structure* is consistent with minimizing the cost of debt and equity funds and maximizing the value of the firm. Substantial deviations from an optimal capital structure, associated with either too little or too much long-term debt, will not minimize the cost of capital. Some amount of long-term debt is valuable to the firm because it will be less costly than equity funds, and interest also is deductible for tax purposes. In contrast, too much long-term debt will cause substantial increases in the cost of both long-term debt and equity funds because of concern over whether the firm will be able to meet its interest and principal payments as they come due. Excessive use of debt also will show up in the assignment of lower bond quality ratings by such organizations as Moody's and Standard and Poor's. Lower quality ratings result in higher interest costs because of greater perceived risk, and vice versa. Thus, internal policy decisions with respect to capital structure and debt ratios must be tempered by a recognition of how outsiders view the strength of the firm's financial position.

The process of calculating the cost of capital which is really a *weighted average cost of capital* can be illustrated using the data for ABC Manufacturing. Let's assume that long-term debt can be sold at a 12 percent interest rate and that ABC has a 40 percent tax rate. In addition, management believes that its stockholders expect a 14 percent rate of return from dividends and stock price appreciation. This is a 2 percentage point premium over the cost of long-term debt.[1] Since interest is deductible for tax purposes, we multiply the 12 percent before-tax rate by .60 (one minus the .40 tax rate) to arrive at an after-tax cost of 7.2 percent. Now, using the previously determined optimal capital structure weights, we calculate the after-tax cost of capital as follows:

	Weight	After-tax Cost	Component Cost
Long-term Debt	.27	.072	.019
Owners' Equity	.73	.140	.102
		Cost of Capital = .121 = 12%	

This 12 percent cost of capital should be used as ABC's discount rate for making future capital budgeting decisions.

Flexibility

As described in the sections relating to short-term financial policies, we saw that one of the important reasons for the use of short-term borrowing was seasonality. If a business needs funds for only six or seven months of the year, it may be far cheaper to engage in short-term borrowing rather than to encumber the firm with long-term funds on which interest would have to be paid throughout the year. By the same token, the business cycle itself results in a change in the financial requirements of the firm. There are always periods in the life of the business in which there will be fewer investment opportunities and in which the market for the firm's products may contract temporarily. It is advantageous to have a capital structure that lends itself to alteration during such periods of time. A large company with many different long-term debt issues with staggered maturities may find during a period of economic contraction that it is wise to simply retire a maturing bond issue out of the increasing liquidity of the firm as working assets move from inventories and accounts receivable into cash.

In other situations the business may engage in temporary ventures that are to be abandoned either at some determinable future date or at the discretion of management. In this case, too, a type of financing that lends itself to elimination if no longer needed becomes appropriate. In both of these cases debt financing holds an important advantage over preferred stock or common stock financing since by the nature of these equity instruments there is no maturity that makes possible their convenient retirement. Debt financing may be accomplished with maturities suited to the expected period of need for funds. It should be mentioned

---

[1]The risk premium approach for estimating the cost of equity capital is based on examining the "spread" between bond and stock returns for firms with comparable business and financial risk characteristics. Two other approaches used to estimate the cost of equity capital are: the dividend yield plus capital appreciation method, and the capital asset pricing method. For a discussion of these methods, see Robert W. Johnson and Ronald W. Melicher, *Financial Management*, 5th ed. (Boston: Allyn and Bacon, Inc., 1982), Chapter 14.

also at this point that the lease arrangement offers as one of its special advantages the fact that the lease term may be established to coincide with the duration of the need for the assets. The lease arrangement is described in Chapter 12.

Corporate Control

Although the control of a corporation is administered generally by its board of directors, ultimate control rests with those stockholders who hold classes of stock with voting rights. The stockholders are responsible for the election of the members of the board of directors, and the members of the board of directors are in turn responsible to the stockholders. Many stockholders in large corporations have little interest in their voting rights, owning such stocks purely for income. Under such circumstances it is possible and generally true that stockholders owning only a small proportion of the total stock are able to control the election of the members of the board of directors and hence effect ultimate control over all activities of the corporation.

The device of classifying common stock as voting and nonvoting shares facilitates the control of corporate affairs by the ownership of only a small part of all capital investment, and the same is true in some cases of the issue of nonvoting preferred stock. Some states require that all stock, regardless of its class, be voting stock, a provision apparently designed to permit participation on the part of all stockholders in corporate activity.

A growing enterprise that has prospered under its existing management may lack the capital necessary to take advantage of the opportunities available. Yet the prospect of bringing additional stockholders into the enterprise may not be attractive to management because of the voting privileges that such new investors in the business would acquire. The volume of additional funds required might make necessary the sale of so much new stock that the existing stockholders would lose control of the affairs of the company because of the concentration of voting power in the hands of the new stockholders. Many firms have avoided expansion rather than risk the loss of control through the sale of stock.

Corporate bonds and notes, on the other hand, provide no voting privilege for their holders; hence, management frequently prefers this form of financing. Although the holders of bonds and notes have no voting privilege, there are frequently contractual provisions that limit the managerial actions of the existing owners of the business. For example, before the loan is made, the borrower may be required to agree that dividends will not be distributed to stockholders if the net working capital of the firm falls below a stipulated minimum. When the debt is retired, of course, the management is freed from such restrictions.

Timing

The sale of securities by a corporation and the type of securities sold depends in large measure upon existing conditions in the capital markets. A wise policy with respect to long-term financial planning makes it possible to capitalize on these changing conditions in the market. For example, during a period of economic recession when business is at a low ebb, interest rates are typically at low levels also. By the same token common stock prices are at low levels. Under these conditions, if additional funds are needed for expansion or to retire maturing debt, it becomes much more attractive to do so through the sale of debt instruments rather than through the sale of common stock.

During the upswing and expansion of the business cycle, when business opportunities and investment plans are increasing, it is also advantageous to borrow on a long-term basis even though interest rates may be rising somewhat. After a long period of economic expansion, however, pressure on capital resources and on the capital markets is such that interest rates reach very high levels and all but the very strongest credit risks may find it difficult to borrow additional funds. At these times common stock prices are typically at very high levels and the corporation that sells stock receives a high price therefor.

The ability of a corporation to take advantage of these changing conditions in the capital markets is a function of the maintenance of a favorable capital structure, one that allows it to maneuver between debt issues and common stock issues on the basis of management's desires. The business that has exhausted its long-term borrowing power may find itself trapped in a situation where it may be forced to sell common stock at a time when the price of the shares is depressed and the return from the sale of the stock is correspondingly low. Long-term financial policy, therefore, must be geared to prospective future needs as well as to the needs of the moment.

Availability

Just as financial management must take into consideration flexibility and timing in its plans, so too it must recognize that sheer availability may dictate the type of securities to be sold. Small firms and medium-sized firms, by virtue of their size, may simply not have access to the capital markets for purposes of selling stock. On the other hand, the ownership of plant and equipment may provide entirely suitable collateral for long-term borrowing. At other times a business may be able to borrow only if it provides the lender with a form of override; that is, a form of additional potential return in the form of stock options or other arrangements by which the lender can participate in the prosperity of the company in future years.

Recently it has become customary for even large institutional lenders such as insurance companies to insist upon additional opportunities for reward in their lending operations. One reason for this has been the strong price inflation of recent years. Lenders try to protect themselves against erosion of the value of the dollar. They try to accomplish this at times by insisting that the borrower make available supplementary benefits. Typically, this takes the form of a percentage of gross or net income and at other times through the use of convertible securities or stock options. With the issuance of convertible bonds or preferred stock, the holder of the security not only has the immediate yield and safety provided by the security, but with the increasing prosperity of the business has an opportunity to convert the securities at a predetermined ratio into the common stock of the company. This in turn makes it possible to enjoy the benefits of the common stockholders as the firm prospers.

Obviously, corporations are not anxious to provide investors with securities that provide the best of all worlds; that is, the protection of a fixed-income security in the case of bonds and preferred stock, but also the opportunity to convert these securities into the common stock of the company if the company prospers. Yet there may be times when the corporation may simply be forced to issue such securities in order to raise the capital necessary to accommodate investment plans.

In other instances very strong corporations may resort to the use of convertible securities when common stock prices are depressed below levels considered to be acceptable to the company. Convertible securities are issued with the expectation that when the price of the company's common stock recovers, these securities will be called for redemption, thus forcing the holders to convert to the common stock of the company. The holders of convertible securities, of course, have a specified time period within which they may convert their securities once they have been called for redemption by the company. The net effect of this action is to sell stock at a price considered satisfactory to the company through the device of first issuing convertible bonds or preferred stock and then at a later date forcing conversion.

QUESTIONS

1. What are the major sources of long-term funds available to business corporations? Indicate their relative importance.
2. Describe the relationship between internal and external financing in meeting the long-term financial needs of the firm.
3. Why is it important to establish dividend payout policies and then maintain consistency in dividend payment practices?
4. List the principal features of a stock certificate. How are such certificates transferred from person to person?
5. List and briefly explain special features that may be associated with preferred stock.
6. Distinguish between the types of corporate debt instruments.
7. Describe the link between a firm's rate of return on equity and its rate of return on total assets as calculated under the Du Pont system of analysis.
8. Explain what is meant by trading on the equity. Also, briefly describe the difference between positive and negative financial leverage.
9. Why is it important for a firm to minimize its weighted average cost of capital?
10. It is sometimes said that long-term debt financing provides a greater degree of flexibility to financial managers than either preferred or common stock. Why?
11. What is meant by the concept of corporate control as it relates to a firm's capital structure?
12. Briefly explain how the factors of timing and availability affect the mix between debt and equity capital.

PROBLEMS

1. The Kolbeck Manufacturing company had the following financial statement results for last year. Net sales were $2 million with net income of $100,000. Total assets at year end amounted to $1,800,000 and total liabilities were $900,000.

a. Calculate Kolbeck's asset turnover ratio and profit margin.
b. Calculate Kolbeck's debt ratio and its equity multiplier ratio.
c. Show how the two ratios in Part A can be

used to determine Kolbeck's rate of return on assets.

d. Expand the return on assets model expressed in Part C to a return on owners' equity model. Comment on the difference between the two rate of return calculations.

2. Next year ABC Manufacturing (discussed in the chapter) expects its sales to reach $900,000 with an investment in total assets of $600,000. Total liabilities are estimated to be $325,000 and net income of $70,000 is anticipated.

a. Estimate ABC's debt ratio and equity multiplier for next year. How do these ratios compare with the 1983 results shown in the chapter?

b. The average industry debt ratio is 50 percent and the equity multiplier is 2.00. How does ABC compare against these averages for 1983 and based on next year's projections?

c. Apply the return on owners' equity model based on the projected data and compare it with the results for 1983.

d. Calculate the rate of return on assets ratio using ABC's projected data. Comment on how it compares with the return on equity ratio results.

3. Following are selected financial data in thousands of dollars for the Solar-Genetics Corporation:

	1982	1983
Current Assets	$ 400	$ 500
Fixed Assets, Net	600	700
Total Assets	$1,000	$1,200
Current Liabilities	$ 200	$ 250
Long-term Debt	200	200
Common Equity	600	750
Total Liabilities and Equity	$1,000	$1,200
Net Sales	$1,200	$1,500
Total Expenses	1,100	1,390
Net Income	$ 100	$ 110

a. Calculate Solar-Genetics' rate of return on owners' equity ratio in 1982 and 1983. Did the ratio improve or get worse?

b. Expand the ratio results in Part A into a return on equity model with its three major components and determine what changes occurred between the two years.

4. Use the data for Solar-Genetics in Problem 3 to work this problem.

a. Determine the percentage weights for long-term debt and common equity in Solar-Genetics capital structures in 1982 and 1983.

b. Assume that Solar-Genetics has to pay a 12 percent interest rate on its long-term debt and is in the 40 percent income tax bracket. The firm believes that its common equity carries a 4 percentage point premium over its interest rate on debt. Based on this information, calculate the firm's after-tax cost of long-term debt and its cost of common equity.

c. If Solar-Genetics' 1983 capital structure is considered optimal, determine the firm's weighted average cost of capital.

SUGGESTED READINGS

Helfert, Erich A. *Techniques of Financial Analysis,* 5th ed. Homewood, Illinois: Richard D. Irwin, Inc., 1982. Chapter 5.

Johnson, Robert W., and Ronald W. Melicher. *Financial Management*, 5th ed. Boston: Allyn and Bacon, Inc., 1982. Parts VI and VIII.

Martin, John D., and David F. Scott, Jr. "A Discriminant Analysis of the Corporate Debt–Equity Decisions." *Financial Management* (Winter, 1974), pp. 71–87.

Melicher, Ronald W., and J. Ronald Hoffmeister. "Issuing Convertible Bonds in the Public and Private Markets." *Financial Executive* (June, 1980), pp. 20–23.

Nantell, Timothy J., and C. Robert Carlson. "The Cost of Capital as a Weighted Average." *Journal of Finance* (December, 1975), pp. 1343–1355.

Pfahl, John K., David T. Crary, and R. Hayden Howard. "The Limits of Leverage." *Financial Executive* (May, 1970), pp. 48–56.

Scott, David F., and John Martin. "Industry Influence on Financial Structure." *Financial Management* (Spring, 1975), pp. 67–73.

12 Sources of Long-term Business Financing

Commercial banks are an important supplier of business loans that extend beyond one year, as well as the major provider of short-term business funds. Institutional investors have played a major role as purchasers of the stocks and bonds issued by corporations over the past several decades. The institutions that have been the primary suppliers of long-term debt and equity capital are investment companies, trust companies, and insurance companies.

Some business corporations also provide long-term capital for other businesses in several ways, as we will see shortly. Other important suppliers of long-term funds include regional development companies, small business investment companies, and investment development companies. Leasing and equipment trust financing, while not provided by a specific form of financial institution, also represent important sources of long-term debt financing.

COMMERCIAL BANK TERM LOANS

The *bank term loan* represents an interesting and significant development in the lending practices of commercial banks. This type of loan differs from the usual bank business loan in that it has a maturity exceeding one year. Also, the term loan may require repayment in installments throughout the life of the loan. Such installment repayments may be on a monthly, a quarterly, or a yearly basis.

Development of Term Loans

Term lending by the commercial banks of the nation appears to have begun during the depression years of the thirties. Although the term loan was contrary to the generally accepted concept of bank lending activity, there were several reasons for its rapid growth and acceptance by the banks of the nation. First, banks utilized the term loan arrangement as a convenient means of investing their surplus funds. These surplus funds accumulated in large part from a decline in the demand on the part of business establishments for short-term credit. Second, a higher return could be realized on the term loans than on the usual business loan.

Third, the Securities Act of 1933 made it more difficult for the corporations of the nation to secure money through public distribution of securities, and the incentive was strong for business corporations to negotiate directly with banks to finance their intermediate-term capital needs. Fourth, the commercial banks were encouraged by the federal government to engage in this type of lending activity. This encouragement took the form of direct recommendations, which were reflected in the reports of bank examiners. Finally, the term loan provided banks with an alternative to investment in the securities of the federal government and of the states and municipalities. The yields on government securities had been reduced to unprecedented lows.

In the post-World War II period, the American Bankers Association lent its support to the term lending arrangement and encouraged its members to explore more fully the potential offered by such loans. By 1940 the tremendous growth and popularity of term loans had established them as one of the most important lending innovations by the banks of the nation. During World War II, term lending declined because of the inability of businesses to establish long-range plans for expansion and because special governmental lending programs were established to care for the financing of war production. In the postwar period, however, the volume of such loans increased at a very rapid rate.

Today term loans represent an important long-term source of funds for businesses. Table 11-1 in Chapter 11 shows that in recent years term bank loans have provided over $10 billion annually in funds to business corporations and often are within a few billions of dollars of the annual supply of short-term bank loans. Term loans rank third behind new bond issues and mortgages as an annual source of long-term funds for business corporations.

The Term Loan Agreement

The *term loan agreement* takes the form of a detailed written contract between the bank and the borrower. Term loans may be secured by specific property as collateral or they may be unsecured, depending upon the situation that prevails in each case. Among other things, the bank frequently requires a business to maintain a certain minimum amount of net working capital. In the event the net working capital of the business should fall below the stipulated amount, dividends or the salaries of executives may be reduced or curtailed until the appropriate level of net working capital is reestablished.

It is also frequently stipulated in the agreement that the business is not to dispose of its fixed assets without the permission of the bank or to incur other indebtedness without specific permission. Another common provision is that insurance must be carried on the lives of key individuals in the business with the bank as beneficiary. Some banks carry blanket insurance policies on the lives of executives of companies receiving term loans. Another requirement may be that changes in management personnel, changes in production methods or items of production, and increases in executive salaries or bonuses be approved by the bank before being undertaken by the business.

Despite the restrictive nature of the many protective covenants that usually accompany the term loan, business people have generally found the arrangement to their advantage. In any event, the protective covenants establish only fair and reasonable protection against undesirable business activities of management. Also, the simplicity of the term loan arrangement, as well as its cost, renders it far more desirable under many circumstances than funds that may be secured through the public sale of securities or through other media.

Determining Term Loan Payments

The standard term loan arrangement calls for a constant periodic payment that will fully amortize or pay off the loan at maturity. In Chapter 10 we discussed the process for determining the periodic payment for an annuity. Our example used a $20,000, 10 percent, 3-year loan requiring annual payments. We solve for the annual payment for this term loan as follows:

$$\text{Annual Payment} = \frac{\text{PV Annuity}}{\text{PVIFA}}$$

$$= \frac{\$20,000}{2.487}$$

$$= \$8,042$$

Based on a present value interest factor of an annuity of 2.487 at 10 percent for 3 years, an annual payment of $8,042 would be needed to amortize the loan. For term loans requiring more frequent payments, such as quarterly or monthly, we would need more detailed present value annuity tables or we could use a financial calculator to determine the appropriate payment.

INVESTMENT COMPANIES

Investment companies engage principally in the purchase of stocks and bonds of other corporations.[1] The investment company permits the pooling of funds of many investors on a share basis for the primary purpose of obtaining expert management and wide diversification in security investments. Both the number and the size of investment companies have been increasing rapidly in recent years.

Development of Investment Companies

Forerunners of the modern investment company existed in the United States during the early part of the 19th century when insurance companies accepted funds from individuals and professionally administered them. Following World War I, the tremendous growth of the industry of the nation and interest in stock market activity in general gave support for the first time to large-scale development of the investment companies. Such companies in the United States were both victim and cause of the speculative excesses in the securities market during the 1920s, much like the situation at the close of the 19th century in Great Britain. Following the depression of the 1930s, the investment companies,

---

[1] Money market mutual funds, a form of investment company, also specialize in holding short-term commercial paper, bank CD's, and U.S. Treasury bills. However, our focus here is on long-term business financing sources.

strengthened by the introduction of a new form of operation, again attracted public attention and increased in numbers and strength.

Investment companies pool the savings of the public, provide professional investment management for such savings, and diversify investments. The funds of investment companies are invested principally in equity shares as well as corporate debt instruments in order to provide an increased return for the investor.

Classification of Investment Companies

The Securities and Exchange Commission classifies investment companies as either *management investment holding companies* or *management investment companies*. The first of these two groups operates for the purpose of influencing or controlling the companies in which it invests. The management investment companies invest for the primary purpose of securing diversification and yield. We are concerned only with the latter classification in this chapter.

Investment companies are also classified into the closed-end fund type and the open-end fund type. Although both types have the common objective of securing intelligent diversification for the pooled funds of individuals, the methods by which this objective is accomplished, as well as the way in which shares are purchased and exchanged, are different.

The Closed-End Fund Investment Company. The *closed-end fund investment company* places great emphasis on portfolio management. Ordinarily, the securities issued by a closed-end fund are sold at one time and additional securities seldom are issued. The total asset value of the closed-end fund increases only through the appreciation in the market value of the securities that is holds or through the retention of a small proportion of the earnings obtained by the company. The holder of the securities of a closed-end fund may liquidate investments much as the holder of a security in any corporation does, that is, through the sale of the securities to other investors.

Bonds and preferred stocks, as well as common stocks, may be issued by the closed-end fund company. The holders of these senior securities have the same relative priority to earnings as the holder of senior securities in any organization. The bonds issued by the closed-end fund, however, seldom represent a claim against specific securities held by the fund but rather take the debenture form. The holders of the debenture bonds of the closed-end funds, therefore, have only a general claim against the assets of the company. This arrangement makes possible the frequent sale and purchase of securities by the investment company without the necessity of securing a release of pledged collateral, as would be required if secured bonds were issued against the portfolio of securities. Today the assets of closed-end fund investment companies total less than $10 billion.

The Open-End Fund Investment Company. The *open-end fund investment companies*, commonly referred to as mutual funds, are of American origin. In contrast with closed-end funds, they generally offer only a single class of shares to investors. These shares, held by the public, may be returned to the company for redemption at any time. The bylaws or trust agreement of the investment company provides for the redemption of such shares at the liquidation or net asset value of the investment company. Hence, the price at which shares tendered for redemption to an investment company will be redeemed depends upon the market value of the securities held by the investment company. New shares are offered to the public continuously. The price of these new shares is determined, as is true for shares that are being redeemed, by the current value of the securities held by the investment company.

The shares of the open-end funds are generally sold at a price that includes a selling charge of from 7 to 9 percent with a prevailing average for all companies of about 8 percent. This means that the purchase of shares having a market value of $1,000 would require an additional fee or premium of approximately $80. As larger volumes of shares are purchased, the selling charge as a percentage of the purchase price is reduced accordingly. An increasing number of open-end funds are now available without a selling charge. Such funds are referred to as "no-loads."

Because the shares of the open-end funds are redeemable with the company, they are not listed on the exchanges. It is unnecessary to find other buyers for the shares when they can be promptly and easily redeemed by the investment company itself. In order to know the price at which shares should be redeemed or sold, the investment company must calculate at frequent intervals the total value of its portfolio of securities. Usually a formula that gives due weight to the amount of securities held in the different companies makes possible a quick and ready calculation of the total value of the portfolio. The legal form of organization taken by the open-end fund is generally that of the corporation or the business trust.

Open-end funds may differ radically with respect to objectives of management. In some cases, an extremely conservative portfolio is maintained, comprised largely of high-grade fixed-income senior securities of well-known companies. In other cases, the objective is to maximize the profits to be obtained through the purchase and sale of securities during changes in the market. Then, the bulk of the fund's investments is placed in common stocks. Between these extremes falls the objective of obtaining a somewhat above-average yield combined with reasonable stability of market value. This type of company objective is generally described as a "balanced-fund operation." Such portfolios generally include both bonds and stocks of leading companies.

Securities and Exchange Commission data indicate that open-end funds hold assets in the form of corporate stocks and bonds well in excess of $100 billion. However, rather than being major annual purchasers of new corporate bond and stock issues, mutual funds trade largely in the secondary securities markets which will be discussed in Chapter 13.

Tax Status of Investment Companies

Under the Revenue Act of 1936, corporations are subject to a tax on the dividends they receive. Strictly applied, this tax would make it difficult for investment companies to function in their present form, since it could mean triple taxation: taxation first of the operating corporation, again when the investment company receives its dividends or interest, and finally when these profits are distributed to the holders of the shares of the investment company. A special supplement (Supplement Q) to the Revenue Act of 1936, however, provides that under certain circumstances investment companies are considered as mere conduits through which earnings of a corporation flow to the ultimate shareholders of the investment companies. In order to be so regarded, the investment company must register with the Securities and Exchange Commission and otherwise qualify as a *regulated investment company*, exempt from federal corporate income taxes on earnings distributed to shareholders.

TRUST INSTITUTIONS

Trust institutions administer and control great amounts of wealth, and account for a significant portion of all securities purchased. A *trust institution* serves in a fiduciary capacity for the administration or disposition of assets and for the performance of specified acts for the beneficiaries of trust arrangements. A *fiduciary* is one who acts in a capacity of trust and undivided loyalty for another. It implies integrity and fidelity of the person or institution trusted, and it contemplates good faith rather than legal obligation as the dominant basis for transactions.

It was not until approximately 100 years ago that the institutional form of trustee became important. In earlier times, trust duties were performed primarily by family friends or attorneys. With the growth of the country and the growing complexity of legal and financial matters, however, it became increasingly difficult to find individuals capable of administering properly the matters required of trustees. The amount of trust business administered by individuals in the United States at the present time is of minor importance compared with that undertaken by trust companies and trust departments of banks.

Most of the estimated 3,000 corporations actively engaged in the trust business of the United States are also engaged in the banking business. This is accounted for by the fact that the experiences and skills required for banking and trust work are very much the same. Nearly half of all the corporations engaged in the trust business are national banks that operate trust departments. State-chartered banks account for most the remaining institutional trustees.

Classifications of Trusts

Trusts may be classified according to their functions. These functions may be broadly grouped between those of a personal trust nature and those of a corporate trust nature. Under both classifications, the functions are of tremendous importance to the financial structure of the economy in that they involve the transfer and the management of huge sums of money and the provision of services that make possible the administration of such wealth on the part of others. The personal trust is established for the direct benefit of one or more persons, while the corporate trust exists to handle certain affairs of corporations.

Personal Trust Business

Personal trust business is confined largely to the care of assets included in trust estates and to settling estates of deceased persons. The three principal types of personal trusts are living trusts, trusteeships under will, and insurance trusts.

Living Trusts.   In recent years there has been a tremendous increase in the number of living trusts, due to many factors. In the first place, a living trust is a convenient means of providing a reasonably assured income for a person's family without immediately conveying the property to the family. Under these circumstances, the beneficiary of the trust, who may be a widow or a minor child, will receive only the income from the trust principal during the term of the trust. The principal itself is conveyed to the beneficiary only upon the happening of some specified event set forth in the trust agreement. The trust agreement is often used by persons of advanced age who have reason to doubt their continuing ability to manage their financial affairs. In other cases, trusts may be established for the benefit of minor children or for persons who are incapable of managing their affairs for reasons of physical disability or mental incompetence. A business person may establish a trust that will provide a reasonably comfortable income for a specified period of years to protect against undue hardship that might result from a particularly risky business venture.

Under the laws of most states, living trusts can be revocable, irrevocable, or something in between that may be referred to as short-term trusts. As the term implies, a *revocable trust* is one in which the maker of the trust has the right to revoke the trust arrangement after its creation. Such an agreement makes it possible to plan the transfer of assets and reduces the time required in passing the property to the beneficiaries when the maker dies. Also, probate expenses may be reduced and the publicity of a will avoided by the use of a revocable trust.

An *irrevocable trust*, on the other hand, provides for the complete and final transfer of assets to the trustee. In addition to the advantages cited for the revocable trust, the irrevocable trust may involve substantial tax advantages. As a rule, the maker of the trust can be freed from taxation on the income from the assets transferred to the trust institution. In addition, the property in trust usually escapes estate taxes upon the death of the maker of the trust. The maker of such a trust must pay a gift tax on amounts placed in trust in excess of $10,000 annually for each beneficiary. Nevertheless, this limit allows a significant amount to be placed in trust over a period of years, free of estate or gift taxes.

A *short-term trust* represents a compromise between the revocable and irrevocable trust. In brief, it is an irrevocable trust established for a specified number of years. The reason for the establishment of the short-term trust is often for tax purposes. If the trust meets all of the requirements of the tax laws, the maker is free of tax on the income derived from the assets while the trust exists, assuming such income is paid to a person or institution other than the maker of the trust; and at the end of the trust term, the maker of the trust gets back the assets that have been placed in trust. Short-term trusts can be used for many purposes, such as the support of parents, contributions to charities, the accumulation of an estate for one's family, or carrying insurance on some other person's life.

Trusteeship Under Will.   The trusteeship under will represents a second major classification of personal trust business. For the person who prefers that his or her estate be maintained and administered for the benefit of heirs rather than be turned over to the heirs directly, a *testamentary trust* may be established. The person establishing such a trust is reasonably assured that beneficiaries will be properly cared for and at the same time will be protected against acts of irresponsibility with respect to administration of the estate. A trust institution may be designated as the executor in a will. The duties of the executor are, of course, handling the estate with respect to the accountability for all the assets, liquidating all of those assets of a perishable nature, paying all debts including tax claims that may exist against the estate, and distributing the assets of the estate in accordance with the provisions of the will. The trust institution may also act as administrator, guardian, or conservator under authority of a court appointment.

Insurance Trusts. The *insurance trust* represents a third classification of personal trust business. These trusts come into existence through the voluntary act of placing in trust one or more insurance policies with an agreement that the proceeds of the insurance will be paid to the trust institution upon the death of the maker of the trust. The trust institution is then, as a rule, bound by the terms of the agreement to administer the benefits of the insurance policies for the specified beneficiaries of the trust. Such an arrangement is generally provided when the maker of the trust has reason to doubt the ability of the beneficiary to handle properly the large sum of money that would otherwise accrue to the beneficiary under the terms of the life insurance policy.

Investment Policies of Trust Institutions

State laws that apply to the administration of trust funds are many and varied and are generally considered to be very restrictive. In addition to the law, the terms of the trust agreement itself may establish restrictive limitations on the trustee's management of the assets placed in trust. Traditionally, trust institutions have been required to limit the investment of assets placed in their trust to the securities on a legal list prepared by the state. Such a list includes only high-grade bonds and other designated fixed-income investments. Only a few states continue to impose restrictions of this nature on trust institutions. Most states now follow the *prudent-man rule*, which requires that a trust institution be held responsible for the same degree of judgment that a prudent person would exercise in investing personal funds, a substantial liberalization from the legal-list concept.

Estimates of trust assets held by commercial banks now exceed $400 billion. About one half of this total is in the form of common stock holdings.

The Common Trust Fund

Of particular importance to the administration of trust assets was the modification of the law to permit national banks to commingle the trust funds of their customers. Since one of the long established legal principles required that assets of separate trusts should not be mingled, this represented a major modification in trust administration activities. Amendments to the federal tax laws were also necessary in order that income from such invested assets would not be taxed as income to both the trust institution and the individuals named as beneficiaries of the trusts.

Although the assets invested under the common trust fund plan are subject to the same regulatory limitations as the investment of individual trust assets, substantial advantages are offered both to the trust institution and to the beneficiaries. One primary advantage is that the common trust fund makes it possible for trust institutions to solicit smaller trusts. Principal amounts of only a few thousand dollars placed under control of the trust institution under common trust agreement receive the same competent supervision as much larger trusts. Costs are reduced and greater diversification is obtained through the common trust arrangement than is possible for the individual handling of assets for small trusts. Total assets of the commingled trusts are administered under the centralized supervision of the investment section of the trust department. The common trust fund was established, as a matter of fact, primarily for the benefit of the smaller trusts. This is evidenced by the fact that originally under the regulations of the Federal Reserve System the maximum amount of any single trust which could be placed in a common trust fund was $25,000. This was raised successively to $50,000, $100,000, and then maximum limits were removed entirely, although few common trust accounts are for amounts in excess of $100,000.

Several trust companies offer three separate common trust funds. One of the funds will ordinarily have all of its assets invested in bonds, the second fund will have all of its assets in common stocks, and the third fund will have its assets in both bonds and common stocks. The person establishing the trust, therefore, may choose between a fund with emphasis primarily on stability of principal and a fund with emphasis on higher income and appreciation possibilities. Under this arrangement of multiple common trust funds, the similarity to the operations of investment companies becomes quite readily apparent.

In addition to the common trust fund operations of national banks, all states authorize state-chartered corporations engaged in trust business to operate common trust funds.

Trust Services for Corporations

Trust service for corporations is an important phase of the trust business since by law all corporations subject to regulation by the Securities and Exchange Commission must seek the services of trust corporations. One of the principal forms of trust service provided for corporations is that of *trusteeship under indenture*, referred to in Chapter 11. The duties of the trust institution when serving in a capacity of trusteeship under indenture generally involve the holding of the mortgage against which bonds are issued by the corporation and the enforcement and accountability of all provisions of the trust indenture.

Trust institutions also serve corporations as transfer agents to handle the details relating to the issuance and recording of stock transfers and as dividend disbursing agents to handle details relating to the distribution of dividends. Trust institutions may also serve corporations as registrars. Many of the stock exchanges require that corporations having stock listed on their exchanges maintain separate registrars and transfer agents. The registrar's responsibility, among other things, involves supervision over issuance of new stock of the corporation in order that the corporation will not issue more stock than is authorized by the charter. The transfer agent and the registrar, therefore, provide an effective check on each other's operations and assure that the security holder's interests are being responsibly administered.

In the event of corporate reorganization, it is customary for creditors, pending the final reorganization, to deposit bonds and other credit instruments with a corporate trustee. In return, they are given transferable certificates of deposit. The property of a corporation in bankruptcy is generally conveyed to a trust institution, which provides, if necessary, for the liquidation and the disbursement of funds to the creditors of the corporation.

Trust institutions maintain safe-deposit facilities, administer security holdings, provide complete records of all security transactions, make monthly reports to customers, and provide investment counsel. The numerous additional services provided by trust institutions for corporations cannot be covered in this text. Further reference, however, is made to trust activities later in this part in connection with corporate financing through the use of equipment trust obligations and in connection with pension funds.

LIFE INSURANCE COMPANIES

This section begins with a brief discussion of the importance of life insurance. Then we cover basic types of life insurance before considering life insurance companies as a source of long-term business funds. The characteristics and operations of life insurance companies are covered in Chapter 18.

Importance of Life Insurance

One of the most important functions of life insurance is that of providing an immediate estate for the dependents of the head of a household in the event of death before sufficient personal resources have been accumulated to provide for dependents. Where the amount of life insurance is quite small, the objective may be that of a "clean-up fund" which will defray the costs incident to the death of the insured.[2]

Life insurance may also play an important role in business affairs. For example, where the business organization is a partnership, it is frequently desirable to insure the lives of the partners and to specify the other members of the partnership as the beneficiaries. This arrangement permits the survivors in a partnership to buy the interest of the heirs of a deceased member without serious cash drain on the business. A business person may carry life insurance for the purpose of settling business debts that may exist at the time of death; and finally life insurance provides a means of minimizing the drain on an individual's estate as a result of taxes imposed upon business assets at the time of death.

Two thirds of the individuals in the United States own some form of life insurance. Life insurance in force now exceeds $4,000 billion—a figure that is diffi-

---

[2]Accident and sickness insurance also is an important form of personal insurance because it provides protection against loss of income and for coverage of hospital and surgical expenses. However, companies specializing in this form of insurance are not major suppliers of long-term business funds.

cult to comprehend in size. There are nearly 2,000 active life insurance companies currently operating in the United States.

Types of Life Insurance

The many applications of life insurance to special requirements and situations require the availability of a wide variety of types of policies. The principal types of contracts sold by life insurance companies are term insurance, whole life insurance, endowment insurance, and annuities.

Term Insurance. The basic feature of *term life insurance* is that the policy is issued for a specified period of time after which time no obligation exists on the part of the insurance company toward the insured. During the period of the insurance contract, however, the insured is entitled to protection to the extent of the face amount of the policy. Term life insurance policies are usually issued for one, five, ten, or twenty years.

Term life insurance is seldom recommended in its basic form as an appropriate contract for general family protection. Modifications of the basic form, including renewal privileges without further physical examination and privileges for conversion to more permanent forms of insurance, have added to the attractiveness of this form of insurance. Because no investment program is combined with term insurance, the annual premiums are less than for other types of insurance. But one of the major disadvantages of term insurance is that the premiums are based on standard mortality tables, and they increase as the age of the insured increases. Term life insurance provides much smaller capital accumulation for the insurance companies than do the other types of insurance discussed in the following pages, since the annual premiums correspond more directly to the basic cost of insurance protection and there is no savings or cash value component.

Whole Life Insurance. The *whole life insurance* policy differs from term insurance in that it combines an investment program with the insurance contract. The premiums are generally for a fixed sum each payment period throughout the life of the insured or for a specified number of years. That portion of the premium which applies toward the protection part of the contract represents only a small part of the annual premium during the early years of the contract. Much of the premium is credited toward the savings accumulation of the policyholder. This savings accumulation is referred to as the cash value of the policy. The accumulation of this investment portion of the insurance contract makes it possible for an individual to pay a level or fixed premium throughout life or a specified number of years despite the higher costs of insurance that accompany advancing age.

Endowment Insurance. Like the term plan of life insurance, *endowment insurance* is written for a specified number of years. In contrast, however, if the insured person survives to the end of the stipulated period, the face amount of the policy is payable to the insured. Such policies may be written as 20- or 30-year endowment contracts, or for such other time spans as may be desired. The endowment policy may involve a single premium to be paid immediately upon the writing of the contract with the endowment to be made at some specified future period. Some endowment policies provide for payments of benefits over a period of years rather than in a single lump sum. Such policies involve a combination of the endowment and annuity contracts.

Annuity Contracts. *Annuity insurance* has often been described as "insurance in reverse." The basic purpose of life insurance is to create an estate, while the annuity contract provides for the disposition of an estate through its systematic liquidation. Under an annuity contract, the annuitant agrees to pay a stipulated sum of money to the insurance company, either in the form of a single lump-sum payment or in a series of regular payments, in return for a regular income from the company for a specified time, such as a number of years or for life. Typically, annuities are purchased to meet the possibility that the buyers may outlive their earning periods and will need a regular income to sustain them in the years beyond retirement.

The Investment of Life Insurance Company Funds

Although life insurance companies usually are able to meet the payments for which they are obligated each year out of funds received from insurance premiums and from earnings on their investments, the companies maintain vast reserves. Through the investment of these reserves, the life insurance companies make their principal contribution to the flow of long-term capital in the economy. The investments customarily made by life insurance companies may be described as a *fixed income type* in which the purpose of investment is primarily one of safety of principal and stability of income. Such investments usually take the form of United States government securities, state and municipal bonds, the securities of business and industry, real estate mortgages, direct investment in real estate, and policy loans.

In recent years, there has been a slow but gradual liberalization of restrictive state laws as they apply to investments of life insurance companies. Among other things, these companies have been permitted to invest directly in such income-producing assets as housing projects, real estate for lease-back purposes, and, to a limited extent, common stocks. Although there has been considerable controversy about the merits of life insurance company investment in common stocks, most states now permit such investments.

Figure 11-1 in Chapter 11 indicated that business corporations annually obtain the majority of their new external long-term funds from mortgage loans and by issuing bonds. Life insurance companies are major purchasers of corporate bonds and business mortgage loans. Corporate bonds comprise over one third of U.S. life insurance company assets. Mortgage holdings account for about one fourth of total assets, with the majority being nonfarm, nonresidential mortgages. In addition, corporate common stocks currently constitute nearly 10 percent of life insurance company assets.[3]

---

[3]*Life Insurance Fact Book* (Washington: American Council of Life Insurance, 1982), pp. 68 and 82.

219

PROPERTY AND CASUALTY INSURANCE COMPANIES

Basically, the purpose of *property insurance* is either to protect the insured against loss arising out of physical damages to property or loss arising from damages to others for which the insured may be held liable. Property and casualty insurance companies currently have assets in excess of $100 billion. We will briefly discuss basic types of property insurance before considering these insurance companies as a source of long-term business funds.

Types of Property Insurance

For purposes of describing the types of property insurance, it will be convenient to follow the broad classification of fire, marine, and casualty and surety insurance.

Fire Insurance. The basic form of *fire insurance* offers protection to the insured against the destruction of physical property as a result of fire. In addition, fire insurance companies may write policies that protect against such related perils to property as explosion, windstorm, and riot. The fire insurance companies find these risks convenient to undertake, since it is often difficult to determine the extent to which damage results from these perils or from the fires that often follow such disasters.

Marine Insurance. Marine insurance is one of the oldest forms of commercial insurance. These policies were written originally to protect against the perils of the sea. Marine insurance later was extended to include protection over transportation of merchandise from the seller to the purchaser, including land transportation as well as marine transportation. A distinction is customarily made between insurance written on shipments over land by such carriers as railroads and trucks, which is referred to as *inland marine insurance*, and those that involve sea perils, referred to as *ocean marine insurance*.

Casualty and Surety Insurance. Casualty and surety insurance is of more recent origin than the other forms of insurance discussed. In brief, *casualty and surety insurance* may be assumed to include all forms of coverage not included as marine, fire, or life insurance. An example of casualty insurance is the well-known automobile liability insurance that owners of vehicles carry as protection against claims resulting from injuries to other persons. Another example of insurance of the casualty type is that offering protection against burglary or robbery. Other forms of casualty insurance include insurance of a business against excessive bad-debt loss as a result of sales to customers on open account and protection against the breakage of plate glass.

Business firms protect themselves against claims resulting from occupational accidents through the purchase of a form of casualty insurance known as *workmen's compensation and employers' liability insurance*. Under workmen's compensation laws of the various states, employers are liable for most of the accidents that take place in connection with their business operations. Workmen's compensation and employers' liability insurance assumes the expenses of compensation and provides for medical, surgical, and hospitalization requirements as determined by the compensation laws of the state.

The *surety contract* generally provides that one party, the surety company, becomes answerable to a third party, the insured, as a result of failure on the part of a second party to perform as required by contract. For example, the business person who contracts for the construction of a new building may secure a surety bond to protect against the failure of the contractor to complete the structure by a certain time, or to protect against unsatisfied claims of laborers or suppliers of materials as a result of failure of the contractor to meet obligations.

The *fidelity bond,* as a special form of surety contract, provides that the surety company reimburse employers for the losses incurred as a result of the dishonest acts of employees. Banks, savings and loan associations, and other businesses in which employees have access to large sums of money invariably carry fidelity bonds for protection.

The Investment of Property Insurance Company Funds

Property insurance, like life insurance, is big business. In order to provide an extra guaranty of ability to pay losses, property insurance companies maintain large capital funds. In addition, they have the reserves accumulated out of premiums that are collected on insurance policies in advance. All of these items provide the funds that must be invested and which in turn produce investment income for the companies.

Property and casualty insurance companies are substantially less active than life insurance companies in the annual purchase of new corporate bond issues. They generally focus more on holding government bonds. Neither do they have much interest in the purchase of business real estate mortgages. However, property and casualty insurance companies usually purchase larger amounts of corporate common stocks each year than do life insurance companies. Nearly one fourth of property insurance company total assets are in the form of common stock holdings.

BUSINESS CORPORATIONS

The business corporations of the nation not only are large users of funds but also play a significant part in providing long-term capital for other businesses. Such capital is provided in several ways. First of all, a corporation may invest capital in a subsidiary company for purposes of control. In other cases, a corporation may invest in the securities of another company when that company is an important supplier of materials to the investing company. Finally, large sums accumulated by the employee pension funds of corporations are invested primarily in long-term securities.

Employee Pension Fund Developments

The establishment of pension funds for the benefit of workers has been a part of the American economy for many years. A major form of pension planning today is that provided by the Social Security Act. Somewhat earlier than this act, the Railroad Retirement Act provided for a retirement benefit for railroad employees; and still other legislation provided for benefits for retired government employees. In recent years employers have shown a willingness to establish private pension plans for employees, generally as a supplement to the Federal Old-Age, Survivors, and Disability Insurance System.

Although the first private pension was adopted by the American Express Company in 1875, a large proportion of the private pension plans now in existence have been established since 1945. Their rapid development since that time has been due in part to union pressure and to the desire of employers to reduce labor turnover by providing greater economic security for their employees. Corporations were encouraged further to contribute toward pension funds because of high corporate profits taxes. Corporate pension contributions are treated as deductible business expenses for corporate income tax purposes.

It is estimated that there are over 500,000 private pension plans in existence in the United States today and they cover about one half of the civilian labor force. Government pension plans also cover many federal and state and local government employees.

The Investment of Pension Funds

The majority of large pension funds are administered by trust companies or trust departments of banks. These are primarily private noninsured pension funds. Life insurance companies handle private insured pension accounts, usually in the form of annuity contracts. In some cases, large private pension funds are administered by the companies directly.

The pools of savings channeled through pension plans are an important source of funds in the capital markets. Private noninsured pension funds and state and local retirement funds are major purchasers of new corporate bond and stock issues. In recent years, state and local government pension plans have focused relatively more on the purchase of corporate bonds than corporate stocks. The reverse has been true for private noninsured pension funds with their greater concentration on corporate stocks. More than one half of the over $200 billion in total assets held by private noninsured pension funds are in the form of common stocks, while corporate bonds make up about one fifth of their assets.

Trust institutions have generally avoided investing substantially in the securities of corporations from which such funds have been derived, partly as a matter of sound financial policy and partly as a result of certain requirements on such investments imposed by the United States Treasury Department. Pension funds managed by life insurance companies are invested largely in corporate debt securities, residential and commercial real estate mortgages, and common stocks.

Recent legislation in most states allows life insurance companies to maintain separate investment accounts, each set up for a given pension plan or group of plans. Considerably more investment latitude is permitted for these separate accounts than in life insurance investments generally.

DEVELOPMENT COMPANIES

There are a variety of organizations which exist for the purpose of providing equity capital or long-term loans to new businesses or to small businesses which would find it difficult to raise capital through other sources. Some of these organizations are organized for profit, while others have the goal of developing the economy of a particular area; some receive the assistance of various levels of government, while others operate entirely on private funds. But a common thread runs through all of these development companies—they are designed to enable businesses with good prospects of success but without adequate financial resources to become established, as well as to permit established companies to expand. Although the total amount of long-term funds provided to business through these development companies is not large compared with the total of business credit, it does represent a strategic outlay of funds for the establishment of new businesses and permits the growth of established businesses that are handicapped by a lack of adequate financial resources.

Regional and *local development companies* are usually funded by local citizens and business firms or associations, and sometimes receive assistance from local governments. Their aim is to improve the economy and promote business growth in their area. State development companies are chartered for similar purposes by special state legislation. Although privately capitalized, both local and state development companies increase their leverage by borrowing, using the proceeds to make long-term loans or purchase equity shares of small businesses. The Small Business Administration has a special loan program to assist local and state development companies.

The Small Business Administration is also authorized to license and regulate privately owned *small business investment companies* (SBIC's). These companies are established for profit, and the securities of many SBIC's are actively traded in the securities markets.

An important attraction to the promoters and owners of the SBIC's is the liberal tax treatment to which they are entitled. An SBIC may exempt from corporate income taxes the dividends it receives from investments in small businesses. Both the SBIC and its stockholders may apply against ordinary income any losses sustained from price decline in debentures purchased from small firms, in stock obtained through conversion of such debentures, or in stock obtained through the exercising of stock purchase warrants. Any profits that have accrued can be taxed as capital gains.

An SBIC may finance a small business through the purchase of debentures that are convertible into stock of the small firm, by the purchase of capital stock or debt securities, or through a long-term loan. Although privately capitalized, an SBIC may increase its financial leverage by borrowing from the SBA.

A small group of similar development companies exists entirely independent of the SBA or other government involvement. These companies, in most cases, represent the association of a few wealthy persons interested in taking advantage of growth opportunities of selected speculative enterprises. These venture capital companies, commonly referred to as *investment development companies*, are privately established profit-seeking organizations whose primary function is to provide venture capital not otherwise available to new and growing business ventures. They usually supply equity capital, but some loan capital has been provided when its use seemed appropriate.

In addition to providing the financial backing for new companies, the investment development companies take an active and continuing interest in the companies they finance although they do not necessarily require voting control. They offer expert management counsel and guidance and continuing financial assistance as the companies pass through the various stages of their development. Investments are usually disposed of by the investment development companies when the success of the venture that has been financed is assured and the securities can be sold at a substantial profit.

LEASE ARRANGEMENTS AND EQUIPMENT TRUST FINANCING

The lease arrangement and equipment trust financing do not represent special types of credit flowing from any single form of financial institution; rather, they represent a type of financing arrangement that may be utilized in connection with existing financial institutions.

The Lease Arrangement

It has been estimated that more than 80 percent of all retail establishments rent their places of business under lease arrangements. Many manufacturing corporations also find it to their advantage to rent their plant facilities. One refinement of the typical lease arrangement is that of the construction of certain facilities for the specific use of a particular company. For example, Safeway Stores tries to interest local real estate groups and other persons with the necessary capital to construct buildings to their specifications. After construction, such buildings are leased to Safeway for a period of years in accordance with a predetermined agreement. Through this means the company is benefited by the acquisition of new retail facilities without having to make an outlay of cash or to increase its corporate indebtedness.

The lease arrangement is not confined to real estate transactions, and its use has now extended far down the line through the equipment and other facilities of some firms. For example, insurance companies and other types of financial institutions now lease fleets of automobiles and trucks to many of the nation's leading corporations. The increasing use of containers for surface ship transportation has resulted in an extraordinary demand for containers and sources of financing for them. Container leasing has now become significant in volume as their use has been extended from an original emphasis on household furniture to such bulk commodities as fertilizers, cotton, hides, and manufactured products.

The lease arrangement has also found an important use in the electric utility industry. More than 20 companies now lease their nuclear fuel supply or "nuclear cores" for their nuclear power production facilities. Nuclear power production facilities cost billions of dollars at this time and the leasing of the fuel supply represents an attractive form of financing a portion of the required investment.

Municipal Leasing. The lease financing of factories through municipal bonds is especially popular. The process involves the construction of plant facilities by a municipality to the specifications of an industrial firm. Financing is arranged through the sale of municipal bonds known as *industrial revenue bonds* to the general public or to individual financial institutions. The plant facilities are leased to the industrial company for a period of years at a rental high enough to cover the interest and retirement of the bonds, plus a small reserve. The advantage to the municipality lies in the attraction of desirable industry. The company is benefited by having at its disposal new and modern physical facilities without an immediate outlay of funds except reasonable rental fees. The fact that interest to the purchasers of municipal bonds is free from federal income tax liability and often from state income tax liability makes it possible for the municipality to sell its bonds at a much lower cost than could a private corporation. This in turn makes it possible for the municipality to establish a low and attractive rental fee for the tenant corporation.

The popularity and rapid growth of this financial device has led to its severe curtailment by the federal government. The tax exemptions in this type of industrial aid enabled many large, prosperous firms to obtain low-cost financing. At the same time, the federal government was losing tax revenues from many well-to-do individuals and corporations who purchased these bonds. Federal legislation now eliminates the tax-exempt status of most new issues of industrial revenue bonds of over $10 million.

The Sale and Lease-Back Arrangement. Another lease arrangement involves the sale of property owned by a company and its lease back to the selling company. One important reason for this sale and lease-back arrangement is to acquire additional working capital for business operations. Funds obtained from the sale of fixed assets may be used to take advantage of opportunities at times when a firm finds it either impossible or undesirable to increase the debt or equity of the business. The earnings resulting from the application of these funds may far outweigh the rental cost of the facilities that the company has sold. Also, the rental that is paid thereafter to the new owner of the property is considered to be an expense and, as such, is chargeable against earnings for income tax purposes. In addition to the benefits that may accrue to a company with respect to its working capital position, the sale of fixed assets often makes possible the retirement of existing debt that may be carried against such assets on the balance sheet. Under these circumstances, the capital structure of the firm is simplified, which may result in a stronger credit position.

As a rule, under the sale and lease-back arrangement, the lessee (the user of the property) is required to carry an appropriate amount of property insurance, to pay property taxes that may be levied upon the property, and otherwise to maintain the property as if he or she were the owner.

Equipment Trust Financing

An important method of financing the purchase of heavy rolling stock, such as locomotives and tank cars, by railroads, and expensive equipment in general by other types of businesses, is that of the *equipment trust arrangement*. As an alternative to the outright purchase of rolling stock, this device provides for the transfer of title to the equipment by the seller to a trustee. The trustee, generally a trust company or a trust department of a commercial bank, holds title to the equipment but leases it to the business that is to make use of it.

The lessee usually pays from 20 to 25 percent of the cost of the equipment as an initial rental payment. This is comparable to the down payment that is customarily made in connection with a direct purchase. The balance of the cost of the equipment is financed through the sale of *equipment trust obligations* issued by the trustee against the collateral value of the equipment to which the trustee holds title.

It is generally the responsibility of the lessee to maintain the equipment properly, to pay all taxes and insurance charges, and to keep the trustee informed of the location and the condition of the equipment. After the stipulated number of rental payments has been made, title to the equipment is turned over to the lessee. The periodic lease or rental payment is used by the trustee to pay interest on and gradually retire outstanding obligations. When a railroad acquires rolling stock under this arrangement, a metal plate showing the name of the trust institution that holds title to the property is usually attached to each piece of equipment.

Equipment trust obligations have an extremely favorable investment rating, and very few losses on them have been recorded in recent decades. This excellent record of equipment trust obligations has resulted in part from the fact that the rolling stock of railroads has been in extremely short supply in recent decades, and a trustee can easily reclaim the equipment for the benefit of the holders of the equipment obligations in the event of a default on the part of the railroads. In earlier years, a great proportion of the railroads of the country found it necessary to default on their other fixed financial charges, but they have been loath to miss the regular rental payments on the equipment acquired through the equipment trust obligations device, since loss of the equipment would generally impair seriously the efficiency of operations.

Although this financial arrangement came into existence originally as a result of the need of the weaker railroads to obtain new rolling stock, it is now the typical process by which railroads acquire rolling stock. Equipment trust financing is also used by oil companies for the purchase of tank cars and by air transport companies for the acquisition of airplanes.

QUESTIONS

1. How do commercial bank term loans differ from loans made under regular lines of credit?
2. What benefits do investment companies offer to investors?
3. Identify basic differences between the closed-end fund and the open-end fund types of investment companies.
4. Briefly describe the three principal types of personal trusts. Also describe the meaning of a common trust fund.
5. What trust services are performed for corporations?
6. Identify and describe the principal types of life insurance.
7. Describe the importance of life insurance companies as suppliers of long-term business funds.
8. What are the major types of property insurance? How do property and casualty insurance companies provide long-term funds to business corporations?
9. To some extent business corporations are both suppliers as well as users of long-term business financing. Explain.
10. Briefly describe the development of pension funds and indicate their investment strategies.
11. What are regional development companies? How do they differ from investment development companies?
12. What are small business investment companies? Distinguish between the activities of SBIC's and those of the Small Business Administration.
13. Describe the special features of municipal leasing as a financial device to attract industry. Also indicate what is meant by a sale and lease-back arrangement.
14. Describe the mechanics of financing long-term equipment requirements through the use of the equipment trust arrangement.

PROBLEMS

1. Assume that you have been asked by the president of your firm to obtain a $50,000 term loan from the Third National Bank. The commercial loan officer agrees to a 5-year loan at a 12 percent interest rate and will require annual payments. Determine the amount that your firm will have to pay at the end of each year. How would the annual payments have changed if the loan had been for 6 years at a 14 percent interest rate? (Use the PVIFA table in the Appendix.)
2. A term loan from a local commercial bank is available in the amount of $100,000. It will be a 16 percent, 4-year loan requiring annual payments.
   a. What would be the size of the annual payment needed to fully amortize the term loan? Make use of the PVIFA table in the Appendix.
   b. Prepare a loan amortization schedule for this loan. Refer to Table 10-5 in Chapter 10.
   c. What will be the total amount of interest and principal repayments over the life of the term loan?

SUGGESTED READINGS

Greene, Mark R., and James S. Trieschmann. *Risk and Insurance,* 5th ed. Cincinnati: South-Western Publishing Co., 1981.

Harless, Doris E. *Nonbank Financial Institutions.* Federal Reserve Bank of Richmond, 1975.

Investment Companies. New York: Wiesenberger Financial Services, published annually by the Wiesenberger Investment Company Service.

Johnson, Robert W., and Ronald W. Melicher. *Financial Management,* 5th ed. Boston: Allyn and Bacon, Inc., 1982. Chapter 17.

Life Insurance Fact Book. Washington: American Council of Life Insurance, published annually.

"The Equipment Leasing Industry and the Emerging Role of Banking Organizations." *New England Economic Review,* Federal Reserve Bank of Boston (November/December, 1973), pp. 3–30.

Vanderwicken, Peter. "The Powerful Logic of the Leasing Boom." *Fortune* (November, 1973), pp. 132–140.

13 Markets for Long-term Business Funds

This chapter explores the processes by which the borrowers and the lenders of long-term capital are brought together. Specifically, it describes the activities of the investment bankers as they relate to the origination, distribution, and sale of long-term corporate securities and the activities of the over-the-counter market and securities exchanges in serving as facilitating media for the transfer of outstanding securities.

INVESTMENT BANKING

The process of marketing to the general public securities issued by private corporations is complicated and time-consuming. Corporations usually find it convenient to use independent distributors in selling their products; they find it even more to their advantage to utilize the services of professional groups whose primary activity is that of marketing securities. The average corporation has infrequent occasion to issue long-term securities, and the technicalities of such issues are so great that it is difficult for corporate executives to keep abreast of legal requirements or investor attitudes.

The groups whose function it is to market long-term securities are generally referred to as *investment bankers*. These investment bankers, therefore, are the middlemen between corporations and the general public in the accumulation of investment funds. The legal form of organization used for investment banking purposes includes both the partnership and the corporation.

Functions of Investment Bankers

Although the specific activities of investment bankers may differ, depending upon the size and the financial resources of the company, the primary functions of investment banking in general are:

1. Originating
2. Purchasing and underwriting
3. Selling

Originating. The investment banker assists the issuing corporation by recommending the types and the terms of securities that should be sold and by aiding the corporation in the registration processes required by the Securities and Exchange Commission. Before an investment banking firm undertakes to originate an issue of securities, it makes a detailed study of the corporation in order to determine the feasibility of security distribution. Most of the larger investment banking firms engage in the originating function.

Purchasing and Underwriting. Investment bankers not only offer the facilities through which securities are channeled to the investing public, but they also assume the risk arising from the possibility that such securities may not be purchased by investors. To accomplish this, they enter into a purchase agreement with the issuing corporation. The securities are purchased in their entirety by the investment bankers, then offered for sale to investors at a price sufficiently higher than their cost to provide a profit from operations.

Under the laws of several states, when a corporation issues additional shares of voting stock or any security that may be converted into voting stock, such securities must be offered for sale first to the existing holders of voting stock in the corporation. The purpose of this regulation is to permit existing stockholders to maintain their proportions of voting power and their claims to assets and earnings of the company. This priority is referred to as the *preemptive right*. Corporate charters may provide for such priority on the part of existing stockholders in states that do not require it. To make the new issues of securities attractive to existing stockholders, the company will generally offer the securities at a discount from the market price.

It may appear, then, that the investment bankers serve their purpose only with respect to the initial issue of securities for public sale by a company and that subsequent issues are simply offered to the holders of the company's earlier issues of voting stock. Despite the discount price at which new issues of securities may be offered to a company's existing stockholders, however, a severe break in the market price of the stock during the period when the additional stock is being issued may eliminate the company-established discount from market price. Under this circumstance, investors will not be inclined to invest further in the company on the basis of the price of the securities set by the company. As a result, the company has an unsuccessful flotation and does not receive the money from the sale of securities on which it may have been depending to carry out its commitments.

In view of the uncertainty of success of an issue of securities, even when offered to existing stockholders at a discount price, the investment bankers may again enter the picture. The investment bankers enter into a *standby underwriting agreement* whereby they agree to purchase from the corporation all securities not taken by the stockholders or the public. This standby function of the investment bankers permits the corporation to proceed with its plans with the assurance of receiving its funds from the sale of securities, notwithstanding the uncertainties of the securities markets. The issuing corporation pays the investment bankers a fee for their assumption of the risk of an unsuccessful flotation of securities. Although there is a clear distinction between the purchasing and the standby underwriting activities of the investment bankers, the term "underwriting" is generally used to include both activities.

Another category of investment banking for corporations issuing securities is that of *best-effort selling*. Under this arrangement, the investment bankers make a best effort to sell the securities of the issuing corporation, but they assume no risk for a possible failure of the flotation. The investment bankers are paid a fee for those securities that they sell. Securities are handled on a best-effort basis for either of two reasons. First, the investment bankers may anticipate so much difficulty in selling the securities that they are unwilling to assume the underwriting risk; and second, the issue of securities may appear to be so certain of successful sale, because of the strength and reputation of the company, that the issuing company itself is willing to assume the risk of an unsuccessful flotation.

Selling. A few of the large investment banking houses confine their activities entirely to originating, underwriting or purchasing, and institutional selling, depending upon retail security dealers for sales to individuals. The majority of large investment banking houses, however, also maintain their own retail outlets for individual sales in the major cities of the country. In addition to the retail outlets maintained by the large investment banking firms, there are many independently owned and operated retail brokerage outlets of insufficient size and strength to engage in major originating and underwriting functions. Like the underwriters, they depend upon the resale of the securities for a price above their cost to cover their expenses and provide profit from operations.

The investment banking firm that is selected by a company to handle the distribution of its securities is called the originating house. It should be kept in mind, however, that much cooperation exists among investment bankers. For larger issues of securities several investment banking firms may work together in the originating function. Beyond cooperation in the originating function is a substantial degree of cooperation in the underwriting and selling functions. For large issues of securities, thirty or forty investment banking firms may be invited by the originating group to assume part of the risk of the underwriting and to share in the profits resulting from the sale of the securities. For very large issues two or three hundred firms may participate in the underwriting and distribution efforts.

Competitive Bidding

In contrast with industrial companies, where arrangements are typically negotiated between the company and the chosen investment banking group, governmental bodies generally require competitive bidding by investment banking houses before awarding issues for underwriting purposes. This is true also of railroad securities and of some public utilities. Under these circumstances, there may be little initial negotiation between the investment houses and the issuer. Rather, the issuer decides upon the size of issue and the type of security which it wishes to sell and invites the investment banking houses to offer bids for handling the securities. The investment banking group offering the highest price for the securities and providing information to indicate its ability to carry through a successful flotation of the securities will generally be awarded the contract. From that point on, the process of security distribution may be much like that of the handling of securities of an industrial corporation.

A great deal of controversy has existed with respect to the relative advantages and disadvantages of competitive bidding by investment banking houses. Investment bankers contend vigorously that the continuing counsel which they make available to the corporations served is essential to an economical and efficient distribution of the securities of such companies. Others contend that competitive bidding results in a higher price being paid to the issuer for the securities than would otherwise be the case. Much evidence has been presented by both sides, and it is safe to say that securities will continue to be distributed under both arrangements. During periods of rapidly rising interest rates and general uncertainty and distress in the capital markets—as we have experienced in recent years—negotiated contracts between the investment bankers and the corporate issuer are generally more desirable than competitive bids.

Market Stabilization

Investment bankers generally consider the stabilization of market prices for the securities they are attempting to sell to be an essential feature of their operations. Because the steady flow of the new securities to the market may depress the price temporarily, it is sometimes necessary to offer to buy back the securities at a fixed price in order to prevent a cumulative price drop. Although the action of investment bankers to stabilize the markets for the issues that they are distributing is sometimes regarded as a form of manipulation, its objective is the elimination rather than the creation of wide price fluctuations.

Although the Securities Exchange Act of 1934 prohibits manipulation of this sort on the part of all others, underwriters are permitted to engage in the activity for purposes of reasonably maintaining the price of the securities that they are marketing. When market stabilization is intended, however, it is necessary to state that fact in the information or *prospectus* that is provided for purchasers of registered securities.

Regulation of Investment Banking

Federal regulation of investment banking is administered primarily under the provisions of the Securities Act of 1933. The chief purposes of the Act are to provide full, fair, and accurate disclosure of the character of securities offered for sale in interstate commerce or through the mails and to prevent fraud in the sale of such securities. Disclosure is achieved by requiring the filing of a registration statement with the Securities and Exchange Commission and the delivery of a prospectus to prospective investors. The Securities and Exchange Commission does not pass upon the investment merits of securities, and it is illegal for a seller of securities to represent the Commission's approval of a registration statement as constituting a recommendation of investment quality. The philosophy underlying the Act is that the most effective regulatory device is the requirement of furnishing complete and accurate information on which investment decisions may be made. Although the Securities and Exchange Commission does not guarantee the accuracy of any statement made by an issuer of securities in a registration statement or prospectus, legal action may be taken against officers and other representatives of the issuing company for any incorrect statements and misrepresentations.

In addition to federal regulation of investment banking, most of the states have blue-sky laws to protect investors from fraudulent security offerings. *Blue-sky laws* apparently receive their name from the efforts of some unscrupulous operators to sell portions of the blue sky—operators for whom the sky is the limit in their security dealings. Because the laws of the various states differ with respect to the specific nature of regulation of security selling, the efforts of the states are limited in their effectiveness by the difficulties of administering interstate security operations. Thus, the regulatory actions of the federal government provide the principal basis for regulation of investment banking.

OVER-THE-COUNTER MARKET

The security houses that make up the over-the-counter market not only distribute new securities to the investing public but also provide a secondary market for securities for the public in general; that is, they stand ready to buy as well as sell securities. It is important at this point to distinguish between over-the-counter operations and security exchange operations.

In the over-the-counter markets, securities are purchased and sold by dealers who act as principals. They buy from and sell to the public, other dealers, and commission brokers for their own account. In a sense, they operate in somewhat the manner of any merchant; they have an inventory, comprised of the securities in which they specialize, which they hope to sell at a figure high enough above the purchase price to provide a profit.

The security exchanges, discussed later in this chapter, provide only facilities where members may buy and sell securities among themselves. The nonmember investor does not have access to the floor of the exchange, and so must secure the services of a person or firm that does have membership and floor-trading privileges. The brokers that represent the public in floor-trading activities on the exchange serve as agents and hence must represent their customers to the best of their ability.

Securities Traded in the Over-the-Counter Market

Among the securities handled exclusively through the over-the-counter market may be included real estate bonds, Federal Land Bank and Federal Home Loan Bank bonds, state bonds, municipal bonds, equipment trust obligations, and bank and insurance company stocks. In addition, the over-the-counter market handles the securities of many industrial and utility corporations. Some securities of industrial, utility, and railroad companies are handled both on the exchanges and through the over-the-counter market.

Making a Market

When an over-the-counter dealer stands ready to buy or sell a particular security or group of securities at specified prices, the dealer is said to be *making a market* for the security. The quotation which is made by a dealer making a market for a given security is referred to as the *bid-and-asked price*, the bid being that price the dealer is willing to pay for the securities and the asked price being the figure at which the dealer is willing to sell the security. Hence, the margin or spread between bid and asked price for a security is readily apparent from its quotations. Quotations shown in Table 13-1 indicate the spread for a few of the over-the-counter issues as of June 23, 1983.

A security that is traded frequently and has a ready market can be expected to have a narrower spread than a security that is traded infrequently. Since an over-the-counter dealer cannot make a market for the many thousands of securities in existence, the dealer's activities are confined to a limited number of securities. In earlier times this meant that the broker, following instructions of the customer to buy or sell a particular stock, may have had to contact several known dealers in a stock for the best possible price. At the present time this may be necessary only for the securities of small companies whose securities are seldom traded. The National Association of Securities Dealers Automatic Quotations, referred to as NASDAQ, serves the over-the-counter market by making available immediately the quotations of all market makers in the principal stocks traded over-the-counter. The broker can now, through this electronic system, identify the dealer that is offering the best price, phone the dealer to determine if the quotation remains

Table 13-1
Selected Over-the-Counter Quotations

	June 23, 1983	
	BID	ASKED
AM Cable TV	11⅜	11½
Bankers Trust	34¾	35
Barber-Greene	15¾	16¼
ChemLawn	48	48¾
Dinner Bell Foods	10	11
Fluorocarbon Co.	14¼	14⅝
Harper & Row, Publishers	17	18⅜
Intertherm, Inc.	20½	21
Laclede Steel	14¼	14⅝
Magma Power	8¼	8⅜
Multimedia, Inc.	42¼	42¾
Otter Tail Power	22⅝	22⅞
Shopsmith, Inc.	10½	11¼
Trico Products	36	37½
Tyson Foods	13	13¼
Vulcan Industrial Packaging	4⅝	4¾
Zenith Labs	18½	19¼

SOURCE: NASDAQ System

firm, and then complete the purchase or sale through that dealer. During 1982 a new National Market System was instituted. This system will eventually accommodate as many as 2,000 NASDAQ securities in which high, low, and closing trade prices and continually updated volume figures will be available to brokers. Such information is made available for publication in newspaper stock tables.

Regulation of the Over-the-Counter Market

Under the Securities Exchange Act of 1934, all brokers and dealers doing business in interstate commerce must be registered with the Securities Exchange Commission. Under the Maloney Act of 1938, brokers and dealers were authorized to form national associations to govern and to establish practices of fair trade for their industry. This was one instance where regulation was requested of the government by business itself, and it appears to stem from the fact that reputable dealers in the investment field had little protection against bad publicity resulting from the unscrupulous practices of a few over-the-counter dealers. Under this provision only one such national association, the National Association of Security Dealers, has been formed.

The National Association of Security Dealers has established a lengthy set of rules and regulations intended to insure fair play and responsibility on the part of the member associations. Any broker or dealer engaged in that type of business is eligible to become a member of the NASD as long as a record of responsible operation can be proved and the broker or dealer is willing to accept the code of ethics provided by the NASD. At present approximately 3,100 registered security firms are members of the Association.

SECURITY EXCHANGES

At present there are 10 security exchanges in the United States including the Chicago Board Options Exchange. These exchanges are outgrowths of informal arrangements for trading in securities at convenient locations in the nation's cities. The New York Stock Exchange, for example, had its beginning under the shade of a certain buttonwood tree on Wall Street. At a later date, because of the popularity of this meeting place, traders began to transact business as agents of others. Eventually these traders moved indoors, and they now enjoy spacious and well-equipped quarters and facilities.

The stock exchanges of the nation have applied the latest developments in electronic communications. The present methods of transmitting information within cities and between cities is in sharp contrast with the devices used before the introduction of the telegraph in 1844. Quotations were conveyed between New York and Philadelphia through semaphore signals in the daytime and light signals at night from high point to high point across the state of New Jersey. Although cumbersome compared with modern methods, quotations were often transmitted in this manner in as short a time as ten minutes.

The stock exchanges appear to have come into existence primarily to facilitate trading in local issues; and although there are now only 10 such exchanges in operation, records indicate the existence of more than 100 exchanges during the nation's history. Of the 10 exchanges, only two may be considered to be truly national in scope: the New York Stock Exchange and the American Stock Exchange, both of which are located in New York City. Together these exchanges account for approximately 90 percent of the dollar volume of security trading on all exchanges. The relative importance of the security exchanges may be observed from Table 13-2, which shows the number of shares and market value of stock traded in a month's operation.

Because of the tremendous relative importance of the New York Stock Exchange and because in most respects its operations are typical of those of the other exchanges, the following description of exchange organization and activities will relate primarily to the New York Stock Exchange.

Exchange Organization

The New York Stock Exchange is a voluntary association of 1,366 members. Like all the stock exchanges of the nation, its objective is to provide a convenient meeting place where buyers and sellers of securities or their representatives may transact business. In addition, the New York Stock Exchange provides facilities for the settlement of exchange transactions, establishes rules relative to the trading processes and the activities of its members, provides publicity for the transactions on the Exchange, and establishes standards for the corporations whose securities are traded on the Exchange. The New York Stock Exchange, then, serves primarily to facilitate the transfer of outstanding securities from investor to investor, and in so doing it contributes significantly to the financial processes of the nation. The existence of a highly efficient secondary market in securities, as in most fields of activity, provides assurance to the purchaser of new securities that the investment can be readily sold should alternative investments appear more attractive or if funds are needed for other purposes.

Although the number of shares, or seats as they are commonly referred to, on the New York Stock Exchange was increased from 1,100 to its present level of

Table 13-2

Market Value and Volume of Equity Sales on U.S. Securities Exchanges, March 1983 (Data in Thousands)

REGISTERED STOCK EXCHANGES	Total Market $Value	Stocks		Options	
		$Value	Shares	$Value	Contracts
American	3,863,243	2,817,665	199,652	1,028,075	3,001
Boston	441,958	441,958	13,550	0	0
Chicago Option	2,170,080	0	0	2,170,080	5,444
Cincinnati	124,102	124,102	3,925	0	0
Midwest	4,255,314	4,255,314	118,576	0	0
New York	70,172,482	70,120,530	2,182,535	0	0
Pacific	2,761,605	2,428,906	107,408	331,144	1,037
Philadelphia	1,477,456	1,124,280	53,130	353,112	1,111
Intermountain	213	213	152	0	0
Spokane	2,071	2,071	1,603	0	0

SOURCE: *Statistical Bulletin*, United States Securities and Exchange Commission, May, 1983, p. 4.

1,366 in 1929, it is improbable that the number will soon be increased because the physical accommodations for trading activities are limited. As might be expected, membership shares carry a considerable value; and in order to purchase a share it is necessary to negotiate with other shareholders who may be willing to dispose of their membership. During the height of stock market activity in 1929, membership shares on the New York Stock Exchange sold for as much as $625,000, while in 1942 shares sold for as low as $17,000. The cost of shares in recent years has been within the range of $100,000 to $300,000. Memberships on the exchanges may be grouped into four classes: commission brokers, floor traders, specialists, and odd-lot dealers.

Commission Brokers. The largest group of members on the New York Stock Exchange, the *commission brokers*, maintain offices for the purpose of soliciting business from investors. Many members maintain offices throughout the country.

Floor Traders. *Floor traders* hold membership on the Exchange primarily for their own use. Not only do the floor traders avoid commission charges on their transactions by virtue of their access to the floor of the exchange, but also they are able to determine by direct contact with traders the temper and strength of the market for a security at a particular time. The speculative advantage of such a position is apparent. Because the floor traders are constantly in search of opportunities for even modest profits, their activities give breadth to the entire market. They provide bids and offers when they may not be available from other sources.

Specialists. *Specialists* buy and sell securities for their own account and generally limit their interest to a very few stocks. They also serve as floor brokers for other brokers who place transactions with them.

Odd-lot Dealers. The *odd-lot dealers* facilitate the purchase and sale of securities in less than round lots. Since the customary trading unit on the Exchange is a round lot of 100 shares of stock, the commission broker who receives an order to buy or sell stock in quantities of less than 100 shares must complete the order in a different way than that used for round-lot orders.[1] The odd-lot dealer "makes" a market for these fractional orders by buying full units of a security through the regular trading facilities and selling these securities in odd lots. Similarly, odd lots that are purchased by these dealers are accumulated until they can be resold as full units. For this service the odd-lot dealers charge a commission which is in addition to the commission that the customer would otherwise pay if dealing in lots of 100 shares.

Listing Securities

The New York Stock Exchange requires that all securities be listed before they may be traded on the Exchange. To qualify for listing its security on the Exchange, a corporation must show evidence of its strength and of interest in its

---

[1] For a very few stocks listed on the New York Stock Exchange, the round lot is 10 shares.

security on the part of investors throughout the nation. The corporation agrees to certain requirements stipulated by the Exchange with regard to the publication of periodic reports and the preparation of such other information for public distribution as will make possible an intelligent analysis of the security. If the security is accepted for listing by the Exchange, the corporation then pays a fee for the privilege. The acceptance of the security for listing on the "big board" does not constitute endorsement of the quality of the security by the Exchange. The common stocks of over 1500 corporations are listed on the New York Stock Exchange.

The American Stock Exchange and all of the regional exchanges permit unlisted trading privileges as well as listed trading privileges. The distinction between these two lies primarily in the method by which the security is placed on the exchange for trading. For unlisted securities, the intiative is taken by the exchange itself instead of the issuing corporation in recommending such securities for trading privileges. Unlisted trading privileges must be approved by the Securities and Exchange Commission. The securities of approximately 1,000 corporations carry unlisted trading privileges on the nation's stock exchanges.

Security Exchange Operations

Orders for the purchase or the sale of securities listed on the New York Stock Exchange may be placed with any one of the approximately 4,750 offices maintained for that purpose by members of the Exchange throughout the nation as well as in some foreign countries. In addition, orders may be placed with approximately 2,700 other firms that have correspondent relations with members of the Exchange. The larger firms maintain an electronic board on which security prices are flashed for the customer's observation. Within the city of New York it is possible to dial the telephone for quotations on leading securities.

Market Orders. The firm that receives an order to purchase shares of stock listed on the New York Stock Exchange at the best price immediately available wires the order to the New York office of the firm, where the order is transmitted to the floor of the Exchange. An order for immediate execution at the best possible price is referred to as a *market order.*

When a transaction takes place, a ticker report is sent to the central computer system via direct electronic signals and, in turn, it is conveyed to display devices across the nation. A section of the ticker report and an explanation of the symbols are shown in Figure 13-1. This ticker report includes all transactions on the New York Stock Exchange as well as those of the Midwest Stock Exchange, Pacific Coast Exchange, Boston Exchange, and Cincinnati Exchange.

Ticker abbreviations appear on the upper line of the tape. Immediately below the last letter of the abbreviation are the number of shares and the price. When the sale is for a round lot of 100 shares, only the price is shown. For multiples of 100 shares from 200 through 900, the first digit of the sales figure is followed by an "s." All volume figures are shown for sales of 1,000 shares and over. The letters "ss" are used to separate the volume from the price for stocks traded in units of 10 rather than 100. Errors and corrections are written out.

Figure 13-1
Section of Ticker Report

DI	HLT	GM	LLT		PE
33	$29\frac{3}{4}$	$62\frac{3}{8}$	2s17		$1000s16\frac{3}{4}$

Explanation: Dresser Industries Incorporated, 100 shares sold at 33; Hilton Hotels, 100 shares sold at 29 ¾; General Motors, 100 shares sold at 62 ⅜; Long Island Lighting, 200 shares sold at 17; Philadelphia Electric Company, 1,000 shares sold at 16 ¾.

The purchase transaction is also sent by memorandum to the central office and then by wire to the brokerage office where the order was originally placed. Later the customer will receive a stock certificate indicating ownership of the stock. If the investor chooses, the stock may be bought in *street name,* that is, in the name of the brokerage firm. By so doing, the investor may sell the securities by simply phoning the broker without the necessity of signing and delivering the certificates.

In common use today in the brokerage houses of the nation are computerized devices that permit brokers to obtain the latest stock information for their customers. These devices, in effect, accumulate and store reported information and provide an immediate retrieval of the information upon call.

Limit Orders

As an alternative to the market order, the customer may establish a maximum price to be paid for the security, or, in the case of the sale of securities, a minimum price at which the security will be sold. When such limitations are placed upon the broker, the transaction is referred to as a *limit order.*

In our example, if a limited purchase order of 43 had been placed by the customer for the security in question, the order could not have been filled at that moment since other brokers were bidding as high as 43¼. The broker then would have waited until such time as a price of 43 or less became available. Usually, such limit orders away from the current market price are turned over to a specialist who enters it in a book and acts upon it for the commission broker when the price comes within the limit. Of course, if the price of the stock progressed upward rather than back down, the order would not be completed. Limit orders may be placed to expire at the end of one day, one week, one month, or on a G.T.C. (good-till-canceled) basis.

Stop-loss Orders. The holder of stock may limit possible loss or protect part of a past increase in the price of stock by placing a *stop-loss order* at a price a few points below the prevailing market price. In this way the stock is automatically offered for sale when the price of the security falls to the stop-loss price. For example, the purchaser of stock in our example may place a stop-loss order on the stock at a price of 40. The commission broker makes no effort to sell the stock until the price falls to that figure, whereupon it is sold for as high a price as possible. This type of order does not guarantee a price of 40 to the seller, since by the time the stock is actually sold, the price may have declined rapidly to well below 40.

Short Sales. The *short sale* may be defined as the sale of securities that the seller does not own but which are borrowed for the purpose in anticipation of a price decline in the security. In the event that a price decline does occur, the short seller covers the resulting short position by buying enough stock to repay the lender.

As an example of the operation of a short sale, assume that a person believes that the price of a certain security is going to fall. If the individual owns that particular stock, it may be disposed of as quickly as possible in order to avoid the loss. In addition, or alternatively, the situation may be turned to advantage by selling short, that is, by selling stock in excess of that held in the individual's portfolio. Short sales may be made by anyone who has established favorable customer relations with a brokerage firm. It is not necessary for the person's portfolio to contain the particular security.

Let us assume that 100 shares of a particular stock are to be sold short. The order is placed through the broker, who in turn arranges to borrow the necessary stock to be sold short. The brokerage house handling the order may secure the stock for the short sale from its other customers, with their permission. When the brokerage house is unable to draw upon its own customers' holdings for this purpose, it generally bargains with another brokerage house.

Having sold the securities which have been borrowed for that purpose, the brokerage house delivers to the lender of the securities the proceeds of the sale of the securities to be held by the lender as collateral. If the price at which the securities were sold was 50, then the proceeds from the sale of 100 shares, $5,000, would be turned over to the lender of the stocks. Regulation T of the Board of Governors of the Federal Reserve System, as well as regulations of the New York Stock Exchange, require the short seller to maintain a margin or deposit with the broker equivalent to a specified percentage of the value of the stock sold short. Loans of stock are callable on 24 hours' notice. If the short seller covers the short position at the end of thirty days by which time the stock has dropped to a price of 40, $4,000 is paid for 100 shares to be returned to the lender of the stock. The short seller receives the $5,000 that was posted as collateral and has a $1,000 profit from the transaction, minus brokerage fees. Should the price of the security move upward rather than downward, the short seller must, of course, cover the short position by paying more for the stock than the price at which it was sold, with the result that a loss rather than a gain is experienced.

Because short sales have an important effect on the market for securities, the SEC now regulates them.

Margin Purchases. Securities may be purchased by delivering to the broker only part of the purchase price and using the securities so purchased as collateral for a loan to make up the balance of the purchase price. This is known as *buying* *on the margin.* The purchaser of the securities need not arrange the financing personally since the brokerage houses have constant contact with banks for this purpose. If the price of the securities that have been offered as collateral begins to decline, the customer may be required to reduce the loan by paying additional cash or by placing additional securities as collateral. In the event of a continuing decline in the market for securities pledged as collateral and the failure of the customer to reestablish the required margin, the bank or brokerage house may sell the securities.

Because of the inflationary aspects of a large volume of margin trading, the federal government has limited the extent to which securities may be purchased under this arrangement. In earlier times it was unusual but possible for a person to buy securities by paying in only 10 percent of the purchase price and borrowing the remainder. The leverage that is obtained from such an action is obvious. If the individual should purchase securities having a market price of $10,000 by contributing only $1,000 in cash and by borrowing $9,000, a 10 percent increase in the price of the securities would increase their value to $11,000, which, if sold, would result in a 100 percent gain to the person making the margin purchase. Of course, if the market price should drop by 10 percent, the purchaser's entire investment is wiped out.

The Board of Governors of the Federal Reserve System has the responsibility for setting margin requirements. Since 1974 they have been set at 50 percent, although at times the requirement has been as high as 100 percent, which prohibits margin trading entirely.

THIRD AND FOURTH SECURITIES MARKETS

It should not be surprising that an activity as broad as the security market would give rise to special arrangements. One of these special arrangements, the so-called *third market* refers to a situation in which an over-the-counter dealer who is not a member of an exchange makes a market for a security listed on an exchange. This activity is limited almost entirely to institutional trading in fewer than two hundred major stocks. The ability of a dealer to compete against exchange trading determines the effectiveness of this type of activity.

The *fourth market* is even further removed from the world of organized securities trading. Under this arrangement certain large institutional investors may arrange purchases and sales of securities among themselves without the benefit of a broker or dealer. A third party is charged with responsibility for maintaining an electronic network among these institutions in which offers to buy or sell are made known to the group. Such offers are made by code and institutions wishing to accept a buy or sell offer know the identity of the other party only upon acceptance of the offer. The third party offering this inter-institutional transfer of securities facility is generally paid a flat fee. It has been argued by advocates of fourth market trading that transfers are often quicker and more economical.

OPTION MARKETS

Closely allied to the secondary markets for the exchange of outstanding securities are the markets for options. Most of us are acquainted with option arrangements of one sort or another. We may pay to the owner of real estate a certain amount of money in return for a contract to purchase the property within a certain time period at a specified price. If the purchaser of the option does not exercise the purchase privilege according to the terms of the contract, the option expires. A contract for the purchase of common stock may be similarly acquired, an arrangement customarily referred to as a *call* contract. In like manner, *put* contracts may be purchased which provide for the sale of a certain amount of stock within a specific time period and at a specified price. Until the Chicago Board Options Exchange introduced formalized trading options, however, the activity in option trading was at a relatively modest level. While the Chicago Board Options Exchange remains the dominant market, the American, Pacific, and Philadelphia Exchanges now deal in option contracts.

Traditionally, most individual investors were limited to put and call option purchases. Through the facilities of the organized exchanges the individual investor can now sell or create the options. The seller of option contracts is referred to as an option *writer*. As a buyer of option contracts, the investor may be looking for a potentially large profit for a relatively small investment. The option buyer knows precisely how much to risk. Sellers of options, however, are seeking an opportunity to increase the income from their investment. Speculation for profit or hedging for minimizing loss both play a role in the motivation of investors. The individual investor may be a writer at one time and a buyer of options at another time, depending on the analysis of market prospects.

CHANGES IN THE STRUCTURE OF THE STOCK MARKET

The Securities and Exchange Commission has for several years actively promoted major changes in the structure of stock market activities and institutions. Many of the changes recommended have met with resistance from existing interests as they attempt to appraise the effect such changes will have on their particular role in market activities. Skepticism also derives from a sincere concern with the desirability of some of the recommended programs.

The Securities and Exchange Commission believes that the technology is now at hand to link registered exchanges and over-the-counter markets electronically. In effect, the Commission would like to see the market for stocks take the form of one giant trading floor, all at the command of the broker. The broker would be able to tell which market has the best quote on each stock by punching the quotation machine. Bid and ask prices on covered stocks would be available in all markets. As of late 1982, 61 of the most active and prominent over-the-counter stocks had been added to the national market system along with stocks of the registered exchanges. It is anticipated that more over-the-counter stocks will be added from time to time.

Opponents of the plan offer strong arguments. It is claimed that not only will many existing market institutions be destroyed but that in the long run costs for the investor may be higher than under present market arrangements. Although many of the recommendations of the Commission have been adopted at this time and many more will be instituted, it is doubtful that the full system as recommended by the Commission will be implemented for many years.

REGULATION OF SECURITY TRADING

At the present time, corporations issuing securities for public distribution are subject to both state and federal regulation. Although state blue-sky laws are generally administered well, the very size of many corporations has rendered it necessary to have some form of national control over their activities. The basis of most federal regulation over security trading is the Securities Exchange Act of 1934. It was the purpose of the Act to facilitate the analysis of securities for investment purposes (1) by requiring that information pertinent to that end be made readily available to investors and other interested parties; (2) by maintaining fair and orderly markets and eliminating fraudulent acts, and by establishing rules for the activities of exchange members and others representing investors in the securities markets; (3) by limiting and regulating the use of credit in security trading; (4) by regulating the activities of officers of corporations and other insiders having access to information not available to the general public. These objectives are accomplished in part by requiring the registration of securities, exchanges, and broker dealers.

QUESTIONS

1. Why do corporations employ the services of investment bankers in distributing new issues of securities rather than distribute such securities through their own efforts?

2. Describe in detail each step of the investment banking process.

3. Discuss the assumption of risk by investment bankers in the process of marketing securities of corporations. How do investment bankers minimize their risks?

4. When additional stock of a company is to be offered to existing stockholders at a discount from the market price, why would the services of investment bankers be utilized?

5. Would competitive price bidding for securities by groups of investment bankers provide a higher price to the issuing company than would result from negotiations with investment bankers that knew in advance they were to be chosen to distribute the securities? Explain.

6. The over-the-counter market has been described as a secondary market. As a secondary market, what is the contribution of the over-the-counter market to the economic growth of the nation?

7. Describe some of the types of securities traded in the over-the-counter market.

8. Describe the steps involved in an over-the-counter transaction.

9. Explain how over-the-counter market operations are regulated.

10. Describe the types and nature of operations of the nation's securities exchanges.

11. List the various reasons for ownership of membership shares on one or more of the nation's stock exchanges.
12. Describe the steps involved in the completion of a round-lot market order on the New York Stock Exchange. How does the completion of an odd-lot order differ from that of a round-lot order?
13. Margin purchases of a security are usually made in expectation of a price rise. Short sales are made in expectation of a price drop. Explain.
14. Explain the motivation for an investor to purchase an option to sell common stock. What would be the motivation for writing or creating such an option?
15. Describe some of the changes taking place in the structure of stock market activities and institutions.

SUGGESTED READINGS

Buckley, Julian G. and Leo M. Loll. *The Over-the-Counter Securities Market*, 4th ed. Englewood Cliffs, New Jersey: Prentice-Hall, Inc., 1981.

Garbade, Kenneth. *Securities Markets*. New York: McGraw-Hill Book Company, 1982. Part 7.

Huang, Stanley. *Investment Analysis and Management*. Cambridge, Massachusetts: Winthrop Publishers, 1981. Chapters 2 and 3.

Johnson, Robert W. and Ronald W. Melicher. *Financial Management*, 5th ed. Boston: Allyn and Bacon, Inc., 1982. Chapters 15 and 16.

Reilly, Frank K. "Markets, Securities." *Encyclopedia of Professional Management*. New York: McGraw-Hill Book Company, 1978, pp. 724–731.

Tallman, Gary D., David F. Rush, and Ronald W. Melicher. "Competitive Versus Negotiated Underwriting Costs for Regulated Industries." *Financial Management* (Summer, 1974), pp. 49–55.

Weston, J. Fred, and Eugene F. Brigham. *Essentials of Managerial Finance,* 7th ed. Hinsdale, Illinois: The Dryden Press, 1982.

PART III

Financing Other Sectors of the Economy

14 Financing the Federal Government

The magnitude of the expenditures of the federal government is such that those of all other institutions and governments seem small in comparison. The financing of these expenditures is equally impressive. The federal government relies primarily on tax revenues to support its various expenditure programs. In addition, revenues for general expenditure purposes are received for the performance of specific services benefiting the person charged. Examples of these revenues include such things as postal receipts, rental receipts from federal housing projects, and charges for subsistence and quarters collected from some government personnel.

The federal government also receives substantial insurance trust revenues from contributions to such programs as Old-Age, Survivors, and Disability Insurance and, in turn, makes large disbursements from these revenues. Although these trust fund receipts and expenditures represent a tremendous flow of funds, it is primarily with the general revenues and expenditures of the federal government that we are here concerned. And finally, the federal government relies on borrowing to bridge the gap between revenues and expenditures. Since 1960 the federal government depended upon borrowed funds to support its program of expenditures in every year but one. The national debt increased accordingly.

EXPENDITURES AND RECEIPTS OF THE FEDERAL GOVERNMENT

For many years national defense expenditures constituted the largest single item in the budget. As a result of the slowdown in defense spending and the growth of general expenditures, however, the proportion of defense expenditures fell to second place in the 1970s. The most important expenditure items are those for the welfare of specific individual groups, under the heading of "income security." It is interesting to note that one of the smallest items in the budget is that of the general operations of the government itself. This item includes the operations of the judicial system, the executive branch, the Congress, all regulatory agencies, and most of the departments of government, with the exception of the Department of Defense. (See Table 14-1.)

As noted in the next chapter, local governments depend primarily on property taxes, while state governments depend largely on sales taxes and such special taxes as those on motor fuel, liquor, and tobacco products. In contrast, the federal government relies primarily on income taxes for its revenues. Personal income taxes provide approximately 46 percent of general revenue, and corporate taxes provide approximately 10 percent.

Table 14-1
Federal Budget Receipts by Source, Outlays by Function, and Total Public Debt (Millions of Dollars)

	Fiscal Years	
	1978	1981
BUDGET RECEIPTS	399,561	588,272
Individual income taxes	180,988	285,917
Corporation income taxes	59,952	61,137
Social insurance taxes	120,967	182,720
Excise taxes	18,376	40,839
Estate and gift taxes	5,285	6,787
Customs duties	6,573	8,083
Miscellaneous receipts	6,641	12,834
All other	778	956
BUDGET OUTLAYS	448,368	657,204
National defense	105,186	159,765
International affairs	5,922	11,130
General science, space, and technology	4,742	6,359
Energy	5,861	10,277
Natural resources and environment	10,925	13,525
Agriculture	7,731	5,572
Commerce and housing credit	3,331	3,946
Transportation	15,445	23,381
Community and regional development	11,070	9,394
Education, employment, and social services	26,463	31,402
Health	41,232	65,982
Income security	146,180	225,099
Veterans benefits and services	18,974	22,988
Administration of justice	3,802	4,698
General government	3,706	4,614
General purpose fiscal assistance	9,601	6,856
Interest	43,966	82,537
Allowances	—	—
Undistributed offsetting receipts	−15,772	−30,320
Total surplus or deficit (−)	−48,807	−57,932
OUTSTANDING DEBT, END OF PERIOD	780,425	1,003,941

SOURCE: Treasury Department and Office of Management and Budget.

THE BUDGET

Until 1968 the form of budget presented annually to Congress did not include the expenditures and receipts of the various trust funds of the federal government, such as those of Old-Age, Survivors, and Disability Insurance. As such it failed to reflect the full effect of government activity on the economy. Many economists preferred to use the so-called "cash budget" for analytical purposes. The cash budget recorded transactions with the public, including such items as trust fund expenditures and receipts. It was concerned primarily with cash transactions between the public and the federal government. But even the cash budget did not include all cash expenditures and receipts. For example, the various enterprises operated by the federal government were reflected on a net earnings or net deficit basis rather than on the basis of total expenditures and receipts.

In October, 1967, the President's Commission on Budget Concepts recommended the use of a new "unified budget" to replace all of the older budget concepts. This change has now been made with the result that the best features of the several previous budget concepts have been incorporated in the new budget. All receipts and expenditures are included on a consolidated cash basis. The "uni-budget" covers lending as well as spending, but these two categories are shown separately to facilitate analysis. Lending is included because of the obvious impact it has on the economy. It is separated from spending because it is believed that these two types of outlays differ significantly in their impact on economic activity.

The excess of total expenditures (excluding net lending) over total receipts reflects the deficit in expenditures. The relationship of total outlays relative to total receipts reflects the total budget surplus or deficit.

OFF-BUDGET FEDERAL OUTLAYS

Although the unified budget concept was designed to be comprehensive in coverage, since 1973 the activities of some federally funded agencies have been excluded from the budget totals. These off-budget agencies are now very large and growing. In 1981, net outlays were more than $23 billion, approximately 40 percent as large as the unified budget deficit for that year. The existence of off-budget agencies prevents the unified budget from completely achieving its objectives. Among the off-budget agencies are the United States Postal Service, the United States Railway Association, the Rural Telephone Bank, and the Federal Financing Bank. The Federal Financing Bank is by far the most important and active of the off-budget agencies, accounting for the bulk of the outlays of these agencies. There is some pressure for the return of outlays of these agencies to the basic budget; while some arguments can be marshaled for their continued off-budget status, a stronger case can be made for their inclusion in the basic budget. The existence of off-budget federal agencies adds confusion to the government's financial statements and it is acknowledged that programs financed outside the unified budget receive less congressional scrutiny than programs contained within the budget. This may explain the off-budget outlays' recent growth rate being higher than that for budget outlays. Lack of control has been of increasing concern.

DEBT FINANCING

As we have observed, the federal government obtains its funds for expenditures primarily through tax revenues. To the extent that such tax and other general revenues fail to meet the expenditures of the federal government, deficits are incurred. Although these deficits in most years have been of modest size relative to the level of government expenditures, their cumulative impact has resulted in a vast increase in the total federal debt. Although statutory debt limits have been set by Congress, it has been necessary to raise such limits at frequent intervals to accommodate the continuing deficits of the federal government. For example, on June 28, 1982, the President signed a bill raising the temporary public debt limit to $1,143.1 billion. Figure 14-1 vividly reveals the frequency of budgetary deficits over the course of the last 30 years.

While the federal debt continues to rise, it is important to recognize that the present debt stems primarily from the financing of war and defense efforts. The financial burden of war has increased with the cost of waging war, and each major conflict has made all previous wars inexpensive by comparison. It has been estimated that the per capita figure for debt following the Civil War was $78; following World War I, $240; and following World War II, $1,720.

In contrast with that of some nations, the federal debt of the United States is owned to a large extent by its own citizens and institutions. Indeed, part of our

Figure 14-1
Federal Budget

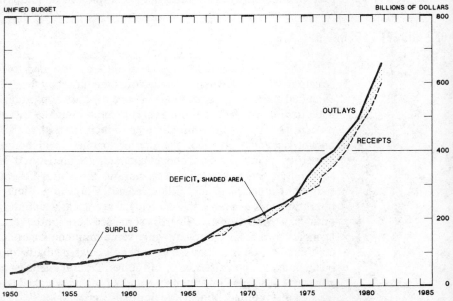

SOURCE: Board of Governors of the Federal Reserve System, *1982 Historical Chart Book*, p. 50.

debt is due to our role as a creditor nation, having advanced many billions of dollars to our foreign allies. This has not always been so, however, and until World War I, this nation depended heavily upon foreign investors for support of both government debt and nongovernment debt.

Nowhere in the economy is the significance of a smoothly functioning financial system more apparent than in connection with the federal debt. Not only does the financial system accommodate the federal government in the financing of its frequent budgetary deficits, but it also provides for the smooth transition from old debt issues that mature to the new issues that take the place of the old. The financial markets face a greater challenge in refunding government issues than in absorption of net new debt. Just as the nation's industrial development has depended upon an equally efficient development of financial institutions, so too, many of the financial activities of modern government depend upon the same institutions.

It is interesting to note that public borrowing is a relatively modern development. During the Middle Ages, governments were forced to borrow from wealthy merchants and others on an individual basis. Often crown jewels were offered as collateral for such advances. Large public borrowing by governments, as for businesses, became possible only with the refinement of monetary systems and the development of efficient financial institutions to facilitate the transfer of monetary savings.

In the following pages of this chapter, we are concerned with the manner in which the federal government finances its debt and the financial system that makes it possible. The impact of the federal debt on the economy of the nation is great indeed. These considerations are discussed at length in Part IV. It is important here to note only that the growth of the federal debt has taken place in the context of an expanding economy and that the burden of the debt is a function of the interest on the debt relative to the ability of the nation to pay.

OBLIGATIONS ISSUED BY THE UNITED STATES

The obligations that constitute the federal debt have become the largest and most important single class of investment instruments. These obligations dominate both short-term and long-term capital markets and play an important role in investment patterns of most financial institutions. Commercial banks, for example, invest heavily in short-term federal government obligations for liquidity and safety. The short-term obligations provide the investor with a near cash position and an income as well. Life insurance companies and pension funds invest heavily in long-term federal obligations for safety and income.

Because the obligations of the federal government are the highest quality available to any investor and because of the breadth of the market for these obligations, interest rates on all securities are geared to those of federal obligations. Table 14-2 reflects the rate structure for both selected short-term and long-term obligations. In both instances, the rate on the federal obligations becomes the base for the spread of rates. As the interest rates on federal obligations increase or decrease, there is pressure on other obligations for movement in a

Table 14-2
Money Market Rates
for Selected Obligations
April 29, 1983

SHORT-TERM OBLIGATIONS		
Three-month federal obligations (Treasury bills)	8.11	Percent
Prime bankers' acceptances—90 days	8.29	"
Prime commercial paper—3 months..............	8.33	"
Prime rate on short-term business loans	10.50	"
LONG-TERM OBLIGATIONS		
Government bonds—10 years....................	10.33	Percent
Aaa corporate bonds (highest grade).............	11.43	"
Baa corporate bonds (medium grade)	13.16	"

SOURCE: *Federal Reserve Bulletin* (May, 1983), pp. A27 and A28.

similar direction. The obligations issued by the federal government may be described as marketable, nonmarketable, and special issues. *Special issues* include those obligations issued specifically for ownership by government agencies and government trust funds. In addition to these direct issues of the federal government, the obligations of certain federal government controlled agencies are either general obligations of or guaranteed by the federal government. The Federal Financing Bank, created by Congress in December, 1973, coordinates under a single agency the marketing of several federal credit programs. Such programs as the Farmers Home Administration, Rural Electrification Administration, and Amtrak may issue their obligations to the Federal Financing Bank which, in turn, issues obligations to the public which are backed by the full faith and credit of the federal government. We are interested here, however, only in the marketable and nonmarketable direct issues of the federal government.

Marketable Obligations

Marketable securities, as the term implies, are those that may be purchased and sold through customary market channels. Markets for these obligations are maintained by large commercial banks and securities dealers. In addition, nearly all securities firms and commercial banks, large or small, will accommodate their customers' requirements for purchase and sale of federal obligations by routing such orders to institutions that do maintain markets in them. The investments of institutional investors and large personal investors in federal obligations are centered almost exclusively in the marketable issues. These marketable issues are bills, notes, and bonds, the differentiating factor being their maturity at time of issue. Although the maturity of an obligation is reduced as it remains in effect, the obligation continues to be referred to by its original descriptive title. Thus, a 30-year Treasury bond continues to be described in the quotation sheets as a bond throughout its life.

Treasury Bills. These Treasury obligations bear the shortest of the maturities and are typically issued for 91 days, with some issues carrying maturities of 182 days. Treasury bills are also issued at auction every 4 weeks with a maturity of one year. Issues of Treasury bills are offered each week by the Treasury to refund the part of the total volume of bills that matures. In effect, the 91-day treasury bills mature and are "rolled over" in 13 weeks, and each week approximately 1/13 of the total volume of such bills is refunded. Insofar as the flow of cash revenues into the Treasury is too small to meet expenditure requirements, additional bills are issued. During those periods of the year when revenues exceed expenditures, Treasury bills are allowed to mature without being refunded. Treasury bills, therefore, provide the Treasury with a convenient financial mechanism to adjust for the lack of a regular flow of revenues into the Treasury. The volume of bills also may be increased or decreased in response to general surpluses or deficits in the federal budget from year to year.

Treasury bills are issued on a discount basis and mature at par. Each week the Treasury bills to be sold are awarded to the highest bidders. Sealed bids are submitted by dealers and other investors. Upon being opened, these bids are arrayed from highest to lowest; that is, those bidders asking the least discount (offering the highest price) are placed high in the array. The bids are then accepted in the order of their position in the array until all bills are awarded. Bidders seeking a high discount (and offering a low price) may fail to receive any bills that particular week. Investors interested in purchasing small volumes of Treasury bills ($10,000 to $500,000) may submit their orders on an "average competitive price" basis. In so doing, the Treasury deducts from the total volume of bills to be sold the total of these small orders. The remaining bills are alloted on the competitive basis described above. These small orders are then executed at a discount equal to the average of the competitive bids that are accepted for the large orders.

Although some business corporations and wealthy individuals invest in Treasury bills, by far the most important holders of these obligations are the commercial banks of the nation.

Treasury Notes. Treasury notes are usually issued for maturities of more than one year but not more than 10 years and are issued at specified interest rates. These intermediate-term federal obligations are also held largely by the commercial banks of the nation.

Treasury Bonds. Treasury bonds may be issued with any maturity but generally have had an original maturity in excess of 5 years. These bonds bear interest at stipulated rates. Many issues of these bonds are callable by the government several years before their maturity. For example, the 25-year issue of 8 percent bonds issued in 1976 is described as having a maturity of 1996–01. This issue may be called for redemption at par as early as 1996 but in no event later than 2001. As of 1983 the longest maturity of Treasury bonds was 28 years. As for the other marketable securities of the government, active markets for the purchase and sale of these securities are maintained by dealers.

All marketable obligations of the federal government, with the exception of Treasury bills, are offered to the public through the federal reserve banks at predetermined prices and yields. Investors place their orders for new issues, and such orders are filled from the available supply of the new issue. If the issue is oversubscribed, investors may be allotted only a part of their original orders.

Nonmarketable Issues

As the name implies, *nonmarketable issues* of federal obligations are those that cannot be transferred to other persons or institutions and can be redeemed only by being turned in to the United States Treasury. Savings bonds comprise the bulk of the nonmarketable issues and as of the end of 1982 were outstanding in the amount of $67.5 billion.

Savings bonds are redeemable at the option of the holder, and their nonmarketability derives from the fact that they may be redeemed only by the person to whom they were issued. Some of the savings bonds are sold at a discount while others pay interest semiannually. Savings bonds sold at a discount earn interest according to a fixed schedule, such interest being paid only upon redemption of the bond. The most popular series of savings bonds has been the Series E. Since January, 1980 a new Series EE savings bond has been sold by the Treasury in place of the Series E bonds. Series E bonds were sold at a discount of 25 percent of their redemption value. The smallest denomination of Series E bonds was $25 and they were sold to the public for $18.75. The new Series EE differs from the older bonds in that the bonds are sold at a 50 percent discount and mature at twice the purchase price. Initially these new Series EE bonds carried a yield of 6½ percent maturing in 11 years. This rate was increased to 9.0 percent with an 8-year maturity by mid-1982. As of November 1, 1982, an entirely new rate structure on these bonds was introduced. The new Series EE bonds have a maturity of 10 years at twice their purchase price but unlike the former system, which set a fixed rate of interest, the new system allows savers to keep pace with market interest rate changes. Every six months, the rate on the bonds is pegged at 85 percent of the average market rate on 5-year Treasury securities. At the end of 5 years the 10 semiannual averages are added, averaged and compounded to determine a bond's 5-year yield. Bonds held longer have additional semiannual market averages added in. Although not knowing in advance what the earnings will be, a saver will be guaranteed a minimum yield of 7½ percent a year, compounded semiannually on bonds held 5 years or longer.

Other savings bonds outstanding are the Series G, H, HH, and K. Although these bonds will remain outstanding until maturity or until redeemed, they are no longer being issued.

The appeal of savings bonds to the small investor stems from their ease of redemption, lack of risk, and ease of replacement in case of loss, theft, or destruction. One of the most significant attractions of these savings bonds, however, is the convenience with which they may be purchased. Commercial banks and other institutions sell and redeem savings bonds without charge. Further, automatic payroll deductions on the part of many employers, now covering approximately 8 million payroll savers, provide a convenient method of budgeting savings out of current income. The fact that more than one half of all savings bonds are more than 10 years old is evidence that many holders consider them to be a part of their retirement program.

Savings bonds were offered to the public as early as 1935. The purpose of this early effort was to democratize the public debt. The program of savings bonds as we know it, however, was begun in May, 1941. Although the program was started exclusively to help finance World War II, it was expanded and adapted to peacetime financial requirements of the federal government. During the war, savings bonds provided nearly 20 percent of all borrowed funds, and they continue to be an important segment of the federal debt.

Tax Status of Federal Obligations

Until March 1, 1941, interest on all obligations of the federal government was exempt from all taxes. The interest on all federal obligations is now subject to ordinary income taxes and tax rates. The Public Debt Act of 1941 terminated the issuance of tax-free federal obligations. Since that time, all issues previously sold to the public have matured or have been called for redemption. Income from the obligations of the federal government is exempt from all taxing authority of state and local governments. Federal bonds, however, are subject to both federal and state inheritance, estate, or gift taxes.

OWNERSHIP OF THE FEDERAL DEBT

The federal debt plays a role in the portfolios of most of the financial institutions of the nation, many business corporations, and millions of individuals. Indeed, the very size of the federal debt dictates that it be represented in almost all investment programs. Ownership of the debt by individual groups is shown as a percentage of the total debt in Table 14-3.

Much of the challenge in managing the federal debt has centered around the individual ownership of obligations, particularly the savings bonds. Throughout World War II, the effective savings bond sales drives resulted in more than $10 billion in sales each year. Following the war, not only did the purchase of bonds slow down markedly, but also vast numbers of bonds were redeemed by individuals anxious to acquire homes and other durable goods that had been in short supply during the war. In addition, alternative investments became more attractive as interest rates increased and as the stock market began to gain the

Table 14-3
Ownership of the
Federal Debt
January 31, 1982

	Percent of Total Debt
U.S. government agencies and trust funds	19.5
Individuals	13.9
Foreign and international	13.7
Federal reserve banks	12.3
Commercial banks...........................	10.7
State and local governments	8.3
Insurance companies........................	1.9
Mutual savings banks........................	.6
Other miscellaneous groups of investors	19.1
	100.0

SOURCE: *Federal Reserve Bulletin* (April, 1982), p. A32.

momentum of a long rising market. Commercial banks, too, were finding profitable alternative investments for their funds, and they reduced their commitments to federal debt obligations. Although the expenditure requirements of the federal government were reduced substantially in the postwar period, they remained relatively high compared with the prewar period. It became necessary for the Treasury to make strong efforts to stabilize the redemption of savings bonds.

The successive actions begun in 1951 by the Treasury to halt the drain of cash due to savings bond redemptions included the first of the 10-year extension privileges on Series E bonds and the introduction of additional series of savings bonds at higher interest rates. Notwithstanding the difficulties of the Treasury in maintaining the volume of savings bonds since World War II, it is obvious that had their sale been terminated at the end of the war, the task of selling other bonds in the financial markets would have been increased greatly. In short, the Treasury has required the investment interest of all possible groups of investors.

MATURITY DISTRIBUTION OF THE FEDERAL DEBT

Early in this chapter the various types of marketable obligations of the federal government are described. The terms "bills," "notes," and "bonds" describe the general maturity ranges, however, only at the time of issue. As time passes, all of these obligations approach maturity. In order to determine the maturity distribution of all obligations, therefore, it is necessary to observe the remaining life of each issue irrespective of its class. The maturity distribution and average length of marketable interest-bearing federal obligations are shown in Table 14-4.

The heavy concentrations of debt in the very short maturity range poses a special problem for the Treasury. This problem is one also for the securities markets in that the government is constantly selling additional securities to replace those that mature. Nor is the solution to the heavy concentration of short-term maturities to be found in the simple issuance of a large number of long-term

Table 14-4

Average Length and Maturity Distribution of Marketable Interest-Bearing Federal Obligations March, 1983

Maturity Class	Percent of Total Marketable Debt
Within 1 year	46.2
1–5 years	33.1
5–10 years	10.9
10–20 years	4.6
20 years and over	5.2
All issues	100.0
Average maturity of all marketable issues	3 years and 10 months

SOURCE: *The Treasury Bulletin* (2nd Quarter, 1983), p. 15.

issues. Like all institutions that seek funds in the financial markets, the Treasury has to offer securities that will be readily accepted by the investing public. Further, the magnitude of federal financing is such that radical changes in maturity distributions can upset the financial markets and the economy in general. The management of the federal debt has become an especially challenging financial problem, and much time and energy are spent in meeting the challenge. The influence of the Treasury's debt management policies on the financial system and on the economy will be described in Chapter 21. We are here concerned only with a general description of the maturity distribution of the debt.

If the Treasury refunds maturing issues with new short-term obligations, the average maturity of the total debt is reduced. As time passes, longer-term issues are brought into shorter-dated categories. Net cash borrowing resulting from budgetary deficits must take the form of maturities that are at least as long as the average of the marketable debt if the average maturity is not to be reduced.

One of the new debt management techniques used to extend the average maturity of the marketable debt without disturbing the financial markets is that of *advance refunding* which involves the offer by the Treasury to owners of a given issue of the opportunity to exchange their holdings well in advance of their regular maturity for new securities of longer maturity.

THE DEALER SYSTEM

The dealer system for marketable U.S. government securities occupies a central position in the nation's financial markets. The smooth operation of the money markets depends on a closely linked network of dealers and brokers. The market for United States government securities centers on the dealers who report activity daily to the Federal Reserve Bank of New York. In 1981 there were 34 such dealers, 12 of which were commercial banks, and the remaining 22, nonbank dealers. New dealers are added only when they can demonstrate a satisfactory responsibility and volume of activity. The dealers buy and sell securities for their own account, arrange transactions with both their customers and other dealers, and also purchase debt directly from the Treasury for resale to investors. Dealers do not typically charge commissions on their trades. Rather they hope to sell securities at prices above the levels at which they were bought. The dealers' capacity to handle large Treasury financings has expanded efficiently in recent years to handle the substantial growth in the government securities market.

In summary, the Treasury is the largest and most active single borrower in the financial markets. The Treasury is continuously in the process of borrowing and refinancing. Its financial actions are tremendous in contrast with all other forms of financing, including that of the largest business corporations. Yet, the financial system of the nation is suitably adapted to the smooth accommodation of these requirements. Indeed, the very existence of a public debt of this magnitude is predicated upon the existence of a highly refined monetary and credit system.

QUESTIONS

1. Identify the various sources of revenues of the federal government.
2. Although the federal government and local governments rely heavily on taxes for their revenues, the type of taxes on which they rely are quite different. Explain.
3. Comment on the evolution of the "unified federal budget."
4. Why is government lending now included in the federal budget? Why is such lending identified and shown separately in the budget?
5. Describe the nature and significance of off-budget federal outlays.
6. Trace the growth of the federal debt and the reasons for its growth pattern.
7. Explain the relevance of the federal debt to a study of the monetary and credit system of the United States.
8. Although we concede that the magnitude of the federal debt poses a problem for the federal budget, the securities represented by this debt do serve a useful purpose in the financial system. Explain why this is true.
9. By reference to the *Federal Reserve Bulletin, Wall Street Journal,* or other such sources of financial information, construct a schedule of interest rates for both short-term and long-term obligations of the federal government and business enterprises.
10. Compare the yields available on high-grade,

corporate obligations with the yields on obligations of the federal government. How do you explain the differential?
11. Explain the mechanics of issuing Treasury bills, indicating how the price of a new issue is determined.
12. What are the factors that determine the volume of Treasury bills in existence at a particular time?
13. The average maturity of obligations of the federal government is quite short at the present time and it would seem desirable to lengthen the maturity in order to remove some of the pressure of refinancing maturing issues. What difficulties are involved in a radical restructuring of the average debt maturity?
14. What have been the special contributions of savings bonds to the financing of the federal government over the years? Has the nature of these contributions changed?
15. Explain the tax status on income from federal obligations.
16. Describe the significant changes in the ownership pattern of the federal debt.
17. Describe the process of advance refunding of the federal debt.
18. Describe the dealer system that exists to accommodate the handling of new issues and the transfer of outstanding government obligations from investor to investor.

SUGGESTED READINGS

Buchanan, James M., and Marilyn R. Flowers. *The Public Finances: An Introductory Textbook*, 5th ed. Homewood, Illinois: Richard D. Irwin, Inc., 1980. Parts 4 and 5.

Gaines, Tilford C. *Techniques of Treasury Debt Management.* New York: The Free Press of Glencoe, 1962. Part III.

Garbade, Kenneth. *Securities Markets.* New York: McGraw-Hill Book Company, 1982. Chapter 1.

Gardner, Wayland D. *Government Finance.* Englewood Cliffs, New Jersey: Prentice-Hall, Inc., 1978. Part 3.

Hyman, David N. *Public Finance.* Hinsdale, Illinois: The Dryden Press, 1983. Part 3.

Pollock, Stephen H. "Off-Budget Federal Outlays." *Economic Review*, Federal Reserve Bank of Kansas City (March, 1981), pp. 3–15.

Tax Foundation, Inc. *Facts and Figures on Government Finance*, 21st ed., 1981. Section III.

"The Dealer Market for U.S. Government Securities." *Instruments of the Money Market*, 5th ed. Federal Reserve Bank of Richmond, 1981, pp. 30–41.

"The Market for Agency Securities," *Quarterly Review,* Federal Reserve Bank of New York, (Spring, 1978), pp. 7–21.

15 Financing State and Local Governments

In this chapter the financing of state governments and all political subdivisions within the state is considered. These political divisions include municipalities, counties, and special tax districts. *Special tax districts* are those governmental units that are set up for the fulfillment of a particular community need. Representative of such districts are school districts, fire districts, and intragovernmental districts which exist for the financing of sewers or watershed areas.

MAGNITUDE OF STATE AND LOCAL GOVERNMENT FINANCING

Total outlays of state and local governments have grown at a very rapid rate since World War II. In fact, outlays at these governmental levels have increased at a greater rate than have the expenditures of the federal government. The magnitude of such outlays and their rapid rate of growth can be seen by comparing year-to-year total state and local government outlays. As measured in national income accounts, outlays increased from $24 billion in 1951 to approximately $280 billion in 1981.

Some of these increased outlays have been due, of course, to the higher cost of providing the same services. For the most part, however, these increasing expenditures represent government's expanded responsibilities and the continuing pressure placed upon existing facilities. Another major factor leading to the post-World War II expansion in state and local government expenditures was the tremendous backlog of projects. The financial pressures of the depression years of the thirties and the shortage of building resources during the war left practically all state and local governments with large accumulations of urgent needs. After this backlog of projects was met, general urban expansion and the movement to suburban areas gave continued support to the upward impetus of governmental expenditure. The suburban movement gave rise to new demands for many kinds of public facilities such as schools, hospitals, and highways. In addition to these reasons for increased state and local government expenditures, there is the fact that the age groups that draw most heavily on governmental services have increased relative to the total population. These factors have led to a rather rapid increase in per capita state and local expenditures as well as total expenditures. Per capita growth in state and local spending is reflected in Table 15-1.

Table 15-1
Per Capita Expenditures by State and Local Governments

(For Twelve Months Ended June 30 for Selected Years)

	Total Expenditures	Education	Highways	Public Welfare	Other
1965	$ 385.30	$147.37	$ 63.05	$ 32.58	$142.30
1973	862.93	331.54	88.71	112.37	330.31
1979	1,488.05	542.70	129.22	190.36	625.77

SOURCE: U.S. Department of Commerce, Bureau of the Census.

Purchases of goods and services by state and local governments constitute a considerable portion of total expenditures for all levels of government. Approximately 84 percent of all governmental units. This represents about 13 percent of the gross national product. Approximately 45 percent of the goods and services purchased by state and local governments are used for education and highways. Health and sanitation, public welfare, and police and fire are the remaining major expenditure areas. More than two thirds of the direct purchases for education are made by local governments, and almost 60 percent of the expenditures for highways by the states. A comparison of the major items in the budgets of state and local governments is shown in Table 15-2.

Table 15-2
Percentage of State and Local Government Direct Expenditures by Function

(For Fiscal Year 1979)

	State	Local Government
Education..................	25.3	43.6
Public Welfare	23.1	5.8
Highways..................	13.7	5.6
Health and Hospitals.......	11.1	7.2
Other......................	26.8	37.8
	100.0%	100.0%

SOURCE: U.S. Department of Commerce, Bureau of the Census.

METHODS OF FINANCING

In its simplest form, government financing is the process of securing funds with which to pay for the goods, services, and benefits governments provide for their citizens. Essentially, this task becomes one of securing enough current revenue to meet the demands of operating expenditures. There are occasions, however, when it becomes necessary or desirable for governments to borrow funds to meet their expenditure needs. One of these occasions arises when a highly uneven flow of receipts is combined with a rather stable governmental expenditure pattern. This often necessitates temporary borrowing on the part of the government in anticipation of the next tax payment period.

The financing of capital expenditures is the second major reason for governmental borrowing. The logic behind such action lies in the fact that capital expenditures are often made to finance improvements which will benefit the community over a long period of time. It is reasoned that because those who will live in the community in the future will benefit from such expenditures, the payment for these improvements should be spread over the useful life of the improvement. This can be accomplished by increasing taxes in the future to finance the repayment of the debt and the interest on the debt.

It may be said that the types of expenditures being made out of current revenues and the capital expenditures being financed through borrowed funds largely dictate the sources of funds for financing governments. In many ways, this can be likened to the financing of a business enterprise. The operating revenues of government are comparable to the internal financing of a business enterprise, while the borrowed funds are much like the external financing of a business. The credit reputations of state and local governments are related to the extent of indebtedness and the ability of the governments to maintain their contractual debt obligations.

Tax Revenues

The major sources of revenue for state and local governments are sales, income, property, and other incidental taxes. With the increase in expenditures mentioned above, it has been a challenge for these governments to increase revenues at the same rate. Many states have enacted an income tax for the first time, while others have either increased the tax rate or started a withholding procedure to achieve greater effectiveness of the existing tax.

Sales taxes, too, have been increased by states and localities to finance the waves of increasing expenditures. Local governments, however, depend largely upon property taxes for their current revenues; and they have relied upon more realistic property assessments, higher tax rates, and a larger tax base arising from new construction. Table 15-3 reveals the relative importance of various sources of revenue for state and local governments.

Intergovernmental Transfers

An increasingly important source of revenue for state and local governments has been advances from one governmental unit to another. In recent years there has been a significant increase in the amount of grants-in-aid made by the federal government to the states for such purposes as unemployment compensation and highway construction. There has also been an increase in the amount of funds given to local governments by the state governments. In addition, there have been

	Fiscal Years		
	1968	1973	1980
	Percent		
STATES			
Total..........................	100.0	100.0	100.0
Sales..............................	28.7	38.2	31.5
Income (personal and corp.)..........	24.1	21.6	36.8
Motor vehicle licenses	6.8	3.5	3.9
Property	2.5	1.4	2.1
Death and gift......................	2.4	1.5	1.5
Other..............................	35.5	33.8	24.2
LOCAL GOVERNMENTS			
Total..........................	100.0	100.0	100.0
Property	56.1	54.1	53.3
Sales..............................	4.0	6.1	9.0
Income (primarily personal)..........	2.2	3.0	3.7
All other taxes......................	2.8	1.8	2.8
Nontaxes	34.9	35.0	31.2

SOURCE: U.S. Department of Commerce, Bureau of the Census.

direct grants-in-aid to municipalities by the federal government for such purposes as public housing and urban renewal.

In 1981, federal grants-in-aid amounted to $90.3 billion and covered about 25 percent of the total direct outlays of the state and local governments.

Debt Financing

In recent years, state and local governments have tended to incur annual deficits, and as a result their total debt has increased. In addition to debt financing to support annual deficits, in recent years large sums have been borrowed on a short-term basis to bridge the time gap between current expenditures and tax collection. For a particular community, such short-term financing is retired out of tax revenues and total debt is not increased. Because of the general increase in operating budgets of state and local governments, however, the amount of short-term borrowing increases from year to year. In 1979, total state debt was $111.7 billion and total local government debt was $192.4 billion.

Notwithstanding the tremendous increases in capital expenditures by state and local governments, the proportion of these expenditures that has been financed through long-term borrowing has dropped steadily since World War II. This has not been due to budgetary surpluses on the part of such governments but rather to the steadily increasing volume of grants by the federal government.

Passage of the Federal Highway Act of 1956 has accounted for a particularly significant increase in grants by the federal government. Although the proportion of capital expenditures financed through long-term borrowing has decreased, state and local governments continue to claim about the same percentage of total funds made available in the capital markets.

STATE AND LOCAL GOVERNMENT BONDS

In investment circles, *municipal bond* is commonly interpreted to mean the obligations of a state itself or of any of its political subdivisions. The description is not technically correct, but it is understood by all parties in the investment world. Municipal bonds are seldom issued with a maturity that exceeds the estimated life of the capital improvement. Exceptions to this rule, such as the issuance of bonds to finance veterans' aid programs, account for a very small part of total long-term debt financing. Specific maturity limits for various types of capital projects have been enacted into law by many states.

Most bonds of state and local governments are issued with *serial maturities*, that is, the bonds mature in installments over the scheduled life of the issue. For example, an issue of bonds for $20,000,000 may have maturities ranging from one to twenty years, with $1,000,000 making up each maturity group. This in effect constitutes 20 separate bond issues, each maturity having its own rate of interest. Typically, the interest rate is lowest on the shortest maturity and increases on the longer maturities. The serial bond arrangement permits the issuing government to pay off its indebtedness on a predetermined schedule. It also serves the investor well in that it makes possible the selection of maturities to meet special requirements or preferences. Serial bonds do have the disadvantage to the issuing government of making the repayment schedule more rigid, resulting in possible embarrassment during years when revenues are unusually low or current expenditures unduly high. The occasional use of *sinking fund bonds* by state and local governments requires the issuer to set aside regularly a certain sum for the purpose of retiring the outstanding bonds. Such sinking fund payments are generally paid to a trustee who may invest such funds pending ultimate redemption of the sinking fund issue. As a more frequent alternative, the trustee may retire the issue regularly through purchases on the market or through the call of selected bonds for sinking fund purposes. Few municipal securities are issued on a sinking fund basis, but this arrangement is typical of corporate bond issues.

Tax Status of State and Local Government Bonds

The interest income on state and local government bonds is not subject to federal income taxes. This freedom is based on the sovereignty of the state and the presumed unconstitutionality of a federal levy. In turn, the states are not free to tax the interest income on the bonds of the federal government. The mutual restriction of such taxing power is based on the burden that each governmental level could impose on the other with respect to deficit financing. Although there is no limitation on the power of the states to tax the income received from obligations of state and local governments, most states do exempt from tax liability the income of their residents from their own obligations or those of their political subdivisions. Because the levels of federal taxation are so much higher than those of the states, the tax status of state and local government bonds is of special significance to investors in the higher income tax brackets.

Major Types of State and Local Government Bonds

The extent of the liability of the issuing governmental unit for the payment of principal and interest and the sources of revenue from which such payments are to be made distinguish the major classes of municipal obligations, the term "municipals" being used here in the customary sense to include all state and local government obligations. The two major classes of municipal obligations bonds are general obligation bonds and limited obligation bonds.

General Obligation Bonds. A *general obligation bond* is secured by the full faith and credit of the issuing governmental unit, that is, the bond is unconditionally supported by the full taxing power of the issuing government. Although such issues have at times resulted in losses to investors, municipalities and other political subdivisions of the states are reluctant to permit such defaults to occur. Very seldom have defaults on municipals resulted from bad faith on the part of the issuing unit. Rather, economic pressure on a community with a resulting inability to meet its financial obligations has been the principal cause of default. The reluctance of governmental units as well as business enterprises to default on their obligations is due to the resulting blemishes to their credit ratings, blemishes not easily nor quickly eliminated. The governmental unit has a special incentive for maintaining its good credit rating because, unlike the business corporation, it cannot reorganize under another name. The credit reputation of most general credit municipals has been strong historically, and such securities have played a prominent role in the investment portfolios of some of the most conservative institutional investors.

Limited Obligation Bonds. The limited obligation bonds of principal importance are the *revenue bonds. Limited obligation bonds* are issued by a state or local governmental unit for the purpose of financing a specific project. Examples of such projects are bridges, transportation terminals, sewer facilities, and general public utilities. These bonds are issued with the understanding that principal and interest will be paid only from the revenues produced by such projects, the issuing governmental unit having no contingent or direct liability otherwise. A much publicized form of revenue bonds has been that sold to make possible the construction of toll roads. The issuance of bonds by states and municipalities to construct industrial plants for lease to private industry may be of the revenue type. This type of financing was described in Chapter 12. Figure 15-1 shows the principal features of a limited obligation bond issue.

The proportion of revenue bonds to total municipal issues has increased greatly since World War II and is now approximately equal to that of general

Figure 15-1

New Issue of Limited Obligation Municipal Bonds

NEW ISSUE

Interest on the 1983 Bonds, in the opinion of Bond Counsel, will be exempt from Federal income taxes under existing laws, court decisions, regulations and rulings except upon the conditions as herein described under the caption "Tax Exemption". In addition, in the opinion of Bond Counsel, under existing laws the interest will be exempt from all present Kentucky income taxes and the principal of the 1983 Bonds will be exempt from ad valorem taxation by the Commonwealth of Kentucky and any political subdivision thereof.

$27,200,000

Regional Airport Authority

of

Louisville and Jefferson County, Kentucky

Airport System Revenue Bonds, 1983 Series A

Dated: April 1, 1983   Due: July 1, as shown below

Principal (payable July 1) and interest (payable January 1, 1984 and each July 1 and January 1 thereafter) are payable at the option of the holder at the principal office of the Mid-America Bank of Louisville and Trust Company, Louisville, Kentucky, the Trustee, or at the principal office of The Chase Manhattan Bank, N.A., New York, New York, paying agent. The 1983 Bonds will be initially issued as coupon bonds in the denomination of $5,000 registrable as to principal only at the principal office of the Trustee, and exchangeable for fully registered 1983 Bonds in the denomination of $5,000 or any multiple thereof. Coupon and fully registered 1983 Bonds may be exchanged as provided in the Bond Resolution.

The 1983 Bonds are subject to redemption on and after July 1, 1993 as more fully described herein.

The payment of principal of and interest on the 1983 Bonds will be insured by the Municipal Bond Insurance Association.

Maturity	Amount	Interest Rate	Maturity	Amount	Interest Rate
1986	$270,000	6¼%	1991	$375,000	7¾%
1987	285,000	6¾	1992	405,000	8
1988	305,000	7	1993	440,000	8.20
1989	325,000	7¼	1994	475,000	8⅜
1990	350,000	7½	1995	515,000	8½

$ 4,210,000 9⅛% Term Bonds due July 1, 2001
$19,245,000 9¼% Term Bonds due July 1, 2013
Price of all Bonds 100%
(Accrued interest to be added)

The 1983 Bonds are offered when, as and if issued and received by the Underwriters, and subject to the approval of legality by Bond Counsel, Harper, Ferguson & Davis, Louisville, Kentucky. Certain matters will be passed upon on behalf of the Authority by Stites & Harbison, Louisville, Kentucky and for the Underwriters by their Counsel, Webster & Sheffield, New York, New York. It is expected that the 1983 Bonds in definitive form will be available for delivery on or about May 10, 1983.

Goldman, Sachs & Co.

Merrill Lynch, White Weld Capital Markets Group
Merrill Lynch, Pierce, Fenner & Smith Incorporated

April 13, 1983

---

obligation bonds. Among the reasons for the increasing volume of revenue bonds may be the expanding scope of state and local governments in the area of public services and the feeling that the cost of new projects should be borne by the users of such facilities. Through the use of revenue bonds the users of new projects pay the fees that support specifically each project.

Special assessment bonds are issued for the purpose of financing improvements that in turn increase adjacent property values. For example, the construction of streets and highways, although for the benefit of all users, is expected to increase the value of nearby properties. These bonds are payable from assessments on the properties that are assumed to have benefited. Since the safety of special assessment bonds depends upon the ability and willingness of individuals and corporations to pay their special assessments, these securities have found less favor with the investing public. Some special assessment bonds have been issued with contingent general liability of the issuing governmental unit, that is, the obligations of an issue are met from general revenues if assessments are not adequate for the purpose. This type is more appropriately classified as a general obligation.

Underwriting State and Local Bond Issues

New issues of municipal obligations are generally sold to investment banking syndicates on the basis of competitive bids. The issuing municipality first secures competent legal opinion. With legality of the issue confirmed, the issuing unit then consults specialists in the field to determine appropriate timing, suitable interest rates, and other technical aspects of the issues.

Having decided upon the appropriate terms and timing of the issue, the governmental unit will advertise such information in local newspapers and financial trade papers (see Figure 15-1) and send special notices to investment banking houses and large commercial banks with bond departments. These notices clearly set forth the terms of the issue and the date by which competitive bids from underwriting firms must be received. After that date, bids are opened, and the award is made to the highest bidder, who then offers the bonds to the public.

The Market for State and Local Government Bonds

The ownership of municipals is most heavily concentrated in commercial banks, personal trusts, and property and casualty insurance companies. Investors are attracted to municipals because of their quality and their exemption from federal income taxes. The investor who is in a 50 percent tax bracket, both corporate and individual, must receive a yield of 14 percent on taxable securities to have an after-tax yield equivalent to the 7 percent from tax-free municipal obligations. As indicated by Figure 15-2, "Aa" grade municipal obligations have averaged a yield of approximately 2 to 3 percent less than the yield on "Aa" grade corporate bonds. Because of the tax-free status of the income from municipal obligations, their yields are closely related to income tax levels and the number of investors in the higher income tax brackets. Yields are also a function of the volume of tax-exempt bonds available and comparative yields on all types of obligations.

The two types of financial institutions that are the principal holders of state and local obligations are the property insurance companies and commercial banks. It is not surprising that these two types of institutions are subject to full corporate income tax liabilities. Property insurance companies and commercial banks provide about three quarters of the total external financing of state and

Figure 15-2

Average Yields of
Long-term Treasury,
Corporate, and
Municipal Bonds

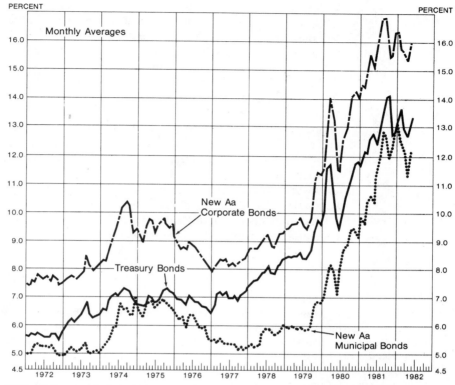

SOURCE: *Treasury Bulletin.* United States Treasury Department, Washington, D.C., July, 1982, p. 69.

local governments.[1] It is interesting also to note that as corporate taxes increased since World War II, the share of these two types of financial institutions in the obligations of state and local governments increased.

CYCLICAL CHANGES IN BORROWING

Although state and local government outlays for construction have until recent years increased at a relatively steady rate, the financing to accommodate such outlays has been very irregular. Further, borrowing by state and local governments has tended to follow a countercyclical pattern. Several factors explain this fluctuation in timing. First, during periods of recession, there is greater availability of bank funds for such investments. This increased availability results from the normally increased excess reserves of the banks during periods of recession without corresponding increases in business demands for funds. Running counter to the availability of bank funds during periods of economic recession, however, is the availability of funds from individuals. Individuals tend

---

[1] *Credit and Capital Markets 1982* (New York: Bankers Trust Company, January 22, 1982), p. 17.

to have greater savings available and higher tax liabilities to face during periods of economic expansion. The increased attractiveness of the tax-exempt municipals does increase individual investment in such securities, but this increase does not offset the countercyclical influence of bank investments.

Another reason for the extensive borrowing of state and local governments during periods of economic recession is the fact that the operating surpluses of these governmental units decline at such times. To the extent that operating surpluses provide only partial financial support for construction outlays in periods of recession, increased borrowing is a necessity. Interest rates, too, influence the willingness of state and local governments to borrow. As interest rates in general decline during periods of economic contraction, the burden of prospective long-term financing is reduced correspondingly. The reduction in interest rates is especially significant in connection with the issuance of revenue bonds since the feasibility of the revenue producing project is, in large measure, related to its debt-servicing capacity. As the interest burden on the financing is decreased, the feasibility of the project is improved.

QUESTIONS

1. Although the expenditures of the federal government seem to be part of the daily news, state and local governments also account for significant expenditures. Comment.

2. In recent decades the pressure on state and local governments to increase expenditures has been great. Describe some of these pressures on state and local budgets.

3. Describe the various sources of financing for state and local governments, and comment on the role that each plays in the overall expenditures of these governmental units.

4. Account for the fact that long-term borrowing has been declining as a percent of the capital expenditures of state and local governments.

5. Describe the general claim to funds of state and local governments as a percent of funds raised by all users. Has any significant trend in such claims taken place in recent years?

6. The term "municipal bond" refers to securities issued by what types of political jurisdictions?

7. The typical municipal bond issue involves serial maturities. How do such maturities differ from those of the typical industrial bond issue?

8. Describe the special appeal of municipal bonds to investors in high income tax brackets.

9. Distinguish between general obligation and limited obligation municipal bonds. Would it be safe to say that general obligation bonds are always to be preferred by investors over limited obligation bonds?

10. Contrast the yields on high-grade municipal bonds with those of federal government bonds. Does the spread in yields seem reasonable?

11. Describe the factors that influence the yield on municipal bonds at any particular time.

12. Describe the cyclical pattern of state and local government borrowing.

SUGGESTED READINGS

Buchanan, James M., and Marilyn R. Flowers. *The Public Finances: An Introductory Textbook,* 5th ed. Homewood, Illinois: Richard D. Irwin, Inc., 1980. Part 8.

Campbell, Tim S. *Financial Institutions, Markets, and Economic Activity.* New York: McGraw-Hill Book Company, 1982. Chapter 14.

Facts and Figures on Government Finance, 21st ed. New York: Tax Foundation, Inc., 1981. Sections IV, V, and VI.

Garbade, Kenneth. *Securities Markets*. New York: McGraw-Hill Book Company, 1982. Chapter 3.

Hyman, David N. *Public Finance*. Hinsdale, Illinois: The Dryden Press, 1983. Part 5.

Jianakoplos, Nancy Ammon. "The Growing Link Between the Federal Government and State and Local Government Financing." *Review*, The Federal Reserve Bank of St. Louis (May, 1977), pp. 13–20.

16 Role of Consumer Credit in the Economy

Consumer credit plays an important role in the financial system of the United States. For example, individuals may purchase automobiles and homes on credit. This permits the use and enjoyment of these consumer assets while they are being paid for. Consumer credit serves to smooth the process between the production or provision of consumer goods and services and their consumption. An exceptionally large amount of consumer credit, however, may be inflationary if it leads to excess demand relative to the available supply of consumer goods and services.

This chapter considers the nature of consumer credit and its role in the financial structure of our economy. Consumer credit is distinguished from other forms of credit. The functions of consumer credit are then considered, showing how development and adaptation took place to meet changing needs. The last section of this chapter discusses the volume of consumer credit and its relationship with economic activity.

NATURE OF CONSUMER CREDIT

Consumer credit may be defined as credit used by consumers to help finance or refinance the purchase of commodities and services for personal consumption. Its use to finance personal consumption distinguishes it from business credit used for production purposes. For example, when an individual uses credit to buy an automobile for personal or family use, the credit extended to the individual is consumer credit; when a cab driver uses credit to buy a similar automobile for use as a taxi, the credit extended is business credit. The distinguishing feature is the use to which the goods or services bought on credit are to be put.

Problems of Classification

Such a definition of consumer credit presents several practical problems. Credit extended to farmers who are operating a family farm may be used for consumption, for production, or for both. It is often difficult for a farmer to know just how the money will be divided among different uses. Banks therefore make no attempt to divide farm loans into loans for production and loans for consumption. Agricultural credit is usually treated as a separate category of credit since it is part consumer and part producer credit, and there are many institutions that loan money exclusively to farmers.

A similar problem of classification of credit arises at times in the nonagricultural sector of the economy. A consumer may use credit to buy an automobile that is intended primarily for personal use. It may be used in part, however, for business purposes. Since there is no practicable way of allocating such credit to consumption and production, all of it is assigned classification as consumer credit.

Long-term Consumer Credit

Our definition of consumer credit includes credit used to purchase residential real estate and to make repairs or to modernize such property, since in each of these cases the purpose is to finance or refinance the purchase of goods or services for personal consumption. The major difference between financing the purchase of an automobile and a home is usually in the time period involved in repayment of the loan. Both are durable goods, but a house obviously lasts much longer than a car and costs considerably more; therefore, payments for a house are made over a longer period of time.

Credit used to purchase homes is treated as long-term consumer credit; that used for other purposes, as intermediate- and short-term credit. Such a distinction is frequently made in practice and in studies of consumer credit. Following such a division, credit for home repairs and modernization is treated as part of short-term and intermediate-term consumer credit. Credit for financing the purchase of a home is, then, the only case of long-term consumer financing and thus will be discussed separately in Chapter 18.

FUNCTIONS OF CONSUMER CREDIT

The basic function of consumer credit is to enable consumers to maximize the satisfaction they obtain by using their income for consumer goods. This assistance to consumers takes several forms: (1) the provision of a convenient form of payment, (2) help in periods of financial stress, and (3) a plan for the payment for durable goods while they are being used.

Convenient Form of Payment

One reason for using consumer credit is the convenience of paying for goods and services. Bank credit cards such as MasterCard and VISA, and other charge accounts, typically are used to make retail purchases on credit. The user makes monthly payments. Since many people are paid monthly or semimonthly, it is a convenience for them to be able to pay for goods as their wages and salaries are paid to them. At times credit cards or charge accounts may carry the consumer for a longer period of time. This is especially true after the heavy purchasing for the Christmas season. Interest is typically charged at a rate of 1½ (or higher) percent per month on the unpaid balance. Credit limits are based upon an analysis of the financial position of the credit card or charge account applicant.

Services are also frequently paid for on a charge basis. This is true of electric, gas, and some telephone services that are billed once a month. As a rule, doctors, dentists, lawyers, and other professional people also send out statements once a month, thus providing a convenient method of monthly payment for their patients and clients.

Aid in Financial Emergencies

A second function of consumer credit is to help consumers through periods of financial stress. This function has been referred to as the safety-valve function of consumer credit. Many families do not have sufficient liquid assets to meet emergencies. They have such assets as homes, life insurance policies, automobiles, and household equipment of considerable value, but they do not have much cash to meet contingencies. When an emergency strikes, such as a serious illness, an accident, loss of a job, or loss of property due to a fire, a tornado, or a theft not covered by insurance, the cash reserves of such families are soon depleted. Consumer credit can perform a valuable function in tiding a family over an emergency. In many cases, the financial difficulty results from poor planning of family expenditures or poor budgeting of family resources. Unpaid bills probably accumulate, and a consumer loan to consolidate these bills may provide a way out of the difficulty.

Buying Durables on Installments

The third function performed by consumer credit is to aid consumers in financing the purchase of durable goods by paying for them in installments. The demand by consumers for housing, refrigeration, transportation, and so on are satisfied in our economy by means of consumer goods that provide such services for a period of time. A house may provide a place to live for 40 to 50 years and an automobile may provide transportation for 5 or more years.

The day-by-day satisfactions from durable goods are made available to consumers in several ways. As is the case with houses, and increasingly with cars and some appliances, it is possible to enjoy them by renting them.

Another way of enjoying durable goods is to purchase them, either new or used. These goods may be bought with cash or on the installment plan. To pay cash, the average consumer would have to save for a period of time until the purchase price has been accumulated. For most consumers, this is not feasible as a method of acquiring a home since by the time a sufficient amount could be saved, the children would be grown and away from home. Therefore, most houses are paid for while the owners are deriving housing services by living in them.

The situation in regard to durables other than housing is similar. Most consumers would take several years to save enough to buy an automobile, furniture, and other major durable goods even if they followed through with a savings program. In the meantime they would have to do without these goods, and the price of waiting could be very high or even prohibitive. It does little good to save enough money to buy a refrigerator two years after the old one has failed to function, or to buy a car to drive to a new job at a place inaccessible to public transportation a year after the job has begun. Therefore, a system of systematically paying for such durables as they are being used is a real service to consumers.

Under most payment plans, these durable goods are paid for in a period that is materially shorter than their useful life. For example, a house that usually is serviceable for 40 years or more is paid for in installments in 25 to 30 years; a refrigerator, which lasts 10 years or more, is usually paid for in 2 years. Financing such purchases on installments, therefore, is also an aid to the consumer in building up a stock of durable goods since, when the article is paid for in full, a substantial period of service still remains.

Another effect of selling durable goods on installments is the acceleration of the movement of manufactured goods, since consumers buy such goods sooner than they could if they first had to save the full purchase price. This effect is especially important in the case of new durable goods because manufacturers are able to achieve volume sales more rapidly than they could in a cash-sale economy.

DEVELOPMENT OF CONSUMER CREDIT

Consumer credit is probably as old as the human race itself. Before money was used, primitive peoples developed credit to make barter more flexible. This was consumer credit because almost all goods were consumer goods in those days. Such a form of consumer credit based on a barter system is still used by primitive societies in remote parts of the world today.

In a primitive economy, no charge was made for the loan of goods because it was a problem for a nomadic people to carry around excess goods, such as food and clothing. If such articles were repaid in kind later on, the borrower and the lender both benefited because the borrower had the goods when needed and the lender did not have to move them around.

Development of Cash Lending

Records indicate that the lending of money for use in buying consumer goods developed almost simultaneously with the development of money as a medium of exchange. The business of lending cash to wage earners in the United States probably began after the Civil War in the cities of the Middle West. Such loans were made for short periods of time, the smallest payable in a week, two weeks, or a month; the largest, in less than a year.

Some degree of specialization developed in this early business of lending cash to consumers. One group of lenders attached wages as security, that is, they had the borrower sign an agreement to have a part of future wages paid to the lender in the event the loan was not paid on time. Another group loaned on unsecured notes, relying on their ability to get a court order to attach wages to collect on defaulted loans. A third group used chattel mortgages on household furniture as security. These loans generally ranged from $15 to $300, and the charges were between 5 percent and 40 percent a month.

This loan business was illegal under the usury laws that existed in most states. But it was difficult to prove the usurious nature of the transactions since interest charges were disguised as fees for services, notes often had to be signed before the loans were completed, the cash being loaned was turned over without witnesses, receipts were not given, and so on. Many borrowers were also so glad to be accommodated that they did not press charges of usury.

As these abuses were brought to light, especially by the Russell Sage Foundation, small-loan legislation was passed in state after state; and legal lending of cash to consumers was subsequently developed by consumer finance companies and still later by commercial banks.

Factors Responsible for the Development of Cash Lending

Several factors account for the development of cash lending to consumers on an organized basis. The structure of our society was undergoing some pronounced changes in the period following the Civil War. One of the most important was the shifting of workers from rural to urban areas. A farmer could get along for a period of time during an emergency with practically no cash. The urban dweller, however, was dependent upon current income, past savings, credit, or charity. Thus, the growing urbanization led to a demand for cash loans to meet emergencies.

This need was further accentuated by the changing character of industry and the position of the laboring class. In 1860 this country was primarily agricultural, but by 1900 it had an established factory system and a permanent body of industrial workers. The average size of the factory increased markedly, and relationships between employer and employee became more and more impersonal. Small independent producers began to disappear, and laborers were organized into plants of a thousand workers or more. In many cases, employers continued to maintain a close relationship with employees and financed them during periods of difficulty. In other cases, there was no such relationship, and emergencies found the workers on their own.

Development of the Financing of Durable Goods Purchases

The use of credit for the payment for durable goods while they were being used also developed early in our economy. At first it was extended in the form of sales credit with long periods for repayment. A very large part of the trade in colonial Philadelphia was carried on by means of credit sales. For example, the records of a cabinetmaker for the period from 1775 to 1811 showed that 92 percent of all sales were on credit. A linen merchant of the same period expected few customers to pay in less than a year. Benjamin Franklin took over nine months, on the average, to pay for the books he bought.

Under such conditions, the volume of bad debts was bound to be high and some people misused credit and got into financial difficulties. The debts of some southern planters to mercantile houses in London were passed from father to son for several generations. Debts that could not be repaid during a lifetime also gave rise to a peculiar marriage custom in colonial days. A man who married a widow whose former husband left unpaid debts was required to have the marriage ceremony take place in the middle of the King's highway with the bride dressed only in her petticoat to avoid taking on her former husband's debts.

The first known examples of installment selling occurred in eastern cities. Stores that sold factory-made furniture on installments were established, but no records remain to show the extent of such trade or the terms of such sales. Early in the nineteenth century, clock manufacturers in New England also began to sell their products on installments. By 1850 a considerable business was done in the sale of pianos and organs on installments. By that year, Singer Sewing Machine Company also had begun to sell its machines through agents on the installment plan, and its competitors soon copied this practice. By the end of the century, the installment system had spread to most of the country east of the Mississippi, and even west in some cases. This plan was used for a wide variety of goods and was made available to consumers with relatively low incomes.

The real giant of installment sales, the automobile, appeared shortly after 1890, but it did not develop into a widely used consumer good until World War I and later. In 1900 fewer than 4,200 cars were built, and the total production of cars and trucks first passed 100,000 in 1909. Sales of cars paid for on installments probably began in 1910, and advertisements offering cars on time payments appeared in New York City in 1914. Thereafter such financing developed at a phenomenal rate, especially after the end of World War I in 1918. As new consumer goods, such as refrigerators, vacuum cleaners, washing machines, and air conditioners, were developed, they also were sold on installments, which helped increase the volume of such financing.

Factors Responsible for the Growth of Installment Buying

One of the basic reasons for the growth of installment credit was the increase in the investment in durable goods by consumers. It is possible to obtain a fairly accurate picture of the durable goods owned by typical families in 1860. In the homes of the better-housed workers in northern cities, a kitchen range was generally the only stove in the house. Candles frequently were the only source of light. Furniture was often homemade or, if factory-made, it was of very poor quality and there was little of it in the house. Dishes, silverware, and cooking utensils were of the cheapest grades. The poor, of course, got by with even less equipment. Farmers, especially those in the West, lived in log houses. What little furniture they had was homemade, and a fireplace served both for cooking and for heat.

The stock of durable equipment in American homes increased between 1860 and 1900, but at the turn of the century it was still not large by today's standards. The moderately well-to-do home in 1900 probably had an original investment of not over $200 in such devices as a sewing machine, an ice refrigerator, a cooking stove, and a few odds and ends of laundry, cleaning, and transportation equipment. Today such a home will probably have one or more automobiles, a refrigerator, a vacuum cleaner, a washing machine and dryer, several radios, television sets and other electronic equipment, many small appliances, and perhaps other items. This increase in the ownership of durable goods has created a large total investment in such goods, as we will see later in the chapter.

Basic Causes of Increased Investment in Durables

This increase in consumer expenditures on durables was the major factor leading to an increase in installment credit. Several factors were responsible for these increased expenditures. Methods of producing durable goods in large quantities at a low price were important. It is, of course, also true that a market had to exist for large quantities of goods to make the economies of large-scale, assembly-line production possible, and the development of installment financing helped to provide such a market.

This mass market was made possible because incomes were increasing and money was available for items other than necessary food, clothing, and shelter. Changing modes of living also provided the incentive to purchase such goods. More and more people moved to the cities and wanted conveniences equal to those of their neighbors. Increased activities put a greater premium on leisure time, thus leading to a demand for labor-saving devices.

Development of Urban Residential Real Estate Financing

Lending money to individuals to buy homes appears to have begun almost as soon as people established communities. The earliest form of real estate financing was through loans by one individual to another, and such direct loans are still one source of financing in this field. The first formal organization to set up a plan for home financing was organized in Frankford (now part of Philadelphia), Pennsylvania, in 1831. It was a cooperative agency for the purpose of lending funds pooled by the shareholders to the members for building or purchasing houses. It was not an American invention but was patterned after similar European institutions with which some of the immigrants were familiar. As time went on, more of these institutions were established; and they developed into the present-day savings and loan associations. Over the years, other agencies have entered the field of home financing.

Factors Responsible for the Development of Lending on Urban Real Estate

The growth of manufacturing and of urbanization after the Civil War led to an increased demand for housing in the cities. In rural areas it was frequently possible to build a log house with the help of the neighbors, but this was impossible in urban areas. The demand for housing was also increased by the large numbers of immigrants entering this country, most of whom were between 15 and 45 years of age. Some of them went onto farms, but most of them remained in cities, especially in the East.

Few families had the necessary cash to buy or build a house. Many rented their homes, but over the years an increasing number became homeowners. The increase in home ownership was possible not only because of increased incomes but also because financial institutions developed procedures by which homes could be paid for while the owners lived in them.

VOLUME OF CONSUMER CREDIT

Consumer credit has become one of the most important segments of financing. We begin our exploration of the importance of credit to consumers today by first examining the consumer balance sheet. Then our attention focuses on installment credit, by type and holder, since this is the most significant portion of short- and intermediate-term consumer credit. The final part of this section focuses on the relationship between consumer credit and economic activity.

The Consumer Balance Sheet

The importance of credit to consumers in recent years is depicted in Table 16-1. Consumers continue to hold well over one half of their total assets in the

Table 16-1

The Consumer Balance Sheet for Selected Years (End of Period in Billions of Dollars)

	1975	1978	1979	1980	1981
ASSETS					
Financial Assets—Subtotal	3,521.8	4,802.7	5,470.1	6,327.9	6,629.0
Demand Deposits and Currency.	170.7	229.5	252.6	268.0	287.9
Time and Savings Accounts.	770.9	1,086.1	1,163.1	1,294.4	1,353.2
Money Market Fund Shares.	3.7	10.8	45.2	74.4	181.9
Life Insurance and Pension Fund Reserves	532.4	729.6	809.6	949.7	1,023.6
Government Securities.	220.2	278.0	333.8	357.0	403.7
Corporate and Foreign Bonds.	69.0	72.8	83.3	86.9	77.8
Corporate Stock at Market Value	660.5	755.5	911.3	1,215.6	1,084.9
Equity in Noncorporate Business. . . .	1,016.4	1,504.4	1,710.7	1,918.7	2,037.7
Other Financial Assets (Net).	78.0	136.0	160.5	163.2	178.3
Tangible Assets—Subtotal	1,835.1	2,777.7	3,101.4	3,465.6	3,720.4
Owner-occupied Housing.	973.8	1,546.0	1,728.5	1,907.1	2,063.1
Land*	276.3	443.7	496.1	585.8	615.1
Consumer Durable Goods	585.0	788.0	876.8	972.7	1,042.2
TOTAL ASSETS (Liabilities + Net Worth)	5,356.9	7,580.4	8,571.5	9,793.5	10,349.4
LIABILITIES—Total	747.0	1,136.4	1,305.9	1,408.9	1,515.8
Home Mortgages.	478.6	740.6	856.5	940.2	1,003.5
Consumer Credit.	223.2	336.4	382.7	385.0	411.4
Bank Loans, Insurance Loans, etc. . . .	45.2	59.4	66.7	83.7	100.9
NET WORTH (of Households)	4,609.9	6,444.0	7,265.6	8,384.6	8,833.6

Note: Parts may not add to totals due to rounding.
*The estimated value of land of the "owner-occupied housing."
SOURCE: National Consumer Finance Association, *Finance Facts Yearbook*, 1982, p. 39.

form of financial assets. Equity held in business proprietorships and partnerships represents the largest type of financial asset. Time and savings accounts are second in importance. Then come major holdings of corporate stock (subject to wide fluctuations in value) and holdings of life insurance and pension fund reserves. As would be expected, owner-occupied housing represents the largest type of tangible or real asset. Furthermore, these housing assets, when coupled with the land values of owner-occupied housing, exceed even consumer equity in business proprietorships and partnerships.

Table 16-1 also shows that consumer liabilities, dominated by home mortgages, more than doubled between 1975 and 1981. Since total assets increased by a lesser amount over the same period, consumer liabilities increased more rapidly than did consumer net worth. This is reflected in the ratio of liabilities to total assets which was 14.6 percent in 1981 compared with 13.9 percent in 1975. Even so, consumer net worth remains at a level that is nearly six times the level of liabilities.

Consumer Installment Credit by Type and Holder

The most important portion of short- and intermediate-term consumer credit is in the form of installment loans. Table 16-2 shows total consumer installment credit outstanding in June, 1982, of $331.9 billion. In contrast, noninstallment consumer credit, which is credit to be repaid in a lump sum (such as charge accounts, service credit, and single-payment loans), averages about one fourth the size of installment credit.

Commercial banks represent the dominant source or holder of consumer installment credit with holdings of about 44 percent of the total. Finance companies are the second most important supplier of installment credit to consumers. Next come credit unions and retailers with about 14 percent and 8 percent of the total, respectively. Savings and loan associations account for less than 4 percent of outstanding consumer installment credit.

Automobile installment credit represents the single most important type of consumer credit, as is shown in Table 16-2. This type of credit is dominated by commercial banks and finance companies. Credit unions rank third in importance as suppliers of automobile installment credit. Rapid growth in bank revolving credit, particularly in the use of credit cards, provides further evidence of the dominance of commercial banks as suppliers of consumer installment credit.

Personal loans, contained within the "other" category in Table 16-2, also represent a significant use of consumer installment credit. Notice that finance companies rank a close second to commercial banks as suppliers of consumer credit in this category. Consumers also rely on short- to intermediate-term installment loans to finance the purchase of mobile homes and to make home improvements.

Consumer Credit and Economic Activity

Consumer credit changes in response to changes or expected changes in economic activity. While the volume of outstanding intermediate-term and home

Table 16-2
Consumer Installment
Credit by Type and
Holder, June 1982

(Millions of Dollars)	Amount	Percent of Total
Total.........................	331,851	100.0%
By major holder		
Commercial banks............	146,775	44.2
Finance companies..........	93,009	28.0
Credit unions	45,882	13.8
Retailers*.....................	26,645	8.0
Savings and loans	12,312	3.7
Gasoline companies	4,398	1.3
Mutual savings banks........	2,830	.9
By major type of credit		
Automobile	128,415	38.7
Commercial banks..........	58,140	
Indirect paper.............	34,903	
Direct loans...............	23,237	
Credit unions	21,940	
Finance companies	48,335	
Revolving....................	59,302	17.9
Commercial banks..........	31,974	
Retailers...................	22,930	
Gasoline companies	4,398	
Mobile home	18,543	5.6
Commercial banks..........	9,924	
Finance companies	4,731	
Savings and loans	3,400	
Credit unions	488	
Other........................	125,591	37.8
Commercial banks..........	46,737	
Finance companies	39,943	
Credit unions	23,454	
Retailers...................	3,715	
Savings and loans	8,912	
Mutual savings banks.......	2,830	

*Includes auto dealers and excludes 30-day charge credit held by
travel and entertainment companies.
SOURCE: *Federal Reserve Bulletin* (September, 1982), p. 42.

mortgage credit takes a relatively long period to extinguish after it has been
granted, new consumer borrowing can fluctuate widely from year to year. Figure
16-1 depicts fluctuations in household borrowing in recent years. For example,
a slowdown in household borrowing, particularly in terms of installment credit

Figure 16-1
Household Borrowing
Percent of Disposable
Personal Income

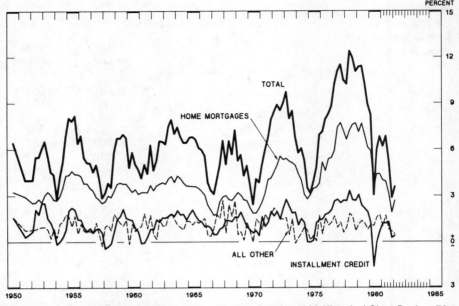

SOURCE: Board of Governors of the Federal Reserve System, *1982 Historical Chart Book,* p. 70.

and home mortgages, occurred during 1969 and 1970. This was a period of tight money characterized by high interest rates and limited credit supplies. The economy also turned down near the end of 1969 and continued in a recession throughout most of 1970.

Another sharp downturn in household borrowing occurred at the beginning of 1973 and preceded the severe economic recession of 1974–75. Consumer borrowing as a percent of disposable personal income then rose rapidly from its low of close to 3 percent in 1975 to exceed 12 percent by 1978. Then in 1979 household borrowing was sharply curtailed until it again reached about 3 percent of disposable personal income by early 1980. This sharp drop in household borrowing again preceded an economic downturn which began in 1980. After a brief period of economic recovery another downturn began and this also is reflected in the household borrowing pattern shown in Figure 16-1.

Considerable concern was voiced by some economists over the ability of consumers to meet their debt obligations when household borrowing reached historically high levels during the latter part of the 1970s. While some of this concern abated at the beginning of the 1980s, recent economic downturns have been associated with substantial increases in the number of consumer or personal bankruptcies.

QUESTIONS

1. How does consumer credit differ from other types of credit?

2. Briefly discuss several problems that arise when describing consumer credit.

3. How does long-term consumer credit differ from other types of consumer credit?
4. What economic functions are performed by consumer credit?
5. Describe the early development of consumer lending.
6. Describe the development of cash lending to consumers in the United States.
7. Briefly trace the development of the financing of durable goods.
8. Discuss the factors responsible for the growth of installment buying.
9. What factors have been responsible for the growth of lending on urban real estate?
10. Briefly describe what has happened in recent years in terms of the "consumer balance sheet."
11. Identify the major types and holders of consumer installment credit.
12. What has been the relationship between consumer credit and economic activity during recent years?

SUGGESTED READINGS

Consumer Credit in the United States. National Commission on Consumer Finance. Washington: U.S. Government Printing Office, 1973.

"Equal Credit Opportunity." *Federal Reserve Bulletin* (February, 1977), pp. 101–107.

Finance Facts Yearbook—1982. Washington: National Consumer Finance Association, 1982.

Greene, Mark R., and Robert R. Dince. *Personal Financial Management.* Cincinnati: South-Western Publishing Co., 1983. Part I.

"Household Borrowing in the Recovery." *Federal Reserve Bulletin* (March, 1978), pp. 153–160.

Luckett, Charles. "Recent Developments in the Mortgage and Consumer Credit Markets." *Federal Reserve Bulletin* (May, 1982), pp. 281–290.

Luckett, Charles. "Recent Financial Behavior of Households." *Federal Reserve Bulletin* (June, 1980), pp. 437–443.

Prell, Michael J. "The Long-Run Growth of Consumer Installment Credit—Some Observations." *Monthly Review,* Federal Reserve Bank of Kansas City (February, 1973), pp. 3–13.

Troelstrup, Arch W., and E. Carl Hall. *The Consumer in American Society,* 6th ed. New York: McGraw-Hill Book Company, 1978.

17 Institutions and Procedures for Financing Consumers

The development and present status of each of the types of institutions that finance the consumer for short-term and intermediate-term needs are analyzed in this chapter. Consideration is also given to their organization and methods of operation, the results of their operations, and their current characteristics.

First to be considered are the institutions in the consumer installment credit industry, which include consumer finance companies, sales finance companies, and industrial banks and loan companies. Next to be discussed are credit unions, followed by commercial banks in their consumer lending role. Also considered are institutions which facilitate consumer financing, including various credit-checking agencies that report on the credit standing of individuals and some specialized insurance companies which insure consumer loans of various types. Recent developments in consumer credit regulation are discussed in the last section of the chapter.

THE CONSUMER INSTALLMENT CREDIT INDUSTRY

Many institutions are involved in making personal loans to consumers and financing consumer purchases of goods and services. Some of the institutions such as banks and credit unions have a basic collateral role, that of serving as a depository for savings of individuals and using such savings as the major source of funds for lending to consumers and others. The consumer installment credit industry includes those finance companies whose primary role is to make installment credit available to consumers. The various types of institutions in this industry began as different types of organizations to meet different needs, but by the 1970s many of the early distinctions had disappeared. The development of each type of institution will be considered first, beginning with consumer finance companies.

Development of Consumer Finance Companies

Consumer finance companies were developed to perform the second function of consumer credit, that is, to provide aid in time of financial emergency. They made loans in the early years of their existence primarily to low-income borrowers who found it impossible to obtain credit elsewhere. As time went on they expanded their scope of operations until today most of them make loans to a cross section of middle-income as well as low-income families.

As was pointed out in the previous chapter, organized cash lending to consumers in this country probably began in cities of the Middle West after the end of the Civil War. Since the laws of the states not only made no provisions for institutions to lend money to consumers but also made profitable legal operation impossible because of usury laws, such lending was carried on in violation of the law. Illegal lending by loan sharks flourished because there was a need for credit for emergencies that was not being met in any other way.

Several steps were taken to combat the loan shark problem in the period before World War I. Late in the nineteenth century, legislation was passed that was designed to encourage the establishment of semiphilanthropic organizations to make small loans to consumers. As a result, in several cities, especially in the East, remedial loan societies were sponsored by social-minded citizens who devoted their time to these organizations without compensation. Although these societies helped many people, they hardly made a dent in the loan shark problem. The first comprehensive small-loan legislation was passed in Massachusetts in 1911, and New Jersey followed suit in 1914. In the next year, such legislation was passed in New York, Ohio, and Pennsylvania. With the experience in these states as a guide, the Russell Sage Foundation published a model Uniform Small Loan Law in 1916.

Several features are basic in a small-loan law if illegal lending is to be eliminated. Maximum charges must be set and these must be high enough to permit profitable operations. The charge is an overall fee for expenses, services, and interest; and it is the only charge permitted. It is computed on the unpaid balance of the loan each month or oftener if payments are made more frequently. Provision must be made for licensing lenders based on character, fitness to conduct the business, and financial responsibility. There must also be state supervision of the business and penalties against nonlicensees and licensees who violate any of the provisions of the law.

Development of Sales Finance Companies

A few years after the development of consumer finance companies, another type of institution, the sales finance company, was developed to finance the sale of durable goods on installments. This is accomplished by purchasing from retail merchants or dealers the promissory notes signed by consumers who have bought goods on time payments. A second function involves the financing of wholesale purchases by the merchant or dealer from the manufacturer. Since cash payment is required by the manufacturer for automobiles and most appliances, the majority of dealers need continuous financing of their stocks. Such financing is business credit, but for convenience it is provided by the same company that finances retail sales.

The sale of durable goods on installments goes back to the early years of the nineteenth century when furniture was sold by some cabinetmakers on that basis.

It received its real impetus in the last part of that century when sewing machines, pianos, and sets of books were frequently sold on installments.

The big growth of sales financing came with the rapid development of the automobile industry. The first corporation to finance auto sales, organized in 1915, was immediately swamped with business. Shortly thereafter, the Commercial Credit Company developed a plan to finance automobile sales. This company had been founded earlier to finance accounts receivable for manufacturers and wholesalers. It developed its automobile sales financing activities rapidly and is today one of the major companies in the sales finance field. General Motors Acceptance Corporation was incorporated in 1919 to do sales financing but also to make wholesale loans to General Motors dealers who were having trouble getting enough funds to finance the purchase of new cars from the manufacturer. Many other sales finance companies were established, especially during the 1920s.

A new type of institution was developed to meet the need for installment sales financing because commercial banks did not engage in sales financing on a large scale until twenty years or more after the sales finance companies pioneered in its development. The basic philosophy under which commercial banks were operating held that they should restrict themselves to short-term business loans that were self-liquidating. Automobile financing was a new type of business that required new methods and a different outlook from regular banking. Risks were likely to be great until a substantial volume was built up. Bankers also had an obligation to depositors that did not exist in sales finance companies. It was not until the depression of the 1930s had run its course that it became clear that sales credit could be extended safely. The ability of sales finance companies to set up branches where they chose also gave them an advantage over banks, which could have no branches in many states and were greatly restricted in others.

A last factor was the usury laws that limited banks to rates lower than those necessary to cover costs of this type of lending. These laws were changed and regulations revised when banks began to enter the field.

Development of Industrial Banking Companies

A third type of institution in the consumer installment loan industry is the industrial banking company. These institutions are at times called *Morris Plan* companies, a name associated with one of the earliest groups of such institutions.

The first financial institution of this type was established in the United States in 1901 when an immigrant from Latvia, David Stein, founded the Merchants and Mechanics Savings and Loan Association at Newport News, Virginia. It was patterned after the consumer banks and loan associations that had been developed in Europe to make loans to workers. Its name is similar to that of present-day organizations granting real estate credit, but it was established to make general consumer loans for small amounts and to provide a means of saving small amounts.

Other banks of this type were not started until 1910, when Arthur J. Morris set up the Fidelity Savings and Trust Company at Norfolk, Virginia. This institution proposed to lend money to people employed in industry; hence the name industrial bank or loan company. Morris also planned to obtain at least part of his funds by selling investment certificates that would carry a definite rate of interest. Since these certificates could be paid for in installments, they also provided a means of saving in small amounts.

In 1911 Mr. Morris copyrighted the name "Morris Plan" and began to promote such units actively in large cities throughout the country. By 1917 he had established over 70 companies in the major cities of the country and also in some smaller ones. While the Morris Plan banks were being developed, other organizations and individuals were setting up similar units. Several other systems of banks were established, but these have all been dissolved.

Over 20 states currently have industrial-loan laws that provide for the chartering or operation of industrial banking companies. However, only 11 states, led by California and Hawaii, have industrial banks with sizable asset holdings. Depending on the state, industrial banking companies operate under such names as industrial loan company, Morris Plan bank, or industrial bank.

Industrial banking companies have both a thrift function and a loan function. While a few state statutes provide for the acceptance of deposits, savings (liabilities) are primarily obtained by issuing thrift investment certificates similar to those issued by thrift depository institutions. Some states also have established guaranty corporations to guarantee depositor savings.

Industrial banking firms continue to emphasize consumer installment loans. In some states they also are active purchasers of retail installment contracts, while in others real estate second mortgage loans and loans for home repair and modernization are important.

Current Status of the Consumer Installment Credit Industry

By the middle 1970s many of the distinctions between consumer finance companies, sales finance companies, and industrial banks and loan companies had disappeared and the trend was clearly toward finance companies with diversified activities. Industrial banks declined as a separate class of institution and often became regular state banks offering a broad group of banking services. As the size of loans which could be made by consumer finance companies was increased, the distinction between them and industrial loan companies disappeared to a large extent. Consumer finance companies and industrial banks and loan companies entered the sales finance field primarily by discounting the sales finance paper of companies selling household durable goods. Sales finance companies also entered the direct cash loan field and the independent companies did so to a significant degree. This happened in part because manufacturers and retail chains established their own sales finance subsidiaries and also because commercial banks entered the automobile financing field in a significant way.

The companies in the consumer installment credit industry vary in size and ownership from one-office concerns to large national chains which operate hundreds of offices. Some companies and chains are independently owned, others are subsidiaries of industrial and commercial firms, bank holding companies, or insurance companies. Today, most finance companies have highly diversified lending operations and obtain funds from a variety of sources.

Organization and Operations

In the early years of licensed lending, most of the lenders were individual proprietorships and partnerships, and most lending was done by individual offices, but since 1920, the corporate form and chain operations have become increasingly important. Chains have grown because they enjoy some advantages over independent offices. They have easier access to capital because they are able to raise funds in the security markets. They also find it easier and cheaper to obtain short-term bank loans. In addition they benefit from the mobility of capital, since they can shift funds from office to office as they are needed. They gain a further advantage from geographic diversification of risks.

Asset and Liability Structures. The Federal Reserve gathers balance sheet data on both consumer finance companies (including sales finance and other firms providing consumer installment credit) and commercial finance companies (including factors).[1] These data are presented in aggregate form for recent years in Table 17-1. Finance company assets are dominated, of course, by accounts

Table 17-1
Finance Company
Assets and Liabilities
for Selected Years.
Billions of Dollars,
End of Period

Account	1975	1977	1979	1981
ASSETS				
Accounts receivable, gross				
Consumer	36.0	44.0	65.7	85.5
Business	39.3	55.2	70.3	80.6
Total.............................	75.3	99.2	136.0	166.1
Less: Reserves for unearned income				
and losses........................	9.4	12.7	20.0	28.9
Accounts receivable, net	65.9	86.5	116.0	137.2
All other	15.7	17.8	24.9	34.2
TOTAL ASSETS	81.6	104.3	140.9	171.4
LIABILITIES				
Bank loans	8.0	5.9	8.5	15.4
Commercial paper	22.2	29.6	43.3	51.2
Other short-term debt.................	4.5	6.2	8.2	9.6
Long-term debt	27.6	36.0	46.7	54.8
Other liabilities......................	6.8	11.5	14.2	17.8
Capital, surplus, and undivided profits ...	12.5	15.1	19.9	22.8
TOTAL LIABILITIES AND CAPITAL	81.6	104.3	140.9	171.4

NOTE—Components may not add to totals due to rounding.
SOURCE: *Federal Reserve Bulletin* (September, 1982), p. A39.

---

[1]Commercial finance companies and factors were discussed in Chapter 9. The importance of finance company loans to business corporations on an annual basis also was depicted in Chapter 12, Table 12-1.

receivable, reflecting the extension of consumer or business credit. Notice the rapid growth in consumer and business loans in recent years.

Finance companies rely very heavily on borrowed funds to finance their loans to consumers and businesses. For example, finance company equity (capital, surplus, and undivided profits) is less than 15 percent of total assets. This heavy reliance on financial leverage is further compounded by the fact that it is not uncommon for one half of the borrowed funds outstanding to be in the form of short-term funds. The major source of short-term funds is commercial paper, most of which is placed directly. Finance companies also rely heavily on short-term loans from commercial banks. Long-term debt continues to average roughly one third of total assets.

As might be expected, finance companies which provide loans to consumers are severely affected during periods of rapidly rising interest rates, particularly short-term rates. This is due to their heavy dependence on short-term funds to finance loans to consumers. Finance rates charged to consumers are relatively stable over time while finance company financing costs fluctuate widely. The result of rising financing costs is a squeeze on profits (or even losses), as occurred in the industry during the 1974–75 period and at the beginning of the 1980s. To counter their profit sensitivity to changes in short-term borrowing costs, some finance companies began offering variable rate loans to consumers and businesses.

Operating Characteristics. The major purpose of cash loans made by finance companies is to tide consumers over a period of financial emergency. Before a loan is made, the complete financial position of the applicant is usually reviewed. It may be possible to plan the applicant's finances in such a way that with a larger loan some of the pressing debts can be paid off and the monthly payments can be reduced to a manageable level.

In the early days of lending, all loans were made with chattel mortgages on automobiles, furniture, or store fixtures as collateral or with a comaker or guarantor of the loan. Today a sizable portion of the loans are being made without security or comaker.

The original plan of consumer finance companies was to have the borrower repay an equal amount of principal each month and a smaller sum as interest each month as the balance was reduced. Most lenders have now changed their loan schedules to provide for equal payments each month.

Rates of charge were stated in the early consumer finance laws as the maximum percent per month on the unpaid balance and often with rates that were higher for the first dollars of a loan. For example, a state's small loan law may have called for a maximum rate of 3 percent per month on the first $150 of a loan, 2½ percent per month on the amount between $150 and $300, and 1 percent per month on the amount between $300 and $2,500. Many states alternately used a maximum dollar add-on to state rates as did commercial banks. An example would be a state law providing for a maximum add-on of $17 per $100 per year up to $300, and $11 per $100 per year on amounts loaned between $300 and $1,800. However, with passage of the Truth in Lending Act in 1968, rate quotations were required to provide the borrower with the actual percentage rate (this will be discussed later in the chapter) on the loan.

Table 17-2 indicates that average finance rates on personal loans have remained in the 20–22 percent range in recent years. At the same time, both the average amount and maturity of such loans have been rapidly increasing since the mid-1970s.

Financing the purchase of consumer durable goods is somewhat different from making cash loans. Since most retailers do not have sufficient capital to carry credit obligations to maturity, they refinance them through sales finance

Table 17-2
Finance Company Consumer Loan Characteristics. Finance Rates, Maturities, and Average Amount Financed by Finance Companies

	1975	1977	1979	1981
Average Finance Rates*				
Personal loans...............	21.0%	20.5%	20.5%	21.7%
Automobiles				
New......................	13.1%	13.1%	13.5%	15.9%
Used	17.6%	17.6%	18.0%	20.0%
Mobile homes	13.6%	13.6%	13.6%	18.1%
Other consumer goods.......	19.8%	19.2%	19.1%	21.6%
Average Maturities*				
Personal loans in months.....	36.3	42.9	50.5	71.1
Automobiles—percent				
New—Total	100.0%	100.0%	100.0%	100.0%
% over 42 months..........	—	26.4	59.2	74.9
% 37 to 42 months	23.6**	21.2	11.0	4.5
% 31 to 36 months	65.3	40.4	21.1	13.9
% 30 months or less........	11.2	11.9	8.7	6.6
% balloon.................	0.1	—	—	—
Used—Total..................	100.0%	100.0%	100.0%	100.0%
% over 36 months..........	—	8.7	40.8	57.5
% 31 to 36 months	54.2	57.3	43.5	31.4
% 25 to 30 months	31.1	23.6	8.5	4.1
% 24 months or less........	14.7	10.4	7.2	7.1
% balloon.................	—	—	—	—
Mobile homes	121.0	126.9	133.4	154.1
Other consumer goods.......	21.1	23.6	25.4	28.7
Average Amount Financed*				
Personal loans...............	$1,260	$1,521	$ 1,684	$ 2,574
Automobiles				
New......................	$4,096	$4,990	$ 6,035	$ 7,313
Used	$2,249	$2,720	$ 3,555	$ 4,354
Mobile homes	$7,686	$9,174	$11,617	$14,625
Other consumer goods.......	$ 464	$ 563	$ 600	$ 833

Note: Parts may not add to totals due to rounding.
*Unweighted means of periodic sample data for each year. Average amount financed excludes precomputed finance charges.
**Over 36 months
SOURCE: National Consumer Finance Association, *Finance Facts Yearbook,* 1982, p. 57.

companies or other financial institutions. The contracts between the seller and the buyer calling for time payments are sold to a financial institution at a discount. The courts held that this sale of the paper is also a sale of a thing rather than a loan of money. Thus, this whole process has been exempted from the usury statutes. Beginning with Indiana in 1935, however, most of the states have passed special statutes dealing with installment sales and financing. About half of these statutes govern the sale of all goods on installments; the rest apply only to the sale of automobiles on time payments. Some of the laws control charges that can be made, while others require only a detailed disclosure of the items added to the cash price to establish the installment sale price. Practically all of the statutes have provisions regarding the refund of charges if the contract is paid in full before final maturity. Some govern repossession practices, and some, charges for delinquency.

Most of the laws require sales finance companies to be licensed. Generally, the licenses are issued on application and the payment of a license fee, but without specific requirements that must be met or investigation of the applicants. The licenses may generally be revoked if a material misstatement is made in the application, for a willful violation of the law, or for fraud.

The basic procedures for financing the sale of automobiles and other consumer goods are the same. The original contract is drawn up between the automobile dealer and the purchaser. The usual procedure is to have the purchaser sign a *conditional sales contract*, which provides that the seller retain title to the car until the agreed purchase price has been paid. In some cases, a separate note is signed for the unpaid balance; in other cases, the sales contract is all that is required. Payments are usually made by the purchaser direct to the sales finance company.

Table 17-2 shows that finance company rates on new and used automobile loans were relatively level during the last half of the 1970s before rising sharply along with the rise in other interest rates at the beginning of the 1980s. As their short-term borrowing costs rise, finance companies must correspondingly charge higher rates in order to maintain their own profitability. Also notice that as automobile prices increased sharply in recent years, in part due to rapid inflation, the average size and maturity of automobile loans increased dramatically. Rates on other consumer goods now approach personal loan rates.

Automobile manufacturers insist on cash payment before delivering cars to dealers, and most dealers must finance their inventories. As part of their service, sales finance companies handle this financing.

The rate for wholesale financing is usually just about equal to costs. It consists of a small flat charge, plus interest for the actual time that the money is used. Low charges for wholesale financing are generally used as a promotional device to obtain retail financing business.

The major difference in appliance wholesale financing from automobile financing is that manufacturers or distributors at times agree to repurchase merchandise that the dealer does not sell. Advances are usually for only 90 percent of the wholesale price, whereas they are almost always 100 percent for cars. Charges are higher, especially the flat charge, and the interest rate may also be somewhat higher.

CREDIT UNIONS

Another type of supplier of credit to consumers is the credit union. The *credit union* is a cooperative nonprofit organization that provides its members with consumer credit. It is comprised of individuals who possess common bonds in terms of occupation, residential ties that are well defined, or some other form of association such as church affiliation. Over three fourths of all credit unions are of the occupational type involving manufacturing industries, government, and educational institutions. The credit union operates as a thrift institution for its members and is designed to provide credit to its members at moderate rates of interest.

Development and Current Status

The American credit union is an adaptation of the cooperative financial institutions that developed in Germany and other parts of Europe in the latter half of the nineteenth century. The first credit union on the American continent was set up in 1900 near Quebec by a member of the Canadian Dominion legislature, Alphonse Desjardins. Some nine years later, he also helped organize one of the first American credit unions among French Canadians residing at Manchester, New Hampshire, which was given a special charter in 1909. Prior to that time, several cooperative credit associations had been operating in Massachusetts, and in 1909 that state passed the first credit union law. Real progress began in 1921 when the late Edward A. Filene, a Boston merchant, became interested in credit union development and set up the Credit Union National Extension Bureau. Filene put a large sum of money into his organization and, under the guidance and outstanding leadership of an excellent promoter, Roy F. Bergengren, adequate credit union laws were subsequently passed in state after state.

In 1934, Congress passed the Federal Credit Union Act. A Credit Union Division was initially created in the Farm Credit Administration to supervise credit unions with United States charters and to render various services to such organizations. At present, the Federal Credit Union Act is administered by the National Credit Union Administration (NCUA) which operates as an independent federal regulatory agency. NCUA is responsible for chartering new federal credit unions and supervising and examining operating practices and financial conditions of existing federal credit unions.

The National Credit Union Administration also administers the National Credit Union Share Insurance Fund which was established by law in 1970. Prior to 1970, no federal insurance program comparable to those provided by the Federal Deposit Insurance Corporation and the Federal Savings and Loan Insurance Corporation was available to credit unions. The maximum amount of deposit insurance is currently set at $100,000. All federal credit unions are required to obtain insurance and state-chartered credit unions may join the National Credit Union Share Insurance Fund.

In addition to federal involvement, as the number of credit unions in a state initially grew, a state credit union league was formed. In 1935 these state leagues formed the Credit Union National Association (CUNA). This Association continues to play an active role by assisting in interlending activities among member credit unions and by providing certain financial market services.

Credit unions grew rapidly after World War II. During the 1950s, credit unions doubled in numbers, more than doubled in membership, and increased their assets by over six times. The 1960s also saw rapid growth with membership nearly doubling and assets increasing over three times. By the end of the 1960s, membership in credit unions was approaching 22 million people and assets were almost $16 billion. Approximately 21,000 credit unions were operating at the end of 1981. These credit unions had 45 million members and held about $78 billion in assets.[2]

The total assets of credit unions, of course, remain small relative to the asset sizes of other thrift institutions, finance companies, and commercial banks. However, their rapid growth in recent years suggests that credit unions will play an increasingly important role in the U.S. financial system—particularly in the consumer credit area.

Organization and Operation

As we alluded to above, credit unions may obtain a federal or state charter. Forty-six states (Alaska, Delaware, South Dakota, and Wyoming are excluded) have provisions for chartering credit unions. Close to 60 percent of all credit unions have federal charters. Over 80 percent of all credit unions are federally insured up to $100,000 per account and 97 percent have either federal or state insurance.

Asset and Liability Structures. Table 17-3 contains some selected asset and liability data for both state-chartered and federally chartered credit unions during recent years. In terms of total size, federally chartered credit unions hold about $7 billion more in assets. Loans outstanding to members dominate the assets of both types of credit unions. Data for 1981 show that approximately 65 percent of

Table 17-3
Credit Union Major Assets and Liabilities for Selected Years. Billions of Dollars, End of Period

Account	1975	1977	1979	1981
TOTAL ASSETS	38.0	54.1	65.8	77.7
Federal.	20.2	29.6	35.9	42.4
State	17.8	24.5	29.9	35.3
LOANS OUTSTANDING	28.2	42.0	53.1	50.5
Federal.	14.9	22.7	28.7	27.5
State	13.3	19.3	24.4	23.0
SAVINGS	33.0	46.8	56.2	68.9
Federal (shares)	17.5	25.8	30.5	37.6
State (shares and deposits) . . .	15.5	21.0	25.7	31.3

SOURCE: *Federal Reserve Bulletin* (September, 1982), p. A29.

---

[2]*Credit Union Report* (Madison: Credit Union National Association, June, 1982), p. 2.

total assets for federally chartered and state-chartered credit unions were in the form of loans to members. At the same time, credit unions rely almost exclusively on savings by members to finance or support assets. In 1981, member savings accounted for 89 percent of the total liabilities and capital held by federal and state credit unions.

Loans made to members are for personal expenses, the purchase of automobiles and other durable goods, residential repair and modernization, and so forth. Credit unions also invest a portion of their assets in U.S. government and federal agency securities, make loans to or hold deposits in other credit unions, and hold cash and miscellaneous assets. On the liability side of their balance sheets, credit unions have experienced a significant change in their savings mix. In 1981, share drafts grew rapidly in importance and thrift certificates began approaching one third of total credit union savings. Debt liabilities in the form of accounts payable and notes payable continue to constitute a small portion of total liabilities and capital. Thus credit unions, in contrast with finance companies that supply consumer credit, rely very little on borrowed funds and financial leverage.

Operating Characteristics. Since the credit union is a cooperative, the power to run it resides in the general meetings of the members. All who have subscribed to at least one share, the par value of which is usually $5, are eligible to vote. The general administration of the credit union is placed in the hands of a board of directors elected at the annual meeting.

A credit committee is the heart of the organization since it must pass on all loan applications. Also elected is a supervisory committee. It is an auditing committee that has the duty of going over the books at frequent intervals to be sure that operations are being carried on in line with the bylaws of the association and the law under which it was chartered. Many credit unions also have an education committee that tries to educate the members in thrift and the proper use of credit.

The funds of the credit union and its financial records are handled by the treasurer, who is elected at the annual meeting. The treasurer may employ clerical assistance to aid in carrying out required duties and may also be paid for the work. The treasurer is the only elected official who may receive any compensation. Since most of the time spent on the credit union affairs is donated by the elected officers and committees and office space is often donated by the firm or organization sponsoring the credit union, total costs can be kept at a relatively low level. These types of subsidies differentiate credit unions from other thrift institutions and commercial banks.

Credit unions also differ because they pay no federal income taxes and generally pay only real property taxes in the form of state taxes. Probably their cooperative nonprofit nature and their relatively small average size have kept them free of income taxation. Other financial institutions have argued against this advantage, and as credit unions become larger and continue to broaden their operations they may find their income tax-exempt status being threatened.

Federal and most state credit unions are legally permitted to charge maximum rates per month on the unpaid balance of a loan. This rate must include the impact of all charges involved in granting the loan. The maximum rate often is charged for small unsecured loans while lower rates often prevail on loans secured by chattel mortgages (on automobiles and other durable goods), pledged shares, and comakers. The maximum amount loaned to one individual cannot exceed 10 percent of the assets of the credit union. Life insurance on the unpaid balance of the loan is provided by most credit unions through a mutual insurance company, Cuna Mutual Insurance Society, at no additional cost to the borrower.

During 1977 major revisions were made in the Federal Credit Union Act. Federal credit union operating powers were substantially broadened by permitting the extension of secured and unsecured loan maturities to 12 years and by allowing credit unions to engage in first-mortgage residential real estate loans for periods not to exceed 30 years. A second major legislative development provided for the establishment and implementation of a permanent share draft program. Under such a program, federal credit union members are permitted to write drafts (similar to checks available through commercial banks) on their share accounts. Credit union share drafts are "cleared" through the banking system as are checks written on commercial banks except that cancelled drafts are not returned to credit union members. Instead, photocopies of the drafts are transmitted to the appropriate credit unions from the bank through which the drafts are paid. Draft writers periodically receive itemized statements.

Passage of the Depository Institutions Deregulation and Monetary Control Act in 1980 also impacts substantially on the operations of credit unions. As was noted in previous chapters, credit unions and other depository institutions can borrow from the Federal Reserve at the discount rate and are being required to hold reserves at a federal reserve bank against their checkable deposits, including share drafts. Likewise, interest-rate and dividend-rate ceilings on savings deposits are being phased out in an orderly manner by the Depository Institutions Deregulation Committee and must be eliminated by early 1986.

COMMERCIAL BANKS

The largest volume of consumer credit is granted by the commercial banks of the country. Banks have achieved this position even though they entered the field of consumer financing after specialized institutions had been developed in this field. Banks now make all types of consumer loans and most banks are competing vigorously for consumer loans.

Development of Consumer Lending and Current Status

Before consumer financing became widespread some banks made loans to consumers on a 30-, 60-, or 90-day basis in the same way that they made commercial loans to business. In the middle 1920s a few smaller banks set up personal loan departments, but the growth was slow. In 1928 impetus was given to the movement when the National City Bank of New York, one of the largest banks in the country, set up a personal loan department. In 1929 the Bank of America in San Francisco, California, which has branches all over the state, entered the field.

In the summer of 1934, the United States Government initiated a program that gave real impetus to the expansion of bank lending to consumers. In an effort to stimulate employment and economic activity in general, the Federal Housing Administration was authorized to guarantee loans to authorized lenders who would extend credit for home repair and modernization. These loans, which had to be repaid in equal monthly installments, were known as FHA Title I loans. During the first couple of years of experience, losses paid to the banks by the FHA were less than 3 percent of the loan volume, and a substantial part of such losses were later recovered by the FHA. The record of FHA loans and their experiences with them convinced many bankers that consumer loans could be made without undue losses so as to yield a reasonable profit.

The Bankers Association for Consumer Credit, which was formed in 1938, gave added impetus to the movement. In 1940 it merged its activities with those of the American Bankers Association, which had recognized the importance of consumer financing by banks. Consumer lending by banks became more widespread, especially during the World War II years.

At the present time almost all commercial banks make consumer loans. As we previously saw in Table 16-2, commercial banks held over 44 percent or nearly one half of the consumer installment credit outstanding as of mid-1982. Approximately 40 percent of the $146.8 billion held by commercial banks was in the form of automobile installment credit. Consumer credit in the form of bank revolving credit (credit cards and check credit) accounted for 22 percent of commercial bank consumer installment credit.

Organization and Operation

The establishment, general organization, and lending operations of commercial banks were initially discussed in Chapter 3. At the end of 1981, commercial banks had total loans and leases outstanding of $981.8 billion. Commercial and industrial loans accounted for 37 percent of this total. This category was followed in importance by real estate loans (29 percent) and loans to individuals (19 percent). These figures indicate the significance of consumer loans to commercial banks.[3]

Banks have generally set up a separate department to handle consumer loans. As personal loan departments have had more experience and have tried to increase their volume, they have shifted from comaker loans to loans on an individual signature. Some personal loans are made with collateral, but banks rely much less on household goods than do other institutions. Collateral may consist of savings accounts, marketable securities, the cash value of life insurance policies that have been assigned to the bank, savings and loan shares, and the like.

The most important field for many of the larger banks is automobile financing. Under an arrangement with a dealer, a bank usually finances the dealer's stock of cars in order to get the note business. The methods used follow closely those developed by the sales finance companies. The practice of making direct loans to

---

[3] *Federal Reserve Bulletin*, September, 1982, p. A15.

individuals to finance car purchases has been developed by many commercial banks into a major outlet for funds. Frequently it is based upon an arrangement between insurance agents or brokers and the bank.

Banks also do a substantial volume of business in financing the purchase of other durable goods. A part of this is direct financing, most of which arises from the purchases of notes from dealers. This financing is done in much the same way as sales financing by sales finance companies.

In the middle 1960s bank credit card plans began spreading throughout the country, but with the largest concentration remaining on the West Coast and in the Chicago and New York areas. Today, the two largest plans (VISA and MasterCard) are national in scope. Check credit or overdraft plans also provide for credit within preset limits; the customer simply writes a check larger than the balance on deposit.

FACILITATING AGENCIES

The merchandising function plays only a minor role in the intermediate- and short-term consumer credit fields. Some selling of consumer paper to other institutions or individuals is done especially by the larger companies. Some sellers of durables carry their own paper for a period and later look for a purchaser for such paper, but there is little organized activity of this kind carried on by brokers or separate institutions.

Credit Exchanges

Several facilitating agencies, however, play a role in the consumer credit field. In most cities of any size the consumer finance companies operating under the small-loan laws have set up a credit exchange to provide information on loans. Some of the earliest of these exchanges operated on a one-loan plan under which an individual or a married couple could have only one loan from a small-loan company outstanding at any time. This was in keeping with the philosophy that one of the functions of a small-loan company is to help a person plan one's finances so as to get out of debt and that this can be done best if the person has to deal with only one company.

The one-loan exchanges met with opposition from new companies entering a territory. When some of the small-loan companies entered the field of durable goods financing, a new problem was created for restricted-loan exchanges since these loans were of a somewhat different nature from the regular loans to help an individual in financial difficulty. As a result, some exchanges amended their rules so as to allow several loans to an individual so long as the same collateral was not used as security for more than one loan. More recently, the consumer finance companies in some cities, for example, St. Louis, have developed clearinghouse exchanges in which no restrictions are placed on loans; but each company furnishes the exchange with complete information on all loans and on all notes they purchase.

Credit Bureaus

Another important facilitating agency is the credit-checking agency or credit bureau. It is organized by local merchants and finance companies to serve as a central exchange for data on the credit extended to individuals. The latest data in the file is usually furnished by telephone or messenger or is transferred electronically. When more detailed information is required, a special report may be prepared which gives data on the applicant, such as age, marital status, family, permanence of residence, mode of living, reputation, estimated income, investments, bank accounts, suits or liens against the applicant, and charge-account buying and paying habits.

For information on an individual who lives out of town, data may be obtained from a credit bureau in that town. Several national concerns also prepare reports on the financial status of individuals, primarily for insurance purposes but also for credit evaluation.

Credit bureaus work well when all important credit-granting agencies cooperate. It is especially difficult to get some used-car dealers to furnish information, and their data is very important since a used-car loan may represent by far the largest debt of a borrower, especially if the person does not own a home.

Insurance Agencies

Insurance of various types, such as fire, theft, and comprehensive, is usually carried on durables when they are financed. This may be handled by regular insurance companies or by special companies writing insurance only in connection with financing. In automobile financing, collision insurance is also required.

To an increasing extent, group life insurance is being used to insure the unpaid balance of consumer loans. Special companies are active in this field and some of the leading life insurance companies have entered it. There is also increasing emphasis on accident and disability insurance on a group basis to protect borrowers against these contingencies.

Even though all types of insurance coverages are growing, there is disagreement as to the advisability of some types. Some feel that although group life insurance is desirable, accident, disability, and similar forms of insurance are of limited usefulness.

RECENT DEVELOPMENTS IN CONSUMER CREDIT REGULATION

Regulation of institutions financing the consumer historically was done by the state governments. Most state consumer installment loan laws evolved out of the Russell Sage Foundation's efforts in the development of the Uniform Small Loan Law and the National Consumer Finance Association's Model Consumer Finance Act prepared in 1948. The U.S. Congress did give the Federal Reserve temporary powers to regulate consumer credit (specifically, regulation of down payments and repayment periods) during World War II, and real estate credit during the Korean War.

In 1968 Congress passed the Consumer Credit Protection Act which regulates the disclosure of consumer credit costs and also garnishment procedures and prohibits exorbitant credit transactions. The regulation to put the Truth in Lending section of the Act into effect was drafted by a Federal Reserve task force and designated as Regulation Z. The purpose of the law and the regulation is to make consumers aware of the cost of credit and to enable them to compare the costs of alternate forms of credit. Regulation Z applies to consumer finance companies, credit unions, sales finance companies, banks, savings and loan associations, residential mortgage brokers, credit card issuers, department stores, automobile dealers, hospitals, craftsmen such as plumbers, doctors, dentists, and any other individuals or organizations which extend or arrange credit for consumers. Credit transactions of more than $25,000 are exempted from the law except for transactions secured by real estate which are covered regardless of amount. The law also instructs the Board of Governors to exempt from federal disclosure requirements classes of consumer credit transactions within a state if the Board finds that state law imposes substantially the same requirements and that the law is enforced.

The law requires disclosure of the total finance charge and the annual percentage rate of charge. The finance charge includes all costs for getting the loan including not only interest or discount but service charges, loan fees, finder fees, insurance premiums, points, and the like. Charges for such items as taxes not included in the purchase price, licenses, certificates of title, and the like may be excluded from the finance charge if they are itemized and disclosed separately. The annual percentage rate of charge is the relationship of total finance charges to the amount financed and must be computed to the nearest one quarter of 1 percent annually. The creditor must also make a series of disclosures to the customer, including such items as the method of determining the balance on which the finance charge is calculated, the conditions under which a creditor may acquire a security interest in any property owned by the customer and the nature of such an interest.

The annual percentage rate (APR) must be calculated in accordance with the actuarial method. Extensive tables are provided by the Federal Reserve for purposes of computing the APR for installment loans involving level monthly payment plans. One needs only to know the dollar amount of the finance charge, the total amount to be financed, and the number of monthly payments. For example, a $200 loan, with finance charges of $35 and requiring 24 monthly payments would have an APR of 16 percent. This is illustrated in Table 17-4.

The APR also can be approximated with the following constant ratio formula:

$$R = \frac{2MI}{P(N + 1)}$$

where

R = annual effective interest rate expressed in decimal form
M = number of installment payments in a year

EXAMPLE
Finance charge = $35.00; Total amount financed = $200; Number of monthly payments = 24.

SOLUTION
Step 1—Divide the finance charge by the total amount financed and multiply by $100. This gives the finance charge per $100 of amount financed. That is, $35.00 ÷ $200 = .1750 × $100 = $17.50.

Step 2—Follow down the left hand column of the table to the line for 24 months. Follow across this line until you find the nearest number to $17.50. In this example $17.51 is closest to $17.50. Reading up the column of figures shows an annual percentage rate of 16%.

NUMBER—ANNUAL PERCENTAGE RATE OF

Payments	14.50%	14.75%	15.00%	15.25%	15.50%	15.75%	16.00%	16.25%
(Finance Charge per $100 of Amount Financed)								
1	1.21	1.23	1.25	1.27	1.29	1.31	1.33	1.35
2	1.82	1.85	1.88	1.91	1.94	1.97	2.00	2.04
3	2.43	2.47	2.51	2.55	2.59	2.64	2.68	2.72
4	3.04	3.09	3.14	3.20	3.25	3.30	3.36	3.41
5	3.65	3.72	3.78	3.84	3.91	3.97	4.04	4.10
6	4.27	4.35	4.42	4.49	4.57	4.64	4.72	4.79
7	4.89	4.98	5.06	5.15	5.23	5.32	5.40	5.49
8	5.51	5.61	5.71	5.80	5.90	6.00	6.09	6.19
9	6.14	6.25	6.35	6.46	6.57	6.68	6.78	6.89
10	6.77	6.88	7.00	7.12	7.24	7.36	7.48	7.60
11	7.40	7.53	7.66	7.79	7.92	8.05	8.18	8.31
12	8.03	8.17	8.31	8.45	8.59	8.74	8.88	9.02
13	8.66	8.81	8.97	9.12	9.27	9.43	9.58	9.73
14	9.30	9.46	9.63	9.79	9.96	10.12	10.29	10.45
15	9.94	10.11	10.29	10.47	10.64	10.82	11.00	11.17
16	10.58	10.77	10.95	11.14	11.33	11.52	11.71	11.90
17	11.22	11.42	11.62	11.82	12.02	12.22	12.42	12.62
18	11.87	12.08	12.29	12.50	12.72	12.93	13.14	13.35
19	12.52	12.74	12.97	13.19	13.41	13.64	13.86	14.09
20	13.17	13.41	13.64	13.88	14.11	14.35	14.59	14.82
21	13.82	14.07	14.32	14.57	14.82	15.06	15.31	15.56
22	14.48	14.74	15.00	15.26	15.52	15.78	16.04	16.30
23	15.14	15.41	15.68	15.96	16.23	16.50	16.78	17.05
➤24	15.80	16.08	16.37	16.65	16.94	17.22	17.51	17.80
25	16.46	16.76	17.06	17.35	17.65	17.95	18.25	18.55
26	17.13	17.44	17.75	18.06	18.37	18.68	18.99	19.30
27	17.80	18.12	18.44	18.76	19.09	19.41	19.74	20.06
28	18.47	18.80	19.14	19.47	19.81	20.15	20.48	20.82
29	19.14	19.49	19.83	20.18	20.53	20.88	21.23	21.58
30	19.81	20.17	20.54	20.90	21.26	21.62	21.99	22.35
31	20.49	20.87	21.24	21.61	21.99	22.37	22.74	23.12
32	21.17	21.56	21.95	22.33	22.72	23.11	23.50	23.89
33	21.85	22.25	22.65	23.06	23.46	23.86	24.26	24.67
34	22.54	22.95	23.37	23.78	24.19	24.61	25.03	25.44
35	23.23	23.65	24.08	24.51	24.94	25.36	25.79	26.23
36	23.92	24.35	24.80	25.24	25.68	26.12	26.57	27.01

SOURCE: *Board of Governors of the Federal Reserve System,* "Truth in Lending—Consumer Credit Cost Disclosure," Exhibit G.

I = total dollar amount of interest charged
P = net principal amount of loan available to the borrower
N = total number of installment payments over the life of the loan

In the above example, the effective interest rate would be estimated as

$$R = \frac{2(12)\$35}{\$200(24+1)} = \frac{\$840}{\$5000} = .168 \text{ or } 16.8 \text{ percent}$$

It should be noted that the formula overstates the "true" APR calculated by the Federal Reserve using the actuarial method. The degree of error increases with higher interest rates and longer loan maturities. However, even with such limitations, the formula does provide the user with a quick estimate of the "true" APR.

Another important development in 1968 (along with 1974 revisions) was the publishing of a Uniform Consumer Credit Code (UCCC) by the National Conference of Commissioners on Uniform State Laws. As of the end of 1981, this Code had been adopted by 8 states (Colorado, Idaho, Indiana, Kansas, Maine, Oklahoma, Utah, and Wyoming). Other states have adopted parts of the UCCC in their own state statutes. It is hoped that the UCCC will eventually replace all existing state consumer credit laws. The UCCC regulates credit transactions to individuals up to $25,000, with possible increases to be based on changes in the Consumer Price Index (CPI). It fixes uniform maximum rates for all types of credit grantors. The maximum rates for installment credit loans or for the financing of credit sales are 36 percent per year on the first $300, 21 percent on the next $700, and 15 percent on the remainder. Maximum rates are subject to change with changes in the CPI.

Several additions and amendments have been made in recent years to improve and strengthen the Consumer Credit Protection Act of 1968. Action was taken by Congress in the fall of 1970 to prohibit the distribution of credit cards which were not requested by a prospective user and to limit the liability of a credit card owner for purchases made by others on lost or stolen cards. In 1971 Congress also passed the Fair Credit Reporting Act which was designed to protect consumers from the distribution by credit agencies of incorrect or outdated information.

The Fair Credit Billing Act was passed in 1974 to aid consumers in having billing errors corrected. The Equal Credit Opportunity Act also was initially passed in 1974 and prohibited creditors from discriminating on the basis of marital status or sex in their credit-granting decisions. Amendments in 1976 extended the list of factors which cannot be used for rejecting credit applications to include religion, race, color, national origin, age, or source of income (such as public assistance programs). Applicants also are not to be discriminated against if they have exercised in "good faith" any rights granted under the Consumer Credit Protection Act including the Truth in Lending section.

Consumer protection legislation also has been passed in the area of long-term consumer financing involving real estate transactions. The Real Estate Settlement Procedures Act was passed by Congress in 1974, amended in 1975, and amended in its current form in mid-1976. Federally regulated lenders must comply with the Act, which is designed to protect purchasers of residential homes and condominiums. Lenders must provide the loan applicant with "good faith" estimates of closing costs (such as loan origination fees, credit reports, and title searches) when a loan application is being made. And, if the borrower requests it, a standard settlements form containing all known settlement costs must be provided by the lender one day before the settlement or closing actually takes place.

Other relevant legislation includes the Community Reinvestment Act of 1977 which was passed to encourage depository institutions to help meet the credit needs of the communities in which they operate and are chartered. In 1979, changes in the National Bankruptcy Act provided for greater protection of assets when personal bankruptcies are filed. Since then personal bankruptcies have soared. The Truth in Lending Act also was modified in 1980 to make it easier for creditors to comply with disclosure requirements and to make the use of annual percentage rates more understandable to borrowers.

QUESTIONS

1. Which institutions are included in the consumer installment credit industry?
2. Why did consumer finance companies develop in the United States? What were the legislative developments that paralleled the growth of consumer finance companies?
3. Briefly describe the functions of sales finance companies and trace their development over time.
4. Discuss the development and current status of industrial banking companies in the consumer financing field.
5. What are the major sources of funds used by finance companies to finance their consumer and business loans?

6. Briefly indicate how average finance rates charged by finance companies differ by type of loan and over time during recent years.
7. Define what is meant by a credit union and briefly trace the development of credit unions.
8. Discuss the operations of credit unions, including information on organizational structure, sources of funds, and recent legislative developments.
9. How important is the role of commercial banks in financing consumers?
10. Identify and briefly describe several facilitating agencies that play a role in the consumer credit field.
11. Describe recent federal legislation in the consumer credit field.

PROBLEMS

1. Assume that you have the opportunity to borrow $10,000 for 4 years. Total finance charges will be $1,000 per year or $4,000 over the 4 years. Use the constant ratio formula to approximate the actual percentage rate if equal quarterly payments are required. Also show how your answer would change if monthly payments had been required.

2. A 1-year, $1,000 loan is offered to you. The finance charge will be $85 and you will be required to make level monthly payments. Use Table 17-4 to determine the annual percentage rate on this loan. How would your answer change if the lender allowed you to make 24 level monthly payments but required a finance charge of $175?

3. Calculate the effective annual rate of interest on the following loan: $850 loaned for a period of 1 ½ years to be repaid with a total loan financing charge of $105 ($70 per year) in equal monthly installments. Use Table 17-4 to determine the annual percentage rate. Also estimate the rate using the constant ratio formula.

SUGGESTED READINGS

Canner, Glenn. "The Community Reinvestment Act: A Second Progress Report." *Federal Reserve Bulletin* (November, 1981), pp. 813–823.

Consumer Credit—Factors Influencing Its Availability and Cost. U.S. Department of Commerce. Washington: U.S. Government Printing Office, 1976.

Consumer Credit in the United States. National Commission on Consumer Finance. Washington: U.S. Government Printing Office, 1973.

"Equal Credit Opportunity." *Federal Reserve Bulletin* (February, 1977), pp. 101–107.

"Exercise of Consumer Rights Under the Equal Credit Opportunity and Fair Credit Billing Acts." *Federal Reserve Bulletin* (May, 1978), pp. 363–366.

Luckett, Charles. "Recent Developments in the Mortgage and Consumer Credit Markets." *Federal Reserve Bulletin* (May, 1982), pp. 281–290.

Melicher, Ronald W. "Managing the Profitability of Finance Companies." *Credit* (January/February, 1978), pp. 18–21.

Melicher, Ronald W. "Profitability Management of Marginal Accounts." *The Credit World* (March, 1978), pp. 20–23.

Prell, Michael J. "The Long-Run Growth of Consumer Installment Credit—Some Observations." *Monthly Review,* Federal Reserve Bank of Kansas City (February, 1973), pp. 3–13.

18 Financing Urban Real Estate

Financing the purchase of residential real estate is classified as long-term consumer financing. Home mortgage debt outstanding is substantially larger than short- and intermediate-term consumer debt, both installment and noninstallment combined. This relative importance of consumer debt components was shown in Chapter 16, Table 16-1.

In this chapter we begin with a discussion of the annual importance of real estate funds raised and also consider the roles of major financial institutions in supplying mortgage funds. Then residential real estate financing procedures are discussed. This is followed by an examination of the major financial institutions and facilitating organizations involved in real estate financing. The final section focuses on the role of government in the financing of urban real estate.

SOURCES AND USES OF MORTGAGE FUNDS

In Chapter 6, Table 6-2, we showed the annual use of funds by nonfinancial sectors in the U.S. economy. Estimates by the Bankers Trust Company indicated that annual amounts of intermediate- and long-term funds raised in the capital markets were substantially larger than short-term funds raised in money markets. Furthermore, the amount of funds raised annually for real estate mortgage financing dominates the amount of funds raised through the issuance of corporate stocks and bonds. Except for periods of major economic downturns, funds raised annually for real estate mortgages represent well over one half of all intermediate- and long-term funds raised.

Table 18-1 shows the amount of mortgage funds raised in recent years by type of mortgage. Residential mortgages, particularly home or one- to four-family mortgages, represent the primary use of mortgage funds and account for well over one half of the total mortgage funds raised annually. Commercial property mortgages rank second in importance.

Thrift institutions and commercial banks are the major private-sector suppliers of mortgage funds. Table 18-1 indicates that savings and loan associations

Table 18-1

Annual Amounts of Mortgage Funds Raised and Supplied (In Billions of Dollars)

	1979	1980	1981	1982 (Est.)	1983 (Proj.)
FUNDS RAISED					
Residential mortgages					
Home	120.4	95.9	73.5	59.5	81.0
Multifamily	7.8	8.7	4.3	6.0	7.5
Total	128.2	104.6	77.8	65.5	88.5
Commercial mortgages	24.1	20.1	24.3	16.3	15.0
Farm mortgages	11.8	9.3	9.7	7.0	5.8
Total	164.2	134.0	111.8	88.8	109.3
FUNDS SUPPLIED					
Insurance companies and pension funds					
Life insurance companies	13.4	13.4	6.8	3.8	5.3
Private noninsured pension funds	1.6	2.3	1.5	1.5	1.6
State and local retirement funds	1.3	1.3	2.3	3.4	4.0
Fire and casualty insurance companies	.3	.3	.3	.5	.3
Total	16.5	17.3	10.9	9.2	11.2
Thrift institutions					
Savings and loan associations	48.8	35.7	22.8	11.5	34.8
Mutual savings banks	5.8	2.6	−.8	−1.5	2.5
Credit unions	.1	−.4	−.4	−.5	—
Total	54.7	37.9	21.5	9.5	37.3
Other financial intermediaries					
Mortgage companies	−1.4	2.8	.2	−2.6	1.7
Real estate investment trusts	−1.0	−.7	−1.1	−.8	−.5
Total	−2.4	2.1	−.9	−3.4	1.2
Commercial banks	32.7	18.3	21.9	17.2	18.5
Government					
U.S. government	6.2	6.9	4.3	2.4	2.9
Federally sponsored agencies	14.4	14.1	12.6	14.0	10.5
State and local general funds	6.5	10.3	7.7	5.0	6.0
Total	27.1	31.3	24.6	21.4	19.4
Individuals and others	35.5	27.1	33.7	34.9	21.7
Total	164.2	134.0	111.8	88.8	109.3
MEMORANDUM					
Mortgage pools*					
Government National Mortgage Association	21.4	18.1	11.9	11.5	12.5
Farmers Home Administration	5.3	3.8	5.1	2.5	2.8
Federal Home Loan Mortgage Corporation	3.3	1.7	3.0	20.8	12.5
Federal National Mortgage Association	—	—	.7	13.2	7.0
Total	30.0	23.6	20.7	48.0	34.8

*Ownership of mortgage pools has been allocated among the investor groups.
SOURCE: Bankers Trust Company, *Credit and Capital Markets,* 1983, p. T10.

historically dominate all other financial institutions as suppliers of mortgage funds. Notice, however, that the combination of economic downturn and disintermediation associated with high interest rates during the beginning of the 1980s resulted in a major curtailment of mortgage funds being supplied by savings and loan associations. Their annual supply of mortgage funds dropped sharply until a low was reached in 1982. Mortgage funds supplied by commercial banks also were curtailed, but to a lesser extent. Commercial bank funds actually exceeded the amount of funds supplied by savings and loan associations during 1982. This development is at least partially related to the greater liquidity problems suffered by savings and loan associations because of their failure to adequately practice the hedging principle as was discussed in Chapter 6. Furthermore, savings and loan associations traditionally have specialized in home (including one- to four-family dwellings) mortgage loans, while commercial banks have been more balanced in their mix between home and other types of mortgage loans.

Life insurance companies also are important suppliers of mortgage funds, particularly as purchasers of commercial property mortgages. Table 18-1 also shows that mutual savings banks were severely affected in their role as suppliers of mortgage funds by the developments of the early 1980s. Their fate was similar to that faced by savings and loan associations; mutual savings banks actually had a net liquidation of mortgage funds in 1981 and 1982. Credit unions have not developed as a thrift institution supplier of mortgage funds.

Individuals have become increasingly important suppliers of mortgage funds in recent years. As a group, many individuals are investing directly in mortgage loans and mortgage "pools" instead of saving in other ways. High interest rates have made such investments attractive, and rapid escalation of property values has resulted in owners being forced to "take back" mortgage loans in order to sell their properties. In addition, a variety of real estate limited partnership arrangements have flourished in recent years. By "pooling" their funds, individuals are able to purchase mortgage loans on large residential and commercial properties.

Mortgage pools provided the basis for the issuance of mortgage pass-through securities beginning in the 1970s. These securities pass through to the holders both interest and principal payments from the underlying pool of mortgages. Table 18-1 shows the importance of these pools, particularly those that underlie the pass-through securities guaranteed by the Government National Mortgage Association. Individuals and financial institutions are major purchasers of mortgage pass-through securities.

Financial intermediaries play an important role in the real estate markets. Some intermediaries are active suppliers of mortgage funds and actually hold the mortgages. Other financial intermediaries, particularly mortgage banking companies, perform an important "merchandising" or facilitating function. The role of these intermediaries will be discussed in a later section.

Finally, the federal government maintains an active role in the financing of urban real estate. A variety of governmental assistance programs have been developed over the years to aid in both the primary and secondary real estate markets. Government efforts extend beyond the direct supply of mortgage funds, as we will see later in the chapter.

PROCEDURES IN RESIDENTIAL REAL ESTATE FINANCING

As in all lending operations, the procedures used in urban residential real estate financing are determined in large part by the characteristics of such financing. The financing traditionally has been long-term except for loans for construction, and even these typically have been replaced by long-term, fixed interest rate mortgage loans. Long-term loans have been possible because houses last for long periods of time, often 40 or 50 or more years. However, because of recently high and volatile interest rates and the liquidity problems faced by savings and loan associations, there has been some trend towards the offering of variable rate mortgages and/or shorter than traditional maturities.

Special Risks

Special risks are involved in real estate financing. The value of the collateral is affected by such factors as the changing economic status of the area, the city, and the neighborhood, as well as by business fluctuations, changing price levels, and the like. There are legal technicalities to consider to insure that the prospective borrower can get a clear title. The property must be maintained adequately if it is to maintain its value. The present and prospective income and other obligations of the borrower are also significant in determining the safety of a loan.

The Mortgage

A loan made to finance the purchase of residential real estate is typically secured by means of a *mortgage* against such property. The real estate mortgage, in one form or another, has probably been used as long as the right of private property has been recognized. The borrower in such a loan transaction is called the *mortgagor*; the lender, the *mortgagee*.[1] The form used in this country is patterned after that of the English common law and equity law. In early England, a borrower of money would actually turn over possession of the land to the lender, and the lender would have use of the land until the debt was paid. The word "mortgage," which stems from the term "mort-gage" or "dead-pledge," was therefore rather appropriate in that the land was, to all intents and purposes, dead so far as the borrower was concerned until such time as the loan was repaid.

Modifications of this form of mortgage arrangement were developed which provided in some cases that the income from the land should apply to the payment of the debt, and in other cases that possession of the land by the lender was not to be obtained unless the borrower failed to abide by the terms of the contractual agreement. Later the English Court of Equity began to take the view that it was unreasonable that a mortgagee should retain the full value of the property if the

---

[1] In some states a *deed of trust* is used as security on a real property loan, whereas in other states a lender has a choice of using either a mortgage or deed of trust. The deed of trust uses three parties: the *beneficiary* (lender), the *trustor* (borrower), and the *trustee* who forecloses on behalf of the beneficiary in the event of default.

borrower defaulted since it was merely conveyed to the mortgagee to secure a debt and, therefore, a mortgagor had a right in equity to redeem the property upon full payment of the obligation, even though the maturity date of the loan had passed. This right is known as the *equity of redemption.*

Along with the development of the equity of redemption came the procedure of *foreclosure.* The foreclosure was necessary to prevent an undue burden upon the lender because of the uncertainty of the period of equity of redemption. It provided that on the petition of the mortgagee the courts would fix a time within which the mortgagor was required to pay the debt. If the mortgagor failed to pay within this time, the decree provided that mortgagor's equity of redemption was thereby "barred and foreclosed."

Junior Mortgages. At times a mortgagor may want to borrow more money on a piece of property than the lender on a mortgage is willing to lend. Then the borrower may find a lender who will lend the additional sum, usually at a higher rate of interest, provided the mortgagor gives the second lender a claim on equity in the property that is not covered by the existing mortgage. When this is done, the existing mortgage is called the first mortgage; the new mortgage, the second or junior mortgage. At times three or more mortgages may be placed on one piece of property.

State laws provide for the recording of mortgages in order to protect the interests of all parties. An unrecorded mortgage is binding between the parties to the agreement, but the law provides that the first mortgage to be recorded is the senior mortgage; so all mortgages should be recorded promptly.

Foreclosure Procedure. In the event of default by the mortgagor, the mortgagee will usually try to work out an arrangement whereby the payments in default may be met. If the mortgagee feels that his or her interests are in jeopardy, a lawsuit asking the court to foreclose on the mortgage and to hold a foreclosure sale will be filed. The mortgagee may bid at the foreclosure sale, and has an advantage because the amount due on the mortgage can be used to pay for the bid while other bidders must pay cash. Foreclosure costs are paid first out of the proceeds of the sale of the property. If a surplus exists after foreclosure costs and the mortgage debt are paid, the mortgagor is entitled to it. If part of the debt is unpaid, the court grants the mortgagee a deficiency judgement for the amount. This may be collected from other assets of the mortgagor. If the mortgagor has insufficient assets, the claim will remain on record for a period of time. Such an unpaid claim makes it almost impossible for the mortgagor to get a mortgage loan in the future.

Land Contracts. In some cases a *land contract* instead of a mortgage is used to finance the sale of real estate. This is a contract for the sale of property in which the deed to the property does not pass to the purchaser until the terms of the contract have been fulfilled. It generally provides for regular payments, usually monthly, of interest and part of the principal. In cases in which the purchaser does not have sufficient money to finance the purchase of property by means of a mortgage, it may be financed by means of a land contract; and in this way a person can build up enough equity to get mortgage financing or to pay the full cost of the property. The seller may be willing to make such an arrangement since seller holds the deed to the property until the terms of the contract have been fulfilled.

Government Guarantees. During the depression of the thirties, the federal government set up the Federal Housing Administration to stimulate home building by insuring mortgages on urban residential real estate. A prospective borrower who wants to obtain an FHA loan applies for such a loan at a savings and loan association, a commercial bank, or other lending institution approved for such loans. The required application papers are sent for approval to the local FHA office which appraises the property and checks the applicant's ability to make payments.

The Servicemen's Readjustment Act, or GI Bill as it is popularly called, authorized the Veterans Administration to guarantee loans on homes purchased by veterans. Such loans were first made available to World War II veterans and later also to veterans of the Korean and Vietnam Wars. Details of FHA and VA loan guarantee programs are covered in the discussion of government agencies and programs in the real estate field.

Amortized Loans. All loans guaranteed by the Federal Housing Administration and by the Veterans Administration must be *amortized loans,* that is, loans on which the borrower agrees to make regular payments on principal as well as on interest. Other amortized mortgage loans that are neither FHA- nor VA-guaranteed are referred to as *conventional mortgage loans.* Today, many of these loans are guaranteed or insured by private mortgage insurance companies. The payments are calculated so that the loan is retired within an agreed period of time. Often the lender also requires that the borrower add to her or his payments an amount equal to one twelfth of the annual property insurance and annual property taxes.

Monthly payments required to repay the principal and to pay interest are reduced materially as the time period of the loan is extended. For example, a $1,000 amortized loan at 12 percent interest requires monthly payments of $14.35 if amortized in 10 years and $10.53 if amortized in 25 years. While these payments could be calculated using formulas, real estate loan amortization tables are readily available for use.

A variation of the fixed interest rate, amortized mortgage loan is known as a *variable rate mortgage.* Instead of agreeing to, say, a 12 percent interest rate, the home buyer agrees to pay the "going rate" which is tied to some "reference" interest rate that changes with changing conditions in the money and capital markets. When market interest rates are rising, the home buyer would expect to pay a higher interest rate on his or her mortgage loan, and vice versa.

SAVINGS AND LOAN ASSOCIATIONS

After the first savings and loan association was established in the Philadelphia area in 1831, the movement spread to surrounding towns and cities and gradually to most of the eastern part of the country. Many of these early associations were called building and loan associations, and this name is still used by some associations today. After 1855, the establishment of new associations spread into the Mississippi and Ohio valleys and also into Texas, California, and a few other states.

Between 1880 and 1890, associations were chartered at a rapid rate in all sections of the country. Up to this time, all associations were local institutions serving their immediate communities. Late in the decade, many national associations were chartered. Many were organized as promotional ventures for the benefit of the organizers. Most of these organizations failed during the several periods of depressed business activity between 1890 and 1901. As a result, several states passed laws preventing national organizations from doing business in their states. This experience has kept the business largely local in character since that time, although a few holding companies have been formed in recent years, especially in California. The big development came after 1920 and again after World War II.

There are about 4,300 savings and loan associations operating approximately 18,000 branch offices in the United States today. However, a small percentage of these associations control over one third of all savings and loan assets.

Regulation and Control

A savings and loan association may be chartered under a state charter or, since 1933, under a federal charter in accordance with the Homeowners Loan Act. At the end of 1981, about 56 percent had state charters. The average size of the federal associations was larger than that of the state associations; the federal group had 61 percent of the total assets of all the associations.[2]

Usually five or more responsible citizens may apply for a charter. To obtain a state charter, they must demonstrate their fitness to receive a charter and the need for the services of the proposed savings and loan association. To obtain a federal charter, they must demonstrate: (1) the good character and responsibility of the applicants, (2) the necessity for such an institution in the community, (3) the reasonable probability of its usefulness and success, and (4) that it can be established without undue injury to properly conducted existing local thrift and home-financing institutions.

Regulation and control of savings and loan associations was conducted solely by state authorities prior to the early 1930s. Federal involvement began in 1932 with the passage of the Home Loan Bank Act, which provided for the creation of the Federal Home Loan Bank System. The FHLB System was structured along the lines of the Federal Reserve System. It has a Federal Home Loan Bank Board and 12 regional banks. Federal savings and loan associations are required to belong to the FHLB System.

State-chartered savings and loan associations, life insurance companies, and mutual savings banks also may join if they meet FHLB System qualifications. At

---

[2]*Savings and Loan Sourcebook* (Chicago: United States League of Savings Associations, 1982), p. 37.

the end of 1981, state-chartered and federal members of the System accounted for over 98 percent of all savings and loan association assets. At the same time, mutual savings banks and two life insurance companies chose to be members of the FHLB System.[3]

The Federal Home Loan Bank System's major responsibility is to provide a central credit facility for its members. A particularly important activity involves providing secondary liquidity in the event certain member institutions are faced with unusually heavy withdrawal demands. The FHLB System, for example, can provide advances or loans to members designed to aid them in maintaining adequate liquidity positions.

All federally chartered and most state-chartered savings and loan associations are insured by the Federal Savings and Loan Insurance Corporation. This governmental agency, formed in 1934 when the Federal Deposit Insurance Corporation was created, will be discussed in greater detail later in the chapter.

Organization and Operation

Savings and loan associations are of two types—mutuals and corporations owned by shareholders. Most of the associations with a federal charter are mutuals. Fewer than 900 savings and loan associations have issued shares of stock and are controlled by shareholders. Over 75 percent of all savings and loan associations are mutual companies.

Both savers and borrowers are members of mutual savings and loan associations. Since these associations are cooperatives, the savings put into them are shares of ownership in the association. This distinguishes them from deposits in a commercial bank, which are liabilities of the bank. Payments on savings and loan shares are *dividends*, not interest. In 1968 the Housing and Urban Development Act authorized federal savings and loan associations to call their savings accounts "deposits." This Act also expanded the types of savings instruments available to federal savings and loan associations by liberalizing the power of the Federal Home Loan Bank Board to authorize new forms of savings accounts and savings certificates. Regulations have been changed periodically to provide for a variety of certificate accounts which pay higher rates of return than passbook accounts but have a minimum balance and maturity restrictions.

The Federal Home Loan Bank Board was given authority under the Interest Rate Adjustment Act passed in 1966 to set maximum interest rates on various types of savings and loan association passbook accounts and savings certificates. The Federal Reserve Board of Governors has had this power over savings accounts and time deposits at member commercial banks since 1933, while the Federal Deposit Insurance Corporation was responsible for setting maximum rates for nonmember, insured commercial banks. However, as we saw in Chapter 6, passage of the Depository Institutions Deregulation and Monetary Control Act (DIDMCA) in 1980 substantially alters the regulation of interest- and dividend-rate ceilings on deposits held at depository institutions. The

---

[3]*Ibid.*, pp. 44 and 48.

Depository Institutions Deregulation Committee is charged with conducting an orderly phaseout of rate ceilings on time and savings deposits. Rate ceilings at all depository institutions must be eliminated by early 1986. The Act further authorizes savings and loan associations and the other depository institutions to issue negotiable order of withdrawal (NOW) accounts and automatic transfer service (ATS) accounts.

The primary source of funds available to savings and loan associations is, of course, in the form of savings deposits. This is shown in Table 18-2 where at the

Table 18-2
Assets and Liabilities of Savings and Loan Associations (In Billions of Dollars)

	1975		1977		1981	
	Amount	Percent	Amount	Percent	Amount	Percent
ASSETS						
Mortgage loans	278.6	82.4	381.2	83.0	518.3	78.1
Cash and investment securities	30.8	9.1	39.2	8.5	62.8	9.5
Real estate owned...........	1.7	.5	1.9	.4	2.8	.4
FHLB stock	2.6	.8	3.2	.7	5.3	.8
Other assets	24.5	7.2	33.8	7.4	74.6	11.2
Total Assets...............	338.2	100.0	459.3	100.0	663.8	100.0
LIABILITIES AND NET WORTH						
Savings deposits.............	285.7	84.5	386.9	84.2	524.4	79.0
FHLB and other advances....	20.6	6.1	27.8	6.1	89.1	13.4
Loans in process............	5.1	1.5	9.9	2.2	6.3	1.0
Other liabilities	7.0	2.0	9.5	2.0	15.6	2.3
Net worth	19.8	5.9	25.2	5.5	28.4	4.3
Total Liabilities and Net Worth	338.2	100.0	459.3	100.0	663.8	100.0

SOURCE: *Savings and Loan Sourcebook,* 1982.

end of 1981 savings deposits accounted for 79 percent of total liabilities and net worth. Of even greater importance is the change in savings mix in recent years. The historical emphasis on passbook savings has been replaced by rate-sensitive deposits such as money market certificates and large certificates of deposit (CD's) that now account for about two thirds of all savings.

Federal Home Loan Bank advances, along with other borrowed money ranks second in importance as a source of funds for savings and loan associations. Net worth represents a relatively small and declining portion of the total source of available funds. This is due in part to the fact that most savings and loan associations are organized as mutual associations. Thus, general reserves set aside to protect savers against possible asset losses, plus undivided profits, account for most of the net worth. Loans in process reflect mortgage-related funds that have been committed but not yet disbursed at the time the underlying mortgage loans have been recorded as assets. Other liabilities include accrued taxes payable and advance payments of taxes and insurance by borrowers.

Loans and Investments

Savings and loan association assets are dominated by mortgage loans, as is shown in Table 18-2. More specifically, residential property loans of the one- to four-family type account for over 80 percent of the total dollar amount of mortgage loans held by savings and loan associations. The remaining loans are roughly equal in size between multifamily residential properties and commercial properties. Savings and loan associations also specialize in conventional mortgage loans. FHA-insured and VA-guaranteed mortgage loans are made infrequently by these associations.

Many savings and loan associations make loans to finance the construction of new homes in addition to making mortgage loans on already completed homes. In recent years, however, construction loans have represented only a small portion of all mortgage loans made. This shorter-term lending, which was dominated by savings and loan associations during the 1950s, has been taken over to a large extent by commercial banks and mortgage banking firms.

Cash and certain investment securities qualify as liquid assets for purposes of meeting liquidity requirements established under the Federal Home Loan Bank Act of 1950. Liquidity ratios (legally acceptable liquid assets to savings deposits and short-term borrowings) can be set between 4 percent and 10 percent. The Federal Home Loan Bank Board specifies required liquidity ratios and determines the composition and maturity of acceptable assets that can be used to meet liquidity requirements. Thus, while savings and loan associations can legally hold many kinds of securities, most of their investments are in the form of short- to intermediate-term U.S. government and federal agency securities, bankers' acceptances, commercial bank time deposits, and relatively short-term state and municipal securities.

Real estate owned reflects the holding of properties acquired due to the default on the part of borrowers. FHLB stock shows up as an asset item because members of the Federal Home Loan Bank System are required to hold stock in their district Banks. Each association purchases stock equal to 1 percent of the principal amount of its outstanding loans.

Table 18-2 indicates that the other assets category as a percentage of total assets has increased since the mid 1970s. This has been due in part to the increase in loans to consumers for purposes other than mortgages. These consumer loans have been largely in the form of mobile home loans, home improvement loans, and education and other loans secured by savings accounts.

Further changes are likely to occur in the asset holdings of savings and loan associations. Under the DIDMCA of 1980, federally chartered savings and loan associations were permitted to invest up to one fifth of their assets in consumer loans, commercial paper, and corporate debt securities.

COMMERCIAL BANKS

State banks have made loans on real estate mortgages almost from their beginning, helping to finance the westward movement of the population. National banks were not permitted to loan money on real property as security under the National Banking Act of 1864, but there was some evasion of this provision. The

Federal Reserve Act allowed loans on farmland, and an amendment in 1916 provided for one-year loans on urban real estate. In later years, much more liberal provisions for real estate loans were enacted. National banks may make FHA and VA loans according to the provisions of these programs.

State banking laws are much more liberal than the national banking laws. Over half of the states have no restriction on the length of the loan or on the loan-to-value ratio. Those states which do have restrictions have more liberal provisions, as a rule, than those of the national banking acts.

The regulation, control, organization, and operation of commercial banks have been discussed in detail in previous chapters. However, commercial banks deserve some additional discussion in this chapter since they represent the second most important annual supplier of mortgage funds. Table 18-3 shows selected assets and liabilities for commercial banks in recent years. Several

Table 18-3

Assets and Liabilities of Commercial Banks (In Billions of Dollars)

	1975		1977		1981	
	Amount	Percent	Amount	Percent	Amount	Percent
ASSETS						
Cash and bank balances.....	133.6	13.8	168.7	14.5	181.1	10.4
Securities investments........	229.6	23.8	257.4	22.1	345.5	19.1
Real estate loans.............	134.8	14.0	177.2	15.2	286.8	15.9
Other loans	411.7	42.7	483.2	41.4	697.7	38.6
Other assets	55.5	5.7	79.6	6.8	288.8	16.0
Total Assets................	965.2	100.0	1,166.1	100.0	1,806.8	100.0
LIABILITIES AND CAPITAL						
Demand deposits	323.6	33.5	383.0	32.8	377.7	20.9
Time and savings deposits ...	462.9	48.0	556.5	47.7	910.9	50.4
Other liabilities	109.6	11.3	146.6	12.6	386.7	21.4
Capital accounts	69.1	7.2	80.0	6.9	131.5	7.3
Total Liabilities and Capital .	965.2	100.0	1,166.1	100.0	1,806.8	100.0

SOURCE: *Federal Reserve Bulletin* (selected issues).

observations can be made. Even though commercial banks are an important supplier of mortgage funds, real estate loan holdings accounted for only about 16 percent of total assets in 1981. Consumer loans and business loans (included within the other loans category) also are very important to banks. In terms of dollar amounts outstanding, commercial and industrial loans rank first followed by real estate loans and then consumer loans. The vast majority of mortgage loans made by commercial banks are of the conventional type rather than FHA or VA. In contrast with savings and loan associations, commercial banks have made a larger commitment in their mortgage loan portfolios to commercial property loans.

In Chapter 6 we first referred to the principle of hedging as providing the fundamental basis for conducting the financial management of financial institutions. The reader should recall that this principle involves matching the average maturities of assets and liabilities. Table 18-3 shows that as of the end of 1981, commercial banks held over 70 percent of their liabilities and capital in demand or time and savings deposits. These short- and intermediate-term liabilities are largely offset, however, by cash and bank balances, large holdings of short-term U.S. government securities, and short- and intermediate-term consumer and business loans. This was not the case for savings and loan associations. Table 18-2 indicates that at the end of 1981, 79 percent of total liabilities and net worth were held in the form of savings deposits, while long-term mortgage loans accounted for 78 percent of total assets. Thus, while commercial banks are reasonably good practitioners of the hedging principle, savings and loan asset maturities are substantially longer than the average maturities on their liabilities. As a result, various forms of U.S. governmental assistance are particularly valuable to savings and loan associations.

MUTUAL SAVINGS BANKS

Mutual savings banks are an important source of real estate credit in a few geographical areas. Of almost 500 such banks in operation, practically all are in the New England states and in New York and New Jersey. They can be traced back to 1812 when savings banks were organized in Boston and Philadelphia. Mutual savings banks have always stressed thrift savings and safety of principal for their members and the making of real estate mortgage loans.

Regulation and Control

Mutual savings banks are all state-chartered and thus are regulated by state authorities within the states where they operate. There are no federal or national charters. However, mutual savings banks may elect to become members of the Federal Home Loan Bank System. They also can elect to be insured under the Federal Deposit Insurance Corporation program which is available to commercial banks. Approximately 70 percent of all mutual savings banks have their savings deposits insured by the FDIC. Virtually all other savings banks are insured under state programs.

Legal restrictions are primarily responsible for the lack of widespread geographical distribution throughout the United States. This is partly offset by the fact that several states permit their mutual savings banks to acquire or participate in mortgages made on properties located in other states.

Operations, Loans, and Investments

Mutual savings banks are organized as mutual organizations as their name implies. They are managed by boards of trustees and are operated for the mutual benefit of their depositor-owners.

Table 18-4 indicates that over 88 percent of the total liabilities and reserves

Table 18-4

Assets and Liabilities of Mutual Savings Banks (In Billions of Dollars)

	1975		1977		1981	
	Amount	Percent	Amount	Percent	Amount	Percent
ASSETS						
Mortgage loans	77.2	63.7	88.2	59.9	100.0	56.9
Other loans	4.0	3.3	6.2	4.2	14.7	8.4
U.S. government, state, and						
municipal securities	6.3	5.2	8.7	5.9	12.1	6.9
Corporate and other securities	27.9	23.1	37.9	25.7	37.8	21.5
Cash and other assets.	5.7	4.7	6.3	4.3	11.1	6.3
Total Assets	121.1	100.0	147.3	100.0	175.7	100.0
LIABILITIES AND RESERVES						
Deposits	109.9	90.8	134.0	91.0	155.1	88.3
Other liabilities	2.8	2.3	3.3	2.2	10.6	6.0
General reserve accounts	8.4	6.9	10.0	6.8	10.0	5.7
Total Liabilities and Reserves	121.1	100.0	147.3	100.0	175.7	100.0

SOURCES: *National Fact Book of Mutual Savings Banking* and *Federal Reserve Bulletin* (selected issues).

are in the form of deposits. These are largely short-term in nature. General reserves of approximately 6 percent are held as protection against possible asset losses. Changes in savings flows, particularly those associated with disintermediation, have been of concern to mutual savings banks, as one might expect. Mutual savings banks that belong to the Federal Home Loan Bank System can, of course, take advantage of the System's credit facilities. Liquidity facilities also are provided by New York and Massachusetts to their own state-chartered savings banks. Passage of the Depository Institutions Deregulation and Monetary Control Act of 1980 should help reduce disintermediation (through elimination of savings rate ceilings) and liquidity problems (through access to the Federal Reserve's discount window).

Table 18-4 also shows that while mortgage loans have been declining as a percentage of total assets in recent years, they still account for about 57 percent of total assets. Well over one half of the mortgage loans made by mutual savings banks are of the one- to four-family residential property type. They also commit a sizable portion of their funds to multifamily and commercial property loans. In contrast with commercial banks and savings and loan associations, approximately one third of the mortgage loans of savings banks are FHA-insured or VA-guaranteed. In contrast, nonmortgage loans have been growing rapidly.

Savings banks have been committing a substantial portion of their funds to the purchase of corporate and other securities in recent years. These are primarily purchases of corporate bonds with some increased commitment to corporate stocks. This category also includes the holding of securities issued by foreign governments and international organizations.

LIFE INSURANCE COMPANIES

A private life insurance company was first established in the United States in 1759. Mutual life insurance companies first began operating during the early 1840s. Life insurance companies have been lending substantial sums on real estate for over a century. In 1890 over 40 percent of their assets were in mortgages. This figure declined, especially after 1929, until it was but 15 percent. Recent levels have been much higher.

Life insurance companies, while an important supplier of mortgage funds, differ substantially from commercial banks and thrift institutions. They were not organized with the primary objective of meeting mortgage needs as were savings and loan associations and mutual savings banks. Savings flows and resulting periods of intermediation and disintermediation are not as important to life insurance companies. Instead, their loans and investment policies are primarily determined by the receipt of premium payments made by their policyholders.

Regulation and Control

All life insurance companies are state-chartered and thus regulated by state authorities, usually insurance commissions. The states providing the charters as well as other states within which the life insurance companies do business are involved in the regulatory process. Many state laws focus on setting detailed standards concerning the types of acceptable investments and the quality of such investments. Many states follow what is considered to be model legislation initially developed in New York.

Corporate bond holdings are regulated as to type and quality while common stocks are tightly restricted in terms of amount and quality. Life insurance companies are permitted to hold FHA and VA mortgage loans. Maximum loan-to-value ratios are generally set on conventional mortgages which can be held. Additional restrictions may also be placed on income-producing real estate investments.

Operations, Loans, and Investments

Life insurance companies may be either stock companies or mutual organizations. Over 90 percent of the approximately 2,000 companies are stockholder owned. Mutual companies, which number less than 150, are much larger than stock companies on average and continue to hold over one half of the life insurance industry's total assets.[4]

Life insurance companies are required by law to hold reserves to back the life, health, and annuity policies written by them. The amount of these policy reserves is actuarially determined to assure that policy obligations can be met as they come due. Table 18-5 shows that policy reserves account for about 81 percent of total liabilities and surplus. Other obligations include policy dividend accumulations, funds set aside to meet next year's policy dividends, incurred expenses,

---

[4]*Life Insurance Fact Book* (Washington: American Council of Life Insurance, 1982), pp. 89–90.

Table 18-5

Assets and Liabilities of Life Insurance Companies (In Billions of Dollars)

	1975		1977		1981	
	Amount	Percent	Amount	Percent	Amount	Percent
ASSETS						
Government securities........	15.2	5.2	23.6	6.7	39.5	7.5
Corporate bonds	105.8	36.6	137.9	39.2	193.8	36.8
Corporate stocks	28.1	9.7	33.8	9.6	47.7	9.1
Mortgages	89.2	30.8	96.8	27.5	137.7	26.2
Real estate owned............	9.6	3.3	11.1	3.2	18.3	3.5
Other assets	41.7	14.4	48.5	13.8	88.8	16.9
Total Assets................	289.3	100.0	351.7	100.0	525.8	100.0
LIABILITIES AND SURPLUS						
Policy reserves...............	235.1	81.3	281.0	79.9	428.0	81.4
Other obligations.............	33.7	11.6	47.1	13.4	60.4	11.5
Surplus funds................	18.6	6.4	21.7	6.2	35.2	6.7
Capital (stock companies)	1.9	.7	1.9	.5	2.2	.4
Total Liabilities and Surplus	289.3	100.0	351.7	100.0	525.8	100.0

SOURCE: *Life Insurance Fact Book,* 1982.

prepaid insurance premiums, and reserves to cover fluctuations in security values. Surplus funds provide extra safeguards against possible unexpected developments such as changes in mortality rates.

Table 18-5 shows that mortgage loans held by life insurance companies rank second only to their holdings of corporate bonds. Of the nearly $138 billion in mortgages held at the end of 1981, 10 percent were farm mortgages, 12 percent were one- to four-family home mortgages, 14 percent were multifamily mortgages, and 64 percent represented nonresidential properties. This latter group included mortgages on office buildings and factories, shopping centers, and medical centers. In the 1950s, one- to four-family residential mortgages accounted for over one half of the total mortgages held by life insurance companies. Since then, these companies have been committing an increasing amount of their funds to multifamily residential mortgages and nonfarm nonresidential mortgages.[5]

Insurance companies make some mortgage loans directly through either the home office or branch offices. Most loans, however, are purchased from brokers, mortgage banking companies, or other institutions. This may be done through branch offices, by appointing a broker or mortgage banking company as a correspondent to bring loans to the attention of the loan department of the insurance company, or by buying mortgages in blocks from mortgage banking

[5]*Ibid.,* pp. 80–81.

companies that have made the loans with the intention of selling the mortgages to permanent investors.

MERCHANDISING AND FACILITATING AGENCIES

The so-called mortgage market actually consists of three parts or activities. The origination or creation of new mortgages is carried out in the *primary mortgage market*. Emphasis to this point in the chapter has focused on the primary market. In some instances, the originators of new mortgage loans are not necessarily the final investors or holders. Instead, they may act as agents in performing the important merchandising function by distributing mortgages to investors. Several agencies and organizations also aid or facilitate the mortgage financing process. Thus, the *merchandising and facilitating functions* represent an important intermediate activity.

The third part or activity involves the *secondary mortgage market* where real estate mortgages can be resold, thus providing some liquidity to mortgage holders. Assistance in this area of the mortgage market will be discussed later in the chapter.

Mortgage Banking Companies

One of the developments that has made possible a national market for real estate mortgages has been the growth of mortgage banking companies. These companies not only negotiate the loans but continue to service them by collecting interest and principal payments and forwarding them to the owners of the mortgage. This requires facilities for receiving such payments and for sending out notices of accounts due and past due. Servicing also includes making sure that proper insurance is carried and that all taxes are paid.

Mortgage banking companies began with the introduction of FHA mortgage insurance in 1934. These companies initially concentrated their activities on FHA loans and later also on VA loans, but they now also handle conventional loans.

Mortgage banking companies are usually closely held private corporations. They have a relatively small capital investment compared with the volume of business they do. They get most of their money for holding mortgages until they are placed with lenders from short-term bank borrowing.

Mortgage brokers sometimes are differentiated from mortgage bankers. Mortgage brokers also perform the loan origination function by bringing borrowers and lenders together. However, in contrast with mortgage banking activities, mortgage brokers generally do not service loans after delivery to the lenders.

Real Estate Investment Trusts

Another type of organization which grew rapidly during the 1968–1973 period was real estate investment trusts, known as REITs. They came into being in 1960, under the Real Estate Investment Trust Act, when Congress extended the same exemption from double taxation which had been granted earlier to mutual funds if they distributed at least 90 percent of their income to shareholders. They engage in a whole series of lending activities in the real estate field and some have taken equity positions in real estate projects. Most activity, however, is in financing construction from land acquisition until completion. At this stage mortgages are often sold to more traditional lenders such as insurance companies.

In the past, REITs have relied very heavily on commercial paper issues and lines of credit and term loans from commercial banks as sources of funds to finance their real estate loans. Thus, REITs have been particularly hard hit during periods of tight money and high interest rates. Table 18-1 shows that REITs have not been important suppliers of mortgage funds in recent years.

Facilitating Agencies

Several agencies also facilitate the process of mortgage financing. One is the professional appraisal concern that makes careful appraisal of all types of property based on such factors as location, the trend of the neighborhood, the type of construction, and the condition of the property. This is done by government appraisers for FHA and VA loans.

Another facilitating agency, the title company, assures the purchaser of real estate or the mortgagee who is loaning money on real estate that the title to the property is clear. The title to most land in the United States was originally held by a state or by the federal government. It has gone through a series of title transfers until it has reached the present owners. Such transfers are recorded in public record books in chronological order. If all titles in the series of sales were defined completely and accurately at the time a transfer was made, if all the proper instruments that might affect the title were properly recorded, and if all complicating factors, such as suits over title arising out of litigation over the bequests in a will, were properly handled, the present title would be clear. There are so many chances for defects in a title that checking the records to be sure a title is clear has become a specialized activity carried on by title companies. They will, for a fee, search the records and issue an opinion on the character of the title being examined.

Important as a clear title to property is, there are very few titles about which there is absolutely no question. Most defects are minor and do not affect the transfer of title. Since it is impossible in most cases to be absolutely sure about a title, some companies have developed title insurance. They, of course, insure only titles that they believe from their examination are sound. The amount of insurance is stated in the policy and is usually the full value of the property at the time the insurance is written. The premium is paid only once, at the time the policy is purchased.

In recent years beginning with the late 1960s private firms have entered the mortgage insurance field on a large scale. Such insurance was developed by the federal government first for FHA loans and then for VA loans. In recent years private insurance of mortgages has grown to such an extent as to rival federal insurance.

In the summer of 1974 a new facilitating agency was set up in the form of a computerized central information system for offers to buy and sell residential mortgage investments. It is called the Automated Mortgage Market Information Network, Inc., or AMMINET. It provides a central data bank on secondary mortgage markets useful to both buyers and sellers of mortgages. It is not an exchange, but provides information to buyers and sellers who conduct their transactions privately, usually by telephone.

GOVERNMENTAL ASSISTANCE IN REAL ESTATE FINANCING

Several agencies of the federal government are instrumental in facilitating the financing of urban residential real estate. One group is the Federal Home Loan Bank Board, and the federal home loan banks and the Federal Savings and Loan Insurance Corporation that are under its jurisdiction. Another group includes the Federal Housing Administration, the Federal National Mortgage Association, the Government National Mortgage Association, and the Federal Home Loan Mortgage Corporation. The Veterans Administration is also engaged in facilitating real estate financing through its program of loan guarantees under the GI Bill and the Farmers Home Administration guarantees loans and makes some loans in rural areas.

Federal Home Loan Bank Board and System

As we saw earlier in the chapter, the Home Loan Bank Act of 1932 established the Federal Home Loan Bank System and Board. The System's primary responsibility is to provide a central credit facility for its savings and loan association (and other) members.

Each of the 12 district banks is administered by a board of 12 directors, 4 of whom are appointed by the Federal Home Loan Bank Board for terms of four years and 8 of whom are elected by the members for terms of two years. The funds of the federal home loan banks are obtained from the proceeds of sales of their capital stock to members, retained earnings, sales of consolidated Federal Home Loan Bank obligations to the public, and deposits of surplus cash by member institutions.

The excess cash of a district federal home loan bank may be deposited with another of the district banks of the system. This is one means by which credit may be transferred from a region of surplus funds to an area of need for funds.

The district banks make long-term or short-term advances to their member institutions on the security of the home mortgages that the members have in turn obtained from their borrowers or on the security of government bonds. These advances to members are particularly important during periods of disintermediation.

The Federal Home Loan Bank Board regulates and supervises its federally chartered and state-chartered members. And, unlike the Federal Reserve System, it evaluates applications for federal charters. The Board also establishes liquidity requirements for its members.

Federal Savings and Loan Insurance Corporation

The Federal Home Loan Bank Board also has supervision over the Federal Savings and Loan Insurance Corporation. Although this agency is entirely separate from the Federal Deposit Insurance Corporation, it functions in much the same manner and has increased public confidence in and encouraged the flow of savings to savings and loan associations. The law requires federal associations to be insured, while state-chartered associations may become insured upon application and approval. Insured associations are subject to annual examination and to the rules and regulations of the Federal Savings and Loan Insurance Corporation (FSLIC). Over 98 percent of all savings and loan association assets are insured by the FSLIC.

The Federal Savings and Loan Insurance Corporation insures the safety of savings against loss up to a maximum of $100,000 for each account. If an insured association must be liquidated because it is in financial difficulties, the Corporation may pay the insured accounts in cash or may make accounts in other insured associations available to the account holders of the association in liquidation.

Besides its function of paying off investors in case an insured association is ordered liquidated, the FSLIC possesses broad preventive powers by coming to the assistance of an association in the early stages of difficulty. For instance, in order to prevent a default or to restore an insured association in default to normal operations, the Insurance Corporation may make a cash contribution or loan to such an institution.

Insured associations other than the federal associations which are required by law to be insured have the right of terminating their insurance, provided they meet certain legal requirements. Also under the provisions of the insurance law, the Corporation has the right to cancel the insurance of any insured association for a violation of the law or the rules and regulations of the Corporation, but it has never found it necessary to do so.

The Federal Housing Administration

The Federal Housing Administration was established under the provisions of the National Housing Act in 1934 for the purposes of stabilizing the mortgage market and making money available to finance both the construction of new homes and needed repairs to homes and other property. This organization was to accomplish its objectives through the insurance against loss of certain types of loans made by private lending institutions.

Insurance of property improvement loans is authorized under Title I of the National Housing Act. The principal activity of the Federal Housing Administration is the insurance of mortgages on both new and existing one- to four-family homes, authorized under Title II of the Act. All FHA loans are amortized loans. The payments include part of the principal, interest, a mortgage insurance premium of ½ percent, fire and other hazard insurance premiums, real property taxes, and special assessments, if any. Maximum interest rates were set by law until 1968 when the Secretary of the Department of Housing and Urban Development was authorized to set ceilings at a level to meet market conditions. The maximum maturity on FHA loans is 30 to 35 years, which the Commissioner of the FHA may reduce when it is desirable. The maximum loan-to-value ratio permitted is 97 percent of appraised value on the first $25,000 and 95 percent on the value over $25,000. On a $50,000 home, for example, the loan may be as high as $48,000 or 96 percent of the appraisal value.

The FHA is also authorized to insure mortgages on cooperative housing projects. The mortgagor must be a nonprofit housing corporation in which the permanent occupancy of the dwellings is restricted to members or a nonprofit corporation organized for the purpose of building homes for its members. Special, more liberal provisions are made if such cooperative housing is for occupancy by elderly persons. FHA insurance is also available to assist in financing the rehabilitation of existing housing, the replacement of slums with new housing, and the construction of housing for essential civilian employees of some defense installations. The Federal Housing Administration also provides insurance on mortgages on certain types of rental property both during and after construction. Beginning in 1965 the FHA was authorized to subsidize some housing in these special categories through interest rate subsidies and rent supplements. The Federal Housing Administration currently operates under the jurisdiction of the Department of Housing and Urban Development (HUD).

Veterans Administration

The "GI Bill" provided for the guarantee of insurance of loans made by private lending institutions to veterans of World War II and subsequent laws have extended the benefits to those veterans serving 181 days or more. The insurance provided by the Veterans Administration was patterned after that of the Federal Housing Administration. The terms, however, are somewhat more liberal than those of the conventional insured loan requiring little or no down payment. The Veterans Administration offers a guarantee for real estate loans to qualified veterans of $27,500 or 60 percent of the total loan, whichever is smaller. No limitation exists on the size of a loan eligible for guaranty but rather on the amount of guaranty.

The large surpluses of loanable funds at the end of World War II resulted in widespread participation in the VA loan insurance program. As these funds were substantially reduced, however, the interest rate limitation on such loans resulted in a lack of interest on the part of many lenders to continue lending on this basis. In 1968 the statutory interest rate ceiling was removed and the VA was given power to set the ceiling.

Farmers Home Administration

The Farmers Home Administration is an agency of the Department of Agriculture which provides insured loans and some grants and direct financing for rural housing programs. To qualify, the real estate must be in a town of not more than 10,000 people and the family must show that credit is not available elsewhere. Most loans are made on an insured basis and then sold to private lenders. Guarantees are also available for loans on commercial and industrial property in small towns. Additional discussion is presented in Chapter 19.

Secondary Mortgage Market Activities

Secondary markets for stocks and bonds are well developed. The New York Stock Exchange, for example, began operating during the 1800s. Because of the absence of such an organized secondary mortgage market, the lack of liquidity was a real problem for mortgage lenders. While some legal provisions for the establishment of a national secondary mortgage market date back to the 1930s, a well-developed secondary mortgage market did not really begin until the beginning of the 1970s. Three major institutions or organizations support and facilitate the secondary mortgage market. These are the Federal National Mortgage Association, the Government National Mortgage Association, and the Federal Home Loan Mortgage Corporation.

The Federal National Mortgage Association was organized in 1938 as a subsidiary of the Reconstruction Finance Corporation and was later transferred to the Housing and Home Finance Agency. It originally was brought into existence to provide an additional market for the FHA-insured mortgages of lenders. In the postwar period its authority was broadened to include mortgages insured by the Veterans Administration and mortgages under special housing programs, such as urban renewal projects, housing for the armed forces, cooperative dwellings, and housing for the elderly. The plan was to help to maintain a more stable construction industry by providing a reservoir of funds that would supplement the flow of mortgage money when it was low and would drain off an excess flow of funds at other times through the sale of mortgages previously purchased.

The Federal National Mortgage Association accumulated a rather substantial portfolio of mortgages prior to World War II, but during the war this process was reversed because construction of new homes was largely curtailed. Following the war, the volume of mortgages purchased by the Association again began to increase as it purchased large sums of mortgages insured by the Veterans Administration and the FHA. As credit became more difficult to obtain from private institutions in the period after 1955, especially at the maximum rates established on FHA and VA loans, the Federal National Mortgage Association increased its activities greatly.

The Housing and Urban Development Act of 1968 divided the Federal National Mortgage Association into two organizations, one of which kept the original title and the other named the Government National Mortgage Association. The GNMA took over the functions of assisting in the financing of special areas which cannot be financed adequately through the usual channels and the management and liquidation operations of the FNMA portfolio acquired under contracts entered into before 1954. As noted earlier, GNMA has developed a highly successful mortgage-backed securities program involving the sale of pass-through securities backed by FHA/VA mortgage pools. GNMA guarantees the passing through to security holders the interest and principal payments from the underlying mortgages. This program has been very important to the development of an effective secondary mortgage market.

The new FNMA is a government-sponsored private corporation which has taken over the secondary market operations in FHA/VA residential mortgages. The 1970 Emergency Home Finance Act also authorized it to operate as a secondary market for conventional loans. It introduced the Free Market System Auction under which it deals in commitments to buy mortgages four or twelve months in the future. The amount of mortgages it will buy is announced; and mortgage holding institutions bid on the price at which they are willing to sell, thus allowing market forces to set the price. In 1981, FNMA initiated a program of conventional mortgage-backed pass-through securities patterned after the GNMA pass-through securities.

FNMA has several sources of funds for its mortgage-buying activity. The principal source is debenture bonds that are sold to private investors and some notes are also sold at a discount. A second source is preferred stock and a third is common stock.

GNMA and FNMA have at times cooperated in a special program called a Tandem Program to absorb some of the risks in investing in mortgages as interest rates rise. When interest rates rise, mortgages sell at a discount as do all fixed-rate obligations. To cushion some of this risk in a period of rising interest rates, GNMA issues a commitment to purchase a mortgage at a fixed price. It is then sold to FNMA at the prevailing market price at the time of such sale, GNMA absorbing any discount from the price paid to seller.

The 1970 Emergency Home Finance Act also provided for the creation of the Federal Home Loan Mortgage Corporation. It is funded by a stock subscription of $100 million held by the regional Federal Home Loan Banks. It gets its funds by issuing bonds backed by GNMA-guaranteed mortgages and by borrowing from the Federal Home Loan Banks. Its declared goal is to establish mechanisms which will make the secondary mortgage market highly liquid so as to make mortgages attractive to investors. The secondary mortgage market is to be provided for savings and loan association members of the Federal Home Loan Bank System. The Federal Home Loan Mortgage Corporation is to do this by purchases of conventional, FHA, and VA mortgages and participation in conventional loans. Such purchases may be over the counter or in the form of commitments for future purchases. It is also to be a major seller of mortgages so as to provide a true secondary market.

QUESTIONS

1. Discuss the importance of mortgage funds by type raised annually in the United States.
2. Indicate the importance of various financial institutions as suppliers of mortgage funds.
3. Describe a typical mortgage and explain its use in real estate financing. How does a mortgage differ from a deed of trust and a land contract?
4. Briefly describe the following real estate terms or concepts: (a) foreclosure procedure, (b) government guarantees, and (c) amortized loans.
5. How are savings and loan associations regulated and controlled?
6. Briefly describe the organization and operation of savings and loan associations today.
7. What is the role of commercial banks in real estate financing? How well do commercial banks and savings and loan associations practice the principle of hedging?
8. Discuss the role of mutual savings banks in real estate financing and describe how their asset structures differ from savings and loan association assets.
9. Describe the activities of life insurance companies as suppliers of mortgage funds by type of mortgage loan and relative to other asset holdings.
10. Identify and briefly describe several merchandising and facilitating agencies that play a role in the real estate field.
11. What is the role of the Federal Home Loan Bank

System and its Board in assisting the process of financing real estate?

12. Briefly discuss the operations of the Federal Savings and Loan Insurance Corporation.

13. What are the home mortgage loan policies of the Federal Housing Administration and the Veterans Administration?

14. Discuss the functions of the Federal National Mortgage Association, the Government National Mortgage Association, and the Federal Home Loan Mortgage Corporation in terms of their secondary mortgage market activities.

PROBLEMS

1. Assume that you can qualify for an FHA mortgage loan on a home that is appraised at $75,000. What is the dollar amount of the maximum loan that you could obtain on the home? What would be the loan-to-value percentage? How would your answers have changed if the appraised value had been $100,000?

2. The Smiths are seeking a mortgage loan of $40,000 on a new house while the Joneses would like a house with a $60,000 mortgage. If both can qualify for VA-guaranteed loans, indicate the dollar amount of guarantee in each case. What percentage of each mortgage loan would be guaranteed?

SUGGESTED READINGS

Harless, Doris E. *Nonbank Financial Institutions.* Federal Reserve Bank of Richmond (October, 1975).

Larkins, Daniel J. "Recent Developments in Mortgage Markets." *Survey of Current Business* (February, 1982), pp. 19–36.

Life Insurance Fact Book. Washington: American Council of Life Insurance, 1982.

Luckett, Charles. "Recent Developments in the Mortgage and Consumer Credit Markets." *Federal Reserve Bulletin* (May, 1982), pp. 281–290.

Peters, Helen F. "The Mortgage Market: A Place For Ceilings." *Business Review*, Federal Reserve Bank of Philadelphia (July/August, 1977), pp. 13–21.

Savings and Loan Sourcebook. Chicago: United States League of Savings Associations, 1982.

Seiders, David F. "Changing Patterns of Housing Finance." *Federal Reserve Bulletin* (June, 1981), pp. 461–472.

Unger, Maurice A., and George R. Karvel. *Real Estate: Principles and Practices,* 7th ed. Cincinnati: South-Western Publishing Co., 1983.

Unger, Maurice A., and Ronald W. Melicher. *Real Estate Finance,* 2nd ed. Cincinnati: South-Western Publishing Co., 1984.

19 Financing Agriculture

The rapid shift of the population of the United States to urban living since the turn of the century has been one of the results of an expanding industrial economy. Agriculture, with a decreasing proportion of the population devoted to it, has had to provide ever-increasing quantities of food and fibers to sustain a rapidly increasing total population. Such production has been made possible by the more skillful utilization of land through the use of modern machinery, and by improved methods of storing and preserving and of transporting farm products to the population centers. Just as industrial productivity has increased based on scientific research and technological experimentation, agriculture has responded in similar fashion. Agriculture has, in fact, become increasingly commercialized.

PROBLEMS IN FINANCING AGRICULTURE

The demands for greater productivity in agriculture have made it necessary for farmers to invest ever-increasing sums of capital in land, buildings, machinery, livestock, fertilizers, and general supplies. Because the typical farm in the United States remains a combination of home and business, funds for operation of the farm must include operation of the home as well.

As an indication of the size of the investment in agriculture in the United States, as of January 1, 1982, total physical assets approximated $1.2 trillion.[1] Table 19-1 reveals the pattern of agricultural assets for selected years. Note that the item of machinery and motor vehicles has increased from 6 percent of total assets in 1940 to more than 9 percent in 1982. As a percentage of non-real estate physical assets, this item has increased from 20 percent in 1940 to more than 45 percent in 1982. Such an increase reflects the increasing capital requirements for mechanization of farms.

---

[1] *Economic Report of the President* (Washington: United States Government Printing Office, 1982), p. 344.

Table 19-1

Comparative Asset
Sheet of Agriculture
United States, January
1, Selected Years,
1940–1982 (In Billions
of Dollars)

Item	1940	1960	1982
ASSETS			
Physical assets:			
Real estate....................................	33.6	130.2	894.5
Non-real estate:			
Livestock	5.1	15.2	63.0
Machinery and motor vehicles..............	3.1	22.2	109.5
Crops stored on and off farms	2.7	7.7	42.8
Household furnishings and equipment......	4.3	9.6	23.7
Financial assets:			
Deposits and currency	3.2	9.2	16.6
United States savings bonds	.2	4.7	3.9
Investments in cooperatives	.8	4.3	22.0
Total.......................................	53.0	203.1	1,176.0

SOURCE: *Economic Report of the President.* Washington: United States Government Printing Office, 1982, p. 344.

Methods of Agricultural Financing

The person who is intent on farming but who has neither a farm nor sufficient capital to acquire one may work for others. As a possible alternative, the farmer may establish partnership relationships with one or more other persons in order to finance the purchase of farmland and equipment. Land may also be leased for farming purposes, either on the basis of a fixed rental or a fixed proportion of the crops grown on the land. Finally, the farmer may borrow. We are concerned here principally with the facilities that are available for borrowing for agricultural production and for the acquisition of farm assets.

Although many farmers own their farms and have adequate financial resources for current farming operations without recourse to borrowing, other farmers spend many years of their lives repaying indebtedness—indebtedness arising from the purchase of land and from the credit purchases of machinery, livestock, and requirements for the home. Nor is such indebtedness by the farmer to be avoided if the farm is to be operated with efficiency. The farmer who has the capacity and the equipment to cultivate 120 acres but who has only 80 acres of land will do well to acquire additional land with borrowed capital, if such land and borrowing are available at a reasonable cost. Too, the farmer with much land but little equipment may be well advised to use credit to acquire equipment in order that the land may be utilized fully.

The farmer who has financial resources sufficient only to carry the family through the year would be foolish to reduce cultivation because of an inability to meet on a cash basis the costs of harvesting crops. Such a farmer would be expected to borrow prior to the harvest period in anticipation of expected income. Without ample credit, farms could no more function efficiently than could the business institutions of the nation. Farming, in fact, is only another form of business activity, operating generally as a single proprietorship. There has, however, been a striking increase in the number of publicly held farm corporations.

Special Considerations in Agricultural Financing

Most farm production is highly seasonal in nature. As such, the bulk of the annual income from farming activities may be received by the farmer within a very few weeks during each year. It may be both necessary and profitable to borrow to meet the operational costs of farming, repaying the loan when the crops have been harvested. The traditional source of such financing for the farmer has been the commercial bank. Banks in the farming regions have at times found it difficult to meet adequately the heavy seasonal demands for operating capital on the part of the farmers. In addition, the term of such loans must be adjusted to the growing period of crops and livestock, a term that is generally longer than that of the typical working capital loan to industry.

The small size of the average farm loan as compared with industrial loans and the difficulty of appraising farm resources have resulted in an interest charge somewhat higher than that to industry. Also the purchase of farmland requires a long amortization period, due to the uncertain year-to-year volume and value of agricultural production.

As a result of the complexities and difficulties of agricultural finance, there have been recurring complaints that agricultural financial facilities were not adequate. This special problem of agricultural financing was recognized as early as World War I by the government. Since that time the government has sponsored several special agencies for the solving of these problems.

SOURCES OF FARM CREDIT

The sources of farm credit may be grouped broadly as private sources and public sources. Although most discussion of farm financing seems to center about the many public agencies established by the government for that purpose, private sources of agricultural credit continue to provide a preponderance of financing required by the farmer for non-real estate purposes. Among the principal sources of private agricultural credit are the commercial banks, life insurance companies, individuals, merchants, and dealers. The governmental facilities for farm financing are almost all within the jurisdiction of the Farm Credit Administration. Both private and governmental facilities for farm financing are discussed here.

Private sources include the following:

1. Commercial banks
2. Life insurance companies
3. Individuals, merchants, dealers, and others

Commercial Banks

The commercial banks of rural areas have been the primary institutional source of short-term agricultural credit throughout the history of this country. In addition, commercial banks provide a substantial amount of long-term farm mortgage credit. Unlike the larger urban communities with many types of financial institutions, the small town in the agricultural area may have the commercial bank as its only private financial institution. It is not surprising then that the commercial banks have played such a dominant role in agricultural financing. There is a possibility, however, that banks may be less capable of serving the agricultural community in the future. A changing regulatory environment and the growing competition for loanable funds fall most heavily on the smaller rural banks.

Because of the high degree of liquidity required of commercial bank assets, short-term loans for production and operating purposes have been the principal contribution of commercial banks to farm finance. Short-term loans are generally based on the current earnings prospects of the farm rather than on land or equipment as mortgage collateral. The restrictive provisions of federal regulation in connection with real estate lending on the part of national banks have made long-term loans secured by real estate less suitable than short-term loans. Also, the banking laws of many states limit long-term lending based on real estate collateral by state-chartered commercial banks. As indicated by Table 19-2,

Table 19-2

Amount of Loans to Farmers and Percent of Total Held by Lenders, January 1, 1981

Lender	Amount (In Billions of Dollars)	Percent of Total
Real Estate Loans		
Federal land banks......................	35.9	39.0
Life insurance companies	12.9	14.0
Commercial banks	8.7	10.0
Farmers Home Administration.............	7.7	8.0
Others (including sellers)	26.7	29.0
Total real estate loans	92.0	100.0
Non-Real Estate Loans		
Production credit associations............	20.0	24.0
Federal intermediate-credit banks.........	0.8	1.0
Commercial banks	31.6	38.0
Farmers Home Administration.............	11.8	14.0
Individuals and others...................	18.4	23.0
Total non-real estate loans..............	82.6	100.0

SOURCE: *Forty-Seventh Annual Report,* 1980, The Farm Credit Administration, Washington, D.C., p. 12.

commercial banks provided only 10 percent of all real estate loans, while they provided over 38 percent of all non-real estate farm loans.

Life Insurance Companies

Life insurance companies have for many years been a significant source of long-term mortgage loans for the farmer. As revealed in Table 19-2, they are one of the most important institutional sources of farm mortgage loans. Life insurance companies of the nation held approximately 14 percent of the farm real estate debt as of January 1, 1981. Yet, because of the tremendous resources of life insurance companies, farm mortgages represent but a small percentage of their total assets.[2]

Since the objective of life insurance companies for most of their investments in farm mortgages is safety of the loan and a modest yield, it is not surprising that the volume of long-term farm mortgage lending by the life insurance companies has diminished during periods of agricultural difficulties. Some authorities believe, however, that the insurance companies have been far more lenient toward distressed mortgagors during periods of economic depression than most other private mortgagees. The emphasis of the life insurance companies on the factor of safety has resulted in their restriction of farm mortgage loans to the better farming areas and to the better farms.

At the present time, long-term life insurance company loans to the farmer carry maturities of up to forty years, with repayment arrangements based upon the farmer's financial position. In some cases the amortization schedule is such that the payments decrease in size from year to year, while in cases where it is expected that ability to repay will increase, the principal payments increase. The fact that insurance companies restrict their mortgage loans to the better risks makes it possible for them to charge lower interest rates than is true of most other private farm mortgage lenders. The low interest rates of life insurance companies on mortgage loans, together with the fact that prepayments of principal are generally permitted without penalty, make these loans very attractive to the farmer.

The large insurance companies, often located far from the agricultural loan areas of their choice, make such loans through branch offices, local banks, or local loan agents. Branch offices are generally established in choice agricultural areas for the purpose of selecting high-grade long-term farm loans. These branch offices must be staffed with personnel trained both in the mortgage loan field and in agriculture. Farmers needing loans are contacted through the company's local underwriters, through casualty and property insurance underwriters who generally receive a fee for such information, or through individuals who may suggest loan prospects. Branch managers are generally responsible to the home office of the company they represent.

In recent years the insurance companies have made funds available to qualifying farmers in less popular lending areas through the establishment of purchase agreements with local banks. Such purchase agreements involve a commitment to purchase qualifying loans from the bank within a two-year period

---

[2]In 1980, approximately 2.7 percent of total life insurance company assets were in farm mortgages. *Life Insurance Fact Book, 1981* (Washington: American Council of Life Insurance, 1981), p. 74.

after the loans are made. To qualify for purchase by the insurance companies, such loans must meet prescribed requirements with regard to appraisal standards, loan-to-value ratios, loan terms, and other pertinent factors. The purchase-agreement arrangement has the advantage to the bank of permitting temporary ownership of long-term investment instruments and the advantage to the insurance company of long-term investments in isolated areas without the trouble of local title and financial settlement details. To the local bank, details of loan settlement and administration are not difficult because they may handle the matters directly rather than by correspondence. The bank generally sells such long-term mortgages to the insurance company at a price somewhat above par as compensation for originating the loan.

Local loan agents also serve the insurance companies in areas where branch offices are not practicable. The loan agents may be real estate agents, contractors, insurance agents, or farm association representatives who have close contact with farmers. Such agents generally receive a fee based on a percentage of the amount of the loan.

Individuals, Merchants, Dealers, and Other Lenders

This group of lenders accounts for well over one fourth of all short- and long-term agricultural loans. Loans from individuals generally arise out of a property sale in which the seller takes a mortgage as part payment for the sale price, or from a sale in which the purchaser borrows from close friends or relatives. As might be expected, there is little standardization of individual lending practices, and there is generally no appraisal of the property by a trained appraiser.

Typical of the loans from merchants and dealers are the equipment loans. Such loans are offered to facilitate the purchase of heavy farm equipment, such as tractors and combines. Although these loans are arranged to permit systematic and periodic repayment, lending agencies rely to a large extent on the collateral value of the equipment for the safety of the loan. While interest rates are usually quite high, the inability of many farmers to secure adequate financing through customary channels often leaves no alternative to the use of such credit. Credit by merchants is sometimes extended for such purchases as fertilizers, feed, farm supplies, and family living.

Within the category of "other lenders" are the mortgage loan companies that make long-term farm mortgage loans with the express purpose of reselling them to institutional investors. Such mortgages are generally at a premium, and the mortgage companies sometimes continue to service the loans by collecting the payments for a fee. Endowment funds of educational and other institutions are in some cases invested in farm mortgages.

THE FARM CREDIT ADMINISTRATION

The Federal Farm Loan Act of 1916 gave rise to the first of many governmental credit institutions that were to be established to aid the farmer. In 1933 most of these federal credit institutions were consolidated in the Farm

Credit Administration, and others have been added since that time. The Farm Credit Administration functioned as an independent agency of the government until 1939, at which time it was placed under the control of the United States Department of Agriculture. Under the provisions of the Farm Credit Act of 1953 the Farm Credit Administration again became an independent agency in the executive branch of the government.

The new act established a 13-member, part-time, policy-making Federal Farm Credit Board to direct, supervise, and control the Farm Credit Administration. Twelve members of the Board, one from each farm credit district, are appointed by the President of the United States, with the advice and consent of the Senate, after giving consideration to nominations made by national farm loan associations, production credit associations, and cooperatives borrowing from the district banks for cooperatives. Thus, farmers through their cooperatives have a voice in the selection of the national board. The thirteenth member is appointed as the Secretary of Agriculture's representative.

The Farm Credit Act of 1953 provides that the Federal Farm Credit Board shall function as a unit without delegating authority to individual members and prohibits the Board from operating in an administrative capacity. All administrative powers, functions, and duties of the Farm Credit Administration are exercised and performed by the Governor of the Farm Credit Administration, its chief, who is appointed by the Federal Farm Credit Board.

The Farm Credit Administration has had a substantial growth of lending activities in recent years. Its share of the lending market has, in fact, increased and it is now the dominant factor in agricultural credit.

The Farm Credit Administration has three principal credit divisions: the Land Bank Service, the Short-Term Credit Service, and the Cooperative Bank Service. The organizational structure of the Farm Credit Administration is shown in Figure 19-1. This diagram will facilitate an understanding of the administrative relationships of the agricultural lending agencies.

THE FEDERAL LAND BANK SERVICE

Under the authority of the Federal Farm Loan Act of 1916, 12 farm credit districts were created. Each farm credit district is served by a federal land bank located, as a rule, in one of the principal cities of the district. The locations of these banks and the district boundaries are shown in Figure 19-2.

Sources of Funds

The original capital of the federal land banks was provided almost entirely by the United States Treasury through the purchase of stock. Each bank was to be capitalized at $750,000 with additional funds to be obtained through the issue of debenture bonds, and these bonds were to be secured by the first mortgages of borrowers or by United States government bonds. With increased subscriptions from other sources, the government-held stock was largely retired by 1932; however, emergency legislation in that year provided for an investment of $125

Figure 19-1

Organization of the Farm Credit Administration

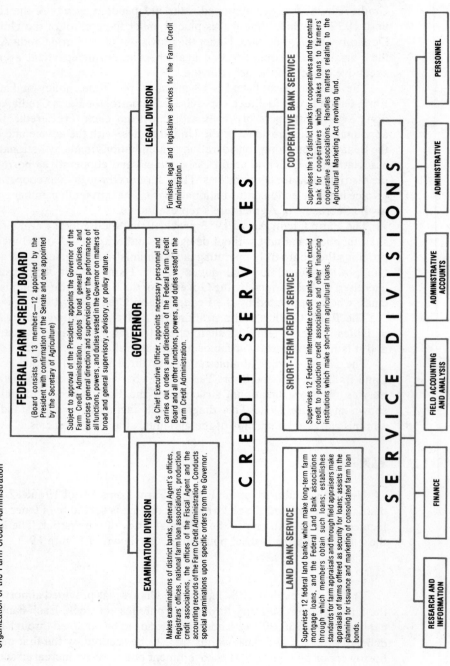

FEDERAL FARM CREDIT BOARD

(Board consists of 13 members—12 appointed by the President with confirmation of the Senate and one appointed by the Secretary of Agriculture)

Subject to approval of the President, appoints the Governor of the Farm Credit Administration, adopts broad general policies, and exercises general direction and supervision over the performance of all functions, powers, and duties vested in the Governor on matters of broad and general supervisory, advisory, or policy nature.

GOVERNOR

As Chief Executive Officer, appoints necessary personnel and carries out orders and directions of the Federal Farm Credit Board and all other functions, powers, and duties vested in the Farm Credit Administration.

EXAMINATION DIVISION

Makes examinations of district banks, General Agent's offices, Registrars' offices, national farm loan associations, production credit associations, the offices of the Fiscal Agent and the accounting records of the Farm Credit Administration. Conducts special examinations upon specific orders from the Governor.

LEGAL DIVISION

Furnishes legal and legislative services for the Farm Credit Administration.

CREDIT SERVICES

LAND BANK SERVICE

Supervises 12 federal land banks which make long-term farm mortgage loans, and the Federal Land Bank associations through which members obtain such loans; establishes standards for farm appraisals and through field appraisers make appraisals of farms offered as security for loans; assists in the planning for issuance and marketing of consolidated farm loan bonds.

SHORT-TERM CREDIT SERVICE

Supervises 12 Federal intermediate credit banks which extend credit to production credit associations and other financing institutions which make short-term agricultural loans.

COOPERATIVE BANK SERVICE

Supervises the 12 district banks for cooperatives and the central bank for cooperatives which makes loans to farmers' cooperative associations. Handles matters relating to the Agricultural Marketing Act revolving fund.

SERVICE DIVISIONS

| RESEARCH AND INFORMATION | FINANCE | FIELD ACCOUNTING AND ANALYSIS | ADMINISTRATIVE ACCOUNTS | ADMINISTRATIVE | PERSONNEL |

SOURCE: Farm Credit Administration

Figure 19-2

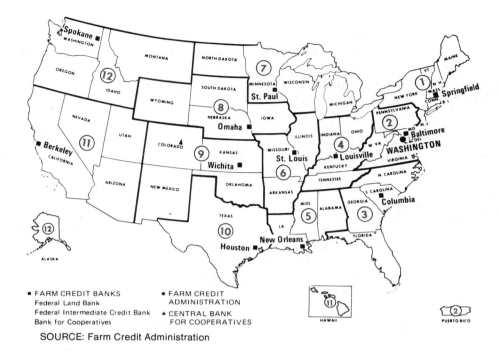

SOURCE: Farm Credit Administration

million in the stock of the banks to increase their supply of loanable funds. No dividends were paid on stock held by the government, and all such stock held by the government has now been retired.

Consolidated federal farm loan bonds, sold to investors, are now the principal source of funds for making land bank loans. These bonds are the joint and several obligations of the twelve federal land banks. They are not guaranteed either as to principal or interest by the United States government. On December 31, 1980, outstanding consolidated federal farm loan bonds amounted to $33.9 billion.[3] In 1976 a new type of security was issued which has proved to be popular with investors. It is called the Federal Farm Credit Banks Consolidated Systemwide Bond and differs from its predecessors in that it is a systemwide obligation backed by all 37 farm credit banks.

Purposes of Federal Land Bank Loans

Federal land bank loans may be made for these purposes: (1) to buy land for agricultural uses; (2) to provide buildings and to improve the farmlands; (3) to buy equipment, fertilizers, and livestock necessary for the proper operation of the farm; (4) to refinance indebtedness of the borrower incurred for agricultural purposes or incurred at least two years prior to the date of the application; and (5) to provide the borrower with funds for general agricultural purposes. A loan

---

[3]*Annual Report of the Farm Credit Administration,* 1980, p. 77.

may not exceed 85 percent of the appraised normal value of the farm to be mortgaged. The Farm Credit Act of 1971, among other things, expanded the lending authority of the Federal Land Banks to include the financing of certain nonfarm rural homes and of businesses providing on-the-farm services.

More than 90 percent of Federal Land Bank loans are made for the purchase of real estate or the refinancing of previous loans. Such loans made to farmers, ranchers, agribusinesses, and rural residents generally have maturities of from 5 to 40 years. They usually specify a fixed number of installments over the life of the loans and all new loans carry a variable interest rate. Depending on changes in the bank's cost of funds, the rate can change during the life of a loan. The loans may be prepaid any time in whole or in part without penalty.

Federal Land Bank Associations

Federal land bank loans are negotiated through the federal land bank associations. These associations exist to provide the connection between the farmer and the land bank and to facilitate the orderly and prompt consideration of loan applications through a system of decentralization of functions and responsibilities.

Federal land bank associations may be described as cooperative credit organizations. They are chartered by and operated under the supervision of the Farm Credit Administration in accordance with the provisions of the Federal Farm Loan Act. The associations are composed of groups of farmers who assume certain mutual responsibilities to provide a source of long-term farm mortgage credit for their community. They are usually organized on a community or county basis. The stockholders of each association elect a board of directors, which in turn appoints a president, a secretary-treasurer, and a loan committee. The secretary-treasurer, upon whom most of the administrative work falls, is not required to be a stockholder. The primary duties of the federal land bank associations consist of assisting the farmer in the determination of loan needs, initiating the loan application, and servicing the loan through collecting payments, placing insurance, and in some cases disposing of property upon nonpayment of debt.

Membership. Each borrower is required to purchase association stock to the extent of 5 percent of the amount of the loan. A stockholder-borrower is entitled to one vote irrespective of the amount borrowed.

Each loan that is made by a federal land bank through a federal land bank association is guaranteed by the association, resulting in a limited guarantee of each member of the association for all of the loans made through the association. This guarantee is made effective through the requirement that the association hold stock of its federal land bank in an amount equal to 5 percent of total loans made through the association. Should mortgage losses of an association exceed normal dividends due from the federal land bank, recourse may be had to the stock held by the borrower-stockholder.

An example of a loan application and approval may best illustrate the functioning of the federal land bank system. Assume that a farmer has applied for a loan of $50,000 for the purchase of land for agricultural use, or for other reasons acceptable to the land bank. The loan committee of the association examines the application to establish a preliminary appraisal of the property to be mortgaged and the acceptability of the applicant as a mortgagor. If the loan application is acceptable to the loan committee, it is presented to the board of directors of the association where, if acceptable to the board, it is forwarded to the federal land bank of that district. The federal land bank then has the property appraised by one of its own appraisers, a requirement established by the Federal Farm Loan Act. If the appraiser submits a favorable report and the application is satisfactory in other respects, the loan may be granted. The maximum nonguaranteed loan-to-value ratio is 85 percent; hence, the property in this example must have an appraised value of at least $58,824.

On the assumption that this loan is approved, upon clearance and transfer of title to the property, the $50,000 is delivered to the federal land bank association through which the loan was initiated. The association in turn brings together the parties to the transaction and delivers the money to the seller of the property after the loan settlement arrangements are completed.

The farmer is required to purchase association stock in the amount of $2,500 (5 percent of $50,000). This amount in turn is paid by the association to the land bank for stock. The farmer is liable, therefore, not only for the $50,000 but also to the extent of $2,500 stock ownership for the loans of other association members. If losses of the association prove to be negligible, the farmer may surrender stock owned in the association upon payment of the loan. Should losses of the association be large because of numerous defaults, the borrower may recover only a part or none of the stock investment, depending on the amount of the stock fund required to offset the loan losses. This system of requiring a joint responsibility for all loans of an association by all borrowers results in a greater selectivity of risks and a local control otherwise difficult to achieve.

Loans, Interest Rates, and Dividends. The federal land banks, through the 491 federal land bank associations, made 92,222 loans for a total of $10.3 billion during the year ending June 30, 1980. The average size of loan was about $112,000. Under the Federal Farm Loan Act, the contract interest rate on loans made through federal land bank associations cannot be more than 1 percent above the interest rate on the last series of bonds issued by the bank making the loans, except with the approval of the Governor of the Farm Credit Administration.

THE FEDERAL SHORT-TERM CREDIT SERVICE

The Federal Short-Term Credit Service supervises and coordinates the operations of the 12 federal intermediate credit banks, which in turn work closely with the 424 production credit associations on all phases of their operations. It provides leadership and guidance in all major phases of the operations of the institutions concerned, including their capitalization, development of credit standards, investment of funds, disposition of earnings, and other factors related to sound lending and management practices. It approves the borrowing of money and the issuance of debentures by the federal intermediate credit banks.

The Federal Intermediate Credit Banks

Federal assistance in the field of long-term credit for the farmer was followed by attempts to provide supplementary sources of intermediate- and short-term credit. This was accomplished through the establishment of 12 federal intermediate credit banks under the Agricultural Credits Act of 1923. Congressional inquiry had revealed that agricultural and livestock industries needed a more adequate and stable supply of intermediate- and short-term credit than was available to them through existing sources.

The federal intermediate credit banks themselves do not make loans directly to farmers; they discount agricultural and livestock paper and make loans to local financial institutions that do finance the credit needs of the farmer. Representative of the kind of institutions receiving such financing are the production credit associations, agricultural credit corporations, livestock loan companies, and commercial banks. These loans are generally made for production and general farm operation purposes, may carry maturities of up to 5 years and may provide for a variable interest rate. The usual loan term is one year or less, based on the time for marketing crops or livestock.

Sources of Funds

The federal intermediate credit banks obtain the bulk of their funds from the sale of consolidated collateral trust debentures in the financial markets to the investing public. Although maturities of up to 5 years are permitted, the average maturity has been from 3 to 42 months. For the year 1980, the average maturity was 12 months. Debentures issued carried an average cost to the banks of 12.4 percent. Each bank's participation in the outstanding debentures must not exceed ten times the amount of its capital and paid-in surplus. The 12 banks are jointly and severally liable for these obligations. The debentures are not guaranteed by the federal government either as to principal or interest. Sales and distribution are usually made through security dealers and dealer banks for delivery on the first of each month. Such sales are made on the basis of estimates of cash needs, but unexpected demands make it necessary from time to time to obtain funds for short periods between sales.

The original capital of each federal intermediate credit bank, $5 million, was supplied by the United States Treasury. The total capital and surplus of the 12 banks as of December 31, 1981, was $1.6 billion. This includes $1.1 billion of stock owned by production credit associations and $68 million of participation certificates owned by other financial institutions which use the services of the federal intermediate credit banks.

Management and Supervision

Each intermediate credit bank operates under its own corporate management and under the direction of a board of directors, which serves as the board for the other permanent credit units of each district. The operations of the banks are supervised by the Intermediate Credit Division Commissioner, who is responsible to the Governor of the Farm Credit Administration.

Interest and Discount Rates

The board of directors of a federal intermediate credit bank together with the Commissioner fix the discount and interest rates. Except with the approval of the Governor of the Farm Credit Administration, however, the rate fixed may not exceed by more than 1 percent per annum the rate of the last preceding issue of debentures in which the bank participated. The rate charged by a bank, therefore, is governed primarily by the cost of money which, in turn, is related closely to the prevailing rates on other prime securities in the market. As of year-end 1980, the interest and discount rate of the federal intermediate credit banks ranged from 10.75 to 12.80 percent.[4]

Institutions that rediscount with an intermediate credit bank are permitted to charge their borrowers on such loans not more than 4 percent per annum in excess of the discount rate of the intermediate credit bank.

Production Credit Associations

The Governor of the Farm Credit Administration is authorized to charter cooperative lending organizations, known as production credit associations, making short-term loans to farmers for agricultural uses. Typically, such loans are used for purposes of breeding, raising, and fattening of livestock and poultry; dairying; the growing, harvesting, and marketing of crops; the purchase and repair of farm machinery; the purchase and repair of rural homes; and the refinancing of short-term debts. Associations now serve every rural county in the United States and Puerto Rico, each association's territory of operation being prescribed by the Governor of the Farm Credit Administration.

Capital Stock. Each production credit association has two classes of capital stock: Class A, which is nonvoting; and Class B, which is voting. Class B stock may be owned only by borrowing farmers. The Class A stock, owned by the Governor of the Farm Credit Administration, is preferred as to assets in case of liquidation of an association, but all stocks share proportionately in dividends. Borrowers are required to purchase Class B stock of an association to the extent of $5 for each $100 of loan. Such stock may be retained and used regularly for borrowing purposes. As in the case of members of the national farm loan associations, each borrower has one vote. Such voting must be accomplished in person, voting by proxy not being permitted. Holders of Class B stock are required to sell their stock in the event that two years elapse after the loan has been repaid and no new loan has been negotiated. The purpose of this limitation is to restrict control of the production credit association to active borrower members.

---

[4] *Ibid.,* p. 45.

Management. Voting stockholders elect their association's board of directors at their annual meetings. The board is generally composed of 5 members, each selected for 3 years on a staggered basis. It is the responsibility of these directors to elect the association officers and appoint its employees.

Source of Funds. The production credit associations secure loan funds by borrowing from the federal intermediate credit bank of their district or by turning over to the intermediate credit banks loans that they have made to their customers. Loans are made to farmers and ranchers for general agricultural purposes to finance sound short-term credit needs. These loans are generally secured by a first lien on crops, livestock, and equipment, and interest is charged only on the amount of the loan actually outstanding.

The production loan associations also charge a loan service fee to cover the cost of appraising, reviewing, and administering the loans. Short-term credit secured from the production credit associations is often sufficient to cover a member's entire credit needs for a season or a year. Farmers usually get their installments as they need the money and repay their loans when they sell the products financed. Budgeted loans of this nature reduce the number of days each dollar is outstanding and reduce correspondingly the amount of interest paid by the borrower. Farmers had loans outstanding for a total of $20 billion from the 424 production credit associations as of January 1, 1981.[5]

THE COOPERATIVE BANK SERVICE

For many years the federal government has encouraged the establishment of farmers' marketing and purchasing cooperatives. Such encouragement has taken the form of immunity from the antitrust laws, tax advantages, and financial assistance. The provision of financial assistance is accomplished through a system of banks for cooperatives.

Under the provisions of the Farm Credit Act of 1933, the Governor of the Farm Credit Administration chartered 12 district banks and 1 Central Bank to provide a permanent system of credit for farmers' cooperatives. One of the banks for cooperatives is located in each of the farm credit districts, and the Central Bank is now located in Denver, Colorado.

Functions of the Banks for Cooperatives

The 13 banks make loans to cooperatives engaged in marketing agricultural products, purchasing farm supplies, and furnishing farm business services. The Central Bank for Cooperatives makes loans that are too large for district banks to handle and loans to cooperatives operating in more than one farm credit district. The Central Bank also participates in many loans made by the district banks. District banks, in turn, participate in loans made by the Central Bank.

------

[5]*Ibid.,* p. 12.

Capital and Other Sources of Loanable Funds

The initial capital for the banks for cooperatives was subscribed by the Governor of the Farm Credit Administration from funds made available by the federal government. Changes in this initial capital have been made from time to time as the demand for credit has varied. All stock originally held by the federal government has now been retired. Borrowing cooperatives must purchase $100 in stock for each $2,000 borrowed.

The banks for cooperatives are authorized to borrow from, or turn their own loans over to, other banks for cooperatives, the federal intermediate credit banks, and commercial banks. The Central Bank for Cooperatives is authorized to issue debentures in an amount not to exceed five times its paid-in capital and surplus.

Management

General supervision of the banks for cooperatives is exercised by the Cooperative Bank Commissioner acting under the direction of the Governor of the Farm Credit Administration. The district banks have as their board of directors the farm credit board of each district. In addition to the officers elected by the board, each of the banks has a staff composed of business analysts, appraisers, accountants, and clerical employees. The Central Bank for Cooperatives has a board of 7 directors, 6 of whom are appointed by the Governor of the Farm Credit Administration. The seventh member is the Cooperative Bank Commissioner, who also acts as chairperson of the board.

Eligible Borrowers

To be eligible to borrow from a bank for cooperatives, an association must be a cooperative operated for the mutual benefit of its members. Farmers must act together in doing one or more of the following: (1) processing, preparing for market, handling, or marketing farm products; (2) purchasing, testing, grading, processing, distributing, or furnishing farm supplies; or (3) furnishing farm business services.

Types of Loans

Three types of loans are made to cooperatives: (1) short-term loans secured by appropriate commodities in storage; (2) operating capital loans to supplement the borrowing cooperatives' working capital; (3) loans for the purpose of assisting in financing the cost of construction, purchase, or lease of land and the acquisition of buildings, equipment, or other physical facilities. Although maturities of 20 years are permitted, in most cases they are for much shorter periods. As of year-end 1980, 3488 cooperatives had loans outstanding from the banks in the amount of approximately $8.1 billion.[6]

---

[6]*Ibid.,* p. 36.

OTHER FEDERAL AGRICULTURAL CREDIT FACILITIES

The trend in recent years has been toward administrative centralization of the many sources of government-sponsored agricultural credit under the Farm Credit Administration. There remain, however, several financial operating organizations directly under the control of the Secretary of Agriculture. Two of these are the Commodity Credit Corporation and the Farmers Home Administration.

The Commodity Credit Corporation

The Commodity Credit Corporation was organized in 1933 to provide a more orderly and stable market for farm products. Loans and loan guarantees are used by the Corporation to support the price of basic commodities, such as wheat, tobacco, corn, and cotton. These basic commodities serve as collateral for Commodity Credit Corporation loans. The maximum loan value on farm products is based on a percentage of "parity" prices established at the beginning of the year. A condition of the availability of such loans, however, is that the borrowing farmer shall have complied with governmental restrictions concerning the number of acres allotted to that farmer for the planting of that crop. A stipulated percentage of the parity value of the crop can be borrowed from the Commodity Credit Corporation even though such parity value is above the prevailing market value of that product. Purchase by the government of the farm products used as collateral for the commodity credit loan becomes effective by default if the loan is not repaid. This amounts to a conditional purchase plan by the government to effect a price floor on farm products.

The Commodity Credit Corporation also gives support to farm prices through the outright purchase and storage of crops, and it has participated in general supply programs in cooperation with other federal agencies, foreign governments, and international relief organizations.

The capital of the Commodity Credit Corporation is provided entirely by the United States government. The Corporation has a capital of $100 million. It is authorized to borrow an additional $20 billion on the credit of the United States government. The Commodity Credit Corporation provided more than $5.8 billion in loans during the fiscal year ending September 30, 1981.[7]

The Farmers Home Administration

The Farmers Home Administration was created in 1946 by the merger of the Farm Security Administration and the Emergency Crop and Feed Loan Division of the Farm Credit Administration. It has been authorized to make loans and to insure loans for farmers who are otherwise unable to obtain credit at appropriate rates of interest and suitable maturities. Preference has been given to veterans to enable them to purchase farms. Loans for terms up to 40 years are made for purposes of purchase, improvement, or repair of farms and farm buildings.

[7]*Commodity Credit Corporation Report of Financial Condition and Operation.* Quarterly Report, Department of Agriculture, Agricultural Stabilization and Conservation Service, September 30, 1981.

Responsibility for the following has been given the Farmers Home Administration: (a) administering of rural resettlement projects; (b) financing the purchase of farm property for tenant farmers; (c) financing emergency loans to low-income farmers; and (d) financing loans to facilitate farmers' community and cooperative enterprises that would be classified as rehabilitation or resettlement projects. Loans of up to $100,000 are made for such purposes as the purchase of livestock, seed, fertilizer, farm equipment, supplies, and other farm needs, as well as for financing indebtedness and family subsistence. Such loans have maturities of from 1 to 7 years. Farm ownership loans are repayable over periods up to 40 years. Farmers Home Administration loans plus other debts against the security property may not exceed $200,000. Borrowers may make advance payments in good years so they will be protected against falling behind in their payments in difficult years. Funds for the loans of the Farmers Home Administration are provided by Congress.

QUESTIONS

1. Explain the increasing capital requirements of agricultural activities.
2. Farm financing is often described as being an especially difficult problem. Explain.
3. Discuss the importance of commercial bank lending for agricultural purposes. Do commercial banks provide credit for all agricultural purposes?
4. To what extent and for what purposes do life insurance companies provide funds for agriculture?
5. How do the life insurance companies of the nation maintain contact with farmers for purposes of extending mortgage loans?
6. Describe some of the private sources of agricultural credit other than commercial banks and life insurance companies.
7. Describe the evolution and present structure of the principal governmental facilities for farm credit.
8. To what extent are the 12 federal farm credit districts similar to the 12 federal reserve districts?
9. Trace the principal steps involved in the making of a federal land bank loan from the original application by the farmer to the receipt of the loan.
10. Discuss the method by which the federal land banks shift part of the risk of mortgage lending to other groups.
11. Describe the role of the federal intermediate credit banks in agricultural financing.
12. Discuss the sources of loan funds for the federal land banks and for the federal intermediate credit banks. To what extent are the obligations of these organizations liabilities of the federal government?
13. Describe the role of the production credit associations in agricultural financing.
14. For what purposes were the banks for cooperatives established?
15. Describe the purposes and operations of the Commodity Credit Corporation.
16. Outline the types of loans available to farmers through the Farmers Home Administration.

SUGGESTED READINGS

Agricultural Finance Review, published annually by the Agricultural Research Service, United States Department of Agriculture.

Agricultural Production Financing. New York: Agricultural Commission, American Bankers Association.

Annual Reports, published by the Farm Credit Administration.

Duncan, Marvin, and Ann Laing Adair. "Sources of Loanable Funds for Agricultural Banks." *Economic Review*, Federal Reserve Bank of Kansas City (March, 1981), pp. 17–28.

Farm Equipment Financing by Banks. New York: Agricultural Commission, American Bankers Association.

Farm Real Estate Financing. New York: Agricultural Commission, American Bankers Association.

Future Sources of Loanable Funds for Agricultural Banks. A Symposium Sponsored by The Federal Reserve Bank of Kansas City (December 8–9, 1980).

Intermediate-Term Bank Credit For Farmers. New York: Agricultural Commission, American Bankers Association.

Webb, Kerry, "The Farm Credit System." *Economic Review*, Federal Reserve Bank of Kansas City (June, 1980), pp. 16–30.

20 International Finance

The productive capacity of the United States economy is the result of many factors, including vast natural resources, suitable climatic conditions, and a population that has had the courage and the ability to profit by these natural advantages. Of equal importance to the productive growth of the nation has been the existence of a form of government that has encouraged this development through stimulation of individual effort. Not the least of the contributions of the government in this respect has been that of facilitating trade between the areas of the nation, in turn making it possible for each geographical area to specialize in those activities for which its individual natural resources best equip it.

It is difficult to imagine the situation that would exist if each of the fifty states tried to be self-sufficient. Under these circumstances, we could expect the northern industrial states to enjoy little of the citrus fruits that they now import from Florida and the West Coast. Nor could we expect the tobacco-growing states to have the full benefit of farm machinery for their operations, since the market for machinery in a single state is hardly sufficient to warrant production on a scale necessary for economical manufacture.

While these principles of specialization with regard to geographical areas of the United States are obvious enough, it may be somewhat more difficult to appreciate the extension of these principles of specialization beyond the borders of the country; yet the basic principles underlying specialization of effort within a nation hold true with equal force among nations. The very size of the United States is such as to lead a person not otherwise familiar with the vast amount of goods and services transported between the United States and foreign countries to believe that the nation is nearly self-sufficient. It is true that many items which were formerly imported are now produced in the country, making us less dependent upon foreign sources; however, there is an effective limit to the self-sufficiency that any nation can attain. For example, the development of sufficient coffee production within the nation to satisfy the current domestic demand for the product would probably be impossible.

In addition to the many items for which other nations possess a natural productive advantage, other items are not available within our own national borders under any circumstances. Such items include tin, magnesium, and extracts from certain tropical plants used in the preparation of medicines. Although there are some legitimate reasons for curtailing temporarily, and in some cases permanently, certain types of trade flows, it is undoubtedly true that a specialized concentration of effort on the part of the nations of the world is to the general benefit of everybody concerned.

The benefits of specialization of effort are made possible only to the extent that the persons participating are assured of a market for the fruits of their effort. A market for goods and services is made effective only if adequate financial facilities exist to enable the settlement of claims between the parties. Just as there has developed within the United States an intricate and smoothly operating system of finance to provide for the exchange of goods and services among persons and institutions, so too a system of international finance has developed whereby settlement of international claims may be effected. It is with this process of settlement of international claims that this chapter is concerned.

INTERNATIONAL PAYMENTS

As a citizen of the United States tours our country during a vacation, lodging bills, gasoline costs, and other vacation expenses are paid with dollars. Similarly, the motel and hotel operators and the service station attendants wish to be paid for their goods and services in the form of dollars. The large mail-order houses located in Chicago also demand dollars for the goods that they are willing to ship to all parts of the country, and the persons ordering such goods are prepared to pay in terms of dollars. On the other hand, a person who orders leather goods from Mexico, glassware from Italy, or a year's subscription to the London *Times*, may arrange for payment for these items not in dollars but rather in the money of the particular country from which the items have been ordered.

Foreign exporters are usually quite willing to accept United States dollars in payment for their goods and services because of the importance of the dollar in international trade and the ease with which it can be converted into the money of the exporter's country. The importers of many countries, however, must arrange payment to foreign exporters in the money of the exporter's country. The importance of the United States dollar in foreign exchange makes it a popular money for the settlement of transactions among other countries as well as between the United States and other countries.

When it is necessary or desirable to make payments in international trade in the money of another country, actual possession of the foreign money is unnecessary. For example, if a person wishes to pay for a year's subscription to the *Times* in sterling, the subscriber need only go to the bank and buy a claim against British pounds equivalent to the subscription cost of the paper. This claim, which is purchased in the United States with American dollars, will be in the form of a bill of exchange, a telegraphic order, or similar instrument. An oversimplified example will illustrate how these claims may be purchased and the actual acquisition of the foreign currency avoided.

If the person who is purchasing a subscription to the *Times* wishes to secure a claim for twenty pounds, a British tourist might be found who at that moment is touring the United States. The tourist might be induced to write a check against a bank in England for twenty pounds, in return for the appropriate number of dollars, which presumably would be spent while touring this country. In addition, of course, the English tourist might expect a slight additional payment to compensate for the trouble of rendering this service. The individual to whom the check is written could then endorse it and send it together with the order for the *Times* to England where the check would be deposited for collection with the bank with which that paper does business. The subscriber to the *Times* purchased, in essence, nothing more than a claim to pounds.

This is rather an awkward process, however, and it is hardly to be expected that an importer would be required to seek out some foreign visitor to this country. Instead, the banking system along with other institutions provides this service for a nominal fee. Although all banks do not have departments that sell foreign exchange to their customers, practically all banks have correspondent relations with banks which do offer that facility. Hence, it is necessary only to go to a local bank in order to secure a claim against foreign money. If the local bank does not itself have a claim to foreign currency, it can purchase such a claim for its customers from a bank with which it deals for that purpose. The banks that deal directly in foreign exchange may do so by maintaining monetary deposits in banks in foreign countries, against which they may draw drafts for sale to their home customers. In other cases, banks may operate branches in the foreign countries. The Federal Reserve Act authorizes banks to establish branches abroad; as of the end of 1981 there were 190 domestic banks with foreign offices. Foreign banking corporations likewise have their own network of foreign contacts. In addition to maintaining correspondent relations with United States banks, foreign banks are permitted to operate agencies and to set up subsidiaries in this country. Subsidiary banking corporations established by foreign banks are not subject to any special restrictions because of foreign ownership.

EXCHANGE RATES

The conversion ratio, or *exchange rate* as it is generally referred to, is the rate at which a given unit of foreign currency is quoted in terms of domestic currency. For example, if the British pound is quoted at $1.60 in the foreign exchange rate section of the daily newspaper, it means that purchases of claims on pounds sterling were made on the basis of a ratio of $1.60 for one British pound. For the individual who cares to buy claims on pounds sterling, this exact ratio would not necessarily prevail since it is a record of the exchange ratio of large unit transfers within the foreign exchange market itself. The prices quoted to the individual are always in favor of the seller of the exchange, which, of course, makes possible a margin of profit for the seller. The seller or dealer in our example is a bank.

The balance in the foreign account of a bank is subject to constant drain as a result of the bank's activities in selling claims to individuals in the United States who wish to import goods or services from other countries. These banks may reestablish a given deposit level with their correspondent banks through either the sale of dollar claims in the foreign country concerned or by buying claims from another dealer in the foreign exchange. The question may arise, however, as to what happens if during a period of time the volume of trading is decidedly unbalanced and the demand for claims against British pounds is substantially greater than the corresponding demand by British businesses and individuals for American dollars. Since the exchange ratio reflects the forces of supply and demand for these two currencies, such a situation would be expected to cause the ratio to rise to a point above $1.60 for each pound sterling. At some point, the number of dollars offered in exchange per pound would become high enough to induce owners of pounds to invest in American dollars.

As do the prices of all commodities, exchange rates vary from one period to another, although the degree of variance is as a rule not large over a short period of time. Changes of a few cents may be noticed in weekly comparisons of the exchange ratios of currencies of other countries and of the United States. As a result of varying exchange rates, the importer or exporter may be financially benefited or hurt in much the same manner as by changes in the price level of the commodity which is purchased or sold. Foreign exchange rates between the United States and the principal countries of the world as of April 15, 1983, are shown in Table 20-1.

Arbitrage

Arbitrage may be defined as the simultaneous, or nearly simultaneous, purchasing, as of commodities, securities, or bills of exchange, in one market and selling in another where the price is higher. In international exchange, variations in quotations between countries at any time are quickly brought into alignment through the arbitrage activities of international financiers.

For example, if the exchange rate in New York was reported at £1 = $1.61 and in London the rate was quoted at £1 = $1.60, alert international financiers would simultaneously sell claims to British pounds in New York at the rate of $1.61 and have London correspondents sell claims on American dollars in London at the rate of $1.60 for each pound sterling. Such arbitrage would be profitable only when dealing in large sums. If an arbitrager, under these circumstances, sold a claim on £100,000 in New York, $161,000 would be received. The corresponding sale of claims on American dollars in London would be at the rate of £100,000 for $160,000. Hence, a profit of $1,000 would be realized on the transaction.

The effect of such arbitrage activities on exchange rates would be the elimination of the variation between the New York and the London quotations. The sale of large amounts of claims to American dollars in London would drive the price for pounds sterling up, and in New York the sale of claims to pounds sterling would force the exchange rate down. A quotation differential of as little as one sixteenth of one cent may be sufficient to encourage arbitrage activities.

Table 20-1

Foreign Exchange Rates, April 15, 1983

Country	U.S. $ Equivalent	Currency per U.S. $	Country	U.S. $ Equivalent	Currency per U.S. $
Argentina (Peso)	.000015	68625.	Lebanon (Pound) . . .	.2418	4.135
Australia (Dollar)	.8695	1.1501	Malaysia (Ringgit). . .	.4335	2.3070
Austria (Schilling) . . .	.0584	17.13	Mexico (Peso)	.00662	151.00
Belgium (Franc).	.0204	48.90	Netherlands (Guilder)	.3640	2.7475
Brazil (Cruzeiro).	.00236	423.16	New Zealand (Dollar)	.6592	1.5170
Britain (Pound).	1.5460	.6468	Norway (Krone)	.1400	7.1430
Canada (Dollar)	.8097	1.2351	Pakistan (Rupee). . . .	.0770	12.99
Chile (Offical-Rate) . .	.0117	85.00	Peru (Sol).	.000798	1252.61
China (Yuan).	.5053	1.9790	Philippines (Peso). . .	.1038	9.63
Colombia (Peso)	.0135	74.19	Portugal (Escudo). . .	.0102	97.65
Denmark (Krone). . . .	.1155	8.6575	Saudi Arabia (Riyal).	.2898	3.45
Ecuador (Sucre)	.0238	42.00	Singapore(Dollar). . .	.4755	2.1030
Finland (Markka). . . .	.1844	5.4220	South Africa (Rand).	.9163	1.0913
France (Franc)	.1367	7.3150	South Korea (Won).	.0013	761.20
Greece(Drachma). . .	.0119	83.85	Spain (Peseta)	.00736	135.80
Hong Kong (Dollar) .	.1479	6.7610	Sweden (Krona).	.1336	7.4850
India (Rupee).	.1003	9.97	Switzerland (Franc).	.4899	2.0410
Indonesia (Rupiah). .	.00103	970.00	Taiwan (Dollar).	.0250	40.03
Ireland (Punt)	1.2970	.7710	Thailand (Baht)	.0434	23.00
Israel (Shekel)	.0254	39.46	Uruguay (New Peso).	.0293	34.12
Italy (Lira).	.000689	1451.00	Venezuela (Bolivar).	.2329	4.2938
Japan (Yen).	.004200	237.80	W. Germany (Mark).	.4101	2.4385

SOURCE: Bankers Trust Company, New York.

Exchange Quotations

On inquiring at the local bank as to the exchange rate for a foreign currency at a specific time, one will generally be given a banker's sight draft rate. A *banker's sight draft,* or *banker's check* as it is more commonly termed, differs from the common bank check only in that it is drawn by one bank on another bank. When the draft is presented for payment at the foreign bank, the balance of the drawing bank is reduced. Several days or weeks may elapse between the time the check is issued by the bank and the time it is presented for payment at the foreign bank or foreign correspondent bank. During this interval, the foreign balance of the issuing bank is not affected by the transaction.

If specifically requested, the quotation may be based on a cable rate. The bank may cable to its foreign correspondent or foreign branch to credit to the account of a specified individual or business establishment a certain amount of money. The cost of a cable order of this sort is more than a banker's check because it reduces the balance of the bank's foreign deposit almost immediately. A rate which is lower than either the banker's check rate or the cable rate is that of the *banker's time draft*, sometimes called long exchange or a long bill. Such instruments are payable at specified future dates, usually thirty days or some multiple thereof. The quotations on these time drafts are, of course, lower because they involve a reduction in the balance of the foreign branch or correspondent only after a specified period of time.

FINANCING INTERNATIONAL TRADE

One of the substantial financial burdens of any industrial firm is that of carrying the cost of the goods being produced through the process of manufacture itself. In the case of a United States manufacturer who ships goods to such far distant places as India or Australia, funds are tied up not only for the period of manufacture but also for a lengthy period of transportation. In order to solve this problem and so reduce the burden of carrying these financial costs, the manufacturers may stipulate that the foreign importer is to provide payment for the goods as soon as the goods are placed in transportation to their destination. In any case, a substantial financial burden exists either on the part of the exporter or on the part of the importer.

Financing by the Exporter

Should the exporter have confidence in the foreign customers and be in a financial position to carry sales to these customers on open-book account, there is no reason why the arrangement should not operate very much as it operates in domestic trade, subject, of course, to the complications involved in any international transaction.

Sight and Time Drafts. As an alternative to the shipment of merchandise on the basis of open-account financing, the exporter may use a collection draft. A *draft* or bill of exchange is an unconditional order in writing, signed by the person drawing it, requiring the person to whom it is addressed to pay on demand or at a fixed or determinable future time a sum certain in money to order or to bearer. A draft may require immediate payment by the importer upon its presentation, or it may require only acceptance on the part of the importer, providing for payment at a specified future time. Those instruments requiring immediate payment are classified as *sight drafts*; those requiring payment later are classified as *time drafts*. These drafts may require remittance in the currency of the country of the exporter or of the importer, depending upon the terms of the transaction. An example of a sight draft form is shown in Figure 20-1.

Drafts may be either documentary or clean. A *documentary draft* is accompanied by an order bill of lading and such other papers as insurance receipts, certificates of sanitation, and consular invoices. The *order bill of lading* represents the written acceptance of goods for shipment by a transportation company and the terms under which the goods are to be conveyed to their destination. In addition, the order bill of lading carries title to the merchandise being shipped, and only its holder may claim the merchandise from the transportation company.

Figure 20-1
Sight Draft or Bill
of Exchange

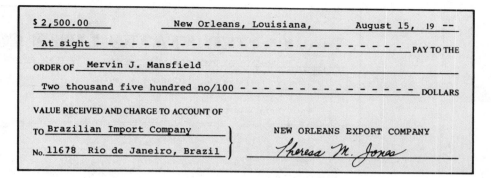

(See Figure 20-2.) The documentary sight draft is generally referred to as a D/P draft (documentary payments draft) while the documentary time draft is referred to as a D/A draft (documentary acceptance draft).

A *clean draft* is one that is not accompanied by any special documents and is generally used when the exporter has confidence in the importer's ability to meet the draft when presented. In such a case, once the merchandise is shipped to the importer, it is delivered by the transportation company irrespective of any action taken with regard to acknowledgment of the draft.

Bank Assistance in the Collection of Drafts. An importer will generally try to avoid making payment for a purchase before the goods are actually shipped because several days and perhaps weeks may elapse before the goods arrive. It is equally true that the exporter is seldom willing to send the draft and documents directly to the importer for payment or acceptance unless there is great confidence in the importer. Therefore, the exporter will work through a commercial bank.

A New York exporter who is dealing with a foreign importer with whom there has been little relationship in the past may ship goods on the basis of a documentary draft that has been deposited for collection with the local bank. That bank, following the specific instructions set out regarding the manner of collection, then forwards the draft together with the accompanying documents to its correspondent bank in the foreign country involved. The correspondent bank is instructed to hold the documents until payment is made if a sight draft is used, or until acceptance is obtained if a time draft is used. Remittance is made to the exporter when collection is made on the sight draft.

Financing Through the Exporter's Bank. It is important to recognize that throughout this transaction the banking system has only provided a service to the exporter and has in no way financed the transaction itself. The exporter's bank, however, may offer considerable assistance in this respect by allowing the exporter to borrow against the security of a documentary draft. The amount of the bank loan under these circumstances is less than the face amount of the draft. Such loans have not only the financial strength of the exporter to support them but also that of the importer, since the documents permitting acquisition of the merchandise are released only after the importer has accepted the draft. The

Figure 20-2
Order Bill of Lading

UNITED STATES LINES CO.

(SPACES IMMEDIATELY BELOW FOR SHIPPERS MEMORANDA — NOT PART OF BILL OF LADING)

FORWARDING AGENT — REFERENCES	EXPORT DEC. No.
John Doe Shipping Co., #E6776 F.M.B. #9786	X67-90687

DELIVERING CARRIER TO STEAMER:	CAR NUMBER — REFERENCE
Penn Central Company	876528

BILL OF LADING
(SHORT FORM)

(NOT NEGOTIABLE UNLESS CONSIGNED "TO ORDER")

SHIP American Banker	FLAG	PIER 61 N.R.	PORT OF LOADING NEW YORK
PORT OF DISCHARGE FROM SHIP Liverpool (Where goods are to be delivered to consignee or On-carrier) If goods to be transhipped beyond Port of Discharge, show destination Here ➡ To	AM.	THROUGH BILL OF LADING	

SHIPPER   Midwest Printing Company

CONSIGNED TO: ORDER OF   M.T. Wilson & Co.

ADDRESS ARRIVAL NOTICE TO   Same at 15 Dock St., Liverpool, E.C. 3

PARTICULARS FURNISHED BY SHIPPER OF GOODS

MARKS AND NUMBERS	NO. OF PKGS.	DESCRIPTION OF PACKAGES AND GOODS	MEASUREMENT	GROSS WEIGHT IN POUNDS
M. T. W. & Co. Liverpool	56	Books		10,145

SPECIMEN

FREIGHT PAYABLE IN   NEW YORK

(10,145) ⦿ ____ PER 2240 LBS.... $ ____	(TERMS OF THIS BILL OF LADING CONTINUED FROM REVERSE SIDE HEREOF)
____ ⦿ ____ PER 100 LBS.... $ ____	IN WITNESS WHEREOF, THE MASTER OR AGENT OF SAID VESSEL HAS SIGNED 3
____ FT. ⦿ ____ PER 40 CU. FT...$ ____	BILLS OF LADING, ALL OF THE SAME TENOR AND DATE, ONE OF WHICH BEING ACCOMPLISHED, THE OTHERS TO STAND VOID.
545 FT. ⦿ $1.05 PER CU. FT. ...... $ 572 25	UNITED STATES LINES COMPANY

BY _____ FOR THE MASTER

B/L No.   ISSUED AT NEW YORK, N.Y.

M-105

TOTAL .... $ ____

January   12   19--
MO.   DAY   YEAR

amount that the exporter can borrow against the draft depends in large measure upon the credit standing of both the exporter and the importer. In some cases, a substantial percentage of the draft may be advanced when the exporter is financially strong, even though the importer may be little known to the exporter's bank, since the credit position of the exporter will offer suitable protection to the bank. In other cases, a substantial advance may be made where the exporter has only modest financial strength but the importer is financially strong.

In addition to the financial strength of the exporter and the importer, the character of the goods shipped will also have an important bearing upon the amount loaned against a draft since the goods shipped offer collateral security for the advance. Goods not subject to breakage or perishability offer a better form of collateral than goods of a highly perishable nature. Also, goods for which there is a ready market are preferred as collateral over those for which the market may be very limited.

Financing by the Importer

As in the case of the exporter, the importer may arrange for the payment of goods without access to bank credit. Payment may be made in full with the order, or a partial payment may be offered. The partial payment offers some protection to both the exporter and the importer. It protects the exporter against arbitrary rejection of the goods so shipped on the part of the importer. It also assures the importer of having some control over the transactions in the event the merchandise purchased is damaged in shipment or does not meet specifications. Where the importer is required to make payment with an order but wishes some protection against failure of the exporter to make shipment in accordance with the provisions of the order, the order may be sent directly to the exporter; but payment therefor is sent to a representative bank in the country of the exporter. The bank is instructed not to release payment until certain documents are presented to the bank to evidence shipment of the goods according to the terms of the transactions. The bank, of course, charges a fee for providing this service.

Financing Through the Importer's Bank. In the field of foreign trade, because of the language barriers that exist and because of the difficulty in obtaining credit information about companies in the various countries, the use of the banker's acceptance is common. The *banker's acceptance* differs from the trade draft in only one respect. The former instrument is drawn on a bank and is accepted by a bank rather than by the importing firm. An example of a banker's acceptance is shown in Figure 20-3. The importer must, of course, make arrangements with the bank in advance of such an action. The exporter, too, must know before shipment is made whether or not the bank in question has agreed to accept such a draft. This arrangement is facilitated through the use of the

Figure 20-3
Banker's Acceptance

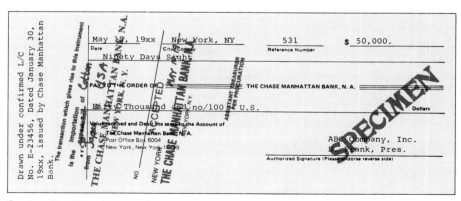

Courtesy The Chase Manhattan Bank. N.A.

commercial letter of credit. The *commercial letter of credit* may be described as a written statement on the part of the bank to an individual or firm guaranteeing acceptance and payment of a draft up to a specified sum if presented to the bank in accordance with the terms of the commercial letter of credit. (See Figure 20-4.)

Importer Bank Financing—An Example. The issuance of the letter of credit and its application to international finance may be observed from the following

Figure 20-4
Irrevocable Commercial
Letter of Credit

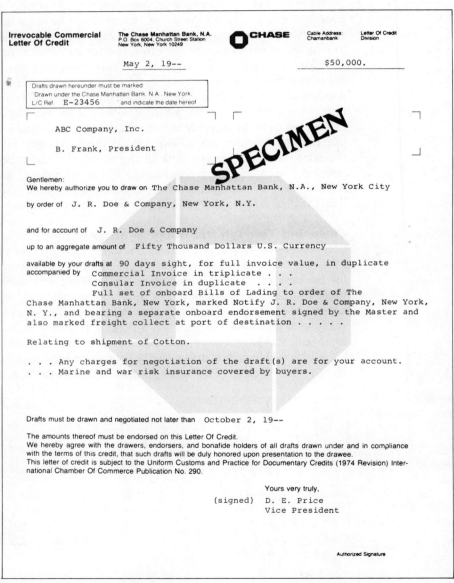

Irrevocable Commercial
Letter Of Credit

The Chase Manhattan Bank, N.A.
P.O. Box 6004, Church Street Station
New York, New York 10249

● CHASE

Cable Address:
Chamanbank

Letter Of Credit
Division

May 2, 19-- $50,000.

Drafts drawn hereunder must be marked
Drawn under the Chase Manhattan Bank, N.A., New York.
L/C Ref   E-23456   and indicate the date hereof

SPECIMEN

ABC Company, Inc.

B. Frank, President

Gentlemen:
We hereby authorize you to draw on The Chase Manhattan Bank, N.A., New York City

by order of   J. R. Doe & Company, New York, N.Y.

and for account of   J. R. Doe & Company

up to an aggregate amount of   Fifty Thousand Dollars U.S. Currency

available by your drafts at 90 days sight, for full invoice value, in duplicate
accompanied by   Commercial Invoice in triplicate . . .
                 Consular Invoice in duplicate . . . .
                 Full set of onboard Bills of Lading to order of The
Chase Manhattan Bank, New York, marked Notify J. R. Doe & Company, New York,
N. Y., and bearing a separate onboard endorsement signed by the Master and
also marked freight collect at port of destination . . . . .

Relating to shipment of Cotton.

. . . Any charges for negotiation of the draft(s) are for your account.
. . . Marine and war risk insurance covered by buyers.

Drafts must be drawn and negotiated not later than   October 2, 19--

The amounts thereof must be endorsed on this Letter Of Credit.
We hereby agree with the drawers, endorsers, and bonafide holders of all drafts drawn under and in compliance
with the terms of this credit, that such drafts will be duly honored upon presentation to the drawee.
This letter of credit is subject to the Uniform Customs and Practice for Documentary Credits (1974 Revision) International Chamber Of Commerce Publication No. 290.

                                        Yours very truly,
                        (signed)   D. E. Price
                                   Vice President

                                                    Authorized Signature

Courtesy The Chase Manhattan Bank. N.A.

example. The owner of a small but exclusive shop located in Chicago may wish to import expensive perfumes from Paris. Although the firm is well known locally, its financial reputation is not known widely enough to permit it to make direct purchases from foreign exporters on the basis of an open-book account arrangement or on the basis of drafts drawn on the firm. Under these circumstances the firm would substitute for its own credit that of its bank through the use of a commercial letter of credit. This would be accomplished by the firm's applying to its bank for a letter of credit. Before the bank will issue such a commitment, it must be entirely satisfied that its customer is in a satisfactory financial condition.

The letter of credit is addressed to a specific French exporter from whom the perfumes are to be purchased. The exporter, upon receipt of the commercial letter of credit, has little reason to hesitate in making the shipment. Although the exporter has perhaps never heard of the firm that has placed the order, the bank which has issued the commercial letter of credit may be well known to the exporter or to the exporter's bank. The French exporter, then, makes shipment of the perfumes and at the same time draws a draft in the appropriate amount on the bank that has issued the letter of credit. The draft is presented to the exporter's bank along with the other papers as required by the commercial letter of credit. The exporter's bank transmits the draft and the accompanying documents to its New York correspondent who forwards them to the importer's bank. The importer's bank, upon receipt of the documents, makes a thorough inspection of the various papers that accompany the draft to determine if all the provisions of the letter of credit have been met. If upon examination of the document the bank is satisfied that the terms of the commercial letter of credit have been met, the draft is accepted and the appropriate officials of the bank enter their signatures on the draft. The accepted draft, now a banker's acceptance, may be held until maturity by the exporter, then rerouted to the accepting bank for settlement or sold to other investors.

After having accepted the draft, the bank notifies its customer that the shipping documents are in its possession and that arrangements should be made to take over the documents. As the merchandise is sold, the firm is able to build up its account with the bank by daily deposits until sufficient deposits are available to retire the acceptance. The bank then is in a position to meet its obligation on the acceptance without advancing its own funds at any time.

In releasing shipping documents to a customer, the bank may prefer to establish an agency arrangement between the firm and the bank whereby the bank retains title to the merchandise. The instrument that provides for the retention of title to the merchandise by the bank is called a *trust receipt*. Should the business fail, the bank would not take the position of an ordinary creditor in order to establish its claim on the business assets, but rather it would be able to repossess the goods and place them with another agent for sale since title had never been transferred to the customer. As the merchandise is sold under the trust receipt arrangement, it is generally required that the business deliver to the bank the proceeds from the sale until such time as the total amount of the acceptance has been deposited with the bank.

In summary, the banker's acceptance and the commercial letter of credit involve four principal parties: the importer, the importer's bank, the exporter, and the exporter's bank. Each benefits to a substantial degree through this arrangement. The importer benefits in that adequate credit is secured. The importer's bank benefits because it has charged a fee for the issuance of the commercial letter of credit and for the other services provided in connection therewith. The exporter has been benefited in that assurance of definite payment is obtained for the shipment of merchandise. A sale is made possible that may otherwise have been rejected because of lack of certainty of payment. Finally, the exporter's bank benefits if it discounts the acceptance for the exporter since it receives a high-grade credit instrument with a definite, short-term maturity. Acceptances held by commercial banks provide a low but certain yield, and a bank can liquidate them quickly if it should need funds for other purposes.

The Volume and Significance of Bankers' Acceptances

The Board of Governors of the Federal Reserve System authorizes member banks to accept drafts that arise in the course of certain types of international transactions. These include the import and export of goods, the shipment of goods between foreign countries, and the storage of readily marketable staples in any foreign country. The maturity of member bank acceptances arising out of such transactions may not exceed six months. This authority to engage in bankers' acceptance financing is designed to encourage banks to participate in the financing of international trade and to strengthen the United States dollar in international exchange.

Bankers' acceptances are used to finance international transactions in a wide variety of items. Such items include coffee, wool, rubber, cocoa, metals and ores, crude oil, jute, and automobiles. Due to the growth of international trade in general and the increasing competition in foreign markets, bankers' acceptances have become increasingly important. Exporters have found it necessary to offer more liberal terms on their sales to compete effectively; the banker's acceptance permits them to do so without exposure to undue risk. Dollar acceptances outstanding as of midyear 1982 arising from imports into and exports from the United States totaled more than $31 billion.[1]

The Cost and Market for Bankers' Acceptances

The cost of financing an international transaction with the banker's acceptance involves not only the interest cost involved in the discounting of the acceptance by the exporter but also the commission charge of the importer's accepting bank. From 1961 through 1982 interest costs on bankers' acceptances moved up steadily from slightly less than 3 percent to more than 10 percent.

Foreign central banks and commercial banks have regarded bankers' acceptances as attractive short-term commitments for their funds. More than half of all

---

[1] *Federal Reserve Bulletin,* October, 1982, p. A25.

dollar acceptances have been held by foreign banks in recent years. Nonfinancial corporations have played a very small role as investors in acceptances.

There are only 14 firms that deal in bankers' acceptances. These dealers arrange nearly simultaneous exchanges of purchases and sales.

THE EXPORT-IMPORT BANK

The Export-Import Bank was authorized in 1934 and became an independent agency of the government in 1945. The purpose of the Bank is to aid in financing and to facilitate exports and imports between the United States and other countries. It is the only agency engaged solely in the financing of the foreign trade of the United States.

The Export-Import Bank is a government-owned corporation with capital of $1 billion in nonvoting stock paid in by the United States Treasury. It may borrow from the Treasury on a revolving basis and sell short-term discount promissory notes. Interest is paid on these borrowings, and dividends are paid on the capital stock. In performing its function of aiding and facilitating the foreign trade of the United States, the Bank makes long-term loans to finance the purchase of United States equipment, goods, and related services for projects undertaken by private enterprises or governments abroad. The Bank also aided substantially in the economic development of foreign countries. Emergency credits are provided to assist other countries in maintaining the level of their imports from the United States when they experience temporary balance-of-payments difficulties. In addition, the Bank finances or guarantees the payment of medium-term commercial export credits extended by exporters and, in partnership with private insurance companies, offers short- and medium-term credit insurance. It lends and guarantees only where there is reasonable assurance of repayment but avoids competition with souces of private capital.

During the fiscal year 1981 the Export-Import Bank supported $18.6 billion of the nation's nearly $250 billion of exports.[2]

TRAVELER'S LETTER OF CREDIT

A purchaser for a firm traveling abroad may not know in advance from which individuals or firms purchases will be made, as, for example, the case of an art buyer who tours several countries. The buyer might carry American currency that could be exchanged in the foreign countries for their currency. This involves the possible physical loss of the money, and occasionally conversion into the currency of the foreign country is accomplished only at a substantial discount. A traveler's letter of credit provides the necessary convenience and protection for this purpose.

---

[2]Export-Import Bank of the United States, *Annual Report,* Fiscal 1981 (Washington: U.S. Government Printing Office), pp. 1 and 3.

The *traveler's letter of credit* is issued by a bank in one country and is addressed to a list of banks abroad. These foreign banks to which the letter of credit is addressed are usually correspondents of the issuing bank and have agreed to purchase upon sight drafts presented to them by persons displaying such letters of credit. At the time a letter of credit is issued by a bank, a copy of the signature of the person to whom the letter of credit is issued is sent to each of the foreign correspondent banks. When the individual presents a draft for payment in foreign currency to one of these foreign correspondent banks, a signature is requested, which is then compared with the signature forwarded directly to these banks by the issuing bank. In addition, the individual presenting the draft may be asked for supplementary identification.

As in the case of the regular letter of credit, a maximum amount is stipulated for draft purposes on the part of the holder of the letter of credit. In order that an individual holding such a letter of credit may not exceed authorized withdrawals, each bank to which the letter of credit is presented will enter on the letter of credit the amount of the draft that it has honored. In this way the individual presenting the letter of credit is unable to draw an amount in excess of that authorized.

TRAVELERS' CHECKS

Travelers' checks, which are offered by banks, express companies, and other agencies, are generally issued in denominations of $10, $20, $50, and $100. These checks, generally purchased by an individual before leaving for a trip, involve a promise to pay on demand even amounts as indicated by the face of the traveler's check. Each check must be signed twice, once at the time it is purchased and again at the time it is presented for payment. In this manner, the firm or institution to which the travelers' checks are presented for payment may be able to determine the authenticity of the signature by requiring the signing in its presence. Such travelers' checks are usually sold for their face amount plus a charge of one percent. The use of the travelers' check is widespread and offers many advantages to the traveler, including protection in the event of loss of the travelers' checks and certainty of acceptance on the part of the firms to which they are presented for payment.

QUESTIONS

1. A smoothly functioning system of international finance makes possible specialization of productive effort by the nations of the world. Why is such specialization of effort desirable?

2. How do commercial banks provide for the financial settlement of international transactions? Describe the institutional arrangements of commercial banks for maintaining deposits in foreign countries.

3. Explain the role of supply and demand as it relates to the establishment of exchange rates between countries.

4. Describe the activities and economic role of the arbitrager in international finance.

5. Foreign exchange quotations may be given in terms of sight drafts, cable drafts, and time drafts. What is the relative cost of these different types of drafts? Why should such cost differentials exist?

6. Describe the various ways by which an exporter

may finance an international shipment of goods. How may commercial banks assist the exporter in the collection of drafts?

7. How may importers protect themselves against improper delivery of goods when they are required to make payment when placing an order?

8. Describe fully the process by which an importing firm may substitute the credit of its bank for its own credit in financing international transactions.

9. How may a bank protect itself after having issued a commercial letter of credit on behalf of a customer?

10. Describe the costs involved in connection with the financing of exports through bankers' acceptances.

11. Describe the ultimate sources of funds for export financing with bankers' acceptances. How are acceptances acquired for investment by these sources?

12. Explain the role played by the Export-Import Bank in international trade. Do you consider this Bank to be in competition with private lending institutions?

13. Commercial letters of credit, travelers' letters of credit, and travelers' checks all have an important role in international finance. Distinguish among these three types of instruments.

SUGGESTED READINGS

Baldwin, Robert E., and J. David Richardson. *Structural Changes in International Financial Relations,* 2nd ed. Boston: Little, Brown & Company, 1981. Part VI.

Eiteman, David K., and Arthur I. Stonehill. *Multinational Business Finance*, 3rd ed. Reading, Massachusetts: Addison-Wesley Publishing Co., Inc., 1982. Chapter 13.

Ritter, Lawrence S., and William L. Silber. *Principles of Money, Banking, and Financial Markets,* 4th ed. New York: Basic Books, Inc., Publishers, 1983. Part 6.

Van Horne, James C. *Financial Management and Policy,* 6th ed. Englewood Cliffs, New Jersey: Prentice-Hall, Inc., 1983. Chapter 25.

Weston, J. Fred, and Bart W. Sorge. *Guide to International Financial Management.* New York: McGraw-Hill Book Company, 1977.

PART IV

Monetary, Fiscal and Debt Management Policies

21 Policy Instruments of the Federal Reserve and Treasury

In Part I of this text the financial system of the United States was described. This description included a discussion of the monetary system, the banking structure, and the operation of the central banking system. The nature and sources of the nation's money supply, along with the savings and investment process, were explained in detail. In Part IV we will examine the way in which the policies of the federal government and the Federal Reserve System influence the operation of the financial system and the economy. In this chapter we will discuss the nature of the decisions these two bodies must make. In the remainder of Part IV we will describe the ways that these decisions influence the economy, including their effect on interest rates and prices. The final chapter illustrates these concepts by reviewing the development of economic policy over the last several decades.

NATIONAL POLICY OBJECTIVES

The broad range of policy objectives for the nation can be described in many ways and with different degrees of emphasis. The sheer size of the government's involvement in the economy influences its course and affects the lives of everyone. While partisans debate the proper application of this influence, there are a number of areas in which there is broad agreement that the decisions of the nation's policymakers have a significant effect. There is also a strong tradition in our system that a given set of objectives should be pursued with minimum infringement on the economic freedom of individuals. There are four areas in which objectives are usually defined, or four general economic goals toward which economic policy actions are directed.

Economic Growth

The standard of living of the nation's citizens has increased dramatically over our history as a result of the growth of the economy and its productivity. But growth consists of more than merely increasing our total output; it requires that output increase faster than the population so that per capita or average output per person expands. Growth has, therefore, been a function of two components: one, an increasing stock of resources for productive services—i.e., a larger labor force and a larger stock of capital; and two, improved technology and skills.

High and Stable Levels of Employment

Unemployment represents a loss of potential output and imposes costs on the entire economy. The economic and psychological costs are especially hard on those who are unemployed. While there is some disagreement over what we should consider full employment, it is a stated objective of the government to promote stability of employment and production at levels close to our potential. We seek to avoid fluctuations in economic activity, minimizing the hardships that accompany loss of jobs and output.

Price Stability

In recent years the importance of stability of prices has become well recognized, as such stability has become more difficult to achieve. Consistently stable prices help create an environment in which the other economic objectives are achieved more easily. Inflation causes inequities and discourages investment by increasing the uncertainty about future returns. And inflation is no longer considered a tolerable price to pay for high levels of employment, as in recent experience the dual evils of high unemployment and high inflation have beset our economy at the same time.

International Financial Equilibrium

The increasing importance of international trade and of the flow of funds in the international capital markets has imposed an emphasis on international affairs that has not always been present. Further, the size of the United States economy is such that the actions that we take with respect to our own affairs inevitably influence the economies of other nations. Economic policymakers therefore must maintain a world view rather than a narrow nationalistic approach in pursuing international policy.

ECONOMIC POLICIES AND GOVERNMENT INFLUENCE ON THE ECONOMY

The federal government plays a dual role in the economy. In its traditional role it engages in economic activity to provide services which cannot be provided as efficiently by the private sector. In this role it acts much like a firm, hiring resources in the marketplace and producing a product. The magnitude of this activity and its influence on economic activity have led to its more modern role, that of guiding or regulating the economy. The government cannot ignore its influence on the course of the economy, and the decisions of a number of policy-making entities must be coordinated in order to achieve the desired economic objectives.

A government may raise the funds to pay for its activities in three ways: it may levy taxes, it may borrow, or it may print money for its own use. Since this last option has proved tempting to some governments, with disastrous results, our government has delegated the power to create money to the Federal Reserve System. Our federal government collects taxes to pay for most of its expenditures, and it borrows, competing for funds in the financial system, to finance its deficits.

As an illustration of the complexity of the government's influence on the economy, consider the many ramifications of the federal deficit. The government competes with other borrowers in the financial system. Financing the deficit absorbs savings, and may raise interest rates and thus reduce private investment by making it more difficult for firms to borrow the funds needed for such investment. On the other hand, a deficit stimulates economic activity; the larger the deficit the more total spending or demand, since the government is spending more or collecting less in taxes, leaving more income for consumers to spend. In some circumstances this stimulation of the economy generates enough extra income and savings to finance both the deficit and additional investment by firms. Furthermore, the Federal Reserve may buy government securities, financing some of the deficit and providing additional reserves to the banking system, thus increasing the money supply. This process is known as *monetizing* the deficit, and is analogous to a government's printing money to pay for its expenditures. The Federal Reserve may be subjected to political pressure to monetize some of a current deficit, even though doing so would be counter to its current monetary policy. Finally, financing a deficit has a significant impact on the financial markets. The competition for funds makes it more difficult for some other borrowers to meet their financing needs. Not all other borrowers will be affected to the same degree. The characteristics and maturities of debt sold by the Treasury will determine which sectors of the financial system will be affected the most.

The Policymakers

The decision of policymakers enter this process at a number of points. The President and the Council of Economic Advisors formulate a program of *fiscal policy*, which sets forth the expenditure and taxation plans of the government. Congress passes legislation authorizing this plan or a variation of it. The Treasury has responsibility for the actual collection of taxes and the disbursement of funds. The Treasury is also responsible for the monumental task of *debt management*, which includes the financing of current deficits and refinancing the outstanding debt of the government. The Federal Reserve System formulates *monetary policy*, using its powers to regulate the growth of the money supply and thus influence interest rates and the availability of credit. Figure 21-1 may help us to visualize the relationship between policymakers and policy objectives.

The principal responsibilities of these policymakers have not always been the same. When the Federal Reserve System was established in 1913, most of the power to regulate money and credit was placed in its hands. However, as the public debt grew during World War I, during the depression of the early thirties, and during World War II, the Treasury became vitally interested in credit conditions. Policies that affect interest rates and monetary ease or stringency

Figure 21-1
Policymakers and Policy Objectives

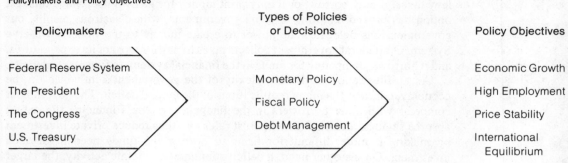

Policymakers	Types of Policies or Decisions	Policy Objectives
Federal Reserve System	Monetary Policy	Economic Growth
The President	Fiscal Policy	High Employment
The Congress	Debt Management	Price Stability
U.S. Treasury		International Equilibrium

affect the Treasury directly, since it is the largest borrower in the nation on both a short-term and a long-term basis. Furthermore, in managing the large public debt and various trust funds placed under its jurisdiction, the Treasury has acquired the power to influence the money market materially. The Federal Reserve System came back into its own in the 1950s and now is the principal architect of monetary policy.

It would be surprising if the policy instruments of the various policymakers did not at times put them at cross-purposes. Such conflicting pressures are reported regularly in the newspapers; for example, when representatives of the Federal Reserve claim that their efforts alone are not enough to solve current problems, that federal deficits must be reduced if monetary efforts are to be successful. A long-standing controversy continues regarding the balance between full employment and price stability. A particular policy that leads toward one may make the other more difficult to achieve, yet each objective has its special advocates. As in all things, governmental policy objectives are necessarily subject to compromise and trade-offs.

Dynamic, Defensive, and Accommodative Functions

Although public discussions in the media of Federal Reserve and Treasury operations are almost universally directed toward such dynamic actions as the stimulation or repression of the level of prices or economic activity, we should recognize that this area is but a minor part of the continuous operation of these systems. Far more significant in terms of time and effort are the defensive and accommodative functions of the Federal Reserve and the Treasury. Defensive activities may be described as those that contribute to the smooth everyday functioning of the economy. Unexpected developments and shocks are continuously imposing themselves upon the economy and unless these events are countered by appropriate monetary actions, cumulative disturbances may develop. Large unexpected shifts of capital out of or into the country and especially large financing efforts by some of the nation's biggest corporations may significantly alter the reserve positions of the banks. Similarly, recent buy-outs and acquisitions of one corporation by another, supported by bank financing, have affected reserve positions.

It should be recognized that in our competitive enterprise system some unexpected developments contribute to the vigor of our evolving economy. Monetary policy, however, has a special responsibility in directing the smooth absorption of these events while at the same time avoiding much of their traumatic short-term effects. The accommodative function of the nation's monetary system involves the provision of stability and flexibility in meeting the requirements of money and credit for an expanding economy.

FEDERAL RESERVE POLICIES

The basic instruments of Federal Reserve action are the establishment of reserve requirements for depository institutions, lending to depository institutions through the discount window, and open market operations. By setting reserve requirements, the Federal Reserve establishes the maximum amount of deposits the banking system can support with a given level of reserves. The amount of reserves can be affected directly through open market operations, thereby effecting a contraction or expansion of deposits and credit by the banking system. Discount policy also affects the availability of reserves to depository institutions, and influences the way they adjust to changes in their reserve positions brought about by open market operations or changes in reserve requirements. Thus the Federal Reserve has a set of tools which collectively enables it to influence the money supply and the availability of credit in striving to attain its broader economic objectives.

Reserve Requirements

Depository institutions are required to hold reserves in the amount of a specified percentage of their deposit liabilities. The assets which may be counted as reserves are vault cash and deposits with the Federal Reserve Banks. If a depository institution holds reserves in excess of the required amount, it may lend them out. This, of course, is how banks earn a profit, and it is also the way in which the money supply is expanded.

In Chapter 5 the mechanics of multiple deposit credit expansion and contraction were explained in detail. We observed that in our system of fractional reserves, control of deposit credit depends primarily on reserve management. Recall that the total deposit credit that can be supported by a given level of reserves can be shown to be the reciprocal of the reserve requirement. Thus, a required reserve ratio of 10 percent can give rise to a tenfold increase in deposit credit for each dollar of additional reserves placed in the system, and a 15 percent ratio can give rise to an increase in deposit credit of 6.67 times.

Thus the ability to determine and enforce reserve requirements is an extremely powerful instrument of monetary control, without which, in fact, the Federal Reserve's other powers would have little effect. Since the reserve requirement establishes the maximum ratio of deposits to reserves, the Federal Reserve can influence the level of deposits by increasing or decreasing reserves in the banking system, which it does primarily through open market operations. Actually, the ability to change reserve requirements is not essential to the Federal Reserve's control, and in fact, changing reserve requirements has been infrequently used as a policy instrument. But the fact that a reserve ratio is established is essential, and the closer to the required minimum the banking system maintains its reserves, the tighter control the central bank has over the money creation process through its other instruments.

If the banking system has close to the minimum of reserves (that is, if excess reserves are near zero), then a reduction of reserves forces the banking system to tighten credit in order to reduce deposits. If substantial excess reserves exist, the pressure of reduced reserves is not felt so strongly. Similarly, when reserves are added to the banking system, the banks are not forced to expand their lending but do so at their own discretion. However, since banks earn no interest on reserves, profit maximization motivates them to lend out excess reserves to the fullest extent consistent with their liquidity requirements. When interest rates are high this motivation is especially strong.

The power to change reserve requirements is a potentially powerful tool that the Federal Reserve has used only very selectively. If reserve requirements are changed, the maximum amount of deposits that can be supported by a given amount of reserves is changed. Total deposits and the money supply can be contracted by holding the amount of reserves constant but raising the reserve requirement. Expansion of money and credit will result from lowering reserve requirements. The Federal Reserve can potentially achieve the same result by doubling reserves or by cutting reserve requirements in half. However, for a number of reasons the central bank has preferred to use open market operations to change reserves rather than changing reserve requirements for most of its policy actions. It has been argued that changing reserve requirements is too powerful a tool, and that its use as a policy instrument would be destabilizing to the banking system. The institutional arrangements through which the banking system adjusts to changing levels of reserves might not respond as efficiently to changing reserve requirements. Another advantage of open market operations is that they can be conducted discretely, while changing of reserve requirements requires a public announcement. The Federal Reserve has often felt that its purposes would be thwarted if public attention were directed toward its actions.

Reserve requirements have been changed on occasion for policy reasons. In the late 1930s reserve requirements were increased substantially in order to absorb huge amounts of excess reserves in the banking system. Excess reserves were so excessive that the central bank could exert no influence on the banking system through its other policy instruments. Reserve requirements were lowered during World War II, in order to assure adequate credit to finance the war effort, but they were raised again in the postwar period to absorb excess reserves. In the fifties and early sixties, reserve requirements were lowered on several occasions during recessions. In each case, the lowering of the reserve requirement made available excess reserves to encourage bank lending, ease credit, and stimulate the economy. At the same time, by using this policy tool, the Federal Reserve was conspicuously announcing its intention to ease credit in order to instill confidence in the economy.

In the late sixties and seventies, reserve requirements were selectively altered to restrain credit as the banking system experimented with new ways to get around Federal Reserve controls. The increased use of negotiable certificates of deposit, Eurodollar borrowings and other sources of reserve funds for banks prompted the Federal Reserve to manipulate the reserve requirements on specific liabilities in order to impose restraint on the banks.

The evolution of the banking system eventually led Congress to pass the Monetary Control Act of 1980, which makes significant changes in reserve requirements throughout the financial system. Up to this time the Federal Reserve had control over the reserve requirements of its members only. Nonmember banks were subject to reserve requirements established by their own states, and there was considerable variation among states. As checks written on member banks were deposited in nonmember banks, and vice versa, funds moved among banks and deposits were subject to different reserve requirements. Thus the average reserve requirement tended to vary as funds moved from bank to bank. This reduced the Federal Reserve's control over the money supply.

The Monetary Control Act applies uniform reserve requirements for all depository institutions with certain types of accounts. These requirements are, in general, lower now for all depository institutions than they were prior to the Act for banks that were members of the Federal Reserve System. These reserve requirements are being phased in over a 3½-year period for member banks starting November, 1980, and over a seven-year period for nonmembers. A schedule of these revised reserve requirements is shown in Table 21-1.

The Discount Rate

One of the most important instruments of Federal Reserve policy, in the minds of the framers of the Act, was the use of the discount rate for making the amount of currency and credit correspond to the needs of business. The discount power was given to the Reserve authorities as a basic part of the monetary and credit system because it was felt that it would be effective in regulating the volume of money and credit in use in the economy. The ability of commercial banks to borrow from their federal reserve banks was the sole mechanism by which the money supply would adjust to the demands of business. A bank could borrow funds to make additional loans by discounting or by using as collateral loans already made to businesses. Thus as business demands for credit increased, banks were able to borrow more from the Federal Reserve, and as business loan demand declined the banks would repay their borrowing and contract both outstanding credit and the money supply.

This process was largely automatic, since the original purpose of the discount mechanism was to insure the flexibility of the monetary system in response to the needs of the economy. The discount rate was the major policy tool of the Federal Reserve in regulating this mechanism. If business were expanding too rapidly, the Federal Reserve could slow the expansion of credit by raising the discount rate. Lowering the rate would encourage borrowing and was expected to stimulate economic activity.

Table 21-1
Revised Reserve Requirements under the Monetary Control Act of 1980

RESERVES REQUIRED FOR TRANSACTION ACCOUNTS[1]

An institution with this amount of net transaction balances...	...must keep this portion in cash or in a reserve account.
$26 million or less	3%
Over $26 million	3% of first $26 million plus 12% of the rest

RESERVES REQUIRED FOR TIME DEPOSITS

Time deposits held by this type of depositor...	...which have this length of maturity...	...must be backed by reserves equal to this portion of the deposits that are transferable...	...and by this portion of the deposits that are not transferable (including personal savings deposits).
Individuals (natural persons, sole proprietors)	Less than 3½ years	3%	0%
	3½ years or more	0%	0%
Businesses (partnerships, corporations, nonprofit organizations, governmental units)	Less than 3½ years	3%	3%
	3½ years or more	0%	0%

[1] Transaction accounts include all deposits on which the account holder is permitted to make withdrawals by negotiable or transferable instruments, payment orders of withdrawal (in excess of three per month) for purposes of making payments to third persons or others.

Stated in somewhat oversimplified terms, discount policy was intended to work in the following fashion. If the Federal Reserve wanted to cool an inflationary boom, it would raise the discount rate. An increase in the discount rate would lead to a general increase in interest rates and a restriction of the extension of credit. This would tend to decrease the demand for short-term credit for additions to inventory and to accounts receivable. This in turn would lead to a postponement of the establishment of new production facilities and therefore to a decreased demand for capital goods. As a consequence, the rate of increase in income would slow down, and in time income would decrease and with it the demand for consumer goods. Holders of inventories carried by means of borrowed funds would liquidate their stocks in an already weak market. The result would be a drop in prices that would tend to stimulate the demand for and reduce the supply of goods, thus restoring economic balance. A reduction in the discount rate was expected to have the opposite effect.

Discount policy is no longer expected to be the major instrument of credit policy and, in fact, is now regarded more as an adjustment mechanism. It has placed the discretion for its use at the option of the banks with the federal reserve banks' actions limited to protecting their "discount windows" by altering the rates charged. As an adjustment mechanism the discount arrangement does provide some protection to depository institutions in that aggressive control actions in other forms may be temporarily moderated by the ability of banks to borrow. For example, the Federal Reserve System may take a strong restrictive stance through open market operations. Individual banks may counter such pressure by borrowing from their federal reserve banks. The federal reserve banks are willing to tolerate what appears to be a circumvention of their efforts while banks are adjusting to the pressure being exerted. Failure of banks to work down their level of borrowing under the discount facility can always be countered by additional open market actions. Discount borrowing fluctuates rapidly, but typically is in a range of 1 percent to 5 percent of total reserves. For several years borrowed reserves have exceeded excess reserves for the banking system as a whole. In other words, nonborrowed reserves have not been large enough to meet requirements. Figure 21-2 shows borrowed reserves and excess reserves in recent years.

Open Market Operations

One of the most important instruments of monetary and credit policy is open market operations, that is, the purchase of securities by the federal reserve banks to put additional reserves at the disposal of the banking system or the sale of securities to reduce bank reserves. The original Federal Reserve Act did not provide for open market operations. This policy instrument developed out of the experience of the early post-World War I period.

From the beginning of their operations, the reserve banks bought government securities with funds at their disposal to earn money for meeting expenses and to show a profit in order that dividends on the stock held by member banks could be paid. All 12 banks usually bought and sold such securities in the New York market, and at times their combined sales were so large that they disorganized that market. Furthermore, the funds used to buy the bonds got into the hands of New York member banks and enabled them to reduce their borrowing at the Federal Reserve Bank of New York. This made it difficult for the Federal Reserve Bank of New York to maintain effective credit control in its area. As a

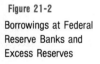

Figure 21-2

Borrowings at Federal Reserve Banks and Excess Reserves

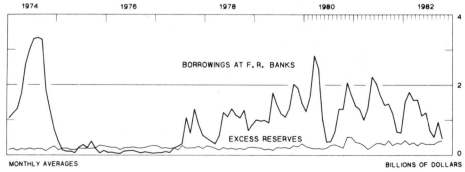

SOURCE: *Federal Reserve Chart Book*, November, 1982, p. 3.

result, an open market committee was set up to coordinate buying and selling of government bonds. In 1933 the Open Market Committee was established by law, and in 1935 it was given its present composition of the Federal Reserve Board of Governors, plus 5 of the presidents of the 12 federal reserve banks, who serve on a rotating basis.

Open market operations differ from discount operations in that they increase or decrease reserves at the initiative of the Federal Reserve, not of individual bankers. The process in simplified form works as follows. If the Open Market Committee wants to buy government securities, it contacts dealers in such securities to ask for offers and then accepts the best offers which meet its needs. The dealers receive checks for the securities from the federal reserve banks, and these checks are deposited with member banks. They in turn deposit the checks at their federal reserve banks, thus adding new reserves that form the basis for additional credit expansion. Since 1966 the Federal Reserve also has had the authority to buy or sell issues of government agencies such as the Federal Home Loan Banks.

If the Federal Reserve wants to reduce reserves, it sells government securities to the dealers. The dealers pay for them by a check in favor of a federal reserve bank drawn on a member bank, and the reserve bank then deducts the amount from the reserves of the member bank.

Open market operations may not lead to an immediate change in the volume of bank credit. This is especially true when bonds are sold to restrict credit. As bonds are sold by the reserve banks, some banks lose reserves and are forced to borrow from their reserve bank. Since they are under pressure from the Federal Reserve to repay the loan, they use funds from loans that mature to repay the reserve bank. Thus, credit is gradually restricted as a result of the adjustments banks make to the open market operations. Although not provided for in the original organization of the Federal Reserve System, open market operations have become the most important and effective means of monetary and credit control. These operations can take funds out of the market and thus raise short-term interest rates and help restrain inflationary pressures. Or they can provide for easy money conditions and lowered short-term interest rates. Of course, such monetary ease will not necessarily start business on the recovery road after a recession. But when used with discount policy, open market operations are an effective way of restricting credit or making it more easily available.

Open market operations are also the instrument used by the Federal Reserve in carrying out its accommodative and defensive functions. Over an extended period, purchases of securities exceed sales, and these net purchases provide for the growth of reserves in the banking system and the growth of money and credit to accommodate a growing economy. On any given day, however, purchases or sales may take place as the Federal Reserve reacts defensively to fluctuations in reserves originating from sources beyond its control. For example, when the U.S. Treasury makes large expenditures from its account at the Federal Reserve, bank reserves are increased substantially. To prevent this sudden increase from having a disruptive impact on the money supply and credit conditions, the Federal Reserve will sell securities to absorb some of the increase in reserves. In fact, a majority of the open market purchases and sales by the Federal Reserve are for defensive purposes.

POLICY INSTRUMENTS OF THE UNITED STATES TREASURY

The Treasury has vast power to affect the supply of money and credit. The very magnitude of Treasury operations, however, has dictated that its principal challenge is that of playing as defensive or neutral a role as possible. The power to regulate money and credit has been placed primarily in the hands of the Federal Reserve System and close cooperation between the Treasury and the Federal Reserve must exist if Treasury operations are not to be disruptive. We need only to contemplate the impact on monetary affairs of a massive withdrawal of taxes from the banking system without offsetting actions. Such a contraction of bank deposits would result in a temporary breakdown of the system's ability to serve the credit needs of the public. Yet, taxes are periodically claimed by the federal government without significant impact on lending institutions' ability to continue their regular lending activities. In like manner, borrowing by the government or the refunding of maturing obligations could be traumatic in their effect on money and credit, but such is not the case. In short, the dynamic aspects of managing money and credit are left to the Federal Reserve System with the Treasury largely limiting its actions to taxing, borrowing, paying bills, and refunding maturing obligations with as little disturbance of money and credit affairs as possible. In view of the substantial potential of the Treasury to interfere with the conduct of monetary affairs by virtue of sheer magnitude of operations, this is no small challenge.

Managing the Treasury's Cash Balances

The operations of the Treasury are carried out on a large scale involving expenditures of nearly $750 billion a year. It is necessary to maintain a large cash balance, especially since funds are not paid into the Treasury at an even rate throughout the year and are not paid out on a regular basis. This makes it imperative for the Treasury to handle its cash balances in such a way that it will not create undesirable credit ease or stringency during the year. The Treasury has developed detailed procedures for handling its cash balances so as to affect bank reserves as little as possible.

Treasury Tax and Loan Accounts. The primary demand accounts of the Treasury for day-to-day Treasury operations are on deposit at the federal reserve banks. Most cash flows into the Treasury through Treasury Tax and Loan Accounts of banks and other depositories. All incorporated banks and trust companies are eligible to have such accounts and about 13,000 banks do. Late in 1977, the President signed a bill that permits savings and loan associations and state-chartered insured credit unions to maintain tax and loan accounts in the same manner as commercial banks. Several types of government receipts are deposited in these Treasury Tax and Loan Accounts. Employers have the option of paying withheld income, old-age insurance, and railroad retirement taxes either to federal reserve banks or to one of the special depositories; and most employers have been making their payments to the latter.

The Treasury may also make payments of income and profits taxes eligible for deposit in Tax and Loan Accounts. Many excise taxes may also be paid either to a federal reserve bank or to a qualified depository with a Tax and Loan Account. The proceeds from a large proportion of the sales of new government securities also flow into the Tax and Loan Accounts. The proceeds from the sale of nonmarketable securities are always eligible for deposit in such accounts. Most marketable issues are also sold with the privilege of credit to these accounts. Sales of Treasury bills, however, have rarely been made eligible for credit to Tax and Loan Accounts. The Treasury can also transfer funds to its account at depositories, if its balances at the federal reserve banks are larger than it feels they should be.

Treasury Receipts and Outlays. The Treasury has sought to handle its cash receipts, outlays, and balances so as to avoid large changes in bank reserves. To do this, the Treasury tries to keep its balances in its accounts at the federal reserve banks relatively stable. Almost all Treasury disbursements are made by checks drawn against its deposits at the federal reserve banks. Most Treasury receipts are deposited in Tax and Loan Accounts at the various depositories, but some are deposited directly in the Treasury accounts at the federal reserve banks. The Treasury adjusts the withdrawal of funds from its accounts at the depositories in such a way as to keep its balances at the federal reserve banks as stable as possible. This means that the funds shifted from depositories and the funds deposited directly in the federal reserve banks must closely correspond to the volume of Treasury checks that are likely to be presented to the federal reserve banks.

When the Treasury account at the reserve banks is kept at the same level, bank reserves are not changed. This is possible only if accurate forecasts are made of the daily receipts and expenditures from the Treasury account so that funds from the Tax and Loan Accounts may be shifted in the right amounts at the right time. If such forecasts and procedures for shifting balances in depository accounts had not been worked out with a reasonable degree of success, the operations of the Treasury would cause bank reserves to fluctuate a great deal over short periods of time. Despite these precautions, the Treasury's account frequently does fluctuate by as much as several billion dollars from day to day. The Federal Reserve closely monitors the Treasury account and takes any fluctuations into consideration in conducting daily open market operations in order to minimize the effect on bank reserves.

Powers Relating to the Government Budget and to Surpluses or Deficits

The government may also influence monetary and credit conditions indirectly through the effects of taxation and expenditure programs, and especially by having a significant cash deficit or surplus. Decisions in the budget-making area rest with Congress and are usually based on the needs of the government and on political considerations without giving much weight to the monetary and credit effects. Because of the magnitude of the government budget, government income and expenditures may be one of the most important factors in determining credit conditions.

General Economic Effects of Fiscal Policy. Economic activity depends to a large extent on aggregate demand or the total amount of spending in the economy. An increase in total spending will generally cause an increase in production and employment, but may also cause upward pressure on prices. If the economy is already close to full employment, further increases in aggregate demand will likely increase prices more than output. Similarly, decreases in total spending will result in lower employment and reduced pressure on prices. Fiscal policy has a significant effect on aggregate demand and economic activity. Not only is government spending itself a large component of aggregate demand, but any change in government spending has a multiplied effect on total spending. Since an increase in government spending increases employment and incomes, it also increases spending on consumption. Changes in taxes also have a direct impact on disposable incomes and thus affect aggregate demand through consumption spending.

Various programs of the federal government act in such a way as to help stabilize disposable income and, in turn, economic activity in general. Some act on a continuing basis as built-in or automatic stabilizers, others depend on specific congressional action in each case.

One of the automatic programs is income security, especially the unemployment insurance program. Under the program, payments are made to workers without jobs, thus providing part of their former incomes. This is also true of relief payments under federal and state aid programs. Not only are expenditures increased in a downturn, but social security tax collections of all types, including those for old-age pensions, decrease when fewer people are at work inasmuch as these taxes are based on payrolls.

Of the programs that act as automatic stabilizers of disposable income, the "pay-as-you-go" progressive income tax is one of the most important. When income rises, tax receipts rise faster than income; when income falls, tax receipts drop faster. The result is to a large degree immediate under our system of tax withholding since, for the large proportion of wages subject to withholding, taxes change as soon as incomes change.

These programs are a regular part of our economy. In severe fluctuations, Congress can go further in stabilizing disposable income. Income tax rates have been raised in prosperity to lower disposable income and to restrain inflationary pressures, and they have been lowered in recession to increase disposable income and spending. Government expenditures have been increased in recession to increase disposable income. They could, of course, be cut in prosperity to reduce disposable income, but for political reasons attempts to cut expenditures have not met with much success.

When a recession is so severe that larger deficits than those resulting from built-in stabilizers or formulas are required to promote recovery, there is seldom complete agreement on the course of action to be followed. A decision must be made changing the level of government spending or the total amount of tax receipts. Increased expenditures, or a tax cut of the same amount, would cost the same number of dollars initially, but the economic effects would not be the same. If income taxes are cut, disposable income is increased almost immediately under our system of tax withholding. This provides additional income for all sectors of the economy and an increase in demand for many types of goods. The amount of the increase in relation to the tax cut depends on the proportion of the funds that are spent by the recipients of the tax cut.

If increased expenditures are decided on, the amount of the expenditures determines the initial increase in income for the economy. But the effects of increased expenditures occur more slowly than those of a tax cut since it takes time to get programs started and to put them in full operation. The increased income arises in the first instance in those sectors of the economy in which the money is spent. Thus, the major effect initially will be on specific areas of the economy, not on the economy as a whole.

The secondary effects of spending from a tax cut or from increased government expenditures depend on what the recipients do with the income. To the extent that they spend it on current consumption, total spending is further increased in the short run. The goods for which they spend it determine the sectors of the economy that receive a boost in income. If they invest the added income and it is used for purchasing capital goods, spending is also increased, but with a time lag and in different sectors of the economy. If the money is saved and is added to idle funds available for investment, there is no secondary effect on spending.

The same general types of effects must be considered if economic activity is to be restrained by a decrease in government expenditures or by a tax increase. A decrease in expenditures by the government will cut expenditures by at least that amount, and the secondary effects may cut it farther. A tax increase may not cut expenditures by the amount of the cut since some taxpayers may keep up their level of spending by reducing saving out of current income or by using past savings. It could, however, cut total expenditures even more if higher taxes discouraged some types of spending that were currently taking place, such as that on home building or on consumer durable goods bought on credit. This could lead to a cut in spending that is substantially greater than the amount of money taken by the higher taxes.

Effects of Tax Policy. The tax policy and tax program of the federal government have a direct effect on monetary and credit conditions which may work in several ways. The level of taxes in relation to national income may affect the volume of saving and thus of the funds available for investment without credit expansion. The tax structure may also help determine whether saving is done largely by upper-income groups, middle-income groups, or by all groups. This fact could affect the amount of funds available for different types of investment. Persons in middle-income groups may be more conservative than those with more wealth, and many tend to favor bonds or mortgages over equity investments. Persons in high tax brackets may on the other hand tend to invest in securities of state and local governments, the income from which is not subject to income taxes. Or they may invest for capital gains since the tax rate on such gains is much lower than that on regular income.

Changes in corporation tax rates may also affect the amount of funds available for short-term investment in government bonds and the balances kept in bank accounts. This is true in part because larger tax payments reduce the amount of money a corporation has available for current expenditures. Also, if tax rates are raised with little advance warning, as has been done at times in the past, a corporation may be forced to use funds it is holding for future use to meet the higher tax payments. Some concerns that are short of funds may be forced to borrow to meet the tax payments. In either case a smaller amount of credit is available for other uses than was available before.

Effects of Deficit Financing. The government spending program affects not only the overall economy but also monetary and credit conditions, especially when cash disbursements exceed receipts. When spending is at a faster rate than collecting of taxes and other funds, the resulting cash deficit will affect the monetary and banking system. The effect will depend on how the deficit is financed. Budgetary deficits result in government competition for private investment funds. At times when credit demands are great there may be a real threat of "crowding out" private borrowers from the capital markets. When credit demands are slack the sale of Treasury obligations puts idle bank reserves to use and total credit is expanded. When deficit financing is so large that the private sector cannot or will not absorb the Treasury obligations offered, the Federal Reserve System may purchase a significant portion of the issues. A total increase in credit availability results.

DEBT MANAGEMENT

Debt management includes determining the types of refunding to carry out, the types of securities to sell, the interest rate patterns to use, and also making decisions on callable issues. Since World War II, federal debt management has become an important Treasury function affecting economic conditions in general and money markets in particular. The economy and the money markets are affected in several ways by the large government debt. Interest must be paid on the debt; and this has become one of the major items in the federal budget, estimated at nearly $125 billion for the fiscal year 1982. Interest payments do not, of course, transfer resources from the private to the public sector; but they do represent a transfer of funds from taxpayers in general to bondholders. When the debt is widely held, there is little or no redistribution of income by income groups. However, the taxes levied to pay the interest may have an adverse effect on the incentives of taxpayers and so affect economic activity. This could lead to less risk taking and so slow down economic growth.

One of the basic objectives of debt management has been to handle the debt in such a way as to help establish an economic climate which would encourage orderly growth and stability. This has been done in an effort to avoid inflation in boom periods, such as World War II, by encouraging saving and bond purchases by large numbers of individuals. During recessions, the Treasury can borrow in ways that are least likely to compete with private demands for funds, for instance, by selling short-term securities so as to attract idle short-term funds and especially idle bank reserves. Thus, there will be no restriction of credit for business and individuals. Credit will be available in larger amounts to the extent that bank purchases of bonds lead to credit expansion.

Some advocate that the Treasury go further in this area and affect the supply of long-term funds so as to promote stability. If long-term bonds are issued at attractive rates, funds can be taken out of the long-term market. This action can reduce the supply of available funds for home construction, capital development, and the like and so help restrain a boom. The Treasury can also do more financing on a short-term basis when it wants to increase the amount of funds available for capital improvements. There is no agreement that the Treasury should use debt management in this way, and no serious attempt has been made to apply such a policy over a period of time.

Another objective of debt management policy is to hold down Treasury interest costs. The influence of Treasury policies may also tend to reduce all interest rates; and lower interest rates tend to stimulate home building, the construction of business plant and equipment, commercial building, and the like. This objective and the first one may, however, conflict at times when higher interest rates may be helpful to restrain inflationary pressures.

A somewhat more restricted objective is to maintain satisfactory conditions in the government securities market. This means that investor confidence should be maintained in government securities. It also means that wide price swings should be discouraged and that buying and selling should be orderly.

More technical objectives are to issue securities of different types so as to fit the needs of various investor groups, and to obtain an evenly spaced scheduling of debt maturities so as to facilitate debt retirement if funds are available, or refunding when that is necessary.

TREASURY PROBLEMS—AN OUTLOOK

Even assuming some budgetary cutbacks, military and otherwise, and a reasonable recovery of the economy, there is a high probability of budgetary deficits of greater than $150 billion per year through 1988. These deficits are huge by any comparison and are likely to be approximately equal to the entire amount of savings by individuals, leaving state and local saving, corporate saving, and foreign saving to finance whatever private capital formation occurs. During a recovery, significant reductions in the absolute size of the deficit are typically an important source of net saving to finance inventory accumulation and fixed capital formation. It is for this reason that so much consternation exists with respect to the budgetary deficit outlook. The intractability of budgetary entitlement programs, the danger of reducing national defense expenditures, the political unattractiveness of tax increases all converge to virtually assure large continuing deficits.

Further, a continuing anti-inflation stance by the Federal Reserve System may serve to moderate a strong recovery in the economy. A strong recovery of the economy is perhaps our best hope of reducing our deficits as tax revenues are increased, but even that possibility is not without its problems. A strong economic recovery could reverse the nation's recent progress in reducing inflationary pressures. All in all, the remaining years of the 1980s will be a challenge to our ingenuity as well as to our patience.

QUESTIONS

1. List and describe briefly the policy objectives of the nation.
2. In what ways does the federal government attempt to promote and attain these objectives?
3. How does the government raise the funds to pay for its activities?
4. Describe the relationship among policymakers, types of policies, and policy objectives.
5. It is sometimes said that policymakers may work at cross-purposes in achieving desirable objectives. Comment.
6. Distinguish among the dynamic, defensive, and accommodative functions of the Federal Reserve System and of the United States Treasury.
7. Evaluate the use of discount policy by the Federal Reserve.
8. How may changes in reserve requirements be used to carry out Federal Reserve policy?
9. Discuss the process by which open market operations affect monetary conditions and evaluate the effectiveness of such operations.
10. Although the United States Treasury has vast power to affect the supply of money and credit, the dynamic aspects of monetary control is delegated to the Federal Reserve. Comment.
11. How do commercial banks accommodate Treasury cash operations as depositories?
12. Describe the effects of tax policy on monetary and credit conditions.
13. Federal government deficit financing may have a profound influence on monetary and credit conditions. Explain.
14. Discuss the various objectives of debt management.

SUGGESTED READINGS

D'Antonio, Louis J., and Ronald W. Melicher. "Changes in Federal Reserve Membership: A Risk-Return Profitability Analysis." *Journal of Finance* (September, 1979), pp. 987–997.

Friedman, Milton. *A Program for Monetary Stability.* New York: Fordham University Press, 1960.

Klein, John J. *Money and the Economy,* 5th ed. New York: Harcourt Brace Jovanovich, Inc., 1982. Chapter 13.

Prager, Jonas. *Fundamentals of Money, Banking, and Financial Institutions.* New York: Harper & Row, Publishers, Inc., 1982. Part 5.

Roth, Howard L., and Diane Seibert. "The Effect of Alternative Discount Mechanisms on Monetary Control." *Economic Review,* Federal Reserve Bank of Kansas City (March, 1983), pp. 16–29.

Smith, Gary. *Money and Banking: Financial Markets and Institutions.* Reading, Mass.: Addison-Wesley Publishing Co., 1982. Chapters 12 and 13.

Webb, Roy H. "Interest Rates and Federal Deficits." *Economic Review,* Federal Reserve Bank of Richmond (July/August, 1982), pp. 16–21.

Wood, John H. "Interest Rates and Inflation: An Old and Unexplained Relationship." *Economic Review,* Federal Reserve Bank of Dallas (January, 1983), pp. 11–23.

22 Interest Rate Levels and Structure

The basic price that equates the demand for and supply of loanable funds in the financial markets is the interest rate. We begin with a discussion of some of the characteristics of interest rates and their patterns over time. Then our attention focuses on theories used to explain the level of interest rates. This is followed by a discussion of the term structure of interest rates which indicates the relationship between maturity and yields. Interest rate relationships in the money market are then covered. The last section of the chapter focuses on inflation expectations and interest rate differentials in the capital markets.

INTEREST RATE CHARACTERISTICS AND PATTERNS

The quoted interest rate for any type of loan is a combination of several factors. Part of it is a fee for the administrative costs of making a loan, and another part of it is a payment for the risk involved. If inflation is anticipated, part of the payment is to offset the expected decline in purchasing power of the borrowed dollars due to inflation during the term of the loan. The remainder is a payment for the use of money itself. This payment is made because the borrower has the use of the money during the period of the loan and can employ it to advantage. It is also in part a compensation to the lender for parting with liquidity. Instead of having money that can be used at will for investment or consumption expenditures the lender now has a claim for repayment at a future date.

Risk, Marketability, and Maturity Factors

Quoted interest rates for different types of loans vary depending upon the use to which the funds are to be put. The costs incurred in making loans to business, loans to governmental units, and loans to consumers to buy real estate, to finance the purchase of durable goods, or to tide them over emergencies vary significantly; and these variations account for differences in quoted interest rates. The same is true of the way in which lenders assess the degree of risk involved in various types of loans. Differences in the quality or credit rating of borrowers will lead to differences in the interest rates which are charged them. Interest rates also differ because of differences in the degree of marketability of the instruments used. For example, the bonds of the United States government are more marketable than those of a major corporation such as IBM; and both of these are more marketable than the bonds of a relatively unknown corporation sold in the over-the-counter market.

Interest rates also differ because of the differences in the maturities of the loans. Interest rates for loans of differing maturities usually are not the same; at times short-term rates are below long-term rates, and at other times the reverse is true. This occurs in part because of differences in the supply of and demand for funds of various types. In other words, the market is partly segmented into submarkets for funds of varying maturities. But funds are shifted between markets even though some lag is involved, and differences in rates are due in part to expectations of lower or higher interest rates in the future. Various factors affect interest rates in different sectors of the market; however, the part of the quoted interest rate that is paid for the use of the money itself and for parting with liquidity, is determined by general supply and demand factors in the market for loanable funds.

Historical Changes in Interest Rate Levels

Interest rates have varied throughout our history as the supply of and demand for loanable funds has shifted. Since just before the end of the Civil War, there have been four periods of rising or relatively high long-term interest rates and three periods of low or falling interest rates on long-term loans and investments. The first period of rising interest rates was from 1864 to 1873 and was based on the rapid economic expansion of the period after the ending of the Civil War. The second period was from 1905 to 1920 and was based on large-scale prewar expansion and after 1914 on the inflation associated with World War I. The third period, from 1927 to 1933, was due to the boom from 1927 to 1929 and the unsettled conditions in the securities markets during the depression from 1929 to 1933. The last period, from 1946 to the present, is based on the rapid expansion in the period following the end of World War II.

Beginning in 1966 interest rates entered a period of unusual increases which led to the highest rates in our history. This increase in rates was due in the early part of the period to demands arising out of the Vietnam War. In the 1970s it was due to dislocations arising out of a policy of on-again, off-again price controls, increased demands for capital arising out of ecological concerns and the energy crisis, and worldwide inflation fueled in part by several periods of poor crops and greatly increased prices for crude oil put into effect by oil-producing nations. Interest rates peaked at the beginning of the 1980s with short-term rates above 20 percent and long-term rates in the high teens. Double-digit inflation, a somewhat restrictive monetary policy, and heavy borrowing demand on the part of businesses contributed to these record levels.

The first period of falling interest rates was from 1873 to 1905. This was a period of falling prices in which there were large-scale savings and funds made available by the redemption of the public debt. Even though the economy moved forward during this period, the supply of funds grew more rapidly than the demand for them; and interest rates fell. The same general factors were at work in the second period, 1920 to 1927, but this period was much shorter than the one after the Civil War. The third period of low interest rates was from 1933 to 1946. Low rates resulted from the actions of the government in fighting the Great Depression and continued when interest rates were "pegged" during World War II.

Short-term interest rates generally move up and down with the business cycle and therefore show many more periods of expansion and contraction. Both long-term and short-term interest rates tend to rise in prosperity periods in which the economy is expanding vigorously. The only major exception was during World War II when interest rates were pegged. During this period the money supply increased rapidly, and this laid the base for the postwar inflation.

Yield and Price Relationships

Most debt instruments and securities carry a stated interest rate. Exceptions include U.S. Treasury bills and commercial paper issued by corporations along with other loans made on a discount basis. U.S. Treasury and corporate bonds have coupon interest rates stated on the certificates. Most bonds are issued in $1,000 denominations and par values also are usually stated in $1,000 denominations. Coupon rates then are expressed as a percentage of the bond's par value. For example, a $1,000 par value bond with a 10 percent coupon rate would pay $100 in interest per year. Typically, interest would be paid in $50 amounts twice a year. The issuing organization also agrees to redeem or "pay off" the bond at its par value at the maturity date.

Because of the fixed characteristics (coupon rates, maturity dates, and par redemption values) on most debt instruments, prices will vary inversely with yields or changes in financial market interest rates. For example, if interest rates were to rise for bonds similar in quality to the one described above, due to changes in economic activity or inflation expectations, the bond's price will fall. The "new" price will reflect the yield being demanded at that time in the market-place as determined by supply and demand factors.

The present value process for determining the value or price of a bond was initially described in Chapter 10. Recall that when the market interest rate is the same as the coupon rate for a particular quality of bond that the bond will be priced at its $1,000 par value. For example, let's assume that the above bond has a 10-year life, the market interest rate is 10 percent, and the bond pays $100 annually. Using present value tables from Chapter 10 or the Appendix for the $100 annuity and the one time receipt of $1,000 at maturity enables us to calculate the bond value or price as follows:[1]

---

[1] For semiannual or twice yearly interest payments of $50 ($100/2), we would use the present value interest factor for a 5% (10%/2), 20 periods (10 years × 2) annuity of 12.462 from Table 4 in the Appendix. Likewise, the $1,000 amount at maturity would be multiplied by the 5%, end of 20 periods factor of .377 taken from Table 3 in the Appendix. Notice that the price would still be $1,000 for this example.

10%; 10 yrs.

$100 × 6.145 = $614
$1,000 × .386 =   386
Bond Value = $1,000

Now let's assume that the bond falls in price to $887 because of rising interest rates. The bond then would have a "current yield" to a new purchaser of 11.3 percent ($100/$887). However, this current yield estimate fails to consider that the bond will be redeemed for $1,000 at maturity even though it costs the new purchaser only $887. To take this cost-versus-maturity price differential into consideration we need to calculate the yield to maturity on the bond. Finding the *yield to maturity* is comparable to finding the internal rate of return as discussed in Chapter 10 because we need to determine the discount rate that will make the present value of the cash inflows (interest and maturity payments) equal to the investment or cost. As before, this requires a trial and error process to find the rate that makes the net present value zero.

For our bond example we would begin by choosing a discount rate greater than 10 percent because the current price is less than $1,000. Let's try 12 percent. Using the appropriate factors from present value Tables 3 and 4 in the Appendix gives us the following:

12%; 10 yrs.

$100 × 5.650 = $565
$1,000 × .322 = 322
                 $887

In this case the internal rate of return or yield to maturity is right at 12 percent because the present value of cash inflows of $887 is equal to the current price or cost of $887. In many instances we would not be so "lucky" to find the yield to maturity so easily. For example, if the current bond price were $800, the yield would be greater than 12 percent. We would try higher discount rates until the present value of cash inflows approached $800. Some interpolation between discount rates might be necessary.

A simple formula also is available for approximating the average annual yield to maturity and can be expressed as follows:

$$YM = \frac{I + \dfrac{PV - CP}{N}}{\dfrac{CP + PV}{2}}$$

where

YM = the approximate yield to maturity
I = annual dollar amount of interest
PV = par value of bond
CP = current price of bond
N = the number of years remaining to maturity

We would estimate the yield to maturity on our $887 bond example as:

$$YM = \frac{\$100 + [(\$1,000 - \$887)/10]}{(\$887 + \$1,000)/2} = \frac{\$100 + \$11.30}{\$1,887/2} = \frac{\$111.30}{\$943.50} = 11.8\%$$

Thus while this formula does not consider the time value of money, the 11.8 percent estimate in this case is reasonably close to the true 12 percent yield to maturity.

Bonds and other debt instruments and securities trade in the marketplace at prices that will reflect yields to maturity being required by investors. As interest rates rise, the prices of existing bonds will fall, and vice versa. An understanding of this relationship is crucial to understanding how debt instruments and securities trade in secondary markets.

DETERMINATION OF INTEREST RATE LEVELS

Two basic theories often are used to explain the level of interest rates. One theory is commonly referred to as the *loanable funds theory* and holds that interest rates are a function of the supply of and demand for loanable funds. This is a "flow" theory in that it focuses on the relative supply and demand of loanable funds during or over a specified period of time. An alternative theory is frequently termed the *liquidity preference theory*. Its proponents contend that interest rates are determined by the supply of and demand for money. This is viewed as a "stock" theory in that it focuses on the amount or stock of money as of a point in time.

These theories are not considered to be incompatible. That is, one is not right and the other wrong. The choice often is made on the basis of objective or convenience. Both theories are considered in the following discussion with the initial and major focus being on the loanable funds theory.

Loanable Funds Theory

The loanable funds theory focuses on the "market" for loanable funds. The interest rate is the price paid by borrowers to lenders of these funds. As is true in any market, the interaction of the supply of and the demand for loanable funds determine this price and the quantity of funds which flows through the market during any period. If the supply of funds available increases, holding demand constant, interest rates will tend to fall. Likewise, an increase in the demand for loans will tend to drive interest rates up.

Supply of Loanable Funds. There are two basic sources of loanable funds—current savings and the creation of new funds through the expansion of credit by depository institutions. The supply of savings comes from all sectors of the economy and most of it flows through our financial institutions. Individuals may save part of their incomes, either as voluntary savings or through a contractual savings program such as that involved in purchasing whole life or endowment insurance policies or in the repayment of installment or mortgage loans. Governmental units at times have funds available in excess of current expenditures, and so do nonprofit institutions. Corporations may have savings available because they are not paying out all their earnings as dividends. Depreciation allowances which are not being used currently for the purchase of new capital equipment to replace that which is wearing out may also be available for lending.

Another source of savings consists of the many pension funds, both governmental and private, in existence in this country. These funds, which are building up large reserves to meet future commitments, are available for investment.

Some savings are invested as ownership equity in businesses either directly in single proprietorships or partnerships or by buying stock in corporations. This is, however, only a small portion of total savings; the bulk of the total volume of savings each year is available as loanable funds.

Some lending is done directly as, for example, when an individual lends money to a friend who is in business to enable the friend to expand operations. As we have seen, however, one of the basic functions of financial institutions is the accumulation of savings, and most savings are made available to borrowers through such institutions.

The other basic source of loanable funds is the creation of money by the banking system. Banks and other depository institutions not only channel savings to borrowers, but they also create deposits which are the most widely used forms of money in our economy. This process was discussed in detail in Chapter 5. Net additions to the money supply are a source of loanable funds, and during periods when the money supply is being contracted, the flow of loanable funds is reduced below the level of current savings.

The supply of loanable funds can be grouped in various ways. They may be divided into short-term funds and long-term funds. The supply of funds can also be grouped by types of credit, such as business credit, consumer credit, agricultural credit, and government credit, and by the institutions supplying each type, as has been done in this book.

Factors Affecting the Supply of Loanable Funds. Many factors affect the supply of loanable funds from savings and from the expansion of depository institution credit. Both sources have some tendency to increase as interest rates rise due to increases in demand. However, this effect is frequently overshadowed by other factors that limit or otherwise affect the volume of savings or the ability of the banking system to expand credit.

Volume of Savings. The major determinant in the long run of the volume of savings, corporate as well as individual, is the level of national income. When income is high, savings are high; when it is low, savings are low. Important in the level of savings, too, is the pattern of income taxes, that is, both the level of the tax and the tax rates in various income brackets. The tax treatment of savings itself influences the amount of income saved, for example, the tax deferral of savings placed in individual retirement accounts (IRA's).

Also important from the standpoint of the individual is the stage in one's life cycle. Little saving is done by young people, especially young married people with children of school age. When the children have finished school, a family usually saves money for a period of time until the retirement of the wage earner or until the wage earner's income is reduced or cut off completely because of physical disability. An economy in which a substantial proportion of the families are young couples with children will have a smaller amount of savings in the aggregate than one in which older people predominate.

The volume of savings is also dependent upon the factors that affect indirect savings. The more effectively the life insurance industry promotes the sale of whole life and endowment insurance policies, the larger will be the volume of savings. The larger the demand for private pension funds in which funds are built up during working years to be used to make payments upon retirement, the larger the volume of savings. The effect of interest rates on such savings is often just the reverse of the normal effect of price on supply. As interest rates decrease, more money must be paid for insurance to provide the same type of coverage since a smaller amount of money is available from the reinvestment of earnings. Inversely, as interest rates rise, less money need be put into reserves to obtain the same objectives. The same thing is true of savings put into annuities and pension funds.

In the case of savings associated with the use of consumer credit, the effect of interest rates is felt only with quite a lag. When, for example, a car is bought on payments over a three-year period, savings must go on for three years to repay the loan. This saving to meet monthly payments is unrelated to current changes in interest rates. There may even be an inverse effect in the case of a loan for the purchase of a house, since if interest rates drop substantially, the loan can be refinanced so that the same dollar payments provide a larger amount for repayment of principal, that is, for saving.

Expansion of Credit by Depository Institutions. The availability of short-term credit depends to a large extent upon the lending policies of commercial banks and other depository institutions, and upon the policies of the Federal Reserve System that affect them. The attitude of these lenders is important, and this is influenced by such factors as present business conditions and future prospects. But the Federal Reserve has significant control over the ability of the banking system to create new funds, through its powers to set reserve requirements and to control the volume of reserves available to the banking system.

The availability of long-term credit of different types depends upon the policies of the many different suppliers of credit. Since depository institutions are by no means dominant in this field, credit is not expanded directly to any appreciable extent to meet long-term credit demands. Indirectly, however, their policies and those of the Federal Reserve are very important because, if funds are being supplied by the banking system for short-term needs, a larger proportion of the supply of loanable funds may be made available for long-term credit.

Liquidity Attitudes. A significant factor at times in determining the available supply of loanable funds, both long-term and short-term, is the attitude of lenders regarding the future. Lenders may feel that the economic outlook is so uncertain that they are reluctant to lend their money, preferring to keep it in liquid form.

This preference may be so strong that large funds lie idle as they did in the Depression of the thirties. Lenders may also have a preference for liquidity because they feel that interest rates will be higher in the near future or opportunities for direct investment will be more favorable, and they will therefore hold funds idle rather than lend them at current rates. Thus, liquidity attitudes may result in the holding of some funds idle that would normally be available for lending.

Demand for Loanable Funds. The demand for loanable funds comes from all sectors of the economy. Business borrows to finance current operations and to buy plant and equipment. Farmers borrow to meet short-term and long-term needs. Institutions such as hospitals and schools borrow primarily to finance new buildings and equipment. Individuals borrow on a long-term basis to finance the purchase of homes and on an intermediate- and short-term basis to purchase durable goods or to tide them over emergencies. Governmental units borrow to finance public buildings, to bridge the gap between expenditures and tax receipts, and to meet budget deficits.

Factors Affecting the Demand for Loanable Funds. The factors affecting the demand for loanable funds are different for different types of borrowers. They have been considered in detail in the analysis of the various types of credit. Therefore, the only factor to be considered here will be the effect of interest rates on the major types of borrowing.

One of the biggest borrowers is the federal government, and Congress is generally little influenced in its spending program by interest rate considerations. Short-term business borrowing is not affected by minor changes in interest rates. However, historical evidence shows that substantial increases in short-term interest rates will lead to a curtailment in the demand for bank loans and other forms of short-term business borrowing.

Fluctuations in long-term interest rates have an effect on long-term business borrowing. Most corporations will defer long-term borrowing when a substantial rise in rates has taken place if prospects are favorable for lower rates in the near future.

Minor changes in interest rates have little effect upon consumer borrowing. For short-term installment loans the monthly repayments of principal are so large in relationship to the interest cost that the total effect of a minor change in interest rates on the repayment schedule is small. Of course, substantial changes in interest rates have decidedly influenced consumer borrowing patterns in the past. This has been particularly noticeable in recent years as home mortgage rates reached historically high levels and new housing starts declined sharply.

Role of the Banking System and the Government. Changes in interest rates do not directly or quickly change the supply of some types of loanable funds. The demand for loanable funds of many types is likewise not directly or immediately affected by interest rates. On the other hand, both the supply of and the demand for loanable funds are affected materially by the actions of the banking system and the government. When credit is expanded through an increase in the total volume of short-term loans made by commercial banks and other depository institutions, the supply of loanable funds is increased; and when credit is contracted, the supply of loanable funds is decreased. All actions of the Federal Reserve in setting discount rates, in buying securities in the open market, and in changing reserve requirements also affect the supply of loanable funds. In fact, all factors that were described in Chapter 5 as affecting the level of banking system reserves and checkable deposit credit affect the supply of loanable funds in the market.

Furthermore, on the demand side government borrowing has now become a major influence and will remain so in the foreseeable future. Government surpluses or deficits make funds available in the market or take them out of the market in substantial amounts. Treasury policies regarding debt management which materially affect the supply-and-demand relationships for short-term, intermediate, and long-term funds were treated in Chapter 21.

The financial markets are thus under the influence of the Treasury and the Federal Reserve and are likely to remain so. The Federal Reserve has a significant influence on the supply of funds, and the Treasury, through tax policies and other government programs, has some role on this side of the market. Currently, however, the Treasury's major influence is on the demand for funds, as it borrows heavily to finance federal deficits.

Liquidity Preference Theory

Some economists prefer to analyze interest rates from the viewpoint of money rather than loanable funds. This is an alternative formulation of the problem rather than an opposing viewpoint. The two approaches are related, since an increase in the demand for money will tend to increase the holding of money balances and thus reduce the flow of loanable funds.

The factors which determine the supply of money were considered in detail in Chapter 5 and therefore need not be reviewed here. Instead, our focus will be on a brief review of the demand for money which was also considered to some extent in Part I. There are three basic motives for holding money: the transactions motive, the speculative motive, and the precautionary motive. The *transactions motive* has already been considered in some detail and refers to the need for money to meet the gap between the receipt of income and the time when payments must be made. The amount of money to be held for the transactions motive varies with the level of national income and is primarily responsive to changes in such income rather than in interest rates. The *speculative motive* refers to the desire to hold money currently in the belief or hope that more profitable investment opportunities will arise in the near future. The *precautionary motive* refers to holding cash for emergency needs. Some money is always held to meet emergencies by many businesses, institutions, and individuals. However, the amount so held varies with the confidence in the future of the economy and of the monetary unit. In a severe depression, large-scale hoarding of cash may take place. On the other hand when inflation is rampant, money is spent as soon as possible to avoid loss. If carried to the extreme, this lack of confidence in money leads to uncontrolled inflation.

The demand for money is also influenced by the existence of "near" money and the markets which exist to buy and sell such highly liquid investments. If short-term investments can be made easily and quickly and can also be converted back into cash quickly and with little or no chance of loss, there is less demand to hold money than when such investment possibilities do not exist.

The interest rate can be analyzed from either point of view, the supply of and demand for money or the supply of and demand for loanable funds. Many economists prefer to use the approach based on the supply of and demand for money since it fits more easily into their analyses of change in national income. Most short-run forecasts by analysts in the financial markets are made from the point of view of the supply of and demand for loanable funds. This approach requires an analysis of the money supply since it is a major factor in the supply of loanable funds. It also involves an analysis of the amount of money to be held in idle balance since this, too, is a factor in determining the supply of loanable funds.

Long-run Relationship Between Changes in Money and Interest Rates

The short-run effect of an increase in money is a decrease in interest rates, but the long-run effect may be different. If there is an increase in the money supply which was not fully anticipated, investors will probably want to make some changes in their portfolios. The holders of the increased cash will have more funds than they planned on and will try to convert some of them into corporate and government securities. This will bid up the price of these securities and so lower the interest rate. Since someone must hold the cash, interest rates will tend to be lowered until there is a new equilibrium between the desire to hold money and the interest rates.

This process may also be viewed from the actions of the Federal Reserve in increasing the money supply. This would ordinarily be done by increased purchases of U.S. government securities. These increased purchases will add to reserves in the banking system which will increase the supply of loanable funds and thus tend to reduce interest rates.

But this short-run effect is not the only effect of an increase in money supply. Lower interest rates and more money will lead to increased economic activity and higher national income to the extent that there is an increase in the demand for goods and services. Initially, inventories will be reduced and production will then increase to replenish stocks of goods. The increase in the level of production will lead to an increased demand for credit to finance it. If the increased demands for credit which result from an expansion of the money supply are greater than the supply of credit which is created, the net result, after some lag, will be upward pressure on interest rates.

If the rate of increase in the money supply and the increase in total demand are faster than the rate at which output can be increased, prices will rise. This increase in prices leads to further increases in demands for credit since more funds are needed to finance the production of a given volume of goods. Wages will also rise with little lag in labor groups having a union contract calling for cost-of-living adjustments and with a lag for other groups. This raises costs and thus increases the demand for credit. The expectation of inflation also has an effect on interest rates. Borrowers are willing to pay higher rates since they expect to repay the loan with cheaper dollars, and lenders will expect higher rates in order to get the same real return as before. In addition, in an inflationary period rising prices increase the cost of holding cash. Therefore, smaller cash balances will be held in relation to income; and more funds are available for spending and investing, thus reinforcing the increase in economic activity which is already in progress.

In summary, rapid increases in the money supply will cause interest rates to be lower in the short run than they otherwise would be. However, a sustained increase in the rate of growth of the money supply will work in the opposite direction if the rate of growth is greater than the supply of money desired to be held as cash balances. The result will be an increase in the demand for goods, services, and credit, and in prices. The rise in prices will be most severe when the economy is operating at capacity levels. As a result, market rates of interest will rise in response to increased credit demands. In the long run, increased money growth does not necessarily lead to lower interest rates.

TERM STRUCTURE OF INTEREST RATES

The term structure of interest rates refers to the impact of loan maturities on interest rates. This relationship is generally described by three basic theories—expectations theory, market segmentation theory, and liquidity premium theory. Empirical evidence suggests that no single theory completely explains the term structure of interest rates. Rather, all three are important in explaining the term structure changes over time.

Before examining each of these theories, we need to describe how the term structure of interest rates is expressed. This is often accomplished through the graphic presentation of *yield curves*. A yield curve must first reflect securities of comparable risk (default risk is another factor that affects interest rate differentials and will be discussed later). Second, the yield curve must be prepared as of a particular point in time and the interest rates should reflect yields to maturity. That is, the yields should include not only stated interest rates but should also consider that instruments and securities could be selling above or below their par values. The third requirement is the need for yields on a number of securities with differing lengths of time to maturity.

U.S. government securities provide the best basis for constructing yield curves in that Treasury securities are considered to be risk-free in terms of default risk and there are a large number of these securities with differing maturities that are outstanding at any point in time. Figure 22-1 shows yield curves or the term structure of interest rates that existed at five different points in time as we entered the 1980s. Although interest rates were historically high in mid-January, 1980, they increased rapidly across all maturities by mid-March, 1980. This was followed by a rapid decline, particularly in short-term rates, by mid-May, 1980. Interest rates then proceeded to rise during the remainder of 1980 and into 1981.

Figure 22-1
Interest Rate Term
Structure

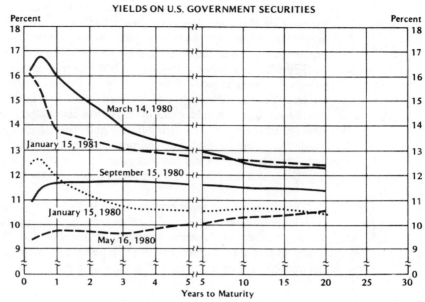

YIELDS ON U.S. GOVERNMENT SECURITIES

SOURCE: Federal Reserve Bank of St. Louis

Historical evidence suggests that interest rates generally rise during periods of economic expansion and fall during periods of economic contraction. This is to say that the term structure of interest rates or yield curves shift upwards or downwards with changes in economic activity with interest rate levels being the lowest at the bottom of a recession and the highest at the top of an expansionary period. Furthermore, as the economy begins moving out of a recessionary period, the yield curve is upward sloping. The yield curve begins to flatten out during the latter stages of an expansionary period and typically becomes downward sloping when economic activity peaks. As the economy turns downward interest rates begin falling and the yield curve again goes through a flattening-out phase and becomes upward sloping as economic activity reaches a bottom point.

The *expectations theory* contends that the long-term interest rates at any point in time reflect the average of the prevailing short-term interest rates plus short-term rates expected in the future. Thus, over the long run, a series of consecutive short-term securities is expected to have the same yield as a long-term security of comparable default risk. This implies that if short-term rates are lower than long-term rates in a given period the relationship is expected to shift in the future, and vice versa. Historical evidence, however, shows that upward sloping yield curves have been more prevalent than downward sloping yield curves, suggesting that the expectations theory does not provide a complete explanation of the term structure of interest rates.

The *liquidity premium theory* is sometimes used in conjunction with the expectations theory. Because of uncertainty in the future, there is reason to believe that the yield curve should be predominantly upward sloping. Investors should be willing to trade off some yield for greater liquidity that is inherent in short-term securities. Likewise, borrowers would prefer to borrow long-term and thus reduce their own liquidity risks associated with maturing securities. These supply and demand pressures suggest that short-term rates should be lower than long-term rates and that the yield curve should be upward sloping.

The *market segmentation theory* is the third theory used to explain the term structure of interest rates. This theory holds that securities of different maturities are less than perfect substitutes for each other. Institutional pressures dominate this theory. For example, commercial banks concentrate their activities in short-term securities because of their demand and other deposit liabilities. On the other hand, the nature of insurance company and pension fund liabilities allows these firms to concentrate their purchases and holdings in long-term securities. Thus supply and demand factors in each segmented market will affect the shape of the yield curve.

The shapes of the yield curves shown in Figure 22-1, and what is historically known about yield curves, suggest that probably all three theories are involved in the explanation of the term structure of interest rates. In any case, we have observed that time to maturity is an important factor in explaining interest rate differentials among securities of comparable quality.

INTEREST RATE RELATIONSHIPS IN THE MONEY MARKET

The money market, in a broad sense, involves the obtaining and trading of credit and debt instruments of one year or less. There are actually both primary and secondary money markets. For example, short-term bank loans are made in the primary money market but seldom are traded in the secondary money market. Short-term debt instruments that do trade in the secondary money market include U.S. Treasury bills, negotiable certificates of deposit, bankers' acceptances, and commercial paper. These money market instruments were first mentioned in Chapter 1 and, while several were discussed in other chapters, they will be summarized in this section.

Several other interest rates, in addition to those established in the money market, are important to an understanding of how the overall money market operates. One such rate is the *prime rate* charged by commercial banks to their "best" business customers. This short-term bank loan rate sets a "floor" interest rate for other loans to less qualified business borrowers. Interest rates charged by commercial banks to security dealers and brokers are also closely tied to other money market rates. The discount rate controlled by the Federal Reserve also is important to the money market. In the past, maximum rates on time and savings deposits set by regulatory agencies directly affected the processes of intermediation and disintermediation. However, with the phasing out of dividend and interest-rate ceilings on depository institution deposits, the impact of regulatory control will diminish and money market operations will depend even more heavily on free market supply and demand factors.

New York Money Market Activities

While informal markets for short-term debt instruments are conducted throughout the United States, major money market activities are carried out in New York City through the use of telephone and electronic transfers. The national money market in New York City is not a definite organization such as the New York Stock Exchange, but an intangible relationship among various participants that demand and supply funds in this market. The New York money market is located primarily in the financial district on lower Manhattan in the general neighborhood of Wall Street.

Wall Street itself is surprisingly short, running only seven blocks from Broadway's old Trinity Church to the East River less than half a mile away. In the area a few hundred yards to the north and south of this Street, which is less than a half-mile square, are most of the purely financial institutions of the New York money market. The buildings house the Federal Reserve Bank of New York, the great stock and commodity exchanges, the head offices of the nation's largest banks, government security dealers, investment bankers, corporate and municipal bond houses, foreign exchange dealers, and many subsidiary financial specialists. This small area is probably the most intensively used land area in the world. So much steel, stone, brick, concrete, and mortar are packed on each square foot of Manhattan bedrock that engineers once feared the island might sink from the weight. So many people work here that they could not all crowd into the streets at one time.

As is to be expected in a market of final money adjustments, most credit is extended for short periods of time, some of it on a day-to-day basis. The procedure is largely impersonal since borrowers and lenders do not have a regular demand for and supply of funds but are in and out of the market so as to adjust their finances.

Money Market Instruments and Rates

U.S. Treasury bills represent the single most important debt instrument bought and sold in the money market. Also important in dollar amount and trading activity are commercial paper, negotiable certificates of deposit (CD's), bankers' acceptances, and Eurodollar time deposits. Federal funds are excess reserves held by banks (or other depository institutions) that are lent on a short-term basis to reserves-short depository institutions. These funds also have a major impact in the money market.

Interest rates on Treasury bills and these other money market instruments fluctuate freely with changing supply and demand forces, with Treasury bill rates setting the floor or minimum for the other instruments. In contrast, the Federal Reserve's discount rate and the bank prime rate do not fluctuate freely but rather are administered or set. The discount rate historically has been kept below the Treasury bill rate while the prime rate has been set above the Treasury bill rate. A higher prime rate is consistent with higher default risk exposure on the bank loans.

U.S. Treasury Bills. As we have previously discussed, Treasury bills are sold at a discount through competitive bidding in a weekly auction. These bills are offered in all parts of the country, but most of them are bought in New York City. In addition to these primary market offerings, Treasury bills are actively traded in secondary money markets with most of the trading again being conducted in New York City.

Figure 22-2 shows the levels and volatility of 3-month Treasury bill yields in recent years. Notice that they were below 5 percent in early 1977, rose sharply to the 15 percent level in early 1980, dropped dramatically to about 7 percent, and then rose above 16 percent in mid-1981 before again dropping sharply by 1982. U.S. Treasury bills are considered to be essentially risk free in that there is virtually no risk of default. Consequently, interest rates would be expected to be higher for other money market instruments of comparable maturity as of any point in time.

Federal Funds. As a result of normal operations some commercial banks and other depository institutions find they have reserves that are temporarily greater than their required reserves. These temporarily excess reserves, or *federal funds* as they are called when loaned, can be lent on a day-to-day basis to depository

Figure 22-2
Selected Money Market
Rates

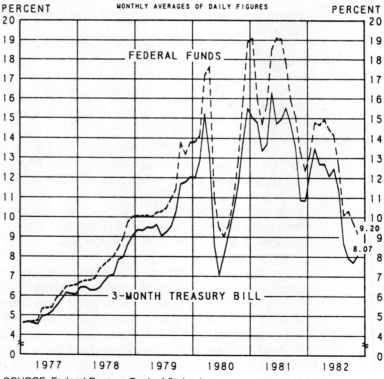

SOURCE: Federal Reserve Bank of St. Louis

institutions that are temporarily short of reserves. This process involves the transfer of reserve balances on the books of the appropriate federal reserve bank from the reserve account of the lending bank or other depository institution to the reserve account of the borrowing depository institution.

The lending for a one-day period is generally done by an electronic funds transfer and can be illustrated with an example involving two commercial banks. The deal may be made by one or more telephone calls from the bank wanting to borrow funds, or it may be arranged through a federal funds broker. Funds are electronically transferred from the lending bank's reserve account to the borrowing bank's reserve account at the federal reserve bank. Repayment of the loan plus interest occurs the next day. Many of these transactions are between New York City banks, but banks in other cities also enter the New York money market, usually as lenders but also as borrowers.

The most common trading unit for federal funds is $1 million, but this is often exceeded. Trades may at times be made for $250,000 or multiples thereof, but they are practically never made for less. The number of banks trading federal funds has increased substantially in recent years and the volume of funds traded has gone up very significantly. Other depository institutions are just beginning to participate.

Federal funds rates usually parallel U.S. Treasury bill rates, as is shown in Figure 22-2. Notice that the federal funds rate has remained above the 3-month Treasury bill rate in recent years. Normally the "spread" or difference between the two rates is narrow. During periods of tight money and credit, however, federal funds rates can be bid up to very high levels as is witnessed by the rates in excess of 19 percent in 1981. Banks and other depository institutions have the option, within limits, of using either the discount window at the Federal Reserve or borrowing federal funds to meet reserve requirements. If they were perfect substitutes, the discount rate set in accordance with monetary policy objectives would set an upper limit for the federal funds rate, since banks would borrow at the lower of the two rates. In practice, however, banks prefer to borrow federal funds, even at the high rates that occur when money is tight, rather than borrow too frequently at the discount window.

Commercial Paper. As was discussed in Chapter 9, commercial paper is the short-term, unsecured notes of well-known business firms. Both major finance companies and nonfinancial corporations have been actively involved in selling commercial paper through dealers or commercial paper houses for many years. More recently many issuers, particularly finance companies, have chosen to directly issue or sell their own commercial paper.

Interest rates on commercial paper tend to closely follow Treasury bill rates over time. Of course, because of somewhat greater default risk, commercial paper rates for comparable maturities will be higher than Treasury bill rates at any specific point in time. Commercial paper rates typically are below bank prime rates, making this a valuable short-term financing source for high quality business firms.

Negotiable Certificates of Deposit. One of the major new developments in the money market in the 1960s was the greatly increased use of negotiable certificates of deposit or CD's. Many banks had issued such certificates as early as the turn of the century, but before 1960 they were rarely issued in negotiable form. A certificate of deposit is in essence a receipt issued by a bank in exchange for a deposit of funds. The bank agrees to pay the amount deposited plus interest to the bearer of the receipt on the date specified on the certificate. Because the certificate is negotiable, it can be traded in the secondary market before maturity.

Within a short time after CD's were issued in substantial amounts, a government securities dealer decided to trade in outstanding negotiable certificates of deposit. This beginning of a secondary market was followed by trading by other security dealers so that by 1969 virtually all of the nonbank dealers and many of the bank dealers in U.S. government securities bought, sold, and maintained an inventory in CD's.

The volume of negotiable CD's (usually issued in denominations of $100,000 or more) has increased dramatically in recent years. Interest rates paid on these CD's usually parallel rates on other money market instruments such as commercial paper and bankers' acceptances, and are above the less risky Treasury bill rates.

Bankers' Acceptances. The origination and use of bankers' acceptances were discussed in Chapter 20. As we know, this form of business paper is used primarily to finance exports and imports and, since it is the unconditional obligation of the accepting bank, it generally has a high quality rating. Yields on bankers' acceptances closely follow yields on commercial paper.

In the mid-1970s, a substantial increase in the volume of bankers' acceptances was associated with their use in domestic transactions. Most of this activity involved commodities in storage or transit within the United States.

Eurodollars. *Eurodollars* are deposits placed in foreign banks that remain denominated in U.S. dollars. A demand deposit in a United States bank becomes a Eurodollar when the holder of such a deposit transfers it to a foreign bank or an overseas branch of an American bank. After the transfer, the foreign bank holds a claim against the U.S. bank, while the original deposit holder (possibly a business firm) now holds a Eurodollar deposit. It is a Eurodollar deposit because it is still denominated in U.S. dollars rather than being denominated in the currency of the country in which the foreign bank operates.

In recent years, and especially since 1966, large commercial banks have raised money by borrowing from the Eurodollar market through their overseas branches. The Eurodollar market is one in which overseas branches of United States banks and banks outside the United States get funds by accepting dollars in interest-bearing time deposit accounts. These dollar deposits are lent almost anywhere in the world, usually on a short-term basis. The transfer of funds is generally made by telephone or teletype and lending between banks is done without collateral in large sums. The transfers of funds usually involve shifts of balances from one bank account in the United States to another account in the United

States. Banks which handle Eurodollars are located in Europe with London as the center, but are also located in financial centers throughout the world, including such places as Singapore and the Bahamas.

Eurodollar deposit liabilities arose because of the widespread use of the dollar as an international currency and the increase in dollar holdings of foreigners due to persistent balance-of-payment problems for the United States. Eurodollars are supplied by national and international corporations, banks, insurance companies, wealthy individuals, and some foreign governments and agencies. Eurodollar loan recipients are also a diverse group, but commercial banks, multinational corporations, and national corporations are heavy users.

There are several major reasons why United States banks have entered the Eurodollar market by means of their overseas branches: to finance business activity abroad, to switch Eurodollars into other currencies, to lend to other Eurodollar banks. The most important reason, and the one which has received the most publicity in the United States, is the lending of Eurodollars by overseas branches to their head banking offices in the United States. This is done to obtain funds at lower costs and to obtain funds during periods of tight money.

Relationship of Monetary Policy to the Money Market

As the final money market, the New York money market is affected directly or indirectly by all factors that affect the supply of and the demand for loanable funds. A demand for additional funds in St. Louis, for example, would first be met locally. If it continued, however, funds would be obtained from balances held by New York correspondent banks and by the sale of short-term government securities, probably in the New York market. Similarly, excess funds of banks and businesses tend to flow to the New York market. The most important determinant of day-to-day conditions in that market is the reserve position of New York City banks. When excess reserves exist, they are made available; when reserves are low or practically nonexistent, credit is tight in this market. Conditions in the New York market and in other markets are also equalized quite rapidly. If reserves are short in New York but plentiful elsewhere, funds will flow to the money market. Likewise, if funds are available in New York, they will be loaned out and find their way into the channels of trade throughout the country. Therefore, any policy that affects the money market will affect the supply of loanable funds throughout the country.

Changes in Federal Reserve policy have a pronounced effect upon this market. In fact, the direct impact upon the economy of changes in Federal Reserve policies is often through this New York money market. Changes in reserve requirements directly affect the market for federal funds. Changing the discount rate affects the rate on federal funds; and by influencing this most sensitive of all rates, it affects the whole market. Open market operations have their first impact almost entirely in the New York money market as government securities are bought and sold here. Treasury financing by means of short-term securities is also largely done in this market. Thus, Treasury policies regarding money and debt management have an important influence. In fact, all types of changes in monetary policy influence the money market materially. Since it is a sensitive market, it does not take major changes to affect it substantially. Monetary policy has a more direct and immediate effect on the availability of funds than it would have if this final market for balancing supply and demand did not exist or was not organized so well.

INFLATION AND INTEREST RATE DIFFERENTIALS IN THE CAPITAL MARKETS

It is important to separate the money and capital markets when discussing long-run inflation expectations and interest rate differences between securities. Supply and demand in the money market is influenced substantially by Federal Reserve actions and objectives. In contrast, interest rates change more slowly in the long-term capital markets and traditionally have been indirectly affected by monetary policy.

Long-term Treasury securities, like Treasury bonds, are viewed as being risk free in a default risk context. Furthermore, at any point in time this risk-free rate is viewed as being composed of a real return component and a long-run inflation expectations component. Economists typically contend that the real return required to cause investors to convert cash into investments is about 3 percent. This, in turn, implies that the remaining portion of the risk-free rate reflects long-run inflation expectations.

Figure 22-3 shows the interest rates on long-term Treasury securities during recent years. Notice that these rates were about 7.5 percent for most of 1977. This suggests that investors then expected long-run inflation to be about 4.5 percent (7.5% − 3.0%) and, in fact, inflation was low at that time. Long-term Treasury rates rose dramatically thereafter as inflation accelerated, until peaking in 1981 at about 14.5 percent suggesting double-digit long-run inflation expectations. Actual inflation rates dropped substantially during 1982. However, long-run inflation expectations declined to a lesser degree because of a continued worry that inflation rates would again accelerate in the future.

Figure 22-3 also shows the interest rate differentials due to differences in quality or risk of default between long-term Treasury securities and Aaa (highest quality) corporate bonds. *Default risk* is the probability that the issuer of a security will fail to make interest or principal payments. Treasury securities are considered to be risk free. The difference between the risk-free rate and the interest rate on a risky corporate bond is referred to as a *risk premium*. Notice that the risk premium typically is far less than one percentage point for Aaa corporate bonds. These interest rate differentials generally narrow during periods of economic expansion and widen during economic downturns when defaults and bankruptcies increase.

Corporate securities that are of lower quality than Aaa would have even higher yields and larger rate differentials when compared with long-term government securities. Bond quality or default risk is affected by such factors as the firm's profitability, its debt to equity ratios, and its ability to cover interest expenses.

FHA mortgage rates are consistently higher than the rates on long-term Treasury bills and Aaa corporate bonds. This substantial rate differential reflects

Figure 22-3

Selected Capital
Market Rates

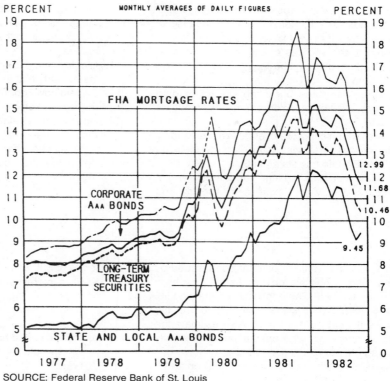

PERCENT   MONTHLY AVERAGES OF DAILY FIGURES   PERCENT

FHA MORTGAGE RATES

CORPORATE
Aₐₐ BONDS

12.99
11.68
10.46
9.45

LONG-TERM
TREASURY
SECURITIES

STATE AND LOCAL Aₐₐ BONDS

1977   1978   1979   1980   1981   1982

SOURCE: Federal Reserve Bank of St. Louis

higher default risk as well as other differences between the bond and real estate
mortgage capital markets.

Interest rate differentials also may be influenced by other factors such as marketability, taxability, and whether or not the issuing organization can call or
refund the debt issue before maturity. The taxability factor, for example, accounts for the much lower interest rates on state and local Aaa bonds shown in
Figure 22-3. Interest on these securities is excluded from federal income taxes.
The marketability factor impacts most heavily on smaller firms which find it difficult to issue debt securities because of their size and the size of their issues.
Small issues usually have little marketability in secondary markets and thus must
carry interest rate premiums.

QUESTIONS

1. Briefly discuss why interest rates for different
   types of loans are likely to vary.
2. Identify major periods of rising interest rates in
   U.S. history and describe some of the underlying
   reasons for these interest rate movements.

3. Describe the relationship between yields and
   prices for debt securities.
4. Identify the two basic theories used to explain
   the level of interest rates. Discuss how these
   theories differ from each other.

5. What are the basic sources of loanable funds? Also indicate and briefly discuss the factors that affect the supply of loanable funds.

6. Indicate the sources of demand for loanable funds and discuss the factors that affect the demand for loanable funds.

7. Discuss the three basic motives for holding money. What other factors affect the demand for money?

8. The short-run effect of a change in money supply on interest rates may differ from its long-run effect. Explain this statement.

9. What is meant by the term structure of interest rates and how is it expressed? Identify and describe the three basic theories used to explain the term structure of interest rates.

10. Define and describe what is meant by the money market.

11. Identify and briefly describe the major debt instruments that trade in the money market.

12. Explain how Federal Reserve policies affect the money market.

13. Describe how inflation has impacted on capital market interest rates in recent years. Indicate and describe other factors that influence interest rate differentials between debt securities trading in the capital markets.

PROBLEMS

1. A $1,000 par value, 9 percent bond issued by the Energy Conservation Corporation is currently selling for $900. The bond has a remaining life of 5 years. What is the coupon rate and the current yield on this bond? Also estimate the approximate average annual yield to maturity using the approximation formula.

2. Assume that interest is paid annually on an 11 percent, $1,000 par value, 10-year bond issued by the Rotary Machine Tool Corporation. If the market rate of interest is 14 percent on bonds of comparable quality, what will be the bond's current price or value? How would the price change if interest payments of $55 occurred semiannually?

3. Two $1,000 par value corporate bonds with 10-year lives are available for investment purposes. The Alpha Corporation bond pays annual in-terest of $90 while the Beta Corporation pays $140 in interest annually on its bond.
   a. Determine the yield to maturity or internal rate of return on Alpha's bond if its current price is $939.
   b. If Beta's bond has a current price of $1,200, what would be the yield to maturity on the bond?

4. Use a current copy of the *Federal Reserve Bulletin* to find interest rates on U.S. government securities and on corporate bonds with different bond ratings.
   a. Prepare a yield curve or term structure of interest rates.
   b. Identify long-run inflation expectations and the size of interest rate differentials between long-term U.S. Treasury securities and corporate bonds.

SUGGESTED READINGS

"Bankers' Acceptances." *Quarterly Review*, Federal Reserve Bank of New York (Summer, 1981), pp. 39–55.

Cook, Timothy Q., and Bruce J. Summers (eds.). *Instruments of the Money Market,* 5th ed. Federal Reserve Bank of Richmond, 1981.

Henning, Charles N., William Pigott, and Robert H. Scott. *Financial Markets and the Economy,* 3rd ed. Englewood Cliffs, New Jersey: Prentice-Hall, Inc., 1981. Part 4.

Hurley, Evelyn M. "The Commercial Paper Market since the Mid-Seventies." *Federal Reserve Bulletin* (June, 1982), pp. 327–334.

Jackson, William D. "Federal Deficits, Inflation, and Monetary Growth: Can They Predict

Interest Rates?" *Economic Review*, Federal Reserve Bank of Richmond (September/October, 1976), pp. 13–25.

LeRoy, Stephen F. "Interest Rates and the Inflation Premium." *Monthly Review,* Federal Reserve Bank of Kansas City (May, 1973), pp. 11–18.

"Repurchase Agreements and Federal Funds." *Federal Reserve Bulletin* (May, 1978), pp. 353–360.

Van Horne, James C. *Financial Market Rates and Flows.* Englewood Cliffs, New Jersey: Prentice-Hall, Inc., 1978.

23 Price Level Changes and Developments

Monetary and fiscal policies attempt to "manage" or "guide" the economy of the United States so as to achieve certain economic goals or objectives. Major economies throughout history have strived to achieve economic growth and high employment while maintaining stable prices. The Employment Act of 1946 stated similar economic goals for the United States. Since then, the increasing interdependence of the world's economies has led to the recognition of international financial balance as a fourth objective.

This chapter is concerned with the relationship of monetary and fiscal policies to price changes and the effects of such changes on the economy in general. The next chapter explores the impact of monetary and fiscal policies on business fluctuations or cycles and on international financial equilibrium.

Any factor that changes the value of the money unit or the supply of money and credit will affect the whole economy by affecting the supply of loanable funds and interest rates and, in time, both the demand for and the supply of goods in general. The price changes that arise from changes in the monetary system are the topic for this chapter. As a background for understanding such changes, we will briefly examine past changes in the price level of an unusual nature, especially in the United States.

SOME OUTSTANDING PAST PRICE MOVEMENTS

Changes in the money supply or in the amount of metal in the money unit have influenced prices materially from time to time since the days of the earliest records of civilization.

The money standard in ancient Babylon was in terms of silver and barley. The earliest available price records show that one shekel of silver was equal to 240 measures of grain. At the time of Hammurabi, which was just before 2000 B.C., a shekel in silver was worth between 150 and 180 measures of grain, while in the following century it declined to 90 measures. After the conquest of Babylonia by Persia in 539 B.C., the value of the silver shekel was recorded as between 15 and 40 measures of grain.

The greatest inflationary period in ancient history was probably initiated by Alexander the Great when he captured the large gold hoards of Persia and brought them to Greece. The effect on prices was pronounced for some years; but twenty years after the death of Alexander, a deflationary period began that lasted over fifty years.

The first recorded instances of deliberate currency debasement occurred in the Greek city states. The government debased currency by calling in all coins and issuing new ones containing less of the precious metals. This must have been a popular form of inflation, for there are many such cases in the records of Greek city states.

Roman Experience

Similar inflationary situations occurred in Roman history. Caesar Augustus brought such large quantities of precious metals from Egypt that prices rose and interest rates fell. During the Punic wars devaluation led to inflation as the heavy bronze coin was reduced in stages from one pound to one ounce. From the time of Nero, debasements were frequent. The weight of gold coins was gradually reduced, and silver coins had baser metals added to them so that they finally were only 2 percent silver. Few attempts were made to arrest or reverse this process of debasement of the coinage. An attempt by Aurelian to improve the coinage by adding to its metallic content was resisted so vigorously that it led to armed rebellion.

Experience in the Middle Ages and Early Modern Times

During the Middle Ages debasement of coinage was frequently used as a source of revenue for princes and kings. The rulers of France used it more than others, and records show that profit from debasement at times exceeded the total of all other revenues.

One of the outstanding examples of inflation followed the discovery of America. Gold and silver poured into Spain from Mexico and Peru; and since they were used to buy goods from other countries, they were distributed over the continent and to England. Prices rose in Spain and in most of Europe, but not in proportion to the increase in gold and silver stocks. This was due to the demands of increased trade resulting from the discovery of America and to large-scale hoarding of the precious metals.

Paper money was not used generally for domestic exchange until the end of the seventeenth century. The first outstanding example of inflation due to the issuing of an excessive amount of paper money was in France where John Law was given a charter in 1719 for a bank that could issue paper money. The note circulation of his bank amounted to almost 2,700 million livres[1] against which he had coin of 21 million livres and bullion of 27 million livres. Prices went up rapidly, but they fell just as fast when Law's bank failed; and the money supply was again restricted.

---

[1] The livre was the monetary unit in use at that time in France.

The next outstanding example of inflation is the American experience during the Revolutionary War. This is considered in the following section, which deals with American monetary experiences. Shortly after this American inflation, the government of the French Revolution issued paper currency in huge quantities. This currency, called assignats, declined to ½ percent of its nominal value.

Inflation During World Wars I and II

The only outstanding case of inflation in the period between the Napoleonic Wars and World War I took place in the United States during the Civil War. Inflation during World War I was widespread, but it was held in check to some degree by government action. The most spectacular inflation took place in Germany when in 1923 prices soared to astronomical heights.

Greater attempts were made to control inflation during World War II, and they met with some measure of success. Runaway inflation occurred, however, especially in China and Hungary.

MAJOR AMERICAN PRICE MOVEMENTS

Prices in the United States have been affected in a pronounced way by monetary factors on several occasions. This has been especially true during major wars.

Revolutionary War

The war that brought this nation into being was financed to a large degree by inflationary means. The Second Continental Congress had no real authority to levy taxes and thus found it difficult to raise money. As a result this Congress decided to issue notes, at first for only $2 million. More and more were issued until the total rose to over $240 million, and the individual states issued $200 million more. Since the notes were crudely engraved, counterfeiting was easy; and this fact helped to swell the total of circulating media. This continental currency depreciated in value so rapidly that the expression "not worth a Continental" has become a part of the American language.

War of 1812

During the War of 1812 attempts were made to avoid the inflationary finance of the Revolutionary War. But since the war was not popular in New England, it was impossible to finance it by taxation and borrowing. Paper currency was issued in a somewhat disguised form by the issuance of bonds of small denomination bearing no interest and having no maturity date. The wholesale price index (based on 1913 as 100) rose from 128 in 1812 to 178 in 1814. Prices declined to about the prewar level by 1816 and continued downward as depression engulfed the economy.

Civil War

The Mexican War did not involve the total economy to any extent and led to no inflationary movements in prices. The Civil War, however, was financed in part through the issuance of paper money. In the early stages, Congress could not raise enough money by taxes and borrowing to finance all expenditures, and therefore it resorted to inflation by issuing United States Notes with no backing, called "greenbacks." In all, $450 million of such paper money was authorized. Even though this was but a fraction of the cost of the war, prices went up substantially. Wholesale prices on a 1913 base increased from 87 in 1860 to 189 in 1865. Atttempts to retire the greenbacks at the end of the war led to deflation and depression in 1866, and as a result the contraction law was repealed. Greenbacks are still a part of our money supply.

World War I

During World War I no resort was made directly to printing-press money, but inflationary policies were nevertheless followed. About one third of the cost of the war was raised by taxes and two thirds by borrowing. A substantial part of this credit was obtained from the banking system, and this added to the supply of purchasing media. Individuals were even persuaded to use Liberty Bonds as collateral for bank loans to buy other bonds. The price index rose from 98 in 1914 to 221 in 1920, and then, as credit expansion was finally restricted in 1921, dropped to 139 in 1922.

World War II and Postwar Period

A much larger proportion of the cost of World War II was met by noninflationary means. Nevertheless, large sums of bonds were still taken up by the banking system. By the end of the war, the debt of the federal government had increased by $207 billion. Bank holdings of government bonds had increased by almost $60 billion. Prices went up by only about a third during the war as they were held in check after the first year by price and wage controls, but they rose rapidly when the controls were lifted after the war. In 1948 wholesale prices had risen to 236 from a level of 110 in 1939, using 1913 as a base (100).

Wholesale prices increased during the Korean War and again during the 1955–57 period of expansion in economic activity as the economy recovered from the 1954 recession. Consumer goods prices continued to move upward during practically the entire postwar period, increasing gradually even in those years in which wholesale prices remained more or less stable.

Recent Decades

Wholesale prices again increased and consumer goods prices increased substantially during the period of escalation of the Vietnam War after mid-1965. Prices continued upward after American participation in the Vietnam War was reduced in the early seventies and especially after American participation in the war ended. Prices rose at the most rapid levels since World War I days in part to correct imbalances and adjust to increases in the money supply during periods of on-again, off-again price controls, and also because of crop failures in many parts of the world and the greatly increased costs of crude oil put into effect by petroleum-producing countries. Inflation in the middle seventies was a worldwide phenomenon which was much worse in many industrial countries than in the United States.

As the decade of the 1970s ended the full impact of a philosophy geared to a high rate of inflation was realized. Many economists had come to the conclusion that a high inflation rate could keep unemployment down permanently, notwithstanding historical evidence to the contrary. The continuing effort to control interest rates by monetary accommodation reinforced the skepticism of the public regarding relief from inflationary pressures and high interest rates. By October, 1979, the Federal Reserve System abandoned this approach and adopted a policy of monetary growth control as opposed to interest rate control. The result was twofold. First, there was a far greater volatility in interest rate movements as the Federal Reserve concentrated on monetary factors. Second, during the first three quarters of 1980 some monetary restraint was exercised. This monetary restraint was accompanied by a depressing effect on production and employment. The Federal Reserve System quickly backed off from this position of restraint and by the end of 1980 interest rates had been driven to new peaks as a result of an unprecedented resurgence of monetary stimulus.

The prime rate had risen to 21½ percent and 3-month Treasury bills had doubled in yield from their midyear lows. These high interest rates had a profound effect on the fortunes of such interest-sensitive industries as housing, automobiles, and related industries. The new Administration reversed the rapid growth of money supply throughout 1981 and until late in 1982. During this period the rate of unemployment climbed as the transitory effects of monetary restraint were imposed on the economy but the back of inflation was broken. See Figure 23-1. By the end of 1982 encouraging signs of recovery were in place—along with an easing of monetary restraint. Specific measures of monetary growth were clouded, however, as a result of the changed composition of the various monetary measures. M1, for example, increased dramatically in November and December, 1982, but M2 and M3 showed stability.

MONETARY AND FISCAL FACTORS THAT AFFECT PRICES

The record of outstanding monetary changes throughout history shows that inflation usually occurred because the supply of money was increased faster than was the supply of goods. In the earliest cases this was true because large stocks of gold and silver were acquired as part of the booty of war. Later on, governments increased the money supply by cutting the metal content of existing coins and using the extra metal to issue more coins. Beginning in the eighteenth century paper money was issued in quantities, which led to higher prices. In the last half of the nineteenth century, and especially in the twentieth century, bank credit expansion was the basis for inflation, and credit contraction was the basis for deflation.

Figure 23-1
Consumer Prices

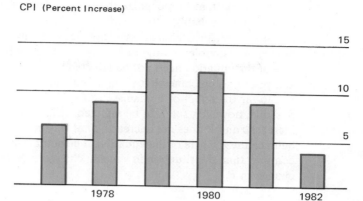

SOURCE: Board of Governors of the Federal Reserve System

Such changes in the volume of money were probably the most important factors affecting prices. They were by no means the only influence, however. Prices did not always go up in proportion to the increases in money supply. This was especially true in connection with the increase in the money supply as gold and silver were brought to the Old World from Mexico and Peru. Trade went up at the same time, and so more money was needed to meet the demands of such commerce. Hoarding of precious metals also took place, or in other words, the rate at which the money was used in the market to buy goods was slowed down.

Following are three concepts or approaches that will aid us in understanding the relationship between monetary and fiscal policies and prices.

Equation of Exchange

Changes in the volume of money, in the rate at which money is used, and in the volume of goods being exchanged must be considered together if we are to understand their relationship to price changes. These factors have been put into an equation, known as the *equation of exchange* or the quantity equation, which serves as a ready frame of reference for analysis: $MV = \Sigma\ pQ$.

In this equation M is the total supply of money in circulation, and V is the velocity of circulation or turnover expressed as the average number of times the money supply is used to purchase goods during the year. On the goods (right) side of the equation there is a summation of the amounts spent on all goods, which is equal to the average price of each article sold, as for example, bushels of wheat, multiplied by the quantity sold. For convenience, the right side of the equation may be written as PT with P a weighted average of all average prices, or p's, and T the sum of all the Q's. The equation then becomes $MV = PT$.

This equation can aid in the understanding of factors involved in general price changes. It views two equal quantities from different points of view. The total money value of goods and services sold is seen from the point of view of the price of the goods by summing the quantities of goods multiplied by a weighted average of prices and frc..i the point of view of the sum of the money transactions to buy such goods. These two magnitudes must of course be equal, but valuable information can be gained from a study of the factors at work on each of them.

It is important to recognize that when one factor such as M changes, other factors will probably also change so that the effect on prices may not be proportionate, or a change may not occur at all. For example, the supply of money may double; but the rate of use, or V, may be cut in half. Then the other side of the equation need not be affected at all. Or, V could decrease somewhat and prices go up somewhat to again balance the situation.

So far the effect of a change in M or V has been assumed to be on P. It is possible, however, for T to be affected. If in a period of unused resources M is increased and V does not decrease, or at least not proportionately, T can go up to balance the PT side of the equation. The actual situation is likely to be far more complex than the situation in which a change in M or V leads to a proportionate change in P.

The Cash Balances Approach

An alternative way of analyzing the effect of money changes on prices is through an analysis of the cash balances held by the public. Several equations are used to explain the relationship of money to prices and trade. One of the most useful is the following: $M = KTP$. In this equation M is the money supply, T is the physical volume of trade to be transacted with money during a year, and P is the price level of the things included in T. The new factor, K, is the amount of money held in the form of cash balances, that is, cash plus bank deposits. It is expressed as the fraction representing the ratio of cash balances to the amount of transactions in a given period of time, such as a year, a quarter, or a month.

K is thus related to the velocity of the circulation of money. If the amount of cash balances held is equal to one fifth of a year's transactions, V is 5 and K is 1/5. In other words, K and V are reciprocals of one another, that is, $K = (1/V)$. The cash balances equation therefore can be written $M = (1/V)(TP)$ or $MV = TP$. Thus, this cash balances equation and the quantity equation are but somewhat different ways of looking at the same thing. There is an advantage, however, to using both equations as alternative approaches to the factors affecting prices. The equation of exchange focuses attention on the rate at which money is spent and the reasons for spending it at that rate. The cash balances equation puts special emphasis on the reasons for holding money as cash balances, as well as on the reasons for spending it, by stating the relationship between the money supply on one side and the demand for money to be held as cash balances and to be used in trade on the other side. It is, therefore, possible to use traditional economic supply and demand analysis to help understand what is happening to prices.

One or two brief examples will show how the cash balances approach can be useful in analysis. For example, increases in the government deficit and the money supply are likely to affect cash balances. If there is less than full employment at that time, the volume of trade will go up, but there may also be an abnormal increase in cash balances. This will occur if business persons do not feel that future prospects for a continuing volume of business at profitable levels are good and, therefore, do not spend normal amounts on replacement of inventory, repairs and maintenance, and capital expenditures. As a result, the increased government expenditures at such a time will not have the same effect on the volume of business as they would have had if the outlook for the future were more optimistic. This was the situation during the thirties when government deficits led to abnormal increases in cash balances.

However, if government deficits and increases in the money supply occur when the expectation is for a continued increase in business at profitable levels and for inflation, as is true during a war, cash balances, or K, will not increase. They may even be reduced as business persons rush to buy raw materials and machinery and equipment before prices advance. On the other hand, if prices are held in check by price controls as they were during World War II, and for a time in the post-Vietnam War period, cash balances, or K, will increase greatly. When price controls are lifted, these additional cash balances will be used to buy goods and services; and prices will rise at that time. Thus, inflation has not been avoided but only repressed for a time and shifted to a period when more goods are available.

The Quantity Theory

One of the oldest, and also one of the newest, theories which attempts to explain the relationship of money to prices is the quantity theory, which holds that changes in the quantity of money are the main causal determinants of changes in the price level. All versions of this theory have relied in part at least on some form of the equation of exchange to develop their relationships. In its crudest form, the quantity theory holds that changes in the money supply lead to equal, proportionate changes in the same direction in the price level. This may have some validity in a free-enterprise economy in which institutional arrangements are such that the full-employment level of output is the norm and the level of V does not change, but such an economy does not exist today and probably never did. Professor Irving Fisher was one of the early exponents in America of a more refined quantity theory. He recognized that V and T might change at times, thus offsetting the effect of changes in the money supply on the price level. But he held that such changes took place primarily during the upswing and downswing of the business cycle and were thus cyclical in nature. At about the same stage in the next cycle he felt that V and T would have about the same level.

The experiences during the Depression, which began in 1929, and the writings of J. M. Keynes convinced most economists that the quantity theory was inadequate as an explanation of general price changes. But it has come back into prominence in recent years, largely as a result of the work of Professor Milton Friedman and some of his colleagues, who refer to themselves as *monetarists*. Friedman holds that the money supply is the major determinant of the value of output, that is, PT, rather than P alone. This means, of course, that the velocity of money or its reciprocal, the demand for cash balances, is a fairly stable, or at least a reasonably predictable, factor.

This version of the quantity theory is based on the premise that an outside influence which changes the prices and quantities of some assets initiates a series of adjustments in the prices and quantities of other assets in such a way that equilibrium is again established. Under a given level of income, interest rates, prices, and services received from holding real assets, spending units will want to hold a given amount of real assets and a given amount of money and other financial assets, and to buy a given amount of goods and services. This is true whether the spending units are businesses, governmental units, or individuals. Any amount of money they receive in excess of the amount they desire to hold is used to acquire real and financial assets and to buy goods and services. Changes in the rate of spending are part of the adjustment, tending to close the gap between desired and actual money balances.

Assets are generally produced in changing quantities in response to changes in demand, but changes in the money stock are in the short run largely independent of changes in the demand for money. When the Federal Reserve increases the money stock by supplying banks with additional reserves, they have more reserves than desired and, therefore, invest them or increase their volume of lending. Spending units will sell securities or borrow as long as the interest rate charged by banks is less than the yield from hiring labor and from buying and using other assets. These spending units in turn use their demand deposits to buy additional services and goods and to invest in real and financial assets; and so other spending units receive additions to money balances in excess of the desired amounts. This process leads to an increase in the rate of spending or investing to eliminate the excess. But spending or investing does not destroy the money balances; it merely passes them on to someone else. The process continues until new levels of income, prices, interest rates, and services received from holding real assets are reached and spending units desire to hold the expanded stock of money.

The demand to hold money need not be the same as it was before the money stock was expanded since the demand to hold money changes in relationship to income and wealth and changes in the price level. The same person usually wants to hold more money when personal income or real wealth is greater than when it is smaller. When the price level increases and the nominal wealth of an individual or of a corporation increases, the desire is to hold more money. When prices have not increased, but are likely to increase in the future, the demand for money will tend to decline since the cost of holding it becomes higher. Interest rates also affect the amount of money an individual or corporation desires to hold, since at higher interest rates the opportunity cost of holding money is higher. These and other factors will affect the equilibrium level of money which the community desires to hold, but changes in the money supply and the desire to hold money will affect the volume of output so as to reach the desired equilibrium levels of money, other assets, and spending.

FACTORS INFLUENCING THE MONEY SUPPLY, VELOCITY, AND THE VOLUME OF TRADE

Since in Chapter 5 we analyzed in detail the factors affecting the supply of money in the American monetary system, they will be reviewed only briefly here. The total currency supply is influenced primarily by the demands of the public for cash. The largest part of the supply of money today is bank credit. The amount of such credit is determined by the demand for holding such credit as deposits in checking accounts and for borrowing such credit by private individuals and the government, and by the policies of the banks and central bank authorities that govern its availability. The basic reasons for holding a certain level of money in checking accounts usually relate to the timing of receipts and disbursements and to expectations about the future.

The velocity of money is the relationship between two factors: the volume of monetary transactions; and the amount of cash balances (cash and bank deposits) that individuals, business units, institutions, and the government feel they must keep on hand to meet demands for funds and to tide them over emergencies. These factors in turn depend upon the organization of the financial system of the community and expectations concerning the future.

The organization of the financial system is an important factor in determining the needs for money and bank credit. If money can be borrowed easily, quickly, and at a reasonable cost, smaller money balances will be kept by individuals, businesses, and government. A highly developed system of savings institutions that provides safety, liquidity, and some income on savings also increases velocity since individuals will place funds in such institutions rather than hoard the money. The degree to which such funds can be kept fully invested by such institutions also affects velocity.

Another major factor affecting velocity is the state of expectations about the future level of economic activity. Consumers will spend more freely when they feel that money income will remain stable or will increase than they will when they expect incomes to decrease. They will also spend their money more rapidly when they feel prices are likely to increase in the near future. Business persons keep smaller sums of money on deposit to meet emergencies when they feel the future outlook is favorable than when it is doubtful or unfavorable. This is especially true when they expect the prices of the goods they have to buy to increase. They also defer expenditures on capital equipment and cut purchases for inventory when expectations are for a decline in business, and this reduces the velocity of money. Expectations regarding interest rates and the future level of security prices may make new financing more or less desirable and so increase or decrease velocity.

Not only the volume and velocity of purchasing media but also the physical volume of trade is subject to many influences, some of which lead to changes in prices. The basic volume of trade is determined by such factors as the size of the population and the labor force and its technical competence, the quantity and the quality of the natural resources and man-made capital, and the techniques of production, distribution, and administration. The extent to which resources are fully used is equally important. This, in turn, depends on the ability of producers to sell their output, or the total demand for goods and services in the economy.

The general price level is thus the result of the interaction of all of these factors that affect M, V, and T. Changes in the money supply can lead to changes in price, but many other factors are involved.

ANALYSIS OF CHANGES IN THE GENERAL PRICE LEVEL

On the basis of all of these factors that affect the price level, it is possible to further analyze various types of changes in the general price level.

Price Changes Initiated by a Change in Costs

The general price level can at times increase without the original impulse coming from either the money supply or its velocity. If costs are increased faster than productivity increases, as in the case of wages, businesses which have some discretion over prices will attempt to raise them in order to cover the increased costs. Such increases are likely to be effective in a period in which the demand for goods is strong in relationship to the supply. The added need for funds to meet production and distribution at higher prices usually leads to increases in the money supply and velocity. But the basic influence on prices comes from the cost side, not from increases in the money supply. It may not go up, however, if the monetary authorities restrict credit expansion, but in that case only the most efficient concerns will have enough demand to operate profitably, and as a result some resources will be unemployed.

This type of inflation has been referred to as the wage-push, or *cost-push*, type of inflation to distinguish it from inflation due to an increase in the money supply, which is called *demand-pull* inflation. In actual practice both aspects of inflation are likely to be operative at the same time since cost-push can occur only in industries in which institutional arrangements are such that labor negotiations are carried out on an industry-wide basis and in which management has a significant amount of discretion over prices. This has led some economists to ascribe this type of inflation to institutional factors rather than to a wage-push.

Inflation may also be initiated by changes in demand in particular industries which are greater in relationship to supply than overall changes in demand. The demand for nonferrous metals, for example, may be greater than demand in general, and prices may rise in this industry before they rise generally. The first raise is likely to be in the basic materials themselves, and such raises will lead to increased profits in the producing industries. Labor will press for wage increases to get its share of the total value of output, and thus labor costs will also rise. Price rises in such basic industries lead to price increases in the industries with administered prices which use their products. Wage increases in one major industry are also likely to lead to demands for similar increases in other industries and among the nonorganized workers in such industries. Thus, a process is set into motion which can lead to general changes in prices, provided the monetary authorities do not restrict credit so as to prevent it.

Price Changes Initiated by a Change in the Money Supply

The interrelationship of the factors that affect prices in actual practice is quite complex. In this topic additional consideration will be given to the adjustments that take place when the primary change is in the money supply or its velocity. In the following chapter the more complex interrelationships arising out of changes in both the money supply and goods side of the equation during business cycles will be considered.

Several types of inflation may be due to an increase in the supply or turnover of money. Inflation may be generated by an increase in the supply of purchasing power. In modern times such inflation is often initiated by government deficits financed by credit creation and at other times by private demands for funds.[2] If this is done in periods of less than full employment of people and resources, the volume of trade will go up; and prices may at first be affected, but slightly, if at all. As unused resources are brought into use, however, prices will be affected. Some items, such as metals, may become scarce while other resources are still in plentiful supply, and the prices of the scarce items will rise. As full use of any resource is approached, expectations of future price rises will force prices up. Attempts to buy before such price rises will also increase demand above current needs and thus force prices up. Since some costs, such as interest costs and wages set by contract, will lag, profits will rise; and this will tend to increase the demand for capital goods. Such changes will be considered more fully in the discussion of monetary factors in business cycles in Chapter 24.

After resources are fully employed, the full effect of the increased money supply will be on prices. It may be more than proportional for a time as expectations of higher prices lead to a faster rate of spending and so raise V. The expansion will continue until trade and prices are in balance at the new levels of the money supply. Velocity will probably drop somewhat from those levels during the period of rising prices since the desire to trade money for goods before they go up in price has disappeared.

Even if the supply of purchasing media is increased in a period of relatively full employment of people and resources, prices may not go up proportionately. Higher prices will increase profits for a time and so lead to a demand for more capital and labor. This may lead to an increase of the labor force by inducing married women, retired workers, and similar groups to enter the labor force. Capital will also probably be utilized more fully by such devices as having two or three shifts use the same machines.

Speculative Type of Inflation

Inflation due to an increased money supply can lead to additional price pressure of the speculative type. Since prices have risen for some time, the idea becomes current that they will keep on rising. This may become self-generating for a time since instead of higher prices resulting in decreased demand, people may buy more to get goods before they go still higher. This may not happen in all sectors of the economy but may be confined to certain areas, as it was to land prices in the Florida land boom in the 1920s or to security prices in the 1928–29 stock market boom. Such a price rise leads to an increase in V since speculators try to turn over their funds as rapidly as possible and many others try to buy ahead of needs in anticipation of further price rises.

---

[2] The traditional view of *demand-pull* inflation exists during periods of economic expansion when the demand for goods and services exceeds the available supply of such goods and services. A second version also associated with increases in the money supply occurs because of "monetization" of the U.S. government debt. The reader should recall from Chapter 21 that the Treasury finances government deficits by selling U.S. government securities to the public, commercial banks, or the Federal Reserve. When the Federal Reserve purchases U.S. government securities, money must be "printed" to pay for the purchases. This, in turn may lead to increased inflationary pressures due to an increase in money supply and bank reserves.

A Long-run Inflationary Bias

Since the end of the Korean War, price pressures and inflation have existed despite frequently stringent policies of credit restraint. In fact prices continued upward in recession periods, though at a slower rate than in prosperity periods. The Federal Reserve was hampered in promoting growth and also in fighting recessions because of the need to restrain price rises. The reaction of prices during this period and other economic developments have led many to feel the economy has developed a long-run inflationary bias.

The following factors are used to varying degrees to substantiate the case for such a bias. Prices and wages tend to rise during periods of boom as is to be expected in a competitive economy. This tendency is reinforced by wage contracts that provide escalator clauses to keep wages in line with prices and by wage increases which are at times greater than increases in productivity. During recessions, prices tend to remain stable rather than to decrease. This is due to the power of major unions not only to resist pay cuts in depressions but also to get pay increases in recession years through long-run contracts calling for annual wage increases irrespective of economic conditions at the time. It is also helped along by the tendency of large corporations to rely on nonprice competition rather than cut prices. Furthermore, if prices do decline drastically in a field, government programs are likely to be used to help take excess supplies off the market. There is little doubt that prices would decline in a severe and prolonged depression. Government takes action to restore employment, however, before such a level of economic activity is reached and the downward price pressure of a depression has been lost.

The inflation resulting from these factors has been referred to as *administrative inflation*. This is to distinguish it from the type of inflation that results from demand exceeding the available supply of goods, either because demand is increasing more rapidly than supply in the early stages of a recovery period, or because demand from monetary expansion by the banking system or the government exceeds available supply.

Traditional monetary policy is not wholly effective to combat administrative inflation. If money supplies are restricted enough, prices can be kept in line; but this will lead to chronic unemployment and slow growth. It also makes it difficult for new firms and small growing firms to get credit since lending policies are likely to be conservative. Administrative inflation calls for potentially new tools of governmental policy if it is to be dealt with effectively.

The Relationship Between Growth in Money Supply and Inflation

We have seen that the interrelationship of the factors that affect prices in actual practice is quite complex. In addition, there are several different types or kinds of inflation at work in the U.S. economy. Even with these complexities, however, we can gain some valuable insights by examining the relationship between money supply growth and inflation over a relatively long period of time.[3]

---

[3]Inflation rates can be estimated in a number of ways. For example, a consumer price index (CPI) or a producer price index could be used. Many economists, however, prefer the use of the GNP price

Figure 23-2 shows a close parallel between inflation rates and money growth until the early 1970s. This suggests that underlying the complex relationship between prices and other factors the inflation rate seems to vary directly with the trend growth rate in money supply or stock.

Substantial deviation in the relationship between money growth and inflation did occur over the 1971–75 time period. Several reasons, however, seem to account for this deviation. First, wage and price controls were instituted in 1971 and mandatory and voluntary versions were maintained until early 1974. Inflation rates seem to have been artificially held below money growth rates

Figure 23-2
Rates of Change of
Money and Prices

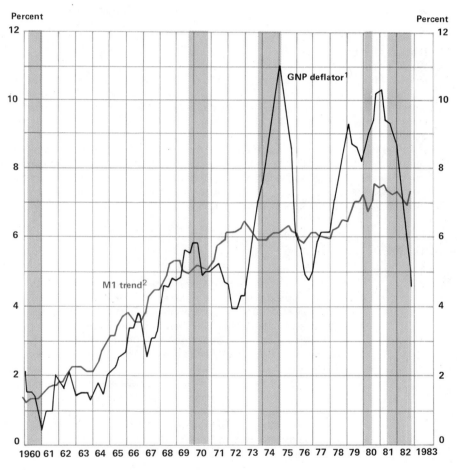

[1]Four-quarter rate of change.
[2]Twenty-quarter rate of change. Shaded areas represent periods of business recessions.
SOURCE: Federal Reserve Bank of St. Louis

deflator because of its comprehensiveness since Gross National Product measures the total output of goods and services in the United States for a specified time period. The GNP deflator reflects the ratio of GNP measured in terms of current prices relative to GNP measured using last year's prices or some base-period prices.

through these controls during 1971 and part of 1972 before "catching up" with the growth in money supply. It also should be noted that a rapid rise in energy costs due to an embargo on oil shipments to the United States contributed to the rapid inflation of 1973 and 1974. Since then the historical relationship between money supply growth and inflation seems to be returning.[4]

QUESTIONS

1. Describe the process by which inflation took place before modern times.
2. Discuss the early periods of inflation based on the issue of paper money.
3. Discuss the basis for inflation during World Wars I and II.
4. Discuss the causes of the major periods of inflation in American history.
5. State the equation of exchange. Identify each factor in it. Why are the two sides of the equation equal?
6. State the cash balances equation and identify each factor in it. Also indicate how this approach can be useful in analyzing the factors affecting the price level.
7. Discuss various formulations of the quantity theory of money. Explain, step by step, how the Friedman version of the quantity theory is supposed to work.
8. Outline and discuss major factors that affect the money supply, the velocity of money, and the physical volume of trade.
9. Explain the process by which price changes may be initiated by a general change in costs.
10. Explain the process by which a change in the money supply leads to a change in the general price level.
11. Discuss the speculative type of inflation.
12. What factors are used to support the case for a long-run inflationary bias?
13. Discuss the relationship between money supply growth and inflation rates.

SUGGESTED READINGS

Davidson, Lawrence S. "Inflation Misinformation and Monetary Policy." *Review*. Federal Reserve Bank of St. Louis (June/July, 1982), pp. 15–26.

Economics of Inflation, Federal Reserve Bank of Philadelphia (October, 1974).

Karnosky, Denis S. "The Link Between Money and Prices—1971–76." *Review*, Federal Reserve Bank of St. Louis (April, 1976), pp. 17–23.

Luckett, Dudley G. *Money and Banking*, 2nd ed. New York: McGraw-Hill Book Company, 1980. Part 7.

Prager, Jonas. *Fundamentals of Money, Banking, and Financial Institutions.* New York: Harper & Row, Publishers, Inc., 1982. Part 5.

Ritter, Lawrence S., and William L. Silber. *Principles of Money, Banking, and Financial Markets*, 4th ed. New York: Basic Books, Inc., Publishers, 1983. Part 4.

Smith, Gary. *Money and Banking: Financial Markets and Institutions.* Reading, Mass.: Addison-Wesley Publishing Co., 1982. Chapter 13.

Tatom, John A. "Does the Stage of the Business Cycle Affect the Inflation Rate?" *Review*, Federal Reserve Bank of St. Louis (September, 1978), pp. 7–15.

---

[4]For further recent empirical evidence on the relationship between money and price levels, see: Denis S. Karnosky, "The Link Between Money and Prices—1971–76," *Review*, Federal Reserve Bank of St. Louis (April, 1976), pp. 17–23; and John A. Tatom, "Does the Stage of the Business Cycle Affect the Inflation Rate?" *Review*, Federal Reserve Bank of St. Louis (September, 1978), pp. 7–15.

24 Business Fluctuations and International Payment Problems

In the two previous chapters, an analysis was made of the effect of changes in monetary and fiscal policies upon interest rates and the money market and upon the price level. Because price changes and fluctuations in interest rates are strategic variables in the continually recurring cycles in business activity, the role of monetary and fiscal policies in the cyclical process is analyzed more thoroughly in the first part of this chapter. The latter part of the chapter explores our nation's international financial relationships. The final chapter in this text traces recent monetary and fiscal policy actions taken in an attempt to achieve the four economic goals of: (1) sustained economic growth, (2) high levels of employment, (3) stable prices, and (4) international financial equilibrium.

BUSINESS FLUCTUATIONS AND CYCLES

Since records have become available, and especially since business activity has been carried on almost exclusively by means of monetary or credit transactions in an economy with highly developed financial institutions, economic activity has not grown at an even rate but has fluctuated between prosperity and recession or depression. These recurring fluctuations in economic activity have come to be known as *business cycles* even though they are not of equal intensity. They have ranged from such mild downturns as those in 1927 and 1960, of which many people were hardly aware, to the deep Depression of the early thirties, in which about a third of the labor force was out of work. They are also of unequal length—from a little over a year to almost nine years.

Sustained economic growth is perceived by most economists and individuals as being desirable, particularly when such growth is not accompanied by rising price levels. This is because "real" economic growth traditionally has led to higher living standards. Emphasis in this section is placed on the impact of monetary and fiscal policies on economic activity in the United States.

The Circular Nature of Economic Activity

Economic activity is a circular process in which income is generated in the act of producing goods and services; this income enables the recipients to buy goods and services; their expenditures lead to production to satisfy their wants; the wants are satisfied by the production of goods; and so on in a continuous circular process. Expenditures of one individual or group are income to another individual or group.

At any given time, a nation has a structure of production and governmental facilities that is set up to produce consumer goods and services of all kinds; producer goods; governmental goods, such as military equipment; and government services, such as fire protection. Some goods and services are produced for export to the rest of the world, and other goods and services are bought from foreign countries. This structure for producing goods and services, called the *structure of production*, has been developed over a long period of time, and only a part of it is in the process of changing at any one time. Various parts of the structure are related to each other. The number and type of steel mills currently in existence, for example, are such as to provide the different types and quantities of steel needed to meet the demands of consumers, producers, and the government. Some parts of the structure of production are being changed constantly as the demand for steel changes. The amounts and types of goods being produced in any period of time in the economy are referred to as *the pattern of production of goods and services*.

In the act of producing goods and services, income is paid to the factors of production in the form of wages, interest, rent, and the distribution of profits. Money is paid to the government in the form of taxes on income, indirect taxes, payments for licenses, etc. Some money is also transferred to other agencies and to individuals in the form of gifts and grants. The remaining funds are kept by businesses, some as depreciation allowances to provide for the replacement of plant and equipment, and some as retained profits to increase the equity of the owners. This pattern of income distribution and other money receipts is referred to as *the pattern of money flow receipts*, and it has developed over a period of time as the economy has developed. Tax structures, for example, have evolved gradually; and business and consumer decisions have been adjusted to them. Wage rates are set by bargaining, which is affected by the relative strengths of business and labor bargaining units in general and in each industry, and so on. Just as in the structure of production of goods and services, only a relatively small part of the pattern of money flow receipts is changing at any one time.

The funds from the pattern of money flow receipts continue in the circular flow when they are spent on goods and services either directly by the recipients or by others to whom they have been made available. The recipients of money flow receipts include individual consumers, nonprofit institutions, businesses, and governmental units. They, in turn, decide how they will spend this money on goods and services of various types, and the proportion of it they will save. They may also make use of credit and, in this way, spend more for a period of time than the money they receive. From time to time, such debts may be paid off faster than new credit is extended. The goods and services that consumers, businesses, governments, and institutions purchase and the prices they are willing and able to pay determine what is produced in the next round.

Money kept in businesses as depreciation allowances and as retained earnings and the savings of individuals and institutions also enter the expenditure stream to complete the circular flow of money. Depreciation allowances and retained earnings may be spent by the business on plant and equipment or additional goods for inventory, and so are entered into the expenditure stream. If the business does not have an immediate need for these funds, it may make them available for investment in the money market; and the borrower will then spend them. Savings may enter the spending stream by being invested directly in real estate, equipment, or other assets; or they may be put into financial institutions and entered into the spending stream when they are spent by a borrower. The amount and type of all expenditures by the recipients of money flow receipts constitute the *pattern of expenditures* in any period of time.

The monetary and banking system is used by individuals, institutions, governments, and businesses to facilitate the transfer of money in the circular flow of activity. The operation of the banking system can create a problem in maintaining equilibrium since money may at times accumulate in the banking system rather than be spent or invested. At other times individuals, businesses, or governments may have money available for an expenditure that did not arise out of the circular flow of economic activity but which came from credit creation by the banking system.

The Role of Monetary and Fiscal Policy in Cyclical Fluctuations

As has already been shown, monetary changes are important in the cyclical process because of their effect on interest rates. Their influence is more pervasive than this, however. In fact, modern business cycles could exist only in an economy with a banking system that has the ability to expand and contract credit. In the analysis of the factors at work in the cyclical process, expansion will be considered first.

Initiating Factors Leading to an Upswing. Many factors can initiate an upswing in economic activity. Any change in the pattern of production, of money flows, or of consumption can be the factor that initiates the upswing. General initiating factors might include unusually good crops or new inventions.

The effects of increased expenditures during periods of defense and war production need no further explanation. Increases in government expenditures except during periods of full employment of resources, even though of a smaller magnitude, initiate increases in economic activity. The same is true of changes in the methods of financing such expenditures. A shift from the payment of government expenditures through taxation to payment by borrowing or credit creation materially affects the economy by increasing the incomes of those individuals whose taxes have been cut. Government activity in regard to the public debt likewise has a pronounced economic effect. Rapid reduction of the public debt through income raised by general taxation has a deflationary effect since it cuts income available for consumer expenditures and results in a reduction in production due to reduced consumer demand.

A change in transfer payments affects the pattern of money flow receipts and, in turn, the patterns of expenditures and production. This happens, for example, when social security taxes are raised and increased sums are paid to those receiving benefits under the social security programs.

The government can also initiate changes in economic activity by actions in the housing field. Making more money available for financing, or making financing easier to obtain, changes the patterns of money flow receipts, expenditures, and production.

Governmental bodies can also influence business conditions and thus initiate upward movements in economic activity by changing the legal rules under which business is carried on as, for example, tariff and banking legislation. The introduction of a high protective tariff after the existence of low rates causes a demand for producer goods with which to produce the items that were formerly imported. The higher prices for the domestically produced goods likewise will lead to a change in consumer expenditure patterns.

Changes in monetary policies can also initiate fluctuations in the economy. If credit is made more easily available at lower rates, investment expenditures for the improvement and expansion of plant and equipment will increase. If the actions of the Federal Reserve restrict credit, the rate of business investment will be slowed down. Monetary policy also has a similar effect on the housing market, which is especially vulnerable to severe credit restriction, and it has some effect on the durable consumer goods market.

Some of these initiating factors have their original impact on business; others have their original impact upon consumers and upon their pattern of expenditures. As business persons operating under the profit motive attempt to adjust to changes in consumer buying habits, there will also be an impact upon the pattern of production and in turn on the pattern of income distribution and money flow receipts. This, in turn, again affects the pattern of consumption.

The Cumulative Process During Expansion. After one of the initiating factors has begun an upswing, various intensifying factors may reinforce the upward movement. One of the most significant of these is the *multiplier*, that is, the process by which an increase in investment expenditures or government expenditures leads to a multiplied effect on national income. For example, as investment expenditures are increased, the level of national income increases, and this leads to an increase in consumption expenditures, which again in turn raises national income, which leads to more expenditures on consumption, and so on. If investment expenditures do not increase, the total effect on income will depend on the marginal propensity to consume, that is, the relationship of consumption expenditures to changes in income. Suppose the increase in investment expenditures is $5 billion and the marginal propensity to consume is .8; that is, 80 percent of the increased income is spent on consumption. This means that in the next round $4 billion is spent on consumption and $1 billion is saved, and this increases national income by $4 billion. Of this amount $3.2 billion is spent in the next round, and so on. If all other factors remained constant, this process would go on until the total change in income would be $25 billion of which $5 billion is the increase in investment expenditures and $20 billion is the increase in consumption expenditures.

A factor that intensifies the upswing as the demand for consumer goods increases is the derived demand for additional producer goods. The demand for producer goods increases by a larger percentage than that for consumer goods due to the operation of the *accelerator principle*. Since capital goods last for a relatively long period of time, only a small proportion needs to be replaced each year. For example, if capital goods last for ten years, 10 percent will be replaced each year on the average. At a time when all of the capital equipment is being utilized fully, a 10 percent increase in consumer demand may lead to a doubling of the demand for capital goods, 10 percent of the current stock for normal replacement, and another 10 percent to meet the added demand for consumer goods.

In the final analysis, all intensifying factors are related to credit creation, the reduction of cash balances, or an increase in the velocity of money, or to the level of interest rates. When business persons build up inventories in anticipation of price rises or expand production as profits increase, they either use previously idle funds or increase short-term borrowing. This borrowing has been an important source of added purchasing media in past cycles.

Speculation in commodity and security markets is also aided by credit expansion. The same has usually been true of government deficit financing during an upturn. Long-term business financing is done primarily from current savings; but in the early stages of an upturn, funds held in short-term investments are drawn into the capital markets. Some funds made available to a business from bank loans may also find their way into permanent investment in plant and equipment.

Initiating Factors Leading to a Downturn. The downturn in business may be brought about by an initiating factor from outside the circular flow of economic activity, such as a decrease in government spending or a reduced availability or higher price for bank credit. Changes, however, are going on during the expansion period that tend to slow business down or even to cause a downturn. Costs tend to rise faster than do selling prices after a period of time, and the cut in profits reduces the motive for expansion. Inefficiency increases, and this in turn reduces profits.

Furthermore, errors of forecast made during the upswing do not show up while activity is expanding rapidly. After a while, however, it becomes apparent that all of the goods that some business people thought would be demanded in their field cannot be sold at prices to yield a reasonable profit, and this factor also slows down the expansion.

During the period of business expansion there is also an increase in interest rates because the demand for funds rises faster than the supply. This makes it less profitable to finance expansion by means of bonds and also makes capital investment less desirable. At the same time that interest rates are rising, the marginal efficiency of capital, that is, the expected rate of return which can be earned by adding units of capital equipment falls, first in a few fields and then in others. This is true because expectations of future profits are reduced as supply becomes larger in relation to demand and costs press against selling prices. The result is a decrease in the expenditures on new plant and equipment.

The Cumulative Process During Contraction. The process of income generation, decreasing profits and future expectations of smaller profits, credit contraction, and increasing pessimism intensify the downturn just as their converse did the upturn. The fall in prices now causes business persons to buy less than is needed to meet current demands since they want to cut inventory losses. Inventories from the past prosperity period are reduced below the point where they are adequate to take care of the current volume of business so as to cut losses from future price declines. Hoarding on the part of individuals and business persons takes funds out of the current economic stream, whereas credit creation adds funds during an upswing. In the Keynesian terminology, liquidity preference is increased during the downturn, and this intensifies the recession. Furthermore, funds that would normally be used to buy consumer goods are used to retire debts because of the fear of the future, and such payments are usually saved by the recipients so that funds which would normally go into consumption now become a part of savings. As profits are reduced and gross errors of forecast become apparent in some fields, there is liquidation of many businesses. This leads to a forced sale of assets to pay off debts and to distress prices, which further complicates the business picture and intensifies the recession.

Factors Leading to Another Upswing. In many past cycles, initiating factors arising outside the circular flow of economic activity have started business on a new upward movement. These have included such things as new inventions leading to increased business spending, new consumer goods leading to increased consumer and business spending, increased foreign purchases in the United States, and increased governmental expenditures. Even in the absence of such outside initiating forces, the economy will gradually generate the momentum for an upturn.

After liquidation has gone so far that only reasonably strong concerns remain and some businesses are again operating at reasonable profits, confidence returns gradually. This leads to an increase in expenditures for repairs and for some replacement of equipment. After a period of time, this replacement demand will become greater because many producer goods do not last more than a few years and have to be replaced if production is to continue. At the same time, the drive for a further reduction in costs is likely to lead to the introduction of cost-cutting devices, thus further augmenting the demand for new capital. Lower interest rates and increased profits will also lead to an increase in investment expenditures.

Monetary and Fiscal Policies and the Level of Economic Activity

The discussion of the cyclical process indicates clearly that monetary actions and fiscal policy play a significant role in the cycle. Either can act as an initiating factor leading to an upturn or a downturn; and they also have a relationship to the intensifying factors.

There are basically two different approaches to the relationship of monetary policy to economic activity, the one holding that the major effect works out through interest rates, the other that it works through changes in the money stock. The standard Keynesian national income analysis puts major emphasis on interest rates. Government expenditures are held to be largely autonomous, and consumer expenditures are determined by the level of income and the consumption function, that is, the relationship of consumption expenditures to income. Investment expenditures depend upon the interaction of the schedule of the marginal efficiency of capital, that is, the demand for investment of the whole economy expressed as a function of the rate of interest, and the interest rate. Different rates of interest induce different rates of investment and, in turn, different equilibrium levels of income. Therefore, the level of interest rates is one of the key variables in the economic process, and a change in interest rates leads to a change in economic activity. When Federal Reserve policy, for example, leads to lower interest rates, the equilibrium level of investment expenditures is increased; and so forces are set in motion through the multiplier and accelerator which increase the level of national income until a new equilibrium is reached at the lower interest rates. Fiscal policy is, of course, of prime significance in the Keynesian framework since government expenditures along with investment expenditures are the major dynamic determinants of the level of national income. No economist holds that the relationships in the real world are as simple as the simplified national income model, but the significance of the rate of interest and of government spending is still basic even after many other factors are taken into consideration.

The alternative approach is the modern quantity theory or monetarist approach, which holds that the most significant factor affecting the economy is the effect of Federal Reserve policies on the money stock.[1] Some aspects of this theory were considered in the previous section in the discussion of the effects of changes in the money supply on prices. This view holds that changes in the money stock result directly and indirectly in increased expenditures on a whole spectrum of capital goods and consumer goods. The most significant factor is the relationship between income and the amount of money individuals and businesses choose to hold. When money supplies change, spending is adjusted to bring money balances to desired levels. Such adjustments affect the relative prices of goods; and such changes in prices, as well as changes in interest rates, are the transmission mechanism according to this point of view. Since someone has to hold the total money supply, changes in income occur until actual money holdings are in line with desired holdings.

---

[1] We first discussed a relationship between changes in money supply or stock and economic activity in Chapter 5. Downturns or recessions in economic activity are preceded by sharp declines in the short-run growth rates of money stock relative to long-run trends or growth rates in money stock. Increasing rates of change in money stock are associated with economic expansion. However, a too rapid rate of increase in money stock may lead to higher inflation rates, as we saw in Figure 23-2.

According to the modern quantity theory, the role of fiscal policy is generally minor when compared with that of monetary policy. The size of the federal budget, or even of a deficit, is not of major importance. There may be some influence on total spending resulting from changes in the interest rate and in real and nominal wealth, but the relationship is not clear. When a deficit is financed by the monetary system, the effect is expansionary. This is true, however, because the money supply expands, not because of the federal deficit itself.

It is impossible at this stage to choose between these conflicting viewpoints since the evidence is not all in. In all probability both interest rates and the size of the money stock play a significant role in determining the level of economic activity. And the role may well be different at different times and under differing conditions. Interest rates may be more significant than the money stock when the economy is operating at levels of less than full employment of resources, and changes in the money stock most important in boom periods of full or overutilization of resources.

The Relationship of Prices, Wages, and Employment

Another unresolved problem is the relationship of the rate of unemployment to wages and prices. The trade-off view holds that it is impossible to have high employment without inflation and that policymakers must choose between some degree of unemployment and some degree of inflation. Theoretically, if such relationships are plotted, the curve slopes downward from left to right and is usually shaped like a rounded "L." This curve is often called the Phillips curve, after the British economist who first stressed the relationship between levels of unemployment and wages. The trade-off view holds that such relationships are stable, and that when the economy reaches a high employment range, excessive wage increases and price inflation result from expansionary fiscal policies rather than further reductions in unemployment.

Figure 24-1 shows the annual relationship between inflation and unemployment in the United States for the 1954–1981 time period. It can be seen that a rounded "L" curve fits rather nicely for the 1954–1969 time period and supports the contention of a somewhat simplified trade-off relationship. However, since 1970 the relationship seems to have dramatically changed. Some economists attempt to explain this change by suggesting that the Phillips curve has shifted upward and to the right in the short run because of higher inflation expectations. Presumably if inflation expectations were to decline to more traditional levels, the relationship would fall in line with the 1954–1969 period.

Opposed to the trade-off view is the long-run equilibrium view which holds that if proper policies are followed, inflation need not result. This view suggests that there is a "natural" rate of unemployment determined by supply and demand factors and that this rate is independent of the rate of inflation. In other words, the long-run Phillips curve would be a vertical line at the "natural" rate of unemployment.

For illustration, assume that the economy is at the stage of a cycle in which there is significant unemployment. Monetary or fiscal action starts an upswing in activity. Spending occurs at first with the anticipation that prices will remain as

Figure 24-1

Inflation and
Unemployment
Relationships,
1954–1981

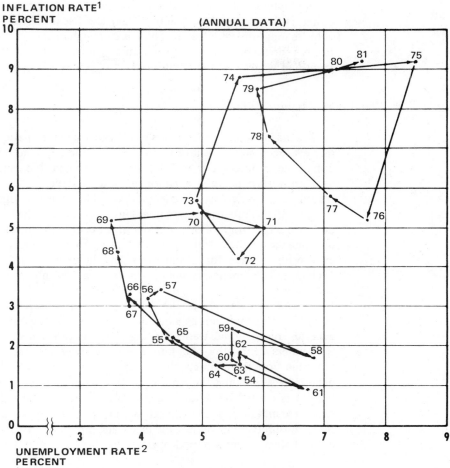

INFLATION RATE[1]
PERCENT
(ANNUAL DATA)

[1] Percentage change in the GNP implicit price deflator.
[2] Percent of civilian labor force.

UNEMPLOYMENT RATE[2]
PERCENT

SOURCE: Keith M. Carlson, "A Monetary Analysis of the Administration's Budget and Economic
Projections," *Review*, Federal Reserve Bank of St. Louis (May, 1982), p. 6.

they are and output and employment rise more rapidly for a time than wages or
prices. But as demand increases and prices rise, real wages are reduced and
workers demand higher wages and get them during periods of high employment. If
inflationary monetary and fiscal policies are pursued, wages will continue to rise
and inflation will result. But as wages rise, employers are no longer ready to hire
workers or raise wages as rapidly as early in the upswing, and they also find it
profitable to use more labor-saving equipment. If some degree of deflationary
action is pursued after the upswing has lost momentum, there will be some
increased unemployment, but it will be temporary. As soon as a new price trend
not only becomes a reality but is anticipated for the future, nominal and real
wages will coincide; and unemployment will again fall. According to this view,
inflationary policy is not necessary or desirable as a way of achieving high levels

of employment. It is impossible to determine at the present time which view, if either, is the correct one, or if monetary and fiscal policies can be so used as to achieve long-run equilibrium. There are enough questions, however, that policymakers should be cautious about assuming any set relationship between employment and wages and the resulting level of prices.

INTERNATIONAL FINANCIAL EQUILIBRIUM

Just as monetary policy plays a strategic role in the nation's stability, growth, interest rates, and price levels, so, too, it is relied upon to relieve the pressure of imbalance in international financial relationships. No nation is a world unto itself, however; nor can a nation pursue whatever policies it desires without regard to the reactions of other nations. This is especially true of the United States with its immense international involvement and the importance of the U.S. dollar in world trade. Policymakers of all economies must recognize the interdependence of their actions in attempting to maintain international financial equilibrium. Since the dollar is widely held as a medium of international exchange, U.S. monetary policy has especially significant effects on the world economy.

Briefly, the nations of the world strive to achieve international financial equilibrium by maintaining a balance in their exchange of goods and services. In general, international trade benefits both countries involved in an exchange. Consumers benefit by obtaining goods at lower cost, since the goods can be imported from the country where they are produced most efficiently. Producers benefit by expanding their markets. Well over one tenth of the U.S. national income is earned by selling our goods to foreigners, and a like amount of our needs are met through imports. However, the decisions to import and export are made by different individuals and firms, and problems arise if they are significantly out of balance over a period of time.

The Nature of the Problem

Exports are sales to foreigners; they represent a source of income to domestic producers. Imports divert expenditures to foreign producers and therefore represent a loss of potential income to domestic producers. When the two are in balance there is no net effect on total income in the economy. However, an increase in exports over imports has an expansionary effect on the economy just as would an increase in investment or government spending. An excess of imports has a contractionary effect. These macroeconomic effects can be quite significant. Furthermore, increasing imports of a particular product may cause loss of jobs and income in the domestic industry that produces that product even if exports are increasing in other industries.

Just as in the domestic economy, goods and services are not exchanged directly in international trade, but payment is made through monetary or financial transactions. Methods of making payments and financing international trade were discussed in Chapter 20. When imports are financed, short-term international liabilities are created. Other short- and long-term lending and investment are conducted across national boundaries on a large scale. In addition, government grants for both military and civilian purposes, and private gifts and grants, are sources of international financial flows. These flows can have a significant impact on domestic economies, and may affect the decisions of monetary policymakers.

Since producers, consumers, and investors in different countries use different currencies, the international financial system requires the existence of a mechanism for establishing the relative values, or exchange rates, between currencies, and for facilitating their actual exchange. Under a system of fixed exchange rates, such as the gold standard which existed in some variation until the early 1970s, the government or central bank of a country agrees to redeem its currency for fixed amounts of gold. If there is a currency outflow, due to excessive imports or lending or grants to foreigners, this currency will be redeemed for gold by the foreign recipients. The loss of gold reserves by the central bank results in a decrease in the money supply, which may lead to recession or deflation unless countered by other monetary policy action. A persistent gold loss may lead to loss of confidence that the central bank will be able to redeem all outstanding currency, and may necessitate *devaluation*, which is an official reduction of the exchange rate.

Under the system of flexible or floating exchange rates which has existed since 1973, central banks are not obligated to redeem their currencies. Exchange rates are determined in the actual process of exchange, by supply and demand in the foreign exchange market. This system puts less pressure on central bank reserves and reduces the impact of international financial transactions on domestic money supplies. Nevertheless, fluctuations in exchange rates affect imports and exports and can thus have an effect on domestic production, incomes, and prices. And international financial markets significantly influence domestic interest rates, and vice versa, so that domestic monetary policy still involves international considerations.

In short, domestic economies are inextricably linked to each other in a worldwide economy and financial system. The United States has played a leading role in the development and growth of that system. Before we take a closer look at that role, it will be helpful to examine the accounting system by which we attempt to keep track of our international financial transactions.

The Balance of Payments Accounts

The United States *balance of payments* involves all of its international transactions including foreign investment, private and government grants, expenditures of United States military forces overseas, and many other items in addition to the purchases and sales of goods and services. The single most important element of the balance of payments is the *balance of trade* which is the net balance of exports and imports. Broadly defined, this concept reflects the balance of goods and services. A more narrow view considers only the import and export of goods and is termed the *merchandise trade balance*. This latter concept is depicted in Figure 24-2. It can be seen that the merchandise trade balance was

Figure 24-2
U.S. International
Transactions

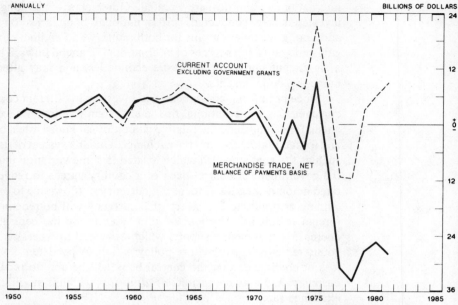

SOURCE: *Historical Chart Book*, Board of Governors of the Federal Reserve System, 1982, p. 100.

consistently favorable between the 1950s and the beginning of the 1970s. In recent years, however, the import of goods has exceeded the export of goods. This imbalance has been particularly severe since 1977, as is shown in Figure 24-2. A major factor has been our dependence on oil imports. In addition, the United States experienced more rapid economic growth during 1977 and 1978 relative to growth abroad, which also contributed to more imports relative to exports.

A more comprehensive understanding of the U.S. balance of payments situation can be developed by examining Table 24-1 below. The merchandise trade balance adjusted for military transactions, investment income earned on foreign investments, and other service transactions that include tourism, transportation, and banking activities, results in a *goods and services balance*. Next, the *current account balance* is obtained by subtracting unilateral transfers from the goods and services balance. These transfers include remittances, pensions, and private gifts and grants as well as U.S. government grants excluding military grants. In essence, the current account balance shows the flow of income into and out of the U.S. during a specified time period.

Deficits or surpluses in the current account must be offset by changes in capital account flows. That is, the two must be equal except for statistical discrepancies due to measurement errors. The *capital account balance* includes changes in foreign government and private investment in the United States in such forms as bank deposits, the purchasing of government and corporate securities, loans, and direct investment in land and buildings. Netted against this would be similar U.S. government and private investments or holdings in foreign

United States Balance of Payments (Millions of Dollars)

Item credits or debits	1980	1981	1982
Merchandise exports	224,237	236,254	211,013
Merchandise imports	−249,575	−264,143	−247,344
Merchandise trade balance	−25,338	−27,889	−36,331
Military transactions, net	−2,472	−1,541	640
Investment income, net	29,910	33,037	28,720
Other service transactions, net	6,203	7,472	6,746
Balance on goods and services	8,303	11,079	−205
Remittances, pensions, and other transfers	−2,101	−2,104	−2,455
U.S. government grants (excluding military)	−4,681	−4,504	−5,413
Balance on current account	1,520	4,471	−8,093
Change in U.S. government assets, other than official reserve assets, net (increase, −)	−5,126	−5,137	−5,766
Change in U.S. official reserve assets (increase, −)	−8,155	−5,175	−4,965
Gold	0	0	0
Special Drawing Rights (SDR's)	−16	−1,823	−1,371
Reserve position in International Monetary Fund (IMF)	−1,667	−2,491	−2,552
Foreign currencies	−6,472	−861	−1,041
Change in U.S. private assets abroad (increase, −)	−72,746	−98,982	−107,535
Change in foreign official assets in the United States (increase, +)	15,442	4,785	3,043
Change in foreign private assets in the United States (increase, +)	39,042	73,136	81,451
Balance on capital account	−31,543	−31,373	−33,772
Statistical discrepancy	28,870	25,809	41,864

SOURCE: *Federal Reserve Bulletin* (May, 1983), p. A54.

countries. The final adjusting factor, excluding the statistical discrepancy amount, would be a change in U.S. official reserve assets as shown in Table 24-1.

This last item, U.S. official reserve assets, consists of gold, Special Drawing Rights, and convertible foreign currencies held by the U.S. Treasury and Federal Reserve. The role of these international reserve assets in the world financial system depends upon the currency exchange mechanism in effect. Under fixed exchange rates the government or central bank is obligated to redeem its currency for fixed amounts of gold or other reserve assets. Thus the official reserve asset account is in fact a balancing factor. The amount of change in this account would exactly offset the net surplus or deficit resulting from all other transactions (again excluding the statistical discrepancy, which arises because it is impossible to keep track of all international transactions).

Under the current system of floating exchange rates, a central bank is not obligated to redeem its currency. However, it may attempt to control or influence its exchange rate by entering the foreign exchange market, using its reserve asset account to buy or sell the currency, thus adding to demand or supply. Such intervention by central banks in the floating exchange rate system is referred to as a managed or "dirty" float. Under a pure floating system in which central banks do not enter the foreign exchange market at all, there would be no change in the official reserve asset account. Note, however, that the rest of the accounts would still balance. Any surplus or deficit in current accounts would be balanced by the capital accounts; for example, a trade deficit might be balanced in part by an increase in foreign assets in the United States, including deposits in U.S. banks transferred to foreigners in payment for imports.

The International Financial System

For many years after World War II the United States enjoyed a favorable balance of trade; that is, it had more exports than imports. During this period, however, the U.S. also engaged in a massive program of international aid to countries whose productive facilities were destroyed by the war and shouldered the preponderance of the burden of military capability and action. The U.S. also gave vast measures of assistance to developing nations of the world. One of the results of these efforts was the large accumulations of foreign claims to United States dollars and the loss of a large amount of gold reserves.

Even with loss of gold reserves, the United States had far greater reserves than any other nation. Too, the large accumulation of claims against United States dollars had long been considered desirable. Indeed, one of the most serious difficulties facing international trade in the early postwar period was the "dollar gap" or dollar shortage, as the dollar became increasingly relied upon as an international currency. Gold had been the international reserve currency of the world and the basic medium of exchange in international commerce. Yet, as the volume of world trade increased over the years, the supply of gold failed to keep pace. Without some form of supplementary international money, the result would have been international deflation.

The unfavorable balance of payments problem of the United States and the world's requirements for a growing monetary base to meet the needs of increasing international liquidity came into sharp focus late in the 1960s. The year-by-year growth in short-term financial claims on the dollar resulting from our continuing unfavorable balance of payments served foreign central banks well. It provided them with a growing base of reserve assets. Since these claims to United States dollars were convertible into gold at a fixed rate, such claims were considered to be as good as gold. But just as the annual growth of the world's monetary gold supply was not increasing at a rapid enough rate to accommodate expanding international commerce, it was inevitable that the United States stock of monetary gold would cease to be adequate to support the vast increase in claims against it.

Special Drawing Rights. Recognizing that the dollar could no longer serve as a steadily increasing international money, in January, 1968, the principal nations of the world agreed to a supplementary world money—Special Drawing Rights. The Rights, sometimes referred to as "paper gold," can be created freely by the International Monetary Fund.[2] The drawing rights are assets that the participating central banks accept from one another up to specified limits. Like gold, they are claims on the world's resources and are allocated to participants in proportion to their International Monetary Fund quotas.

The End of the Gold Standard. In 1971, as a result of strong inflationary pressures in the United States, our trade balance swung into deficit. Further, higher interest rates in Europe than in the United States created a torrent of capital outflows to Europe. The resulting deterioration of the dollar became so great that on August 15, 1971, the President suspended convertibility of the dollar into gold in an effort to protect our declining gold stock.

Floating International Exchange Rates. Suspension of dollar convertibility in the fall of 1971 was a monumental milepost in the deteriorating United States international monetary situation. At the same time an equally significant event was that of allowing the dollar to "float" in relation to its exchange rate with other currencies of the world. Under the previous rules of the International Monetary Fund a nation was to alter the established (or pegged) exchange ratio with other currencies only with the Fund's approval. The arguments for and against flexible exchange rates had been debated in academic circles for a dozen years. Under flexible exchange rates, it was contended, supply and demand would establish appropriate exchange rates between nations, and cost and price structures as well as changing monetary policy would be reflected in such supply and demand relationships.

One of the principal objections to flexibility in exchange rates is the possibility of wide swings in exchange rates in response to changes in supply and demand with a resulting uncertainty in international trade. After only four months of floating exchange rates, this concern for international monetary stability resulted in a meeting of a group of ten representatives of central banks of leading industrial nations at the Smithsonian Institution in Washington in December, 1971. Out of

---

[2]The United Nations Monetary and Financial Conference, meeting at Bretton Woods, New Hampshire, in the summer of 1944, proposed the establishment of the International Monetary Fund and the International Bank for Reconstruction and Development (The World Bank). The International Monetary Fund attempts to provide for balanced growth of international trade and exchange stability. The "World Bank," in contrast, promotes long-term capital loans between nations for productive purposes. Approximately 142 member nations make up the membership of these two organizations.

this so-called Smithsonian Agreement came a new alignment of fixed exchange rates. Major currencies were officially revalued against the dollar and the dollar was devalued in terms of gold. However, the Smithsonian Agreement became completely inoperative by March 1, 1973, and rather than attempt to establish another realignment of fixed exchange rates the leading industrial nations decided to again let their currencies float.

Recent Foreign Exchange Developments. The dollar remains the principal currency for international commercial and financial transactions. Because of this, both the United States and the rest of the world benefit from a strong and stable U.S. dollar. The strength and stability of the dollar depend directly on the ability of the United States to pursue noninflationary economic policies. In the late 1960s and the 1970s the United States failed to meet this objective. A continuing high and varying rate of inflation led to a dollar crisis in 1978, which, in turn, threatened the stability of international financial markets. As inflationary pressures were brought under control in 1982, the dollar rose against other major currencies to its highest level since the beginning of floating exchange rates in 1973. The renewed strength of the dollar provided some benefits to the U.S economy by reducing import prices and thus accelerating progress against inflation. On the other hand, the increasing strength of the dollar caused problems by decreasing the cost competitiveness of exported U.S. goods. It is hoped that inflationary pressures in the United States will remain under control in the long-term interests of a stable international medium of exchange.

QUESTIONS

1. Describe the circular nature of economic transactions.
2. Describe the circular flow of money in the total economy.
3. Identify and analyze various factors that may initiate an upswing in economic activity.
4. Discuss possible intensifying factors that may reinforce expansion in economic activity.
5. Discuss the factors that may lead to a downturn in economic activity.
6. Briefly describe the cumulative process during contraction and the factors that will lead to another upswing.
7. Identify and describe the two different approaches used to explain the relationship of monetary and fiscal policies to economic activity.
8. Discuss the two views concerning the relationship of unemployment rates to wages and prices.
9. Briefly indicate the problems facing the United States in its attempt to maintain international financial equilibrium.

10. The U.S. international balance of payments position is measured in terms of the current account balance. Describe the current account balance and indicate its major components. Also indicate developments in the current account balance during recent years.
11. Discuss the meaning of the capital account balance and identify its major components.
12. Considerable concern has been expressed about the lack of international monetary stability in recent years. In conjunction with this concern, describe some of the developments in terms of gold and floating exchange rates in relation to the U.S. dollar.
13. Discuss some of the recent foreign exchange developments as they relate to the United States and its recent balance of payments deficits. What seems to have caused the decline in the foreign exchange value of the U.S. dollar and its recently renewed strength?

SUGGESTED READINGS

Dauten, Carl A., and Lloyd M. Valentine. *Business Cycles and Forecasting.* 6th ed. Cincinnati: South-Western Publishing Co., 1983. Parts 2 and 3.

Hoehn, James G. "Back to Gold?" *Voice*, Federal Reserve Bank of Dallas (March, 1981), pp. 1–10.

Levi, Maurice. *International Finance.* New York: McGraw-Hill Book Company, Inc., 1983. Chapter 4.

Pearce, Douglas K. "Alternative Views of Exchange-Rate Determination." *Economic Review*, Federal Reserve Bank of Kansas City (February, 1983), pp. 16–30.

Prager, Jonas. *Fundamentals of Money, Banking, and Financial Institutions.* New York: Harper & Row, Publishers, Inc., 1982. Part 6.

Ritter, Lawrence S., and William L. Silber. *Principles of Money, Banking, and Financial Markets*, 4th ed. New York: Basic Books, Inc., Publishers, 1983. Chapter 6.

"Treasury and Federal Reserve Foreign Exchange Operations." *Federal Reserve Bulletin* (October, 1982), pp. 579–607.

25 Monetary and Fiscal Policy Efforts and Actions

Monetary and fiscal policies have been important factors in the economy since World War II. There has frequently been a difference of opinion about the types of policies to follow. This led to open disagreement for a time between the Treasury and the Board of Governors of the Federal Reserve System. Even after they reached an accord, opinion was still divided at times as to the proper course to follow. In order to understand the issues involved, it is necessary to look at the financing of World War II which, in the early postwar period, gave rise to the problems that created this divergence of viewpoints.

MONETARY POLICY DURING WORLD WAR II

When the international situation worsened in the spring of 1939, the Federal Reserve System took steps to meet any serious disturbances in the securities markets. The Open Market Committee authorized its executive committee to make large purchases of government securities to prevent disorderly conditions in the market. When war broke out later in the year, the System purchased almost a half billion dollars of government bonds and announced that all the federal reserve banks stood ready to make advances on government securities at par to both member and nonmember banks. These actions helped to maintain an orderly market in government securities.

Interest Rate Pattern

In order to meet the needs of the government for funds an agreement was made with the Treasury on a pattern of interest rates that would be maintained by Federal Reserve open market operations. It was decided to stabilize rates to keep down the cost of borrowing and also to remove an incentive to wait for higher rates later instead of buying bonds when funds were available.

The pattern agreed on was much the same as that prevailing during the depressed period of the thirties. The rate was fixed at ⅜ percent on 90-day bills, ⅞ percent on certificates of indebtedness, 2 percent on 8-year to 10-year bonds, and 2½ percent on the 15-year maturities.

Having agreed on this pattern for financing the war, the Federal Reserve System took steps to maintain such a pattern. To maintain the ⅜ percent rate on bills, the federal reserve banks announced that they would purchase any quantity of such bills offered in the market at a price necessary to maintain that rate. They also agreed to give the seller an option to repurchase the bills at the same rate. This, in effect, made bills as liquid as cash and enabled the banks to invest their excess reserves at ⅜ percent. This kept excess reserves in banks at a minimum. Rates on other securities were prevented from rising by open market purchases of securities of all issues in amounts large enough to keep the price at par or above. To help encourage bank participation in war financing, discount rates were set at 1 percent.

Federal Reserve System Bond Purchases

The process of maintaining rates forced the Reserve System to buy large quantities of short-term securities. The large volume of short-term securities issued by the Treasury also led to almost continuous refunding operations. To sell all of the securities needed required either interest rates high enough to meet the demands of the market or a continuous increase in the money supply. The latter course was followed as reserves were supplied by open market purchases, especially of short-maturity securities.

The details of this process are interesting since they show how the banking system was used to inflate the money supply. Many banks were designated as special depositories in which the Treasury kept war-loan accounts. Such a bank could pay for new issues of government securities purchased for its own account or for the account of its customers by crediting the war-loan account rather than transferring the funds to the federal reserve bank. These accounts were made exempt from reserve requirements and were not assessed for deposit insurance in order to encourage their use to the fullest extent. After this was done, a bank no longer needed additional reserves against deposits resulting from its own purchases of government securities. When its customers bought bonds, reserves were freed as the funds were shifted out of regular deposit accounts to reserve-free war-loan accounts. These excess reserves were used by the banks to buy government securities. As the government spent its funds, deposits were shifted from war-loan accounts to regular deposit accounts requiring reserves. To get the necessary reserves, banks sold securities, especially the short-term ones. These were bought by the Federal Reserve System to maintain the pattern of rates, and thus new reserves were created and the money supply increased.

This was a case of wartime money inflation just as definitely as the continental currency or greenback inflation, but the process was more complex and, hence, less generally understood. It is true that the Federal Reserve discouraged banks from participating unnecessarily in the absorption of government securities. As long as the pattern of interest rates made expansion of bank credit profitable, however, it was not unusual that many bonds were bought by the commercial banks and the Federal Reserve System when individuals and institutions found it desirable to dispose of them at premium.

POSTWAR MONETARY POLICY AND THE ACCORD OF 1951

It may seem in retrospect that at the end of World War II steps should have been taken to reduce the money supply or at least not to allow it to increase further. Many governmental officials were afraid to tighten credit, however, because of the fear of a major depression. It had taken the demands of all-out war to eliminate the persistent large-scale unemployment of the thirties. Now government spending was to be cut from $100 billion a year to $40 billion or even less. Predictions were common that as many as eight million would be unemployed in 1946.

The Economy after the War

The rapid reconversion from war production to consumer goods production, however, was almost as miraculous an achievement as the rapid buildup of production to meet the needs of war. Consumers had buying power and pent-up desires for goods from the wartime period and spent it on goods as fast as they were available. The government also failed to cut expenditures as fast or as far as some had predicted. As a result, there was no depression in the early postwar period.

Practically all economic controls were abandoned in 1946, however, and prices went up sharply through 1947 and until the fall of 1948. Price controls had held prices in check sufficiently so that wholesale prices rose from 79 to only 107 (1926 = 100) during the war. By early 1948, they had increased to 170.

Even though economic controls were abandoned quickly, monetary policies changed slowly. This was due in part to economic uncertainty and to fears of a postwar depression. The new situation in which government bonds dominated the market also led to cautious action as both the Federal Reserve System and the Treasury Department were working out policies under these changed conditions. There was also a reluctance to do anything that might unsettle the security markets since the large volume of government securities with short maturities called for frequent large refunding operations.

The action of Congress was also on the inflationary side. In 1948 taxes were cut sufficiently to increase the amount of money available for consumer spending by over $5 billion. Inflationary pressures were intense. To restrain these pressures somewhat, the Federal Reserve raised reserve requirements in 1948.

Inflationary pressures abated late in 1948 as the increase in government expenditures slowed down and as private borrowing for capital expansion and especially for increasing inventories decreased. There was a minor recession in business activity in 1949, but consumer expenditures did not decrease appreciably. To ease money conditions, reserve requirements were reduced in May and June of 1949 and again in August. This reduction in required reserves freed bank funds, and the demand for government bonds on the part of banks increased.

Bond prices rose, and yields on short-term securities fell. The Federal Reserve System moderated this adjustment by selling a part of its portfolio of securities.

When the Korean War started in June of 1950, the increased demand for goods led to renewed inflationary pressures. Government deficits were not the cause of price rises in the last half of 1950, since the Treasury had an excess of cash income over cash outgo in the last half of the year of almost a billion dollars. The explanation lies in private spending. Consumers, fearing the shortages of World War II, spent large sums on various types of durable and semidurable goods. Business also spent heavily for inventories and for capital investment. The annual rate of gross private domestic investment went up over $12 billion from the second to the fourth quarter of 1950.

Treasury-Federal Reserve Controversy

Under these conditions, reserve bank credit increased materially. The Board of Governors of the Federal Reserve System wanted to act to restrict expansion, but it could not so long as it felt obligated to support the bond market by buying all government securities at par or better. The Treasury wanted to follow a pattern of low rates as it did in World War II; and this, of course, required price-support operations, since interest rates would have gone up in a free market as the demand for funds increased.

The controversy between the Treasury and the Federal Reserve System developed into an open conflict in the summer of 1950, especially after the Reserve System had to engage in larger-scale open market operations to assure the success of some financing at a rate the market did not find attractive. When the Secretary of the Treasury stated in a speech in January, 1951, that the Treasury had not changed its position and was not willing to allow even fractional increases in interest rates, the controversy became acute. Not only Federal Reserve officials but the press and the members of Congress entered it. Such a situation could not last long, and the President appointed a committee to study ways and means to provide the necessary restraint on private credit expansion and at the same time to maintain stability in the market for government securities. Before this committee could report, however, an agreement between the Treasury and the Federal Reserve System was announced in March, 1951.

Basis of the Opposing Viewpoints

Before looking at this agreement, it is desirable to see the basis of the opposing viewpoints. Treasury officials were interested in keeping interest rates on the debt at a low level. They favored low rates not only to keep the cost of servicing the debt at a minimum but also from a belief that low interest rates were necessary to keep investment in plant, equipment, housing, local public works, and the like at high levels. The Treasury also emphasized orderly conditions in the bond markets since stable interest rates were as important for debt management as low interest rates. The Treasury officials believed that the emergency arising out of the Korean War should be met by direct controls such as material allocation, rationing, and price controls.

Federal Reserve officials felt that in the absence of all-out war such controls were unnecessary if proper monetary and fiscal policies were followed. They believed that if the government kept cash outgo and income reasonably in balance, monetary controls would be sufficient to prevent inflation. Such a course would also prevent the building up of idle funds by consumers as was done during World War II, causing inflationary pressures when controls were taken off.

The Accord

The accord that was announced in March, 1951, was designed to check credit expansion without the use of direct controls. The accord returned to the Federal Reserve the power to use open market operations as an instrument of monetary policy. After this time government bonds were no longer automatically bought in the market by the Federal Reserve whenever their prices began to fall. The Federal Reserve did not stay out of the market completely but continued to buy and sell some securities so as to maintain an orderly market. For the first time since the beginning of World War II, as the private demand for funds increased, interest rates rose and long-term securities prices fell.

MONETARY AND FISCAL POLICIES DURING THE 1950s AND 1960s

The accord of 1951 marked the beginning of an era in which monetary policy became an independent force in the management of the economy. By releasing the restrictions that had impaired the central bank's use of open market operations, the accord restored the Federal Reserve's use of all its instruments of monetary control. Although it proceeded cautiously at first, the Federal Reserve had clearly asserted its independence from the Treasury. Since then, the primary responsibilities for monetary and fiscal policies have resided in different decision-making bodies.

The following two decades were relatively placid ones for the United States economy. This provided the opportunity for the increasing use of economic policy to manage the economy. Both fiscal policy and monetary policy were used in attempts to stabilize the economy by influencing the level of aggregate demand. The Federal Reserve described its role as "leaning against the wind," countercyclically easing credit when the economy was contracting and applying monetary restraint when inflationary pressures built up. Figure 25-1 indicates the rate of change in economic activity, as measured by real GNP, since 1950. Note that when the rate of change is below zero, the economy is contracting. Recessions or contractions lasting more than one quarter are indicated by shaded areas. It is instructive to refer to this figure during the following discussion in order to relate policy actions to the behavior of the economy.

Policies from the Accord to the 1957 Recession

The Federal Reserve acted to restrict credit in the early part of 1953. There was much debate about the correctness of monetary policies during this period. Many felt that credit was restricted too severely and that the Federal Reserve would be forced to return to a policy of fixed interest rates. Therefore, the Federal

Figure 25-1

Rate of Change in
Real GNP, 1950–1982

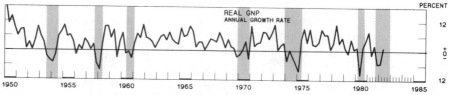

Shaded areas represent periods of business recessions.
SOURCE: *Historical Chart Book,* Board of Governors of the Federal Reserve System, 1982, p. 12,
and the National Bureau of Economic Research.

Reserve acted in early 1953 to convince investors and dealers in government securities that it was not undertaking to peg interest rates and especially not rates on intermediate- and long-term securities. It did so by announcing in April, 1953, that until further notice open market operations would be carried on only in the short-term area (this became known as the "bills-only" policy) where operations would have the least market impact. Operations in other markets would be undertaken only when disorderly conditions arose and then only to the extent needed to correct such conditions.

Since it was not the policy of the Federal Reserve authorities to force deflation, reserve requirements were lowered in the early summer to provide the funds needed to meet a sizable government deficit. As funds were needed for seasonal use, the Federal Reserve System bought government securities to provide such funds. When signs appeared during the summer that a business readjustment was in prospect, credit was eased still further. As business turned down somewhat in a minor recession, the Federal Reserve used all the instruments at its command to reverse the recession. The reserve banks reduced discount rates, the Board of Governors reduced member bank reserve requirements, and the Open Market Committee acted to maintain more than adequate reserves. Under this policy of "active ease," the free reserves of member banks rose materially.

This policy of active ease was followed during most of 1954. As a result, interest rates dropped to the lowest level in several years. This reduction did not prevent a slight decline in short-term business loans or consumer loans during the year, but it did help increase loans on real estate materially and, thus, activity in the home building field.

Business started to expand late in 1954 and continued upward in 1955. When it became apparent that a business boom was developing, steps were again taken to restrict credit. The Open Market Committee reduced the holdings of government securities. Discount rates were increased in April and May and again several times later in the year. Margin requirements on stock purchases were also raised, first to 60 percent and then to 70 percent. By the last quarter of the year, borrowing from the federal reserve banks exceeded reserves by $350 million. As credit became more and more restricted, interest rates rose, especially short-term and intermediate-term rates. There was little question raised about this reversal of policy from credit ease to credit restraint during most of 1955.

Beginning in 1956 and through 1957, wholesale prices and prices of consumer goods began to advance after having been more or less stable for several years. To hold inflationary forces in check, the Federal Reserve followed a policy of active restraint through open market operations and also by raising the discount rate on several occasions. Their policies were designed to curb the price rises and speculative excesses at the top of a cycle.

The inflation during this expansion period was of a somewhat different nature from that in the early postwar period. It did not result from a demand pull in the main but was a result of a cost push and primarily a wage push. This made traditional tools of monetary policy less effective that they would have been against inflation of the more usual type. In trying to stem this type of inflation by the use of its regular monetary instruments, the Federal Reserve was forced to use more active restraint than many felt was in the best interest of the economy. Even with such restraint it was impossible to halt inflation completely, and a significant rise in prices took place. Federal Reserve policy during the whole period of expansion was marked by an independence from the policies and actions of the Treasury. It was also carried on without regard to criticism that was at times vociferous in the business community and in Congress.

In the late fall of 1957 business began to decline, and Federal Reserve policy shifted from restraining credit to making credit easier and cheaper to obtain. The policy was applied cautiously, however, since price rises continued in the early stages of the downturn.

Policies from 1958 to Mid-1965

The recession which began in 1957 was a short one, and by late spring of 1958 the economy was again moving forward. By late summer the Federal Reserve began to restrict credit expansion and continued to do so in the first half of 1959 when it appeared for a time that a real boom would develop. The economy suffered a severe setback when the longest steel strike on record began shortly after midyear. When the strike ended in November, there was a new surge of economic activity, and the economy reached new highs. In the second half of 1960, a fourth postwar recession began, but it was also short and mild. The Federal Reserve relaxed pressures on the money supply early in 1960, and again in the second half of 1961. Monetary policy remained expansionary throughout the period until mid-1965.

Federal Reserve policy in the period from 1958 to 1963 was governed by the changing nature of economic developments. Inflation was no longer the major economic problem, at least not in the short run. All basic commodities were in good supply, and business and consumers had a good stock of durable goods. Excess capacity existed in many industrial fields, and labor was not fully utilized. The wholesale price level in the spring of 1965 stood at about the same level as in 1958, and consumer prices had increased only about one percent a year during this period. Part of this small increase was probably spurious since the consumer price index cannot accurately measure short-run changes in the quality of goods and services.

Two major factors governed Federal Reserve policy during this period and especially after 1960. The first was the recurring deficits in the United States balance of payments, and the second was the problem of underutilization of resources and especially the problem of unemployment. The United States had a sizable deficit in its balance of payments in each year during this period. In 1960 this problem was aggravated by a substantial flow of short-term funds from the United States to foreign money centers. This outflow was due, in part at least, to lower interest rates here than abroad. Interest rates had dropped here as a result of the policy of monetary ease to combat the recession.

This situation presented a dilemma for Federal Reserve policymakers. If they continued to buy Treasury bills, they might drive short-term interest rates so low as to encourage a greater outflow of funds. But if no additional funds were provided to the banking system, the Federal Reserve could not make its maximum contribution to stimulating the domestic economy. This led the Federal Reserve in late October, 1960, to provide additional reserves to stimulate the economy by buying certificates, notes, and bonds maturing within 15 months instead of buying Treasury bills. In 1961 the Federal Reserve initiated "operation twist" activities and essentially abandoned the "bills-only" policy (since then a "bills-preferable" or "bills-usually" policy has been employed). Operation twist involved purchasing longer-term Treasury securities with some selling of Treasury bills by the Federal Reserve in an attempt to keep long-term rates up to help solve the balance of payments problem.

The second major influence on Federal Reserve policy was the problem of unemployment and underutilization of other resources, especially capital equipment in many industries. The problem was more than a cyclical one since, as industrial output increased during this period, the number of jobs declined. Increased technology was replacing people with machines at a faster rate than the economy was growing to absorb them. Monetary policy alone could not solve this problem, and the situation was complicated by the balance of payments problem. This problem cannot be solved only by stimulating growth, even though this is essential; it requires retraining and upgrading of large segments of the labor force. Therefore, the Federal Reserve kept credit relatively easy but did not flood the banking system with reserves since to do so would have led to renewed inflation. Fiscal policy was also used to expand the level of economic activity during this period. In 1962 the investment tax credit was enacted, and depreciation guidelines were liberalized to stimulate investment expenditures. In early 1964 personal and corporate income taxes were cut significantly, part of the cut becoming effective in 1964 and part in 1965. In response to expansionary monetary and fiscal policies during this period, real gross national product rose at an average rate somewhat over 5 percent per year, while prices rose only a little over one percent. Unemployment dropped gradually, but was still 4.5 percent of the labor force in 1965.

The Vietnam War to the End of 1969

In mid-1965 the economy entered a new period of inflationary pressures due to increased military spending resulting from the escalation of the war in Vietnam. These expenditures, added to rising expenditures for plant and equipment and to increased spending for inventories, led to greatly increased demands for funds, to labor shortages, and to price increases. The Federal Reserve took steps to restrict bank credit expansion, and interest rates moved up. Since little was done to impose fiscal restraint, the burden of restraining inflation fell on monetary policy. Monetary policy became progressively tighter during the first half of 1966, and interest rates reached their highest levels in forty years. Savings which normally were deposited in savings and loan associations and mutual savings banks were, to a large extent, invested directly into money market securities which paid a higher rate; as a result, the mortgage market was seriously short of funds. Residential construction was cut sharply and some unemployment developed in the construction field. This period has been referred to as the period of the "credit crunch."

There were some signs in the fall that the overheated economy was beginning to cool off, but prices continued to rise. In October, 1966, the investment tax credit was suspended to help restrict expansion of plant and equipment expenditures. Economic activity began to moderate and GNP remained about level during the first quarter of 1967 and rose little during the second quarter, and industrial production dropped somewhat. Monetary policy became progressively easier beginning in November, 1966, and fiscal policy also played a counter-cyclical role in 1967 when funds that had been withheld from the highway program were released. The investment tax credit was reinstated, more mortgage funds were made available through FNMA, and veterans' insurance dividend payments were speeded up. There was a very sharp recovery in economic activity in the second half of 1967. Monetary policy remained relatively easy until late in the year when a move was made to moderate restraint to help restrain price advances.

Inflationary pressures became greater in 1968 due to increased private spending but primarily due to greatly increased federal government expenditures, which resulted in a deficit in excess of $25 billion in the federal budget in fiscal 1968. The President asked for a surtax to be added to personal and corporate income taxes in the summer of 1967, but Congress took no action until June, 1968. At this time a 10 percent surtax was enacted and a ceiling was placed on federal government expenditures. There was a general feeling that this fiscal action would lead to a substantial reduction in economic activity, and monetary policy was eased after midyear to cushion the blow. The economy continued to expand rapidly, however, and prices continued upward. The consumer price index rose over 5 percent during 1968. Beginning in December, 1968, the Federal Reserve again moved to a policy of active restraint since it was now apparent that fiscal policy was having little, if any, restraining effect on economic activity.

Inflation continued in 1969 at an accelerated rate. Wholesale prices rose sharply in the first quarter, and the consumer price index rose at its sharpest level in years. This renewed inflation was not due primarily to federal government spending, since the budget for fiscal 1969 showed a small surplus. But business expenditures on new plant and equipment were up sharply; and private spending, in general, continued to increase rapidly. By midyear the Federal Reserve was following a policy of severe restraint on the money and credit markets, which in some respects was greater than the restraint in 1966. Interest rates rose to higher levels than in 1966 and in some cases were the highest since Civil War days. Capital spending was decreased somewhat from plans announced earlier in the year, but continued at very high levels. Credit for mortgage financing was again decreased and housing starts declined.

The economy suffered a period of recession beginning in late 1969 and continuing through almost all of 1970. This recession was to a large extent due to the restrictive credit policy followed in late 1968 and 1969 in an attempt to slow the rate of inflation. It appears in retrospect that monetary policy was too restrictive in 1966 and too easy in 1967. It should have been much more restrictive during most of 1968 when it was relaxed to partially cushion the effects of fiscal policy. As a result monetary policy had to be too restrictive in 1969 and the effects of this policy helped bring on a recession.

MONETARY AND FISCAL ACTIVITIES SINCE 1970

The situation at the end of the 1960s was an omen for the coming years. The demand management approach to monetary and fiscal policies had achieved satisfactory results in the preceding two decades when applied to either inflation or recession. But when both problems existed simultaneously, attacking either with the old tools would only make the other worse. The history of economic policies since 1970 is marked by a variety of attempts to deal with these and other problems faced by policymakers.

The First Half of the 1970s

The recession of 1969–1970 was unusually mild and recovery began near the end of 1970. The Federal Reserve had adopted a policy of credit ease to slow the 1970 decrease in economic activity and to stimulate recovery. Inflationary pressures were so strong, however, that prices continued to increase even during the recession. The economy entered a period of slow recovery in 1971 under the stimulus of a rapidly increasing money supply in the first half of the year. Prices moved up sharply, the consumer price index increasing by more than five percent during the year. To combat inflation, the President ordered a 90-day price freeze in mid-August and set up wage and price controls when the freeze ended. The goal was to cut price increases to an average of 2.5 percent per year while wages rose on an average by 5.5 percent. This was based on the assumption that average productivity in the economy would increase at a 3-percent rate per year. To help restrain prices, the growth rate of the money supply was cut materially after midyear.

The economy continued to have balance of payments problems which had persisted for several years. In order to correct what appeared to be a basic imbalance in the relationship of the dollar to major foreign currencies, the dollar was devalued in December of 1971 by 12 percent.

Recovery in economic activity accelerated in 1972 and by the end of the year real growth was increasing at a rapid rate. Consumer prices went up by only about 3.5 percent, the best year for price restraint since 1967. This was due in large measure to price and wage controls. Federal Reserve monetary policy was expansive in the early part of the year, but late in 1972 money growth was slowed due to renewed inflationary pressures.

These inflationary pressures continued and became greater in 1973, a year in which consumer prices increased some 9 percent. It looked early in the year as if 1973 might be a good year for the economy. American involvement in the Vietnam War ended early in the year. The dollar was devalued by 10 percent in February and was allowed to float against other currencies in March, and the balance-of-payments problem seemed to be on the way to solution as America again developed a surplus in its trade balance with the rest of the world. Price controls of a mandatory nature were replaced in January with more or less voluntary controls. The growth of Federal Reserve credit was slowed and the federal government had a surplus by the second quarter of the year.

However, economic activity increased at a rapid rate and demand in many fields was in excess of supply. The unemployment rate which was about 6 percent at the beginning of 1972 dropped below the 5 percent level in 1973. Price controls also led to dislocations in many sectors of the economy, thus adding to shortages in some areas. Prices moved up so rapidly that a new 60-day price freeze was put into effect in June, and at the end of this period prices were again frozen but were allowed to be increased for the exact amount of higher costs. Provisions were made for decontrol on an industry-by-industry basis.

The price situation got worse as the year progressed, for several reasons. There were poor crops in many parts of the world, which raised the prices of food products. Large amounts of wheat were sold to Russia and China and this led to rapid increases in grain prices. In October another Arab-Israeli War broke out, but it was of short duration. The Arabs, however, in order to put pressure on the United States and other countries to support their cause put an embargo on oil shipments and raised oil prices. The embargo was lifted after a time but prices were raised to several times their prewar levels. As the demand for credit remained high, the supply of credit was restricted, and investors feared continued inflation as interest rates reached unprecedented levels.

High interest rates and tighter credit would probably have led to some slowing in economic activity in 1974; but the oil crisis compounded the problem since it affected production in many industries based on petroleum products. The gasoline shortage also led to reduced automobile sales, especially of full-sized cars. High interest rates led to a major decrease in residential construction and slowed some other plans for expansion.

Price controls were removed in April, not because inflation was under control, but because of the widespread belief that controls were a failure. Prices moved up after decontrol and price pressures intensified when the Midwest farm belt was hit by a severe drought. By summer, prices were increasing at a faster rate than at almost any time since World War I days and interest rates reached new historic highs. The economy suffered a decline in real growth and was in a deep recession during 1974. Interest rates peaked at record highs and inflation rates reached double-digit levels also during the 1974 economic downturn.

From the End of 1974 to 1979

Unemployment levels which were under 5 percent in 1973 reached above 9 percent in 1975 before they started to drop as the economy began recovering. Fiscal policy moved to stimulate the economy in 1975. Corporate income taxes were reduced and the investment tax credit was increased from 7 percent to 10 percent. In addition, individuals received certain tax cuts and a rebate on some of their 1974 taxes. The result of these tax cuts and increased government spending was a substantial deficit budget in 1975.

Monetary policy also became somewhat easier during 1975. The Federal Reserve, which allowed the money stock to increase only at a 3.4 percent rate between the second quarter of 1974 and the first quarter of 1975, began increasing the money stock at a rate in excess of 5 percent.

Fiscal policy continued to stimulate the economy in 1976. The Tax Reform Act of 1976 was passed by Congress and provided tax credits for individuals and extended the corporate income tax changes enacted in 1975. In 1977, the Tax Reduction and Simplification Act extended for one year the temporary provisions passed in the 1976 Act. This legislation was followed by the Revenue Act of 1978 which reduced capital gains tax rates for individuals, liberalized investment tax credits, and reduced corporate income tax rates. The results of these various income tax policies, along with U.S. government spending programs, produced fiscal year budget deficits of $66.0 billion in 1976, $45 billion in 1977, and $49 billion in 1978.

The Federal Reserve also stimulated the U.S. economy by increasing the money stock at an 8 percent rate between the third quarter of 1976 and the third quarter of 1978. As a result of these stimulative monetary and fiscal policies, inflation rates began accelerating during 1978, economic activity continued to grow, and the unemployment rate fell below 6 percent. However, as we discussed in Chapter 24, the relatively greater rate of U.S. economic expansion resulted in imports exceeding exports and produced very large current-account deficits in the U.S. balance of payments in 1977 and 1978. These deficits, coupled with an accelerating U.S. inflation rate relative to the rates in many other major countries, also resulted in a very large reduction in the exchange rate value of the U.S. dollar in 1978, 1979, and 1980.

By the latter part of 1978, the Federal Reserve had moved to a much tighter monetary policy and the Federal Reserve and U.S. Treasury were attempting to support the U.S. dollar in foreign exchange markets. The Carter administration also was proposing less stimulative fiscal policy in the form of smaller budget deficits through a reduction in government spending. As the United States entered 1979, growth in economic activity continued while inflation and interest rates returned to high levels.

New Directions for the 1980s

As indicated in Chapter 23, the Federal Reserve System in October, 1979, abandoned its long-standing efforts to control interest rates by monetary accommodation. Emphasis was placed on monetary growth control as opposed to interest rate control. The vigor of this approach not only reduced interest rates but also precipitated a brief recession. The real Gross National Product declined at a rapid rate in the second quarter of 1980 but advanced rapidly thereafter as a result of a quick reversal of restrictive monetary control. Both interest rates and prices increased to record levels. Figure 25-2 reflects a decline in Gross National Product in early 1980 as measured in both current and 1972 dollars. It should be recalled that the difference between the growth rates of these two Gross National Product measures reflects inflation as measured by the Gross National Product price deflator.

The redirection of economic policy of the new Administration coming into power in 1981 attempted to increase aggregate supply by promoting economic

Figure 25-2

Gross National Product

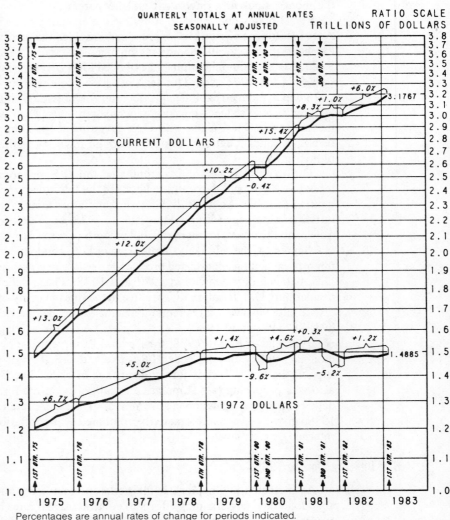

Percentages are annual rates of change for periods indicated.
SOURCE: *National Economic Trends,* Federal Reserve Bank of St. Louis, April, 1983, p. 13, and U.S. Department of Commerce.

growth and efficiency. Inflation was to be held in check by monetary restraint, and tax reductions were intended to stimulate investment and production. The expected stimulative effects of the tax cuts were not immediately felt, but the Federal Reserve substantially reduced the rate of growth of the money supply relative to the record high rate of growth in late 1980. This monetary restraint reduced inflation and short-term interest rates but also influenced the decline in economic activity in late 1981. As reflected in Figure 25-2, real output fell at an annual rate of 5.2 percent in the final quarter of 1981. The Administration stated its belief that this recession would be over by the second quarter of 1982.[1] Such was not the case. The recovery did not begin until much later in the year, by which time the unemployment rate had surged to nearly 11 percent, as indicated in Figure 25-3. The effects of the recession, the reduced tax rates, and the failure of the government to reduce its expenditures combined to produce enormous federal budget deficits.

Although the substantial decline in the rate of growth of the money supply was the principal contributor to the decline in economic activity, this decline was compounded by a marked reduction in the velocity of money. The decline in velocity was the largest since 1959, the earliest year for which the Federal Reserve

Figure 25-3
Unemployment Rate

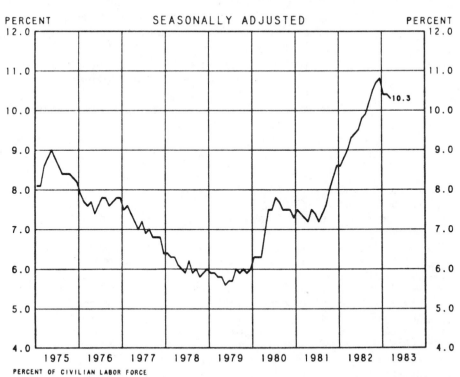

SOURCE: *National Economic Trends*, Federal Reserve Bank of St. Louis, April 1983, p. 3, and U.S. Department of Labor.

---

[1] *Economic Report of the President* (Washington, D.C.: Government Printing Office, 1982), p. 25.

System has published data on currently defined monetary aggregates. The causes of this decline in velocity are still not completely known, but it appears that major changes in asset demands of individuals and businesses played an important role. The introduction of nationwide interest-bearing negotiable order of withdrawal accounts and the increasing popularity of money market funds offer a partial explanation. The attractive yields on these investments apparently induced savings that otherwise would have been spent. The authorities had not anticipated such a decline in velocity and were not inclined to increase the money supply to offset it for fear of creating excessive liquidity and a return to high interest rates and prices.

While economic activity had advanced in early 1983, and inflation had not yet reawakened, several disturbing and seemingly intractable problems remained. First, the substantial level of excess business productive capacity inhibited investment in plant and equipment. Furthermore, although nominal interest rates had decreased dramatically, so too had inflationary pressures. The real interest rate as measured by the difference between nominal interest rates and the rate of price inflation therefore remained high. Since it is on the basis of real interest rates that business investment decisions are made, this further inhibited any resurgence of capital investment. The failure of nominal rates to decline further was attributed to the expectation of a return to price inflation and high interest rates. This expectation was buttressed by the recent increases in the money supply and the prospect of record high budgetary deficits. The monetary aggregates expanded rapidly, with both M1 and M2 growing at about a 15 percent rate over an eight-month period beginning in July of 1982, compared to rates of 4.6 and 9.1 percent, respectively, over the previous 15 months. This increase in the money supply undoubtedly contributed to the rebound in economic activity. Whether prices and interest rates would return to the high levels of recent years remained to be seen.

QUESTIONS

1. Describe the interest rate pattern the Federal Reserve System and the Treasury agreed on for financing World War II. How was this pattern maintained?

2. Describe the process by which bond sales led to credit creation and expansion of the money supply during World War II.

3. Describe the economic and financial situation in the immediate post-World War II period. What was the role of monetary policy in this period?

4. Describe the Treasury-Federal Reserve controversy during the Korean War. Discuss the opposing viewpoints and indicate the nature of the accord that was reached.

5. Briefly describe the monetary policies followed by the Federal Reserve System during 1953 and 1954. Also indicate how Federal Reserve policy was conducted during the prosperity period from late 1954 to late 1957.

6. How did Federal Reserve policy in the 1958–1963 period differ from that in 1954–1957? Why?

7. Review monetary and fiscal policy during the period from mid-1965 to the 1969–1970 recession. Evaluate policy decisions during this period.

8. Briefly describe the economic developments during the 1971–1973 expansionary period. Also, indicate the factors that contributed to the severity of the economic downturn during 1974 and early 1975.

9. Tax legislation in the years 1975, 1976, 1977, and 1978 provided both a stimulus for the economy and an increase in the budgetary deficit. Describe the nature of this tax legislation.

10. The recession of early 1980 is reported to have been one of the shortest on record. How do you account for its brevity?

11. Describe the nature and principal cause of the recession starting in 1981.

12. Although price inflation had been brought to a very low level in 1983, real interest rates remained very high. Explain.

SUGGESTED READINGS

Batten, Dallas S., and James E Kamphoefner. "The Strong U.S. Dollar: A Dilemma for Foreign Monetary Authorities." *Review*, Federal Reserve Bank of St. Louis (August/September, 1982), pp. 3–12.

Bedford, Margaret E. "The Federal Reserve and the Government Securities Market." *Economic Review,* Federal Reserve Bank of Kansas City (April, 1978), pp. 15–31.

Bowsher, Norman N. "The Early 1960s: A Guide to the Late 1970s." *Review*, Federal Reserve Bank of St. Louis (October, 1977), pp. 12–18.

Carlson, Keith M. "The Mix of Monetary and Fiscal Policies: Conventional Wisdom vs. Empirical Reality," *Review,* Federal Reserve Bank of St. Louis (October, 1982), pp. 7–21.

Ritter, Lawrence S., and William L. Silber. *Principles of Money, Banking, and Financial Markets,* 4th ed. New York: Basic Books, Inc., Publishers, 1983. Chapter 6.

Webb, Roy H. "Interest Rates and Federal Deficits," *Economic Review,* Federal Reserve Bank of Richmond (July/August, 1982), pp. 16–21.

Wood, John H. "Interest Rates and Inflation: An Old Unexplained Relationship," *Economic Review,* Federal Reserve Bank of Dallas (January, 1983), pp. 11–23.

APPENDIX

Table 1
Future Value of $1 (FVIF)

Year	1%	2%	3%	4%	5%	6%	7%	8%	9%	10%	12%	14%	15%	16%	18%	20%	25%	30%
1	1.010	1.020	1.030	1.040	1.050	1.060	1.070	1.080	1.090	1.100	1.120	1.140	1.150	1.160	1.180	1.200	1.250	1.300
2	1.020	1.040	1.061	1.082	1.102	1.124	1.145	1.166	1.188	1.210	1.254	1.300	1.322	1.346	1.392	1.440	1.563	1.690
3	1.030	1.061	1.093	1.125	1.158	1.191	1.225	1.260	1.295	1.331	1.405	1.482	1.521	1.561	1.643	1.728	1.953	2.197
4	1.041	1.082	1.126	1.170	1.216	1.262	1.311	1.360	1.412	1.464	1.574	1.689	1.749	1.811	1.939	2.074	2.441	2.856
5	1.051	1.104	1.159	1.217	1.276	1.338	1.403	1.469	1.539	1.611	1.762	1.925	2.011	2.100	2.288	2.488	3.052	3.713
6	1.062	1.126	1.194	1.265	1.340	1.419	1.501	1.587	1.677	1.772	1.974	2.195	2.313	2.436	2.700	2.986	3.815	4.827
7	1.072	1.149	1.230	1.316	1.407	1.504	1.606	1.714	1.828	1.949	2.211	2.502	2.660	2.826	3.185	3.583	4.768	6.276
8	1.083	1.172	1.267	1.369	1.477	1.594	1.718	1.851	1.993	2.144	2.476	2.853	3.059	3.278	3.759	4.300	5.960	8.157
9	1.094	1.195	1.305	1.423	1.551	1.689	1.838	1.999	2.172	2.358	2.773	3.252	3.518	3.803	4.435	5.160	7.451	10.604
10	1.105	1.219	1.344	1.480	1.629	1.791	1.967	2.159	2.367	2.594	3.106	3.707	4.046	4.411	5.234	6.192	9.313	13.786
11	1.116	1.243	1.384	1.539	1.710	1.898	2.105	2.332	2.580	2.853	3.479	4.226	4.652	5.117	6.176	7.430	11.642	17.922
12	1.127	1.268	1.426	1.601	1.796	2.012	2.252	2.518	2.813	3.138	3.896	4.818	5.350	5.936	7.288	8.916	14.552	23.298
13	1.138	1.294	1.469	1.665	1.886	2.133	2.410	2.720	3.066	3.452	4.363	5.492	6.153	6.886	8.599	10.699	18.190	30.288
14	1.149	1.319	1.513	1.732	1.980	2.261	2.579	2.937	3.342	3.797	4.887	6.261	7.076	7.988	10.147	12.839	22.737	39.374
15	1.161	1.346	1.558	1.801	2.079	2.397	2.759	3.172	3.642	4.177	5.474	7.138	8.137	9.266	11.974	15.407	28.422	51.186
16	1.173	1.373	1.605	1.873	2.183	2.540	2.952	3.426	3.970	4.595	6.130	8.137	9.358	10.748	14.129	18.488	35.527	66.542
17	1.184	1.400	1.653	1.948	2.292	2.693	3.159	3.700	4.328	5.054	6.866	9.276	10.761	12.468	16.672	22.186	44.409	86.504
18	1.196	1.428	1.702	2.026	2.407	2.854	3.380	3.996	4.717	5.560	7.690	10.575	12.375	14.463	19.673	26.623	55.511	112.46
19	1.208	1.457	1.754	2.107	2.527	3.026	3.617	4.316	5.142	6.116	8.613	12.056	14.232	16.777	23.214	31.948	69.389	146.19
20	1.220	1.486	1.806	2.191	2.653	3.207	3.870	4.661	5.604	6.728	9.646	13.743	16.367	19.461	27.393	38.338	86.736	190.05
25	1.282	1.641	2.094	2.666	3.386	4.292	5.427	6.848	8.623	10.835	17.000	26.462	32.919	40.874	62.669	95.396	264.70	705.64
30	1.348	1.811	2.427	3.243	4.322	5.743	7.612	10.063	13.268	17.449	29.960	50.950	66.212	85.850	143.371	237.376	807.79	2620.00

Note: The basic equation for finding the future value interest factor (FVIF) is:

$$FVIF_{i,n} = (1 + i)^n$$

where i is the interest rate and n is the number of periods in years.

Table 2
Future Value of a $1 Ordinary Annuity (FVIFA)

Year	1%	2%	3%	4%	5%	6%	7%	8%	9%	10%	12%	14%
1	1.000	1.000	1.000	1.000	1.000	1.000	1.000	1.000	1.000	1.000	1.000	1.000
2	2.010	2.020	2.030	2.040	2.050	2.060	2.070	2.080	2.090	2.100	2.120	2.140
3	3.030	3.060	3.091	3.122	3.152	3.184	3.215	3.246	3.278	3.310	3.374	3.440
4	4.060	4.122	4.184	4.246	4.310	4.375	4.440	4.506	4.573	4.641	4.779	4.921
5	5.101	5.204	5.309	5.416	5.526	5.637	5.751	5.867	5.985	6.105	6.353	6.610
6	6.152	6.308	6.468	6.633	6.802	6.975	7.153	7.336	7.523	7.716	8.115	8.536
7	7.214	7.434	7.662	7.898	8.142	8.394	8.654	8.923	9.200	9.487	10.089	10.730
8	8.286	8.583	8.892	9.214	9.549	9.897	10.260	10.637	11.028	11.436	12.300	13.233
9	9.369	9.755	10.159	10.583	11.027	11.491	11.978	12.488	13.021	13.579	14.776	16.085
10	10.462	10.950	11.464	12.006	12.578	13.181	13.816	14.487	15.193	15.937	17.549	19.337
11	11.567	12.169	12.808	13.486	14.207	14.972	15.784	16.645	17.560	18.531	20.655	23.044
12	12.683	13.412	14.192	15.026	15.917	16.870	17.888	18.977	20.141	21.384	24.133	27.271
13	13.809	14.680	15.618	16.627	17.713	18.882	20.141	21.495	22.953	24.523	28.029	32.089
14	14.947	15.974	17.086	18.292	19.599	21.015	22.550	24.215	26.019	27.975	32.393	37.581
15	16.097	17.293	18.599	20.024	21.579	23.276	25.129	27.152	29.361	31.772	37.280	43.842
16	17.258	18.639	20.157	21.825	23.657	25.673	27.888	30.324	33.003	35.950	42.753	50.980
17	18.430	20.012	21.762	23.698	25.840	28.213	30.840	33.750	36.974	40.545	48.884	59.118
18	19.615	21.412	23.414	25.645	28.132	30.906	33.999	37.450	41.301	45.599	55.750	68.394
19	20.811	22.841	25.117	27.671	30.539	33.760	37.379	41.466	46.018	51.159	63.440	78.969
20	22.019	24.297	26.870	29.778	33.066	36.786	40.995	45.762	51.160	57.275	72.052	91.025
25	28.243	32.030	36.459	41.646	47.727	54.865	63.249	73.106	84.701	98.347	133.334	181.871
30	34.785	40.568	47.575	56.805	66.439	79.058	94.461	113.283	136.308	164.494	241.333	356.787

Note: the basic equation for finding the future value interest factor of an ordinary annuity (FVIFA) is:

$$FVIFA_{i,n} = \sum_{t=1}^{n} (1 + i)^{t-1} = \frac{(1 + i)^n - 1}{i}$$

where i is the interest rate and n is the number of periods in years.

(continued)

Table 2
Future Value of a $1 Ordinary Annuity (FVIFA) (continued)

Year	16%	18%	20%	25%	30%
1	1.000	1.000	1.000	1.000	1.000
2	2.160	2.180	2.200	2.250	2.300
3	3.506	3.572	3.640	3.813	3.990
4	5.066	5.215	5.368	5.766	6.187
5	6.877	7.154	7.442	8.207	9.043
6	8.977	9.442	9.930	11.259	12.756
7	11.414	12.142	12.916	15.073	17.583
8	14.240	15.327	16.499	19.842	23.858
9	17.518	19.086	20.799	25.802	32.015
10	21.321	23.521	25.959	33.253	42.619
11	25.733	28.755	32.150	42.566	56.405
12	30.850	34.931	39.580	54.208	74.327
13	36.786	42.219	48.497	68.760	97.625
14	43.672	50.818	59.196	86.949	127.91
15	51.660	60.965	72.035	109.69	167.29
16	60.925	72.939	87.442	138.11	218.47
17	71.673	87.068	105.931	173.64	285.01
18	84.141	103.740	128.117	218.05	371.52
19	98.603	123.414	154.740	273.56	483.97
20	115.380	146.628	186.688	342.95	630.17
25	249.214	342.603	471.981	1054.80	2348.80
30	530.312	790.948	1181.882	3227.20	8730.00

Future Value of a $1 Annuity Due (FVIFAD)

The future value interest factor of an annuity due (FVIFAD) may be found by using the following formula to convert FVIFA values found in Table 2:

$$FVIFAD_{i,n} = FVIFA_{i,n+1} - 1$$

where i is the interest rate and n is the number of periods in years.

Example: You are planning to deposit $100 at the beginning of each year for five years in a savings account that pays 7 percent. The value of this account at the end of the fifth year is $100 × FVIFAD_{i,n}$ where i is 7 percent and n is 5.

$$FVIFAD_{7\%,5} = FVIFA_{7\%,(5+1)} - 1$$

Table 2 gives the value of the FVIFA at 7 percent for six years as $FVIFA_{7\%,6} = 7.153$, so

$$FVIFAD_{7\%,5} = 7.153 - 1 = 6.153$$

Your account after five years will be worth

$$\$100 \times 6.153 = \$615.30$$

Table 3

Present Value of $1 (PVIF)

Year	1%	2%	3%	4%	5%	6%	7%	8%	9%	10%	12%	14%	15%	16%	18%	20%	25%	30%
1	.990	.980	.971	.962	.952	.943	.935	.926	.917	.909	.893	.877	.870	.862	.847	.833	.800	.769
2	.980	.961	.943	.925	.907	.890	.873	.857	.842	.826	.797	.769	.756	.743	.718	.694	.640	.592
3	.971	.942	.915	.889	.864	.840	.816	.794	.772	.751	.712	.675	.658	.641	.609	.579	.512	.455
4	.961	.924	.888	.855	.823	.792	.763	.735	.708	.683	.636	.592	.572	.552	.516	.482	.410	.350
5	.951	.906	.863	.822	.784	.747	.713	.681	.650	.621	.567	.519	.497	.476	.437	.402	.328	.269
6	.942	.888	.837	.790	.746	.705	.666	.630	.596	.564	.507	.456	.432	.410	.370	.335	.262	.207
7	.933	.871	.813	.760	.711	.665	.623	.583	.547	.513	.452	.400	.376	.354	.314	.279	.210	.159
8	.923	.853	.789	.731	.677	.627	.582	.540	.502	.467	.404	.351	.327	.305	.266	.233	.168	.123
9	.914	.837	.766	.703	.645	.592	.544	.500	.460	.424	.361	.308	.284	.263	.225	.194	.134	.094
10	.905	.820	.744	.676	.614	.558	.508	.463	.422	.386	.322	.270	.247	.227	.191	.162	.107	.073
11	.896	.804	.722	.650	.585	.527	.475	.429	.388	.350	.287	.237	.215	.195	.162	.135	.086	.056
12	.887	.788	.701	.625	.557	.497	.444	.397	.356	.319	.257	.208	.187	.168	.137	.112	.069	.043
13	.879	.773	.681	.601	.530	.469	.415	.368	.326	.290	.229	.182	.163	.145	.116	.093	.055	.033
14	.870	.758	.661	.577	.505	.442	.388	.340	.299	.263	.205	.160	.141	.125	.099	.078	.044	.025
15	.861	.743	.642	.555	.481	.417	.362	.315	.275	.239	.183	.140	.123	.108	.084	.065	.035	.020
16	.853	.728	.623	.534	.458	.394	.339	.292	.252	.218	.163	.123	.107	.093	.071	.054	.028	.015
17	.844	.714	.605	.513	.436	.371	.317	.270	.231	.198	.146	.108	.093	.080	.060	.045	.023	.012
18	.836	.700	.587	.494	.416	.350	.296	.250	.212	.180	.130	.095	.081	.069	.051	.038	.018	.009
19	.828	.686	.570	.475	.396	.331	.276	.232	.194	.164	.116	.083	.070	.060	.043	.031	.014	.007
20	.820	.673	.554	.456	.377	.312	.258	.215	.178	.149	.104	.073	.061	.051	.037	.026	.012	.005
25	.780	.610	.478	.375	.295	.233	.184	.146	.116	.092	.059	.038	.030	.024	.016	.010	.004	.001
30	.742	.552	.412	.308	.231	.174	.131	.099	.075	.057	.033	.020	.015	.012	.007	.004	.001	.000

Note: The basic equation for finding the present value interest factor (PVIF) is:

$$PVIF_{i,n} = \frac{1}{(1 + i)^n}$$

where i is the interest or discount rate and n is the number of periods in years.

Table 4

Present Value of a $1 Ordinary Annuity (PVIFA)

Year	1%	2%	3%	4%	5%	6%	7%	8%	9%	10%	12%	14%
1	0.990	0.980	0.971	0.962	0.952	0.943	0.935	0.926	0.917	0.909	0.893	0.877
2	1.970	1.942	1.913	1.886	1.859	1.833	1.808	1.783	1.759	1.736	1.690	1.647
3	2.941	2.884	2.829	2.775	2.723	2.673	2.624	2.577	2.531	2.487	2.402	2.322
4	3.902	3.808	3.717	3.630	3.546	3.465	3.387	3.312	3.240	3.170	3.037	2.914
5	4.853	4.713	4.580	4.452	4.329	4.212	4.100	3.993	3.890	3.791	3.605	3.433
6	5.795	5.601	5.417	5.242	5.076	4.917	4.767	4.623	4.486	4.355	4.111	3.889
7	6.728	6.472	6.230	6.002	5.786	5.582	5.389	5.206	5.033	4.868	4.564	4.288
8	7.652	7.325	7.020	6.733	6.463	6.210	5.971	5.747	5.535	5.335	4.968	4.639
9	8.566	8.162	7.786	7.435	7.108	6.802	6.515	6.247	5.995	5.759	5.328	4.946
10	9.471	8.983	8.530	8.111	7.722	7.360	7.024	6.710	6.418	6.145	5.650	5.216
11	10.368	9.787	9.253	8.760	8.306	7.887	7.499	7.139	6.805	6.495	5.938	5.453
12	11.255	10.575	9.954	9.385	8.863	8.384	7.943	7.536	7.161	6.814	6.194	5.660
13	12.134	11.348	10.635	9.986	9.394	8.853	8.358	7.904	7.487	7.103	6.424	5.842
14	13.004	12.106	11.296	10.563	9.899	9.295	8.745	8.244	7.786	7.367	6.628	6.002
15	13.865	12.849	11.938	11.118	10.380	9.712	9.108	8.559	8.061	7.606	6.811	6.142
16	14.718	13.578	12.561	11.652	10.838	10.106	9.447	8.851	8.313	7.824	6.974	6.265
17	15.562	14.292	13.166	12.166	11.274	10.477	9.763	9.122	8.544	8.022	7.120	5.373
18	16.398	14.992	13.754	12.659	11.690	10.828	10.059	9.372	8.756	8.201	7.250	6.467
19	17.226	15.678	14.324	13.134	12.085	11.158	10.336	9.604	8.950	8.365	7.366	6.550
20	18.046	16.351	14.877	13.590	12.462	11.470	10.594	9.818	9.129	8.514	7.469	6.623
25	22.023	19.523	17.413	15.622	14.094	12.783	11.654	10.675	9.823	9.077	7.843	6.873
30	25.808	22.397	19.600	17.292	15.372	13.765	12.409	11.258	10.274	9.427	8.055	7.003

(continued)

Note: The basic equation for finding the present value interest factor of an ordinary annuity (PVIFA) is:

$$PVIFA_{i,n} = \sum_{t=1}^{n} \frac{1}{(1+i)^t} = \frac{1 - \frac{1}{(1+i)^n}}{i}$$

where i is the interest or discount rate and n is the number of periods in years.

Table 4

Present Value of a $1 Ordinary Annuity (PVIFA) (continued)

Year	16%	18%	20%	25%	30%
1	0.862	0.847	0.833	.800	.769
2	1.605	1.566	1.528	1.440	1.361
3	2.246	2.174	2.106	1.952	1.816
4	2.798	2.690	2.589	2.362	2.166
5	3.274	3.127	2.991	2.689	2.436
6	3.685	3.498	3.326	2.951	2.643
7	4.039	3.812	3.605	3.161	2.802
8	4.344	4.078	3.837	3.329	2.925
9	4.607	4.303	4.031	3.463	3.019
10	4.833	4.494	4.193	3.571	3.092
11	5.029	4.656	4.327	3.656	3.147
12	5.197	4.793	4.439	3.725	3.190
13	5.342	4.910	4.533	3.780	3.223
14	5.468	5.008	4.611	3.824	3.249
15	5.575	5.092	4.675	3.859	3.268
16	5.668	5.162	4.730	3.887	3.283
17	5.749	5.222	4.775	3.910	3.295
18	5.818	5.273	4.812	3.928	3.304
19	5.877	5.316	4.843	3.942	3.311
20	5.929	5.353	4.870	3.954	3.316
25	6.097	5.467	4.948	3.985	3.329
30	6.177	5.517	4.979	3.995	3.332

Present Value of a $1 Annuity Due (PVIFAD)

The present value interest factor of an annuity due (PVIFAD) may be found by using the following formula to convert PVIFA values found in Table 4:

$$PVIFAD_{i,n} = PVIFA_{i,n-1} + 1$$

where i is the interest or discount rate and n is the number of periods in years.

Example: The present value of a ten year lease with annual payments of $1000, with the first payment due immediately and the remaining nine payments due at the beginning of each year, discounted at 9 percent rate, is $1000 × PVIFAD_{i,n} where i is 9 percent and n is 10.

$$PVIFAD_{9\%,10} = PVIFA_{9\%,(10-1)} + 1$$

Table 4 gives the value of the PVIFA at 9 percent and nine years as $PVIFA_{9\%,9} = 5.995$, so

$$PVIFAD_{9\%,10} = 5.995 + 1 = 6.995$$

The present value of the ten year lease discounted at 9 percent is $1000 × 6.995 = $6995.

GLOSSARY

Accelerator principle. A concept expressing the relationship between investment in real capital assets such as plant and equipment and demand for output from such assets. If demand for consumer goods is growing, new producer assets must be added to meet this new demand plus worn-out (depreciated) equipment must be replaced. This, in turn, leads to accelerated economic activity.

Accounts payable. Accounts arising primarily from the purchase of goods by a business on credit terms.

Accounts receivable. Accounts arising from the sale of products, merchandise, or services on credit and which reflect an oral promise of the customer to pay.

Accrued liabilities. Amounts owed but not yet paid for such items as wages and salaries, taxes, and interest on notes.

Acid-test ratio. A liquidity ratio that is calculated by dividing the residual of current assets minus inventories by the firm's current liabilities.

Advance refunding. A technique sometimes used by the United States Treasury in lengthening the average maturity of the national debt. Securities of extended maturities are offered to holders of government obligations before the specified maturity of the obligations.

Amortized loans. Loans on which the borrower agrees to make regular payments on principal as well as on interest.

Annuity. A constant or level cash flow amount in each time period.

Annuity insurance. Described as "insurance in reverse," and provides for the disposition of an estate through its systematic liquidation. The annuitant agrees to pay a stipulated sum of money to the insurance company, in return for a regular income from the company for a specified time, such as a number of years or for life.

Arbitrage. The simultaneous, or nearly simultaneous, purchasing, as of commodities, securities, or bills of exchange, in one market and selling in another where the price is higher. In international exchange, variations in quotations between countries at any time are quickly brought into alignment through the arbitrage activities of international financiers.

Asset utilization ratios. Financial ratios that show how well the firm uses its assets to support or generate sales.

Balance of payments. A summary of all international transactions including foreign investment, private and government grants, expenditures of the U.S. military forces overseas, and many other items in addition to the purchases and sales of goods and services.

Balance of trade. The net balance of exports and imports of goods and services and the single most important element in the balance of payments.

Balance sheet. The summary or report that shows the assets and the sources of financing of a business at a particular point in time. It reveals two broad categories of information: the properties owned by a business (assets); and the creditors' claims (liabilities) and the owners' equity in the business.

Bankers' acceptances. Instruments used to finance exports and imports arising from foreign trade and representing the unconditional obligation of the accepting or guaranteeing bank. These financial claims to wealth may be traded in secondary money markets.

Banker's sight draft (banker's check). A draft differing from the common bank check only in that it is drawn by one bank on another bank. As might be expected, there is also a banker's time draft which is payable at a specified future date.

Bank holding company. A company which directly

or indirectly owns, controls, or holds the power to vote 25 percent or more of the voting shares of each of two or more banks.

Bank term loan. A loan which differs from the usual bank business loan in that it has a maturity exceeding one year. Also, the term loan may require repayment of principal and interest in installments throughout the life of the loan.

Barter. The process of directly trading or exchanging goods and services without the use of money in such transactions.

Best-effort selling. An arrangement whereby the investment bankers make a best-effort to sell the securities of the issuing corporation, but they assume no risk for a possible failure of the securities issue.

Bid-and-asked price. The quotation which is made by a dealer making a market for a given security. The "bid" is that price the dealer is willing to pay for the securities and the "asked price" is the figure at which the dealer is willing to sell the security.

Bimetallic standard. A monetary standard based upon two metals such as silver and gold.

Blue-sky laws. State laws to protect investors from fraudulent security offerings.

Branch banks. Banking offices that are controlled by a single parent bank. One board of directors and one group of stockholders control the home office and the branches.

Business cycles. Economic activity has not grown at an even rate but has fluctuated between prosperity and recession or depression. These recurring fluctuations in economic activity have come to be known as "business cycles" even though they are not of equal intensity or equal length.

Business risks. Risks associated with the operation of the business itself and those from outside economic forces.

Business trust (also called Massachusetts trust). A trust which combines the advantage of limited liability with convenience in raising capital. Assets of the company are held by a trustee and the beneficiaries hold trust certificates. Profits are distributed to the holders of the trust certificates.

Call contract. An option to buy a security at a specified price during a specified period of time.

Capital account balance. Includes changes in foreign government and private investment in the United States. Netted against this would be similar U.S. government and private investments in foreign countries.

Capital formation. The creation of physical productive facilities such as buildings, tools, equipment, and roads.

Capital markets. Markets where longer-term (in excess of one year maturities) debt securities (notes and bonds) and instruments (mortgages) as well as corporate stocks are traded.

Capital notes. Long-term obligations issued by some commercial banks to supplement capital accounts. Such notes are issued as substitutes for common stock and are always subordinated to the claims of depositors. Although liabilities of the bank, no legal reserves are required against outstanding capital notes.

Casualty and surety insurance. Includes all forms of coverage not included as marine, fire, or life insurance. Examples would be automobile liability insurance and insurance protection against burglary or robbery.

Check. A written order to a depository institution to transfer money to the party who received the check or written order.

Closed-end mortgage. Prevents further sale of bonds using the same real property in contrast with the provisions in an open-end mortgage which allow continuing bond sales against the same mortgage.

Commercial finance companies. Organizations without bank charters that make loans to business firms by: advancing funds to business firms by discounting accounts receivable; making loans secured by chattel mortgages on machinery or liens on inventory; and financing deferred-payment sales of commercial and industrial equipment.

Commercial letter of credit. A written statement on the part of the bank to an individual or firm guaranteeing acceptance and payment of a draft up to a specified sum if presented to the bank in accordance with the terms of the commercial letter of credit.

Commercial paper. Short-term unsecured promissory notes of well-known business concerns with strong credit ratings.

Commercial paper houses. Organizations which purchase the promissory notes of reputable business organizations for the purposes of resale to other lenders (i.e., individuals and organizations desiring to invest in or hold commercial paper).

Commission brokers. The members of the securities exchanges that serve the public in effecting purchases and sales of securities on the exchanges.

Commodity standard. A monetary unit based on a fixed quantity of a group of commodities such as wheat, coffee, sugar, petroleum, and coal.

Common stock. Shares representing an ownership claim in the assets of a business corporation and a claim to the profits of the business that remain after the holders of all other classes of debt and equity instruments have received their stipulated returns. Also, the common stockholders vote to select the board of directors of a corporation.

Compensating balance. The portion of a loan that must be kept on deposit with the lending bank by the borrowing business.

Compounding. Interest earned each period plus the principal will be reinvested at the stated interest rate such that interest will be earned on interest as well as on the principal.

Conditional sales contract. An agreement which provides that the seller retain title to assets until the agreed purchase price has been paid.

Consumer credit. Credit used by consumers to help finance or refinance the purchase of goods and services for personal consumption. Its use to finance personal consumption distinguishes it from business credit used for production purposes.

Consumer finance companies. Organizations providing credit to consumers which were originally developed to provide aid in time of financial emergency.

Contractual savings. Savings accumulated on a regular schedule by prior agreement, such as pension fund contributions, life insurance premiums, or loan repayments.

Conventional mortgage loan. Amortized mortgage loans that are neither FHA-insured nor VA-guaranteed. Today, many of these loans are guaranteed or insured by private mortgage insurance companies.

Corporation. An artificial being that exists as a legal entity with limited stockholder liability and other advantages over other forms of business organizations.

Cost of capital. The combined rate of return neces-

sary for a firm to cover its cost of debt and equity funds.

Cost of goods sold. The costs associated with producing or manufacturing the products sold to produce the revenues shown on the income statement. These expenses are largely variable and reflect the cost of raw materials, labor, and overhead directly involved in producing the products that were sold.

Cost-push inflation. If costs are increased faster than productivity increases, as in the case of rising wages, businesses which have some discretion over prices will attempt to raise them in order to cover the increased costs. The result is wage-push or cost-push inflation.

Countercyclical policies. Any economic policy that attempts to stabilize economic activity by countering the current tendency of the economy; i.e., policies that stimulate the economy during recessions and restrain it during inflationary periods.

Credit bureaus. Organizations set up by local merchants and finance companies to serve as central exchanges for data on the credit extended to individuals.

Credit crunch. A period of "tight" money and a lack of loanable funds except at possibly very high interest rates. This occurs when the demand for money and available credit exceeds the available supply.

Credit money. Money which has a greater value than the value of the material out of which it is made.

Credit unions. Cooperative nonprofit organizations that provide their members with consumer credit. They are comprised of individuals who possess common bonds in terms of occupation, residential ties that are well-defined, or other forms of association such as church affiliation.

Cumulative preferred stock. Shares requiring that before common stock dividends may be paid, preferred dividends must be paid not only for the dividend period in question but also for all previous periods in which no preferred dividends were paid.

Current account balance. Shows the flow of income into and out of the United States during a specified time period. It is calculated by subtracting unilateral transfers from the goods and services balance.

Current assets. Cash and other assets (such as accounts receivable and inventory) of a business that may be reasonably expected to be converted into cash, sold, or used in the near future through the normal operations of the business.

Current liabilities. Business obligations that must be satisfied within a period of one year. They are the liabilities that usually are to be met out of current funds and operations of the business.

Current ratio. A relationship determined by dividing total current assets by total current liabilities.

Debenture bonds. Bonds which are dependent upon the general credit and strength of the corporation for their security. They represent no specific pledge of property, but rather their holders are classed as general creditors of the corporation.

Debt capital. Business funds obtained from creditors rather than from owners. Such capital may be obtained through direct negotiation with a lender or the sale of notes or bonds to many lenders.

Debt management. A Treasury function affecting economic conditions and money markets through the refunding of debt issues. Decisions with respect to advance refunding, types of securities to sell, interest rate patterns to use, and call provisions are involved in connection with debt management.

Debt ratio. Calculated as total liabilities divided by total assets.

Deed of trust. Used as security on a real property loan. It differs from a mortgage in that three parties, the beneficiary, the trustor, and the trustee, are involved.

Default. The failure to fulfill a contractual obligation when it comes due such as the failure to make interest and/or principal payments.

Default risk. The likelihood or probability that a bond issuer will fail to meet its interest or principal payment obligations.

Demand deposits. The checking accounts of individuals, businesses, and other organizations held at commercial banks.

Demand-pull inflation. This type of inflation occurs when the demand for goods and services exceeds the available supply of such goods and services.

Depreciation. The using up of some of the economic value of the plant and equipment. Depreciation is charged off against the original cost of plant and equipment.

Depreciation expense. An expense reflecting the reduction in the economic value of the firm's plant and equipment incurred by manufacturing the firm's products during the time period covered by the income statement.

Derivative deposits. Deposits that occur when reserves created from primary deposits are made available through bank loans to borrowers who leave them on deposit in order to write checks against the funds.

Devaluation. Action taken by the central bank of a nation to reduce the official exchange rate of its monetary unit relative to that of other nations.

Direct securities. Contracts between savers and borrowers themselves such as corporate stocks and bonds.

Disability income insurance. Insurance which provides protection against loss of income because of accident or sickness. Under such insurance, a person may receive weekly payments for total or partial disability.

Discount. A loan on which interest is paid in advance, i.e., the borrower receives only the discounted value of the loan, but repays the full face amount.

Discounting. The opposite of compounding whereby the focus is on finding the present value of cash flows that are to be received in future time periods by discounting or reducing them by a stated interest rate.

Disintermediation. The process whereby savings are withdrawn from thrift institutions and commercial banks and are channeled into alternative investments.

Dissaving. Liquidation of accumulated savings for consumption uses.

Documentary time draft. The time draft, in contrast with the sight draft, requires payment at a fixed or determinable future time. The documentary draft, in contrast with a "clean draft" is accompanied by an order bill of lading and such other papers as insurance receipts and consular invoices.

Draft (bill of exchange). An unconditional order in writing, signed by the person drawing it, requiring the person to whom it is addressed to pay on demand or at a fixed or determinable future time a sum certain in money to order or to bearer.

Electronic funds transfer systems. EFTS provide for the receiving and disbursing of funds electronically instead of through the use of checks.

Eleemosynary institutions. Nonprofit organizations such as educational institutions, charitable organizations, philanthropic institutions, hospitals, and religious bodies.

Eligible paper. Short-term promissory notes of commercial, industrial, and agricultural customers of banks, eligible for discounting with the federal reserve banks. Such paper may also be used as collateral against advances from the federal reserve banks, although in practice U.S. government and agency securities are generally used.

Endowment insurance. Insurance written for a specified number of years. If the insured person survives to the end of the stipulated period, the face amount of the policy is payable to the insured.

Equipment trust arrangement. A device providing for the transfer of title to the equipment by the seller to a trustee. The trustee, generally a trust company or a trust department of a commercial bank, holds title to the equipment but leases it to the business that is to make use of it.

Equity capital. The capital supplied by the owner of an enterprise such as a proprietorship, partnership, or business corporation.

Equity multiplier. Shows the extent to which a firm's assets are financed by borrowed funds by dividing total assets by owners' equity.

Equity of redemption. A mortgagor's right in equity to redeem property even though there has been a default on a mortgage loan against the property. Payment in full must take place within a time period specified by a decree of foreclosure.

Eurodollars. Deposits placed in foreign banks that remain denominated in U.S. dollars. A demand deposit in a United States bank becomes a Eurodollar when the holder of such a deposit transfers it to a foreign bank or an overseas branch of an American bank. After the transfer the foreign bank holds a claim against the U.S. bank, while the original deposit holder (possibly a business firm) now holds a Eurodollar deposit.

Excess reserves. The difference between the total reserves of the banking system and those required to be held at the federal reserve banks. These constitute the excess reserves available for credit expansion.

Exchange rate. The rate at which a given unit of foreign currency is quoted in terms of domestic currency and vice versa.

Expectations theory. Theory contending that the long-term interest rates at any point in time reflect the average of the prevailing short-term interest rates plus short-term rates expected in the future. Thus, over the long-run, short-term and long-term interest rates should be equal for securities that have comparable default risks.

Export-import bank. A bank authorized in 1934 which became an independent agency of the government in 1945. The purpose of the Bank is to aid in financing and to facilitate exports and imports between the United States and other countries. It is the only agency engaged solely in the financing of the foreign trade of the United States.

Factors. Organizations which engage in accounts receivable financing for business enterprises by purchasing the accounts outright and by assuming all credit risks.

Federal Deposit Insurance Corporation (FDIC). An agency which insures deposits and supervises member commercial banks.

Federal funds. Temporary excess reserves that are loaned on a day-to-day basis to banks that are temporarily short on reserves. This process involves the transfer of reserve balances on the books of the federal reserve bank from the reserve account of the lending bank to the reserve account of the borrowing bank.

Federal Home Loan Bank Board. An agency which regulates and supervises its federally-chartered and state-chartered members. It evaluates applications for federal charters and also establishes liquidity requirements for its members.

Federal Home Loan Bank System. A system whose primary responsibility is to provide a central credit facility for its savings and loan association (and other) members. It also supervises and regulates its members.

Federal Home Loan Mortgage Corporation (FHLMC). An agency providing a secondary market for the mortgages written by savings and loan associations that are members of the Federal Home Loan Bank System.

Federal Housing Administration (FHA). An agency providing mortgage loan insurance on homes that meet FHA requirements and standards.

Federal National Mortgage Association (FNMA). A corporation which purchases and sells mortgages in the secondary mortgage market. Although privately owned, the corporation is government regulated.

Federal Reserve System. The central banking system in the United States; it performs important functions for the banking system and it establishes and administers monetary policy.

Federal Savings and Loan Insurance Corporation (FSLIC). An agency which insures deposits and supervises member savings and loan associations.

FHA-insured mortgage. A mortgage loan that is insured by the Federal Housing Administration.

Fiat money. Money based on the general credit of an issuing government and proclaimed to be money by law or fiat.

Fiduciary. One who acts in a capacity of trust and undivided loyalty for another.

Fiduciary money. Paper money issued by central banks under the authority of the government.

Field warehouses. Warehouses set up on the premises of the borrowing business firms.

Financial assets. Claims against (obligations or liabilities of) individuals, businesses, financial institutions, and governments who issued them. Examples would be debt obligations issued by businesses and savings accounts held at commercial banks by individuals.

Financial leverage ratios. Financial ratios that indicate the extent to which assets are financed by borrowed funds and other liabilities.

Fire insurance. Insurance offering protection to the insured against the destruction of physical property as a result of fire. Such insurance does not provide for protection against loss to the insured of the use of such facilities.

Fiscal policy. The exercise of influence on economic activity through government expenditure and taxation programs.

Fixed assets. Physical facilities used in the production, storage, display, and distribution of the products of a firm. These assets normally provide many years of service to the firm. The principal fixed assets are equipment, land, and buildings.

Fixed costs. Expenses such as general and administrative expenses that must be incurred regardless of the volume of sales generated by the firm.

Float. The amount payable on checks already written but not yet deducted from the accounts on which drawn. Federal Reserve float is the temporary increase in bank reserves that results when checks are credited to the reserve accounts of banks that deposited them before they are debited to the accounts of banks on which they are drawn.

Foreclosure. Provides that a mortgagor's equity of redemption right is "barred and foreclosed" after a court specified time period.

Fractional certificate. Stock certificates representing less than one hundred shares of ownership in a corporation.

Fractional reserve system. A system whereby banks are required to hold reserves equal to some portion or fraction of their deposits rather than on a dollar-for-dollar basis.

Full-bodied money. Circulating coins that have their full monetary value of metal in them, under a gold, silver, or bimetallic standard. Their value as a commodity thus is as great as their value as money.

General obligation bonds. Bonds secured by the full faith and credit of the issuing governmental unit, that is, the bond is unconditionally supported by the full taxing power of the issuing government. General obligation bonds constitute by far the largest class of municipal obligations.

Government National Mortgage Association (GNMA). A government owned corporation that participates in the secondary mortgage market.

Greenbacks. Paper money officially known as United States notes authorized by Congress to help finance the Civil War.

Gresham's law. Law stating that when several types of money exist in an economy, the one which is most overvalued as money in relationship to the others will circulate while the other types will disappear from circulation. Sometimes it is expressed by saying that *bad* money drives *good* money out of circulation.

Group banking. Method of banking which involves the use of the holding-company device, whereby two or more individual banks are controlled through a company that holds the voting control of the individual banks.

Hedging. Concept involving the matching of the average maturities of an organization's assets and liabilities.

High employment budget. An estimate of the surplus or deficit of the federal government at a level of gross national product which provides for high employment and economic activity, but does not lead to inflationary pressures.

High-leverage company. A company that is engaged heavily in trading on the equity.

Housing and Urban Development, Department of (HUD). This department, created in 1965, has a wide range of responsibilities including the regulation of the Federal Housing Administration and the Government National Mortgage Association.

Income statement. A statement reflecting the change in a firm's financial position over a specified accounting time period. It shows the net profit or income (or loss) available to the owners of the business.

Inconvertible paper standard. A monetary system based upon paper money as the standard as set up by governments. The paper currency cannot be exchanged for gold or other metals.

Indirect instruments. An intermediary creates and is a party to separate instruments with the ultimate lenders and the borrowers. Examples would be time deposits held in a financial institution and a business loan made by that institution.

Industrial banking company (Morris Plan company). A company established to make general consumer loans for small amounts and to provide individuals a means of saving small amounts.

Industrial revenue bonds. Bonds issued by municipalities to provide lower-cost financing for construction of plant facilities for business firms as an incentive for the firms to locate in their areas.

Industry comparative analysis. A method that compares financial ratios for a firm against industry ratios.

Inflation. A condition which occurs when a rise or increase in the prices of goods and services is not offset by increases in the quality of those goods and services.

Insurance trust. One or more insurance policies placed in trust with the agreement that the proceeds of the insurance be paid to the trust institution upon death of the maker of the trust to be administered for the beneficiaries of the trust.

Intangible assets. Assets which include patent rights and a firm's "goodwill."

Interest rate. The basic price that equates the demand for and the supply of loanable funds in the financial markets. The quoted interest rate for any type of loan is a combination of several factors. Part of it is a fee for the administrative costs of making a loan, and another part of it is payment for the risk involved. The remainder is a payment for the use of money itself.

Interest risk premium. The difference between the interest rate on a comparable maturity U.S. government security (that is viewed as being risk-free) and the interest rate on a risky security.

Intermediation. The process by which savings are accumulated in financial institutions and, in turn, lent or invested by them.

Internal rate of return. The rate of return when the net present value is zero. This occurs when the present value of the cash inflows equals a project's investment or initial outlay.

Inventories. The materials and products that a manufacturing enterprise has on hand. Generally, a manufacturing firm categorizes its inventories in terms of raw materials, goods in the process of manufacture, and finished goods.

Inventory turnover. A financial ratio measured as the cost of goods sold divided by inventories.

Investment banking firms. Financial intermediaries which developed to help businesses to market and distribute their bonds and stocks in the primary securities market.

Investment companies. Institutions which engage principally in the purchase of stocks and bonds of other corporations. This permits the pooling of funds of many investors on a share basis for the primary purpose of obtaining expert management and wide diversification in security investments.

Junior mortgages. Mortgages recorded after the first mortgage. At times three or more mortgages may be placed on one piece of property.

Land contract. A contract for the sale of property in which the deed to the property does not pass to the purchaser until the terms of the contract have been fulfilled.

Life insurance. Insurance whose main function is providing an immediate estate for the dependents of the head of the household in the event of death before sufficient personal resources have been accumulated to provide for the dependents.

Limited partnership. A statutory modification of

the common-law partnership in which one or more general partners combine with one or more limited partners. Limited partners have limited liabilities in terms of the partnership organization.

Limit orders. An order placed with a broker providing a maximum price that is to be paid for a particular security or a minimum price at which a security may be sold.

Line of credit. The loan limit that a bank establishes for each of its business customers.

Liquidity. The ease with which an asset can be exchanged for money or other assets.

Liquidity preference theory. A theory which holds that interest rates are determined by the supply of and demand for money. This is viewed as a "stock" theory in that it focuses on the amount or stock of money as of a point in time.

Liquidity premium theory. A theory which holds that investors should be willing to trade off some yield for greater liquidity that is inherent in short-term securities. Likewise, borrowers would prefer to lend long-term and thus reduce their own liquidity risks associated with maturing securities. These supply and demand pressures suggest that short-term rates should be lower than long-term rates and that the yield curve should be upward sloping.

Liquidity ratios. Financial ratios that indicate the ability of the firm to meet its short-term debt obligations as they come due.

Loanable funds theory. A theory which holds that interest rates are a function of the supply of and demand for loanable funds. This is a "flow" theory in that it focuses on the relative supply and demand of loanable funds during or over a specified time period.

Long-term liabilities. Business debts with maturities greater than one year.

Macroeconomic business risk. The extent to which changes in the economy and the firm's industry impact on the business operations of the firm.

Making a market. The willingness of dealers to buy and/or sell a particular security or group of securities. As such, the dealer is acting as a principal in the transaction in much the same manner as any merchant.

Margin purchases. The use of borrowed funds to support part of the purchase price of a security. The security so purchased serves as the collateral for the borrowed funds.

Marine insurance. Provides protection over transportation of merchandise from the seller to the purchaser and includes land and marine transportation.

Marketable security. An investment that is highly liquid (short maturity and an active secondary market) and of high quality such that there is little chance that the borrower will default.

Market order. An order placed with a commission broker requesting the purchase or sale of a particular security at the best possible price that can be negotiated at the time the order is received.

Market segmentation theory. A theory which holds that securities of different maturities are less than perfect substitutes for each other. Institutional pressures dominate this theory. For example, commercial banks concentrate their activities in short-term securities because of their demand and other deposit liabilities. On the other hand, the nature of insurance company and pension fund liabilities allows these firms to concentrate their purchases and holdings in long-term securities. Thus supply and demand factors in each segmented market will affect the shape of the yield curve.

Medium of exchange. The basic function of the money in any economy. Money also serves as a store of purchasing power and as a standard of value.

Merchandise trade balance. The net difference between the import and export of goods between one nation and the rest of the trading world.

Monetary base. Reserve deposits held in federal reserve banks, vault cash or currency held by banks and other depository institutions, and currency held by the nonbank public. The monetary "base" (MB) times the money multiplier (m) produces the M1 definition of the money supply and can be expressed in formula form as $MBm = M1$.

Monetary policy. The formulation of policy by the Federal Reserve System to regulate the growth of the money supply and influence interest rates and the availability of credit.

Monetizing the debt. The process of increasing the money supply by the Federal Reserve System purchasing government debt obligations. The result is essentially equivalent to the government's printing money to pay for its expenditures.

Money. Anything that is generally accepted as a

means of paying for goods and services and of discharging debts.

Money markets. Markets where debt instruments of one year or less are traded.

Money supply or stock. The basic definition (M1) includes: currency held by the nonbank public (i.e., outside depository institutions, the Federal Reserve System, the federal government, and foreign banks and governments); demand and other checkable deposits at depository institutions; and travelers' checks. M2, M3, and L measures broaden this basic definition.

Mortgage. An interest in real property used as security for payment of a debt. Two parties, a mortgagee and a mortgagor, are involved.

Mortgage banking companies. Companies which originate or negotiate real estate mortgage loans and often service the mortgages by collecting interest and principal payments and then forwarding them to the owners of the mortgage. These firms are usually closely held private corporations. They have relatively small capital investment compared with the volume of business they do.

Mortgage bonds. Bonds that are secured by the pledge of specific real property.

Mortgagee. The lender in a mortgage transaction.

Mortgagor. The borrower in a mortgage transaction.

Multiple-line insurance companies. Companies which make possible the writing of insurance at lower cost for different specified risks. The complete property insurance requirement of an individual or business may be handled in a single contract.

Multiplier (in terms of economic activity). The process by which an increase in investment expenditures leads to a multiplied effect on national income. For example, as investment expenditures or government expenditures are increased, the level of national income increases, and this leads to an increase in consumption expenditures, which again in turn raises national income, which leads to more expenditures on consumption, and so on.

Municipal bond. In investment circles, commonly interpreted to mean the obligations of a state itself or of any of its political subdivisions. The description is not technically correct, but it is understood by all parties in the investment world.

Negative financial leverage. Situation which occurs when the interest cost of borrowing is more than the return being earned on the investment in assets. And, if the earnings before interest falls below the amount needed to meet interest obligations on the borrowed funds, the firm might be forced into bankruptcy.

Negotiable certificate of deposit. In essence, a receipt issued by a bank in exchange for a deposit of funds. The bank agrees to pay the amount deposited plus interest to the bearer of the receipt on the date specified on the certificate. Because the certificate is negotiable ($100,000 or more in amount), it can be traded in the secondary market before maturity.

Negotiable orders of withdrawal (NOW) accounts. Accounts that pay interest and against which checks can be written.

Net present value. The present value of cash inflows less the initial investment or outlay for the fixed assets which generate the inflows.

Net working capital. An amount determined by subtracting the total of current liabilities shown on the balance sheet from the total of current assets.

Nonmarketable government security issues. Instruments that cannot be transferred to other persons or institutions and can be redeemed only by being turned in to the United States Treasury. Savings bonds comprise the bulk of nonmarketable issues.

Note payable. A written promise to pay a specified amount of money to the order of a creditor on or before a certain date.

Note receivable. A written promise by a debtor of the business to pay a specified sum of money on or before a stated date.

Odd-lot dealers. Dealers who facilitate trading by the general public for orders of less then 100-share "round lots."

Open-end fund investment company. Commonly referred to as a mutual fund where the public buys shares in the fund directly from the investment company and redeems shares with the company. This contrasts with a closed-end fund investment company which has a fixed number of shares that are bought and sold in securities markets.

Optimal capital structure. Reflects the ideal mix

between long-term debt and equity funds that minimizes the cost of capital and maximizes the value of the firm.

Option. A contract which gives its holder the right to buy (call option) or sell (put option) a security at a specified price before a specified date.

Option writer. The seller of put and call contracts.

Order bill of lading. This instrument carries title to the merchandise being shipped and only its holder may claim the merchandise at the transportation terminal. The order bill of lading represents the written acceptance and terms of goods for shipment by a transportation company.

Paid-in capital (or surplus) account. Part of the owners' equity of a corporation; it reflects the issuing of shares of common stock above a stated or par value.

Participating preferred stock. Preferred stock that participates, on a share-for-share basis with common stock, in any residual profits of a corporation after basic preferred and common stock dividend payments.

Partnership. A form of business organization that exists when two or more persons own a business operated for profit.

Par value. A fixed or stated value assigned for common stock in the certificate of incorporation.

Payback period. A method that determines the time it will take in years to recover the initial investment in fixed assets.

Positive financial leverage. Situation which occurs when the interest cost of borrowing is less than the return being earned on the investment in assets. Trading on equity thus is favorable to the firm's stockholders.

Precautionary motive. Demand for marketable securities or cash to handle disruptive developments that otherwise could cause severe short-term liquidity problems.

Preemptive rights. A requirement in some states and in some corporate charters providing for the sale of new issues of voting stock to existing stockholders. Such entitlement, if exercised, permits existing stockholders to maintain their proportion of voting power and claims to assets.

Preferred stock. Equity capital in a corporation that has a prior claim relative to common stock on a firm's assets but generally carries a limited dividend.

Primary deposits. Deposits that add new reserves to the bank where deposited and generally arise when cash and checks drawn against other banks are placed on deposit in a bank.

Primary mortgage market. The market where the origination or creation of new mortgages is carried out.

Primary securities markets. Those markets involving the creation and issuance of new securities, mortgages, and other claims to wealth.

Prime rate. The interest rate charged by commercial banks to their "best" business customers. This short-term bank loan rate sets a "floor" interest rate for other loans to less qualified business borrowers.

Profitability ratios. Financial ratios that indicate the degree to which firms have been able to generate profits relative to sales, assets, or stockholders' equity.

Property insurance. Insurance whose purpose is either to protect the insured against loss arising out of physical damages to insured's property or loss arising from damages to others for which the insured may be held liable.

Prospectus. The document that describes the terms and conditions of a new security issue. The Securities Exchange Act of 1934 requires the distribution of prospectuses to buyers of securities coming under regulation of the Securities and Exchange Commission.

Prudent-man rule. Rule which requires that a trust institution be held responsible for the same degree of judgment that a prudent person would exercise in investing personal funds.

Purchasing power risk. A risk which results from changes in the price level. For example, a rise or increase in prices in the form of inflation in the U.S. results in a decline in the purchasing power of the dollar.

Put contract. An option to sell a security at a specified price during a specified period of time.

Quantity theory. One of the oldest, and also one of the newest, theories which attempts to explain the relationship of money to prices and which holds that changes in the quantity of money are the main causal determinants of changes in the price level. This theory relies on the use of the equation of exchange.

Real assets. Assets which include direct ownership

of land, buildings, machinery, inventory, and precious metals.

Real Estate Investment Trust (REIT). A trust authorized to invest in real estate that is managed and controlled by trustees and is exempt from federal corporate income taxes.

Regional and local development companies. Established to improve the economy and to promote business growth in their area by providing long-term funds to businesses. Their funding comes from private community sources and possibly local governments.

Regulation Z. The Truth in Lending section of the Consumer Credit Protection Act. It regulates the disclosure of consumer credit costs and also garnishment procedures and prohibits exorbitant credit transactions. Its purpose is to make consumers aware of the cost of credit and to enable them to compare the costs of alternate forms of credit.

Representative full-bodied money. Paper money with full metallic backing.

Retained earnings. Reflects the retention or accumulation of earnings or profits of a corporation and is part of the owners' equity.

Revenue bonds. Obligations issued by state or local governments to finance specific projects. The revenues from these specific projects are to provide the funds to service the obligations with liability of the governmental unit being limited to those specific sources of funds.

Revocable trust. A trust in which the maker of the trust has the right to revoke the trust arrangement after its creation. This contrasts with an irrevocable trust, which provides for the complete and final transfer of assets to the trustee.

Revolving credit agreement. A standby agreement for a guaranteed line of credit that a business firm may obtain from a commercial bank.

Risk-adjusted discount rate. Determined by adding a risk premium to the firm's cost of capital for purposes of discounting riskier than average projects.

Risk premium. The difference between the risk-free interest rate on a Treasury security and the interest rate on a risky corporate debt security.

Sales finance companies. Organizations developed to finance the sale of durable goods on installments, and also to finance the wholesale purchases by merchants or dealers from manufacturers.

Savings. The accumulation of cash and other financial assets such as savings accounts and corporate securities.

Savings surplus unit. An economic unit, such as individuals taken as a group, which has current savings that exceed the group's direct investment in real assets. Savings deficits occur when an economic unit's investment exceeds its income. This often is the case for business firms as a group or economic unit.

Secondary mortgage market. Market where real estate mortgages can be resold thus providing some liquidity to mortgage holders.

Secondary securities markets. Markets involving the transfer of existing securities from old investors to new investors. A secondary market also exists for real estate mortgages.

Secured loan. Loan for which specific property is pledged as collateral.

Serial maturities. An issue of bonds that matures in installments, permitting investors to choose the maturity best suited to their needs.

Short sales. The sale of securities that the seller does not own but which are borrowed in anticipation of a price decline in the security. The securities must be bought back at a future time.

Sinking fund bonds. Bond contracts that require the setting aside on a regular basis of funds to retire all or a part of an issue during the life of the issue.

Small Business Administration. An agency established by the federal government to provide financial assistance to small firms that are unable to obtain loans through private channels on reasonable terms.

Small business investment companies (SBICs). Privately owned, profit seeking firms licensed and regulated by the Small Business Administration that provide long-term funds to other businesses.

Sole proprietorship. A business venture that is owned by a single individual who personally receives all of the profits and assumes all the responsibility for the debts and the losses of the business.

Special assessment bonds. Generally issued by local governments to finance community improvements. Since such improvements are expected to improve the value of properties adjacent to the improvements, special tax assessments may be levied to provide the funds to service the obligations.

Special Drawing Rights (SDR's). A form of reserve asset or "paper gold" as they are called. They are account entries in the books of the International Monetary Fund which are separate from all other accounts and are divided among the members in accordance with their quotas in the fund. The SDR's can be used to meet balance-of-payments deficits with other countries.

Specialists. Members of the exchanges that buy and sell for their own accounts, generally limiting their attention to only a few stocks. They also serve as floor brokers for other brokers who place transactions with them.

Speculative motive. Demand for marketable securities or cash to be able to take advantage of unusual cash discounts or other price bargains.

Stock certificate. Provides evidence of an ownership claim in a corporation.

Stock power or bond power. Authorizes a lender to sell or otherwise dispose of assignable stocks and bonds, provided as collateral for a loan by the borrower, should it become necessary to do so to protect the loan.

Straight-line depreciation. Writing-off the value of an asset in equal amounts over the life of the asset. This assumes a level decline in the value of the asset over time.

Street name. Securities owned by investors that are issued and retained in the name of the brokerage firm serving the customer. This arrangement facilitates the sale of securities with only a telephone call and eliminates the requirement of careful safekeeping of the securities.

Tax anticipation bills. Short-term bills offered periodically by the U.S. Treasury to smooth out its flow of tax receipts. These securities are offered at a discount and can be submitted at par to meet tax payments when they are due.

Term life insurance. Insurance whose basic feature is that the policy is issued for a specified period of time after which time no obligation exists on part of the insurance company toward the insured.

Term loan agreement. A detailed written contract between the bank and a borrower.

Term structure of interest rates. The impact of loan maturities on interest rates at a point in time. The "term structure" is reflected in a "yield curve" which is constructed by plotting yields versus maturity for securities of comparable risk. U.S. government securities generally are used to construct yield curves and show the term structure of interest rates as of a specified date.

Testamentary trust. A trust that provides that an estate be maintained and administered for the benefit of heirs rather than be turned over to the heirs directly.

Token coins. Coins made with less than their full weight of metal.

Total bank reserves. Member bank deposits held in Federal Reserve Banks and vault cash or currency held by member and nonmember banks.

Trade credit. The open accounts receivable, together with notes receivable, taken by manufacturers, wholesalers, jobbers, and other business units as sellers of goods and services to other businesses.

Trading on the equity. The process of using borrowed funds in an attempt to increase the percentage return on the investment of existing stockholders in a business.

Transactions motive. Demand for cash needed to carry on day-to-day operations.

Transfer payments. Payments for which no current productive service is rendered. Examples of government transfer payments include pensions, direct relief, and veterans' allowances and benefits.

Traveler's letter of credit. An instrument issued by a bank in one country and addressed to a list of banks abroad. These foreign banks to which the letter is addressed are usually correspondents of the issuing bank and have agreed to purchase upon sight the drafts presented to them by persons displaying such letters of credit.

Treasury bills. Treasury obligations of the shortest maturities which are typically issued for 91 days, with some issues carrying maturities of 182 days or one year. They are sold at a discount from their value at maturity.

Treasury bonds. Obligations which may be issued with any maturity but generally have had an original maturity in excess of five years. These bonds bear interest at stipulated rates. Many issues of these bonds are callable by the government several years before their maturity.

Treasury notes. Obligations which are usually issued for maturities of more than one year but not more than ten years and are issued at specified interest rates.

Trend (or time series) analysis. A method that compares financial ratios over several years for the same firm.

Trust indenture. A document that spells out in detail the contractual terms associated with a bond issue.

Trust institution. Serves in a fiduciary capacity for the administration or disposition of assets and for the performance of specified acts for the beneficiaries of trust arrangements.

Trust receipt. An instrument used by lenders in releasing merchandise to a customer but in which title to the merchandise is retained by the lender. In the event of failure of the business the lender claims possession of the merchandise and does not take the position of an ordinary creditor of the business.

Unsecured loan. A loan that represents a general claim against the assets of the borrower.

VA-guaranteed mortgage. A mortgage where a portion of an eligible veteran's loan is guaranteed in terms of repayment to the lender by the Veterans Administration.

Variable costs. The types of business expenses that vary directly with sales such as cost of goods sold.

Variable rate mortgage. A mortgage where instead of agreeing to a certain fixed interest rate, the home buyer agrees to pay the "going rate" which is tied to some "reference" interest rate that changes with changing conditions in the financial markets. When market interest rates are rising, the home buyer would expect to pay a higher interest rate on his or her mortgage loan, and vice versa.

Velocity of money. A measure of the rate of circulation of the money supply, expressed as the average number of times each dollar is spent on purchases of goods and services and calculated by dividing gross national product (GNP) in current dollars by the money supply.

Voluntary savings. Financial assets set aside for use in the future.

Weighted average cost of capital. The after-tax cost of a firm's long-term debt and equity capital weighted on the basis of the optimal capital structure mix.

Whole life insurance. Insurance which combines an investment program with the insurance contract. The premiums are generally for a fixed sum each payment period throughout the life of the insured.

Working capital. A firm's current assets and current liabilities.

Yield curve. A graphic representation of the term structure of interest rates. Interest rates for securities of comparable quality for various maturities are compared as of a point in time.

Yield to maturity. The rate of return based on interest and principal payments that will be received on a bond held to its maturity.

INDEX